REDEMPTION SONGS

A

REDEMPTION SONGS

SONGS

A CHOICE COLLECTION OF

1000

HYMNS AND CHORUSES

FOR

EVANGELISTIC MEETINGS

SOLO   SINGERS   CHOIRS

AND   THE   HOME

LONDON

PICKERING & INGLIS LTD.

PICKERING & INGLIS LTD.

29 LUDGATE HILL, LONDON, E.C.4

229 BOTHWELL STREET, GLASGOW, C.2

Home Evangel Books Ltd., 1 Waterman Avenue, Toronto, 16

Made and Printed in Great Britain

Acknowledgments

THE following are gratefully thanked for permission given to use the hymns or tunes of which they hold the copyright.

The Charles M. Alexander Copyrights Trust, for Nos. 142, 158, 190, 236, 321, 327, 340, 362, 366, 391, 438, 605, 672, 694, 726, 748, 798, 817, 882.

Mr. Cecil J. Allen, for the chorus, I am the Door (1).

Mr. David J. Beattie, for the tune, Stanwix (133).

Mr. H. Ford Benson, for the tune, Light (652).

Miss M. Beveridge, for Nos. 90, 452, 712, 928, 938.

The Bible Institute Colportage Association, for No. 859.

Messrs. Bilhorn Brothers, for Nos. 88, 211, 246, 349, 378, 763, 834, 837, 838.

Messrs. J. Blakemore & Sons, for the tune, Ellan Vannin (562).

Mr. Clifford Booth, for the tune, True Hearted (339).

The Bullinger Publications Trust, for the tune, Pax Tecum (437 and 577).

Mr. E. Bunnett, for the tune, Heathside (480).

The Canadian General Synod, for the tune, Galilee (6).

The Canieddyd Committee of the Union of Welsh Independents, for the tunes, Rachie (8 and 668), Merthyr Tydfil (253).

The Chatauqua Press, for the words of No. 2.

The Church Book Room Press, for the tune, Pax Tecum (437 and 577).

The Church Hymnal for the Christian Year, for the tune, Hispania (577).

The Congregational Union of England and Wales, for the tune, Greenwood (580).

Messrs. J. Curwen & Sons, Ltd., for the words and tune of No. 892; the Faux Bourdon setting of St. Anne (47), from Curwen Edition, No. 6300; and for the tune, Marching (492), from Curwen Edition, No. 80631.

Mr. Francis Duckworth, for the tunes, Swanside (502), Rimington (646), Autumn (950).

Mrs. Evans, for the tune, Glaston (563).

Mr. E. M. Farrar, for the words of No. 71.

Messrs. A. W. Ford & Co., Ltd., for the tune, Eventide (948).

The Adam Geibel Music Company, for Nos. 52, 311, 354, 358, 454, 751, 822, 915.

Mr. C. A. Hammond, for the tune, Dursley (475), from The Botley Tune Book.

Mr. John J. Hood, for the words and music of No. 240.

Miss Constance Morley Horder, for the words of No. 661; and for the tunes, Westenhanger (398), Tavy Cleave (579), Vesper No. 3 (831).

Mrs. John Hughes, Tregarth, for the tune, Cwm Rhondda (33).

Messrs. Hughes A'I Fab Publishers, Ltd., for the tune, Aberystwyth (428).

Hymns Ancient and Modern, for the tune, St. Andrew (489).

The International Music Board of The Salvation Army, for Nos. 185, 276, 286, 293, 341, 343, 424, 552, 593, 692, 820.

Miss M. E. Janvrin, for the words of No. 647.

Miss T. C. M. Legge, for the tune, Theodora (45).

Mr. G. Tom Lewis, for the tune, Blaencefn (649).

The Lillenas Publishing Company, for No. 624.

The London Missionary Society, for Nos. 625, 640.

The Lorenz Publishing Company, for Nos. 386, 592, 762, 850.

Mr. Michael Maclagan, for the tune, Showers of Blessing (277).

Mr. F. C. Maker, for the tune, Melrose (498).

Mrs. Evelyn H. Manwell, for the tune, Newcastle (14).

Messrs. Marshall, Morgan & Scott, Ltd., for the music of Nos. 336 and 418.

The Methodist Conference, for the tunes, Frogmore (148), Even Me (277).

The Methodist Youth Department, for the tunes, Cliftonville (658), Athlone (683).

Mr. Alexander Morris, for the tune, Llef (602).

The National Council of the Christian Endeavour Unions, for the words and harmonization of No. 889.

The National Sunday School Union, for the tune, Greenwell (395); and for the words and tune of No. 895.

The National Young Life Campaign, for Nos. 830, 865.

Mr. Ernest W. Naylor, for the tune, From Strength to Strength (482).

Mrs. Richard S. Newman, for the tune, Land of Rest (114).

Messrs. H. E. Nichol & Son, for Nos. 636, 873, 886, 888, 901, 909, 912, 917.

Messrs. William Nicholson & Sons, for the tune, Consort (678).

Messrs. Novello & Co., Ltd., for the tunes, St. Margaret (16), Mendelssohn (42), Day of Rest (51), Laudate Dominum (74), Nichomadus (81), Chilton Foliat (148), Grace (500), Ludborough (540), and a tune by F. H. Cowen (484).

The Oxford University Press, for the tunes, Il Buon Pastor (491), Tiltey Abbey (505), Fingal (596), Randolph (942), Birling (947), from Songs of Praise (Enlarged Edition); and the tunes, Sidon (205), St. Mabyn (224), from The Church Hymnary (Revised Edition).

Mr. John T. Park (Geo. Taylor), Stainland, for the tunes, Lloyd (322), Te Laudant Omnia (330)

Miss Millicent Pickersgill-Cunliffe, for the tune, St. Petrox (500).

The Psalms and Hymns Trust, for the tune, Silksworth (914).

Messrs. Randle & Sons, for No. 403.

Mr. Charles Reeves, for the tunes, Harlesden (261), Timios (904).

Messrs. Reid Brothers, Ltd., for the words and tune of Chorus No. 2.

The Rodeheaver Hall-Mack Company, for Nos. 209, 318, 409, 458, 479, 607, 612, 687, 689, 690, 696, 703, 736, 738, 807, 920,

Messrs. Seeley, Service & Co., Ltd., for the tune, Ne Derelinquas Me (602).

Messrs. Snell & Sons, Ltd., for the tune, Penlan (149).

The South Africa General Mission, for Nos. 693, 831, 923.

Messrs. Stainer & Bell, Ltd., for the tune, St. Columba (394).

Mr. Bayford Stone, for the tune, Angel's Story (656).

Mr. E. H. Swinstead, for the tunes, Nos. 443, 461, 513, 739, 746, 747, 749, 762, 773, 875.

Dr. Sybil Tremellen, for the words of 132 and 606.

The Tullar-Meredith Company, for Nos. 138, 184, 421, 673, 709, 713, 786, 804, 843, 844, 877, 910.

Messrs. A. Weeks & Co., Ltd., for the tune, Regnabit (646).

Messrs. Joseph Williams, Ltd., for the tune of No. 71.

The words of Nos. 575, 588, 630, 637; the tunes, Overtown (2), Harbour (455), Bright Gems (659), Ellison (908); the second tunes to Nos. 10, 146, 159, 349, 442, 534; the arrangements of 27, 637, 651; and the Faux Bourdon settings of 23, 485, 486, 487; are the copyright of the Publishers.

INDEX OF SUBJECTS

1

All Hail the Power

EDWARD PERRONET   MILES LANE C.M.   W. SHRUBSOLE

1 All hail the pow'r of Je - su's Name! Let an - gels prostrate fall; Bring forth the roy-al
2 Crown Him, ye martyrs of your God, Who from His al - tar call; Ex - tol the stem of
3 Ye cho-sen seed of Is-rael's race, A rem-nant weak and small, Hail Him who saves you
4 Ye Gen-tile sin-ners ne'er for - get The worm-wood and the gall; Go, spread your trophies

1 di - a - dem, And crown Him, crown Him, crown Him, Crown Him Lord of all.
2 Jes - se's rod, And crown Him, crown Him, crown Him, Crown Him Lord of all.
3 by His grace, And crown Him, crown Him, crown Him, Crown Him Lord of all.
4 at His feet! And crown Him, crown Him, crown Him, Crown Him Lord of all.

5 Let every kindred, every tribe,
  On this terrestrial ball,
  To Him all majesty ascribe,
  And crown Him Lord of all.

6 O that with yonder sacred throng
  We at His feet may fall,
  Join in the everlasting song,
  And crown Him Lord of all.

Optional Refrain after Last Verse

And crown . . Him Lord of all, And crown . . . Him Lord of all,

And crown Him Lord of all,   And crown Him Lord of all,

And crown Him Lord of all, And crown Him Lord of all.

1

TUNES DIADEM and CORONATION are overleaf

1 All Hail the Power!

EDWARD PERRONET   DIADEM   JAMES ELLOR, *Arr.* P. J. MANSFIELD

1. All hail the pow'r of Jesus' Name! Let
2. Crown Him ye martyrs of your God Who
3. Ye chos-en seed of Is-rael's race, A
4. Ye Gen-tile sin-ners ne'er for-get The
5. Let ev-'ry kin-dred, ev-'ry tribe On
6. O that with yon-der sa-cred throng We

1. an - gels pros-trate fall; Let an - gels pros - trate fall; Bring
2. from His al-tar call, Who from His al - tar call, Ex-
3. rem - nant weak and small, A rem - nant weak and small, Hail
4. worm - wood and the gall; The worm - wood and the gall; Go,
5. this ter-res-trial ball, On this ter - res - trial ball, To
6. at His feet may fall! We at His feet may fall! Join

REFRAIN

And crown

1. forth the roy - al di - a - dem   And crown
2. tol the stem of Jes - se's rod
3. Him who saves you by His grace,
4. spread your tro - phies at His feet,
5. Him all maj - es - ty a - scribe,
6. in the ev - er - last - ing song,   And crown Him,

And crown Him,

Him,   crown Him,

crown Him,   crown Him,   crown Him,   crown Him,

crown Him,   crown Him,   Crown

All Hail the Power!—*Continued*

crown Him,   crown Him   Lord . of all.

(ff)

crown Him,   crown Him, And   crown   Him Lord . of all!

Him, And   crown   Him Lord . of all.

EDWARD PERRONET   CORONATION 8.6.8.6.8.6   OLIVER HOLDEN

1 All hail the pow'r of Je-sus' Name! Let an-gels pros-trate fall;
2 Crown Him ye mar-tyrs of your God Who from His al-tar call;
3 Ye cho-sen seed of Is-rael's race, A rem-nant weak and small,
4 Ye gen-tile sin-ners ne'er for-get The worm-wood and the gall;
5 Let ev-'ry kin-dred, ev-'ry tribe On this ter-res-trial ball,
6 O that with yon-der sa-cred throng We at His feet may fall!

1 Bring forth the roy-al di-a-dem And crown Him Lord of all!
2 Ex-tol the stem of Jes-se's rod And crown Him Lord of all!
3 Hail Him who saves you by His grace, And crown Him Lord of all!
4 Go, spread your troph-ies at His feet, And crown Him Lord of all!
5 To Him all ma-jes-ty a-scribe, And crown Him Lord of all!
6 Join in the ev-er-last-ing song, And crown Him Lord of all!

1 Bring forth the roy-al di-a-dem And crown Him Lord . of all!
2 Ex-tol the stem of Jes-se's rod And crown Him Lord . of all!
3 Hail Him who saves you by His grace, And crown Him Lord . of all!
4 Go, spread your troph-ies at His feet, And crown Him Lord . of all!
5 To Him all maj-est-y a-scribe, And crown Him Lord . of all!
6 Join in the ev-er-last-ing song, And crown Him Lord . of all!

For tune MILES LANE see two pages previous to this one

2   Break Thou the Bread

MARY A. LATHBURY   BREAD OF LIFE 6.4.6.4.D   W. F. SHERWIN

1 Break Thou the bread of life, Dear Lord, to me,
2 Break Thou the bread of life, O Lord, to me,
3 O - pen Thy Word of Truth, That I may see
4 Bless Thou the truth, dear Lord, To me, to me,

1 As Thou didst break the loaves Be - side the sea.
2 That hid with - in my heart Thy Word may be;
3 Thy mes - sage writ - ten clear And plain for me;
4 As Thou didst bless the bread By Gal - i - lee;

1 Be - yond the sa - cred page I seek Thee, Lord;
2 Mould Thou each in - ward thought, From self set free,
3 Then in sweet fel - low - ship Walk - ing with Thee,
4 Then shall all bond - age cease, All fet - ters fall;

1 My spi - rit pants for Thee, O Liv - ing Word!
2 And let my steps be all Con - trolled by Thee.
3 Thine im - age on my life En - graved will be.
4 And I shall find my peace, My All in All!

By permission of the CHATAUQUA PRESS   Tune OVERTOWN is on next page

2   Break Thou the Bread

MARY A. LATHBURY   OVERTOWN 6.4.6.4.D   GEORGE ALLAN

1 Break Thou the bread of life, Dear Lord, to me,
2 Break Thou the bread of life, O Lord, to me,
3 O - pen Thy Word of Truth, That I may see
4 Bless Thou the truth, dear Lord, To me, to me,

1 As Thou didst break the loaves Be - side the sea.
2 That hid with - in my heart Thy Word may be ;
3 Thy mes - sage writ - ten clear And plain for me ;
4 As Thou didst bless the bread By Gal - i - lee ;

1 Be - yond the sa - cred page I seek Thee, Lord ;
2 Mould Thou each in - ward thought, From self set free,
3 Then in sweet fel - low - ship Walk - ing with Thee,
4 Then shall all bond - age cease, All fet - ters fall ;

1 My spi - rit pants for Thee, O Liv - ing Word!
2 And let my steps be all Con - trolled by Thee.
3 Thine im - age on my life En - graved will be.
4 And I shall find my peace, My All in All!

Tune BREAD OF LIFE is on previous page

3

Send Thy Blessing

Irvin H. Mack

Maurice A. Clifton

1 We come be-fore Thy throne to-day, Thy prom-ised pre-sence claim:
2 We know that Thou art pre-sent here, Thy grace to us re-veal;
3 O send to us Thy quick-'ning pow'r, All guilt and dross re-move:
4 Ac-cept the hom-age that we bring, O Lord, we hum-bly pray:

1 O come and en-ter now our hearts, And set our souls a-flame.
2 We fain would know Thy bles-sed will, Thy ho-ly pres-ence feel.
3 O let our wait-ing hearts be fill'd, Dear Sa-viour, with Thy love.
4 Be-stow Thy rich-est bless-ings now, And meet with us to-day.

REFRAIN

Lord, send Thy bless-ing, Lord, send Thy bless-ing,

Lord, send Thy bless-ing On our wait-ing souls!

4 The Name of Jesus

W. C. Martin

E. S. Lorenz

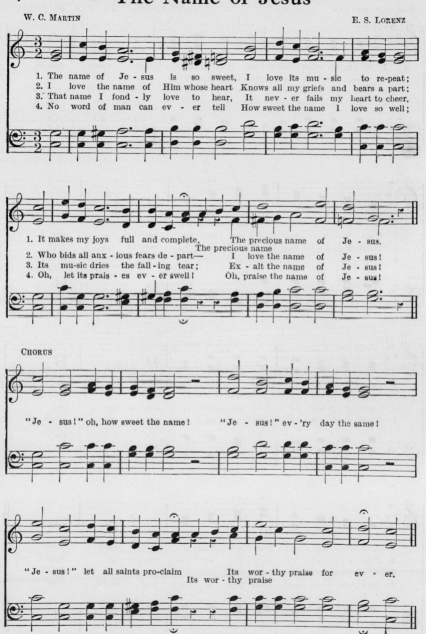

1. The name of Je - sus is so sweet, I love its mu - sic to re-peat;
2. I love the name of Him whose heart Knows all my griefs and bears a part;
3. That name I fond - ly love to hear, It nev - er fails my heart to cheer,
4. No word of man can ev - er tell How sweet the name I love so well;

1. It makes my joys full and complete, The precious name of Je - sus.
   The precious name
2. Who bids all anx - ious fears de - part— I love the name of Je - sus!
3. Its mu - sic dries the fall - ing tear; Ex - alt the name of Je - sus!
4. Oh, let its prais - es ev - er swell! Oh, praise the name of Je - sus!

CHORUS

"Je - sus!" oh, how sweet the name! "Je - sus!" ev - 'ry day the same!

"Je - sus!" let all saints pro-claim Its wor - thy praise for ev - er.
Its wor - thy praise

5 Count Your Blessings

JOHNSON OATMAN

E. O. EXCELL. *Arr.* P. J. MANSFIELD

1 When up - on life's bil - lows you are tem - pest - toss'd,
2 Are you ev - er bur - den'd with a load of . care?
3 When you look at o - thers with their lands and . gold,
4 So a - mid the con - flict, wheth - er great or . small,

1 When you are dis - cour - ag'd, think-ing all is . lost,
2 Does the cross seem hea - vy you are call'd to . bear?
3 Think that Christ has prom - is'd you His wealth un - told,
4 Do not be dis - cour - ag'd, God is o - ver . all,

1 Count your ma - ny bless - ings, name them one by . one,
2 Count your ma - ny bless - ings, ev' - ry doubt will . fly,
3 Count your ma - ny bless - ings, mon - ey can - not . buy
4 Count your ma - ny bless - ings, an - gels will at - tend,

1 And it will sur - prise you what the Lord hath . done.
2 And you will be sing - ing as the days go . by.
3 Your re - ward in hea - ven, nor your home on . high.
4 Help and com - fort give you to your jour - ney's . end.

Count Your Blessings—*Continued*

REFRAIN

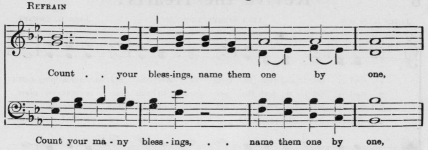

Count . . your bless-ings, name them one   by   one,

Count your ma - ny bless - ings, . . name them one by   one,

Count . . your bless-ings, see what God   hath   done ;

Count your ma - ny bless - ings, . . see what God hath   done ;

Count . . your bless - ings, . name them one by   one,

Count your ma - ny bless - ings, . name them one by   one,

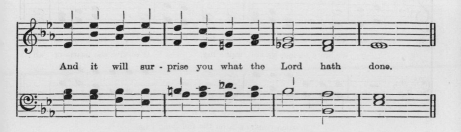

And it will sur - prise you what the Lord   hath   done.

6 Revive the Hearts!

JAMES L. BLACK   ARCH STREET 8.7.8.7.D   JOHN R. SWENEY

1 God is here! and that to bless us With the Spi-rit's quick-'ning pow'r;
2 God is here! we feel His pre-sence In this con-se-crat-ed place;
3 God is here! O then, be-liev-ing, Bring to Him our one de-sire!
4 Sa-viour, grant the pray'r we of-fer, While in sim-ple faith we bow,

1 See! the cloud al-read-y bend-ing Waits to drop the grate-ful show'r.
2 But we need the soul re-fresh-ing Of His free, un-bound-ed grace.
3 That His love may now be kind-led, Till its flame each heart in-spire.
4 From the win-dows of Thy mer-cy Pour us out a bless-ing now.

REFRAIN

Let it come, . . O Lord we pray Thee! Let the show'r . . of bless-ing fall;

. . Let it come, O Lord we pray Thee! . . Let the show'r of bless-ing fall;

We are wait - ing, we are wait-ing, O re-vive . . the hearts of all!

. . We are wait-ing, we are wait - ing, . . O re-vive the hearts of all!

The tune GALILEE is on the following page

6   Revive the Hearts!

JAMES L. BLACK   GALILEE 8.7.8.7.D   F. E. J. LLOYD

1 God is here! and that to bless us   With the Spi-rit's quick-'ning pow'r;
2 God is here! we feel His pre-sence   In this con-se-crat-ed place;
3 God is here! O then, be-liev-ing,   Bring to Him our one de-sire!
4 Sa-viour, grant the pray'r we of-fer,   While in sim-ple faith we bow,

1 See! the cloud al-read-y bend-ing   Waits to drop the grate-ful show'r.
2 But we need the soul re-fresh-ing   Of His free, un-bound-ed grace.
3 That His love may now be kind-led,   Till its flame each heart in-spire.
4 From the win-dows of Thy mer-cy   Pour us out a bless-ing now.

REFRAIN

Let it come, O Lord we pray Thee! Let the show'r of bless-ing fall;'

We are wait-ing, we are wait-ing, O re-vive the hearts of all!

The music by permission of THE CANADIAN GENERAL SYNOD
The tune ARCH STREET is on the preceding page

7 To God be the Glory

FANNY J. CROSBY   WILLIAM H. DOANE

1 To God   be the glo - ry, great things He   hath done,
2 O   per - fect re - demp-tion! the pur - chase of   blood,
3 Great things   He hath taught us, great things He   hath done,

1 So   lov'd He   the world that He gave us   His   Son,
2 To   ev - 'ry be - liev - er   the pro - mise of   God;
3 And great our   re - joic - ing thro' Je - sus   the   Son;

1 Who yield - ed His life   an   a - tone - ment for   sin,
2 The vil - est of - fen - der   who tru - ly   be - lieves
3 But pur - er, and high - er,   and great - er   will be

1 And o - pen'd the   life gate that all   may   go   in.
2 That mo - ment from Je - sus   a   par - don re - ceives.
3 Our won - der, our   trans - port when Je - sus   we   see.

To God be the Glory—*Continued*

REFRAIN

Praise the Lord! praise the Lord! Let the earth hear His voice,

Praise the Lord! praise the Lord! Let the peo - ple re - joice;

O come to the Fa - ther through Je - sus the Son!

And give Him the glo - ry, great things He hath done.

8 On the Lord's Side

FRANCES R. HAVERGAL   HERMAS 6.5.6.5.6.5.D   FRANCES R. HAVERGAL

1 Who is on the Lord's side? Who will serve the King? Who will
2 Not for weight of glo - ry, Nor for crown and palm, En - ter
3 Je - sus, Thou hast bought us Not with gold or gem, But with
4 Fierce may be the con - flict, Strong may be the foe; But the

1 be His help - ers O - ther lives to bring? Who will leave the
2 we the arm - y, Raise the war - rior psalm; But for love that
3 Thine own life - blood For Thy di - a - dem; With Thy bless - ing
4 King's own arm - y None can o - ver - throw: Round His stand - ard

1 world's side? Who will face the foe? Who is on the Lord's side?
2 claim - eth Lives for whom He died: He whom Je - sus nam - eth
3 fill - ing All who come to Thee, Thou hast made us will - ing,
4 rang - ing Vic - t'ry is se - cure, For His truth un - chang - ing

1 Who for Him will go? By Thy call of mer - cy, By Thy
2 Must be on His side! By Thy love con - strain - ing, By Thy
3 Thou hast made us free: By Thy grand re - demp - tion, By Thy
4 Makes the tri - umph sure: Joy - ful - ly en - list - ing By Thy

1-4 grace di - vine, We are on the Lord's side, Sa - viour, we are Thine!

The tunes ARMAGEDDON and RACHIE are on the pages following

8 On the Lord's Side

F. R. HAVERGAL   ARMAGEDDON 6.5.6.5.6.5.D   L. REICHARDT (*Arr.* GOSS)

1 Who is on the Lord's side? Who will serve the King? Who will be His
2 Not for weight of glo - ry, Nor for crown and palm, En - ter we the
3 Je-sus, Thou hast bought us, Not with gold or gem, But with Thine own
4 Fierce may be the con - flict, Strong may be the foe; But the King's own

1 help - ers, O - ther lives to bring? Who will leave the world's side?
2 ar - my, Raise the war-rior psalm; But for love that claim - eth
3 life - blood For Thy di - a - dem; With Thy bless-ing fill - ing
4 arm - y None can o - ver - throw: Round His stand-ard rang - ing,

1 Who will face the foe? Who is on the Lord's side? Who for
2 Lives for whom He died: He whom Je - sus nam - eth Must be
3 All who come to Thee, Thou hast made us will - ing, Thou hast
4 Vic - t'ry is se - cure, For His truth un - chang-ing Makes the

1 Him will go? By Thy call of mer - cy, By Thy grace di-
2 on His side! By Thy love con - strain - ing, By Thy grace di-
3 made us free. By Thy grand re - demp - tion, By Thy grace di-
4 tri - umph sure. Joy - ful - ly en - list - ing, By Thy grace di-

1-4 vine, We are on the Lord's side, Sa - viour, we are Thine!

The tune HERMAS is on the preceding page and RACHIE on the following page

8 On the Lord's Side

FRANCES R. HAVERGAL   RACHIE 6.5.6.5.6.5. D   CARADOG ROBERTS

1   Who is on the Lord's side?   Who will serve the King?   Who will be His
2   Not for weight of glo - ry,   Nor for crown and palm,   En - ter we the
3   Je - sus, Thou hast bought us,   Not with gold or gem,   But with Thine own
4   Fierce may be the con - flict,   Strong may be the foe;   But the King's own

1   help - er's O - ther lives to . bring?   Who will leave the world's side?
2   ar - my, Raise the war - rior psalm;   But for love that claim - eth
3   life - blood For Thy di - a - dem;   With Thy bless - ing fill - ing
4   ar - my None can o - ver - throw;   Round His stand - ard rang - ing,

1   Who will face the foe?   Who is on the Lord's side? Who for Him will go?
2   Lives for whom He died: He whom Je - sus na - meth Must be on His side!
3   All who come to Thee,   Thou hast made us will - ing, Thou hast made us free.
4   Vic - t'ry is se - cure,   For His truth un-chang-ing Makes the tri - umph sure.

For ORGAN ONLY.   The Voice Parts are on the following page

By Thy call of mer - cy, . . By Thy grace di - vine, . .

We are on the Lord's side, Sav - iour, we are Thine.

On the Lord's Side—*Continued*

Sop.

1 By Thy call of mer - cy, . By Thy grace di - vine, . .
2 By Thy love con - strain - ing, . By Thy grace di - vine, . .
3 By Thy grand re - demp - tion, . By Thy grace di - vine, . .
4 Joy - ful - ly en - list - ing . By Thy grace di - vine, . .

Alto

1 . . By Thy call of mer - cy, . . By Thy grace di - vine, .
2 . . By Thy love con - strain - ing, . . By Thy grace di - vine, .
3 . . By Thy grand re - demp - tion, . . By Thy grace di - vine, .
4 . . Joy - ful - ly en - list - ing . . By Thy grace di - vine, .

Tenor

1 By Thy call of mer - cy, . By Thy grace di - vine, . .
2 By Thy love con - strain - ing, . By Thy grace di - vine, . .
3 By Thy grand re - demp - tion, . By Thy grace di - vine, . .
4 Joy - ful - ly en - list - ing . By Thy grace di - vine, . .

Bass

1 . . By Thy call of mer - cy, . . By Thy grace di - vine, .
2 . . By Thy love con - strain - ing, . . By Thy grace di - vine, .
3 . . By Thy grand re - demp - tion, . . By Thy grace di - vine, .
4 . . Joy - ful - ly en - list - ing . . By Thy grace di - vine, .

1-4 We are on the Lord's side, Sav - iour, we are Thine.

Music by permission of the Caniedydd Committee, Swansea

The tunes Hermas and Armageddon are on the preceding pages

9 The Saviour with Me

LIZZIE EDWARDS   JOHN R. SWENEY

1 I must have the Sa-viour with me For I dare not walk a-
2 I must have the Sa-viour with me For my faith at best is
3 I must have the Sa-viour with me In the on - ward march of
4 I must have the Sa-viour with me, And His eye the way must

1 lone, I must feel His pre-sence near me, And His arm a-
2 weak; He can whis - per words of com - fort That no o - ther
3 life, Thro' the tem - pest and the sun - shine, Thro' the bat - tle
4 guide Till I reach the vale of Jor - dan, Till I cross the

REFRAIN

Then my soul . . . shall fear no

1 round me thrown.
2 voice can speak.
3 and the strife.
4 rol - ling tide.

. . Then my soul shall fear no

ill, . . . Let Him lead . . . me where He

ill, fear no ill, . . . Let Him lead me where He

The Saviour with Me—*Continued*

will, . . . I will go . . . with-
out a mur-mur, And His foot-steps fol-low still.

will, where He will, . . . I will go with-
out a mur-mur, And His foot-steps fol-low still.

In this Tune the Refrain is sung as the last verse

LIZZIE EDWARDS   SEFTON 8.7.8.7   HOWARD A. CROSBIE

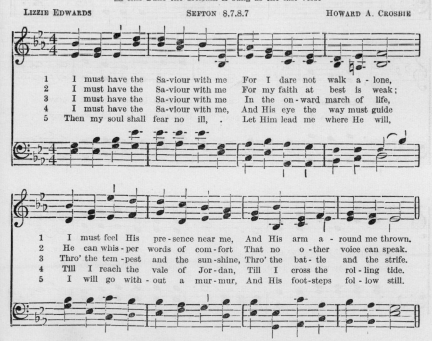

1   I must have the   Sa-viour with me   For I dare not walk a-lone,
2   I must have the   Sa-viour with me   For my faith at best is weak;
3   I must have the   Sa-viour with me   In the on-ward march of life,
4   I must have the   Sa-viour with me,   And His eye the way must guide
5   Then my soul shall fear no ill, .   Let Him lead me where He will,

1   I must feel His   pre-sence near me,   And His arm a-round me thrown.
2   He can whis-per   words of com-fort   That no o-ther voice can speak.
3   Thro' the tem-pest   and the sun-shine,   Thro' the bat-tle and the strife.
4   Till I reach the   vale of Jor-dan,   Till I cross the rol-ling tide.
5   I will go with-out   a mur-mur,   And His foot-steps fol-low still.

10 Showers of Blessing

JENNIE GARNETT JOHN R. SWENEY

1 Here in Thy Name we are ga -ther'd, Come and re - vive us, O Lord !
2 O that the show - ers of bless - ing Now on our souls may de - scend !
3 There shall be show - ers of bless - ing, Pro-mise that ne - ver can fail;
4 Show-ers of bless-ing, we need them, Show - ers of bless-ing from Thee;

1 There shall be show - ers of bless - ing Thou hast de-clar'd in Thy Word.
2 While at the foot-stool of mer - cy Plead-ing Thy prom-ise we bend.
3 Thou wilt re - gard our pe - ti - tion, Sure - ly our faith will pre - vail.
4 Show-ers of bless-ing, O grant them! Thine all the glo - ry shall be.

REFRAIN

O gra-cious-ly hear . . us ! Gra-cious-ly hear us, we pray: .

O gra-cious-ly, gra-cious-ly hear us! Gra-cious-ly hear us, we pray; .

Pour from Thy win-dows up - on . . us Show-ers of bless-ing to - day. .

Pour from Thy win-dows, Lord, pour up-on us, Show-ers of bless-ing to - day. .

10   Showers of Blessing

JENNIE GARNETT   DAVID CARYLL

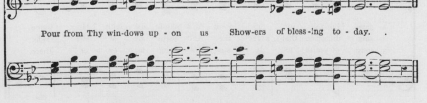

1 Here in Thy Name we are ga - ther'd, Come and re - vive us, O   Lord! .
2 O that the show - ers of bless - ing   Now on our souls may de - scend! .
3 There shall be show - ers of bless - ing,   Pro - mise that ne - ver can   fail; .
6 Show - ers of bless - ing, we need them, Show - ers of bless - ing from Thee; .

1 There shall be show - ers of bless - ing   Thou hast de - clar'd in Thy   Word. .
2 While at the foot-stool of mer - cy   Plead-ing Thy prom-ise we   bend. .
3 Thou wilt re - gard our pe - ti - tion,   Sure - ly our faith will pre - vail. .
4 Show - ers of bless-ing, O grant them!   Thine all the glo - ry shall be. .

REFRAIN

O gra - cious - ly hear us! Gra - cious - ly hear us, we   pray;

Pour from Thy win-dows up - on   us   Show - ers of bless - ing to - day. .

An Alternative Tune is on the preceding page

11   My Song of Jesus

FANNY J. CROSBY   ENDLESS PRAISE 7.6.7.6.D   W. H. DOANE

1 My song shall be of Je - sus, His mer - cy crowns my days, He
2 My song shall be of Je - sus, When sit - ting at His feet I
3 My song shall be of Je - sus, While press - ing on my way, To

1 fills my cup with bless - ings, And tunes my heart to praise ; My
2 call to mind His good - ness, In med - i - ta - tion sweet : My
3 reach the bliss - ful re - gion Of pure and per - fect day ; And

1 song shall be of Je - sus, The pre - cious Lamb of God, Who
2 song shall be of Je - sus, What - ev - er ill be - tide ; I'll
3 when my soul shall en - ter The gate of E - den fair. A

ritard

1 gave Him-self my ran - som, And bought me with His blood.
2 sing the grace that saves me, And keeps me at His side.
3 song of praise to Je - sus I'll sing for ev - er there.

Tune HERRNHUT is on next page

11 My Song of Jesus

FANNY J. CROSBY   HERRNHUT 7.6.7.6.D   JOHANN CRÜGER

1 My song shall be of Je - sus, His mer - cy crowns my days,
2 My song shall be of Je - sus, When sit - ting at His feet
3 My song shall be of Je - sus While pres-sing on my way

1 He fills my cup with bless - ings, And tunes my heart to praise;
2 I call to mind His good - ness, In med - i - ta - tion sweet:
3 To reach the bliss - ful re - gion Of pure and per - fect day;

1 My song shall be of Je - sus, The pre-cious Lamb of God,
2 My song shall be of Je - sus, What-ev - er ill be - tide;
3 And when my soul shall en - ter The gate of E - den fair.

1 Who gave Him-self my ran - som, And bought me with His blood.
2 I'll sing the grace that saves me, And keeps me at His side.
3 A song of praise to Je - sus I'll sing for ev - er there.

The tune ENDLESS PRAISE is on the previous page

12

Praise Him !

FANNY J. CROSBY   JOYFUL PRAISE 12.10.12.10.D   CHESTER G. ALLEN

1 Praise Him! praise Him! Je-sus, our bless-ed Re-deem-er,
2 Praise Him! praise Him! Je-sus, our bless-ed Re-deem-er,
3 Praise Him! praise Him! Je-sus, our bless-ed Re-deem-er,

1 Sing, O earth, His won-der-ful love pro-claim,
2 For our sins He suff-'red and bled and died;
3 Heav'n-ly por-tals loud with ho-san-nahs ring,

1 Hail Him! hail Him! high-est arch-an-gels in glo-ry,
2 He, our Rock, our hope of e-ter-nal sal-va-tion,
3 Je-sus, Sa-viour, reign-eth for e-ver and e-ver,

1 Strength and hon-our give to His ho-ly Name.
2 Hail Him! hail Him! Je-sus, the Cru-ci-fied.
3 Crown Him, crown Him, Pro-phet and Priest and King!

Praise Him!—*Continued*

1 Like a shep - herd Je - sus will guard His chil - dren,
2 Lov - ing Sa - viour, meek - ly en - dur - ing sor - row,
3 Death is van - quish'd! tell it with joy, ye faith - ful.

1 In His arms He car - ries them all day long.
2 Crown'd with thorns that cru - el - ly pierc'd His brow ;
3 Where is now thy vic - to - ry, boast - ing grave ?

1 O ye saints that dwell on the moun-tain of Zi - on,
2 Once for us re - ject - ed, de-spis'd, and for - sak - en,
3 Je - sus lives ! no lon - ger thy por - tals are cheer - less,

1 Praise Him! praise Him! e - ver in joy - ful song.
2 Prince of Glo - ry, e - ver tri-umph-ant now.
3 Je - sus lives, the might - y and strong to save.

13   The Promises of God

R. Kelso Carter

R. Kelso Carter

1 Stand - ing on the prom - is - es of Christ our King,
2 Stand - ing on the prom - is - es that can - not fail,
3 Stand - ing on the prom - is - es I now can see
4 Stand - ing on the prom - is - es of Christ the Lord,

1 Thro' e - ter - nal a - ges let His prais - es ring:
2 When the howl - ing storms of doubt and fear as - sail,
3 Per - fect, pres - ent, cleans - ing in the blood for me;
4 Bound to Him e - ter - nal - ly by love's strong cord,

1 Glo - ry in the high - est I will shout and sing
2 By the liv - ing word of God I shall pre - vail,
3 Stand - ing in the li - ber - ty where Christ makes free,
4 O - ver - com - ing dai - ly with the Spi - rit's sword,

1-4 Stand - ing on the prom - is - es of God.

The Promises of God—*Continued*

REFRAIN—Stand - - ing, stand - - ing,

Stand - ing on the pro - mise, Stand - ing on the prom - ise,

Stand - ing on the prom - is - es of God my Sa - viour,

Stand - - - ing, Stand - - - ing,

Stand - ing on the prom - ise, Stand - ing on the prom - ise,

I'm stand - ing on the prom - is - es of God.

14   A Song of Praise

S. C. KIRK

J. G. WILSON

1 The won-drous work the Lord has done Let ev - 'ry
2 Un - to the Lord doth praise be - long, O tell it
3 We'll sing the pow'r of Je - sus' Name And His a -
4 Let ev - 'ry heart and ev - 'ry tongue As one u -

1 voice pro - claim! And for the work of grace be - gun, The
2 ev - 'ry - where! Let ev - 'ry ran - som'd soul pro - long The
3 ton - ing blood: To - day and ev - er - more the same, The
4 nit - ed host Praise God for what His arm hath done; Praise

1 won-drous bat - tle fought and won, Give glo - ry to His Name!
2 loud ho - san - nah of the song, The Lord doth an - swer pray'r!
3 vi - lest sin - ner to re - claim, And bring him back to God.
4 God the Fa - ther, God the Son, And God the Ho - ly Ghost!

REFRAIN

We plead - ed for the Spi - rit, He came in might - y pow'r;

A Song of Praise—*Continued*

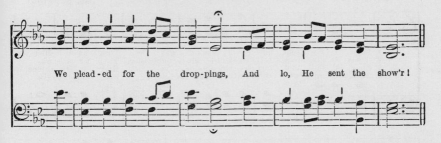

We plead-ed for the drop-pings, And lo, He sent the show'r!

In the Tune below the REFRAIN is omitted

S. C. KIRK   NEWCASTLE 8.6.8.8.6   HENRY K. MORLEY

1 The won-drous work the Lord has done Let ev-'ry voice pro-claim! And for the work of grace be-gun, The won-drous bat-tle fought and won, Give glo-ry to His Name!

2 Un-to the Lord doth praise be-long, O tell it ev-'ry-where! Let ev-'ry ran-som'd soul pro-long The loud ho-san-nah of the song, The Lord doth an-swer pray'r!

3 We'll sing the pow'r of Je-sus' Name And His a-ton-ing blood: To-day and ev-er-more the same, The vi-lest sin-ner to re-claim, And bring him back to God.

4 Let ev-'ry heart and ev-'ry tongue As one u-nit-ed host Praise God for what His arm hath done; Praise God the Fa-ther, God the Son, And God the Ho-ly Ghost!

15 The Everlasting Song

LIZZIE EDWARDS

JNO. R. SWENEY

1. Come, O my soul, my ev'-ry pow'r a - wak - ing, Look un-to Him
2. Think, O my soul, how pa-tient-ly He sought thee, Far, far a - way
3. Sing, O my soul, and let thy pure de - vo - tion Rise to His throne,
4. Soon, O my soul, thine earth-ly house for - sak - ing, Soon shalt thou rise

1. whose good-ness crowns thy days; While in - to song an - gel - ic choirs are
2. up - on the moun-tain steep, Then in His arms how ten - der - ly He
3. thy Sav-iour, Friend, and Guide; Sing of His love that, like a might-y
4. the bet - ter land to see; Then will thy harp, a no - bler strain a-

1. break - ing, O let thy voice its thank - ful tri - bute raise.
2. brought thee, Home to His fold a wea - ry, wand - 'ring sheep.
3. o - cean, Flows un - to thee, and all the world be - side.
4. wak - ing, Praise Him who died to pur - chase life for thee.

CHORUS

Tell how a - lone the path of death He trod; Tell how He

lives, thine Ad - vo - cate with God; Lift up thy voice, while

The Everlasting Song—*Continued*

heav'n's tri-umph-ant throng, Swell at His feet the ev-er-last-ing song.

16   Jesus, All and in All

GEORGE MATHESON   ST. MARGARET 8.8.8.8.6.   A. L. PEACE

1. O Love that wilt not let me go,   I rest my wea-ry soul in
2. O Light that fol-low'st all my way,   I yield my flick-'ring torch to
3. O Joy that seek-est me through pain, I can-not close my heart to
4. O Cross that lift-est up my head,   I dare not ask to fly from

1. Thee: I give Thee back the life I owe,   That
2. Thee: My heart re-stores its bor-rowed ray, That
3. Thee: I trace the rain-bow through the rain, And
4. Thee: I lay in dust life's glo-ry dead,   And

1. in Thine o-cean depths its flow May rich-er, full-er be.
2. in Thy sun-shine's blaze its day May bright-er, fair-er be.
3. feel the prom-ise is not vain, That morn shall tear-less be.
4. from the ground there blos-soms red Life that shall end-less be.

By permission of Novello & Co., Ltd.

17 My Redeemer

PHILIP BLISS   MY REDEEMER 8.7.8.7. D   J. MCGRANAHAN

1 I will sing of my Re-deem-er, And His
2 I will tell the won-drous sto-ry, How my
3 I will praise my dear Re-deem-er, His tri-
4 I will sing of my Re-deem-er, And His

1 won - drous love to me; On the
2 lost es - tate to save. In His
3 umph - ant pow'r I'll tell, How the
4 heav'n - ly love to me; He from

1 cru - el Cross He suf - fer'd, From the
2 bound - less love and mer - cy, He the
3 vic - tor - y He giv - eth O - ver
4 death to life hath brought me, Son of

1 curse to set me free.
2 ran - som free - ly gave.
3 sin, and death, and hell.
4 God, with Him to be.

My Redeemer—*Continued*

Sing, O sing . . . . of my Re - deem -
Sing, O sing of my Re - deem - er! Sing, O sing of

blood . . . .

er, With His blood He pur - chas'd me, He
my Re - deem - er! With His blood, ...

pur - chas'd me, ... On the Cross . . . . .
with His blood He pur - chas'd me, On the Cross He seal'd my par -

He seal'd my par - don, Paid the
don, On the Cross He seal'd my par - don, Paid the

Repeat pp after last verse

debt, ... And made me free.
debt, and made me free, And made me free, and made me free.

2   For tune HYFRYDOL see No. 66

18   The God of Abram Praise

THOMAS OLIVERS   LEONI 6.6. 8.4. D   HEBREW MELODY

With vigour

1 The God of A - bram praise, Who reigns en - thron'd a - bove,
2 The God of A - bram praise, At whose su - preme com - mand
3 He by H m - self hath sworn; I on His oath de - pend;
4 There dwells the Lord our King, The Lord our right - eous - ness!
5 The whole tri - umph - ant host Give thanks to God on high;

1 An - cient of ev - er - last - ing days, And God of love!
2 From earth I rise, and seek the joys At His right hand.
3 I shall, on eag - le's wings up - borne, To heav'n a - scend.
4 Tri - um - phant o'er the world and sin: The Prince of Peace!
5 "Hail, Fa - ther, Son, and Ho - ly Ghost!" They ev - er cry.

1 Je - ho - vah! great I AM! By earth and heav'n con - fest,
2 I all on earth for - sake, Its wis - dom, fame, and pow'r;
3 I shall be - hold His face, I shall His pow'r a - dore,
4 On Zi - on's sa - cred height His king - dom still main - tains,
5 Hail, A - bram's God and mine! I join the heav'n - ly lays;

1 I bow, and bless the sa - cred Name, For ev - er blest.
2 And Him my on - ly por - tion make, My shield and tow'r.
3 And sing the won - ders of His grace For ev - er - more.
4 And glor - ious with His saints in light, For ev - er reigns.
5 All might and ma - jes - ty are Thine, And end - less praise.

Tune COVENANT is on the next page

18   The God of Abram Praise

THOMAS OLIVERS   COVENANT 6.6. 8.4. D   JOHN STAINER

1 The God of A-bram praise, Who reigns en-thron'd a-bove,
2 The God of A-bram praise, At whose su-preme com-mand
3 He by Him-self hath sworn; I on His oath de-pend;
4 There dwells the Lord our King, The Lord our right-eous-ness!
5 The whole tri-umph-ant host Give thanks to God on high;

1 An-cient of ev-er-last-ing days, And God of love!
2 From earth I rise, and seek the joys At His right hand.
3 I shall, on eag-le's wings up-borne, To heav'n a-scend.
4 Tri-um-phant o'er the world and sin: The Prince of Peace!
5 "Hail, Fa-ther, Son, and Ho-ly Ghost!" They ev-er cry.

1 Je-ho-vah! great I AM! By earth and heav'n con-fest,
2 I all on earth for-sake, Its wis-dom, fame, and pow'r;
3 I shall be-hold His face, I shall His pow'r a-dore,
4 On Zi-on's sa-cred height His king-dom still main-tains,
5 Hail, A-bram's God and mine! I join the heav'n-ly lays;

1 I bow, and bless the sa-cred Name, For ev-er blest.
2 And Him my on-ly por-tion make, My shield and tow'r.
3 And sing the won-ders of His grace For ev-er-more.
4 And glor-ious with His saints in light, For ev-er reigns.
5 All might and ma-jes-ty are Thine, And end-less praise.

The tune LEONI is on the previous page

19   My Shepherd is the Lamb

JOHN BEAUMONT   PRIORY 6.6. 8.4. D   ANON

1 My Shep-herd is   the Lamb, The liv-ing Lord, who died;
2 My soul He doth re-store When e'er I go a-stray;
3 When faith and hope shall cease, And love a-bides a-lone,

1 With all good things I ev-er am By Him sup-plied.
2 He makes my cup of joy run o'er From day to day;
3 Then shall I see Him face to face, And know as known.

1 He rich-ly feeds my soul With bless-ings from a-bove,
2 His love, so full, so free, A-noints my head with oil;
3 Still shall I lift my voice, His praise my song shall be;

1 And leads me where the ri-vers roll Of end-less love.
2 Mer-cy and good-ness fol-low me, Fruit of His toil.
3 And I will in His love re-joice, Who died for me.

FROM THE BOTLEY TUNE BOOK

The New Song

20

A. T. PIERSON   THE NEW SONG 11.12.12.12   PHILIPP BLISS

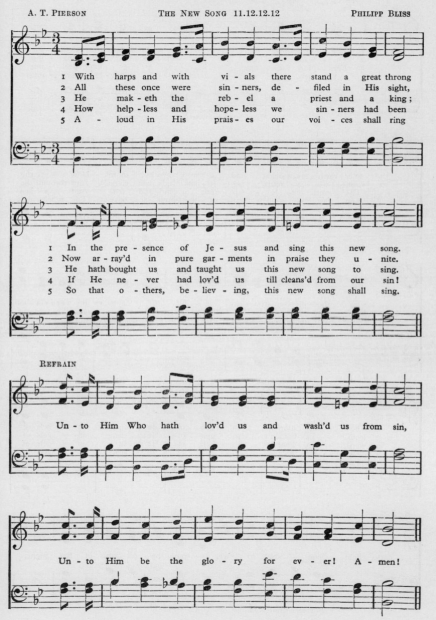

1 With harps and with vi - als there stand a great throng
2 All these once were sin - ners, de - filed in His sight,
3 He mak - eth the reb - el a priest and a king;
4 How help - less and hope - less we sin - ners had been
5 A - loud in His prais - es our voi - ces shall ring

1 In the pre - sence of Je - sus and sing this new song.
2 Now ar - ray'd in pure gar - ments in praise they u - nite.
3 He hath bought us and taught us this new song to sing.
4 If He ne - ver had lov'd us till cleans'd from our sin!
5 So that o - thers, be - liev - ing, this new song shall sing.

REFRAIN

Un - to Him Who hath lov'd us and wash'd us from sin,

Un - to Him be the glo - ry for ev - er! A - men!

21 Hark, Hark, My Soul

F. W. FABER   PILGRIMS 11.10.11.10.9.10   HENRY SMART

1 Hark, hark, my soul! an - gel - ic songs are swell - ing,
2 On - ward we go, for still we hear them sing - ing,
3 Far, far a - way, like bells at ev' - ning peal - ing,
4 An - gels, sing on, your faith - ful watch - es keep - ing;

1 O'er earth's green fields and o-cean's wave-beat shore: How sweet the
2 'Come, wea - ry souls, for Je - sus bids you come'; And through the
3 The voice of Je - sus sounds o'er land and sea, And la - den
4 Sing us sweet frag - ments of the songs a - bove: Till morn-ing's

1 truth those bless-ed strains are tell - ing Of that new life when sin shall
2 dark, its e-choes sweet-ly ring - ing, The mus-ic of the Gos-pel
3 souls, by thou-sands meek-ly steal - ing, Kind Shep-herd turn their wea - ry
4 joy shall end the night of weep - ing, And life's long sha-dows break in

1 be no more: An - gels of Je - sus, an - gels of
2 leads us home: An - gels of Je - sus, an - gels of
3 steps to Thee: An - gels of Je - sus, an - gels of
4 cloud - less love: An - gels of Je - sus, an - gels of

1-4 light, Sing - ing to wel - come the pil-grims of the night.

For the Choir Setting by ADAM GEIBEL see No. 931

22 Ceaseless Praise

CHARLES H. GABRIEL

CHARLES H. GABRIEL

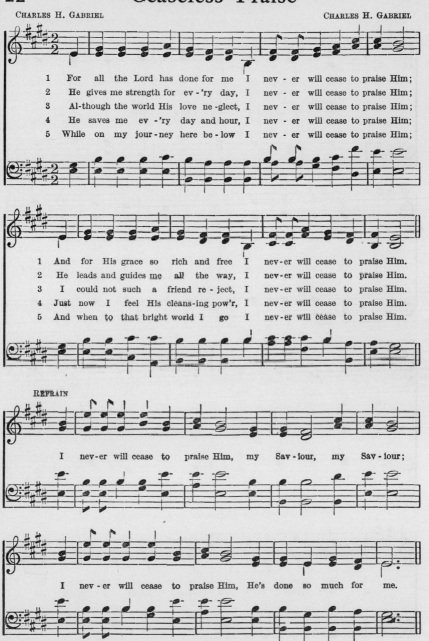

1 For all the Lord has done for me I nev - er will cease to praise Him;
2 He gives me strength for ev -'ry day, I nev - er will cease to praise Him;
3 Al-though the world His love ne -glect, I nev - er will cease to praise Him;
4 He saves me ev -'ry day and hour, I nev - er will cease to praise Him;
5 While on my jour - ney here be - low I nev - er will cease to praise Him;

1 And for His grace so rich and free I nev - er will cease to praise Him.
2 He leads and guides me all the way, I nev - er will cease to praise Him.
3 I could not such a friend re - ject, I nev - er will cease to praise Him.
4 Just now I feel His cleans-ing pow'r, I nev - er will cease to praise Him.
5 And when to that bright world I go I nev - er will cease to praise Him.

REFRAIN

I nev - er will cease to praise Him, my Sav - iour, my Sav - iour;

I nev - er will cease to praise Him, He's done so much for me.

23   O God of Bethel!

PARAPHRASE 2   ST. PAUL C.M.   CHALMERS' COLLECTION, 1749

1 O God of Beth - el! by whose hand Thy
2 Our vows, our pray'rs, we now pre - sent Be -
3 Through each per - plex - ing path of life Our
4 O spread Thy cov - 'ring wings a - round Till
5 Such bless - ings from Thy grac - ious hand Our

1 peo - ple still are fed; Who through this wea - ry
2 fore Thy throne of grace: God of our fa - thers!
3 wand' - ring foot - steps guide; Give us each day our
4 all our wand' - rings cease, And at our Fa - ther's
5 hum - ble pray'rs im - plore; And Thou shalt be our

1 pil - grim - age Hast all our fa - thers led.
2 be the God Of their suc - ceed - ing race.
3 dai - ly bread, And rai - ment fit pro - vide.
4 loved a - bode Our souls ar - rive in peace.
5 cho - sen God And por - tion ev - er - more.

FAUX BOURDON SETTING BY P. J. MANSFIELD

2 Our vows, our pray'rs, we now pre - sent Be -
4 O spread Thy cov' - ring wings a - round Till

O God of Bethel! — *Continued*

2 fore Thy throne of grace: God of our fa-thers!
4 all our wand'-rings cease, And at our Fa-ther's

2 be the God Of their suc-ceed-ing race.
4 loved a-bode Our souls ar-rive in peace.

PARAPHRASE 2　　　SALZBURG C.M.　　　JOHANN M. HAYDN

1 O God of Beth-el! by whose hand Thy peo-ple still are fed;
2 Our vows, our pray'rs, we now pre-sent Be-fore Thy throne of grace.
3 Thro' each per-plex-ing path of life Our wand'-ring foot-steps guide;
4 O spread Thy cov'-ring wings a-round Till all our wand'-rings cease!
5 Such bless-ings from Thy gra-cious hand Our hum-ble pray'rs im-plore;

1 Who thro' this wea-ry pil-grim-age Hast all our fa-thers led.
2 God of our fa-thers! be the God Of their suc-ceed-ing race.
3 Give us each day our dai-ly bread, And rai-ment fit pro-vide.
4 And at our Fa-ther's lov'd a-bode Our souls ar-rive in peace.
5 And Thou shalt be our cho-sen God And por-tion e-ver-more.

The tunes STRACATHRO and BURFORD are on the following pages

23 O God of Bethel!

PARAPHRASE 2   STRACATHRO C.M.   CHARLES HUTCHESON

1 O God of Beth - el! by . whose hand Thy
2 Our vows, our pray'rs, we now . pre - sent Be-
3 Through each per - plex - ing path . of life Our
4 O spread Thy cov - 'ring wings . a - round Till
5 Such bless - ings from Thy gra - cious hand Our

1 peo - ple still are fed; Who through this wea - ry
2 fore Thy throne of grace; God of our fa - thers!
3 wand' - ring foot - steps guide; Give us each day our
4 all our wand' - rings cease, And at our Fa - ther's
5 hum - ble pray'rs im - plore; And Thou shalt be our

1 pil - grim - age Hast all our fa - thers led.
2 be the God Of their suc - ceed - ing race.
3 dail - y bread, And rai - ment fit pro - vide.
4 lov'd a - bode Our souls ar - rive in peace.
5 cho - sen God And por - tion e - ver - more.

FAUX BOURDON SETTING by PURCELL J. MANSFIELD

2 Our vows, our pray'rs, we now pre - sent Be-
4 O spread Thy cov' - ring wings a - round Till

O God of Bethel!—*Continued*

2 fore — Thy throne of grace: God of our fa — thers!
4 all our wand - rings cease, And at our Fa - ther's

2 be the God Of their suc - ceed - ing race.
4 lov'd a - bode Our souls ar - rive in peace.

Copyright by Pickering & Inglis, Ltd.

PARAPHRASE 2   Burford C.M.   Henry Purcell

1 O God of Beth - el! by whose hand Thy peo - ple still are fed;
2 Our vows, our pray'rs, we now pre - sent Be - fore Thy throne of grace:
3 Through each per - plex - ing path of life Our wand' - ring foot - steps guide;
4 O spread Thy cov' - ring wings a - round Till all our wand' - rings cease,
5 Such bless - ings from Thy gra - cious hand Our hum - ble pray'rs im - plore;

1 Who through this wea - ry pil - grim - age Hast all our fa - thers led.
2 God of our fa - thers! be the God Of their suc - ceed - ing race.
3 Give us each day our dail - y bread, And rai - ment fit pro - vide.
4 And at our Fa - ther's loved a - bode Our souls ar - rive in peace.
5 And Thou shalt be our cho - sen God And por - tion e - ver - more.

The tunes St. Paul and Salzburg are on the preceding pages

24   Awake, my Soul

THOMAS KEN   MORNING HYMN L.M.   F. H. BARTHELEMON

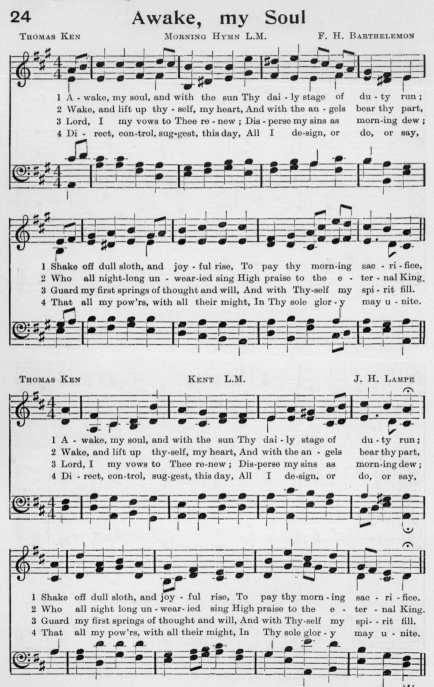

1 A - wake, my soul, and with the sun Thy dai - ly stage of   du - ty run ;
2 Wake, and lift up thy - self, my heart, And with the an - gels bear thy part,
3 Lord, I   my vows to Thee re - new ; Dis - perse my sins as   morn-ing dew ;
4 Di - rect, con-trol, sug-gest, this day, All I   de-sign, or   do, or say,

1 Shake off dull sloth, and joy - ful rise, To pay thy morn-ing sac - ri - fice,
2 Who   all night-long un - wear-ied sing High praise to the   e - ter - nal King.
3 Guard my first springs of thought and will, And with Thy-self my   spi - rit fill.
4 That all my pow'rs, with all their might, In Thy sole glor - y   may u - nite.

THOMAS KEN   KENT L.M.   J. H. LAMPE

1 A - wake, my soul, and with the sun Thy dai - ly stage of   du - ty run ;
2 Wake, and lift up thy-self, my heart, And with the an - gels bear thy part,
3 Lord, I   my vows to Thee re-new ; Dis-perse my sins as   morn-ing dew ;
4 Di - rect, con-trol, sug-gest, this day, All I   de-sign, or   do, or say,

1 Shake off dull sloth, and joy - ful rise, To pay thy morn - ing sac - ri - fice.
2 Who   all night long un - wear- ied sing High praise to the   e - ter - nal King.
3 Guard my first springs of thought and will, And with Thy-self my   spi - rit fill.
4 That   all my pow'rs, with all their might, In Thy sole glor - y   may u - nite.

25   Holy, Holy, Holy

REGINALD HEBER   NICÆA 11.12.12.10.   J. B. DYKES

1 Ho - ly, ho - ly, ho - ly,   Lord   God Al - might - y!
2 Ho - ly, ho - ly, ho - ly!   all the saints a - dore Thee,
3 Ho - ly, ho - ly, ho - ly!   tho' the darkness hide Thee,
4 Ho - ly, ho - ly, ho - ly,   Lord   God Al - might - y!

1 Ear - ly in the morn - ing our song shall rise to Thee;
2 Cast - ing down their gold-en crowns a - round the glas - sy sea,
3 Tho' the eye of sin - ful man Thy glo - ry may not see,
4 All Thy works shall praise Thy name in earth and sky and sea;

1 Ho - ly, ho - ly, ho - ly, mer - ci - ful and might - y,
2 Cher - u - bim and ser - a - phim fall - ing down be - fore Thee,
3 On - ly Thou art ho - ly; there is none be - side Thee,
4 Ho - ly, ho - ly, ho - ly, mer - ci - ful and might - y,

1 God in Three Per - sons, bless - ed Trin - i - ty!
2 Which wert, and art, and ev - er - more shalt be.
3 Per - fect in power, in love, and pur - i - ty.
4 God in Three Per - sons, bless - ed Trin - i - ty!

26 Psalm 100

WILLIAM KETHE   OLD HUNDREDTH L.M.   *French Psalter, 1551*

1. All peo - ple that on earth do dwell, Sing to the Lord with cheer-ful voice;
2. Know that the Lord is God in - deed; With-out our aid He did us make;
3. O en - ter then His gates with praise, Ap-proach with joy His courts un - to;
4. For why the Lord our God is good; His mer - cy is for ev - er sure;

1. Him serve with mirth, His praise forth tell; Come ye be - fore Him and re - joice.
2. We are His flock, He doth us feed, And for His sheep He doth us take.
3. Praise, laud, and bless His Name al - ways, For it is seem - ly so to do.
4. His truth at all times firm - ly stood, And shall from age to age en - dure.

CONGREGATION   ALTERNATIVE VERSION   J. DOWLAND

1. All peo - ple that on earth do dwell, Sing to the Lord with cheer - ful voice;
2. Know that the Lord is God in - deed; With-out our aid He did us make;
3. O en - ter then His gates with praise, Ap-proach with joy His courts un - to;
4. For why the Lord our God is good; His mer - cy is for ev - er sure;

CHOIR OR ORGAN

1. Him serve with mirth, His praise forth tell; Come ye be - fore Him and re - joice.
2. We are His flock, He doth us feed, And for His sheep He doth us take.
3. Praise, laud, and bless His Name al - ways, For it is seem - ly so to do.
4. His truth at all times firm - ly stood, And shall from age to age en - dure.

27 ## Glory to Jesus

BATISTE 10.10.10.10

J. W. MACGILL

BATISTE, *Har.* E. MACGILL

1 Je - sus has lov'd me— won - der - ful Sa - viour! Je - sus has lov'd me, I
2 Je - sus has sav'd me— won - der - ful Sa - viour! Je - sus has sav'd me, I
3 Je - sus will lead me— won - der - ful Sa - viour! Je - sus will lead me, I
4 Je - sus will crown me— won - der - ful Sa - viour! Je - sus will crown me, I

1 can - not tell why : Came He to res - cue sin - ners all worth-less, My heart He
2 can - not tell how ; All that I know is He was my ran - som, Dy - ing on
3 can - not tell where ; But I will fol - low through joy or sor - row, Sun - shine or
4 can - not tell when ; White throne of splen - dour hail I with glad - ness, Crown'd with the

REFRAIN

1 con - quered, for Him I would die.
2 Cal - v'ry with thorns on His brow.   Glo - ry to Je - sus, won - der - ful
3 tem - pest, sweet peace or de - spair.
4 plau - dits of an - gels and men.

Sa - viour! Glo - ry to Je - sus, the One I a - dore. Glo - ry to

Je - sus, won - der - ful Sa - viour! Glo - ry to Je - sus, and praise ev - er - more.

28 Hallelujah!

W. SPENCER WALTON — JOYFUL SOUND 8.8.8.8 — D. B. TOWNER

1 Cleans'd in our Sav-iour's prec-ious Blood, Fill'd with the ful-ness of our God,
2 Lean-ing our heads on Je-sus' breast, Know-ing the joy of that sweet rest,
3 Kept by His pow'r from day to day, Held by His hand, we can-not stray,
4 Liv-ing in us His own pure life, Giv-ing us rest from in-ward strife,
5 O what a Sav-iour we have found! Well may we make the world re-sound,

1 Walk-ing by faith the path He trod, Hal-le-lu-jah! Hal-le-lu-jah!
2 Find-ing in Him the chief, the best, Hal-le-lu-jah! Hal-le-lu-jah!
3 Glo-ry to glo-ry all the way, Hal-le-lu-jah! Hal-le-lu-jah!
4 From strength to strength, from death to life, Hal-le-lu-jah! Hal-le-lu-jah!
5 With one con-tin-ual joy-ous sound, Hal-le-lu-jah! Hal-le-lu-jah!

W. SPENCER WALTON — LAUDAMUS 8.8.8.8.4 — Melody from VULPIUS

1 Cleans'd in our Sav-iour's prec-ious Blood, Fill'd with the ful-ness
2 Lean-ing our heads on Je-sus' breast, Know-ing the joy of
3 Kept by His pow'r from day to day, Held by His hand, we
4 Liv-ing in us His own pure life, Giv-ing us rest from
5 O what a Sav-iour we have found! Well may we make the

1 of our God, Walk-ing by faith the path He trod,
2 that sweet rest, Find-ing in Him the chief, the best,
3 can-not stray, Glo-ry to glo-ry all the way,
4 in-ward strife, From strength to strength, from death to life,
5 world re-sound, With one con-tin-ual joy-ous sound,

Hallelujah !—*Continued*

Hal - le - lu - jah! Hal - le - lu - jah! Hal - le - lu - jah!

29 ## Grateful Praise

SAMUEL MEDLEY GRATEFUL PRAISE L.M. ANON

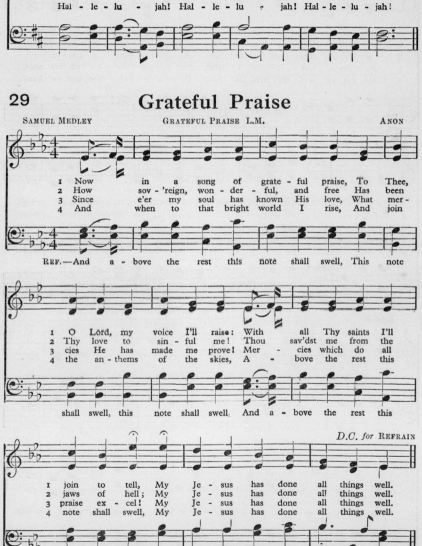

1 Now in a song of grate - ful praise, To Thee,
2 How sov - 'reign, won - der - ful, and free Has been
3 Since e'er my soul has known His love, What mer -
4 And when to that bright world I rise, And join

REF.—And a - bove the rest this note shall swell, This note

1 O Lord, my voice I'll raise: With all Thy saints I'll
2 Thy love to sin - ful me! Thou sav'dst me from the
3 cies He has made me prove! Mer - cies which do all
4 the an - thems of the skies, A - bove the rest this

shall swell, this note shall swell. And a - bove the rest this

D.C. for REFRAIN

1 join to tell, My Je - sus has done all things well.
2 jaws of hell; My Je - sus has done all things well.
3 praise ex - cel! My Je - sus has done all things well.
4 note shall swell, My Je - sus has done all things well.

note shall swell, My Je - sus has done all things well.

30 Redemption Ground

DANIEL W. WHITTLE   REDEMPTION GROUND L.M.D.   JAMES M'GRANAHAN

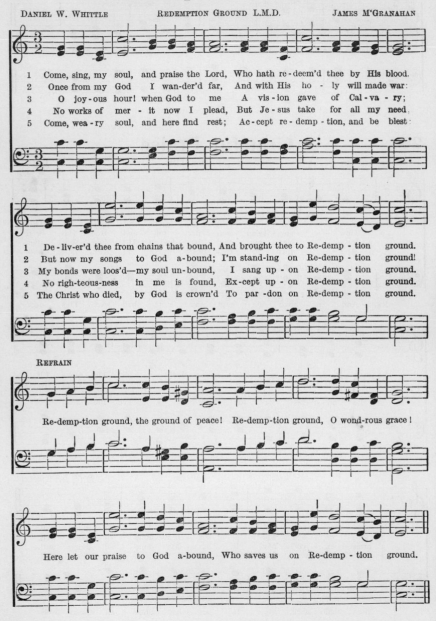

1 Come, sing, my soul, and praise the Lord, Who hath re-deem'd thee by His blood.
2 Once from my God I wan-der'd far, And with His ho - ly will made war:
3 O joy-ous hour! when God to me A vis-ion gave of Cal-va-ry;
4 No works of mer-it now I plead, But Je-sus take for all my need.
5 Come, wea-ry soul, and here find rest; Ac-cept re-demp-tion, and be blest:

1 De-liv-er'd thee from chains that bound, And brought thee to Re-demp-tion ground.
2 But now my songs to God a-bound; I'm stand-ing on Re-demp-tion ground!
3 My bonds were loos'd—my soul un-bound, I sang up-on Re-demp-tion ground.
4 No righ-teous-ness in me is found, Ex-cept up-on Re-demp-tion ground.
5 The Christ who died, by God is crown'd To par-don on Re-demp-tion ground.

REFRAIN

Re-demp-tion ground, the ground of peace! Re-demp-tion ground, O wond-rous grace!

Here let our praise to God a-bound, Who saves us on Re-demp-tion ground.

31 ## Worthy is the Lamb!

WILLIAM P. MACKAY   WORTHY 7.7.7.3.6.6.6.3   OLD MELODY

1 Worth - y, worth - y is the Lamb! . Worth - y, worth - y
2 We the crown of life shall wear, . We the palm of
3 And when land - ed safe a - bove . In the king - dom
4 Now re - vive Thy work, O Lord! . By Thy Spi - rit
5 Strike the stout - est sin - ner through, . Start the cry, 'What

1 is the Lamb! Worth - y, worth - y is the Lamb . That was slain!
2 vic - t'ry bear, All our Fa - ther's bless - ings share . In the Lamb,
3 of His love, We shall all the ful - ness prove . Of the Lamb.
4 and Thy Word; Now re - vive Thy work, O Lord! . Through the Lamb.
5 must I do?' Make him weep till born a - new . Through the Lamb.

REFRAIN

Praise Him, hal - le - lu - jah! Praise Him, hal - le - lu - jah!

Praise Him, hal - le - lu - jah! Praise the Lamb!

32 Praise, My Soul

H. F. LYTE PRAISE MY SOUL 8.7.8.7.8.7 JOHN GOSS

1 Praise, my soul, the King of hea - ven; To His
2 Praise Him for His grace and fa - vour; To our
3 Fa - ther - like He tends and spares . us; Well our
4 An - gels, help us to a - dore Him; Ye be -

1 feet thy tri - bute bring; Ran - som'd, heal'd, re - stor'd, for - giv - en,
2 fa - thers in dis - tress; Praise Him, still the same as ev - er,
3 fee - ble frame He knows; In His hands He gent - ly bears us,
4 hold Him face to face; Sun and moon, bow down be - fore Him;

1 Who like thee His praise shall sing? Praise Him! Praise Him!
2 Slow to chide and swift to bless; Praise Him! Praise Him!
3 Res - cues us from all our foes; Praise Him! Praise Him!
4 Dwell - ers all in time and space; Praise Him! Praise Him!

1 Praise Him! Praise Him! Praise the e - ver - last - ing King.
2 Praise Him! Praise Him! Glo - rious in His faith - ful - ness.
3 Praise Him! Praise Him! Wide - ly as His mer - cy flows.
4 Praise Him! Praise Him! Praise with us the God of grace.

The tune TRIUMPH is on the following page

32 Praise, My Soul

H. F. LYTE   TRIUMPH 8.7.8.7.8.7   H. J. GAUNTLETT

1 Praise, my soul, the King of hea - ven; To His feet thy tri - bute bring; Ran - som'd, heal'd, re - stor'd, for - giv - en, Who like Thee His praise shall sing? Praise Him! Praise Him! Praise Him! Praise Him! Praise the e - ver - last - ing King.

2 Praise Him for His grace and fa - vour To our fa - thers in dis - tress; Praise Him, still the same as ev - er, Slow to chide and swift to bless; Praise Him! Praise Him! Praise Him! Praise Him! Glo - rious in His faith - ful - ness.

3 Fa - ther - like He tends and spares us; Well our fee - ble frame He knows; In His hands He gen - tly bears us, Res - cues us from all our foes; Praise Him! Praise Him! Praise Him! Praise Him! Wide - ly as His mer - cy flows.

4 An - gels, help us to a - dore Him; Ye be - hold Him face to face; Sun and moon, bow down be - fore Him; Dwell - ers all in time and space Praise Him! Praise Him! Praise Him! Praise Him! Praise with us the God of grace.

The tune PRAISE MY SOUL is on the preceding page

33

Look, Ye Saints!

THOMAS KELLY   REGENT SQUARE 8.7.8.7.8.7   HENRY SMART

1 Look, ye saints! the sight is glor - ious; See the Man of
2 Crown the Sav - iour! an - gels, crown Him; Rich the tro - phies
3 Sin - ners in de - ris - ion crown'd Him, Mock - ing thus the
4 Hark, those bursts of ac - clam - a - tion! Hark, those loud tri -

1 Sor - rows now! From the fight re - turn vic - tor - ious,
2 Je - sus brings; In the seat of pow'r en - throne Him,
3 Sav - iour's claim; Saints and an - gels crowd a - round Him,
4 umph - ant chords! Je - sus takes the high - est sta - tion:

1 Ev - 'ry knee to Him shall bow; Crown Him! Crown Him!
2 While the vault of hea - ven rings; Crown Him! Crown Him!
3 Own His ti - tle, praise His Name; Crown Him! Crown Him!
4 O what joy the sight af - fords! Crown Him! Crown Him!

1 Crown Him! Crown Him! Crowns be - come the Vic - tor's brow.
2 Crown Him! Crown Him! Crown the Sav - iour King of kings!
3 Crown Him! Crown Him! Spread a - broad the Vic - tor's fame!
4 Crown Him! Crown Him King of kings, and Lord of lords!

The tune CWM RHONDDA is on the following page

33
Look, Ye Saints!

THOMAS KELLY   CWM RHONDDA, 8.7.8.7.8.7   JOHN HUGHES

1 Look ye saints! the sight is glor-ious; See the Man of Sor-rows now
2 Crown the Sav-iour! an-gels, crown Him! Rich the tro-phies Je-sus brings;
3 Sin-ners in de-ris-ion crown'd Him, Mock-ing thus the Sav-iour's claim;
4 Hark, those bursts of ac-clam-a-tion! Hark, those loud tri-umph-ant chords!

1 From the fight re-turn vic-tor-ious, Ev-'ry knee to Him shall bow;
2 In the seat of pow'r en-throne Him, While the vault of hea-ven rings;
3 Saints and an-gels crowd a-round Him, Own His ti-tle, praise His Name;
4 Je-sus takes the high-est sta-tion; O what joy the sight af-fords!

1 Crown Him! Crown Him! Crown Him! Crown Him! Crowns be-come the Vic-tor's
2 Crown Him! Crown Him! Crown Him! Crown Him! Crown the Sav-iour King of
3 Crown Him! Crown Him! Crown Him! Crown Him! Spread a-broad the Victor's
4 Crown Him! Crown Him! Crown Him! Crown Him! King of kings, and Lord of

1 brow! Vic-tor's brow! Crowns be-come the Vic-tor's brow!
2 kings! King of kings! Crown the Sav-iour King of kings!
3 fame! Vic-tor's fame! Spread a-broad the Vic-tor's fame!
4 lords! Lord of lords! King of kings, and Lord of lords!

By permission of Mrs. JOHN HUGHES, Tregarth, Pontypridd, Glam.
The tune REGENT SQUARE is on the preceding page

34   Who is He?

B. R. HANBY   LOWLINESS 7.7.8.8.7.7.   B. R. HANBY

1. Who is He in yon-der stall, At whose feet the shep-herds fall?
2. Who is He in deep dis-tress Fast-ing in the wil-der-ness?
3. Who is He the peo-ple bless For His words of gen-tle-ness?
4. Who is He to whom they bring All the sick and sor-row-ing?
5. Who is He that stands and weeps At the grave where Laz'-rus sleeps?

REFRAIN *Joyful*

'Tis the Lord! oh, wond-rous sto-ry! 'Tis the Lord, the King of glo-ry!

At His feet we hum-bly fall— Crown Him! crown Him, Lord of all!

VERSES 6 to 10

6. Who is He the gath'ring throng Greet with loud tri-umph-ant song?
7. Lo! at mid-night, who is He Prays in dark Geth-sem-an-e?
8. Who is He on yon-der tree Dies in grief and a-gon-y?
9. Who is He who from the grave Comes to suc-cour, help, and save?
10. Who is He who from His throne Rules through all the worlds a-lone?

The tune TIBERIAS is on the following page

Who is He?

34

B. R. Hanby

Tiberias 7.7. 8.8. 7.7.

J. Schmeidlin
Arr. P. J. Mansfield

1 Who is He in yon - der stall At whose feet the shep-herds fall?
2 Who is He in deep dis - tress Fast - ing in the wil - der - ness?
3 Who is He the peo - ple bless For His words of gen - tle - ness?
4 Who is He to whom they bring All the sick and sor - row - ing?
5 Who is He that stands and weeps At the grave where Laz'-rus sleeps?

REFRAIN

'Tis the Lord! O wond-rous sto - ry! 'Tis the Lord, the King of glo - ry!

At His feet we hum - bly fall— Crown Him! crown Him, Lord of all!

VERSES 6 TO 10

6 Who is He the gath'ring throng Greet with loud tri - umph-ant song?
7 Lo! at mid - night, who is He Prays in dark Geth - sem - an - e?
8 Who is He on yon - der tree Dies in grief and a - gon - y?
9 Who is He who from the grave Comes to suc - cour, help, and save?
10 Who is He who from His throne Rules thro' all the worlds a - lone?

The tune LOWLINESS is on the preceding page

35 Glory to God, Hallelujah!

Fanny J. Crosby

William J. Kirkpatrick

1 We are nev-er, nev-er wear-y of the grand old
2 We are lost a-mid the rap-ture of re-deem-ing
3 We are go-ing to a pal-ace that is built of
4 There we'll shout re-deem-ing mer-cy in a glad new

1 song; Glo - ry to God, . hal - le - lu - jah!
2 love; Glo - ry to God, . hal - le - lu - jah!
3 gold; Glo - ry to God, . hal - le - lu - jah!
4 song; Glo - ry to God, . hal - le - lu - jah!

1 We can sing it loud as ev-er with our faith more strong;
2 We are ris-ing on its pin-ions to the hills a - bove;
3 Where the King in all His splen-dour we shall soon be - hold;
4 There we'll sing the praise of Je-sus with the blood-wash'd throng;

1-4 Glo - ry to God, . hal - le - lu - jah!

Glory to God, Hallelujah!—*Continued*

REFRAIN

O the chil - dren of the Lord have a right to

shout and sing! For the way is grow - ing bright,

and our souls are on the wing; We are go - ing

by - and - bye to the pal - ace of a King;

Glo - ry to God, . hal - le - lu - jah!

Revive Us Again

36

WM. P. MACKAY   MORNINGSIDE   English Air

1. We praise Thee, O God, for the Son of Thy love,
2. We praise Thee, O God, for Thy Spir - it of light,
3. All glo - ry and praise to the Lamb that was slain,
4. All glo - ry and praise to the God of all grace,
5. Re - vive us a - gain; fill each heart with Thy love;

1. For Je - sus who died, and is now gone a - bove.
2. Who has shown us our Sav - iour, and scat - tered our night.
3. Who has borne all our sins, and has cleansed ev - 'ry stain.
4. Who has bought us, and sought us, and guid - ed our way.
5. May each soul be re - kin - dled with fire from a - bove.

CHORUS

Hal - le - lu - jah! Thine the glo - ry, Hal - le - lu - jah, A - men.

Hal - le - lu - jah! Thine the glo - ry, Re - vive us a - gain.

37 Thrice Blessed Ground

JOHN GAMBOLD   MORNINGSIDE   *Irregular*   *English Air*

1. My God, I have found The thrice bles - sed ground,
2. 'Tis found in the blood Of Him who once stood
3. He bore on the tree The sen - tence for me,
4. And though here be - low 'Mid sor - row and woe,
5. And this I shall find For such is His mind

1. Where life and where joy and true com - fort a - bound.
2. My re - fuge and safe - ty, my sure - ty with God.
3. And now both the sure - ty and sin - ner are free.
4. My place is in hea - ven with Je - sus I know.
5. "He'll not be in glo - ry and leave me be - hind,"

REFRAIN

Hal - le - lu - jah! Thine the glo - ry, Hal - le - lu - jah! A - men.

Ha - le - lu - jah! Thine the glo - ry, Re - vive us a - gain!

38 Sound His Praises

H. BONAR   MORNINGSIDE   English Air

1. Re - joice and be glad! the Re - deem - er has come!
2. Re - joice and be glad! it is sun - shine at last!
3. Re - joice and be glad! for the blood hath been shed;
4. Re - joice and be glad! now the par - don is free!
5. Re - joice and be glad! for the Lamb that was slain
6. Re - joice and be glad! for our King is on high;
7. Re - joice and be glad! for He com - eth a - gain;

1. Go, look on His cra - dle, His Cross, and His tomb.
2. The clouds have de - part - ed, the sha - dows are past.
3. Re - demp - tion is fin - ished, the price hath been paid.
4. The Just for the un - just has died on the tree.
5. O'er death is tri - um - phant, and liv - eth a - gain.
6. He plead - eth for us on His throne in the sky.
7. He com - eth in glo - ry the Lamb that was slain.

CHORUS

Sound His prais - es, tell the sto - ry of Him who was slain!

Sound His prais - es, tell with glad - ness, He liv - eth a - gain!
(*Last verse*) He com - eth a - gain!

We Plough the Fields

39

M. CLADIUS   WIR PFLÜGEN 7.6.7.6.D   J. A. P. SCHULZ

1 We plough the fields, and scat - ter The good seed o'er the land, But it is fed
2 He on - ly is the Ma - ker Of all things near and far; He paints the way-
3 We thank Thee then, O Fa - ther, For all things bright and good, The seed-time and

1 and wa - ter'd By God's al-might-y hand; He sends the snow in win - ter,
2 side flow - er, He lights the ev-'ning star; The winds and waves o - bey Him,
3 the har - vest, Our life, our health, our food: Ac - cept the gifts we of - fer

1 The warmth to swell the grain, The breez-es and the sun-shine, And soft re-fresh-ing rain.
2 By Him the birds are fed; Much more to us His chil-dren He gives our dai - ly bread,
3 For all Thy love im-parts, And, what Thou most de-sir-est, Our hum-ble, thank-ful hearts.

REFRAIN

All good gifts a - round us Are sent from heav'n a - bove,

Then thank the Lord. O thank the Lord, For all . . . . His love.

40 Come, All Ye Faithful

WM. MERCER (*tr.*)   ADESTE FIDELES *Irregular*   18th Century Melody

1 O come, all ye faith - ful! Joy - ful - ly tri - umph - ant,
2 Raise, raise, choirs of an - gels, Songs of loud - est tri - umph,
3 A - men! Lord, we bless Thee, Born for our sal - va - tion!

1 To Beth - le - hem has - ten now with glad ac - cord;
2 Thro' hea - ven's high arch - es be your prais - es pour'd:
3 O Je - sus! for ev - er be Thy Name a - dor'd;

1 Lo! in a man - ger Lies the King of an - gels;
2 Now to our God be Glo - ry in the high - est;
3 Word of the Fa - ther, Late in flesh ap - pear - ing;

REFRAIN :||:

O come, let us a - dore Him, O come, let us a - dore Him,

O come, let us a - dore Him, Christ the Lord!

41 A Firm Foundation

RICHARD KEEN   MONTGOMERY 11.11.11.11   J. STANLEY

1. How firm a found - a - tion, ye saints of the Lord,
2. Fear not, I am with thee, O be not dis - mayed!
3. When through the deep wat - ers I call thee to go,
4. The soul that on Je - sus hath leaned for re - pose,

1. Is laid for your faith in His ex - cel - lent Word!
2. I, I am thy God and will still give thee aid:
3. The riv - ers of grief shall not thee o - ver - flow:
4. I will not, I will not, de - sert to its foes!

1. What more can He say than to you He hath said,
2. I'll strength - en thee, help thee, and cause thee to stand,
3. For I will be with thee in trou - ble to bless;
4. That soul, though all hell should en - deav - our to shake,

1. You who un - to Je - sus for re - fuge have fled?
2. Up - held by My right - eous, om - ni - po - tent hand.
3. And sanc - ti - fy to thee thy deep - est dis - tress.
4. I'll nev - er, no, nev - er, no, nev - er for - sake!

May also be sung to ADESTE FIDELES, No. 40

3

42 The Herald Angels

CHARLES WESLEY   MENDELSSOHN 7.7.7.7.7.7.D.   MENDELSSOHN

1 Hark! the her-ald ang-els sing, "Glo-ry to the new-born King.
2 Christ, by high-est heav'n a - dored, Christ, the ev - er - last-ing Lord.
3 Hail, the heav'n-born Prince of Peace! Hail, the Sun of Right-eous-ness!

1 Peace on earth and mer-cy mild, God and sin-ners re - con-ciled."
2 Late in time be - hold Him come, Off-spring of a Vir-gin's womb.
3 Light and life to all He brings, Ris'n with heal-ing in His wings.

1 Joy-ful, all ye na-tions rise, Join the tri - umph of the skies;
2 Veil'd in flesh the God-head see! Hail, the Incarnate De - i - ty!
3 Mild He lays His glo-ry by, Born that man no more may die.

1 With th' an - gel - ic host pro - claim, "Christ is born in Beth-le-hem.
2 Pleased as Man with man to dwell, Je - sus our Em - man - u - el.
3 Born to raise the sons of earth, Born to give them se - cond birth.

REFRAIN

Hark! the her-ald an - gels sing, "Glo-ry to the new-born King."

Org.

By permission of NOVELLO & CO., LTD.

43 Ten Thousand Times

HENRY ALFORD   ALFORD 7.6.8.6.D   J. B. DYKES

1 Ten thous-and times ten thous-and, In spark-ling rai-ment bright,
2 What rush of Al - le - lu - ias Fills all the earth and sky!
3 O then what rap-tur'd greet-ings On Ca-naan's hap - py shore,

1 The arm - ies of the ran-som'd saints Throng up the steps of light;
2 What ring - ing of a thous-and harps Be - speaks the tri-umph nigh!
3 What knit - ting se - ver'd friend-ships up Where part - ings are no more!

1 'Tis fin-ish'd! all is fin-ish'd, Their fight with death and sin;
2 O day, for which cre - a - tion And all its tribes were made!
3 Then eyes with joy shall spar - kle That brimm'd with tears of late:

1 Fling o - pen wide the gold - en gates, And let the vic - tors in.
2 O joy, for all its form - er woes A thous-and-fold re - paid!
3 Or - phans no long - er fa - ther-less, Nor wi - dows des - o - late.

44 Prince of Peacemakers

F. W. WARE   PEACEMAKERS 12.12.12.12. D   J. E. GLINES

1. He hath spo-ken, Be still! the Re-bu-ker of seas:
2. He hath quick-en'd my soul by a life from a-bove,
3. He's a won-der-ful Je-sus, this Sav-iour of mine;
4. I will love Him and serve Him from now till I die;

1. The com-mand was for me, and my heart is at ease;
2. It was done by the Spi-rit, its es-sence is love;
3. He's the great Son of God, a Re-deem-er di-vine;
4. For His love fills my heart, and His beau-ty my eye;

p rall.   *cres.*

1. He hath hush'd in-to si-lence the waves and the winds
2. He hath par-don'd and wash'd me as white as the snow,
3. He's my Strength and my Wis-dom, my Life and my Lord,
4. He's the fair-est and dear-est of all to my soul,

1. By ap-ply-ing His blood, and re-mov-ing my sins.
2. And my heart with His love does this mo-ment o'er-flow.
3. And en-thron'd in my heart to be lov'd and a-dor'd.
4. And our lives shall be one while e-ter-ni-ties roll.

Prince of Peacemakers—*Continued*

REFRAIN   *Faster*

He's the Prince of Peace - mak - ers, all glo - ry to God!

To re - deem me and cleanse me He shed His own blood;

My a - dop - tion is seal'd, I'm a child of the King,

And for e - ver and e - ver of Je - sus I'll sing.

45 Rest of the Weary

JOHN S. B. MONSELL   THEODORA 5.4.5.4.D   ALFRED LEGGE

1 Rest of the wea - ry, Joy of the sad;
2 Pil - low where, ly - ing, Love rests its head;
3 When my feet stum - ble I to Thee cry,
4 E - ver con - fess - ing Thee, I will raise

1 Hope of the drea - ry, Light of the glad;
2 Peace of the dy - ing, Life of the dead;
3 Crown of the hum - ble, Cross of the high;
4 Un - to Thee bless - ing, Glo - ry, and praise:

1 Home of the strang - er, Strength to the end;
2 Path of the low - ly, Prize at the end;
3 When my steps wan - der O - ver me bend,
4 All my en - deav - our, World with - out end,

1 Re - fuge from dan - ger, Sav - iour and Friend!
2 Breath of the ho - ly, Sav - iour and Friend!
3 Tru - er and fond - er, Sav - iour and Friend!
4 Thine to be ev - er, Sav - iour and Friend!

Music by permission of Miss T. C. M. LEGGE

The tune ST. CECILIA NEW is on the following page

45 Rest of the Weary

JOHN S. B. MONSELL   ST. CECILIA NEW 5.4.5.4.D   M. A. SIDEBOTHAM

1 Rest of the wea - ry, . Joy of the sad;
2 Pil - low where, ly - ing, . Love rests its head;
3 When my feet stum - ble . I to Thee cry,
4 E - ver con - fess - ing . Thee, I will raise

1 Hope of the drea - ry, . Light of the glad; .
2 Peace of the dy - ing, . Life of the dead; .
3 Crown of the hum - ble, . Cross of the high; .
4 Un - to Thee bless - ing, . Glo - ry, and praise: .

1 Home . of the strang - er, . Strength to the
2 Path . of the low - ly, . Prize . at the
3 When . my steps wan - der . O - ver me
4 All . my en - deav - our, . World with - out

1 end; . . Re - fuge from dan - ger, Sav - iour and Friend !
2 end; . . Breath of the ho - ly, Sav - iour and Friend !
3 bend, . . Tru - er and fond - er, Sav - iour and Friend !
4 end, . . Thine to be ev - er, Sav - iour and Friend !

The tune THEODORA is on the preceding page

46 # Joyful Pilgrims

CARRIE M. WILSON

JNO. R. SWENEY

1 Sing on, ye joy-ful pil-grims, Nor think the mo-ments long;
2 Sing on, ye joy-ful pil-grims, While here on earth we stay
3 Sing on, ye joy-ful pil-grims, The time will not be long

1 My faith is heav'n-ward ris — ing with ev-'ry tune-ful song;
2 Let songs of home and Je — sus Be-guile each fleet-ing day;
3 Till in our Fa-ther's king — dom We swell a no-bler song,

1 Lo! on the mount of bless — ing, The glo-rious mount I stand.
2 Sing on the grand old sto — ry Of His re-deem-ing love,
3 Where those we love are wait — ing To greet us on the shore,

1 And, look-ing o-ver Jor — dan, I see the prom-is'd land.
2 The ev-er-last-ing cho — rus That fills the realms a-bove.
3 We'll meet be-yond the ri — ver Where sur-ges roll no more.

Joyful Pilgrims—*Continued*

REFRAIN

Sing on; O bliss - ful mu - sic! With ev - 'ry

note you raise My heart is filled with rap - ture,

My soul is lost in praise; Sing on; O
Sing on; bliss - ful,

bliss - ful mu - sic! With ev - 'ry note you raise
bliss - ful mu - sic!

My heart is filled with rap - ture, My soul is lost in praise.

47 O God, our Help!

ISAAC WATTS ST. ANNE C.M. WILLIAM CROFT

1 O God, our help in a-ges past, Our hope for years to come.
2 Un-der the sha-dow of Thy throne Thy saints have dwelt se-cure;
3 Be-fore the hills in or-der stood, Or earth re-ceiv'd her frame,
4 A thou-sand a-ges in Thy sight Are like an ev-'ning gone,
5 Time, like an e-ver-roll-ing stream, Bears all its sons a-way;
6 O God, our help in a-ges past, Our hope for years to come,

1 Our shel-ter from the storm-y blast, And our e-ter-nal home!
2 Suf-fi-cient is Thine arm a-lone, And our de-fence is sure.
3 From e-ver-last-ing Thou art God, To end-less years the same.
4 Short as the watch that ends the night Be-fore the ris-ing sun.
5 They fly for-got-ten, as a dream Dies at the op-'ning day.
6 Be Thou our guard while trou-bles last, And our e-ter-nal home!

ISAAC WATTS FAUX BOURDON SETTING MARTIN SHAW

1 O God, our help in a-ges past, Our hope for years to come,
2 Un-der the sha-dow of Thy throne Thy saints have dwelt se-cure;
3 Be-fore the hills in or-der stood, Or earth re-ceive'd her frame,
4 A thou-sand a-ges in Thy sight Are like an ev-'ning gone,
5 Time, like an e-ver-roll-ing stream, Bears all its sons a-way;
6 O God, our help in a-ges past, Our hope for years to come,

1 Our shel-ter from the storm-y blast, And our e-ter-nal home!
2 Suf-fi-cient is Thine arm a-lone, And our de-fence is sure.
3 From e-ver-last-ing Thou art God, To end-less years the same.
4 Short as the watch that ends the night Be-fore the ris-ing sun.
5 They fly for-got-ten, as a dream Dies at the op-'ning day.
6 Be Thou our guard while trou-bles last, And our e-ter-nal home!

By permission of J. CURWEN & SONS, LTD., Edition No. 6300

48

Eternal Father

WILLIAM WHITING   MELITA 8.8 8.8 8.8   J. B. DYKES

1 E - ter - nal Fa - ther, strong to save, Whose arm hath bound the
2 O Christ! Whose voice the wa - ters heard, And hush'd their rag - ing
3 O Ho - ly Spi - rit! Who did'st brood Up - on the wa - ters
4 O Trin - i - ty of love and pow'r! Our breth-ren shield in

1 rest - less wave, Who bidd'st the might - y o - cean deep Its
2 at Thy word; Who walk - edst on the foam - ing deep, And
3 dark and rude, And bid their an - gry tu - mult cease, And
4 dan - ger's hour; From rock and tem - pest, fire and foe, Pro -

p

1 own ap - point - ed li - mits keep: O hear us when we
2 calm a - mid the storm did'st sleep: O hear us when we
3 give, for wild con - fus - ion, peace: O hear us when we
4 tect them where - so - e'er they go: Thus e - ver - more shall

1-3 cry to Thee For those in per - il on the sea!
4 rise to Thee Glad hymns of praise from land and sea.

49   O Lord of Heaven!

CHRISTOPHER WORDSWORTH   ALMSGIVING 8.8.8.4   JOHN B. DYKES

1. O Lord of heav'n and earth and sea!
   To Thee all praise and glo-ry be;
   show our love to Thee, Who giv-est all?
2. Thou didst not spare Thine on-ly Son,
   But gav'st Him for a world un-done;
   with the bless-ed One Thou giv-est all.
3. We lose what on our-selves we spend,
   We have as treas-ure with-out end
   Lord, to Thee we lend, Who giv-est all.
4. To Thee, from whom we all de-rive
   Our life, our gifts, our pow'r to give;
   e-ver with Thee live! Who giv-est all.

50   The One Foundation

SAMUEL J. STONE   AURELIA 7.6.7.6. D   SAMUEL S. WESLEY

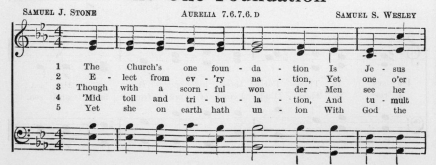

1. The Church's one foun-da-tion Is Je-sus
2. E-lect from ev-'ry na-tion, Yet one o'er
3. Though with a scorn-ful won-der Men see her
4. 'Mid toil and tri-bu-la-tion, And tu-mult
5. Yet she on earth hath un-ion With God the

The One Foundation—*Continued*

1 Christ her Lord: She is His new cre - a - tion By
2 all the earth, Her char - ter of sal - va - tion One
3 sore op - press'd, By schisms rent a - sun - der, By
4 of her war, She waits the con - su - ma - tion Of
5 Three in One, And mys - tic sweet com - mun - ion With

1 wa - ter and the Word; From heav'n He came and
2 Lord, one faith, one birth: One ho - ly Name she
3 her - e - sies dis - tress'd; Yet saints their watch are
4 peace for e - ver - more, Till with the vis - ion
5 those whose rest is won. O hap - py ones and

1 sought her To be His ho - ly bride; With His own
2 bless - es, Par - takes one ho - ly food, And to one
3 keep - ing, Their cry goes up, 'How long?' And soon the
4 glor - ious Her long - ing eyes are blest, And the great
5 ho - ly! Lord, give us grace that we, Like them, the

1 blood He bought her, And for her life He died.
2 hope she press - es, With ev - 'ry grace en - dued.
3 night of weep - ing Shall be the morn of song.
4 Church vic - tor - ious Shall be the Church at rest.
5 meek and low - ly, On high may dwell with Thee.

51 O Jesus, I have Promised

J. E. BODE   DAY OF REST 7.6. 7.6. D   J. W. ELLIOTT

1 O Je - sus, I have prom - ised To serve Thee to the end;
2 O let me feel Thee near me; The world is ev - er near;
3 O let me hear Thee speak - ing In ac - cents clear and still,
4 O Je - sus, Thou hast prom - ised, To all who fol - low Thee,

1 Be Thou for ev - er near me, My Mas - ter and my Friend:
2 I see the sights that daz - zle, The tempt-ing sounds I hear;
3 A - bove the storms of pas - sion, The mur - murs of self - will;
4 That where Thou art in glo - ry There shall Thy ser - vant be;

1 I shall not fear the bat - tle If Thou art by my side,
2 My foes are ev - er near me, A - round me and with - in;
3 O speak to re - as - sure me, To hast - en or con - trol;
4 And, Je - sus, I have prom - ised To serve Thee to the end;

1 Nor wan - der from the path - way If Thou wilt be my Guide,
2 But, Je - sus, draw Thou near - er, And shield my soul from sin,
3 O speak, and make me list - en, Thou Guard-ian of my soul,
4 O give me grace to fol - low, My Mas - ter and my Friend.

52   Stand Up for Jesus

GEORGE DUFFIELD   MORNING LIGHT 7.6.7.6.D.   G. J. WEBB

1. Stand up! stand up for Jesus, Ye soldiers of the Cross!
2. Stand up! stand up for Jesus! The trumpet call obey;
3. Stand up! stand up for Jesus! Stand in His strength alone:
4. Stand up! stand up for Jesus! The strife will not be long;

1. Lift high His royal banner; It must not suffer loss.
2. Forth to the mighty conflict, In this His glorious day;
3. The arm of flesh will fail you, Ye dare not trust your own;
4. This day the noise of battle, The next the victor's song:

1. From vict'ry unto vict'ry His army shall He lead,
2. Ye that are men now serve Him Against unnumbered foes;
3. Put on the gospel armour, Each piece put on with prayer;
4. To Him that overcometh, A crown of life shall be;

1. Till ev'ry foe is vanquished, And Christ is Lord indeed.
2. Let courage rise with danger, And strength to strength oppose.
3. Where duty calls, or danger, Be never wanting there.
4. He with the King of glory Shall reign eternally.

The tune by ADAM GEIBEL is on the following page

52 Stand Up for Jesus

GEORGE DUFFIELD

ADAM GEIBEL

1 Stand up! stand up for Je - sus, Ye sol - diers of the Cross
2 Stand up! stand up for Je - sus, The trum - pet call o - bey
3 Stand up! stand up for Je - sus, Stand in His strength a - lone
4 Stand up! stand up for Je - sus, The strife will not be long

1 Lift high His roy - al ban - ner, It must not suf - fer loss:
2 Forth to the migh - ty con - flict, In this His glo - rious day:
3 The arm of flesh will fail you, Ye dare not trust your own;
4 This day the noise of bat - tle, The next the vic - tor's song:

1 From vic - t'ry un - to vic - t'ry His ar - my shall He lead,
2 Ye that are men now serve Him A - gainst un - num - ber'd foes;
3 Put on the Gos - pel ar - mour, And watch - ing un - to pray'r,
4 To him that o - ver - com - eth, A crown of life shall be

Stand Up for Jesus—*Continued*

1 Till ev-'ry foe is van-quish'd, And Christ is Lord in-deed.
2 Let cou-rage rise with dan-ger, And strength to strength op-pose.
3 Where du-ty calls, or dan-ger, Be nev-er want-ing there.
4 He with the King of glo-ry Shall reign e-ter-nal-ly.

REFRAIN *Harmony*

Stand up for Je-sus, Ye sol-diers of the

Stand up, stand up for Je-sus,

Cross! Lift high His roy-al ban-ner, It

must not! It must not suf-fer loss!

The tune MORNING LIGHT precedes this one

53 Thine Arm, O Lord

E. H. PLUMPTRE   ST. MATTHEW, C.M.D   WILLIAM CROFT

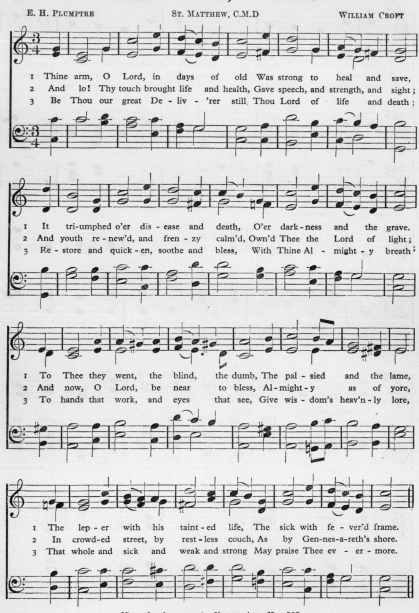

1 Thine arm, O Lord, in days of old Was strong to heal and save,
2 And lo! Thy touch brought life and health, Gave speech, and strength, and sight;
3 Be Thou our great De-liv-'rer still, Thou Lord of life and death;

1 It tri-umphed o'er dis-ease and death, O'er dark-ness and the grave.
2 And youth re-new'd, and fren-zy calm'd, Own'd Thee the Lord of light;
3 Re-store and quick-en, soothe and bless, With Thine Al-might-y breath;

1 To Thee they went, the blind, the dumb, The pal-sied and the lame,
2 And now, O Lord, be near to bless, Al-might-y as of yore,
3 To hands that work, and eyes that see, Give wis-dom's heav'n-ly lore,

1 The lep-er with his taint-ed life, The sick with fe-ver'd frame.
2 In crowd-ed street, by rest-less couch, As by Gen-nes-a-reth's shore.
3 That whole and sick and weak and strong May praise Thee ev-er-more.

May also be sung to NORSE AIR, No. 332

The Angel's Song

54

ROBERT LOWRY

ROBERT LOWRY (*Arr.*)

1 Roll - ing down-ward   through the mid - night   Comes a glo - rious
2 Won-d'ring shep-herds   see   the glo - ry,   Hear   the word   the
3 Christ the Sa - viour,   God's A-noint - ed,   Comes to earth   our

1 burst of heav'n - ly   song;   'Tis   a cho - rus   full   of sweet-ness—
2 shin - ing ones de - clare;   At   the man - ger   fall   in wor-ship,
3 fear - ful debt   to   pay;   Man   of sor-rows,   and   re - ject - ed,

REFRAIN

1 And the sing - ers   are an an - gel   throng.
2 While the mu - sic fills the quiv-'ring   air.   } 'Glo - ry! glo - ry
3 Lamb of God, that takes our sin   a - way.   } 'Glo-ry! glo-ry! glo-ry!

in   the high-est!   On   the earth good-will and peace to men!'   Down the

a - ges   send the e - cho; Let   the glad earth shout   a - gain!
a-ges, down the a-ges

55 Mighty to Save

F. BOTTOME

W. B. BRADBURY

1 O bliss of the pu-ri-fied! bliss of the free! I
2 O bliss of the pu-ri-fied! Je-sus is mine, No
3 O bliss of the pu-ri-fied! bliss of the pure! No
4 O Je-sus the cru-ci-fied! Thee will I sing! My

1 plunge in the crim-son tide o-pen'd for me; O'er sin and un-
2 long-er in dread con-dem-na-tion I pine; In con-scious sal-
3 wound hath the soul that His blood can-not cure; No sor-row-bow'd
4 bless-ed Re-deem-er, my God, and my King! My soul, filled with

1 clean-ness ex-ult-ing I stand, And point to the print of the
2 va-tion I'll sing of His grace, Who lift-ed up-on me the
3 head but may sweet-ly find rest; No tears, but may dry them on
4 rap-ture, shall shout o'er the grave, And tri-umph in death in the

REFRAIN

1 nails in His hand.
2 light of His face.
3 Je-sus-'s breast.
4 Might-y to Save.
} O sing of His might-y love; Sing of His

might-y love! Sing of His might-y love, Might-y to Save!

56 Sing the Love of Jesus

HARRIET E. JONES   MATCHLESS LOVE 8.7.8.7.D   CHAS. H. GABRIEL

1 Sing, O sing, the dear old story Of our Sa-viour's match-less love;
2 Sing of love to you so pre-cious, Tell, in song, how Je-sus died;
3 Ye re-deem'd ones, sing the sto-ry! Sing it o'er and o'er a - gain,

1 Sing of Je - sus and His glo-ry With the ran-som'd host a - bove.
2 Let sweet mu - sic draw the mill-ions to the dear Re-deem-er's side.
3 Un - til ev - 'ry tribe and na-tion Join to sing the glad re - frain.

REFRAIN

Sing, O sing . . . . the love of Je - sus, Sound His
Sing, O sing the love, the love of Je - sus,

prais - es far and near, . . Sing the won - drous sto-ry
Sound His prais - es, prais - es far and near, Sing the won-drous sto-ry

o - ver, Till the whole . . . wide world shall hear.
o - ver, Till the whole wide world shall hear.

57 A Thousand Tongues

CHARLES WESLEY   Evan C.M.   W. H. HAVERGAL

1 O for a thous-and tongues to sing My great Re-deem-er's praise!
2 My gra-cious Mas-ter and my God As-sist me to pro-claim,
3 Je-sus! the Name that charms our fears, That bids our sor-rows cease:
4 He breaks the pow'r of can-cell'd sin, He sets the pris'-ner free;

1 The glo-ries of my God and King, The tri-umphs of His grace.
2 And spread thro' all the earth a-broad The hon-ours of Thy Name.
3 'Tis mu-sic in the sin-ner's ears, 'Tis life and health and peace.
4 His blood can make the foul-est clean, His blood a-vail'd for me.

CHARLES WESLEY   LYDIA C.M.   THOMAS PHILLIPS

1 O for a thous-and tongues to sing My great Re-
2 My gra-cious Mas-ter and my God! As-sist me
3 Je-sus! the Name that charms our fears, That bids our
4 He breaks the pow'r of can-cell'd sin, He sets the

1 deem-er's praise! The glo-ries of my God and King, The
2 to pro-claim And spread thro' all the earth a-broad The
3 sor-rows cease; 'Tis mu-sic in the sin-ner's ears, 'Tis
4 pris'-ner free; His blood can make the foul-est clean, His

A Thousand Tongues—*Continued*

CHARLES WESLEY   TIVERTON C.M.   F. T. GRIGG

1 tri-umphs of His grace, The tri-umphs of His grace.
2 hon-ours of Thy Name, The hon-ours of Thy Name.
3 life and health and peace, 'Tis life and health and peace.
4 blood a-vail'd for me, His blood a-vail'd for me.

1 O for a thous-and tongues to sing My
2 My grac-ious Mas-ter and my God As-
3 Je-sus! the Name that charms our fears, That
4 He breaks the pow'r of can-cell'd sin, He

1 great Re-deem-er's praise! The glo-ries of my
2 sist me to pro-claim, And spread thro' all the
3 bids our sor-row's cease; 'Tis mu-sic in the
4 sets the pris'-ner free; His blood can make the

1 God and King, The tri-umphs of His grace.
2 earth a-broad The hon-ours of Thy Name.
3 sin-ner's ears, 'Tis life and health and peace.
4 foul-est clean, His blood a-vail'd for me.

For the two CHOIR SETTINGS see No. 936

58 O for a Faith!

W. H. BATHURST   ST. LEONARD C.M.   HENRY SMART

1 O for a faith that will not shrink, Tho' press'd by many a foe,
2 That will not mur-mur nor com-plain Be-neath the chast-'ning rod,
3 A faith that shines more bright and clear When tem-pests rage with-out,
4 A faith that keeps the nar-row way Till life's last spark is fled,
5 Lord, give me such a faith as this! And then, what-e'er may come,

1 That will not trem-ble on the brink Of pov-er-ty or woe!
2 But, in the hour of grief and pain, Can lean up-on its God.
3 That when in dan-ger knows no fear, In dark-ness feels no doubt.
4 And with a pure and heav'n-ly ray Lights up a dy-ing bed!
5 I taste e'en now the hal-low'd bliss Of an e-ter-nal home.

59 Come, let us Return

JOHN MORISON   CHELSEA C.M.   THOMAS ATTWOOD

1 Come, let us to the Lord our God With
2 His voice com-mands the tem-pest forth, And
3 Long hath the night of sor-row reign'd, The
4 Our hearts, if God we seek to know, Shall
5 As dew up-on the ten-der herb Dif-
6 So shall His pres-ence bless our souls, And

1 con-trite hearts re-turn; Our God is grac-ious,
2 stills the storm-y wave; And though His arm be
3 dawn shall bring us light; God shall ap-pear, and
4 know Him, and re-joice; His com-ing like the
5 fus-ing fra-grance round; As show'rs that ush-er
6 shed a joy-ful light; That hal-low'd morn shall

Come, let us Return—*Continued*

```
1 nor    will   leave   The   des - o - late   to   mourn.
2 strong to     smite,  'Tis  al - so  strong  to   save.
3 we     shall  rise    With  glad - ness  in  His  sight.
4 morn   shall  be,     Like  morn - ing  songs His  voice.
5 in     the    spring, And   cheer  the  thirs - ty ground.
6 chase  a - way The    sor - rows  of   the  night.
```

JOHN MORISON   KALTENTHAL C.M.   JOHANN G. FRECH

```
1 Come,  let   us    to    the   Lord  our   God   With
2 His    voice com - mands the   tem - pest forth, And
3 Long   hath  the   night of    sor - row  reign'd, The
4 Our    hearts, if  God   we    seek  to    know,  Shall
5 As     dew   up - on    the   ten - der  herb  Dif -
6 So     shall His   pres - ence bless our   souls, And
```

```
1 con - trite hearts re - turn;   Our   God   is   grac - ious,
2 stills the   storm - y  wave;    And   though His  arm   be
3 dawn  shall  bring  us   light;   God   shall  ap - pear, and
4 know  Him,   and   re - joice;   His   com - ing  like the
5 fus - ing   fra - grance round;  As   show'rs that ush - er
6 shed  a     joy - ful light;     That  hal - low'd morn shall
```

```
1 nor    will   leave   The   des - o - late   to   mourn.
2 strong to     smite,  'Tis  al - so  strong  to   save
3 we     shall  rise    With  glad - ness  in  His  sight.
4 morn   shall  be,     Like  morn - ing  songs His  voice.
5 in     the    spring, And   cheer  the  thirs - ty ground.
6 chase  a - way The    sor - rows  of   the  night.
```

60 Hark, the Glad Sound!

PHILIP DODDRIDGE   BELGRAVE C.M.   WILLIAM HORSLEY

1 Hark, the glad sound! the Sa-viour comes, The   Sa - viour prom-ised long;
2 He comes, the pris'-ners to re-lease, In   Sa - tan's bond-age held;
3 He comes, from thick-est films of vice, To   clear the men-tal ray;
4 He comes, the bro-ken heart to bind, The   bleed-ing soul to cure;
5 Our glad hos-an-nas, Prince of Peace, Thy   wel - come shall pro-claim;

1 Let ev-'ry heart pre-pare a throne, And ev-'ry voice a song.
2 The gates of brass be-fore Him burst, The i-ron fet-ters yield.
3 And on the eye-balls of the blind To pour ce-lest-ial day.
4 And with the treas-ures of His grace To enrich the hum-ble poor.
5 And heaven's e-ter-nal arch-es ring With Thy be-lov-ed Name.

61 O Thou My Soul!

T. STERNHOLD   FRENCH C.M.   SCOTTISH PSALTER, 1615

1 O Thou, my soul, bless God the Lord, And all that in me is,
2 Bless O my soul, the Lord thy God, And not for-get-ful be,
3 All thine in-i-qui-ties Who doth Most gra-cious-ly for-give;
4 Who doth re-deem thy life, that thou To death may'st not go down:

1 Be stirr-ed up, His ho-ly Name To mag-ni-fy and bless.
2 Of all His gra-cious ben-e-fits He hath be-stow'd on thee.
3 Who thy dis-eas-es all and pains Doth heal and thee re-lieve.
4 Who thee with lov-ing kind-ness doth And ten-der mer-cies crown.

An Alternative Tune is on the following page

61 O Thou My Soul!

T. STERNHOLD

JAS. McGRANAHAN

1 O Thou, my soul, bless God the Lord, And all that in me is,
2 Bless, O my soul, the Lord thy God, And not for - get - ful be,
3 All thine in - i - qui - ties Who dost Most gra - cious - ly for - give;
4 Who doth re - deem thy life, that thou To death may'st not go down:

1 Be stirr - ed up, His ho - ly Name To mag - ni - fy and bless!
2 Of all His gra - cious ben - e - fits He hath be - stow'd on thee.
3 Who thy dis - eas - es all and pains Doth heal and thee re - lieve.
4 Who thee with lov - ing kind - ness doth And ten - der mer - cies crown.

REFRAIN

Bless the Lord, . . . O my soul! . . Bless the Lord, O my soul!
Bless the Lord, O my soul!

And all that is with - in me Bless His ho - ly Name!
Bless His ho - ly Name!

The tune FRENCH is on the preceding page

62   I to the Hills

W. Whittingham   Kilmarnock C.M.   Neil Dougall

1 I to the hills will lift mine eyes, From whence doth come mine aid.
2 Thy foot He'll not let slide, nor will He slum-ber that thee keeps.
3 The Lord thee keeps, the Lord thy shade On thy right hand doth stay:
4 The Lord shall keep thy soul; He shall Pre-serve thee from all ill.

1 My safe-ty com-eth from the Lord, Who heav'n and earth hath made.
2 Be-hold, He that keeps Is-ra-el, He slum-bers not, nor sleeps.
3 The moon by night thee shall not smite, Nor yet the sun by day.
4 Hence-forth thy go-ing out and in God keep for ev-er will.

W. Whittingham   Lunenburg C.M.   G. F. Handel

1 I to the hills will lift mine eyes, From whence doth come mine aid. My saf-ety
2 Thy foot He'll not let slide, nor will He slum-ber that thee keeps. Be-hold, He
3 The Lord thee keeps, the Lord thy shade On thy right hand doth stay: The moon by
4 The Lord shall keep thy soul; He shall Pre-serve thee from all ill. Hence-forth thy

1 com-eth from the Lord, Who heav'n and earth hath made. Who heav'n and earth hath made.
2 that keeps Is-ra-el, He slum-bers not, nor sleeps. He slum-bers not, nor sleeps.
3 night thee shall not smite, Nor yet the sun by day. Nor yet the sun by day.
4 go-ing out and in God keep for ev-er will. God keep for ev-er will.

63 To Him that Loved

ISAAC WATTS   MIRFIELD C.M.   ARTHUR COTTMAN

1 To Him that lov'd the souls of men, And wash'd us in His blood,
2 To Him let ev - ry tongue be praise, And ev - ry heart be love!
3 Be - hold, on fly - ing clouds He comes! His saints shall bless the day;
4 I am the First, and I the Last; Time cen - tres all in Me;

1 To roy - al hon-ours rais'd our head, And made us priests to God.
2 All grate-ful hon-ours paid on earth, And no - bler songs a - bove.
3 While they that pierc'd Him sad - ly mourn In an - guish and dis - may.
4 Th' Al-mighty God, who was, and is, And ev - er - more shall be.

64 What though no Flowers

P. DODDRIDGE   BISHOPTHORPE C.M.   JEREMIAH CLARK

1 What though no flow'rs the fig - tree clothe, Tho' vines their fruit de - ny,
2 Though from the fold, with sad sur - prise, My flock cut off I see;
3 Yet in the Lord will I be glad, And glo - ry in His love;
4 He to my tard - y feet shall lend The swift-ness of the roe;
5 God is the treas - ure of my soul, The source of last - ing joy;

1 The lab - our of the ol - ive fail, And fields no meat sup - ply?
2 Tho' fam - ine pine in emp - ty stalls, Where herds were wont to be;
3 In Him I'll joy, who will the God Of my sal - va - tion prove;
4 Till, rais'd on high, I safe - ly dwell Be - yond the reach of woe.
5 A joy which want shall not im - pair, Nor death it - self des - troy.

65 Revive Thy Work

ALBERT MIDLANE   REVIVAL S.M.D   W. H. DOANE

1 Re - vive Thy work, O Lord ! O Lord ! Thy might-y arm make bare ; make bare ;
2 Re - vive Thy work, O Lord ! O Lord ! Dis - turb this sleep of death ; of death ;
3 Re - vive Thy work, O Lord ! O Lord ! Cre - ate soul-thirst for Thee ; for Thee ;
4 Re - vive Thy work, O Lord ! O Lord ! Ex - alt Thy precious name; precious name;

rall.

1 Speak with the voice that wakes the dead, And make Thy peo - ple hear !
2 Quick - en the smoul-d'ring em - bers now By Thine Al - might - y breath.
3 And hung'ring for the bread of life, Oh, may our spi - rits be !
4 And by the Ho - ly Ghost, our love For Thee and Thine in - flame.

REFRAIN

Re - vive Thy work, O Lord !........ While here to Thee we bow ;........
O Lord ! we bow ;

rall.

De - scend, O gra - cious Lord, de - scend! O come and bless us now.............
now, us now.

molto rall.

The Wondrous Story

66

F. H. ROWLEY   HYFRYDOL 8.7.8.7.D   R. H. PRICHARD

1. I will sing the won-drous sto - ry Of the Christ who
2. I was lost, but Je - sus found me; Found the sheep that
3. I was bruised, but Je - sus healed me; Faint was I from
4. Days of dark - ness still come o'er me; Sor - row's paths I
5. He will keep me till the riv - er Rolls its wa - ters

1. died for me; How He left His home in glo - ry, For the
2. went a - stray; Threw His lov - ing arms a - round me, Drew me
3. man - y a fall; Sight was gone and fears pos - sess'd me; But He
4. of - ten tread; But the Sa - viour still is with me, By His
5. at my feet; Then He'll bear me safe - ly o - ver, Where the

REFRAIN

1. cross on Cal - va - ry.
2. back in - to His way.
3. freed me from them all.   } Yes, I'll sing the won - drous sto - ry
4. hand I'm safe - ly led.
5. lov'd ones I shall meet.

Of the Christ who died for me; Sing it with the

saints in glo - ry, Ga - ther'd by the crys - tal sea.

67 Love Divine

CHARLES WESLEY   BETHANY 8.7. 8.7. D.   HENRY SMART

1 Love di - vine, all love ex - cel - ling, Joy of heav'n, to earth come down!
2 Breathe, O breathe Thy lov - ing Spi - rit In - to ev - 'ry troub - led breast!
3 Come, al - might - y to de - liv - er; Let us all Thy grace re - ceive!
4 Fin - ish then Thy new cre - a - tion: Pure and spot - less may we be;

1 Fix in us Thy hum - ble dwell - ing, All Thy faith - ful mer - cies crown:
2 Let us all in Thee in - her - it, Let us find the prom - is'd rest;
3 Sud - den - ly re - turn, and ne - ver, Ne - ver more Thy tem - ples leave:
4 Let us see our whole sal - va - tion Per - fect - ly se - cur'd by Thee!

1 Je - sus, Thou art all com - pas - sion, Pure, un - bound - ed love Thou art!
2 Take a - way the love of sin - ning; Al - pha and Om - e - ga be;
3 Thee we would be al - ways bless - ing, Serve Thee as Thy hosts a - bove,
4 Chang'd from glo - ry in - to glo - ry, Till in heav'n we take our place;

1 Vis - it us with Thy sal - va - tion, En - ter ev - 'ry trem - bling heart.
2 End of faith, as its be - gin - ning, Set our hearts at lib - er - ty.
3 Pray, and praise Thee, with - out ceas - ing, Glo - ry in Thy per - fect love.
4 Till we cast our crowns be - fore Thee, Lost in won - der, love, and praise.

The tune BEECHER is on the following page

67 Love Divine

CHARLES WESLEY BEECHER 8.7.8.7.D JOHN ZUNDEL

1 Love Di - vine, all love ex - cel - ling, Joy of heav'n, to earth come down!
2 Breathe, oh, breathe Thy lov - ing Spi - rit In - to ev' - ry troub-led breast!
3 Come, al - might - y to de - liv - er; Let us all Thy grace re - ceive!
4 Fi - nish then Thy new cre - a - tion: Pure and spot-less may we be;

1 Fix in us Thy hum - ble dwell - ing, All Thy faith-ful mer - cies crown.
2 Let us all in Thee in - her - it, Let us find the prom-is'd rest;
3 Sud - den - ly re - turn, and ne - ver, Ne - ver more Thy tem - ples leave.
4 Let us see our whole sal - va - tion Per - fect - ly se - cur'd by Thee!

1 Je - sus, Thou art all com - pas - sion, Pure, un-bounded love Thou art!
2 Take a - way the love of sin - ning; Al - pha and Om - e - ga be;
3 Thee we would be al - ways bless-ing, Serve Thee as Thy hosts a - bove,
4 Chang'd from glo-ry in - to glo - ry, Till in heav'n we take our place;

1 Vis - it us with Thy sal - va - tion, En - ter ev' - ry trem - bling heart.
2 End of faith, as its be - gin - ning, Set our hearts at lib - er - ty.
3 Pray, and praise Thee with-out ceas - ing, Glo - ry in Thy per - fect love.
4 Till we cast our crowns be - fore Thee, Lost in won-der, love, and praise.

The tune BETHANY is on the preceding page

4

68 Crowned with Glory

THOMAS KELLY   ST. MAGNUS C.M.   JEREMIAH CLARK

1 The head that once was crown'd with thorns Is crown'd with glo-ry 'now,
2 The high-est place that heav'n af-fords Is His by sov'-reign right:
3 The joy of all who dwell a-bove, The joy of all be-low
4 To them the Cross, with all its shame, With all its grace, is giv'n,

1 A roy-al di-a-dem a-dorns The might-y Vic-tor's brow.
2 The King of kings, and Lord of lords, He reigns in per-fect light.
3 To whom He man-i-fests His love, And grants His Name to know.
4 Their name an e-ver-last-ing name, Their joy the joy of heav'n.

A LOWER SETTING

1 The head that once was crown'd with thorns Is crown'd with glo-ry now,
2 The high-est place that heav'n af-fords Is His by sov'-reign right;
3 The joy of all who dwell a-bove, The joy of all be-low
4 To them the Cross, with all its shame, With all its grace, is giv'n,

1 A roy-al di-a-dem a-dorns The might-y Vic-tor's brow.
2 The King of kings, and Lord of lords, He reigns in per-fect light.
3 To whom He man-i-fests His love, And grants His Name to know
4 Their name an e-ver-last-ing name, Their joy the joy of heav'n.

69

Arise, My Soul!

CHARLES WESLEY   LENOX 6.6.6.6.8.8.8   LEWIS EDSON

1 A - rise, my soul, a - rise! Shake off thy guil - ty fears,
2 He ev - er lives a - bove, For me to in - ter - cede;
3 Five bleed - ing wounds He bears, Re - ceiv'd on Cal - va - ry;
4 My God is re - con - cil'd, His pard-'ning voice I hear;

1 The bleed - ing Sac - ri - fice In my be - half ap - pears;
2 His all - re - deem - ing love, His pre - cious blood to plead;
3 They pour ef - fect - ual pray'rs, They strong - ly plead for me;
4 He owns me for His child, I can no long - er fear;

1 Be - fore the throne my Sure - ty stands, Be - fore the throne
2 His blood a - ton'd for all our race, His blood a - ton'd
3 'For - give him, O for - give!' they cry, 'For - give him, O
4 With con - fi - dence I now draw nigh, With con - fi - dence

1 my Sure - ty stands, My name is writ - ten on His hands.
2 for all our race, And sprin - kles now the throne of grace.
3 for - give!' they cry, 'Nor let that ran - som'd sin - ner die.'
4 I now draw nigh, And 'Fa - ther, Ab - ba, Fa - ther!' cry.

70 The Sweetest Name

GEORGE W. BETHUNE   DULCE NOMEN 8.7.8.7.D   WILLIAM B. BRADBURY

1 There is no name so sweet on earth, No name so sweet in hea - ven,
2 And when He hung up - on the tree They wrote this name a - bove Him,
3 So now, up - on the Fa-ther's throne, Al - might-y to re - lease us
4 O Je - sus! by that match-less Name Thy grace shall fail us nev - er;

1 The name, be - fore His won-drous birth, To Christ the Sa - viour giv - en.
2 That all might see the rea - son we For ev - er - more must love Him.
3 From sin and pain, He ev - er reigns, The Prince and Sa - viour, Je - sus.
4 To - day as yes - ter - day the same; Thou art the same for ev - er!

REFRAIN

We love to sing of Christ our King, And hail Him bless - ed Je - sus;

For there's no word ear ev - er heard So dear, so sweet, as Je - sus.

The tune BISHOPSGARTH is on the following page

The Sweetest Name

70

GEORGE W. BETHUNE   BISHOPSGARTH 8.7.8.7.D   ARTHUR S. SULLIVAN

1 There is no name so sweet on earth, No name so
2 And when He hung up - on the tree They wrote this
3 So now, up - on the Fa - ther's throne, Al - might - y
4 O Je - sus! by that match - less Name Thy grace shall

1 sweet in . hea - ven, The name, be - fore His won-drous birth, To
2 name a - bove Him, That all might see the rea - son we For
3 to re - lease us From sin and pain, He ev - er reigns, The
4 fail us . nev - er; To - day as yes - ter - day the same; Thou

REFRAIN

1 Christ the Sa - viour giv - en.
2 ev - er-more must love Him.
3 Prince and Sa - viour, Je - sus,
4 art the same for ev - er!

We love to sing of

Christ our King, And hail Him bless - ed Je - sus; For there's no

word ear ev - er heard So dear, so sweet, as Je - sus.

The tune DULCE NOMEN is on the preceding page

71 With Their Flocks Abiding

F. W. Farrar

J. Farmer

1 In the field with their flocks a - bid - ing, They
2 'To you in the Ci - ty of Da - vid, A
3 And the shep - herds came to the man - ger, And

1 lay on the dew - y ground; And glim - mer-ing un - der the
2 Sa - viour is born to - day!' And sud - den a host of the
3 gaz'd on the Ho - ly Child; And calm - ly o'er that rude

1 star - light The sheep lay white a - round, When the
2 heav'n - ly ones Flash'd forth to join the lay; O
3 cra - dle The Vir - gin Mo - ther smil'd; And the

1 light of the Lord stream'd o'er them, And lo! from the heav - en a
2 nev - er hath sweet - er mess - age Thrill'd home to the souls of
3 sky, in the star - lit si - lence, Seem'd full of the an - gel

With Their Flocks Abiding—*Continued*

1 bove, An an-gel lean'd from the glo-ry And
2 men, And the heav'ns them-selves had nev-er heard A
3 lay: 'To you in the Ci-ty of Da-vid, A

1 sang his song of love: He sang. that first sweet
2 glad-der choir, till then, For they sang that Christ-mas
3 Sa-viour is born to-day'; O they sang— and I ween that

1 Christ-mas, The song that shall nev-er cease, 'Glo-
2 car-ol, That nev-er on earth shall cease, 'Glo-
3 nev-er The car-ol on earth shall cease, 'Glo-

1-3 ry to God in the high-est, On earth good-will and peace.'

Words by permission of E. M. FARRAR. Music by permission of J. WILLIAMS, LTD.

72 We Sing the Praise

Thomas Kelly   Warrington L.M.   Ralph Harrison

1 We sing the praise of Him who died, Of
2 In - scrib'd up - on the Cross we see, In
3 The Cross, it takes our guilt a - way, It
4 It makes the cow - ard spi - rit brave, And

1 Him who died up - on the Cross,
2 shin - ing let - ters, 'God is love!'
3 holds the faint - ing spi - rit up;
4 nerves the fee - ble arm for fight;

1 The sin - ner's hope— tho' men de - ride; For
2 The Lamb who died up - on the tree Has
3 It cheers with hope the gloom - y day, And
4 It takes its ter - ror from the grave, And

1 Him we count the world but loss.
2 brought us mer - cy from a - bove.
3 sweet - ens ev - 'ry bit - ter cup.
4 gilds the bed of death with light.

The tunes Mainzer and Oxford are on the following page

We Sing the Praise—*Continued*

THOMAS KELLY   MAINZER L.M.   JOSEPH MAINZER

1 We sing the praise of Him who died, Of Him who died up - on the Cross,
2 In-scrib'd up - on the Cross we see, In shin - ing let - ters, 'God is Love!'
3 The Cross, it takes our guilt a - way, It holds the faint-ing spi - rit up;
4 It makes the cow - ard spi - rit brave, And nerves the fee - ble arm for fight;

1 The sin-ner's hope—tho' men de - ride, For Him we count the world but loss.
2 The Lamb who died up - on the tree Has brought us mer - cy from a - bove
3 It cheers with hope the gloom - y day, And sweet-ens ev - 'ry bit - ter cup.
4 It takes its ter - ror from the grave, And gilds the bed of death with light.

THOMAS KELLY   OXFORD L.M.   JOHN STAINER

1 We sing the praise of Him who died, Of Him who died up - on the Cross,
2 In - scrib'd up - on the Cross we see, In shin - ing let - ters, 'God is love!'
3 The Cross, it takes our guilt a - way, It holds the faint-ing spi - rit up;
4 It makes the cow - ard spi - rit brave, And nerves the fee-ble arm for fight;

1 The sin-ner's hope—tho' men de - ride; For Him we count the world but loss.
2 The Lamb who died up - on the tree Has brought us mer - cy from a - bove.
3 It cheers with hope the gloom - y day, And sweet-ens ev - 'ry bit - ter cup.
4 It takes its ter - ror from the grave, And gilds the bed of death with light.

73   O Worship the King!

ROBERT GRANT   HANOVER 10.10.11.11.   WILLIAM CROFT

1 O wor-ship the King all glor-ious a-bove!
2 O tell of His might, O sing of His grace!
3 This earth with its store of won-ders un-told,
4 Thy boun-ti-ful care what tongue can re-cite?

1 O grate-ful-ly sing His pow'r and His love!
2 Whose robe is the light, Whose can-o-py space,
3 Al-might-y, Thy pow'r hath found-ed of old,
4 It breathes in the air; it shines in the light;

1 Our Shield and De-fend-er, the An-cient of Days,
2 His char-iots of wrath the deep thun-der-clouds form,
3 Hath 'stab-lish'd it fast by a change-less de-cree,
4 It streams from the hills; it de-scends to the plain,

1 Pa-vil-ion'd in splen-dour, and gird-ed with praise.
2 And dark is His path on the wings of the storm.
3 And round it hath cast, like a man-tle, the sea.
4 And sweet-ly dis-tils in the dew and the rain.

The tune HOUGHTON is on the following page

O Worship the King!

73

ROBERT GRANT   HOUGHTON 10.10.11.11   H. J. GAUNTLETT

1 O wor - ship the King all glor - ious a - bove!
2 O tell of His might, O sing of His grace!
3 This earth with its store of won - ders un - told,
4 Thy boun - ti - ful care what tongue can re - cite?

1 O grate - ful - ly sing His pow'r and His love!
2 Whose robe is the light, Whose can - o - py space,
3 Al - might - y, Thy pow'r hath found - ed of old,
4 It breathes in the air; it shines in the light;

1 Our Shield and De - fend - er, the An - cient of Days,
2 His char - iots of wrath the deep thun - der - clouds form,
3 Hath 'stab - lish'd it fast by a change - less de - cree,
4 It streams from the hills; it de - scends to the plain,

1 Pa - vil - ion'd in splen - dour, and gird - ed with praise.
2 And dark is His path on the wings of the storm.
3 And round it hath cast, like a man - tle, the sea.
4 And sweet - ly dis - tils in the dew and the rain.

The tune HANOVER is on the preceding page

74 Ye Servants of God

CHARLES WESLEY   LAUDATE DOMINUM 10.10.11.11.   CHARLES H. PARRY

1 Ye ser - vants of God, Your Mas - ter pro - claim,
2 God ru - leth on high, Al - might - y to save;
3 Sal - va - tion to God, Who sits on the throne;
4 Then let us a - dore And give Him His right;

1 And pub - lish a - broad His won - der - ful Name;
2 And still He is nigh, His pres - ence we have!
3 Let all cry a - loud, And hon - our the Son:
4 All glo - ry and pow'r, All wis - dom and might;

1 The Name all vic - tor - i - ous Of Je - sus ex - tol;
2 The great con - gre - ga - tion His tri - umph shall sing,
3 The prais - es of Je - sus All an - gels pro - claim,
4 All hon - our and bless - ing, With an - gels a - bove;

1 His King - dom is glor - i - ous, And rules ov - er all.
2 As - crib - ing sal - va - tion To Je - sus our King.
3 Fall down on their fa - ces, And wor - ship the Lamb.
4 And thanks ne - ver ceas - ing, And in - fin - ite love.

    Tune WORSHIP is on following page

74 Ye Servants of God

CHARLES WESLEY WORSHIP 10.10. 11.11. E. P. CRAWFORD

1 Ye ser - vants of God, Your Mas - ter pro - claim,
2 God ru - leth on high, Al - might - y to save;
3 Sal - va - tion to God, Who sits on the throne!
4 Then let us a - dore And give Him His right:

1 And pub - lish a - broad His won - der - ful Name;
2 And still He is nigh, His pres - ence we have;
3 Let all cry a - loud, And hon - our the Son:
4 All glo - ry and pow'r, All wis - dom and might;

1 The Name all vic - tor - ious Of Je - sus ex - tol;
2 The great con - gre - ga - tion His tri - umph shall sing,
3 The prais - es of Je - sus All an - gels pro - claim,
4 All hon - our and bless - ing, With an - gels a - bove;

1 His King - dom is glor - ious, And rules ov - er all.
2 As - crib - ing sal - va - tion To Je - sus our King.
3 Fall down on their fa - ces, And wor - ship the Lamb.
4 And thanks ne - ver ceas - ing, And in - fin - ite love.

The tune LAUDATE DOMINUM is on the preceding page

75 The King's Business

E T. CASSEL

FLORA H. CASSEL

1 I am a stran-ger here with-in a for-eign land,
2 This is the King's com-mand, that all men ev-'ry-where
3 My home is bright-er far than Sha-ron's ros-y plain,

1 My home is far a-way up-on a gold-en strand;
2 Re-pent and turn a-way from sin's se-duc-tive snare;
3 E-ter-nal life and joy through-out its vast do-main:

1 Am-bas-sa-dor to be of realms be-yond the sea,
2 That all who will o-bey with Him shall reign for aye,
3 My Sov-'reign bids me tell how mor-tals there may dwell,

The King's Business—*Continued*

1 I'm here on busi - ness for my King. . .
2 And that's my busi - ness for my King. . .
3 And that's my busi - ness for my King. . .

REFRAIN

This is the mes - sage that I bring, . . A mes - sage

an - gels fain would sing; . . 'O be ye re - con - ciled!' Thus saith my

Lord and King, 'O be ye re - con - ciled to God!' . .

76 That Grand Word

E. E. HEWITT

E. E. HEWITT

1 That grand word Who-so-ev-er is ring-ing thro' my soul, Who-so-ev-er
2 When-ev-er this sweet message in God's own Word I see, Who-so-ev-er
3 I heard the lov-ing message, and now to o-thers say, Who-so-ev-er
4 To God be all the glo-ry, His on-ly Son He gave, Who-so-ev-er

1 will may come; In riv-ers of sal-va-tion the liv-ing wa-ters roll,
2 will may come; I know 'tis meant for sin-ners, I know 'tis meant for me,
3 will may come; Seek now the pre-cious Sav-iour, and He'll be yours to-day,
4 will may come; And those who come be-liev-ing, He'll to the ut-most save,

REFRAIN

1-4 Who-so-ev-er will may come. O that 'Who so

Who-so-ev-er will,

ev-er!' Who-so-ev-er will may come; The Sa-viour's in-vi-

who-so-ev-er will,

-ta-tion is free-ly sound-ing still, Who-so-ev-er will may come.

77 Abundant Life

WILLIAM LESLIE

Arr. JAS. M‘W. BONNAR

1 Un - der the bur - dens of guilt and care Ma - ny a
2 Bur - den'd one, why will you lon - ger bear Sor - rows from
3 Leav - ing the moun - tain, the stream - let grows, Flood - ing the
4 O for the floods on the thirs - ty land! O for a

1 spi - rit is griev - ing, . Who in the joy of the
2 which He re - leas - es? . O - pen your heart, and re -
3 vale with a riv - er; . So from the hill of the
4 might - y re - vi - val! . O for a sanc - ti - fied,

1 Lord might share, Life ev - er - last - ing re - ceiv - ing.
2 joic - ing share Life more a - bun - dant in Je - sus.
3 Cross there flows Life more a - bun - dant for ev - er.
4 fear - less band! Read - y to hail its ar - ri - val.

REFRAIN

Life! life! e - ter - nal life! Je - sus a - lone is the Giv - er;

Life! life! a - bun - dant life! Glo - ry to Je - sus for ev - er!

78 Power in the Blood

L. E. Jones   L. E. Jones

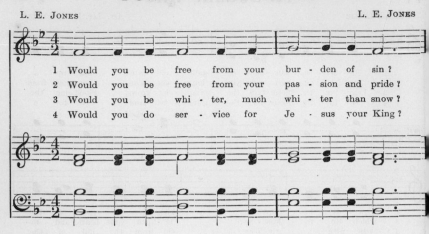

1 Would you be free from your bur - den of sin?
2 Would you be free from your pas - sion and pride?
3 Would you be whi - ter, much whi - ter than snow?
4 Would you do ser - vice for Je - sus your King?

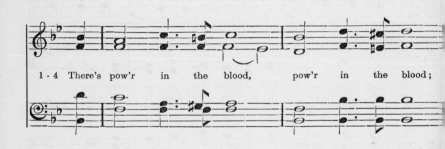

1-4 There's pow'r in the blood, pow'r in the blood;

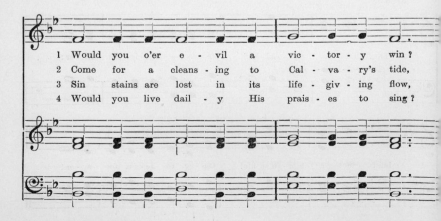

1 Would you o'er e - vil a vic - tor - y win?
2 Come for a cleans - ing to Cal - va - ry's tide,
3 Sin stains are lost in its life - giv - ing flow,
4 Would you live dail - y His prais - es to sing?

Power in the Blood—*Continued*

1 - 4 There's won - der - ful pow'r in the blood.

REFRAIN

There is pow'r, pow'r, Won - der - work - ing
There is pow'r,

pow'r in the blood of the Lamb,
in the blood of the Lamb,

There is pow'r, pow'r, Won - der - work - ing pow'r,
There is pow'r,

In the pre - cious blood of the Lamb.

The Joy-Bells

WM. J. KIRKPATRICK

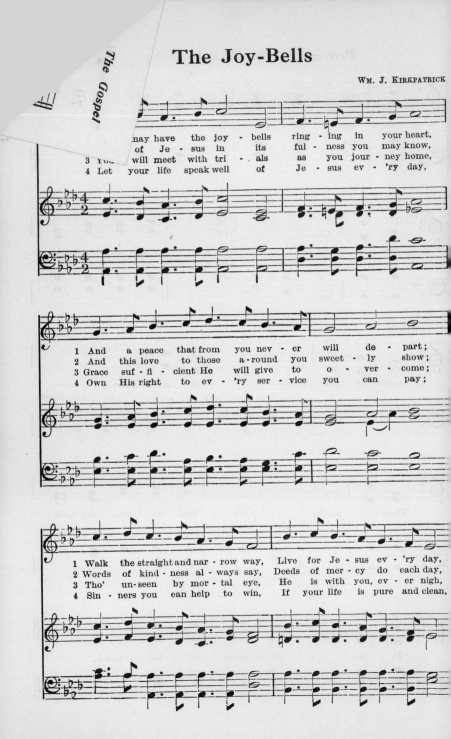

may have   the joy - bells   ring - ing in   your heart,
of   Je - sus in   its   ful - ness you   may know,
3 You will meet with tri - als   as   you jour - ney home,
4 Let   your life speak well   of   Je - sus ev - 'ry day,

1 And   a peace   that from   you nev - er   will   de - part;
2 And   this love   to those   a - round you   sweet - ly   show;
3 Grace   suf - fi - cient He   will give   to   o - ver - come;
4 Own   His right   to ev - 'ry ser - vice you   can   pay;

1 Walk   the straight and nar - row way,   Live   for Je - sus ev - 'ry day,
2 Words   of kind - ness al - ways say,   Deeds   of mer - cy   do   each day,
3 Tho'   un - seen   by mor - tal eye,   He   is with you, ev - er nigh,
4 Sin - ners you   can help to win,   If your life   is   pure and clean,

The Joy-Bells—*Continued*

1 He will keep the joy - bells ring - ing in your heart.
2 Then He'll keep the joy - bells ring - ing in your heart.
3 And He'll keep the joy - bells ring - ing in your heart.
4 And you keep the joy - bells ring - ing in your heart.

REFRAIN

Joy - - bells ring-ing in your heart, Joy - - bells
Ring-ing in your heart, You may have the joy - bells

ring-ing in your heart; Take the Sa-viour here be-low, With you ev - 'ry-

where you go; He will keep the joy - bells ring-ing in your heart.

80   The Story of Jesus

D. W. WHITTLE

MAY WHITTLE MOODY

1 They tell me the sto - ry of Je - sus is old,
2 Yet the sto - ry is old, as the sun - light is old,
3 For what can we tell to the wea - ry of heart
4 So with sor - row we turn from the wise of this world

1 And they ask that we preach some - thing new; . .
2 Though it's new ev - 'ry morn all the same; . .
3 If we preach not sal - va - tion from sin? . .
4 To the wan - der - ers far from the fold; . .

1 They say that the Babe and the Man of the Cross
2 As it floods all the world with its glad - ness and light,
3 And how can we com - fort the souls that de - part
4 With hearts for the mess - age they'll join in our song,

The Story of Jesus—*Continued*

1 For the wise of this world will not do. . .
2 Kind-ling far a - way stars by its flame. . .
3 If we tell not how Christ rose a - gain? . .
4 That the sto - ry can nev - er grow old. . .

REFRAIN

It can nev - er grow old, It can nev - er grow old, Though a

mil - lion times o - ver the sto - ry is told; While sin lives un-van-quish'd,

rit.

And death rules the world, The sto - ry of Je - sus can nev-er grow old.

81 Was it for Me?

J. M. WHYTE   J. M. WHYTE

1 Was it for me, for me a - lone, The Sa - viour
2 Was it for me sweet an - gel strains Came float - ing
3 Was it for me the Sa - viour said, 'Pil - low thy
4 Was it for me He wept and pray'd, My load of
5 Was it for me He bow'd His head Up - on the

1 left His glo - rious throne ; The dazz - ling splen - dours of the
2 o'er Ju - de - a's plains ? That star - light night so long a -
3 wea - ry, ach - ing head, Trust-ing - ly on thy Sa - viour's
4 sin be - fore Him laid ; That night with - in Geth - sem - an -
5 Cross, and free - ly shed His pre - cious blood—that crim - son

1 sky, Was it for me He came to die ?
2 go, Was it for me God plann'd it so ?
3 breast ?' Was it for me, Can I thus rest ?
4 e, Was it for me that a - gon - y ?
5 tide, Was it for me the Sa - viour died ?

REFRAIN

It was for me, yes, all for me, O love of

It was for me, yes, all for me, O love of

Was it for Me?—*Continued*

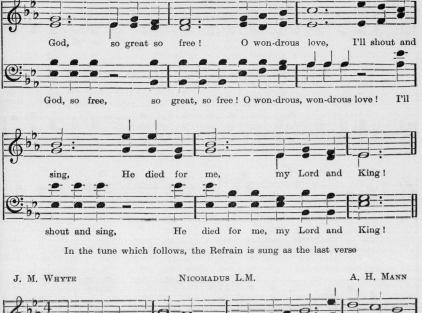

God, so great so free! O won-drous love, I'll shout and

God, so free, so great, so free! O won-drous, won-drous love! I'll

sing, He died for me, my Lord and King!

shout and sing, He died for me, my Lord and King!

In the tune which follows, the Refrain is sung as the last verse

J. M. WHYTE NICOMADUS L.M. A. H. MANN

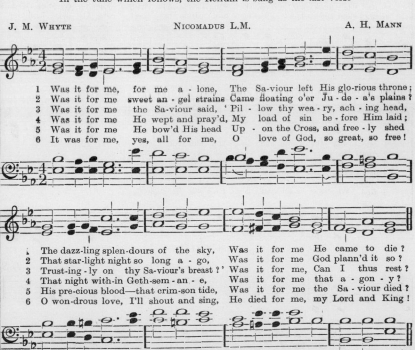

1 Was it for me, for me a - lone, The Sa - viour left His glo-rious throne;
2 Was it for me sweet an - gel strains Came floating o'er Ju - de - a's plains?
3 Was it for me the Sa - viour said, 'Pil - low thy wea - ry, ach - ing head,
4 Was it for me He wept and pray'd, My load of sin be - fore Him laid;
5 Was it for me He bow'd His head Up - on the Cross, and free - ly shed
6 It was for me, yes, all for me, O love of God, so great, so free!

1 The dazz-ling splen-dours of the sky, Was it for me He came to die?
2 That star-light night so long a - go, Was it for me God plann'd it so?
3 Trust-ing - ly on thy Sa-viour's breast?' Was it for me, Can I thus rest?
4 That night with-in Geth-sem - an - e, Was it for me that a - gon - y?
5 His pre-cious blood—that crim-son tide, Was it for me the Sa - viour died?
6 O won-drous love, I'll shout and sing, He died for me, my Lord and King!

The music by permission of NOVELLO & CO., LTD.

82 A Hill Lone and Grey

R. Carradine

Jno. B. Bryant

1 There's a hill lone and grey in a land far a-way, In a coun-try be-
2 Be-hold! faint on the road, 'neath a world's hea-vy load, Comes a thorn-crown-ed
3 Hark! I hear the dull blow of the ham-mer swung low; They are nail-ing my
4 How they mock Him in death, to His last lab-'ring breath! While His friends sad-ly
5 Then the dark-ness came down and the rocks rent a-round, And a cry pierc'd the
6 Let the sun hide its face, let the earth reel a-pace, O-ver men who their

1 yond the blue sea, Where be-neath that fair sky went a Man forth to
2 Man on the way, With a cross He is bowed, but still on thro' the
3 Lord to the tree, And the cross they up-raise while the mul-ti-tude
4 weep o'er the way; But tho' lone-ly and faint, still no word of com-
5 grief-la-den air; 'Twas the voice of our King who re-ceiv'd death's dark
6 Sa-viour have slain; But be-hold from the sod comes the blest Lamb of

D.S.—For 'twas there on its side, Je-sus suf-fer'd and

FINE REFRAIN

1 die For the world and for you and for me.
2 crowd He's as-cend-ing that hill lone and grey.
3 gaze On the blest Lamb of dark Cal-va-ry.
4 plaint Fell from Him on the hill lone and grey.
5 sting, All to save us from end-less des-pair.
6 God, Who was slain and is ris-en a-gain.

O it bows down my

died To re-deem a poor sin-ner like me.

D.S.

heart and the tear-drops will start, When in mem-'ry that grey hill I see,

83 ## They Crucified Him

J. M. WHYTE   J. M. WHYTE

1 Come, sin - ner, be - hold what Je - sus hath done, Be - hold how He suf - fer'd for

2 From heav - en He came, He loved you—He died: Such love as His nev - er was

3 No pi - ty - ing eye, a sav - ing arm, none. He saw us and pi - tied us

4 They cru - ci - fied Him, and yet He for - gave, 'My Fa - ther, for - give them!' He

5 So what will you do with Je - sus your King? Say, how will you meet Him at

1 thee: They cru - ci - fied Him, God's in - no - cent Son, For - sak - 'n, He died on the tree.

2 known; Be - hold, on the Cross your King cru - ci - fied, To make you an heir to His throne.

3 then; A - lone, in the fight, the vic - t'ry He won; O praise Him, ye chil - dren of men!

4 cried; What must He have borne, the sin - ner to save, When un - der the bur - den He died!

5 last? What plea in the day of wrath will you bring, When of - fers of mer - cy are past?

REFRAIN

They cru - ci - fied Him, they cru - ci - fied Him, They nail'd Him to the tree, . .

And so there He died, A King cru - ci - fied To save a poor sin - ner like me, like me.

84 The Atoning Blood

C. R. Hurditch

J. J. Sims

1 Th'a-ton-ing blood is flow-ing, Let all the tid-ings hear, The Gos-pel word is show-ing
2 Th'a-ton-ing blood is sav-ing Sin-ners of deep-est dye, And mul-ti-tudes are hav-ing
3 Th'a-ton-ing blood is bring-ing Poor lost ones to the fold, And heav'nly hosts are sing-ing
4 Th'a-ton-ing blood is stay-ing The great a-veng-ing rod, While men are still de-lay-ing

1 How sin-ners may draw near. Th'a-ton-ing blood's re-liev-ing The pris'ners from their chains.
2 Free ti-tles to the sky. Th'a-ton-ing blood is heal-ing The souls that sin had slain;
3 O'er mul-ti-tudes un-told. Th'a-ton-ing blood is speak-ing To ev-'ry pre-cious soul
4 To yield themselves to God. Th'a-ton-ing blood is seal-ing The world's e-ter-nal doom;

REFRAIN. *Faster*

1 And sin-ners in be-liev-ing Lose all their guilt-y stains. }
2 Re-joic-ing saints are feel-ing The prom-is'd lat-ter rain. }
3 Who is sal-va-tion seek-ing, 'Be-lieve, and be made whole.' }
4 But, to Thy soul ap-peal-ing, Says, 'Lost one, to Me come.' }

It is the blood,.................

It is the blood,

the pre-cious blood,................. It is the blood,................. the pre-cious blood,

the pre-cious blood, It is the blood, the pre-cious blood,

rit.

It is the blood that mak-eth an a-tone-ment for the soul.

The Love of Jesus

85

W. E. LITTLEWOOD

T. E. PERKINS

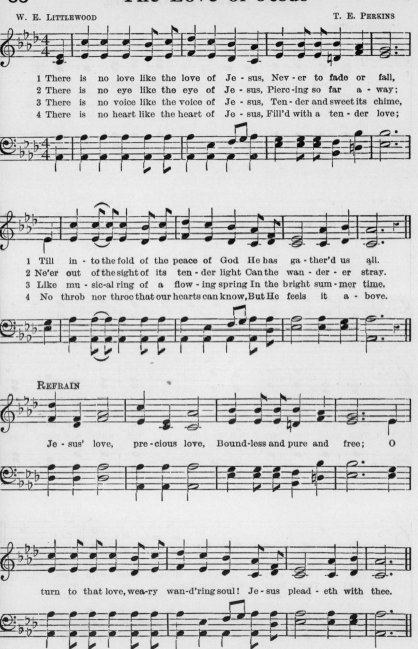

1 There is no love like the love of Je - sus, Nev - er to fade or fall,
2 There is no eye like the eye of Je - sus, Pierc - ing so far a - way;
3 There is no voice like the voice of Je - sus, Ten - der and sweet its chime,
4 There is no heart like the heart of Je - sus, Fill'd with a ten - der love;

1 Till in - to the fold of the peace of God He has ga - ther'd us all.
2 Ne'er out of the sight of its ten - der light Can the wan - der - er stray.
3 Like mu - sic-al ring of a flow - ing spring In the bright sum - mer time.
4 No throb nor throe that our hearts can know, But He feels it a - bove.

REFRAIN

Je - sus' love, pre - cious love, Bound-less and pure and free; O

turn to that love, wea - ry wan-d'ring soul! Je - sus plead - eth with thee.

Hear Him Knocking

Johnson Oatman   J. Howard Entwisle

1 A hand all bruis'd and bleed-ing is knock-ing at the door,
2 How of - ten when in sick-ness, your bod - y rack'd with pain,
3 While stand-ing by the cask - et of some de - part - ed friend,
4 Why will you keep Him knock-ing? why don't you let Him in?

1 Is knock - ing at the door .. of your heart; ..
2 This knock - ing re - - sound - ed in your ears; ..
3 With sor . row your . . heart was sick and sore; ..
4 He'll fill . . your . . path - way with de - light; ..

1 It is the hand of Je - sus, who long has knock'd be -
2 How of - ten in the night-time the knock would come a -
3 What caus'd that train of think-ing of how your life would
4 That hand so torn and bleed-ing will wash a - way your

1 fore, Though oft you have told Him to de - part.
2 gain, So loud it would fill your soul with fears.
3 end? That hand was then knock-ing at the door.
4 sin, O wel - come the Sa-viour in to - night!

Hear Him Knocking—*Continued*

O don't you hear Him knock-ing, knock-ing at the door?

He's knock-ing at the door to come in;

He wants an in - **vi** - ta - tion to cross your thres - hold o'er,

Then Je - sus will save you from all sin.

87 He'll Do Better for You

E. E. Hewitt

Jno. R. Sweney

1 Come a-way to Je-sus; He is will-ing to for-give,
2 Come a-way to Je-sus; let il-lus-ive tri-fles go,
3 Come a-way to Je-sus; from your earth-ly i-dols part,

1 His love will shine a-round you ev-'ry mo-ment that you live;
2 For ev-er-last-ing bless-ing He is a-ble to be-stow;
3 And take His great sal-va-tion for it sat-is-fies the heart;

1 You'll find Him good and true, The .. pil-grim jour-ney thro',
2 He'll an-swer when you pray, He'll . take your sins a-way,
3 He'll o-pen to your view His .. treas-ures ev-er new,

1 He'll do bet-ter for you than this world can do.
2 Lead you up and on-ward to His per-fect day.
3 He'll do bet-ter for you than this world can do.

He'll Do Better for You—*Continued*

REFRAIN   *With spirit*

He'll do bet - ter for you than this world can do,

He's a might - y Sa - viour, He is good and true;

He'll .. save you by His grace, Un - til you see His face,

He'll do bet - ter for you than this world can do.

5

The Best Friend

88

P. P. BILHORN

P. P. BILHORN

DUET, SOPRANO (or TENOR) and ALTO

1 O the best friend to have is Je - sus! When the
2 What a friend I have found in Je - sus! Peace and
3 Tho' I pass thro' the night of sor - row, And the
4 When at last to our home we gath - er, With the

1 cares of life up - on you roll; He will heal the wound-ed heart, He will
2 com-fort to my soul He brings; Lean-ing on His might-y arm, I will
3 chill - y waves of Jor - dan roll, Nev - er need I shrink or fear, For my
4 lov'd ones who have gone be - fore, We will sing up-on the shore, Prais-ing

1 strength and grace impart; O the best friend to have is Je - sus!
2 fear no ill or harm; O the best friend to have is Je - sus!
3 Sa - viour is so near; O the best friend to have is Je - sus!
4 Him for ev - er-more; O the best friend to have is Je - sus!

The Best Friend—*Continued*

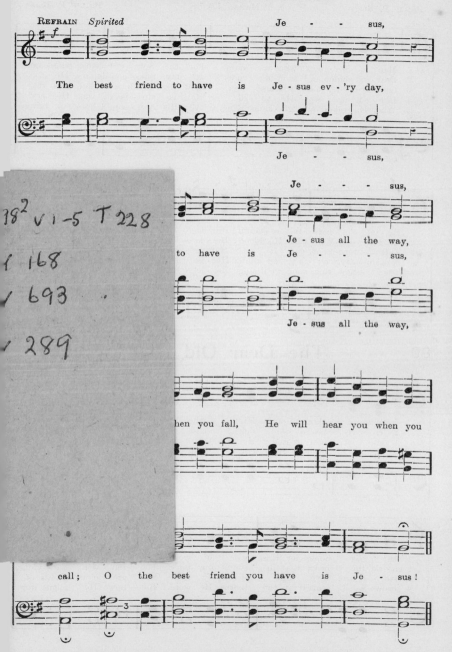

89 Man of Sorrows

Philip P. Bliss   Marah 7.7. 7.8   Philip P. Bliss

1 Man of sor-rows! what a name For the Son of God, who came
2 Bear-ing shame and scoff-ing rude, In my place con-demn'd He stood;
3 Guil-ty, vile, and help-less, we; Spot-less Lamb of God was He!
4 Lift-ed up was He to die, 'It is fin-ish'd,' was His cry;
5 When He comes, our glo-rious King, All His ran-som'd home to bring,

1 Ru-in'd sin-ners to re-claim! Hal-le-lu-jah! what a Sa-viour!
2 Seal'd my par-don with His blood: Hal-le-lu-jah! what a Sa-viour!
3 Full a-tone-ment, can it be? Hal-le-lu-jah! what a Sa-viour!
4 Now in heav'n ex-alt-ed high; Hal-le-lu-jah! what a Sa-viour!
5 Then a-new this song we'll sing: Hal-le-lu-jah! what a Sa-viour!

90 The Dear Old Story

James Fraser   William Fraser

1 When I think of Him who hath lov'd me so, Who
2 How He heal'd the sick and re-stor'd the blind, And
3 As wea-ried He sat at Sa-ma-ria's well, The
4 My griefs He car-ried, my sor-rows bore, His

1 left His home for this vale of woe, Was cra-dled in a
2 cheer'd the heart that in sor-row pin'd, The ten-der Sa-viour,
3 sto-ry of love did sweet-ly tell, His gra-cious words of
4 brow was scarr'd by the thorns He wore, But now He reigns for

The Dear Old Story—*Continued*

1 man - ger low, O it's a pre - cious old sto - ry!
2 lov - ing kind, O it's a pre - cious old sto - ry!
3 mer - cy fell, O it's a pre - cious old sto - ry!
4 ev - er - more, O it's a pre - cious old sto - ry!

REFRAIN

O the dear old sto - ry, the pre - cious sto - ry, That

O the dear old sto - ry, the pre - cious old sto - ry, That

fills my heart with grace and glo - ry, The sweet - est song in

fills, that fills my heart, with grace and glo - ry, The sweet - est song in

heav'n I'll sing, 'Twill be the old, old sto - ry!

glo - ry I shall sing, 'Twill be, 'twill be. the old, old sto - ry!

By permission of R. F. BEVERIDGE

91

He's the One

J. B. MACKAY

J. B MACKAY

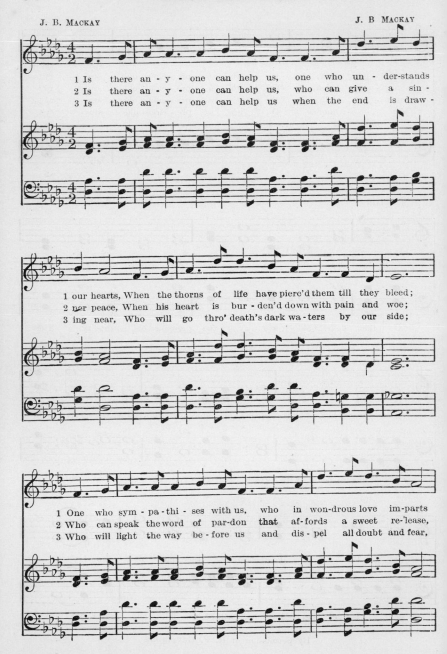

1 Is there an-y-one can help us, one who un-der-stands
2 Is there an-y-one can help us, who can give a sin-
3 Is there an-y-one can help us when the end is draw-

1 our hearts, When the thorns of life have pierc'd them till they bleed;
2 ner peace, When his heart is bur-den'd down with pain and woe;
3 ing near, Who will go thro' death's dark wa-ters by our side;

1 One who sym-pa-thi-ses with us, who in won-drous love im-parts
2 Who can speak the word of par-don that af-fords a sweet re-'lease,
3 Who will light the way be-fore us and dis-pel all doubt and fear,

He's the One—*Continued*

1 Just the ver - y, ver - y bless-ing that we need?
2 And whose blood can wash and make us white as snow?
3 And will bear our spir - its safe - ly o'er the tide?

REFRAIN

Yes, there's One, on - ly One! The bless-ed, bless-
Yes, there's One, on - ly One!

ed Je - sus, He's the One! When af - flic - tions press the soul, when

waves of trou - ble roll, And you need a friend to help you, He's the One!

92   The Old Fountain

EMMA M. JOHNSTON

WM. J. KIRKPATRICK

1 By Sa - ma - ria's way - side well, Once a bless - ed mes -
2 And a lit - tle cap - tive maid, By a lep - er un -
3 And a wo - man in a crowd, With - out word or cry
4 As the eu - nuch tried to read, Phil - ip taught him of

1 sage fell On a wo - man's thirs - ty soul, Long a - go;
2 dis - may'd, Told to him a sim - ple sto - ry Long a - go;
3 a - loud, Just stoop'd down and touch'd His gar - ment Long a - go;
4 his need, And bap - tized him in the stream, Long a - go;

1 And to eyes that long were seal'd Was the glo - rious light re -
2 That the stream where he might lave Had a - lone the pow'r to
3 As her ur - gent need ap - peal'd, So her sin - ful soul was
4 As the out - ward seal and sign Of an in - ward work di -

1 veal'd Thro' a foun - tain that was o - pen'd Long a - go.
2 save, Thro' his trust in that old foun - tain, Long a - go.
3 heal'd In that foun - tain that was o - pen'd Long a - go.
4 vine, That was wrought thro' that old foun - tain, Long a - go.

The Old Fountain—*Continued*

REFRAIN

There's a foun - tain that was o - pen'd Long a - go, Long a - go;

For the heal - ing of the na - tions is its flow; . . A -

long the line of a - ges The pro-phets and the sa - ges Caught the

sing - ing of its wa - ters, Long a - go, Long a - go.

93 Whosoever Will

PHILIP P. BLISS   PHILIP P. BLISS

1 Who - so - ev - er hear - eth! shout, shout the sound! Send the bless-ed tid - ings
2 Who - so - ev - er com - eth need not de - lay; Now the door is o - pen,
3 Who - so - ev - er will! the pro-mise is se - cure; Who - so - ev - er will! for

1 all the world a-round! Spread the joy-ful news wher - ev - er man is found:
2 en - ter while you may; Je - sus is the true and on - ly Liv - ing Way,
3 ev - er shall en - dure; Who - so - ev - er will— 'tis life for ev - er-more!

REFRAIN

1-3 Who - so - ev - er will may come! Who - so - ev - er will! who - so - ev - er

will! Send the pro - cla - ma - tion o - ver vale and hill: 'Tis the lov-ing

Fa - ther calls the wan-d'rer home; Who - so - ev - er will may come!

Sins as Scarlet

94

Fanny J. Crosby

W. H. Doane

DUET

1st time | 2nd time

1 Tho' your sins be as scar-let, They shall be as white as snow ; as snow;
2 Hear the voice that en-treats you, O re-turn ye un-to God ! to God !
3 He'll for-give your trans-gressions, And re-mem-ber them no more : no more :

QUARTET

1 Tho' they be red . . . like crim-son, They shall be as woo
2 He is of great . . . com-pas-sion, And of won-d'rous love ;
3 'Look un-to Me, . . . ye peo-ple,' Saith the Lord your God;

Tho' they be red

DUET p   QUARTET f

1 Tho' your sins be as scar-let, Tho' your sins be as scar-let,
2 Hear the voice that en-treats you, Hear the voice that en-treats you,
3 He'll for-give your trans-gres-sions, He'll for-give your trans-gres-sions,

p ritard

1 They shall be as white as snow, They shall be as white as snow.
2 O re-turn ye un-to God ! O re-turn ye un-to God !
3 And re-mem-ber them no more, And re-mem-ber them no more.

95 Softly and Tenderly

WILL L. THOMPSON   WILL L. THOMPSON

1 Soft - ly and ten - der - ly Je - sus is call - ing, Call - ing for
2 Why should we tar - ry when Je - sus is plead-ing, Plead-ing for
3 Time is now fleet-ing, the mo-ments are pass-ing, Pass - ing from
4 Oh! for the won-der - ful love He has pro-mised, Pro-mised for

1 you and for me, See, on the por-tals He's wait-ing and watch-ing,
2 you and for me? Why should we lin - ger and heed not His mer-cies,
3 you and from me; Sha-dows are gath-er - ing, death-beds are com-ing,
4 you and for me; Though we have sinn'd, He has mer-cy and par-don,

REFRAIN

1 Watch-ing for you and for me........ Come home,........ come home,...........
2 Mer - cies for you and for me?....... Come home, come home,
3 Com - ing for you and for me........
4 Par - don for you and for me........

cres.   pp   ppp

Ye who are wea - ry come home,............ Earn - est - ly, ten - der - ly,

rit.   pp

Je - sus is call - ing, Call - ing, O sin - ner, "Come home!"

96 The Very Same Jesus

L. H. EDMONDS   WM. J. KIRKPATRICK

1 Come sin - ners to the liv - ing One, He's just the same Je - sus
2 Come, feast up - on the liv - ing bread, He's just the same Je - sus
3 Come, tell Him all your griefs and fears, He's just the same Je - sus
4 Still fol - low Him for clear - er light, He's just the same Je - sus
5 Then calm 'midst waves of trou - ble be, He's just the same Je - sus
6 Some day our rap-tur'd eyes shall see He's just the same Je - sus,

1 As when He rais'd the wi - dow's son, The ve - ry same Je - sus.
2 As when the mul - ti - tudes He fed, The ve - ry same Je - sus.
3 As when He shed those lov - ing tears, The ve - ry same Je - sus.
4 As when He gave the blind their sight, The ve - ry same Je - sus.
5 As when He hush'd the rag - ing sea, The ve - ry same Je - sus.
6 O bless - ed day for you and me! The ve - ry same Je - sus.

REFRAIN

The ve - ry same Je - sus, The won - der - work - ing Je - sus;

O praise His Name, He's just the same! The ve - ry same Je - sus.

97 Whosoever Means Me

J. G. BADGER

Arr. EMMA PEARCE

1 Won - d'rous love of Je - sus, spread the news a - round; . .
2 Who - so - ev - er means me bet - ter than my name, . .
3 Who - so - ev - er com - eth may the prom - ise claim, . .
4 Do not trust your feel - ings, trust His word a - lone, . .

1 Par - don free - ly of - fer'd, what a joy - ful sound! Je - sus, lov - ing
2 An - y - one, ev - 'ry - one, is not that the same? Be - lieving is sal -
3 Pre - cious blood of Je - sus cleans - eth ev - 'ry stain: The Son of God has
4 Pray'rs can nev - er save you, tears can - not a - tone: Fin - ish'd! cried the

1 Sa - viour, died to set me free; O that bles - sed Who - so - ev - er!
2 va - tion, pre - sent, full and free; Who - so - ev - er is the mes - sage,
3 lov'd me, won - der, can it be? Who - so - ev - er, saith the Sa - viour,
4 Sa - viour; no - thing now to do, Come, be - lieve this Who - so - ev - er

Whosoever Means Me—*Continued*

REFRAIN

1 that means me.
2 that means me.
3 that means me.
4 that means me.

Par - don free - ly of - fer'd all who will be - lieve;

Who - so - ev - er com - eth Je - sus will re - ceive;

Je - sus, lov - ing Sa - viour, died to set us free:

Hal - le - lu - jah! Who - so - ev - er! that means me.

98 Look and Live

WILLIAM A. OGDEN

WM. A. OGDEN, *Arr.* GEO. ALLAN

1 I've a mes-sage from the Lord, Hal - le - lu - jah! The
2 I've a mes-sage full of love, Hal - le - lu - jah! A
3 Life is of-fer'd un - to you, Hal - le - lu - jah! E -

1 mes-sage un - to you I'll give; 'Tis re - cord-ed in His Word,
2 mes-sage, O my friend, for you; 'Tis a mes-sage from a - bove,
3 ter-nal life your soul shall have; If you'll on - ly look to Him,

1 Hal - le - lu - jah! It is on - ly that you look and live.
2 Hal - le - lu - jah! Je - sus said it, and I know 'tis true.
3 Hal - le - lu - jah! Look to Je - sus, who a - lone can save.

REFRAIN

Look and live! my bro - ther, live,

Look and live! my bro - ther, live, Look and live!

Look to Je - sus now and live; 'Tis re - cord-ed in His Word,

Look and Live—*Continued*

Hal - le - lu - jah! It is on - ly that you look and live.

99 Nothing but the Blood

ROBERT LOWRY

ROBERT LOWRY

1 What can wash a - way my stain? Noth-ing but the blood of Je - sus!
2 For my cleans-ing this I see— Noth-ing but the blood of Je - sus!
3 Noth-ing can for sin a - tone, Noth-ing but the blood of Je - sus!
4 This is all my hope and peace— Noth-ing but the blood of Je - sus!
5 Now by this I ov - er - come— Noth-ing but the blood of Je - sus!

1 What can make me whole a - gain? Noth-ing but the blood of Je - sus!
2 For my par - don this my plea— Noth-ing but the blood of Je - sus!
3 Nought of good that I have done— Noth-ing but the blood of Je - sus!
4 He is all my right-eous - ness— Noth-ing but the blood of Je - sus!
5 Now by this I'll reach my home— Noth-ing but the blood of Je - sus!

REFRAIN

Oh, pre - cious is the flow That makes me white as snow!

No o - ther fount I know, Noth-ing but the blood of Je - sus!

Seeking for Thee

FANNY J. CROSBY   JOHN R. SWENEY

1 Out in the des - ert, seek - ing, seek - ing, Sin - ner, 'tis Je - sus
2 Still He is wait - ing, wait - ing, wait - ing, O what com - pas - sion
3 Lov - ing - ly plead-ing, plead-ing, plead-ing, Mer - cy, tho' slight-ed,
4 Spi - rits in glo - ry, watch-ing, watch-ing, Long to be - hold thee

1 seek - ing for thee; Ten - der - ly call - ing, call - ing, call - ing,
2 beams in His eye! Hear Him re - peat-ing gent - ly, gent - ly,
3 bears with thee yet; Thou canst be hap - py, hap - py, hap - py,
4 safe in the fold; An - gels are wait - ing, wait - ing, wait - ing,

REFRAIN

1 Hi - ther, thou lost one, O come un - to Me!
2 Come to thy Sa-viour, O why wilt thou die?
3 Come, ere thy life star for ev - er shall set.
4 When shall thy sto - ry with rap - ture be told?

Je - sus is seek - ing,

Je - sus is call - ing, Why dost thou lin - ger, why tar - ry a - way?

Run to Him quick-ly, say to Him glad-ly, Lord, I am com-ing, com-ing to - day!

The Eden Above

101

ANON

OLD MELODY

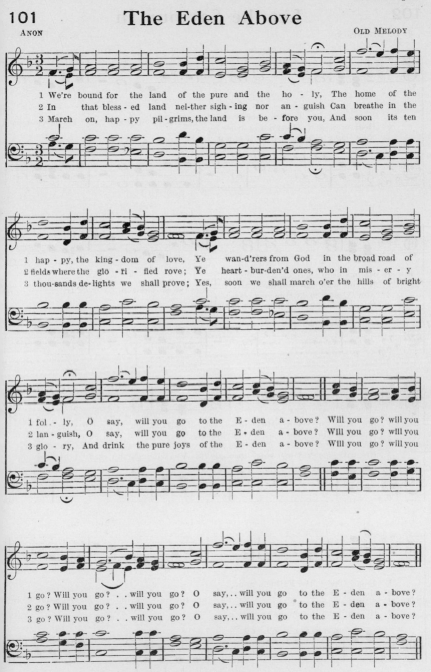

1 We're bound for the land of the pure and the ho - ly, The home of the
2 In that bless - ed land nei-ther sigh-ing nor an - guish Can breathe in the
3 March on, hap - py pil - grims, the land is be - fore you, And soon its ten

1 hap - py, the king - dom of love, Ye wan-d'rers from God in the broad road of
2 fields where the glo - ri - fied rove; Ye heart - bur-den'd ones, who in mis - er - y
3 thou-sands de - lights we shall prove; Yes, soon we shall march o'er the hills of bright

1 fol - ly, O say, will you go to the E - den a - bove? Will you go? will you
2 lan - guish, O say, will you go to the E - den a - bove? Will you go? will you
3 glo - ry, And drink the pure joys of the E - den a - bove? Will you go? will you

1 go? Will you go? . . will you go? O say, .. will you go to the E - den a - bove?
2 go? Will you go? . . will you go? O say, .. will you go to the E - den a - bove?
3 go? Will you go? . . will you go? O say, .. will you go to the E - den a - bove?

Let the Saviour In

J. B. Aitchison

E. O. Excell

Let Him in,

1 There's a stran-ger at the door,
2 O - pen now to Him your heart,
3 Hear you now His lov-ing voice?
4 Now ad - mit the heav'n-ly Guest,
Let the Sa-viour in, let the Sa-viour in;

Let Him in,

1 He has been there oft be - fore,
2 If you wait He will de - part,
3 Now, O now make Him your choice,
4 He will make for you a feast,
Let the Sa-viour in, let the Sa-viour in.

1 Let Him in, ere He is gone, Let Him in, the Ho - ly One,
2 Let Him in, He is your Friend, He your soul will sure de - fend,
3 He is stand - ing at the door, Joy to you He will re - store,
4 He will speak your sins for - giv'n, And when earth ties all are riv'n.

Let Him in,

1 Je-sus Christ, the Father's Son,
2 He will keep you to the end,
3 And His Name you will a - dore,
4 He will take you home to heav'n,
Let the Sa-viour in, let the Sa-viour in.

103   What a Wonderful Saviour!

E. A. HOFFMAN

Arr. J. M'W. BONNAR

1 Christ has for sin a - tone - ment made, What a won -
2 I praise Him for the cleans - ing blood, What a won -
3 He dwells with - in me day by day, What a won -
4 He gives me o - ver - com - ing pow'r, What a won -
5 To Him I've giv - en all my heart, What a won -

1 der - ful Sa - viour! We are re-deem'd, the price is paid,
2 der - ful Sa - viour! That re - con - cil'd my soul to God,
3 der - ful Sa - viour! And keeps me faith - ful all the way,
4 der - ful Sa - viour! And tri - umph in each con - flict hour,
5 der - ful Sa - viour! The world shall ne - ver share a part,

REFRAIN

1 - 5 What a won - der - ful Sa - viour! What a won - der - ful

Sa - viour is Je - sus, my Je - sus! What a

won - der - ful Sa - viour is Je - sus, my Lord!

104 Whiter than the Snow

E. R. LATTA

H. S. PERKINS

1 Bless-ed be the Foun-tain of blood To a world of sin-ners re-veal'd;
2 Thorn-y was the crown that He wore, And the cross His bod-y o'er-came;
3 Fa-ther, I have wan-der'd from Thee, Oft-en has my heart gone a-stray;

1 Bless-ed be the dear Son of God, On-ly by His stripes are we heal'd:
2 Griev-ous were the sor-rows He bore, But He suf-fer'd thus not in vain:
3 Crim-son do my sins seem to me: Wa-ter can-not wash them a-way;

1 Tho' I've wander'd far from His fold, Bring-ing to my heart pain and woe,
2 May I to that Foun-tain be led, Made to cleanse my sins here be-low;
3 Je-sus, to that Foun-tain of Thine, Lean-ing on Thy pro-mise I go,

1 Wash me in the blood of the Lamb, And I shall be whit-er than snow.
2 Wash me in the blood that He shed, And I shall be whit-er than snow.
3 Cleanse me by Thy wash-ing di-vine, And I shall be whit-er than snow.

Whiter than the Snow—*Continued*

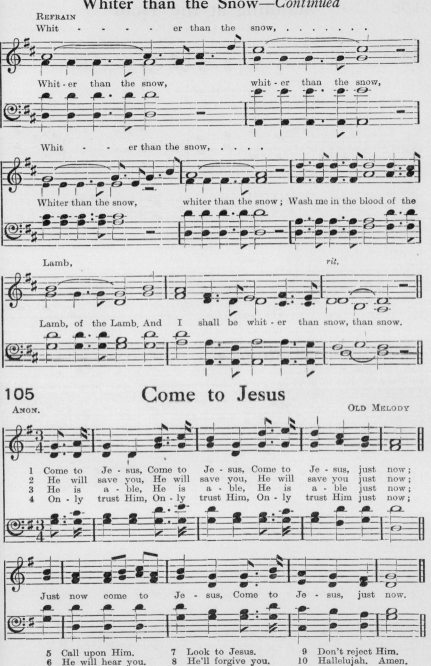

REFRAIN

Whit - - - - er than the snow, ...

Whit - er than the snow, whit - er than the snow,

Whit - - er than the snow, ...

Whiter than the snow, whiter than the snow; Wash me in the blood of the

Lamb, *rit.*

Lamb, of the Lamb. And I shall be whit - er than snow, than snow.

105 Come to Jesus

ANON.

OLD MELODY

1 Come to Je - sus, Come to Je - sus, Come to Je - sus, just now;
2 He will save you, He will save you, He will save you just now;
3 He is a - ble, He is a - ble, He is a - ble just now;
4 On - ly trust Him, On - ly trust Him, On - ly trust Him just now;

Just now come to Je - sus, Come to Je - sus, just now.

5 Call upon Him.   7 Look to Jesus.   9 Don't reject Him.
6 He will hear you.   8 He'll forgive you.   10 Hallelujah. Amen.

106 Standing at the Door

FANNY J. CROSBY PORTAL 8.8. 8.8.D J. F. KNAPP

1 Be - hold . . Me stand-ing at the door, And hear Me
2 I bore . . the cru - el thorns for thee, I wait - ed
3 I would . . not plead with thee in vain; Re - mem - ber
4 I bring . . thee joy from heav'n a - bove, I bring thee

1 plead-ing ev - er - more, With gen - tle voice : O heart of
2 long and pa - tient - ly : Say, wea - ry heart, op - prest with
3 all My grief and pain ! I died to ran - som thee from
4 par - don, peace, and love : Say, wea - ry heart, op - prest with

1-4 sin, . . May I come in, may I come in ?

REFRAIN

Be - hold Me stand-ing at the door, And hear Me pleading ev - er-more ; Say,

wea - ry heart, op-prest with sin, May I come in ? may I come in ?

107 Old, Yet Ever New

W. A. WILLIAMS   W. A. WILLIAMS

1 There is a sto-ry sweet to hear, I love to tell it too;
2 It tells me God the Son came down From glo-ry's throne to die,
3 It says He bore the Cross for me, And suf-fer'd in my place,
4 O wondrous love, so great, so vast, So bound-less and so free!

1 It fills my heart with hope and cheer, 'Tis old, yet ev-er new.
2 That I might live and wear a crown, And reign with Him on high.
3 That I from sin might ran-som'd be, And praise Him for His grace.
4 Lord, at Thy feet my-self I cast: My all I give to Thee!

REFRAIN

'Tis old, yet ev-er new, 'Tis old, yet ev-er new,
'Tis old, 'tis old, yet ev-er new, 'Tis old, 'tis old, yet ev-er new,

I know, I feel 'tis true, 'Tis old, yet ev-er new.
I know, I know, I feel 'tis true, 'Tis old, yet ev-er new.

108 Oh, How He Loves!

MARIANNE NUNN   CARITAS 8.4.8.4.8.8.8.4   R. W. BEATY

1 One there is a - bove all o - thers, Oh, how He loves!
2 'Tis e - ter - nal life to know Him, Oh, how He loves!
3 We have found a Friend in Je - sus, Oh, how He loves!
4 Through His Name we are for - giv - en, Oh, how He loves!

1 His is love be - yond a broth - er's, Oh, how He loves!
2 Think, oh, think how much we owe Him! Oh, how He loves!
3 'Tis His great de - light to bless us, Oh, how He loves!
4 Back-ward shall our foes be driv - en, Oh, how He loves!

1 Earth-ly friends may fail or leave us, One day soothe, the next day grieve us,
2 With His prec-ious blood He bought us, In the wil - der - ness He sought us,
3 How our hearts de - light to hear Him, Bid us dwell in safe - ty near Him!
4 Best of bless - ings He'll pro - vide us, Nought but good shall e'er be - tide us,

1 But this Friend will ne'er de - ceive us: Oh, how He loves!
2 To His fold He safe - ly brought us: Oh, how He loves
3 Why should we dis - trust or fear Him? Oh, how He loves:
4 Safe to glo - ry He will guide us: Oh, how He loves!

Tune GOODREST is on next page

108

Oh, How He Loves!

MARIANNE NUNN   GOODREST 8.4. 8.4. 8.8. 8.4.   C. E. KETTLE

1 One there is a - bove all oth - ers, Oh, how He loves!
2 'Tis e - ter - nal life to know Him, Oh, how He loves!
3 We have found a Friend in Je - sus, Oh, how He loves!
4 Thro' His Name we are for - giv - en, Oh, how He loves!

1 His is love be - yond a broth-er's, Oh, how He loves!
2 Think, oh, think how much we owe Him! Oh, how He loves!
3 'Tis His great de - light to bless us, Oh, how He loves!
4 Back-ward shall our foes be driv - en, Oh, how He loves!

1 Earth-ly friends may fail or leave us, One day soothe, the next day grieve us,
2 With His prec-ious blood He bought us, In the wil - der - ness He sought us,
3 How our hearts de - light to hear Him, Bid us dwell in safe - ty near Him!
4 Best of bless-ings He'll pro-vide us, Nought but good shall e'er be - tide us,

1 But this Friend will ne'er de - ceive us, Oh, how He loves!
2 To His fold He safe - ly brought us, Oh, how He loves!
3 Why should we dis - trust or fear Him? Oh, how He loves!
4 Safe to glo - ry He will guide us, Oh, how He loves!

Tune CARITAS is on opposite page

109 Bring Them In

ALEXCENAH THOMAS

A. OGDEN

1 Hark! 'tis the Shep-herd's voice I hear, Out in the de - sert
2 Who'll go and help this Shep-herd kind, Help Him the wan-d'ring
3 Out in the de - sert hear their cry: Out on the moun-tain

1 dark and drear, Call - ing the lambs who've gone a - stray,
2 lambs to find? Who'll bring the lost ones to the fold,
3 wild and high; Hark! 'tis the Mas - ter speaks to thee,

REFRAIN

1 Far from the Shep-herd's fold a - way.
2 Where they'll be shel - ter'd from the cold? } Bring them in,
3 "Go, find My lambs, where - e'er they be!"

bring them in, Bring them in from the fields of sin:

Bring them in, bring them in, Bring the wan-d'ring ones to Je - sus.

No, Not One!

110

JOHNSON OATMAN

GEORGE G. HUGG

1 There's not a friend like the low - ly Je - sus, No, not one! no, not one!
2 No friend like Him is so high and ho - ly, No, not one! no, not one:
3 There's not an hour that He is not near us, No, not one! no, not one!
4 Did ev - er saint find this Friend for - sake him? No, not one! no, not one!
5 Was e'er a gift like the Sa - viour giv - en? No, not one! no, not one!

1 None else could heal all our soul's dis - eas - es, No, not one! no, not one!
2 And yet no friend is so meek and low - ly, No, not one! no, not one!
3 No night so dark but His love can cheer us, No, not one! no, not one!
4 Or sin - ner find that He would not take him? No, not one! no, not one!
5 Will He re - fuse us a home in hea - ven? No, not one! no, not one!

REFRAIN

Je - sus knows all a - bout our strug-gles, He will guide till the day is done;

There's not a friend like the low - ly Je - sus, No, not one! no, not one!

111 What's the News?

ANON. GOOD NEWS 8.6.8.6.8.8.8.6. OLD MELODY

1 When-e'er we meet you al - ways say— 'What's the news? What's the news?
2 The Lamb was slain on Cal - va - ry— That's the news! That's the news!
3 The Lord has par - don'd all my sin— That's the news! That's the news!
4 And Je - sus Christ can save you too— That's the news! That's the news!
5 And then if an - y one should say— 'What's the news? What's the news?'

1 Pray, what's the or - der of the day— What's the news? What's the news?'
2 To set a world of sin - ners free— That's the news! That's the news!
3 I feel the wit - ness now with - in— That's the news! That's the news!
4 Your sin - ful heart He can re - new— That's the news! That's the news!
5 O tell them you've be - gun to pray!— That's the news! That's the news!

1 O I have got good news to tell! My Sav - iour hath done all things well,
2 For us He bow'd His sa - cred head, For us His prec - ious blood was shed,
3 And since He took my guilt a - way, And taught me how to watch and pray,
4 This mo - ment, if for sin you grieve, This mo - ment, if you do be - lieve,
5 That you have join'd the con - qu'ring band, And now, with joy, at God's com - mand,

1 And tri - umph'd ov - er death and hell— That's the news! That's the news!
2 And now He's ris - en from the dead— That's the news! That's the news!
3 I'm hap - py now from day to day— That's the news! That's the news!
4 A rea - dy par - don you'll re - ceive— That's the news! That's the news!
5 You're march - ing to the Bet - ter Land— That's the news! That's the news!

The tune TIDINGS is on the following page

111 What's the News?

ANON   TIDINGS 8.6.8.6.8.8.8.6   *Arr.* GEORGE ALLAN

1 When-e'er we meet you al-ways say— 'What's the news? What's the news?
2 The Lamb was slain on Cal-va-ry—   That's the news! That's the news!
3 The Lord has par-don'd all my sin—   That's the news! That's the news!
4 And Je-sus Christ can save you too—   That's the news! That's the news!
5 And then if a - ny one should say— 'What's the news? What's the news?'

1 Pray what's the or-der of the day— What's the news? What's the news?'
2 To set a world of sin-ners free—   That's the news! That's the news!
3 I feel the wit-ness now with-in—   That's the news! That's the news!
4 Your sin-ful heart He can re-new—   That's the news! That's the news!
5 O tell them you've be-gun to pray!   That's the news! That's the news!

1 O I have got good news to tell! My Sav-iour hath done all things well,
2 For us He bow'd His sac-red head, For us His pre-cious blood was shed:
3 And since He took my guilt a-way, And taught me how to watch and pray,
4 This mo-ment, if for sin you grieve, This mo-ment, if you do be-lieve,
5 That you have join'd the con-qu'ring band, And now with joy, at God's com-mand,

1 And tri-umph'd o - ver death and hell— That's the news! That's the news!
2 And now He's ris - en from the dead— That's the news! That's the news!
3 I'm hap-py now from day to day— That's the news! That's the news!
4 A rea-dy par-don you'll re-ceive— That's the news! That's the news!
5 You're march-ing to the bet-ter land— That's the news! That's the news!

The tune GOOD NEWS is on the preceding page

112 Will You Go?

ANON.   BETTER WORLD 8.6. 8.6. 8.8. 8.6.   H. P. MAIN (*Adapted*)

1 We're march-ing on to heav'n a - bove,   Will you go?   Will you go?
2 The   way to heav'n is strait, but plain,   Will you come? Will you come?
3 How   bless - ed 'tis to serve Him here!   Praise the Lord! Praise the Lord!
4 And   when our day of fight-ing's o'er;   Home at last! Home at last!

1 To   sing the Sa - viour's dy - ing love— Will you go?   Will you go?
2 Re -   pent, be - lieve, be born a - gain,   Will you come? Will you come?
3 Re -   deem'd from ev - 'ry doubt and fear, Praise the Lord! Praise the Lord!
4 We'll praise Him on the oth - er   shore, Home at last! Home at last!

1 Mill - ions have reach'd that bliss-ful shore, Their tri - als and their lab-ours o'er,
2 Christ of - fers par - don free to all, Who will ac - cept His lov - ing call,
3 Tho' trib - u - la - tion cross our way, Af - flic - tion or ad - ver - si - ty,
4 We'll join a - gain in songs of praise With those who see the Mas-ter's face.

1 And   yet there's room for mill-ions more— Will   you go?   Will   you go?
2 And   at His feet re - pent-ant fall—   Will   you come? Will   you come?
3 Yet   Je - sus saves us ev - 'ry day,   Praise the Lord! Praise the Lord!
4 And   ev - er sing re - deem-ing grace— Home at last! Home at last!

For alternative tunes see No. 111

113   The Feast is Spread

HENRY BURTON   FEAST 6.4.6.4.6.6.6.4.   PHILIPP BLISS

1 Come, for the feast is spread; Hark to the call!
2 Come where the foun-tain flows— Riv - er of life—
3 Come to the throne of grace, Bold - ly draw near;
4 Je - sus, we come to Thee, Oh, take us in!

1 Come to the Liv - ing Bread, Bro - ken for all;
2 Heal - ing for all thy woes, Doubt - ing, and strife;
3 He who would win the race Must tar - ry here;
4 Set Thou our spir - its free; Cleanse us from sin!

1 Come to His house of wine, Low on His breast re - cline,
2 Mill - ions have been sup - plied, No one was e'er de - nied;
3 What - e'er thy want may be Here is the grace for thee,
4 Then, in yon land of light, All clothed in robes of white,

1 All that He hath make thine; Come, sin - ner, come!
2 Come to the crim - son tide, Come, sin - ner, come!
3 Je - sus, thy on - ly plea; Come, Christ - ian, come!
4 Rest - ing not day nor night, Thee will we sing.

5

114 God Loved the World

MARTHA M. STOCKTON   WONDROUS LOVE C.M.D.   WILLIAM G. FISCHER

1 God lov'd the world of sin - ners lost And ru - in'd by the fall,
2 E - ter - nal prai - ses, Lord, to Thee, Thou bless - ed Son of God,
3 E'en now by faith I know I'm Thine, 'Tis in Thy faith - ful Word;
4 O help me, Lord, to spread Thy fame! And tell of all Thy grace,

1 Sal - va - tion full, at high - est cost, He off - ers free to all.
2 For Thy deep love in cleans - ing me In Thy most prec - ious blood.
3 O height! O depth of love di - vine In Thee, the ris - en Lord!
4 To all the world Thy love pro-claim Un - til I see Thy face.

REFRAIN

O 'twas love, 'twas won - drous love! The love of God to me:

rit.

It brought my Sa - viour from a - bove To die on Cal - va - ry.

The tune LAND OF REST is on the following page

114 God Loved the World

MARTHA M. STOCKTON LAND OF REST C.M.D. RICHARD S. NEWMAN

1 God lov'd the world of sin - ners lost And ru - in'd by the fall,
2 E - ter - nal prai - ses, Lord, to Thee, Thou bless - ed Son of God,
3 E'en now by faith I know I'm Thine, 'Tis in Thy faith - ful Word;
4 O help me, Lord, to spread Thy fame! And tell of all Thy grace,

1 Sal - va - tion full, at high - est cost, He off - ers free to all.
2 For Thy deep love In cleans - ing me In Thy most prec - ious blood.
3 O height! O depth of love di - vine In Thee, the ris - en Lord!
4 To all the world Thy love pro - claim Un - til I see Thy face,

REFRAIN

O 'twas . love, 'twas won - drous love! The love . of God to me:

It brought my Sa - viour from a - bove To die on Cal - va - ry.

The tune WONDROUS LOVE is on the preceding page

115 **Seeking for Me**

A. N.

Arr. E. E. HASTY

1 Je - sus, my Sa - viour, to Beth - le -hem came, Born in a
2 Je - sus, my Sa - viour, on Cal - var - y's tree Paid the great
3 Je - sus, my Sa - viour, the same as of old, While I was
4 Je - sus, my Sa - viour, shall come from on high; Sweet is the

1 man - ger to sor - row and shame; O it was won - der-ful— blest
2 debt, and my soul He set free; O it was won - der-ful— how
3 wan - d'ring a - far from the fold Gent - ly and long did He plead
4 prom - ise as wea - ry years fly; O I shall see Him de - scend-

REFRAIN

1 be His Name! Seek-ing for me, for me! . . Seek-ing for me!
2 could it be? Dy -ing for me, for me! . . Dy -ing for me!
3 with my soul, Call-ing for me, for me! . . Call-ing for me!
4 ing the sky! Com-ing for me, for me! . . Com-ing for me!

For me! . .   For me! . .

1 . Seek-ing for me! . Seek-ing for me! . Seek-ing for me! . O it
2 . Dy -ing for me! . Dy -ing for me! . Dy -ing for me! . O it
3 . Call-ing for me! . Call-ing for me! . Call-ing for me! . Gent - ly
. Com-ing for me! . Com-ing for me! . Com-ing for me! . O 1

Seeking for Me—*Continued*

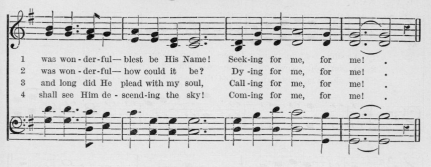

1 was won-der-ful— blest be His Name! Seek-ing for me, for me!
2 was won-der-ful— how could it be? Dy-ing for me, for me!
3 and long did He plead with my soul, Call-ing for me, for me!
4 shall see Him de-scend-ing the sky! Com-ing for me, for me!

In the following Tune the REFRAIN is omitted

A. N   CLARE MARKET 10.10.10.8   MARY PALMER

1 Je - sus, my Sa - viour, to Beth - le-hem came, . Born in a
2 Je - sus, my Sa - viour, on Cal - var - y's tree , Paid the great
3 Je - sus, my Sa - viour, the same as of old, . While I was
4 Je - sus, my Sa - viour, shall come from on high: . Sweet is the

1 man - ger to sor - row and shame; O it was won - der - ful— blest be His
2 debt, and my soul He set free; O it was won - der - ful— how could it
3 wan - d'ring a - far from the fold Gent - ly and long did He plead with my
4 pro - mise as wea - ry years fly; O I shall see Him de - scend - ing the

1 Name! . Seek - ing for me, . Seek - ing for me!
2 be? . Dy - ing for me, . Dy - ing for me!
3 soul, . Call - ing for me, . Call - ing for me!
4 sky! . Com - ing for me, . Com - ing for me!

I'm Redeemed

T. C. O'Kane

T. C. O'Kane

1 O sing of Je - sus, Lamb of God, Who died on Cal - va - ry!
2 O wondrous pow'r of love di - vine! So rich, so full, so free,
3 All glo - ry now to Christ the Lord, And ev - er - more shall be,

1 And for a ran - som shed His blood For you, and e - ven me.
2 It reach - es out to all man-kind, Em - brac - es e - ven me.
3 He hath re - deem'd a world of sin, And ran-som'd e - ven me.

REFRAIN

I'm re - deem'd . . . I'm re - deem'd, . . . Thro' the
I'm re-deem'd, I'm re-deem'd,

blood of the Lamb that was slain; . . . I'm re - deem'd, . . .
of the Lamb that was slain, I'm re-deem'd,

I'm re - deem'd, . . Hal - le - lu - jah to God and the Lamb!
I'm re-deem'd,

117 One Who Loves Thee

H. C. AYRES

W. H. DOANE

1 One there is who loves thee, Wait-ing still for thee; Canst thou yet re-
2 Gra-cious-ly He woos thee, Do not slight His call; Tho' thy sins are
3 Je-sus still is wait-ing; Sin-ner, why de-lay? To His arms of

1 ject Him? None so kind as He! Do not grieve Him long-er,
2 ma-ny, He'll for-give them all. Turn to Him, re-pent-ing,
3 mer-cy Rise and haste a-way! On-ly come be-liev-ing,

1 Come and trust Him now! He has wait-ed all thy days: Why wait-est thou?
2 He will cleanse thee now; He is wait-ing at thy heart: Why wait-est thou?
3 He will save thee now; He is wait-ing at the door: Why wait-est thou?

REFRAIN

One there is who loves thee, O re-ceive Him now!

He has wait-ed all thy days; Why wait-est thou?

118 ## Ye Must be Born Again

W. T. SLEEPER

GEO. C. STEBBINS
Arr. P. J. MANSFIELD

1 A rul-er once came to Je-sus by night To ask Him the way
2 Ye chil-dren of men! at-tend to the word So sol-emn-ly ut-
3 O ye who would en-ter the glo-ri-ous rest! And sing with the ran-
4 A dear one in hea-ven thy heart yearn to see, At the beau-ti-ful gates

1 of sal-va-tion and light; The Mas-ter made an-swer in words true and plain,
2 ter'd by Je-sus, the Lord, And let not this mes-sage to you be in vain,
3 som'd the song of the blest; The life ev-er-last-ing if ye would ob-tain,
4 may be watch-ing for thee; Then list to the note of this sol-emn re-frain,

a - gain. . . REFRAIN

1-4 'Ye must be born a-gain, a-gain.' 'Ye must be

a - gain, . . a - gain!' . .

born a-gain, a-gain,' 'Ye must be born a-gain, a-gain!' I ver-i-ly,

a - gain!' . .

ver-i-ly say un-to you—'Ye must be born a-gain, a-gain!'

119 Jesus will Give you Rest

FANNY CROSBY JNO. R. SWENEY

1 Will you come, will you come with your poor brok-en heart, Bur-den'd and sin op -
2 Will you come, will you come? there is mer - cy for you, Balm for your ach - ing
3 Will you come, will you come? you have no-thing to pay; Je - sus who loves you
4 Will you come, will you come? how He pleads with you now! Fly to His lov - ing

1 press'd ? Lay it down at the feet of the Sa - viour and Lord,
2 breast: On - ly come as you are and be - lieve on His Name,
3 best. By His death on the Cross pur-chas'd life for your soul;
4 breast; And what - ev - er your sin or your sor - row may be,

REFRAIN

1-4 Je - sus will give you rest. O hap-py rest, sweet hap-py rest !

Je - sus will give you rest. O why won't you come in

hap-py rest,

sim - ple, trust - ing faith ! Je - sus will give you rest.

120 Able to Deliver

W. A. OGDEN

W. A. OGDEN, *arr.* P. J. MANSFIELD

1 'Tis the grandest theme thro' the a - ges rung, 'Tis the grandest theme for a mortal tongue,
2 'Tis the grandest theme in the earth or main, 'Tis the grandest theme for a mortal strain,
3 'Tis the grandest theme, let the tid-ings roll To the guilt-y heart, to the sin-ful soul;

1 'Tis the grandest theme that the world e'er sung, Our God is a - ble to de - liv - er thee.
2 'Tis the grandest theme, tell the world a - gain, Our God is a - ble to de - liv - er thee.
3 Look to God in faith, He will make thee whole, Our God is a - ble to de - liv - er thee.

REFRAIN

He is a - - - ble to de - liv - er thee, He is
a - ble, He is a - ble

a - - - ble to de - liv - er thee; Tho' by sin op-prest, Go to
a - ble, He is a - ble

Him for rest; Our God is a - ble to de - liv - er thee.

121 There is a Green Hill

C. F. ALEXANDER   STEBBINS C.M.D.   GEO. C. STEBBINS

1 There is   a green hill far a - way, With-out a cit - y   wall,
2 We may not know, we can - not tell What pains He had   to   bear;
3 He died that we might be for-giv'n, He died to do   us   good,
4 There was no o - ther good e - nough To pay the price of   sin;

1 Where the dear Lord was cru - ci - fied, Who died to save us   all.
2 But we be - lieve it   was for us He hung and suf - fer'd there.
3 That we might go at   last to heav'n, Sav'd by His pre - cious blood.
4 He   on - ly could un - lock the gate Of heav'n, and let us   in.

REFRAIN

O   dear - ly, dear - ly has He lov'd! And we must love Him too;

rit.

And trust in His re - deem - ing love, And try His works to   do.

The tunes HORSLEY and MEDITATION are on the following page

121 There is a Green Hill

C. F. ALEXANDER   HORSLEY C.M.   WM. HORSLEY

1 There is a green hill far a-way, With-out a ci-ty wall,
2 We may not know, we can-not tell, What pains He had to bear,
3 He died that we might be for-giv'n, He died to make us good,
4 There was no o-ther good e-nough To pay the price of sin:
5 Oh, dear-ly, dear-ly has He loved, And we must love Him too,

1 Where the dear Lord was cru-ci-fied, Who died to save us all.
2 But we be-lieve it was for us He hung and suf-fer'd there.
3 That we might go at last to heav'n, Saved by His pre-cious blood.
4 He on-ly could un-lock the gate Of heav'n, and let us in.
5 And trust in His re-deem-ing blood, And try His works to do.

Tune STEBBINS is on previous page

C. F. ALEXANDER   MEDITATION C.M.   JOHN H. GOWER

1 There is a green hill far a-way, With-out a ci-ty wall,
2 We may not know, we can-not tell, What pains He had to bear,
3 He died that we might be for-giv'n, He died to make us good,
4 There was no o-ther good e-nough To pay the price of sin:
5 Oh, dear-ly, dear-ly has He loved, And we must love Him too,

1 Where the dear Lord was cru-ci-fied, Who died to save us all.
2 But we be-lieve it was for us He hung and suf-fer'd there.
3 That we might go at last to heav'n, Saved by His pre-cious blood.
4 He on-ly could un-lock the gate Of heav'n, and let us in.
5 And trust in His re-deem-ing blood, And try His works to do.

122 Any Room for Jesus?

Daniel W. Whittle   Room for Jesus 8.7.8.7.D   C. C. Williams

1 Have you an-y room for Je-sus, . He who bore your load of
2 Room for pleas-ure, room for busi-ness, . But for Christ the cru-ci-
3 Have you an-y time for Je-sus, . As in grace He calls a-
4 Room and time now give to Je-sus, . Soon will pass God's day of

1 sin? . . As He knocks and asks ad-mis-sion,
2 fied; . . Not a place that He can en-ter
3 gain? . . O to-day is time ac-cep-ted! . . To-
4 grace; . . Soon thy heart left cold and si-lent,

REFRAIN

1 Sin-ner, will you let Him in?
2 In your heart for which He died!
3 mor-row you may call in vain.
4 And thy Sa-viour's plead-ing cease.

Room for Je-sus, King of

glo-ry, Has-ten now, His word o-bey, . . Swing the

heart's door wide-ly o-pen, Bid Him en-ter while you may. .

123   Come to the Saviour

GEORGE F. ROOT   INVITATION 9.9.9.6. D   GEORGE F. ROOT

1 Come to the Sa - viour, make no de - lay, Here in His Word He has
2 "Suf - fer the chil-dren!" oh, hear His voice! Let ev - 'ry heart leap
3 Think once a - gain, He's with us to - day; Heed now His blest com -

1 shown us the way; Here in our midst He's stand - ing to - day,
2 forth and re - joice; And let us free - ly make Him our choice,
3 mand, and o - bey: Hear now His ac - cents ten - der - ly say,

REFRAIN

1 Ten - der - ly say - ing, "Come!"
2 Do not de - lay, but come.
3 "Will you, My chil - dren, come?"   Joy - ful, joy - ful

will the meet-ing be, When from sin our hearts are pure and free,

And we shall ga - ther, Sa-viour, with Thee, In our e - ter - nal home.

124   Oh, be Saved !

Fanny J. Crosby   Jura   8.7. 8.7. 7.7.7.   S. J. Vail

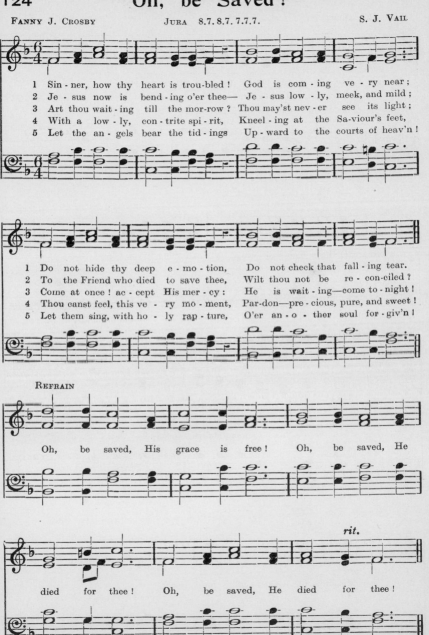

1 Sin - ner, how thy heart is trou-bled !   God is com - ing   ve - ry near ;
2 Je - sus now is   bend - ing o'er thee— Je - sus low - ly,   meek, and mild ;
3 Art thou wait - ing   till the mor-row ? Thou may'st nev - er   see its light ;
4 With a   low - ly,   con - trite spi - rit,   Kneel - ing at the Sa-viour's feet,
5 Let the an - gels bear the tid - ings   Up - ward to the courts of heav'n !

1 Do not hide thy deep   e - mo - tion,   Do not check that fall - ing tear.
2 To the Friend who died   to save thee,   Wilt thou not be   re - con - ciled ?
3 Come at once ! ac - cept His mer - cy :   He is wait - ing—come to - night !
4 Thou canst feel, this ve - ry mo - ment,   Par-don—pre - cious, pure, and sweet !
5 Let them sing, with ho - ly rap - ture,   O'er an - o - ther soul for - giv'n !

Refrain

Oh, be saved, His grace is free !   Oh, be saved, He

rit.

died for thee !   Oh, be saved, He died for thee !

125 Calling the Prodigal

CHAS. H. GABRIEL

CHAS. H. GABRIEL

1 God is call-ing the prod-i-gal, come with-out de-lay, . . .
2 Pa-tient, lov-ing, and ten-der-ly still the Fa-ther pleads, . .
3 Come, there's bread in the house of thy Fa-ther, and to spare, . .

1-3 Hear, O hear Him call-ing, call-ing now for thee ! . . .
for thee,

1 Tho' you've wan-der'd so far from His pres-ence, come to-day, . . .
2 O re-turn while the Spir-it in mer-cy in-ter-cedes ! . .
3 Lo ! the ta-ble is spread and the feast is wait-ing there, . .

1-3 Hear His lov-ing voice call-ing still, ...
call-ing still.

Calling the Prodigal—*Continued*

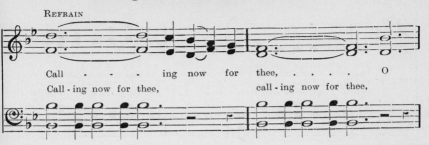

Call - - - ing now for thee, ... O
Call - ing now for thee, call - ing now for thee,

wea - - - - ry pro-di-gal, come! . . .
wea - ry pro-di-gal, come! wea - ry pro-di-gal, come!

Call - - - ing now for thee, . . . O
Call - ing now for thee, call - ing now for thee,

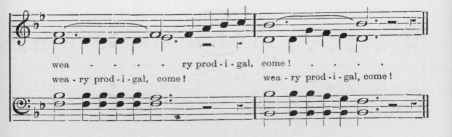

wea - - - - ry prod-i-gal, come! . . . .
wea - ry prod-i-gal, come! wea - ry prod-i-gal, come!

Than Tongue can Tell

J. E. Hall   Tongue Can Tell 8.8. 8.6.D.   J. E. Hall

1 The love that Je-sus had for me   To suf-fer on the cru-el tree,
2 The bit-ter sorrow that He bore,   And O that crown of thorns He wore!
3 The peace I have in Him, my Lord,   Who pleads be-fore the throne of God
4 The joy that comes when He is near,   The rest He gives, so free from fear,

1 That I a ran-som'd soul might be,   Is more than tongue can tell!
2 That I might live for ev-er-more,   Is more than tongue can tell!
3 The mer-it of His pre-cious blood,   Is more than tongue can tell!
4 The hope in Him so bright and clear,   Is more than tongue can tell!

Refrain

His love is more than tongue can tell!   His
than tongue can tell!

love is more than tongue can tell!   The
than tongue can tell!

love that Je-sus had for me . . Is more than tongue can tell!

The tune SAGINA is on the following page

126 Than Tongue can Tell

J. E. HALL   SAGINA 8.8. 8.8.D.   T. CAMPBELL

1 The love that Je - sus had for me To suf - fer on the
2 The bit - ter sor - row that He bore, And O that crown of
3 The peace I have in Him, my Lord, Who pleads be - fore the
4 The joy that comes when He is near, The rest He gives, so

1 cru - el tree, That I a ran - som'd soul might be, Is more, is
2 thorns He wore! That I might live for ev - er - more, Is more, is
3 throne of God The mer - it of His pre - cious blood, Is more, is
4 free from fear, The hope in Him so bright and clear, Is more, is

REFRAIN

1-4 more than tongue can tell! His love is more than tongue can tell!

His love is more than tongue can tell! The love that Je - sus
His love is more than tongue can tell! His love is more

had for me Is more than tongue can tell, than tongue can tell!
than tongue can tell! His love is more than tongue can tell!

The tune TONGUE CAN TELL is on the preceding page

127   The Wonderful Story

CHARLES H. GABRIEL   CHARLES H. GABRIEL

1 O . sweet . is the sto - ry of Je - sus!
2 He . came . from the bright - est of glo - ry;
3 His . mer - cy flows on like a riv - er,

1 The . won - der - ful Sa - viour of men, .
   His . blood . as a ran - som He gave .
3 His . love . is un - mea - sur'd and free; .

1 Who suf - fer'd and died for the sin - ner;
2 To . pur - chase e - ter - nal re - demp - tion,
3 His . grace - is for - ev - er suf - fi - cient,

1 I'll . tell . it a - gain and a - gain! .
2 And . O . He is might - y to save! .
3 It . reach . es and pu - ri - fies me. .

The Wonderful Story—*Continued*

REFRAIN

O . won - - der-ful, won-der-ful sto - - ry ! .
O . won-der-ful sto - - ry! . O won-der-ful sto - ry !

The dear - - est that ev - er was told, . .
The dear-est that ev - - er, . that ev - er was told,

I'll re-peat it in glo - - ry, The won-der-ful sto -
. . . I'll re-peat it in glo-ry, The won-der-ful

rit.

ry, . Where I . . . shall His beau-ty be - hold. . .
sto - ry, Where I shall His beau - - ty, . His beau-ty be-ho·d.

128

Power to Save

W. A. Ogden

W. A. Ogden

1 There's a song my heart is sing-ing; In my soul its tones are ring-ing,
2 O that song my soul is thrill-ing! Je - sus saves the soul that's will-ing,
3 Sin - ner, come! if thou'lt re - ceive Him, Look to Je - sus and be - lieve Him;

1 Peace and rest and joy 'tis bring-ing: Je - sus Christ has pow'r to save!
2 Pre-cious truth my heart 'tis fill - ing: Je - sus Christ has pow'r to save!
3 All your life and ser - vice give Him: Je - sus Christ has pow'r to save!

REFRAIN

Sing it o - ver and o - ver a - gain to me

Sing it o'er . . . a - gain to me . . . In its

cres.

In it's won-der-ful sweet sim - pli - ci - ty; Tell it o'er . . the

Tell it o'er the

sweet . . sim - pli - ci - ty; . . .

o - cean wave, Je - sus Christ . . has pow'r to save.
o - cean wave, Je-sus Christ has pow'r to save.

129 Salvation!

P. P. Bliss

P. P. Bliss

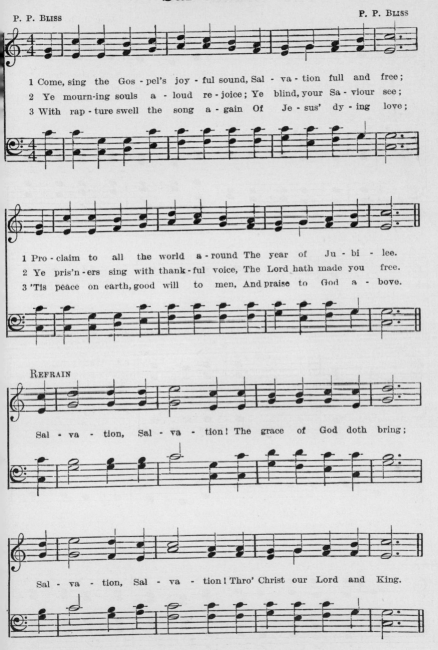

1 Come, sing the Gos - pel's joy - ful sound, Sal - va - tion full and free;
2 Ye mourn-ing souls a - loud re - joice; Ye blind, your Sa - viour see;
3 With rap - ture swell the song a - gain Of Je - sus' dy - ing love;

1 Pro - claim to all the world a - round The year of Ju - bi - lee.
2 Ye pris'n - ers sing with thank - ful voice, The Lord hath made you free.
3 'Tis peace on earth, good will to men, And praise to God a - bove.

REFRAIN

Sal - va - tion, Sal - va - tion! The grace of God doth bring;

Sal - va - tion, Sal - va - tion! Thro' Christ our Lord and King.

130 The Grand Old Story

E. E. Hewitt

Wm. J. Kirkpatrick

1 We tell it as we jour - ney toward the man - sions built a -
2 His hand can lift the fall - en and His blood can make them
3 We'll sing it in the bat - tle, and its notes shall vic - t'ry
4 The an - gels look with won - der, yet their harps can nev - er

1 bove, The grand old sto - ry of sal - va - tion;
2 white, The grand old sto - ry of sal - va - tion;
3 be, The grand old sto - ry of sal - va - tion;
4 tell The grand old sto - ry of sal - va - tion;

1 We sing it out with glad - ness in the mel - o - dies of
2 His love can pierce the dark - ness with a ne - ver - fad - ing
3 We'll sing it in our tri - als till the pass - ing sha - dows
4 His ran-som'd, cloth'd with beau - ty, shall the praise of Je - sus

The Grand Old Story—*Continued*

1 love, The grand old sto - ry of sal - va - tion.
2 light, The grand old sto - ry of sal - va - tion.
3 flee, The grand old sto - ry of sal - va - tion.
4 swell, The grand old sto - ry of sal - va - tion.

REFRAIN

Ring it out, ring it out! Ring to
Ring it out, ring it out!

ev - 'ry tribe and na - tion, Ring it out ev - 'ry-where,

Ring it out! The grand old sto - ry of sal - va - tion.
ev - 'ry-where!

131

Come, Ye Sinners

JOSEPH HART ROUSSEAU 8.7.8.7. D JEAN J. ROUSSEAU

1 Come, ye sin - ners, poor and need - y, Weak and wound - ed,
2 Let not con - science make you ling - er, Nor of fit - ness

1 sick and sore, Je - sus read - y stands to save you, Full of
2 fond - ly dream; All the fit - ness He re - quir - eth Is to

1 pi - ty, love, and pow'r: Now, ye need - y, come and
2 feel your need of Him: Come, ye wea - ry, heav - y

1 wel - come, God's free boun - ty glo - ri - fy; True be -
2 la - den, Bruis'd and man - gled by the fall: If you

1 lief and true re - pen - tance, Ev - 'ry grace that brings you nigh.
2 tar - ry till you're bet - ter You will nev - er come at all.

The tune NORMANDY is on the following page

Come, Ye Sinners

131

JOSEPH HART NORMANDY 8.7.8.7.D. A. BOST

1 Come, ye sin-ners, poor and need-y, Weak and wound-ed sick and sore,
2 Let not con-science make you ling-er, Nor of fit-ness fond-ly dream,

1 Je - sus read-y stands to save you, Full of pi - ty, love, and pow'r:
2 All the fit-ness He re - quir-eth Is to feel your need of Him:

1 Now, ye need-y, come and wel - come, God's free boun - ty glo - ri - fy;
2 Come, ye wea - ry, heav-y la - den, Bruis'd and man - gled by the fall:

1 True be - lief and true re - pen-tance, Ev - 'ry grace that brings you nigh,
2 If you tar - ry till you're bet - ter, You will nev - er come at all.

The tune ROUSSEAU is on the preceding page

132   The Old, Old Story

KATE HANKEY   EVANGEL   W. H. DOANE

1 Tell me the old, old sto - ry Of un - seen things a - bove.
2 Tell me the sto - ry slow - ly That I may take it in—
3 Tell me the sto - ry soft - ly, With ear - nest tones, and grave:
4 Tell me the same old sto - ry, When you have cause to fear

1 Of Je - sus and His glo - ry, Of Je - sus and His love:
2 That won - der - ful re - demp - tion, God's rem - e - dy for sin:
3 Re - mem - ber I'm the sin - ner Whom Je - sus came to save:
4 That this world's emp - ty glo - ry Is cost - ing me too dear:

1 Tell me the sto - ry sim - ply, As to a lit - tle child,
2 Tell me the sto - ry of - ten For I for - get so soon;
3 Tell me that sto - ry al - ways If you would real - ly be
4 Yes, and when that world's glo - ry Is dawn - ing on my soul.

1 For I am weak and wea - ry, And help - less, and de - fil'd.
2 The ear - ly dew of morn - ing Has pass'd a - way at noon.
3 In a - ny time of trou - ble A com - fort - er to me.
4 Tell me the old, old sto - ry, Christ Je - sus makes thee whole.

The Old, Old Story—*Continued*

REFRAIN

Tell me the old, old sto - ry, Tell me the old, old sto - ry,

Tell me the old, old sto - ry Of Je - sus and His love.

Words by permission of LONGMAN'S, GREEN & CO.

An Alternative Tune when the REFRAIN is used alone

KATE HANKEY   AULE 7.6.7.6.   OLD MELODY

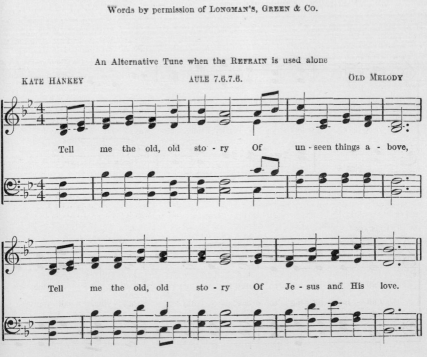

Tell me the old, old sto - ry Of un - seen things a - bove,

Tell me the old, old sto - ry Of Je - sus and His love.

133 Jesus is Calling

FANNY J. CROSBY   GEORGE C. STEBBINS

1 Je - sus is ten - der - ly call - ing thee home,   Call - ing to - day!
2 Je - sus is call - ing the wea - ry to rest,   Call - ing to - day!
3 Je - sus is wait - ing, O come to Him now!   Wait - ing to - day!
4 Je - sus is plead - ing, O list to His voice!   Hear Him to - day!

1 call - ing to - day!   Why from the sun - shine of love wilt
2 call - ing to - day!   Bring Him thy bur - den and thou shalt
3 wait - ing to - day!   Come with thy sins— at His feet low -
4 hear Him to - day!   They who be - lieve on His Name shall

a - way? . . . .
a - way. . . . .
de - lay. . . . .
a - way! . . . .

1 thou roam,   Far - ther and far - ther, and far - ther a - way?
2 be blest,   He will not turn thee, not turn thee a - way.
3 ly bow,   Come and no long - er, no long - er de - lay.
4 re - joice, Quick - ly a - rise, come a - way, come a - way!

a - way? . . . .
a - way. . . . .
de - lay. . . . .
a - way! . . . .

REFRAIN

Call - ing to - day!   Call - ing to -
Call - ing, call - ing to - day, to - day!   Call - ing, call - ing to -

Jesus is Calling—*Continued*

day   Je - sus is call -

day, to - day!   Je - sus is call - ing, is ten - der - ly call -

ing, is ten - der - ly call - ing to - day.

ing, is ten - der - ly call - ing, is call - ing to - day!

An Alternative Tune for the Refrain

FANNY J. CROSBY   STANWIX 8.9.11.9.   DAVID J. BEATTIE

Call - ing to - day,   Call - ing to - day,

Je - sus is call - ing,   call - ing to - day;   Je - sus is call - ing, is

ten - der - ly call - ing;   Je - sus is call - ing,   call - ing to - day.

Music by permission of DAVID J. BEATTIE

134 The Conquering Saviour

HENRY Q. WILSON   LION OF JUDAH 11.11.11.11.   *Arr.* HENRY TUCKER

1 'Twas Je - sus, my Sa - viour, who died on the tree
2 And when I was will - ing with all things to part,
3 Tho' round me the storms of ad - ver - si - ty roll,
4 And when with the ran - som'd of Je - sus, my head,
5 Come, sin - ners, to Je - sus! no lon - ger de - lay;

REFRAIN.—For the con - quer - ing Sa - viour shall break ev - 'ry chain,

1 To o - pen a foun - tain for sin - ners like me; His
2 He gave me my boun - ty, His love in my heart; So
3 And the waves of de - struc - tion en - com - pass my soul, In
4 From foun - tain to foun - tain I then shall be led, I'll
5 A full free sal - va - tion He of - fers to - day; A -

And give us the vic - t'ry a - gain and a - gain; For the

1 blood is the foun - tain that par - don be - stows,
2 now I am join'd with the con - quer - ing band,
3 vain this frail ves - sel the tem - pest shall toss,
4 fall at His feet and His mer - cy a - dore,
5 rouse your dark spi - rits, a - wake from your dream,

con - quer - ing Sa - viour shall break ev - 'ry chain,

D.C. for REFRAIN.

1 And cleans - es the foul - est wher - ev - er it flows.
2 Who are march - ing to glo - ry at Je - sus' com - mand.
3 My hopes rest se - cure on the blood of the Cross.
4 And sing of the blood of the Cross ev - er - more.
5 And Christ will sup - port you in com - ing to Him.

And give us the vic - t'ry a - gain and a - gain.

The tune ST. DENIO is on the following page

134 The Conquering Saviour

HENRY Q. WILSON   ST. DENIO 11.11.11.11.   WELSH HYMN MELODY

1 'Twas   Je - sus,   my   Sa - viour,   who   died   on   the   tree
2 And   when I   was   will - ing   with   all   things to   part,
3 Tho'   round me   the   storms of   ad - ver - si - ty   roll,
4 And   when with   the   ran - som'd   of   Je - sus,   my   head,
5 Come, sin - ners,   to   Je - sus !   no   lon - ger de -   lay;

REFRAIN.—For the con - quer - ing   Sa - viour shall   break ev - 'ry   chain.

1 To   o - pen   a   foun - tain for   sin - ners like   me;
2 He   gave   my   boun - ty,   His   love   in   my   heart;
3 And   the waves of de - struc - tion en - com - pass my   soul,
4 From foun - tain to   foun - tain I   then shall be   led,
5 A   full free   sal - va - tion He   of - fers to -   day;

And give us   the   vic - t'ry a -   gain and a - gain;

1 His   blood is   the   foun - tain that   par - don be - stows,
2 So   now   I   am   join'd with the   con - quer - ing band
3 In   vain this   frail ves - sel   the   tem - pest shall toss,
4 I'll fall at   His   feet and   His   mer - cy a -   dore,
5 A - rouse your dark   spi - rits, a -   wake from your dream,

D.C. for REFRAIN

1 And   cleans - es   the   foul - est   wher - ev - er   it   flows.
2 Who are march - ing to   glo - ry   at   Je - sus' com - mand.
3 My   hopes rest se - cure   on   the   blood of   the   Cross.
4 And   sing   of   the   blood of   the   Cross ev - er - more.
5 And   Christ will sup - port you   in   com - ing to   Him.

135   # The Half Never Told

PHILIP P. BLISS   PHILIP P. BLISS

1 Re - peat the sto - ry o'er and o'er Of grace so full and free; I
2 Of peace I on - ly knew the name, Nor found my soul its rest, Un -
3 My high - est place is— ly - ing low At my Re - deem - er's feet; No
4 And O what rap - ture will it be! With all the hosts a - bove, To

1 love to hear it more and more Since grace has res - cued me.
2 til the sweet-voic'd an - gel came To soothe my wea - ry breast.
3 re - al joy in life I know But in His ser - vice sweet.
4 sing thro' all e - ter - ni - ty The won - ders of His love.

REFRAIN

1,2 The half .. was nev-er told, The half .. was nev-er told; Of
3,4 The half was nev - er, nev-er told, The half was nev - er, nev-er told; Of

1 grace
2 peace di - vine, so won - der - ful, The half .. was nev-er told.
3 joy
4 love di - vine, so won - der - ful, The half was nev - er .. told.

136 Come, Sinner, Come!

W. E. WITTER   H. R. PALMER

1 While Je - sus whis - pers to you, Come, sin - ner, come!
2 Are you too hea - vy la - den? Come, sin - ner, come!
3 O hear His ten - der plead - ing! Come, sin - ner, come!

1 While we are pray - ing for you, Come, sin - ner, come!
2 Je - sus will bear your bur - den, Come, sin - ner, come!
3 O now re - ceive the bless - ing! Come, sin - ner, come!

1 Now is the time to own Him, Come, sin - ner, come!
2 Je - sus will not de - ceive you, Come, sin - ner, come!
3 While Je - sus whis - pers to you, Come, sin - ner, come!

1 Now is the time to know Him, Come, sin - ner, come!
2 Je - sus will now re - ceive us, Come, sin - ner, come!
3 While we are pray - ing for you, Come, sin - ner, come!

137 There is a Fountain

WILLIAM COWPER   FOUNTAIN C.M.   OLD MELODY

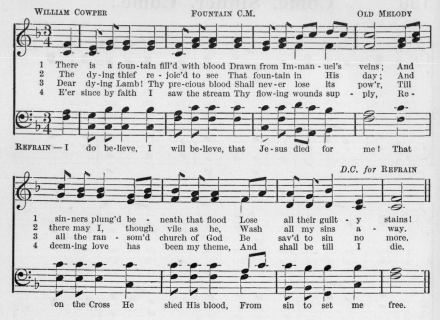

1 There is a foun-tain fill'd with blood Drawn from Im-man-uel's veins; And
2 The dy-ing thief re-joic'd to see That foun-tain in His day; And
3 Dear dy-ing Lamb! Thy pre-cious blood Shall nev-er lose its pow'r, Till
4 E'er since by faith I saw the stream Thy flow-ing wounds sup - ply, Re -

REFRAIN — I do be-lieve, I will be-lieve, that Je-sus died for me! That

D.C. for REFRAIN

1 sin-ners plung'd be - neath that flood Lose all their guilt - y stains!
2 there may I, though vile as he, Wash all my sins a - way.
3 all the ran - som'd church of God Be sav'd to sin no more.
4 deem-ing love has been my theme, And shall be till I die.

on the Cross He shed His blood, From sin to set me free.

In the following tune the Refrain is sung as verse 5

WILLIAM COWPER   UXBRIDGE C.M.   *Dibdin's Psalm Tune Book,* 1857

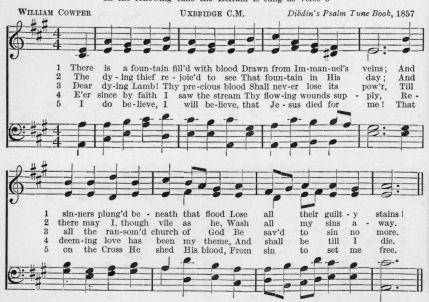

1 There is a foun-tain fill'd with blood Drawn from Im-man-uel's veins; And
2 The dy-ing thief re - joic'd to see That foun-tain in His day; And
3 Dear dy-ing Lamb! Thy pre-cious blood Shall nev-er lose its pow'r, Till
4 E'er since by faith I saw the stream Thy flow-ing wounds sup - ply, Re-
5 I do be-lieve, I will be-lieve, that Je - sus died for me! That

1 sin-ners plung'd be - neath that flood Lose all their guilt - y stains!
2 there may I, though vile as he, Wash all my sins a - way.
3 all the ran-som'd church of God Be sav'd to sin no more.
4 deem-ing love has been my theme, And shall be till I die.
5 on the Cross He shed His blood, From sin to set me free.

The tunes CLEANSING FOUNTAIN and FLOWING STREAM are on the following pages

There is a Fountain

137

WILLIAM COWPER CLEANSING FOUNTAIN OLD MELODY, *Arr.* P. J. MANSFIELD

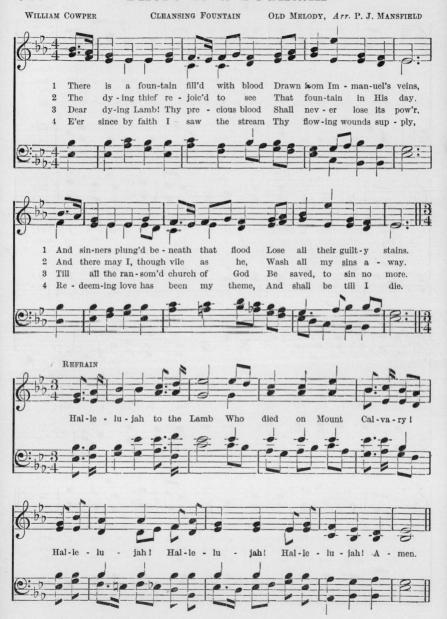

1 There is a foun-tain fill'd with blood Drawn from Im - man-uel's veins,
2 The dy - ing thief re - joic'd to see That foun-tain in His day,
3 Dear dy-ing Lamb! Thy pre - cious blood Shall nev - er lose its pow'r,
4 E'er since by faith I saw the stream Thy flow-ing wounds sup - ply,

1 And sin-ners plung'd be - neath that flood Lose all their guilt-y stains.
2 And there may I, though vile as he, Wash all my sins a - way.
3 Till all the ran - som'd church of God Be saved, to sin no more.
4 Re - deem-ing love has been my theme, And shall be till I die.

REFRAIN

Hal - le - lu - jah to the Lamb Who died on Mount Cal - va - ry!

Hal - le - lu - jah! Hal - le - lu - jah! Hal - le - lu - jah! A - men.

The tunes FOUNTAIN and UXBRIDGE precede, and FLOWING STREAM follows this tune

137 There is a Fountain

WILLIAM COWPER   FLOWING STREAM C.M.D.   OLD MELODY

1 There is a foun-tain fill'd with blood Drawn from Im-man-uel's veins,
2 The dy-ing thief re-joic'd to see That foun-tain in His day;
3 Dear dy-ing Lamb! Thy pre-cious blood Shall nev-er lose its pow'r,
4 E'er since by faith I saw the stream Thy flow-ing wounds sup-ply,

1 And sin-ners plung'd be-neath that flood Lose all their guilt-y stains;
2 And there may I, though vile as he, Wash all my sins a-way;
3 Till all the ran-som'd church of God Be sav'd, to sin no more;
4 Re-deem-ing love has been my theme, And shall be till I die,

1 Lose all their guilt-y stains, Lose all their guilt-y stains;
2 Wash all my sins a-way, Wash all my sins a-way;
3 Be sav'd to sin no more, Be sav'd to sin no more;
4 And shall be till I die, And shall be till I die;

1 And sin-ners plung'd be-neath that flood Lose all their guilt-y stains.
2 And there may I, though vile as he, Wash all my sins a-way.
3 Till all the ran-som'd church of God Be sav'd to sin no more.
4 Re-deem-ing love has been my theme, And shall be till I die.

The tunes FOUNTAIN, UXBRIDGE, and CLEANSING FOUNTAIN precede this tune

All the Way to Calvary

138

W. G. MOYER

I. H. MEREDITH

1 O how dark the night that wrapt my spi-rit round! O how deep the
2 Tremb-ling-ly a sin-ner bow'd be-fore His face, Naught I knew of
3 O 'twas won-drous love the Sa-viour show'd for me! When He left His

1 woe my Sa-viour found! When He walk'd a-cross the wa-ters of my soul,
2 par-don, God's free grace; Heard a voice so melt-ing, 'Cease thy wild re-gret,
3 throne for Cal-va-ry, When He trod the wine-press, trod it all a-lone;

REFRAIN

1 Bade my night dis-perse and made me whole.
2 Je-sus bought thy par-don, paid thy debt,' } All the way to Cal-va-
3 Praise His Name for ev-er, make it known,

ry He went for me, He went for me, He went for me; All the

way to Cal-va-ry He went for me, He died to set me free.

139   # Mercy is Free

HENRIETTA E. BLAIR   WM. J. KIRKPATRICK

1 Praise be to Je-sus! His mer-cy is free; Mer-cy is free,
2 Why on the moun-tains of sin wilt thou roam? Mer-cy is free,
3 Think of His good-ness, and pa-tience and love; Mer-cy is free,
4 Yes, there is par-don for all who be-lieve; Mer-cy is free,

REFRAIN—Je-sus, the Sa-viour is look-ing for thee. Look-ing for thee

1 Mer-cy is free: Sin-ner, that mer-cy is flow-ing for thee,
2 Mer-cy is free: Gent-ly the Spi-rit is call-ing, 'Come home,'
3 Mer-cy is free: Plead-ing thy cause with His Fa-ther a-bove,
4 Mer-cy is free: Come and this mo-ment a bless-ing re-ceive,

Look-ing for thee; Lov-ing-ly, ten-der-ly call-ing for thee,

FINE

1 Mer-cy is bound-less and free. . If thou art will-ing on Him to
2 Mer-cy is bound-less and free. . Thou art in dark-ness, O come to
3 Mer-cy is bound-less and free. . Come, and re-pent-ing, O give Him
4 Mer-cy is bound-less and free. . Je-sus is wait-ing, O hear Him

Call-ing and look-ing for thee. .

1 be-lieve, Mer-cy is free, mer-cy is free: Life ev-er-last-
2 the light! Mer-cy is free, mer-cy is free: Je-sus is wait-
3 thy heart! Mer-cy is free, mer-cy is free: Grieve Him no long-
4 pro-claim! Mer-cy is free, mer-cy is free: Cling to His mer-

Mercy is Free—*Continued*

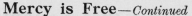

D.C. for REFRAIN

1 ing thy soul may re-ceive, Mer-cy is bound-less and free.
2 ing, He'll save thee to-night, Mer-cy is bound-less and free.
3 er, but come as thou art, Mer-cy is bound-less and free.
4 cy, be-lieve on His Name, Mer-cy is bound-less and free.

140 The Hem of His Garment

GEORGE F. ROOT

GEORGE F. ROOT

1 She on-ly touch'd the hem of His gar-ment As to His side she stole,
2 She came in fear and trem-bling be-fore Him, She knew her Lord had come;
3 He turn'd with, 'Daugh-ter, be of good com-fort, Thy faith hath made thee whole;'

1 A - mid the crowd that gath-er'd a-round Him, And straight-way she was whole.
2 She felt that from Him vir-tue had heal'd her, The might-y deed was done.
3 And peace that pass - eth all un-der-stand-ing With glad-ness fill'd her soul.

REFRAIN

O touch the hem of His gar - ment, And thou, too, shalt be free!

His sav - ing pow'r this ver - y hour Shall give new life to thee.

141 The Love that Sought Me

W. SPENCER WALTON   A. J. GORDON

1 In ten-der-ness He sought me, Wea-ry and sick with sin, And
2 He wash'd the bleed-ing sin-wounds, And pour'd in oil and wine; He
3 He point-ed to the nail-prints, For me His blood was shed, A
4 I'm sit-ting in His pres-ence, The sun-shine of His face, While
5 So while the hours are pass-ing, All now is per-fect rest; I'm

1 on His shoul-ders brought me Back to His fold a-gain; While an-gels
2 whis-per'd to as-sure me, 'I've found thee, thou art Mine;' I nev-er
3 mock-ing crown so thorn-y Was placed up-on His head: I won-der'd
4 with a-dor-ing won-der His bless-ings I re-trace: It seems as
5 wait-ing for the morn-ing, The bright-est and the best, When He will

1 in His pres-ence sang Un-til the courts of hea-ven rang.
2 heard a sweet-er voice, It made my ach-ing heart re-joice.
3 what He saw in me To suf-fer such deep ag-o-ny.
4 if e-ter-nal days Are far too short to sound His praise.
5 call us to His side To be with Him, His spot-less bride.

REFRAIN

O the love that sought me! O the blood that bought me! O the grace that

brought me to the fold! Won-drous grace that brought me to the fold!

142 O It is Wonderful !

CHARLES H. GABRIEL   CHARLES H. GABRIEL

1 I stand all a-maz'd at the love Je-sus of-fers me, Con-fus'd at the
2 I mar-vel that He would de-scend from His throne di-vine To res-cue a
3 I think of His hands, pierc'd and bleed-ing to pay the debt, Such mer-cy, such

1 grace that so ful-ly He prof-fers me; I trem-ble to know that for me He was
2 soul so re-bell-ious and proud as mine; That He should ex-tend His great love un-to
3 love and de-vo-tion can I for-get? No, no! I will praise and a-dore at the

1 cru-ci-fied, That for me, a sin-ner, He suf-fer'd, He bled and died.
2 such as I, Suf-fi-cient to own, to re-deem, and to jus-ti-fy.
3 mer-cy seat, Un-til at the glo-ri-fied throne I kneel at His feet.

REFRAIN

O it is won-der-ful that He should care for me E-nough to
won-der-ful!

die for me! O it is won-der-ful, won-der-ful to me!
won-der-ful!

143 Depending on the Blood

Johnson Oatman

J. Howard Entwisle
Arr. P. J. Mansfield

1 On the gold-en streets of hea-ven all men hope to walk some day,
2 Some will tell us that God's mer-cy is their on-ly hope and plea,
3 As we look back thro' the a-ges where the kings and pro-phets trod,
4 'Tis the bur-den of that cho-rus o-ver on the streets of light,

1 Yet so ma-ny are not will-ing to ac-cept the liv-ing way;
2 That a soul He could not pun-ish thro'-out all e-ter-ni-ty;
3 We may see their al-tars reek-ing with the sa-cri-fice and blood;
4 That the blood from Cal-v'ry's moun-tain hath wash'd all their gar-ments white;

1 But while o-thers build on good works or o-pin-ions if they may,
2 But I read that my dear Sa-viour died for sin-ners just like me,
3 But those types were on-ly point-ing to the Pas-chal Lamb of God,
4 So I'll shout a-long life's path-way till I reach that land so bright,

Depending on the Blood—*Continued*

1-4 Hal-le - lu - jah! hal-le - lu - jah! I'm de - pend-ing on the blood.

REFRAIN

In the soul - cleans-ing blood of the Sa - viour, I've been

wash'd in the crim - son flood; Tho' the world may say There is

hope some o - ther way, I'm de - pend - ing on the blood.

144 The Cleansing Wave

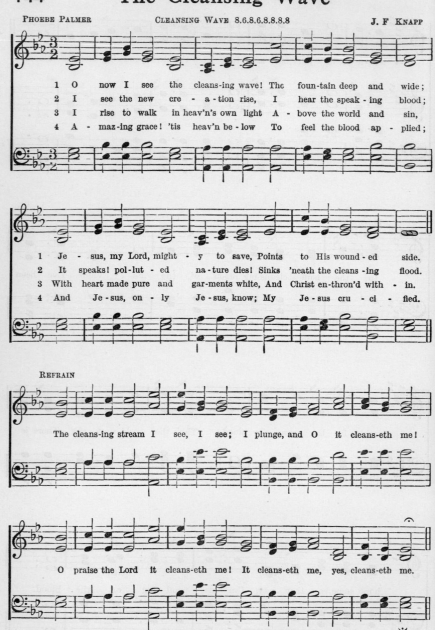

PHOEBE PALMER   CLEANSING WAVE 8.6.8.6.8.8.8.8   J. F KNAPP

1 O now I see the cleans-ing wave! The foun-tain deep and wide;
2 I see the new cre - a - tion rise, I hear the speak - ing blood;
3 I rise to walk in heav'n's own light A - bove the world and sin,
4 A - maz-ing grace! 'tis heav'n be - low To feel the blood ap - plied;

1 Je - sus, my Lord, might - y to save, Points to His wound - ed side.
2 It speaks! pol -lut - ed na - ture dies! Sinks 'neath the cleans -ing flood.
3 With heart made pure and gar-ments white, And Christ en-thron'd with - in.
4 And Je - sus, on - ly Je - sus, know; My Je - sus cru - ci - fied.

REFRAIN

The cleans-ing stream I see, I see; I plunge, and O it cleans-eth me!

O praise the Lord it cleans-eth me! It cleans-eth me, yes, cleans-eth me.

The tune FAITH is on the following page

The Cleansing Wave

144

PHOEBE PALMER   FAITH 8.6.8.6.8.8.8.6.   GERMAN AIR

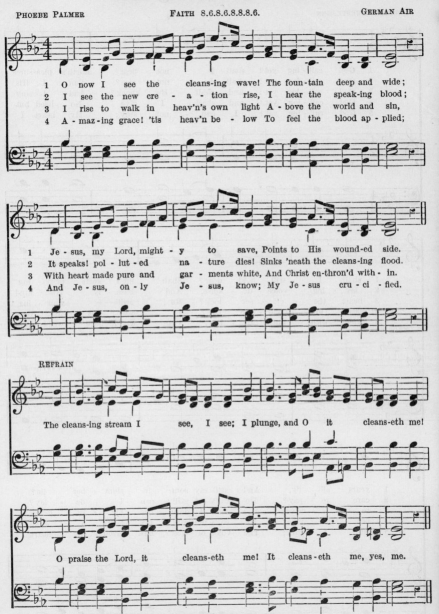

1. O now I see the cleans-ing wave! The foun-tain deep and wide;
2. I see the new cre - a - tion rise, I hear the speak-ing blood;
3. I rise to walk in heav'n's own light A - bove the world and sin,
4. A - maz-ing grace! 'tis heav'n be - low To feel the blood ap - plied;

1. Je - sus, my Lord, might - y to save, Points to His wound-ed side.
2. It speaks! pol - lut - ed na - ture dies! Sinks 'neath the cleans-ing flood.
3. With heart made pure and gar - ments white, And Christ en-thron'd with - in.
4. And Je - sus, on - ly Je - sus, know; My Je - sus cru - ci - fied.

REFRAIN

The cleans-ing stream I see, I see; I plunge, and O it cleans-eth me!

O praise the Lord, it cleans-eth me! It cleans-eth me, yes, me.

The tune CLEANSING WAVE is on the preceding page

145   God is Calling Yet

GERHARD TERSTEEGEN

E. O. EXCELL

1 God call-ing yet! shall I not hear? Earth's plea-sures
2 God call-ing yet! shall I not rise? Can I His
3 God call-ing yet! and shall He knock? And I my
4 God call-ing yet! and shall I give No heed but
5 God call-ing yet! I can-not stay; My heart I

1 shall I still hold dear? Shall life's swift pass-ing
2 lov-ing voice de-spise, And base-ly His kind
3 heart the clo-ser lock? He still is wait-ing
4 still in bond-age live? I wait; but He does
5 yield with-out de-lay: Vain world, fare-well! from

1 years all fly, And still my soul in slum-ber lie?
2 care re-pay? He calls me still: can I de-lay?
3 to re-ceive; And shall I dare His Spi-rit grieve?
4 not for-sake; He calls me still: my heart, a-wake!
5 thee I part; The voice of God has reach'd my heart.

God is Calling Yet—*Continued*

146 Why Do You Wait?

GEORGE F. ROOT   GEORGE F. ROOT

1 Why do you wait, dear bro-ther?   O why do you tar -ry so long!
2 What do you hope, dear bro-ther,   To gain by a furth-er de -lay?
3 Do you not feel, dear bro-ther,   His Spi - rit now striv-ing with-in?
4 Why do you wait, dear bro-ther?   The har-vest is pass-ing a -way,

1 Your Sa-viour is wait-ing to give you   A place in His sanc-ti -fied throng.
2 There's no one to save you but Je-sus,   There's no o-ther way but His way.
3 O why not ac-cept His sal - va-tion!   And throw off your bur-den of sin.
4 Your Sa-viour is long-ing to bless you,   There's dan-ger and death in de -lay!

REFRAIN

Why not? why not? Why not come to Him now?

Why not? why not? Why not come to Him now?

An Alternative Tune is on the following page

146 Why Do You Wait?

GEORGE F. ROOT   PURCELL J. MANSFIELD

1 Why do you wait, dear bro - ther? O why do you
What do you hope, dear bro - ther, To gain by a
3 Do you not feel, dear bro - ther, His Spi - rit now
4 Why do you wait, dear bro - ther? The har - vest is

1 tar - ry so long! Your Sa - viour is wait - ing to
2 furth - er de - lay? There's no one to save you but
3 striv - ing with - in? O why not ac - cept His sal -
4 pass - ing a - way, Your Sa - viour is long - ing to

1 give you A place in His sanc - ti - fied throng.
2 Je - sus, There's no o - ther way but His way.
3 va - tion! And throw off your bur - den of sin.
4 bless you, There's dan - ger and death in de - lay!

REFRAIN

Why not? why not? Why not come to Him now?

An Alternative Tune is on the preceding page

Sowing the Seed

Emily S Oakey   P. P. Bliss, *Arr.* P. J. Mansfield

1 Sow-ing the seed by the day-light fair,   Sow-ing the seed by the noon-day glare,
2 Sow-ing the seed by the way-side high,   Sow-ing the seed on the rocks to die,
3 Sow-ing the seed of a ling-'ring pain,   Sow-ing the seed of a mad-den'd brain,
4 Sow-ing the seed with an ach - ing heart,   Sow-ing the seed while the tear-drops start,

1 Sow-ing the seed by the fad - ing light,   Sow-ing the seed in the sol - emn night;
2 Sow-ing the seed where the thorns will spoil,   Sow-ing the seed in the fer - tile soil;
3 Sow-ing the seed of a tar-nish'd name,   Sow-ing the seed of e - ter - nal shame;
4 Sow-ing in hope till the reap - ers come   Glad-ly to gath-er the har - vest home:

1-4 O what shall the har - vest be ! . . . O what shall the har-vest be ! . . .

Sowing the Seed—*Continued*

REFRAIN

Sown . . in the dark - ness or sown . . . in the

Sown in the dark - ness or sown in the light, Sown in the dark-ness or

light, ... Sown . . . in our weak - - ness or

sown in the light, Sown in our weak-ness or sown in our might,

sown . . . in our might, . . . Gath- - er'd in

Sown in our weak-ness or sown in our might, Gath - - er'ed in

time . . . or e - ter - - - ni - ty, . . .

time . . . or e - ter - - ni - ty, . . .

Sure, . . ah, sure will the har . . . vest be. . .

har - - - vest, har - vest be

Sure, ah sure will the har . . . vest be. . .

148 To-day the Saviour Calls

SAMUEL F. SMITH   NAIN 6.4.6.4.   LOWELL MASON

1 To - day the Sa - viour calls; Ye wan - d'rers come:
2 To - day the Sa - viour calls; O hear Him now!
3 To - day the Sa - viour calls; For re - fuge fly;
4 The Spi - rit calls to - day; Yield to His pow'r;

1 O ye be - night - ed souls! Why long - er roam?
2 Be - fore your day is gone, To Je - sus bow.
3 The storm of ven - geance falls; Ru - in is nigh,
4 O grieve Him not a - way, 'Tis mer - cy's hour!

SAMUEL F. SMITH   FROGMORE 6.4.6.4.   WALTER PARRATT

1 To - day the Sa - viour calls; Ye wan - d'rers come;
2 To - day the Sa - viour calls; O hear Him now!
3 To - day the Sa - viour calls: For re - fuge fly;
4 The Spi - rit calls to - day: Yield to His pow'r;

1 O ye be - night - ed souls! Why long - er roam?
2 Be - fore your day is gone, To Je - sus bow.
3 The storm of ven - geance falls; Ru - in is nigh.
4 O grieve Him not a - way, 'Tis mer - cy's hour!

Music by permission of the METHODIST CONFERENCE
The tune CHILTON FOLIAT is on the following page

148 ## To-day the Saviour Calls

Samuel F. Smith   Chilton Foliat 10.10.10.10.   George C. Martin

1 To - day the Sa - viour calls; Ye wan - d'rers come,
2 To - day the Sa - viour calls; For re - fuge fly;

1 O ye be - night - ed souls! Why lon - ger roam?
2 The storm of ven - geance falls; Ru - in is nigh:

1 To - day the Sa - viour calls; O hear Him now!
2 The Spi - rit calls to - day; Yield to His pow'r;

1 Be - fore your day is gone, To Je - sus bow.
2 O grieve Him not a - way, 'Tis mer - cy's hour!

Music by permission of Novello & Co., Ltd.
The tunes Nain and Frogmore are on the preceding page

149 ## Thy Mercy Calls Me

Oswald Allen   Penlan 7.6.7.6.d.   David Jenkins

1 To-day Thy mer-cy calls me To wash a-way my sin; How-ever great my tres-pass, What-e'er I may have been. However long from mer-cy I may have turned a-way, ... Thy blood, O Christ, can cleanse me, And make me white to-day.

2 To-day Thy gate is o-pen, And all who en-ter in Shall find a Fa-ther's wel-come, And par-don for their sin; The past shall be for-got-ten, A pre-sent joy be giv'n, ... A fu-ture grace be pro-mised, A glo-rious crown in heav'n.

3 To-day the Fa-ther calls me; The Ho-ly Spi-rit waits; The bless-ed an-gels ga-ther A-round the heav'n-ly gates. The ques-tion will be asked me, How of-ten I have come: ... Al-though I oft have wan-dered, It is my Fa-ther's home.

4 O all-em-brac-ing mer-cy! Thou ev-er o-pen door! What should I do with-out thee, When heart and eyes run o'er? When all things seem a-gainst me, To drive me to des-pair, ... I know one gate is o-pen, One ear will hear my prayer.

Music by permission of Snell & Sons, Ltd.

The tune Eden Grove is on the following page

149 **Thy Mercy Calls Me**

OSWALD ALLEN   EDEN GROVE 7.6.7.6. D   SAMUEL SMITH

1 To - day Thy mer - cy calls me To wash a - way my sin;
2 To - day Thy gate is o - pen, And all who en - ter in
3 To - day the Fa - ther calls me; The Ho - ly Spi - rit waits;
4 O all - em - brac - ing mer - cy! Thou ev - er o - pen door!

1 How - ev - er great my tres - pass, What - e'er I may have been.
2 Shall find a Fa - ther's wel - come, And par - don for their sin;
3 The bless - ed an - gels ga - ther A - round the heav'n-ly gates:
4 What should I do with - out thee When heart and eyes run o'er?

1 How - ev - er long from mer - cy I may have turned a - way,
2 The past shall be for - got - ten, A pre - sent joy be giv'n,
3 No ques - tion will be asked me, How of - ten I have come:
4 When all things seem a - gainst me To drive me to des - pair,

1 Thy blood, O Christ, can cleanse me, And make me white to - day.
2 A fu - ture grace be pro - mised, A glo - rious crown in heav'n.
3 Al - though I oft have wan - der'd, It is my Fa - ther's home.
4 I know one gate is o - pen, One ear will hear my prayer.

The tune PENLAN is on the preceding page

150 Jesus is Passing By

ELIZA E. HEWITT

JOHN R. SWENEY

1 Come, con-trite one, and seek His grace, Je-sus is pass-ing
2 Come, hun-gry one, and tell your need, Je-sus is pass-ing
3 Come, wea-ry one, and find sweet rest, Je-sus is pass-ing
4 Come, bur-den'd one, bring all your care, Je-sus is pass-ing

1 by! See in His re-con-cil-ed face The sun-shine
2 by! The Bread of Life your soul will feed, And ful-ly
3 by! Come where the long-ing heart is bless'd, And on His
4 by! The love that list-ens to your pray'r Will no good

REFRAIN

1 of the sky.
2 sat-is-fy.
3 bo-som lie.
4 thing de-ny.

Pass - ing by, ...
Pass - ing by, pass - ing by,

pass - ing by; . . . Hast-en to meet Him on the
pass - ing by, pass - ing by;

Jesus is Passing By—*Continued*

way, Je - sus is pass - ing by to - day; Pass - -
Pass - ing by,

mp

p *rit.*

ing by, ... pass - ing by. . . . .
pass - ing by, pass - ing by, pass - ing by.

AN ALTERNATIVE ARRANGEMENT

ELIZA E. HEWITT   JACKSON C.M.   THOMAS JACKSON

1 Come, con - trite one, and seek His grace, Je - sus is pass - ing by!
2 Come, hun - gry one, and tell your need, Je - sus is pass - ing by!
3 Come, wea - ry one, and find sweet rest, Je - sus is pass - ing by!
4 Come, bur - den'd one, bring all your care, Je - sus is pass - ing by!
5 Je - sus is pass - ing by to - day, O hear - ken to His cry!

1 See in His re - con - cil - ed face The sun - shine of the sky.
2 The Bread of Life your soul will feed, And ful - ly sat - is - fy.
3 Come where the long - ing heart is bless'd, And on His bo - som lie.
4 The love that list - ens to your pray'r Will no good thing de - ny.
5 Has - ten to meet Him on the way, The great Phy - si - cian's nigh!

151 The Gospel Bells

S. WESLEY MARTIN

S. WESLEY MARTIN

1 The Gos-pel bells are ring-ing O - ver land from
2 The Gos-pel bells in - vite us To a feast pre-
3 The Gos-pel bells give warn-ing As they sound from
4 The Gos-pel bells are joy - ful As they e - cho

1 sea to sea; Bless-ed news of free sal-va-tion Do they
2 par'd for all; Do not slight the in - vi - ta - tion, Nor re-
3 day to day, Of the fate which doth a - wait them Who for
4 far and wide, Bear-ing notes of per-fect par-don Thro' a

1 of - fer you and me: For God so lov'd the world That His
2 ject the gra - cious call: 'I am the bread of life; Eat of
3 ev - er will de - lay: Es - cape thou for thy life; Tar - ry
4 Sa - viour cru - ci - fied: Good tid - ings of great joy To all

1 on - ly Son He gave, Who-so - e'er be - liev - eth
2 Me, thou hun - gry soul, Tho' your sins be red as
3 not in all the plain, Nor be - hind thee look, O
4 peo - ple do I bring, Un - to you is born a

The Gospel Bells—*Continued*

1 in Him Ev-er-last-ing life shall have.
2 crim-son They shall be as white as wool.'
3 nev-er! Lest thou be con-sum'd in pain.
4 Sa-viour, Which is Christ the Lord and King.

REFRAIN

Gos-pel bells . . . how they ring! . . . O-ver
. . . Gos-pel bells . . . how they ring! O-ver

land from sea to sea; Gos-pel bells . . . free-ly
land from sea to sea; . . . Gos-pel bells . .

bring . . . Bless-ed news to you and me.
. free-ly bring Bless-ed news to you and me.

152 Art Thou Weary?

JOHN M. NEALE   STEPHANOS 8.5.8.3   HENRY W. BAKER

1 Art thou wea-ry, art thou lan-guid, Art thou sore dis-tress'd?
2 Hath He di-a-dem, as mon-arch, That His brow a-dorns?
3 If I ask Him to re-ceive me Will He say me nay?
4 Find-ing, follow-ing, keep-ing, strug-gling, Is He sure to bless?

1 'Come to me,' saith One, 'and com-ing, Be at rest.'
2 Yes, a crown in ve-ry sure-ty, But of thorns!
3 Not till earth, and not till hea-ven, Pass a-way.
4 An-gels, mar-tyrs, saints, and pro-phets An-swer, 'Yes.'

153 Calvary

W. M'K. DARWOOD   CALVARY'S BROW L.M.D.   JOHN R. SWENEY

1 On Cal-v'ry's brow . . . . my Sa-viour died, ...
2 'Mid rending rocks . . . . and dark-'ning skies, ...
3 O Je-sus, Lord! . . . . how can it be . . . . .

1 'Twas there my Lord . . . . was cru-ci-fied: . . . .
2 My Sa-viour bows . . . . His head and dies; . . . .
3 That Thou shouldst give . . . . Thy life for me? . . . .

Calvary—*Continued*

1 'Twas on the Cross . . . He bled for me, . . .
2 The op-'ning veil . . . re-veals the way . . .
3 To bear the Cross . . . and ag-o-ny . . .

1 And pur-chas'd there . . . my par-don free.
2 To hea-ven's joys . . . and end-less day.
3 In that dread hour . . . on Cal-va-ry!

REFRAIN

O Cal-va-ry! dark Cal-va-ry! Where Je-sus shed

His blood for me, for me: O Cal-va-ry! blest

Cal-va-ry! 'Twas there my Sa-viour died for me.

154 The Royal Road

JENNIE WILSON

POLEMOS 8.7.8.7.D

WELSH MELODY
Arr. P. J. MANSFIELD

1 There's a roy-al high-way lead-ing To the King's su-blime a-bode;
2 O'er the high-way Je-sus trav-ell'd, Up the hill of Cal-v'ry trod,
3 As I jour-ney o'er the high-way To the coun-try of my king,
4 Oft a glad, en-tranc-ing vis-ion To my spi-rit is be-stow'd;

1 And I seek a home in glo-ry, Walk-ing in that roy-al road.
2 That He might a path make o-pen, Lead-ing to the throne of God.
3 Oft by faith I hear the e-cho From the land where an-gels sing.
4 'Tis the cit-y, bright, e-ter-nal, Whi-ther leads the roy-al road.

REFRAIN

O the bless-ed roy-al road! O the bless-ed roy-al road! Will you go with me to glo-ry Walk-ing in that roy-al road?

An Alternative Tune is on the following page

154 The Royal Road

JENNIE WILSON

L. E. JONES

1 There's a roy-al high-way lead-ing To the King's su-blime a-bode;
2 O'er the high-way Je-sus trav-ell'd, Up the hill of Cal-v'ry trod,
3 As I jour-ney o'er the high-way To the coun-try of my king,
4 Oft a glad, en-tranc-ing vis-ion To my spi-rit is be-stow'd;

1 And I seek a home in glo-ry, Walk-ing in that roy-al road.
2 That He might a path make o-pen, Lead-ing to the throne of God.
3 Oft by faith I hear the e-cho From the land where an-gels sing.
4 'Tis the cit-y, bright, e-ter-nal, Whi-ther leads the roy-al road.

REFRAIN

O the bless-ed roy-al road! . . . O the
. Bless-ed, roy-al road, . . bless-ed, roy-al road, . .

bless-ed, roy-al road! . . Will you go
Bless-ed, roy-al road, . bless-ed, roy-al road, Will you go with me to glo-

with me to glo-ry, Walk-ing in . that roy-al road?
ry, Will you go with me to glo-ry, . Walk-ing in that roy-al road?

The tune POLEMOS is on the preceding page

8

155 Seeking to Save

PHILIP P. BLISS

PHILIP P. BLISS

1 Ten - der - ly the shep - herd, O'er the moun - tains cold,
2 Pa - tient - ly the ow - ner Seeks with ear - nest care,
3 Lov - ing - ly the Fa - ther Sends the news a - round:

1 Goes to bring his lost one Back to the fold.
2 In the dust and dark - ness, Her trea - sure rare.
3 He once dead now liv - eth— Once lost is found.

REFRAIN

Seek - ing to save, seek - ing to save; Lost one, 'tis Je -

sus Seek - ing to save! Seek - ing to save, Seek -

ing to save; Lost one, 'tis Je - sus Seek - ing to save!

156 Whiter than Snow

JAMES NICHOLSON

WM. G. FISCHER

1 Lord Je - sus, I long to be per - fect - ly whole, I want Thee for ev -
2 Lord Je - sus, let no - thing un - ho - ly re - main, Ap - ply Thine own blood
3 Lord Je - sus, look down from Thy throne in the skies, And help me to make
4 Lord Je - sus, for this I most hum - bly en - treat; I wait, bless - ed Lord,
5 Lord Je - sus, Thou see - est I pa - tient - ly wait; Come now, and with - in

1 er to live in my soul; Break down ev - 'ry i - dol, cast out ev - 'ry foe:
2 and ex - tract ev - 'ry stain; To get this blest cleans - ing I all things fore - go;
3 a com - plete sac - ri - fice; I give up my - self and what - ev - er I know;
4 at Thy cru - ci - fied feet; By faith, for my cleans - ing I see Thy blood flow:
5 me a new heart cre - ate; To those who have sought Thee Thou ne - ver saidst, No:

1-5 Now wash me, and I shall be whit - er than snow.

REFRAIN

Whit - er than snow; yes, whit - er than snow;

Now wash me and I shall be whit - er than snow.

157 The Light of the World

PHILIP P. BLISS

PHILIP P. BLISS

1 The whole world was lost in the dark-ness of sin,
2 No dark-ness have we who in Je-sus a-bide,
3 Ye dwell-ers in dark-ness with sin-blind-ed eyes,
4 No need of the sun-light in heav-en, we're told,

1-4 The Light of the world is Je-sus!

1 Like sun-shine at noon-day His glo-ry shone in,
2 We walk in the light when we fol-low our Guide,
3 Go, wash at His bid-ding, and light will a-rise,
4 The Lamb is the Light in the Ci-ty of Gold,

The Light of the World—*Continued*

1-4 The Light of the world is Je - sus!

REFRAIN

Come to the Light, 'tis shin - ing for thee; Sweet - ly the

Light has dawn'd up - on me; . Once I was blind, but

now I can see; The Light of the world is Je - sus!

158 Would you Believe?

Caroline Sawyer

Arr. Daniel B. Towner

1 If you could see Christ stand-ing here to - night— His thorn-crown'd
2 If you could see that face so calm and sweet, Those lips that
3 He whis - pers to your heart, turn not a - way, For He's be -

1 head and pier - ced hands could view; Could see those eyes that
2 spake words on - ly pure and true; Could see the nail - prints
3 side you in your nar - row pew; If you will lis - ten

1 beam with heav'ns own light, And hear Him say, 'Be - lov - ed, 'twas for you:'
2 in His ten - der feet, And hear Him say, 'Be - lov - ed, 'twas for you:'
3 you will hear Him say In lov - ing tones, 'Be - lov - ed, 'twas for you:'

REFRAIN

1-2 Would you be - lieve, ... and Je - sus re -
3 Will you be - lieve, , , . . . and Je - sus re -

1-2 Would you be - lieve,
3 Will you be - lieve.

Would you Believe?—*Continued*

1-2 ceive, ... If He were stand -
3 ceive? . . . . . For He is stand -

1-2 and Je - sus re - ceive,
3 and Je - sus re - ceive?

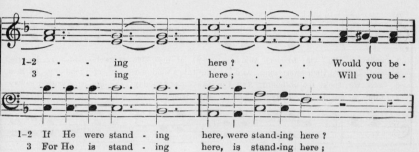

1-2 - - ing here? . . . Would you be -
3 - - ing here; . . . Will you be -

1-2 If He were stand - ing here, were stand-ing here?
3 For He is stand - ing here, is stand-ing here;

1-2 lieve, . . . and Je - sus re - ceive, . . .
3 lieve, . . . and Je - sus re - ceive? . . .

1-2 Would you be - lieve, . . and Je - sus re - ceive,
3 Will you be - lieve, . . and Je - sus re - ceive?

1-2 If He were stand - ing . . here? . .
3 For He is stand - ing . . here. . .

159 The Old Ship of Zion

M. J. CARTWRIGHT

DANIEL B. TOWNER

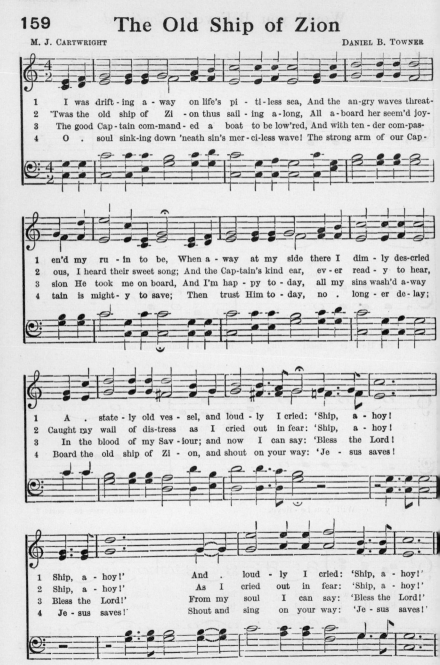

1   I was drift-ing a-way   on life's pi - ti-less sea, And the an-gry waves threat-
2   'Twas the old ship of Zi - on thus sail - ing a - long, All a - board her seem'd joy-
3   The good Cap-tain com-mand-ed a   boat to be low'red, And with ten - der com-pas-
4   O . soul sink-ing down 'neath sin's mer-ci-less wave! The strong arm of our Cap-

1   en'd my ru - in to be, When a - way at my side there I   dim - ly des-cried
2   ous, I heard their sweet song; And the Cap-tain's kind ear, ev - er read - y to hear,
3   sion He took me on board, And I'm hap - py to - day, all my sins wash'd a - way
4   tain is might- y to save; Then trust Him to - day, no . long - er de - lay;

1   A . state - ly old ves - sel, and loud - ly I cried: 'Ship, a - hoy!
2   Caught my wail of dis-tress as I cried out in fear: 'Ship, a - hoy!
3   In the blood of my Sav - iour; and now I can say: 'Bless the Lord!
4   Board the old ship of Zi - on, and shout on your way: 'Je - sus saves!

1   Ship, a - hoy!'   And . loud - ly I cried: 'Ship, a - hoy!'
2   Ship, a - hoy!'   As I cried out in fear: 'Ship, a - hoy!'
3   Bless the Lord!'   From my soul I can say: 'Bless the Lord!'
4   Je - sus saves!'   Shout and sing on your way: 'Je - sus saves!'

An Alternative Tune is on the following page

159 # The Old Ship of Zion

M. J. CARTWRIGHT

DAVID CARYLL

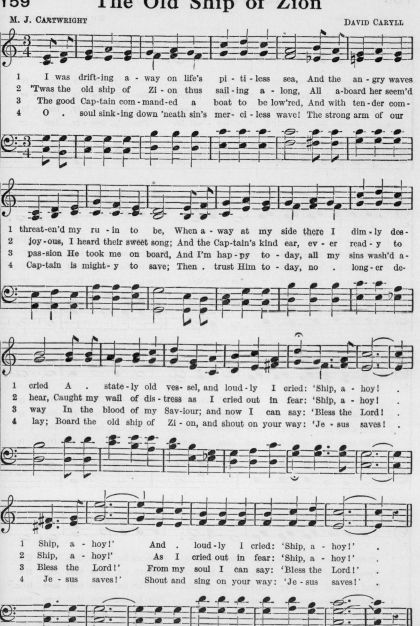

1 I was drift-ing a - way on life's pi - ti - less sea, And the an - gry waves
2 'Twas the old ship of Zi - on thus sail-ing a - long, All a-board her seem'd
3 The good Cap-tain com - mand-ed a boat to be low'red, And with ten - der com -
4 O . soul sink-ing down 'neath sin's mer - ci - less wave! The strong arm of our

1 threat-en'd my ru - in to be, When a - way at my side there I dim - ly des -
2 joy-ous, I heard their sweet song; And the Cap-tain's kind ear, ev - er read - y to
3 pas-sion He took me on board, And I'm hap - py to - day, all my sins wash'd a -
4 Cap-tain is might - y to save; Then . trust Him to - day, no . long - er de -

1 cried A . state - ly old ves - sel, and loud - ly I cried: 'Ship, a - hoy!
2 hear, Caught my wail of dis - tress as I cried out in fear: 'Ship, a - hoy!
3 way In the blood of my Sav-iour; and now I can say: 'Bless the Lord!
4 lay; Board the old ship of Zi - on, and shout on your way: 'Je - sus saves!

1 Ship, a - hoy!' And . loud - ly I cried: 'Ship, a - hoy!'
2 Ship, a - hoy!' As I cried out in fear: 'Ship, a - hoy!'
3 Bless the Lord!' From my soul I can say: 'Bless the Lord!'
4 Je - sus saves!' Shout and sing on your way: 'Je - sus saves!'

An **Alternative Tune** is on the preceding page

160 The Water of Life

FANNY J. CROSBY

WILLIAM B. BRADBURY

1 Je-sus the wa-ter of life will give Free-ly, free-ly, free-ly;
2 Je-sus has pro-mis'd a home in heav'n Free-ly, free-ly, free-ly;
3 Je-sus has pro-mis'd a robe of white Free-ly, free-ly, free-ly;
4 Je-sus has pro-mis'd e-ter-nal day Free-ly, free-ly, free-ly

1 Je-sus the wa-ter of life will give Free-ly to those who love Him:
2 Je-sus has pro-mis'd a home in heav'n Free-ly for those that love Him:
3 Je-sus has pro-mis'd a robe of white Free-ly for those that love Him:
4 Je-sus has pro-mis'd e-ter-nal day Free-ly for those that love Him:

1 Come to that foun-tain, O drink and live! Free-ly, free-ly, free-ly;
2 Trea-sures un-fad-ing will there be giv'n Free-ly, free-ly, free-ly;
3 King-doms of glo-ry and crowns of light, Free-ly, free-ly, free-ly;
4 Plea-sures that nev-er shall pass a-way, Free-ly, free-ly, free-ly;

1 Come to that foun-tain, O drink and live! Flow-ing for those that love Him.
2 Trea-sures un-fad-ing will there be giv'n Free-ly for those that love Him.
3 King-doms of glo-ry and crowns of light, Free-ly for those that love Him.
4 Plea-sures that nev-er shall pass a-way, Free-ly for those that love Him.

The Water of Life—*Continued*

DUET **CHORUS**

The Spi - rit and the Bride say, Come; Free - ly, free - ly, free - ly:

DUET **CHORUS**

And he that is thirst - y let him come And drink of the

FULL CHORUS

wa - ter of life. . . The foun-tain of life is flow - ing,

Flow - ing, free - ly flow - ing; The foun-tain of life is

rit.

flow - ing, is flow - ing for you and for me. .

161   O Christ, What Burdens !

ANNE ROSS COUSIN   SPOHR 8.6. 8.6. 8.6.   LUDWIG SPOAR

1 O Christ, what bur - dens bow'd Thy head ! Our load was
2 Death and the curse were in our cup, O Christ, 'twas
3 The tem - pest's aw - ful voice was heard, O Christ, it
4 For me, Lord Je - sus, Thou hast died, And I have

1 laid on Thee ; Thou stood - est in the sin - ner's
2 full for Thee ! But Thou hast drain'd the last dark
3 broke on Thee ! Thy o - pen bo - som was my
4 died in Thee : Thou'rt ris'n— my bands are all un

1 stead, Didst bear all ill for me. A Vic - tim
2 drop, 'Tis emp - ty now for me. That bit - ter
3 ward, It braved the storm for me : Thy form was
4 tied ; And now Thou liv'st in me ; When pur - -

1 led, Thy blood was shed, Now there's no load for me.
2 cup, love drank it up, Now bless - ing's draught for me.
3 scarr'd, Thy vis - age marr'd ; Now cloud - less peace for me.
4 fied, made white, and tried, Thy glo - ry then for me !

162 The Gospel of Thy Grace

A. T. Pierson

James McGranahan

1 The gos-pel of Thy grace My stub-born heart has won,
2 The ser-pent "lift-ed up" Could life and heal-ing give,
3 "The soul that sin-neth dies:" My aw-ful doom I heard;
4 "Not to con-demn the world" The "Man of Sor-rows" came;
5 "Lord, help my un-be-lief!" Give me the peace of faith,

1 For God so lov'd the world He gave His on-ly Son, That
2 So Je-sus on the Cross Bids me to look and live; For
3 I was for e-ver lost, But for Thy gra-cious word That
4 But that the world might have Sal-va-tion thro' His Name; For
5 To rest with child-like trust On what Thy gos-pel saith, That

REFRAIN

"Who-so-ev-er will be-lieve Shall ev-er-last-ing life re-ceive!

Shall ev-er-last-ing life re-ceive!"

163 # At Even

HENRY TWELLS

ANGELUS L.M.

GEORG JOSEPH

1 At e - ven, ere the sun was set, The sick, O
2 Once more 'tis e - ven - tide, and we, Op - press'd with
3 O Sa - viour Christ, our woes dis - pel! For some are
4 And some are press'd with world - ly care, And some are
5 And some have found the world is vain, Yet from the
6 O Sa - viour Christ, Thou too art Man! Thou hast been
7 Thy touch has still its an - cient pow'r; No word from

1 Lord, a - round Thee lay; O in what di - vers
2 var - ious ills, draw near; What if Thy form we
3 sick, and some are sad, And some have nev - er
4 tried with sin - ful doubt, And some such griev - ous
5 world they break not free; And some have friends who
6 trou - bled, tempt - ed, tried, Thy kind but search - ing
7 Thee can fruit - less fall; Hear in this sol - emn

1 pains they met! O with what joy they went a - way!
2 can - not see, We know and feel that Thou art here.
3 lov'd Thee well, And some have lost the love they had.
4 pass - ions tear, That on - ly Thou canst cast them out;
5 give them pain, Yet have not sought a friend in Thee.
6 glance can scan The ve - ry wounds that shame would hide.
7 ev'n - ing hour, And in Thy mer - cy heal us all.

The tune EDEN is on the following page

At Even

163

HENRY TWELLS

EDEN L.M.

TIMOTHY B. MASON

1 At e - ven, ere the sun was set, The sick, O
2 Once more 'tis e - ven - tide, and we, Op - press'd with
3 O Sa - viour Christ, our woes dis - pel! For some are
4 And some are press'd with world - ly care, And some are
5 And some have found the world is vain, Yet from the
6 O Sa - viour Christ, Thou too art Man! Thou hast been
7 Thy touch has still its an - cient pow'r; No word from

1 Lord, a - round Thee lay; O in what di - vers
2 var - ious ills, draw near; What if Thy form we
3 sick, and some are sad, And some have nev - er
4 tried with sin - ful doubt, And some such griev - ous
5 world they break not free; And some have friends who
6 trou - bled, tempt - ed, tried; Thy kind, but search - ing
7 Thee can fruit - less fall; Hear in this sol - emn

1 pains they met! O with what joy they went a - way!
2 can - not see, We know and feel that Thou art here.
3 lov'd Thee well, And some have lost the love they had.
4 pass - ions tear, That on - ly Thou canst cast them out;
5 give them pain, Yet have not sought a friend in Thee.
6 glance can scan The ve - ry wounds that shame would hide.
7 ev'n - ing hour, And in Thy mer - cy heal us all.

The tune ANGELUS is on the preceding page

164 Rock of Ages

A. M. TOPLADY   PETRA 7.7.7.7.7.7   RICHARD REDHEAD

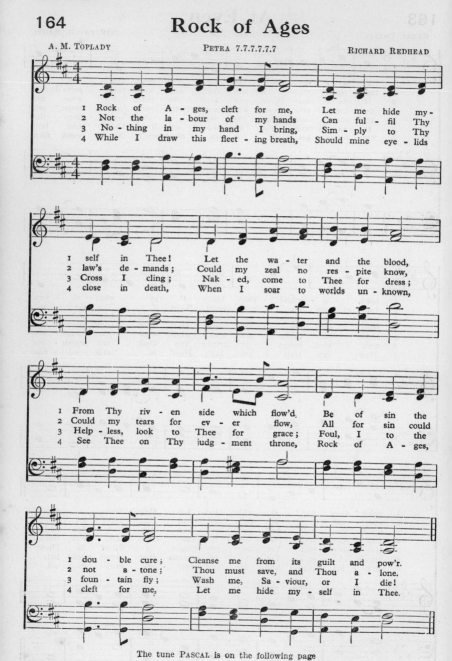

1. Rock of A - ges, cleft for me, Let me hide my-
2. Not the la - bour of my hands Can ful - fil Thy
3. No - thing in my hand I bring, Sim - ply to Thy
4. While I draw this fleet - ing breath, Should mine eye - lids

1. self in Thee! Let the wa - ter and the blood,
2. law's de - mands; Could my zeal no res - pite know,
3. Cross I cling; Nak - ed, come to Thee for dress;
4. close in death, When I soar to worlds un - known,

1. From Thy riv - en side which flow'd, Be of sin the
2. Could my tears for ev - er flow, All for sin could
3. Help - less, look to Thee for grace; Foul, I to the
4. See Thee on Thy judg - ment throne, Rock of A - ges,

1. dou - ble cure; Cleanse me from its guilt and pow'r.
2. not a - tone; Thou must save, and Thou a - lone.
3. foun - tain fly; Wash me, Sa - viour, or I die!
4. cleft for me, Let me hide my - self in Thee.

The tune PASCAL is on the following page

Rock of Ages

164

A. M. TOPLADY   PASCAL 7.7.7.7.7.7   *Katholisches Gesangbuch*

1 Rock of A - ges, cleft for me, Let me hide my-
2 Not the la - bour of my hands Can ful - fil Thy
3 No - thing in my hand I bring, Sim - ply to Thy
4 While I draw this fleet - ing breath, Should mine eye - lids

1 self in Thee! Let the wa - ter and the blood,
2 law's de - mands; Could my zeal no res - pite know,
3 Cross I cling; Nak - ed, come to Thee for dress;
4 close in death, When I soar to worlds un - known,

1 From Thy riv - en side which flow'd, Be of sin the
2 Could my tears for ev - er flow, All for sin could
3 Help - less, look to Thee for grace; Fou, I to the
4 See Thee on Thy judg - ment throne, Ro.k of A - ges,

1 dou - ble cure; Cleanse me from its guilt and pow'r.
2 not a - tone; Thou must save and Thou a - lone.
3 foun - tain fly; Wash me, Sa - viour, or I die!
4 cleft for me, Let me hide my - self in Thee.

The tune PETRA is on the preceding page.

165 It Reaches Me

MARY D. JAMES ATTAINMENT 8.7. 8.7. D JOHN R. SWENEY

1 Oh, this ut - ter-most sal - va - tion! 'Tis a foun - tain full and free,
2 How a - maz - ing God's com - pas - sion, That so vile a worm should prove
3 Je - sus, Sa - viour, I a - dore Thee! Now Thy love I will pro - claim;

1 Pure, ex - haust-less, ev - er flow - ing, Won-drous grace! it reach-es me!
2 This stu - pend - ous bliss of hea - ven, This un - meas-ur'd wealth of love!
3 I will tell the bless-ed sto - ry, I will mag - ni - fy Thy Name!

REFRAIN

It reach-es me! it reach-es me! Won-drous grace! it reach-es me!

Pure, ex - haust - less, ev - er flow - ing, Won-drous grace! it reach-es me!

The tune CHELSEA BRIDGE is on the following page

165 It Reaches Me

Mary D. James   Chelsea Bridge 8.7.8.7. d   Arr. Geo. Allan

1 Oh, this ut-ter-most sal-va-tion! 'Tis a foun-tain full and free,
2 How a-maz-ing God's com-pas-sion, That so vile a worm should prove
3 Je-sus, Sa-viour, I a-dore Thee! Now Thy love I will pro-claim;

1 Pure, ex-haust-less, ev-er flow-ing, Won-drous grace! it reach-es me!
2 This stu-pend-ous bliss of hea-ven, This un-meas-ur'd wealth of love!
3 I will tell the bless-ed sto-ry, I will mag-ni-fy Thy Name!

Refrain

It reach-es me! it reach-es me! Won-drous grace! it reach-es me!

Pure, ex-haust-less, ev-er flow-ing, Won-drous grace! it reach-es me!

The tune Attainment is on the preceding page

166 Away Over Jordan

ANON

OLD MELODY

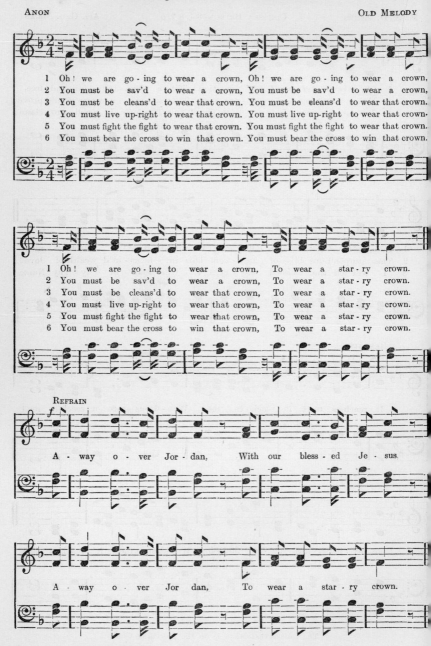

1 Oh! we are go-ing to wear a crown, Oh! we are go-ing to wear a crown.
2 You must be sav'd to wear a crown, You must be sav'd to wear a crown.
3 You must be cleans'd to wear that crown, You must be cleans'd to wear that crown.
4 You must live up-right to wear that crown, You must live up-right to wear that crown.
5 You must fight the fight to wear that crown, You must fight the fight to wear that crown.
6 You must bear the cross to win that crown, You must bear the cross to win that crown.

1 Oh! we are go-ing to wear a crown, To wear a star-ry crown.
2 You must be sav'd to wear a crown, To wear a star-ry crown.
3 You must be cleans'd to wear that crown, To wear a star-ry crown.
4 You must live up-right to wear that crown, To wear a star-ry crown.
5 You must fight the fight to wear that crown, To wear a star-ry crown.
6 You must bear the cross to win that crown, To wear a star-ry crown.

REFRAIN

A-way o-ver Jor-dan, With our bless-ed Je-sus.

A-way o-ver Jor-dan, To wear a star-ry crown.

167 Will You be There?

M. C. Wilson

ANON

1 We know there's a bright and a glo-ri-ous home, A-
2 In robes of white o'er streets of gold, Be-
3 If we find the lov-ing Sa-viour now, And
4 If we are shel-ter'd by the Cross, And

1 way in the hea-vens high, Where all the re-
2 neath a cloud-less sky, They'll walk in the
3 fol-low Him faith-ful-ly, When He ga-thers His
4 through the blood brought nigh; Our ut-most

FINE

1 deem'd shall with Je-sus dwell, Will you be there, and I?
2 light of their Fa-ther's love, Will you be there, and I?
3 chil-dren in that bright home, Will you be there, and I?
4 gain we'll count but loss, Since you'll be there, and I.

REFRAIN

D.S. al Fine

1 Will you be there and I?......... Will you be there and I?
2 Will you be there and I?......... Will you be there and I?
3 Will you be there and I?......... Will you be there and I?
4 Since you'll be there and I, ... Since you'll be there and I;

168 The Saviour Calling

Fanny J. Crosby

W. H. DOANE

1 Hark! there comes a whisper, Steal-ing on thine ear;
2 With that voice so gen-tle, Dost thou hear Him say?
3 Would'st thou find a re-fuge For thy soul op-prest?
4 At the Cross of Je-sus Let thy bur-den fall;

1 'Tis the Sa-viour call-ing, Soft, soft and clear.
2 "Tell Me all thy sor-rows; Come, come a-way!"
3 Je-sus kind-ly an-swers, "I am thy rest."
4 While He gent-ly whis-pers, "I'll bear it all."

REFRAIN

"Give thy heart to Me, to Me, Once I died for thee, for thee";

Hark! hark! thy Sa-viour calls: Come, sin-ner, come!

169 Life for a Look

Asa M. Hull

E. G. Taylor

1 There is life for a look at the Cru-ci-fied One, There is
2 It is not thy tears of re-pen-tance, or pray'rs, But the
3 We are heal'd by His stripes; wouldst thou add to the word? And
4 Then doubt not thy wel-come, since God has de-clar'd There re-
5 But take, with re-joic-ing, from Je-sus at once The

1 life at this mo-ment for thee, Then look, sin-ner, look un-to
2 blood that a-tones for the soul; On Him then be-lieve, and a
3 He is our right-eous-ness made; The best robe of hea-ven He
4 main-eth no more to be done: That once in the end of the
5 life ev-er-last-ing He gives: And know with as-sur-ance thou

1 Him and be sav'd! Un-to Him who was nail'd to the tree.
2 par-don re-ceive, For His blood now can make thee quite whole.
3 bids thee to wear, Oh, couldst thou be bet-ter ar-rayed?
4 world He ap-pear'd, And com-ple-ted the work He be-gun.
5 nev-er canst die, Since Je-sus thy right-eous-ness lives.

REFRAIN

Look! look! look and live! There is life for a look at the
Cru-ci-fied One, There is life at this mo-ment for thee.

170 Seeking the Lost

W. A. Ogden

W. A. Ogden

1 Seek - ing the lost, yes, kind - ly en - treat - ing Wan - der-ers on the
2 Seek - ing the lost, and point-ing to Je - sus, Souls that are weak and
3 Thus I would go on miss-ions of mer - cy, Fol - low-ing Christ from

1 moun-tain a - stray; 'Come un - to Me,' His mess-age re - peat - ing,
2 hearts that are sore; Lead-ing them forth in ways of sal - va - tion,
3 day un - to day; Cheer-ing the faint, and rais-ing the fall - en;

REFRAIN

1 Words of the Mas - ter speak-ing to - day.
2 Show-ing the path to life ev - er - more.
3 Point-ing the lost to Je - sus the way.

{ Go - ing a-far   Up-on the moun-tain,   Bring-ing the
{ In - to the fold   Of my Re-deem-er.   Je - sus the

{ far . . . up-on the moun - tain, . . Bring-ing the wan - -
{ fold . . . of my Re-deem - er, . . Je-sus the Lamb - -

1st time

2nd time

{ wan - d'rer back a - gain, back a - gain, } sin - ners slain, for sin-ners slain.
{ Lamb for (Omit)

{ d'rer back a - gain, } sin - ners slain. . .
{ for (Omit)

171 ## Washed in the Blood

ELISHA A. HOFFMAN   ELISHA A. HOFFMAN

1 Have you been to Je - sus for the cleans - ing pow'r? Are you wash'd in
2 Are you walk - ing dai - ly by the Sa - viour's side? Are you wash'd in
3 When the Bride - groom com-eth will your robes be white? Pure and white in
4 Lay a - side the gar-ments that are stain'd by sin, And be wash'd in

1 the blood of the Lamb? Are you ful - ly trust-ing in His grace this hour?
2 the blood of the Lamb? Do you rest each mo-ment in the Cru - ci - fied?
3 the blood of the Lamb? Will your soul be rea - dy for the man - sions bright?
4 the blood of the Lamb; There's a foun - tain flow-ing for the soul un - clean,

REFRAIN

1 Are you
2 Are you } wash'd in the blood of the Lamb? Are you wash'd   in the
3 And be
4 O be
         Are you wash'd

blood,   In the soul-cleans-ing blood of the Lamb?   Are your
     in the blood   of the Lamb?

gar-ments spot-less? Are they white as snow? Are you wash'd in the blood of the Lamb?

172 That Old Story is True

D. B. WATKINS

E. O. EXCELL

1. There's a won - der - ful sto - ry I've heard long a - go, 'Tis
2. They told of a Sav-iour so love - ly and pure, That
3. He a - rose and as - cend - ed to hea - ven, we're told, Tri-
4. Oh, that won - der - ful sto - ry I love to re - peat, Of

1. called "The sweet sto - ry of old," I hear it so oft - en, wher-
2. came to the earth to dwell, To seek for His lost ones, and
3. umph - ant o'er death and hell; He's pre - par - ing a place in that
4. peace and good - will to men; There's no sto - ry to me that is

1. ev - er I go, That same old sto - ry is told; And I've
2. make them se - cure From death and the pow - er of hell! That
3. ci - ty of gold, Where loved ones for ev - er may dwell. Where our
4. half so sweet, As I hear it a - gain and a - gain. He in-

1. thought it was strange that so oft - en they'd tell That sto - ry as if it were
2. He was des-pised and with thorns He was crowned, On the Cross was ex - tend - ed to
3. kin - dred we'll meet, and we'll nev - er more part, And oh, while I tell it to
4. vites you to come—He will free - ly re - ceive, And this mes - sage He send-eth to

That Old Story is True—*Continued*

REFRAIN

1. new;   But I've found out the reas-on they loved it so   well,   That
2. view;   But   oh, what sweet peace in my heart since I've found   That
3. you,   It is   peace to my soul, it is joy to my   heart,   That
4. you,   "There's a man-sion in glo-ry for all who be - lieve"   That

1. old,   old sto-ry is   true.   That old,   old sto-ry is   true,
2. old,   old sto-ry is   true.   That old,   old sto-ry is   true,
3. old,   old sto-ry is   true.   That old,   old sto-ry is   true,
4. old,   old sto-ry is   true.   That old,   old sto-ry is   true,

1. That old,   old sto-ry is   true,   But I've found out the reas-on they
2. That old,   old sto-ry is   true,   But   oh, what sweet peace in my
3. That old,   old sto-ry is   true,   It is peace to my soul, it is
4. That old,   old sto ry is   true,   "There's a man-sion in glo-ry for

1. loved   it   so   well,   That old,   old sto - ry is   true.
2. heart since I've found   That old,   old sto - ry is   true.
3. joy   to   my   heart,   That old,   old sto - ry is   true.
4. all who be - lieve"   That old,   old sto - ry is   true.

173 Verily, Verily

J. McGranahan

J. McGranahan

1 O what a Sa-viour that He died for me ! From con-dem-na-tion
2 All my in-i-qui-ties on Him were laid, All my in-debt-ed-
3 Tho' poor and need-y I can trust my Lord, Tho' weak and sin-ful
4 Tho' all un-worth-y, yet I will not doubt, For him that com-eth,

1 He hath made me free ; 'He that be-liev-eth on the Son', saith He, 'Hath
2 ness by Him was paid ; All who be-lieve on Him, the Lord hath said, 'Hath
3 I be-lieve His word ; O glad mes-sage! ev'-ry child of God, 'Hath
4 He will not cast out, 'He that be-liev-eth,' O the good news shout, 'Hath

REFRAIN

ev-er-last-ing life.' 'Ver-i-ly, ver-i-ly, I say un-

to you, Ver-i-ly, ver-i-ly,' mes-sage e-ver new ; 'He that

be-liev-eth on the Son' 'tis true, 'Hath ev-er-last-ing life.'

174 I Heard the Voice

HORATIUS BONAR VOX DILECTI D.C.M. J. B. DYKES

1. I heard the voice of Je - sus say, "Come un - to Me and rest:
2. I heard the voice of Je - sus say, "Be - hold, I free - ly give
3. I heard the voice of Je - sus say, "I am this dark world's Light;

1. Lay down, thou wea - ry one, lay down Thy head up - on My breast."
2. The liv - ing wa - ter; thirs - ty one, Stoop down and drink, and live."
3. Look un - to Me, thy morn shall rise, And all thy day be bright."

1. I came to Je - sus as I was, Wea - ry, and worn, and sad;
2. I came to Je - sus, and I drank Of that life - giv - ing stream;
3. I looked to Je - sus, and I found In Him my Star, my Sun;

1. I found in Him a rest - ing place, And He has made me glad.
2. My thirst was quench'd, my soul re-vived, And now I live in Him.
3. And in that light of life I'll walk, Till trav-'lling days are done.

Tunes EVAN, NOX PRAECESSIT, and KNIGHTSWOOD are on the next two pages

174   I Heard the Voice

HORATIUS BONAR   EVAN C.M.   W. H. HAVERGAL

1. I heard the voice of Je - sus say, "Come un - to Me and rest;
2. I came to Je - sus as I was, Wea - ry, and worn, and sad;
3. I heard the voice of Je - sus say, "Be - hold, I free - ly give
4. I came to Je - sus, and I drank Of that life - giv - ing stream;

1. Lay down, thou wea - ry one, lay down Thy head up - on My breast."
2. I found in Him a rest - ing place, And He has made me glad.
3. The liv - ing wa - ter; thirs - ty one, Stoop down and drink, and live."
4. My thirst was quench'd, my soul re - vived, And now I live in Him.

5. I heard the voice of Jesus say,
    "I am this dark world's Light;
Look unto Me, thy morn shall rise,
    And all thy day be bright."

6. I looked to Jesus, and I found
    In Him my Star, my Sun;
And in that light of life I'll walk,
    Till travelling days are done.

HORATIUS BONAR   NOX PRAECESSIT C.M.   J. B. CALKIN

1. I heard the voice of Je - sus say, "Come un - to Me and rest;
2. I came to Je - sus as I was, Wea - ry, and worn, and sad;
3. I heard the voice of Je - sus say, "Be - hold, I free - ly give
4. I came to Je - sus, and I drank Of that life - giv - ing stream;

1. Lay down, thou wea - ry one, lay down Thy head up - on My breast."
2. I found in Him a rest - ing place, And He has made me glad.
3. The liv - ing wa - ter; thirs - ty one, Stoop down and drink, and live."
4. My thirst was quench'd, my soul re - vived, And now I live in Him.

5. I heard the voice of Jesus say,
    "I am this dark world's Light;
Look unto Me, thy morn shall rise,
    And all thy day be bright."

6. I looked to Jesus, and I found
    In Him my Star, my Sun;
And in that light of life I'll walk,
    Till travelling days are done.

The tune VOX DILECTI is on previous page. The tune KNIGHTSWOOD is on the following page.

174   I Heard the Voice

HORATIUS BONAR   KNIGHTSWOOD   D.C.M.   F. H. HUTCHINS

1 I heard the voice of Je-sus say, "Come un-to Me and rest; Lay
2 I heard the voice of Je-sus say, "Be-hold, I free-ly give The
3 I heard the voice of Je-sus say, "I am this dark world's Light; Look

1 down, thou wea-ry one, lay down, Thy head up-on My breast." I came to Je-sus
2 liv-ing wa-ter, thirst-y one, Stoop down, and drink, and live." I came to Je-sus
3 un-to Me, thy morn shall rise, And all thy day be bright." I look'd to Je-sus

1 as I was, Wea-ry, and worn, and sad; I found in Him a
2 and I drank Of that life-giv-ing stream; My thirst was quench'd, my
3 and I found In Him my Star, my Sun; And in that light of

1 rest-ing place, And He has made me glad, And He has made me glad.
2 soul re-viv'd, And now I live in Him, And now I live in Him.
3 life I'll walk, Till trav-'lling days are done, Till trav-'lling days are done.

The tunes VOX DILECTI, EVAN, and NOX PRAECESSIT precede this tune

175 Come, O Come!

J. G. JOHNSON

JAMES McGRANAHAN

1 O word! of words the sweet-est, O word! in which there lie
2 O soul! why shouldst thou wan-der From such a lov-ing Friend?
3 O each time draw me near-er! That soon the Come may be,

1 All pro-mise, all ful-fil-ment, And end of mys-ter-y;
2 Cling clo-ser, clo-ser to Him, Stay with Him to the end;
3 Nought but a gen-tle whis-per To one close, close to Thee;

1 La-ment-ing, or re-joic-ing, With doubt or ter-ror nigh,
2 A-las! I am so help-less, So ve-ry full of sin,
3 Then, o-ver sea and moun-tain, Far from, or near my home,

1 I hear the Come! of Je-sus, And to His Cross I fly.
2 For I am e-ver wand-'ring, And com-ing back a-gain.
3 I'll take Thy hand and fol-low, At that sweet whis-per, Come!

Come, O Come!—*Continued*

REFRAIN

Come! . O come to Me! . . Come! O come to
Come! come! come! come! come! . Come! come! come!

Me! . . Wear-y, heav-y-la - den, Come! O come to
come! come! . Wear-y, heav-y-la - den, Come! O come to

Me! . . Come! . O come to Me! . . Come! O come to
Me! . O come! come! come! come! come! Come! come! come!

Me! . . Wear-y, heav-y-la - den, come, O come to Me! .
come! come! . Wear-y, heav-y-la - den, come, O come to Me! .

rit.

176 # O Turn Ye!

JOSIAH HOPKINS   CLARENDON STREET 11.11.11.11   ADONIRAM J. GORDON

1. O turn ye! O turn ye! for why will ye die
2. How vain the de-lu-sion that, while you de-lay,
3. In rich-es, in plea-sures, what can you ob-tain

1. When God in great mer-cy is draw-ing so nigh?
2. Your hearts may grow bet-ter by stay-ing a-way!
3. To soothe your af-flic-tion or ban-ish your pain,

1. Now Je-sus in-vites you, the Spi-rit says, Come!
2. Come wret-ched, come thirst-y, come just as you be,
3. To bear up your spi-rits when sum-mon'd to die,

1. And an-gels are wait-ing to wel-come you home.
2. While streams of sal-va-tion are flow-ing so free.
3. Or take you to Christ in the clouds of the sky?

The tune ST. DENIO on the following page

176 O Turn Ye!

JOSIAH HOPKINS   ST. DENIO 11.11.11.11   WELSH HYMN MELODY

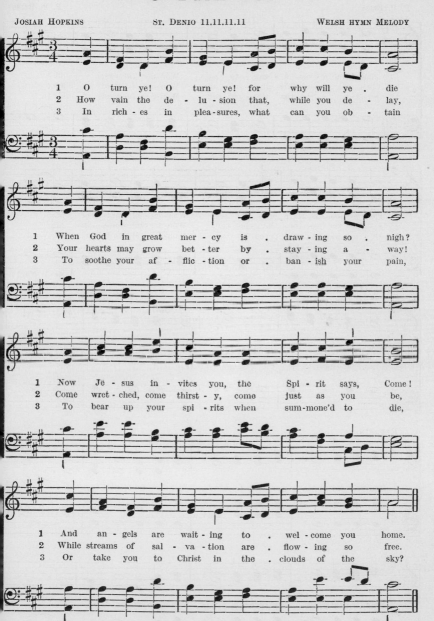

1 O turn ye! O turn ye! for why will ye . die
2 How vain the de - lu - sion that, while you de - lay,
3 In rich - es in plea - sures, what can you ob - tain

1 When God in great mer - cy is . draw - ing so . nigh?
2 Your hearts may grow bet - ter by . stay - ing a - way!
3 To soothe your af - flic - tion or . ban - ish your pain,

1 Now Je - sus in - vites you, the Spi - rit says, Come!
2 Come wret - ched, come thirst - y, come just as you be,
3 To bear up your spi - rits when sum - mone'd to die,

1 And an - gels are wait - ing to . wel - come you home.
2 While streams of sal - va - tion are . flow - ing so free.
3 Or take you to Christ in the . clouds of the sky?

The tune CLARENDON STREET is on the preceding page

177 Wonderful Words of Life

P. P. BLISS   P. P. BLISS

1 Sing them o-ver a-gain to me, Won-der-ful words of life!
2 Christ, the bless-ed One, gives to all Won-der-ful words of life!
3 Sweet-ly e-cho the Gos-pel call, Won-der-ful words of life!

1 Let me more of their beau-ty see, Won-der-ful words of life!
2 Sin-ner, list to the lov-ing call, Won-der-ful words of life!
3 Of-fer par-don and peace to all, Won-der-ful words of life!

1 Words of life and beau-ty, Teach me faith and du-ty,
2 All so free-ly giv-en, Woo-ing us to hea-ven,
3 Je-sus, on-ly Sa-viour, Sanc-ti-fy for ev-er,

REFRAIN

Beau-ti-ful words, won-der-ful words, Won-der-ful words of life!

Beau-ti-ful words, won-der-ful words, Won-der-ful words of life!

178 Spread the News

ANON.

PHILIP P. BLISS

1 Sound the Gos-pel of grace a-broad, There's life in the ris - en Lord!
2 All by na-ture are doom'd to die, So saith the Ho - ly Word;
3 Saints, a-pos-tles, and pro-phets, all Pub - lish'd with one ac - cord
4 Par - don, pow-er, and per - fect peace The words of this life af - ford;

1 Spread the news of the gift of God, There's life in the ris - en Lord!
2 Wel-come, there-fore, the joy - ful cry, There's life in the ris - en Lord!
3 This de-liv-er-ance from the fall, This life in the ris - en Lord!
4 Nev - er then let the tid - ings cease Of life in the ris - en Lord:

1 God a - bove de - sires it, Sin - ful man re - quires it:
2 Wel - come news of glad - ness, An - ti - dote of sad - ness;
3 Glo - ry be to Je - sus, Who from bon - dage frees us;
4 Op - en wide the por - tal Un - to ev - 'ry mor - tal;

REFRAIN

Tell it a - round, let it a-bound, There's life in the ris - en Lord!

Tell it a - round, let it a-bound, There's life in the ris - en Lord!

179 Is Thy Heart Right?

ELISHA A. HOFFMAN   ELISHA A. HOFFMAN

1 Have thy af-fec-tions been nail'd to the Cross ?   Is thy heart right with God ?
2 Hast thou do-min-ion o'er self and o'er sin ?   Is thy heart right with God ?
3 Is there no more con-dem-na-tion for sin ?   Is thy heart right with God ?
4 Are all thy pow'rs under Je-sus' con-trol ?   Is thy heart right with God ?
5 Art thou now walk-ing in hea-ven's pure light ?   Is thy heart right with God ?

1 Dost thou count all things for Je-sus but loss ?   Is thy heart right with God ?
2 O-ver all e-vil with-out and with-in ?   Is thy heart right with God ?
3 Does Je-sus rule in the tem-ple with-in ?   Is thy heart right with God ?
4 Does He each mo-ment a-bide in thy soul ?   Is thy heart right with God ?
5 Is thy soul wear-ing the gar-ment of white ?   Is thy heart right with God ?

REFRAIN

Is thy heart right with God,   Wash'd in the crim-son flood,   Cleans'd and made

ho-ly,   hum-ble and low-ly,   Right in the sight of God ?
of God ?

180 Will Your Anchor Hold?

PRISCILLA J. OWENS WILLIAM J. KIRKPATRICK

1 Will your an-chor hold in the storms of life When the clouds un-
2 It is safe-ly moor'd, 'twill the storm with-stand, For 'tis well se-
3 It will firm-ly hold in the straits of fear When the break-ers
4 It will sure-ly hold in the floods of death When the wa-ters
5 When our eyes be-hold thro' the gath-'ring night The ci-ty of

1 fold their wings of strife? When the strong tides lift, and the ca-bles
2 cur'd by the Sa-viour's hand; And the ca-bles, pass'd from His heart to
3 have told the reef is near; Tho' the tem-pest rave and the wild winds
4 cold chill our lat-est breath; On the ris-ing tide it can nev-er
5 gold, our har-bour bright, We shall an-chor fast by the heav'n-ly

REFRAIN

1 strain, Will your an-chor shift or firm re-main?
2 mine, Can de-fy the blast through strength di-vine.
3 blow Not an an-gry wave shall our bark o'er-flow, | We have an
4 fall While our hopes a-bide with-in the veil.
5 shore With the storms all past for ev-er-more.

an-chor that keeps the soul Stead-fast and sure while the bil-lows roll; Fas-ten'd

to the Rock which can-not move, Ground-ed firm and deep in the Sa-viour's love.

181 The Ninety and Nine

ELIZABETH C. CLEPHANE

IRA D. SANKEY

1 There were nine - ty and nine that safe - ly lay In the
2 'Lord, Thou hast here Thy nine - ty and nine, Are
3 But none of the ran - som'd e - ver knew How
4 'Lord, whence are those blood - drops all the way That
5 But all through the moun - tains, thun - der riv'n, And

1 shel - ter of the fold; But one was out
2 they not e - nough for Thee?' But the Shep - herd made
3 deep were the wa - ters cross'd, Nor how dark was the night
4 mark out the moun - tain's track? They were shed for one
5 up from the rock - y steep, There a - rose a cry

1 on the hills a - way, Far off from the gates of
2 an - swer: 'This of Mine Has wan - der'd a - way from
3 that the Lord pass'd through, Ere He found His sheep that was
4 who had gone a - stray, Ere the Shep - herd could bring him
5 to the gates of heav'n, 'Re - joice! I have found My

The Ninety and Nine—*Continued*

182 Christ has Power to Save

J. B. TROWBRIDGE   J. B. TROWBRIDGE

1 When toss'd on Gal - i - lee's rough wave, And fear their an-xious hearts op-
2 When he who sight had ne - ver known Came to the Lord with plead-ing
3 When cru - ci - fied on Cal - va - ry, And in the tomb was laid a -
4 When tri - als thick my path sur - round, When hope de - parts and gloom de -

1 press'd, The Mas - ter's voice spoke firm and clear, And calm'd the an - gry
2 voice, That word and touch made dark-ness flee, And bade the sor - row-
3 way, He rose tri - um-phant o'er the grave, And lives and reigns with
4 scends, A gen - tle voice speaks from a - bove, And ev - 'ry dark fore-

REFRAIN

1 waves to rest.) It was His voice that still'd the wave, . . His
2 ful re - joice.
3 bound-less sway.
4 bod - ing ends.) It was His voice that still'd the wave, His

heal - ing touch new vis - ion gave; . . His might has
heal - ing touch new . vis - ion gave; His might has

tri-umph'd o'er the grave, . . Our Christ a - lone has pow'r to save.
tri - umph'd o'er the grave, Our Christ . . has pow'r to save.

183 The Marriage Supper

F. A. BRECK   H. L. GILMOUR

1 In the soul's bright home be - yond the sky, In a land where the ran - som'd
2 O the bride shall shine in bright ar - ray, With her tears all for - ev - er
3 From all sin for ev - er - more re - leas'd, They will come from the west and
4 We shall praise Him by the crys - tal tide, When the Lamb that was slain is

1 nev - er die, There will be a roy - al ban - quet by and by, 'Tis
2 wiped a - way; There will be a great re - joic - ing on that day, At
3 from the east, For all na - tions will be ga - ther'd at the feast Of
4 glo - ri - fied; And the ran - som'd Church of God shall be the bride At

Slow and recitative   REFRAIN

1-4 the great mar - riage sup - per of the Lamb. Are you go - ing to be there?

Are you go - ing to be there? At the great mar - riage sup - per of the Lamb;

Ritard.

With your wed - ding gar - ment on, }
Will you meet the lov'd ones gone? } At the great mar - riage sup - per of the Lamb.

184   The Spirit says, Come!

GRANT COLFAX TULLAR   I. H. MEREDITH

1 A glo-rious in-vi-ta-tion, Now calls you to the feast;
2 That bles-sed in-vi-ta-tion! Oh, hear to-day and heed!
3 Re-peat the in-vi-ta-tion! Pass on the bless-ed news;

1 Each soul is now in-vi-ted, The great-est and the least.
2 The Spi-rit now is call-ing, Why long-er dwell in need?
3 Let none for-sake His mer-cy, Or par-don now re-fuse.

1 Come all ye hea-vy bur-den'd With sor-row or with care—
2 Thy soul to-day is faint-ing For Christ the liv-ing Bread;
3 'Tis Je-sus that is call-ing—All things are read-y, come—

1 To-day you are in-vi-ted, Your bur-dens Christ will bear.
2 Ac-cept the in-vi-ta-tion, Come while the feast is spread.
3 The Spi-rit will di-rect you, The Bride will wel-come home.

The Spirit says, Come!—*Continued*

REFRAIN

The Spi - - rit says, Come; .... The Bride............... says,

The Spir - it says, Come; says, Come; The Bride says,

Come; .... Let him that hear - eth say, Come; .... Let

Come; says, Come;

him that thirst-eth come,........ And who - so - ev - er will let him

take of the wa - ter of life............... free - - - ly...............

take of the wa - ter of life free - - ly...............

185   He was Found Worthy

ANON   OLD MELODY

SOLO ... CHORUS

1 When none was found to ran-som me, He was found worth-y.
2 To take the Book and loose the seal, He was found worth-y.
3 To bridge the gulf 'twixt man and God, He was found worth-y.
4 To o-pen wide the gates of heav'n, He was found worth-y.
5 To reign o'er all the ran-som'd race, He was found worth-y.
6 His blood has wash'd me white as snow, He was found worth-y.

SOLO ... CHORUS

1 To set a world of sin-ners free, He was found worth-y.
2 To bruise the head that bruised His heel, He was found worth-y.
3 And save the re-bels by His blood. He was found worth-y.
4 To Him all ma-jest-y is giv'n. He was found worth-y.
5 I've tas-ted of His sav-ing grace. He was found worth-y.
6 And all His ful-ness I shall know. He was found worth-y.

REFRAIN

Oh, the bleed-ing Lamb! Oh, the bleed-ing Lamb!

Oh, the bleed-ing Lamb! He was found worth-y.

By permission of the INTERNATIONAL MUSIC BOARD OF THE SALVATION ARMY

186

Once for All

PHILIP P. BLISS

PHILIP P. BLISS

1. Free from the law, oh, hap-py con-di-tion, Je-sus hath
2. Now we are free— there's no con-dem-na-tion, Je-sus pro-
3. "Chil-dren of God," oh, glo-ri-ous call-ing, Sure-ly His

1. bled, and *there* is re-mis-sion, Curs'd by the law and bruised by the
2. vides a per-fect sal-va-tion; "Come un-to *Me*," oh, hear His sweet
3. grace will keep us from fall-ing; Pass-ing from death to life at His

CHORUS.

1. fall, Grace hath redeemed us once for all.
2. call, Come, and He saves us once for all.
3. call, Bles-sed sal-va-tion once for all.
} Once for all, oh, sin-ner re-

ceive it, Once for all, oh, bro-ther, be-lieve it; Cling to the

Cross, the bur-den will fall, Christ hath redeemed us once for all.

187

Honey in the Rock

F. A. G.

F. A. GRAVES

1. O my brother do you know the Sa - viour, Who is won - drous
2. Have you "tasted that the Lord is gra - cious," Do you walk in the
3. Do you pray un - to God the Fa - ther, "What wilt Thou have
4. Then go out thro' the streets and bye - ways, Preach the word to the

1. kind and true? He's the "Rock of your sal - va - tion!"
2. way that's new? Have you drunk from the liv - ing foun - tain?
3. me to do?" Nev - er fear, He will sure - ly an - swer;
4. man - y or few; Say to ev - 'ry fal - len broth - er,

CHORUS

There's Honey in the Rock for you. Oh, there's Honey in the Rock, my

broth-er, ... There's Honey in the Rock for you; Leave your
my broth-er, for you;

sins for the blood to cov - er, There's Honey in the Rock for you, for you.

188

Let Him In

L. H. PARTHEMORE

L. H. PARTHEMORE

1 Hear the Sa-viour at the door, Let Him in, ... Let Him in, ...
2 He's your best and tru-est Friend, Let Him in, Let Him in,
3 Do not let Him knock in vain, Let Him in, Let Him in,
4 Hear His gen-tle, lov-ing voice, Let Him in, Let Him in,

1 Let Him in; .... He has of-ten knocked be-fore, Let Him in, ...
2 Let Him in; One who al-ways will de-fend, Let Him in,
3 Let Him in; He may nev-er come a-gain, Let Him in,
4 Let Him in, Bid Him wel-come, and re-joice, Let Him in,

REFRAIN

Let Him in, Let Him in. 'Tis the Sa-viour stand-ing at the door,
Let Him in,

at the door, He's been watch-ing, wait-ing there be-fore; yes, be-fore; O-pen wide the

heart of sin, Let the bless-ed Sa-viour in; Let Him in, Let Him in.
Let Him in,

189 Come to Him Now

KATHARINE E. PURVIS

C. F. GREEN

1 Je - sus is wait - ing, O sin - ner, for thee, Call - ing so ten - der - ly,
2 Come from the path that seems pleas-ant and wide, Nar - row the way if thou
3 Come to the Sa-viour whose grace is so free, Come to Him now while He

1 'Come un - to Me,' Wait - ing His mer - cy and peace to im - part,
2 walk by His side, Nar - row, yet bright-en'd with bless-ings un - told,
3 call - eth for thee; En - ter the fold by the on - ly true door,

REFRAIN

1 Come then, O wan - der - er, give Him thy heart.
2 Lead - ing thee home to the ci - ty of gold.   } Come to Him now, He's
3 Come, quick-ly come, lest He call thee no more.

wait-ing for thee, Turn not a-way from His mer-cy so free, Je - sus is

wait - ing, wait-ing for thee, Call-ing so ten-der-ly, 'Come un - to Me.'

190 # How they Sing Up Yonder!

H. E. JONES   HEAVENLY HOME 7.6.7.6.7.7.7.6.   D. B. TOWNER

1. When the sin - ner turns from sin,   How they sing   up yon - der!
2. When the wand - 'rer seeks his home, How they sing   up yon - der!
3. Broth - er, would you join the song, In   the home   up yon - der!

1. Comes to Christ sweet peace to win, How they sing   up yon - der!
2. Just a ser - vant to be - come,   How they sing   up yon - der!
3. Sing while a - ges roll a - long,   In   the home   up yon - der!

1. Asks for cleans - ing in the blood, Sinks be - neath the heal - ing flood,
2. Leaves the by - ways cold and bare, Seeks a - gain a Fath - er's care,
3. Then for - sake the paths so cold,   Fly to Je - sus and His fold,

1. Ris - es, cleansed and owned of God, How they sing   up yon - der!
2. All His wealth of love to share, How they sing   up yon - der!
3. That your name may be en - rolled, In   the home   up yon - der!

191

Come Away to Jesus

J. M. W.

J. M. WHYTE.

1. Oh, why thus stand with re-luc-tant feet, Just on the verge of this
2. The Spi-rit strives, and yet there you stand, In sight of bliss and the
3. Your lov'd ones gone to the o-ther shore, With un-seen hands seem to

1. rest so sweet, While God in-vites and your steps will greet?
2. glo-ry land; Re-treat is death in the sink-ing sand,
3. beck-on o'er; Their voi-ces hush'd, yet they still im-plore,

CHORUS.

Come a-way to Je-sus now. Come a-way to Je-sus, Come a-
Come away to Je-sus, come away,

way to Je-sus, Come a-way to
Come a-way to Je-sus, come a-way, Come a-way to

Je-sus, Come a-way to Je-sus now.
Je-sus, come a-way,

192 Glory to His Name !

E. A. HOFFMAN

J. H. STOCKTON

1 Down at the Cross where my Sa-viour died, Down where for cleans-ing from sin I cried;
2 I am so won-drous-ly sav'd from sin! Je - sus so sweet-ly a-bides with-in;
3 O pre-cious foun-tain that saves from sin! I am so glad I have en-ter'd in;
4 Come to this foun-tain, so rich and sweet; Cast thy poor soul at the Saviour's feet;

1 There to my heart was the blood ap - plied; Glo - ry to His Name !
2 There at the Cross where He took me in; Glo - ry to His Name !
3 There Je - sus saves me, and keeps me clean; Glo - ry to His Name !
4 Plunge in to - day, and be made com-plete; Glo - ry to His Name !

REFRAIN

Glo - ry to His Name !............ Glo - ry to His Name !............

There to my heart was the blood ap - plied; Glo - ry to His Name !

193 This is the Day

Isaac Watts   Dublin C.M.   J. A. Stevenson

1 This is the day the Lord hath made, He calls the hours His own;
2 To-day He rose and left the dead, And Satan's empire fell;
3 Ho-san-na to th'a-noint-ed King, To David's ho-ly Son!
4 Blest be the Lord, who comes to men With mes-sa-ges of grace,
5 Ho-san-na, in the high-est strains The church on earth can raise.

1 Let heav'n re-joice, let earth be glad, And praise sur-round the throne.
2 To-day the saints His tri-umph spread, And all His won-ders tell.
3 Help us, O Lord! des-cend and bring Sal-va-tion from Thy throne.
4 Who comes in God His Fa-ther's name, To save our sin-ful race.
5 The high-est heav'ns in which He reigns Shall give Him no-bler praise.

Isaac Watts   Jerusalem C.M.   S. Grosvenor

1 This is the day the Lord hath made, He calls the hours His own;
2 To-day He rose and left the dead, And Satan's empire fell;
3 Ho-san-na to th'a-noint-ed King, To David's ho-ly Son!
4 Blest be the Lord, who comes to men With mes-sa-ges of grace
5 Ho-san-na, in the high-est strains The church on earth can raise;

1 Let heav'n re-joice, let earth be glad, And praise sur-round the throne.
2 To-day the saints His tri-umph spread, And all His won-ders tell.
3 Help us, O Lord! des-cend and bring Sal-va-tion from Thy throne.
4 Who comes in God His Fa-ther's name, To save our sin-ful race.
5 The high-est heav'ns in which He reigns Shall give Him no-bler praise.

194 Jesus is Passing this Way

ANNIE L. JAMES

WILLIAM H. DOANE

1 Is there a heart that is wait - ing, Long-ing for par-don to - day?
2 Is there a heart that has wan-der'd? Come with thy bur-den to - day;
3 Is there a heart that is bro - ken, Wea - ry and sigh-ing for rest?
4 Come to thy on - ly Re - deem - er, Come to His in - fin - ite love;

rit.

1 Hear the glad mes-sage pro - claim - ing, Je - sus is pass-ing this way.
2 Mer - cy is ten - der - ly plead - ing, Je - sus is pass-ing this way,
3 Come to the arms of thy Sa - viour, Pil - low thy head on His breast.
4 Come to the gate that is lead - ing Home-ward to man-sions a - bove,

REFRAIN

Je - sus is pass-ing this way, . . This way, . . . to - day; . .
Je - sus is pass-ing, is pass-ing this way, Is pass-ing this way, is pass-ing to-day;

Je - sus is pass-ing this way, . . Is pass-ing this way to - day.
Je - sus is pass-ing this way to-day, Is pass-ing this way to - day.

195 The Heart of the Shepherd

Mary B. Wingate

Wm. J. Kirkpatrick

DUET

1 Dear to the heart of the Shep - herd, Dear are the sheep of His fold;
2 Dear to the heart of the Shep - herd, Dear are the lambs of His fold;
3 Dear to the heart of the Shep - herd, Dear are the "nine-ty and nine."

1 Dear is the love that He gives them; Dear-er than sil - ver or gold.
2 Some from the pas-tures are stray - ing, Hung-ry and help-less and cold.
3 Dear are the sheep that have wan - der'd Out in the des - ert to pine.

1 Dear to the heart of the Shep - herd, Dear are His "oth-er" lost sheep;
2 See, the Good Shep-herd is seek - ing, Seek-ing the lambs that are lost;
3 Hark! He is earn-est-ly call - ing, Ten-der-ly plead-ing to - day;

1 O - ver the moun-tains He fol - lows, O - ver the wa-ters so deep.
2 Bring-ing them in with re - joic - ing, Saved at such in - fin - ite cost.
3 "Will you not seek for My lost ones, Far from My shel-ter a - stray?"

REFRAIN

poco rit.

Out in the des - ert they wan - der, Hung-ry and help-less and cold;.........

The Heart of the Shepherd—*Continued*

f a tempo

Off to the res-cue He hast - ens, Bring-ing them back to the fold.

196 Only Trust Him

J. H. STOCKTON   J. H. STOCKTON

1 Come, ev - 'ry soul by sin op-press'd, There's mer - cy with the Lord,
2 For Je - sus shed His pre - cious blood, Rich bless-ings to be - stow:
3 Yes, Je - sus is the Truth, the Way, That leads you in - to rest!
4 Come, then, and join this ho - ly band, And on to glo - ry go,

1 And He will sure - ly give you rest, By trust - ing in His word.
2 Plunge now in - to the crim - son flood, That wash - es white as snow.
3 Be - lieve in Him with - out de - lay, And you are ful - ly blest,
4 To dwell in that ce - les - tial land, Where joys im - mor - tal flow.

REFRAIN

On - ly trust Him, on - ly trust Him, On - ly trust Him now;

He will save you, He will save you, He will save you now.

197 The Sweet Old Story

W. C. MARTIN   POWELL G. FITHIAN

Voices in Unison Not too fast

1. O tell me o'er and o'er a-gain the tale I love so well, Of
2. I am both weak and sin-ful but one thing I sure-ly know, That
3. O tell a-gain the sto-ry of His mer-cy and His grace, The

1. how the King of glo-ry left His throne, And came a hum-ble man a-
2. Je-sus fills my heart with grace and love, That He will guide me safe-ly
3. sto-ry that is told of Him a-lone; Of how He died in tor-ment,

1. mong our sin-ful race to dwell, That He might save and claim us for His own.
2. thro' my journey here be-low, And then will take me to Himself a-bove.
3. in the helpless sinner's place, And conquered and is now u-pon His throne.

CHORUS.

O tell the sweet old sto-ry once a-gain,   Of how the Sa-viour

PARTS

loved the sons of men, . . .   He loved them, oh, so well, He

The Sweet Old Story—*Continued*

came on earth to dwell, O tell the sweet old sto-ry once a-gain.

198 All to Christ I Owe

ELVINA M. HALL

JOHN T. GRAPE

1 I hear the Sa-viour say, "Thy strength in-deed is small;
2 For noth-ing good have I Where-by Thy grace to claim—
3 When from my dy-ing bed My ran-som'd soul shall rise,
4 And when be-fore the Throne, I stand in Him com-plete,

1 Come to Me—I'll be thy stay, Find in Me thine all in all."
2 Je-sus died my soul to save, And bless-ed be His Name!
3 "Je-sus died my soul to save," Shall rend the vault-ed skies.
4 "Je-sus died my soul to save," My lips shall still re-peat.

REFRAIN

Je-sus paid it all, All to Him I owe—

Sin had left a crim-son stain; He wash'd it white as snow.

199   Tell it Far and Wide

MARY A. CROCKER   WM. A. MAY

1. Tell it! let the peo-ple hear it, "Je-sus saves from sin!" Let the
2. Tell it to the lone and wea-ry, To the blithe and gay; To the
3. Free the mer-cy, full the par-don, Je-sus died to give! Sweet the

1. bree-zes bear the mes-sage, "Je-sus makes men clean; That He shed His
2. a-ged with their bur-dens, To the child at play. "There is full and
3. welcome that the sin-ner Sure-ly will re-ceive. Wea-ry, weak and

1. blood to save us!" Tell it far and wide, "In no o-ther is re-demp-tion
2. free sal-va-tion!" Hear the bless-ed word, "There is mer-cy and true heal-ing
3. hea-vy la-den, Come to Him to-day, Let the cleans-ing blood of Je-sus

REFRAIN.

1. Save the cru-ci-fied!"
2. In the Sa-viour's blood!" } Tell it far and wide, Tell it far and wide,
3. Wash your sins a-way.

"In no o-ther is re-demp-tion, Save the Cru-ci-fied!"

200 ## Jesus Saves

PRISCILLA J. OWENS   JESUS SAVES 7.6.7.6.7.7.7.6   WM. J. KIRKPATRICK

1 We have heard a joy-ful sound, Je-sus saves, Je-sus saves;
2 Waft it on the roll-ing tide, Je-sus saves, Je-sus saves;
3 Sing a-bove the bat-tle's strife, Je-sus saves, Je-sus saves;
4 Give the winds a might-y voice, Je-sus saves, Je-sus saves;

1 Spread the glad-ness all a-round, . Je-sus saves, Je-sus saves;
2 Tell to sin-ners far and wide, . Je-sus saves, Je-sus saves;
3 By His death and end-less life . Je-sus saves, Je-sus saves;
4 Let the na-tions now re-joice, . Je-sus saves, Je-sus saves;

1 Bear the news to ev'-ry land, Climb the steeps and cross the waves,
2 Sing, ye is-lands of the sea, E-cho back, ye o-cean caves,
3 Sing it soft-ly thro' the gloom, When the heart for mer-cy craves,
4 Shout sal-va-tion full and free, High-est hills and deep-est caves.

1 On-ward, 'tis our Lord's com-mand, Je-sus saves, Je-sus saves,
2 Earth shall keep her Ju-bi-lee, Je-sus saves, Je-sus saves,
3 Sing in tri-umph o'er the tomb, Je-sus saves, Je-sus saves,
4 This our song of vic-tor-y, Je-sus saves, Je-sus saves.

201

Able to Save

E. A. HOFFMAN

P. P. BLISS

1 Who-ev-er re-ceiv - eth the Cru-ci-fied One,
2 Who-ev-er re-ceiv - eth the mes-sage of God,
3 Who-ev-er re-pents and for-sakes ev-'ry sin,

1 Who-ev-er be-liev - eth on God's on-ly Son,
2 And trusts in the pow'r of the soul-cleans-ing blood,
3 And o-pens his heart for the Lord to come in,

1 A free and a per - fect sal-va-tion shall have,
2 A full and e-ter - nal re-demp-tion shall have,
3 A pres-ent and per - fect sal-va-tion shall have,

1 For He is a-bun - dant-ly a-ble to save.
2 For He is both a - ble and will-ing to save.
3 For Je-sus is read - y this mo-ment to save.

Able to Save—*Continued*

REFRAIN

My bro - ther, the Mas - - - - ter is call - ing for
Bro - ther, the Mas - ter is come and is

thee ; . . . . His grace and His mer - - - - cy
call - ing for thee ; Bro - ther, His grace and

are won - drous - ly free, ... His blood as a
His mer - cy are won - drous - ly free,

ran - - - - - som for sin - ners He gave . . . . .
Bro - ther, His blood as a ran - som for sin - ners He gave,

And He is a - bun - - - dant - ly a - ble to save.
And He is a - bun - dant - ly a - ble to save.

202 That Man of Calvary

M. P. FERGUSON

M. P. FERGUSON

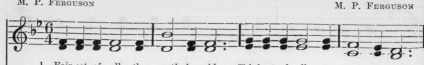

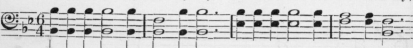

1 Fair-est of all the earth be-side, Chief-est of all un-to Thy bride,
2 Grant-ing the sin-ner life and peace, Grant-ing the cap-tive sweet re-lease,
3 Giv-ing the gifts ob-tain'd for men, Pour-ing out love be-yond our ken,
4 Com-fort of all my earth-ly way, Je-sus, I'll meet Thee some sweet day;

1 Ful-ness di-vine in Thee I see, Won-der-ful Man of Cal-va-ry!
2 Shed-ding His blood to make us free, Mer-ci-ful Man of Cal-va-ry!
3 Giv-ing us spot-less pu-ri-ty, Boun-ti-ful Man of Cal-va-ry!
4 Cen-tre of glo-ry Thee I'll see, Won-der-ful Man of Cal-va-ry!

REFRAIN

That Man of Cal-va-ry Has won my heart from me,

rit.

And died to set me free; Blest Man of Cal-va-ry!

203

Shout the Tidings!

ANON

ANON

1 Shout the tid-ings of sal - va - tion   To   the a - ged and the   young!
2 Shout the tid-ings of sal - va - tion   North and south and east and west!
3 Shout the tid-ings of sal - va - tion!   Ming - ling with the ocean's roar,
4 Shout the tid-ings of sal - va - tion   O'er   the is-lands of the   sea!

1 Till   the pre-cious in - vi - ta - tion   Wa - ken ev-'ry heart and   tongue.
2 Till   each gath'ring con-gre - ga - tion   With the Gos-pel sound   is blest.
3 Till   the ships of ev - 'ry   na - tion   Bear the news from shore to shore.
4 Till, in hum-ble a - dor - a - tion,   All to Christ shall bow the knee.

REFRAIN

Send the word the earth a-round, From the ris-ing to the set-ting of the   sun,

Till each gath'ring crowd shall pro-claim a - loud, 'The glo-rious work is   done.'

204 As When the Prophet

ISAAC WATTS   FRENCH C.M.   SCOTTISH PSALTER, 1615

1 As when the He-brew pro-phet rais'd The bra - zen ser - pent high,
2 So from the Sa-viour on the Cross A heal-ing vir - tue flows:
3 For God gave up His Son to death, So gen-'rous was His love,
4 Not to con-demn the sons of men The Son of God ap-pear'd;

1 The wound-ed look'd and straight were cur'd, The peo-ple ceas'd to die:
2 Who looks to Him with live-ly faith Is sav'd from end-less woes.
3 That all the faith-ful might en-joy E-ter-nal life a-bove.
4 No wea-pons in His hand are seen, Nor voice of ter-ror heard.

5 He came to raise our fallen state,
And our lost hopes restore;
Faith leads us to the mercy-seat,
And bids us fear no more.

6 But vengeance just for ever lies
Upon the rebel race,
Who God's eternal Son despise,
And scorn His offered grace.

ISAAC WATTS   WETHERBY C.M.   SAMUEL S. WESLEY

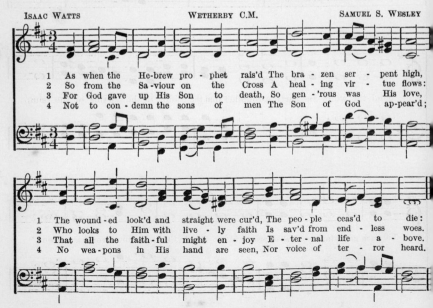

1 As when the He-brew pro-phet rais'd The bra - zen ser - pent high,
2 So from the Sa-viour on the Cross A heal-ing vir - tue flows:
3 For God gave up His Son to death, So gen-'rous was His love,
4 Not to con-demn the sons of men The Son of God ap-pear'd;

1 The wound-ed look'd and straight were cur'd, The peo-ple ceas'd to die:
2 Who looks to Him with live-ly faith Is sav'd from end-less woes.
3 That all the faith-ful might en-joy E-ter-nal life a-bove.
4 No wea-pons in His hand are seen, Nor voice of ter-ror heard.

The tune ST. URSULA is on the following page

204   As When the Prophet

ISAAC WATTS   ST. URSULA C.M.D.   FREDERICK WESTLAKE

1 As when the He-brew pro-phet rais'd The bra - zen ser - pent high
2 For God gave up His Son to death; So gen-'rous was His love,
3 He came to raise our fal - len state, And our lost hopes re - store;

1 The wound - ed look'd and straight were cur'd, The peo - ple ceas'd to die;
2 That all the faith - ful might en-joy E - ter - nal life a - bove;
3 Faith leads us to the mer - cy seat, And bids us fear no more:

1 So from the Sa - viour on the Cross A heal - ing vir - tue flows:
2 Not to con-demn the sons of men The Son of God ap - pear'd
3 But ven-geance just for ev - er lies up - on the re - bel race,

1 Who looks to Him with live - ly faith is sav'd from end - less woes.
2 No wea - pons in His hand are seen, Nor voice of ter - or heard,
3 Who God's e - ter - nal Son de - spise And scorn His of - fer'd grace.

The tunes FRENCH and WETHERBY are on the preceding page

205 **Father of Peace**

PHILIP DODDRIDGE · PALESTRINA C.M. · GIOVANNI DA PALESTRINA

1 Fa-ther of peace, and God of love! We own Thy pow'r to save,
2 Him from the dead Thou brought'st a-gain, When by His sa - cred blood,
3 O may Thy Spi - rit seal our souls, And mould them to Thy will!
4 That to per - fec-tion's sa - cred height We near-er still may rise,

1 That pow'r by which our Shep - herd rose Vic-to-rious o'er the grave.
2 Con-firm'd and seal'd for ev - er - more, Th'e-ter-nal cov'-nant stood.
3 That our weak hearts no more may stray, But keep Thy pre-cepts still.
4 And all we think, and all we do, Be pleas-ing in Thine eyes.

PHILIP DODDRIDGE · SIDON C.M. · WILLIAM CROTCH

1 Fa - ther of peace, and God of love! We
2 Him from the dead Thou brought'st a - gain, When
3 O may Thy Spi - rit seal our souls, And
4 That to per - fec - tion's sa - cred height We

1 own Thy pow'r to save, That pow'r by which our
2 by His sa - cred blood, Con - firm'd and seal'd for
3 mould them to Thy will! That our weak hearts no
4 near - er still may rise, And all we think, and

Father of Peace—*Continued*

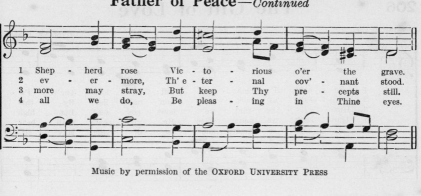

1 Shep - herd rose Vic - to - rious o'er the grave.
2 ev - er - more, Th' e - ter - nal cov' - nant stood.
3 more may stray, But keep Thy pre - cepts still.
4 all we do, Be pleas - ing in Thine eyes.

Music by permission of the OXFORD UNIVERSITY PRESS

PHILIP DODDRIDGE ORLINGTON C.M. JOHN CAMPBELL
Arr. P. J. MANSFIELD

1 Fa - ther of peace, and God of love! We own Thy
2 Him from the dead Thou brought'st a - gain, When by His
3 O may Thy Spi - rit seal our souls, And mould them
4 That to per - fec - tion's sa - cred height We near - er

1 pow'r to save, That pow'r by which our Shep - herd rose, That
2 sa - cred blood, Con - firm'd and seal'd for ev - er - more, Con -
3 to Thy will! That our weak hearts no more may stray, That
4 still may rise, And all we think, and all we do, And

Org.

1 pow'r by which our Shep - herd rose Vic - to - rious o'er the grave.
2 firm'd and seal'd for ev - er - more, Th' e - ter - nal cov' - nant stood.
3 our weak hearts no more may stray, But keep Thy pre - cepts still.
4 all we think, and all we do, Be pleas - ing in Thine eyes.

206   # The Gift of Love

ISAAC WATTS   ST. STEPHEN C.M.   WILLIAM JONES

1 Be - hold th' a - maz - ing gift of love The Fa -
2 Con - ceal'd as yet this hon - our lies By this
3 High is the rank we now pos - sess, But high -
4 Our souls, we know, when He ap - pears, shall bear
5 A hope so great, and so di - vine, May tri -

1 ther hath be - stow'd On us, the sin - ful
2 dark world un - known, A world that knew not
3 er we shall rise; Though what we shall here -
4 His im - age bright; For all His glo - ry,
5 als well en - dure; And purge the soul from

1 sons of men, To call us sons of God.
2 when He came, Ev'n God's e - ter - nal Son.
3 af - ter be Is hid from mor - tal eyes.
4 full dis - clos'd, shall o - pen to our sight.
   sense and sin, As Christ Him - self is pure.

ISAAC WATTS   COBLENZ C.M.   F. MENDELSSOHN—BARTHOLDY

1 Be - hold th' a - maz - ing gift of love The Fa - ther hath be - stow'd
2 Con - ceal'd as yet this hon - our lies By this dark world un - known,
3 High is the rank we now pos - sess, But high - er we shall rise;
4 Our souls, we know, when He ap - pears, Shall bear His im - age bright;
5 A hope so great, and so di - vine, May tri - als well en - dure;

The Gift of Love—*Continued*

1 On us, the sin - ful sons of men, To call us sons of God.
2 A world that knew not when He came, Ev'n God's e - ter - nal Son.
3 Though what we shall here - af - ter be Is hid from mor - tal eyes.
4 For all His glo - ry, full dis - clos'd, shall o - pen to our sight.
5 And purge the soul from sense and sin, As Christ Him - self is pure.

ISAAC WATTS   BURGATE C.M.   M. A. SIDEBOTHAM

1 Be - hold th' a - maz - ing gift of love The Fa -
2 Con - ceal'd as yet this hon - our lies By this
3 High is the rank we now pos - sess, But high -
4 Our souls, we know, when He ap - pears, shall bear
5 A hope so great, and so di - vine, May tri -

1 ther hath be - stow'd .... On us, the sin - ful
2 dark world un - known .... A world that knew not
3 er we shall rise; .... Though what we shall here -
4 His im - age bright; .... For all His glo - ry,
5 als well en - dure; .... And purge the soul from

1 sons of men, to call us sons of God.
2 when He came, Ev'n God's e - ter - nal Son.
3 af - ter be Is hid from mor - tal eyes.
4 full dis - clos'd, shall o - pen to our sight.
5 sense and sin, As Christ Him - self is pure.

207 Him that is Thirsty

LUCY J. RIDER   LUCY J. RIDER

1 Ho! ev-'ry one that is thirs-ty in spi - rit, Ho! ev-'ry one that is
2 Child of the world, are you tir-d of your bon - dage? Wea-ry of earth-joys, so
3 Child of the King-dom, be fill'd with the Spi - rit! Noth-ing but ful-ness thy

1 wea-ry and sad; Come to the foun-tain, there's ful-ness in Je - sus,
2 false, so un - true? Thirst-ing for God and His ful-ness of bless-ing?
3 long-ing can meet: 'Tis the en-due-ment for life and for ser-vice;

REFRAIN

1 All that you're long-ing for, come and be glad.
2 List to the pro-mise, a mes-sage for you! } I will pour wa-ter on
3 Thine is the pro-mise, so cer-tain, so sweet.

him that is thirs-ty, I will pour floods up-on the dry ground; O-pen your

heart for the gift I am bring-ing; While ye are seek-ing Me, I will be found.

208   The Lamb upon Calvary

JOHN NEWTON   OLD MELODY

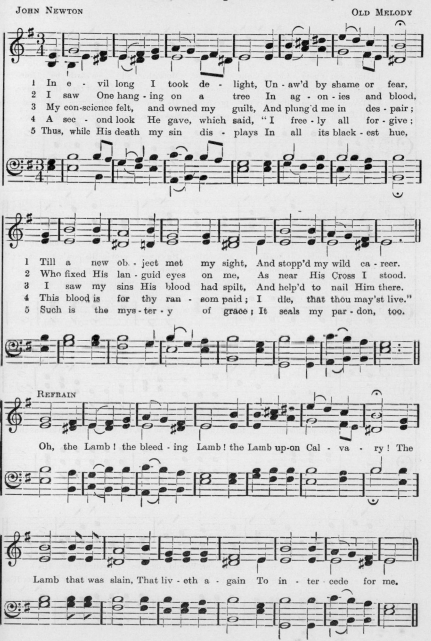

1 In e - vil long I took de - light, Un - aw'd by shame or fear,
2 I saw One hang - ing on a tree In ag - on - ies and blood,
3 My con-science felt, and owned my guilt, And plung'd me in des - pair;
4 A sec - ond look He gave, which said, "I free - ly all for - give;
5 Thus, while His death my sin dis - plays In all its black - est hue,

1 Till a new ob - ject met my sight, And stopp'd my wild ca - reer.
2 Who fixed His lan - guid eyes on me, As near His Cross I stood.
3 I saw my sins His blood had spilt, And help'd to nail Him there.
4 This blood is for thy ran - som paid; I die, that thou may'st live."
5 Such is the mys - ter - y of grace; It seals my par - don, too.

REFRAIN

Oh, the Lamb! the bleed - ing Lamb! the Lamb up-on Cal - va - ry! The

Lamb that was slain, That liv - eth a - gain To in - ter - cede for me.

209 Have You Found the Saviour?

IDA L. REED   J. LINCOLN HALL

1. Have you found the Sa-viour pre-cious, More than all on earth be - side,
2. Have you found the Sa-viour pre-cious, Who for you passed thro' the grave,
3. Have you found the Sa-viour pre-cious? Do you know the peace and rest
4. Have you found the Sa-viour pre-cious? Seek Him then with-out de-lay,

1. He who gave His life to save you, Who for your trans-gress-ions died?
2. Broke the bonds of death a - sun - der, Have you "prov'd His pow'r to save?"
3. That doth fill each soul that trusts Him; Who in His deep love is blest?
4. Taste the sweet - ness of His par - don, He will take our sins a - way.

CHORUS.

Have you found the Sa-viour pre-cious? Can you slight such love as this?
Have you found, found this friend? Can you, can you slight such love as this?

Sure-ly there can be no great - er, Would you give your life for His?
Sure-ly there can be no greater love, Would you give your life for His? (for His.)

210

Tell Me the Story

J. W. Van de Venter

C. Austin Miles

1 When sor-row and trou-ble like sea bil-lows roll, Tell me the sto-ry of Je - sus;
2 When wea-ry from la-bour I rest by the way, Tell me the sto-ry of Je - sus;
3 In times of af-flic-tion, when suff-'ring from pain, Tell me the sto-ry of Je - sus;
4 When life here is o-ver and time is no more, Tell me the sto-ry of Je - sus;

1 When e - vil as-sails me and doubts fill my soul, Tell me the sto-ry of Je - sus.
2 It strength-ens my pur-pose and brigh-tens the day, Tell me the sto-ry of Je - sus.
3 It soft-ens my pil-low, re - vives me a - gain; Tell me the sto-ry of Je - sus.
4 O tell it a-gain on the beau - ti - ful shore! Tell me the sto-ry of Je - sus.

O tell it to me!

REFRAIN

Tell . . . . it to me, ... Tell . . . . it to me, ...
Tell it to me, tell it to me, Tell it to me, tell it to me,

Tell me the sto-ry of Je - sus; Tell . . . . . it to me. . . . . . .
Tell me the sto-ry, O tell it to me!

211

Good News

P. P. BILHORN

P. P. BILHORN

1. Je - sus died for you and me, Is it not good news? Now there's
2. 'It is fin-ish'd,' Je - sus said, Is it not good news? Sin and
3. From the grave the Sa - viour rose, Is it not good news? Gain'd the
4. Now He pleads for us on high, Is it not good news? Pleads that

1. par - don full and free, Is it not good news? On the Cross our sins
2. death are cap - tive led, Is it not good news? In the grave our Lord
3. vic - t'ry o'er His foes, Is it not good news? Christ the law did sat -
4. we may nev - er die, Is it not good news? Soon He'll come to claim

1. He bore, That on heav'n's e - ter - nal shore, We might live for ev - er-more,
2. was laid, And the last great tri - bute paid, Free the sa - cri - fice He made,
3. is - fy, Christ as-cend - ed up on high, We shall meet Him by - and-bye,
4. His own, All who trust in Him a - lone, We shall ga - ther round His throne,

REFRAIN *Faster*

1-4. Is it not good news? Is it not good news? Is it not good

1. news? On the Cross our sins He bore, Oh, is it not good news?
2. news? Free the sac - ri - fice He made, Oh, is it not good news?
3. news? We shall meet Him by-and-bye, Oh, is it not good news?
4. news? We shall gath-er round His throne, Oh, is it not good news?

The Gospel News

212

H. BOURNE and W. SANDERS

R. KELSO CARTER

1 Hark! the Gos - pel news is sound-ing, Christ has suf - fer'd on the tree;
2 O es - cape to yon-der moun-tain! Re-fuge find in Him to-day;
3 Grace is flow - ing like a riv - er, Mil-lions there have been sup-plied;
4 Christ a - lone shall be our por-tion; Soon we hope to meet a - bove;

1 Streams of mer - cy are a - bound-ing, Grace for all is rich and free.
2 Christ in - vites you to the foun-tain, Come and wash your sins a - way;
3 Still it flows as fresh as ev - er From the Sa-viour's wound-ed side;
4 Then we'll bathe in the full o - cean Of the great Re - deem-er's love;

REFRAIN

1 Now, poor sin - ner, Now, poor sin - ner,
2 Do not tar - ry, Do not tar - ry,
3 None need per - ish, None need per - ish,
4 All His ful - ness, All His ful - ness,

1 Now, poor sin-ner, Now, poor sin-ner, Now, poor sin-ner,
2 Do not tar-ry, Do not tar-ry, Do not tar-ry,
3 None need per-ish, None need per-ish, None need per-ish,
4 All His ful-ness, All His ful-ness, All His ful - ness,

1 Come to Him who died for thee, Come to Him who died for thee.
2 Come to Je - sus while you may, Come to Je - sus while you may.
3 All may live for Christ hath died, All may live for Christ hath died.
4 We shall then for - ev - er prove, We shall then for - ev - er prove.

213
Come Unto Me

E. E. HEWITT

F. DEGEN *Arr. by* P. P. BILHORN

1. Come un-to Je - sus, all ye that la - bour, All that are wea - ry,
2. Bring Him the bur - den, hea - vi - ly press - ing, Tell Him the sor - row
3. Lose not a mo - ment, haste to your Sa - viour, Ere the bright day-beams
4. Come un - to Je - sus, Sa - viour and Bro - ther, Sure - ly you need Him,

1. sad and op-pressed; Still He is call - ing, oh, friend and neigh - bour,
2. hid in your breast; Sin and trans-gres - sion free - ly con - fess - ing,
3. fade in the west; Ask - ing His mer - cy, seek - ing His fa - vour,
4. pur - est and best; Tru - er than fa - ther, fond - er than mo - ther,

f CHORUS.

1. Come un - to Me, and I will give you rest.
2. Come un - to Him and He will give you rest.
3. Come un - to Him and He will give you rest.
4. Come un - to Him and He will give you rest.

Down thro' the a - ges,

cres.

sweet - ly 'tis ring - ing, This word of Je - sus, come and be blest; Sweet - er than

rit.

car - ols an - gels are sing - ing, "Come un - to me, and I will give you rest."

214

Give Me Thy Heart

E. E. HEWITT

ANNIE F. BOURNE

1. "Give me thy heart," says the Fa-ther a-bove, No gift so pre-cious to
2. "Give me thy heart," says the Sa-viour of men, Call-ing in mer-cy a-
3. "Give me thy heart," says the Spi-rit di-vine, "All that thou hast, to my

1. Him as our love, Soft-ly He whis-pers wher-ev-er thou art,
2. gain and a-gain; "Turn now from sin, and from e-vil de-part,
3. keep-ing re-sign; Grace more a-bound-ing is mine to im-part,

CHORUS.

1. "Grate-ful-ly trust me, and give me thy heart." }
2. Have I not died for thee? give me thy heart." } "Give me thy heart,
3. Make full sur-ren-der and give me thy heart." }

Give me thy heart," Hear the soft whis-per, wher-ev-er thou art; From this dark

rit.

world He would draw you a-part, Speaking so ten-der-ly, "Give me thy heart."

215 No One Like My Saviour

Eliza E. Hewitt

E. E. Satterlee

1 There's no one like my Sa - viour, No friend can be like Him;
2 There's no one like my Sa - viour; In sea - sons of dis - tress
3 There's no one like my Sa - viour; He par - dons all my sin,
4 There's no one like my Sa - viour, Come now, and find it true;

1 My nev - er fail - ing sun - shine When earth - ly lights grow dim;
2 He draws me clos - er to Him, To com - fort and to bless;
3 And gives His Ho - ly Spi - rit A spring - ing well with - in;
4 He gave His life a ran - som, His blood was shed for you;

1 When sum - mer flow'rs are bloom - ing, The bright - ness of my joy;
2 He gives me in temp - ta - tion The strength of His right arm;
3 He leads me out to ser - vice With gen - tle touch and mild;
4 Then when we reach the Ci - ty Of ev - er - last - ing light,

No One Like My Saviour—*Continued*

1 O may His hap - py ser - vice   My heart and life em - ploy!
2 His an - gels camp a - round me   To keep me from all harm.
3 O won - der of all won - ders   That I should be His child!
4 We'll sing with saints and an - gels,   All hon - our, pow'r, and might.

REFRAIN

No one, no one like my pre-cious Sa - viour, No one, no one,

such a friend can be; No one, no one like my pre-cious

rit.

Sa - viour, Glo - ry, glo - ry, Je - sus cares for me.

216 The Words of Love

HORATIUS BONAR   ST. MICHAEL S.M.   LOUIS BOURGEOIS

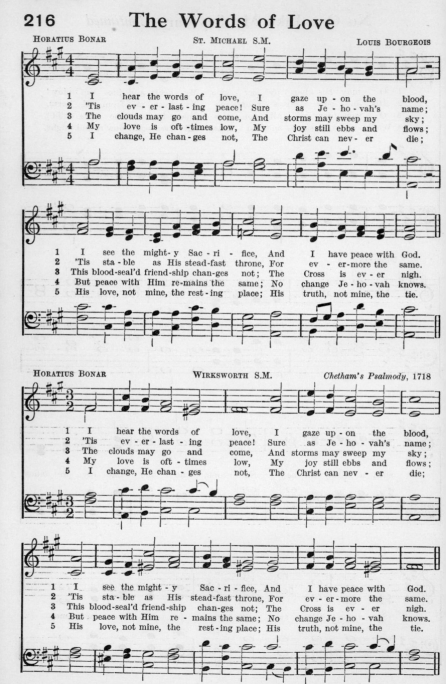

1 I hear the words of love, I gaze up-on the blood,
2 'Tis ev-er-last-ing peace! Sure as Je-ho-vah's name;
3 The clouds may go and come, And storms may sweep my sky;
4 My love is oft-times low, My joy still ebbs and flows;
5 I change, He chan-ges not, The Christ can nev-er die;

1 I see the might-y Sac-ri-fice, And I have peace with God.
2 'Tis sta-ble as His stead-fast throne, For ev-er-more the same.
3 This blood-seal'd friend-ship chan-ges not; The Cross is ev-er nigh.
4 But peace with Him re-mains the same; No change Je-ho-vah knows.
5 His love, not mine, the rest-ing place; His truth, not mine, the tie.

HORATIUS BONAR   WIRKSWORTH S.M.   *Chetham's Psalmody*, 1718

1 I hear the words of love, I gaze up-on the blood,
2 'Tis ev-er-last-ing peace! Sure as Je-ho-vah's name;
3 The clouds may go and come, And storms may sweep my sky;
4 My love is oft-times low, My joy still ebbs and flows;
5 I change, He chan-ges not, The Christ can nev-er die;

1 I see the might-y Sac-ri-fice, And I have peace with God.
2 'Tis sta-ble as His stead-fast throne, For ev-er-more the same.
3 This blood-seal'd friend-ship chan-ges not; The Cross is ev-er nigh.
4 But peace with Him re-mains the same; No change Je-ho-vah knows.
5 His love, not mine, the rest-ing place; His truth, not mine, the tie.

217 The Heavenly Lamb

ISAAC WATTS   BOYLSTON S.M.   LOWELL MASON

1 Not all the blood of beasts On Jew-ish al-tars slain
2 But Christ, the heav'n-ly Lamb, Takes all our sins a-way;
3 My faith would lay her hand On that dear head of Thine,
4 My soul looks back to see The bur-dens Thou didst bear,
5 Be-liev-ing, we re-joice To see the curse re-move;

1 Could give the guil-ty con-science peace, Or wash a-way the stain.
2 A sac-ri-fice of no-bler name And rich-er blood than they.
3 While like a pen-i-tent I stand, And there con-fess my sin.
4 When hang-ing on the cur-sed tree, And knows her guilt was there.
5 We bless the Lamb with cheer-ful voice, And sing His bleed-ing love.

ISAAC WATTS   BEN RHYDDING S.M.   A. R. REINAGLE

1 Not all the blood of beasts On Jew-ish al-tars slain
2 But Christ, the heav'n-ly Lamb, Takes all our sins a-way;
3 My Faith would lay her hand On that dear head of Thine,
4 My soul looks back to see The bur-dens Thou didst bear,
5 Be-liev-ing, we re-joice To see the curse re-move;

1 Could give the guil-ty con-science peace, Or wash a-way the stain.
2 A sac-ri-fice of no-bler name And rich-er blood than they.
3 While like a pen-i-tent I stand, And there con-fess my sin.
4 When hang-ing on the cur-sed tree, And knows her guilt was there.
5 We bless the Lamb with cheer-ful voice, And sing His bleed-ing love.

218 Unto You is Everlasting Life

W. A. O

W. A. OGDEN

1. Hear the prom-ise of the Lord, As re-cord-ed in His word,
2. Wea-ry pil-grim on the road To the judg-ment seat of God,
3. Cast on Je-sus all your care, And your bur-den He will bear,

1. "Un-to you is ev-er-last-ing life!" Hea-vy la-den and distress'd,
2. "Un-to you is ev-er-last-ing life!" If on Je-sus you be-lieve,
3. "Un-to you is ev-er-last-ing life!" In the strait and nar-row way,

1. Come, and I will give you rest, "Un-to you is ev-er-last-ing life!"
2. And His bless-ed word re-ceive, "Un-to you is ev-er-last-ing life!"
3. He will lead you day by day! "Un-to you is ev-er-last-ing life!"

CHORUS.

"Ev-er-last-ing life," the promise reads, While at God's right hand the Saviour pleads;

Will you come to-day, making Christ your stay? For with Him is ev-er-last-ing life.

219 Grace is Free

EMMA M. JOHNSTON   WM. J. KIRKPATRICK

1 There's noth-ing like the old, old sto - ry, Grace is free, grace is free!
2 There's on - ly hope in trust-ing Jes - us, Grace is free, grace is free!
3 From age to age the theme is tell - ing, Grace is free, grace is free!

REF.—*There's noth-ing like the old, old sto - ry, Grace is free, grace is free!*

FINE

1 Which saints and mar - tyrs tell in glo - ry, Grace is free, grace is free!
2 From sin that doom'd He died to free us, Grace is free, grace is free!
3 From shore to shore the strains are swell-ing, Grace is free, grace is free!

Which saints and mar - tyrs tell in glo - ry, Grace is free, grace is free!

1 It brought them thro' the flood and flame, By it they fought and o - ver-came,
2 Who would not tell the sto - ry sweet Of love so won-drous, so com-plete,
3 And when that time shall cease to be, And faith is crown'd with vic - to - ry,

D.C. for REFRAIN

1 And now they cry thro' His dear Name, Grace is free, grace is free!
2 And fall in rap - ture at His feet? Grace is free, grace is free!
3 'Twill sound thro' all e - ter - ni - ty, Grace is free, grace is free!

220 Would I Know Him?

NELLIE MONTGOMERY   E. O. EXCELL

1. Would I know Him if He stood here By my side, by my side;
2. When to Sa-tan thou dost an-swer, "Flee from me, flee from me!"
3. Could I hear Him if He called me, Wait-ing here, wait-ing here;
4. When thou cri-est in thine an-guish, "Sa-viour hear, Sa-viour hear!"

1. Doth the cru-el, cru-el nail-prints Yet a-bide, yet a-bide?
2. When be-tween thee and the Mas-ter Naught shall be, naught shall be;
3. Would His words of ma-gic sweetness Pierce my ear, pierce my ear?
4. It will reach Him thro' the cla-mour, Nev-er fear, nev-er fear!

1. Would He show me in His beau-ty So di-vine, so di-vine,
2. On thine eyes shall flash a vis-ion, Wondrous fair, won-drous fair—
3. Could the world with all its lur-ings, Drown that tone, drown that tone,
4. Tho' some-times thine ears are deaf-ened By the din, by the din;

1. That in rap-ture I would feel Him To be mine, to be mine?
2. Lo! a pierced and thorn-crowned Sa-viour Stand-eth there, stand-eth there.
3. And He pass me by and leave me All a-lone, all a-lone?
4. He is list-'ning for the sum-mons, "Lord, come in, Lord, come in!"

221

Counted In

J. M. W.

J. M. WHYTE.

1. I had wander'd far a - way In the land of might - y foes, And my
2. But I found it writ - ten down, Who - so - ev - er will be - lieve In the
3. When the par - don full and free, That is pro - mis'd in His word, Is re -
4. Oh, my sin - ner friend, be - ware, A re - veal - ing day is near That will

1. soul had felt the bit - ter - ness of sin; I was marching with the hosts
2. Son of God is sav'd from ev - 'ry sin; And I bless His ho - ly name,
3. ceiv'd by faith and Je - sus en - ters in; What a ju - bi - lee of joy
4. show the se - crets of thy heart with - in; Have it cleans'd by grace di - vine

D.S.—What a ju - bi - lee of joy

1. That the truth of God op - pose, And a - mong the sav'd I was not
2. That the pro mise I re - ceive,— In that "who - so - ev - er" I am
3. In the hea - vens then is heard, And a soul a - mong the sav'd is
4. And when Je - sus shall ap - pear, He will then a - mong His jew - els

In the hea - vens then is heard, When a soul a - mong the sav'd is

FINE. CHORUS.

1. count - ed in.)   Count - ed in,   Count - ed in,
2. count - ed in.
3. count - ed in.
4. count you in.)   Count - ed in,   Count - ed in,

count - ed in.

D S.

Who - so - ev - er will be - lieve is count - ed in, count - ed in.

222
Crucified!

C. Austin Miles

C. Austin Miles

1 They nail'd my Lord up - on the tree And left Him, dy - ing, there:
2 Up - on His head a crown of thorns, Up - on His heart my shame;
3 'For - give him, O for-give!' He cried, Then bow'd His sa - cred head;
4 His voice I hear, His love I know; I wor-ship at His feet;

1 Thro' love He suf - fer'd there for me; 'Twas love be-yond com - pare.
2 For me He pray'd, for me He died, And, dy - ing, spoke my name.
3 O Lamb of God! my sac - ri - fice! For me Thy blood was shed.
4 And kneel-ing there, at Calv-'ry's cross, Re - demp-tion is com - plete.

REFRAIN

Cru - ci - fied! cru - ci - fied! And nail'd up - on the tree:

rit

With pier - céd hands and feet and side; For you, For me.
For you, For me.

223 ## Step Out on the Promise

E. F. MILLER, *Arr.*   E. F. MILLER

1 O mourn - er in Zi - on, how bless - ed art thou!
2 O ye that are hun - gry and thirst - y, re - joice!
3 Who sighs for a heart from in - i - qui - ty free?
4 Step out on this pro - mise, and Christ thou shalt win,

1 For Je - sus is wait - ing to com - fort thee now:
2 For ye shall be fill'd; do you hear that sweet voice
3 O poor trou - bled soul! there's a prom - ise for thee:
4 The blood of His Son cleans - eth us from all sin:

1 Fear not to re - ly on the word of thy God;
2 In - vit - ing you now to the ban - quet of God?
3 There's rest, wea - ry one, in the bo - som of God;
4 It cleans - eth me now, hal - le - lu - jah to God!

1 Step out on the promise, get un - der the blood.
2 Step out on the promise, get un - der the blood.
3 Step out on the promise, get un - der the blood.
4 I rest on His promise, I'm un - der the blood.

224   Souls of Men!

FREDERICK W. FABER   ST. MABYN 8.7.8.7.   ARTHUR HENRY BROWN

1 Souls of men! why will ye scat-ter Like a crowd of fright-en'd sheep?
2 Was there ev-er kind-est shep-herd Half so gen-tle, half so sweet,
3 There's a wide-ness in God's mer-cy Like the wide-ness of the sea;
4 For the love of God is broad-er Than the mea-sures of man's mind;
5 There is plen-ti-ful re-demp-tion In the blood that has been shed;

1 Fool-ish hearts! why will ye wan-der From a love so true and deep?
2 As the Sa-viour who would have us Come and ga-ther round His feet?
3 There's a kind-ness in His jus-tice Which is more than li-ber-ty:
4 And the heart of the E-ter-nal Is most won-der-ful-ly kind.
5 There is joy for all the mem-bers In the sor-rows of the Head.

Music by permission of the OXFORD UNIVERSITY PRESS

6 Pining souls! come nearer Jesus,
And O come, not doubting thus,
But with faith that trusts more bravely
His great tenderness for us.

7 If our love were but more simple,
We should take Him at His word;
And our lives would be all sunshine
In the sweetness of our Lord.

FREDERICK W. FABER   OMNI DIE 8.7.8.7.   *Corner's Gesangbuch*, 1631

1 Souls of men! why will ye scat-ter Like a crowd of fright-en'd sheep?
2 Was there ev-er kind-est shep-herd Half so gen-tle, half so sweet,
3 There's a wide-ness in God's mer-cy Like the wide-ness of the sea;
4 For the love of God is broad-er Than the mea-sures of man's mind;
5 There is plen-ti-ful re-demp-tion In the blood that has been shed;

Souls of Men!—*Continued*

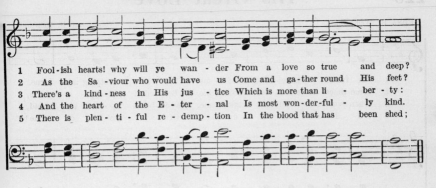

1 Fool-ish hearts! why will ye wan - der From a love so true and deep?
2 As the Sa -viour who would have us Come and ga - ther round His feet?
3 There's a kind - ness in His jus - tice Which is more than li - ber - ty:
4 And the heart of the E - ter - nal Is most won-der-ful - ly kind.
5 There is plen - ti - ful re - demp - tion In the blood that has been shed;

6 Pining souls! come nearer Jesus,
   And O come, not doubting thus,
   But with faith that trusts more bravely
   His great tenderness for us.

7 If our love were but more simple,
   We should take Him at His word:
   And our lives would be all sunshine
   In the sweetness of our Lord.

FREDERICK W. FABER   FIRENZE 8.7.8.7.   GIOVAMMARIA CASIMI

1 Souls of men! why will ye scat - ter Like a crowd of fright-en'd sheep?
2 Was there ev - er kind-est shep - herd Half so gen - tle, half so sweet,
3 There's a wide - ness in God's mer - cy Like the wide - ness of the sea;
4 For the love of God is broad - er Than the mea - sures of man's mind;
5 There is plen - ti - ful re - demp - tion In the blood that has been shed;

1 Fool-ish hearts! why will ye wan - der From a love so true and deep?
2 As the Sa -viour who would have us Come and ga - ther round His feet?
3 There's a kind- ness in His jus - tice Which is more than li - ber - ty:
4 And the heart of the E - ter - nal Is most won-der-ful - ly kind.
5 There is joy for all the mem - bers In the sor - rows of the Head.

225   His Great Love

EDNA R. WORRELL   CLARENCE B. STROUSE

1. A friend I have call'd Je - sus Whose love is strong and true,
2. Some-times the clouds of trou - ble Be - dim the sky a - bove,
3. When sor - row's clouds o'er - take me, And break up - on my head,
4. O I could sing for - ev - er Of Je - sus' love di - vine!

1. And nev - er fails how - e'er 'tis tried, No mat - ter what I do:
2. I can - not see my Sa - viour's face, I doubt His won - drous love:
3. When life seems worse than use - less, And I were bet - ter dead;
4. Of all His care and ten - der - ness For this poor life of mine:

1. I've sinn'd a - gainst this love of His, But when I knelt to pray,
2. But He, from hea - ven's mer - cy seat Be - hold - ing my des - pair,
3. I take my grief to Je - sus then, Nor do I go in vain,
4. His love is in and o - ver all, And wind and waves o - bey,

His Great Love—*Continued*

1 Con - fess - ing all my guilt to Him, The sin - clouds roll'd a - way.
2 In pi - ty bursts the clouds be - tween, And shows me He is there.
3 For heav'n - ly hope He gives that cheers, Like sun - shine af - ter rain.
4 When Je - sus whis - pers 'Peace, be still!' And rolls the clouds a - way.

REFRAIN

It's just like Je - sus to roll the clouds a - way, It's

just like Je - sus to keep me day by day; It's just like

Je - sus all a - long the way, It's just like His great love.

226 Come to the Saviour !

ANON

OLD SCOTTISH MELODY

1 Come to the Sa - viour! come to the Sa - viour! Thou
2 Par - don is of - fer'd, par - don is of - fer'd, A
3 Plunge in the foun - tain, plunge in the foun - tain, The

REFRAIN — I do be - lieve it ! I do be - lieve it! I'm

1 sin - strick - en off - spring of man; He left His throne a - bove To re -
2 par - don full, pres - ent, and free; The might - y debt was paid When on
3 foun - tain which clean - ses the soul; 'Tis clean-sing far and near, And its

sav'd thro' the blood of the Lamb; My hap - py soul is free, For the

1 veal His won-drous love, And to o - pen a foun - tain for sin.
2 Cal - v'ry Je - sus died To a - tone for a re - bel like thee.
3 streams are flow-ing here, O be - lieve it, and thou art made whole

Lord has par-don'd me. Hal - le - lu - jah to His bless - ed Name!

227 Him that Cometh

ELIZA E. HEWITT

WM. J. KIRKPATRICK
Arr. P. J. MANSFIELD

1 List - en to the bless - ed in - vi - ta - tion, Sweet - er
2 Wea - ry toil - er, sad and hea - vy la - den, Joy - ful -
3 Come, ye thirs - ty, to the liv - ing wa - ters, Hun - gry,
4 Who - so com - eth, blind or maim'd or sin - ful, Com - eth
5 Com - ing hum - bly dai - ly to this Sa - viour, Breath - ing

Him that Cometh—*Continued*

1 than the notes of an - gel song; .... Chim - ing soft - ly with a
2 ly the great sal - va - tion see; .... Close be - side thee stands the
3 come and on His boun - ty feed; .... Not thy fit - ness is the
4 for His heal - ing to the Lord, ... Claims the cleans - ing of the
5 all the heart to Him in pray'r; ... Com - ing some day to the

1 heav'n - ly ca - dence, Call - ing to the pass - ing throng.
2 Bur - den-Bear - er, Strong to bear thy load and thee.
3 plea to bring Him, But Thy press - ing ut - most need.
4 blood so pre - cious, Proves a - new this gra - cious word.
5 heav'n - ly man - sions, He will give thee wel - come there.

REFRAIN

Him that com - eth un - to Me; .... Him that
un - to Me,

com - eth un - to Me, ... Him that com - eth un - to
un - to Me;

Me, ... I will in no .... wise cast out.
un - to Me,

228 Why Not Say Yes To-night?

EFFIE WELLS LOUCKS

DUET

LOUIS D. EICHHORN

1. O why not say Yes to the Sa-viour to-night? He's ten-der-ly
2. For with you the Spi-rit will not al-ways plead— O do not re-
3. Take Christ as your Sa-viour, then all shall be well, The mor-row let

1. plead-ing with thee . To come to Him now with thy sin-burden'd heart
2. ject Him to-night! . To-mor-row may bring you the darkness of death,
3. bring what it may; . His love shall pro-tect you, His Spi-rit shall guide,

CHORUS.

1. For par-don so full and so free (so free). Why not say Yes to-
2. Un-bro-ken by hea-ven-ly light. heavenly light.
3. And safe-ly keep you in His way (His way). Why not say Yes to the

night? . . Why not? Why not? While He so gen-tly, so
Saviour to-night? Sav Yes! Say Yes!

Why not say Yes? Why not to-night?

ten-der-ly pleads, O ac-cept Him to-night!
ac-cept Him to-night!

229 Drifting Away from God

F. A. S   Frank A. Simpkins

1. Drift-ing a-way from the Sa - viour,   Drift-ing to lands un-known,
2. Drift-ing a-way from the Sa - viour,   He who would bear your load;
3. Drift-ing a-way from the Sa - viour,   Fear-less-ly on you go;
4. Drift-ing a-way from the Sa - viour,   E - ven the an-gels weep;

1. Drift-ing a-way by night and by day,   Drifting, yes, drifting a-lone.
2. Drift-ing a-way by night and by day,   Drift-ing, yes, drifting from God.
3. Drift-ing a-way by night and by day,   Drift-ing to re-gions of woe.
4. Still you drift on with mirth and with song,   Out on the fa-thom-less deep.

REFRAIN.

Drift-ing a-way from the Sa - viour,   Drifting a-way from His love,   While the

Sa - viour is ten-der-ly call - ing, You are drifting a-way from God.

230 Over the Dead-Line

VIRGINIA W. MOYER

H. L. GILMOUR

1 O sin - ner, the Sa - viour is call - ing for
2 O sin - ner, thine ears have been deaf to His
3 O sin - ner, the Spir - it is striv - ing with
4 O sin - ner, God's pa - tience may wear - y some

1 thee! Long, long has He call'd thee in vain.........
2 voice! Thine eyes to His glo - ry been dim.........
3 thee! What if He should strive ne - ver - more.......,..
4 day! And leave thy sad soul in the blast.......

1 He call'd thee when joy lent its crown to thy
2 The calls of thy Sa - viour have so wear - ied
3 But leave thee a - lone in thy dark - ness to
4 By wil - ful re - sis - tance you've drift - ed a -

Over the Dead-Line—*Continued*

1 days, He call'd thee in sor - row and pain. . . . .
2 thee, O what if they should wear - y Him! . . . .
3 dwell, In sight of the heav - en - ly shore? . . . . .
4 way, ... O - ver the dead - line at last. . . . .

REFRAIN

O turn, while the Sa - viour in mer - cy is wait - ing, And

steer for the har - bour light! For how do you know but your

ritard

soul may be drift - ing O - ver the dead - line to - night? . . . .

231 Be in Time!

ANON WM. J. KIRKPATRICK

1 Life at best is ve - ry brief, Like the falling of a leaf, Like the binding of a sheaf, Be in time! Fleeting days are telling fast That the die will soon be cast, And the fa - tal line be pass'd,

2 Fair - est flow - ers soon de - cay, Youth and beau - ty pass a - way; O you have not long to stay, Be in time! While God's Spi - rit bids you come, Sin - ner, do no long - er roam, Lest you seal your hope - less doom,

3 Time is glid - ing swift - ly by, Death and judg-ment draw-eth nigh, To the arms of Je - sus fly, Be in time! O I pray you count the cost! Ere the fa - tal line be cross'd, And your soul in hell be lost,

4 Sin - ner, heed the warn - ing voice, Make the Lord your fin - al choice, Then all hea - ven will re - joice, Be in time! Come from dark - ness in - to light, Come, let Je - sus make you right, Come, and start for heav'n to - night.

Be in time!—*Continued*

Be in time!

Be in time! Be in time!

Be in time!

Be in time! While the voice of Je - sus

calls you, Be in time! If in

Be in time!

sin you long - er wait You may find no o - pen gate,

And your cry be just too late, Be in time!

232 Meet Me There!

Anon

Wm. J. Kirkpatrick

1 On the hap - py gol - den shore, Where the
2 Here our fon - dest hopes are vain, Dear - est
3 Where the harps of an - gels ring, And the

1 faith - ful part no more, When the storms of life are o'er, Meet me
2 links are rent in twain, But in heav'n no throb of pain, Meet me
3 blest for ev - er sing, In the pal - ace of the King, Meet me

1 there! Where the night dis - solves a - way In - to
2 there! By the ri - ver spark - ling bright, In the
3 there! Where in sweet com - mun - ion blend, Heart with

1 pure and per - fect day I am go ing home to stay;
2 ci - ty of de - light, Where our faith is lost in sight;
3 heart, and friend with friend, In a world that ne'er shall end;

Meet Me There!—*Continued*

233 Drifting Down

JESSIE BROWN POUNDS

W. E. M. HACKLEMAN

1 You are drift-ing far from shore, lean-ing on an i - dle oar,
2 Lights up - on the home-land shore give you warn-ing o'er and o'er,
3 Voi - ces from the home-land shore faint - er grow as they im - plore,

1-3 You are drift - ing, slow - ly drift - ing, drift - ing down;

1 You are drift - ing with the tide to the o - cean wild and wide,
2 Soon be - yond the har - bour bar will your boat be car - ried far,
3 O my bro - ther, do not wait! heed them ere it be too late,

rit. ad lib.

1 You are drift - ing, slow - ly drift - ing, drift - ing down.
2 You are drift - ing, slow - ly drift - ing, drift - ing down.
3 Ere for - ev - er you have drift - ed, drift - ed down.

Drifting Down—*Continued*

REFRAIN *rit.* *a tempo.* *rit.*

You are drift - ing down, drift - ing down

You are drift - ing, slow - ly drift - ing, you are slow - ly drift-ing down

a tempo. *rit.* *a tempo.*

To the dark and aw - ful sea; You are drift - ing down

To the dark and aw - ful sea; You are drift - ing, slow - ly drift - ing

From a Fa - ther's lov - ing care To the black-ness of de - spair,

rit. ad lib.

You are drift - ing, slow - ly drift - ing, drift - ing down. (drift-ing down.)

234 ## Still Out of Christ.

H. E. BLAIR

WM. J. KIRKPATRICK

1. Still out of Christ, when so oft He has call'd you, Why will you long-er re-
2. Still out of Christ, and the mo-ments so pre-cious, Night is approach-ing, oh,
3. Still out of Christ, yet for you there is mer-cy, If you are will-ing to,
4. Still out of Christ, and the love He has promis'd: How you are long-ing that

1. fuse to be-lieve? What can you hope from the world or its plea-sure?
2. what will you do? Still out of Christ, yet there's room at the foun-tain,
3. turn from your sin; Yon-der He stands at the door of sal-va-tion,
4. love to re-ceive! Haste where the star of your faith is di-rect-ing,

REFRAIN.

1. How can you trust them when both will de-ceive?
2. Free are its wa-ters, and flow-ing for you.
3. Wait-ing to par-don and wel-come you in.
4. Haste, and this mo-ment re-pent and be-lieve.

Come, come to Je - sus, wea-ry, hea-vy-heart-ed, Come, come to Je-sus while you may; Now He is wait-ing, wait-ing to receive you, Hark! He is call-ing you to-day.

235 No Room in the Inn

A. L. Skilton

E. Grace Updegraff

1, No beau-ti-ful cham-ber, No soft cra-dle bed, No place but a
2. No sweet con-se-cra-tion, No seek-ing His part, No hu-mil-i-
3. No one to re-ceive Him, No welcome while here, No balm to re-

1. man-ger, Nowhere for His head; No prais-es of glad-ness, No thought of their
2. a-tion, No place in the heart; No thought of the Sa-viour, No sor-row for
3. lieve Him, No staff but a spear; No seek-ing His trea-sure, No weeping for

1. sin, No glo-ry but sad-ness, No room in the inn.
2. sin, No prayer for His fa-vour, No room in the inn.
3. sin, No do-ing His plea-sure, No room in the inn.

CHORUS.

No room, no room for Je-sus! Oh, give Him wel-come free, Lest

you should hear at hea-ven's gate, There is no room for thee!

236 Looking this Way

J. W. VAN DE VENTER   LOOKING THIS WAY 9.9.9.9. D   J. W. VAN DE VENTER

1. O - ver the riv - er fa - ces I see, Fair as the morn - ing,
2. Fa - ther and mo - ther, safe in the vale, Watch for the boat - man,
3. Bro - ther and sis - ter, gone to that clime, Wait for the oth - ers,
4. Sweet lit - tle dar - ling, light of the home, Look - ing for some one,
5. Je - sus the Sa - viour, bright morn - ing star, Look - ing for lost ones

1. look - ing for me: Free from their sor - row, grief, and de - spair, Wait - ing and
2. wait for the sail, Bear - ing the lov'd ones o - ver the tide, In - to the
3. com - ing some - time: Safe with the an - gels, whi - ter than snow, Watch - ing for
4. beck - on - ing come Bright as a sun - beam, pure as the dew, An - xious - ly
5. stray - ing a - far: Hear the glad mes - sage, why will you roam? Je - sus is

REFRAIN

1. watch - ing pa - tient - ly there.
2. har - bour, near to their side.
3. dear ones wait - ing be - low.
4. look - ing, mother, for you.
5. call - ing, 'Sin - ner, come home.'

Look - ing this way, yes, look - ing this way:

Lov'd ones are wait - ing, look - ing this way; Fair as the morn - ing.

bright as the day, Dear ones in glo - ry look - ing this way.

237   O Lay It Down!

FANNY J. CROSBY   W. H. DOANE

1. O come ,sin-ner ,come! 'tis mer-cy's call: Here at   Je-su's feet
2. O come, and be-liev-ing, seek thy rest,   Here at   Je-su's feet
3. O come where thy faith can make thee whole,   Here at   Je-su's feet
4. O come! bless the Lord, there's room for thee   Here at   Je-su's feet

1. O come, and, re-pent-ing, lay thy all   Down at Je-sus' feet
2. Thy heart, with its hea-vy weight op-prest,   Lay at Je-su's feet.
3. O come, and thy wea-ry, troub-led soul   Lay at Je-su's feet
4. Thy bur-den of sin, what-e'er it be,   Lay at Je-su's feet

REFRAIN

O lay it down   lay it down.   Lay thy wea-ry bur-den down

O lay it down,   lay it down,   Down at Je-sus' feet

238 The Stranger at the Door

JOSEPH GRIGG

T. C. O'KANE

1 Be - hold a Stran - ger at the door! He gen - tly knocks, has
2 O love - ly at - ti - tude! He stands With melt - ing heart and
3 But will He prove a Friend in - deed? He will— the ver - y
4 Rise, touch'd with gra - ti - tude di - vine, Turn out His en - e -
5 Ad - mit Him ere His an - ger burn; His feet, de - part - ed,

1 knock'd be - fore; Has wait - ed long, is wait - ing still: You treat
2 o - pen hands; O match - less kind - ness! and He shows The match -
3 Friend you need! The Friend of sin - ners? Yes, 'tis He! With gar -
4 my and thine, That soul - de - stroy - ing mon - ster, sin, And let
5 ne'er re - turn: Ad - mit Him, or the hour's at hand You'll at

REFRAIN

1 no o - ther friend so ill.
2 less kind - ness to His foes.
3 ments dyed on Cal - va - ry.
4 the heav'n - ly Stran - ger in.
5 His door re - ject - ed stand.

O let the dear Sa - viour come

in! .... He'll cleanse the heart from sin .... O keep Him
come in; from sin;

The Stranger at the Door—*Continued*

no more out at the door! But let the dear Sa-viour come in ....

come in.

In the following Tune the REFRAIN is omitted

JOSEPH GRIGG   BERA L.M.   JOHN E. GOULD

1 Be - hold a Stran - ger at the door! He gen - tly
2 O love - ly at - ti - tude! He stands With melt - ing
3 But will He prove a Friend in - deed? He will— the
4 Rise, touch'd with gra - ti - tude di - vine, Turn out His
5 Ad - mit Him ere His an - ger burn; His feet, de -

1 knocks, has knock'd be - fore; Has wait - ed long, is wait -
2 heart and o - pen hands; O match-less kind - ness! and
3 ver - y Friend you need! The Friend of sin - ners? Yes,
4 en - e - my and thine, That sou' - de - stroy - ing mon -
5 part - ed, ne'er re - turn: Ad - mit Him, or the hour's

1 ing still: You treat no o - ther friend so ill!
2 He shows The match-less kind - ness to His foes.
3 'tis He! With gar - ments dyed on Cal - va - ry.
4 ster, sin, And let the heav'n - ly Stran - ger in.
5 at hand You'll at His door re - ject - ed stand.

239 Let the Master In!

SYLVANUS D. PHELPS

ROBERT LOWRY

1. Once I heard a sound at my heart's dark door, And was
2. Then He spread a feast of re - deem - ing love, And He
3. In the ho - ly war with the foes of truth, He's my
4. He will feast me still with His pre - sence dear, And the

1. roused from the slum - ber of sin: It was Je - sus knock'd, He had
2. made me His own hap - py guest: In my joy I thought that the
3. shield; He my ta - ble pre - pares, He re - stores my soul, He re -
4. love He so free - ly hath giv'n; While His pro - mise tells, as I

CHORUS.

1. knock'd be-fore; Now I said, "Blessed Mas-ter, come in!"
2. saints a-bove Could be hard - ly more favour'd or blest.   Then o - - pen!
3. news my youth, And gives triumph in an - swer to pray'rs.   Then o - pen to Him!
4. serve Him here, Of the ban-quet of glo - ry in heav'n.

o - - pen!   o - pen, let the Mas-ter in! . . . . For the
o - pen to Him!   let Him in!

heart will be bright with a heav'n-ly light, When you let the Mas-ter in.

240   Out of Christ

F. M. DAVIS and R. F. BEVERIDGE   FRANK M. DAVIS

1 Out of Christ, with-out a Sa-viour, Oh! can it, can it be?
2 Out of Christ, with-out a Sa-viour, Lone-ly and dark the way;
3 Out of Christ, with-out a Sa-viour, No help nor re-fuge nigh;
4 Out of Christ, with-out a Sa-viour, Dark will the voy-age be;
5 Out of Christ, with-out a Sa-viour, Give to Him now your heart,

1 Like a ship with-out a rud-der, On a wild and storm-y sea!
2 With no light, no hope in Je-sus, Mak-ing bright the cheer-less day.
3 How can you, my friend and bro-ther, Dare to live or dare to die?
4 Clouds will ga-ther, storms sur-round you, Oh, to Christ for re-fuge flee!
5 Ere the door of mer-cy clo-ses, And you hear His word, "de-part."

REFRAIN

Oh, to be with-out a Sa-viour! With no hope or re-fuge nigh;

Can it be, O bless-ed Sa-viour, One with-out Thee dares to die!

By permission of JOHN J. HOOD

241 A Great Day Coming

W. L. T.　　　　　　　　　　　　　　　　　　　　W. L. Thompson

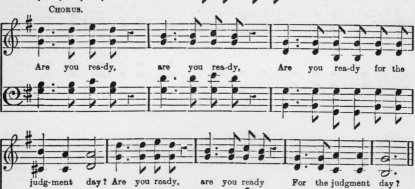

1. There's a great day com-ing, A great day com-ing, There's a great day com-ing by and by, When the saints and the sin-ners shall be part-ed right and left. Are you rea-dy for that day to come?

2. There's a bright day com-ing, A bright day com-ing, There's a bright day com-ing by and by, But its bright-ness shall on-ly come to them that love the Lord. Are you rea-dy for that day to come?

3. There's a sad day com-ing, A sad day com-ing, There's a sad day com-ing by and by, When the sin-ner shall hear his doom, "De-part, I know you not." Are you rea-dy for that day to come?

CHORUS.

Are you ready, are you rea-dy, Are you rea-dy for the judg-ment day? Are you ready, are you ready For the judgment day?

242 Whither will You Wander?

ANON   HIGHWAY 8.5.8.5.D   *Arr.* J. M. BONNAR

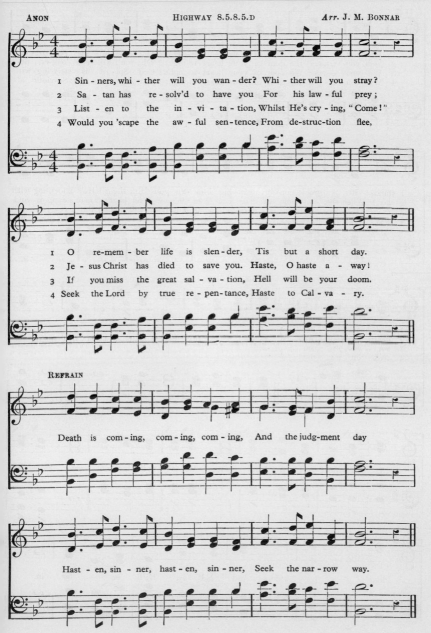

1 Sin - ners, whi - ther will you wan - der? Whi - ther will you stray?
2 Sa - tan has re - solv'd to have you For his law - ful prey;
3 List - en to the in - vi - ta - tion, Whilst He's cry - ing, "Come!"
4 Would you 'scape the aw - ful sen - tence, From de - struc - tion flee,

1 O re - mem - ber life is slen - der, Tis but a short day.
2 Je - sus Christ has died to save you. Haste, O haste a - way!
3 If you miss the great sal - va - tion, Hell will be your doom.
4 Seek the Lord by true re - pen - tance, Haste to Cal - va - ry.

REFRAIN

Death is com - ing, com - ing, com - ing, And the judg - ment day

Hast - en, sin - ner, hast - en, sin - ner, Seek the nar - row way.

243 The Door of your Heart

J. F. K. M.

J. F. K. MACPHERSON

1 Will you o-pen the door of your heart to-night? Out-side Je-sus pa-tient-ly
2 Will you o-pen the door of your heart to-night? Oh, soul, will you long-er de-
3 Will you o-pen the door of your heart to-night? God's Spi-rit is striv-ing with-
4 Will you o-pen the door of your heart to-night? Do not send the dear Sa-viour a-

1 stands; He is grac-ious-ly wait-ing, how can you Him slight? He's knock-ing with
2 lay? When the Sa-viour can free you from sin's aw-ful blight, There's dang-er and
3 in; He may nev-er a-gain with your stub-born will fight, But leave you to
4 way; Lest He leave you for ev-er con-demn'd in God's sight, On the aw-ful

REFRAIN

1 nail-pierc-ed hands.
2 death in your way.
3 per-ish in sin.
4 reck-on-ing day.

Just o-pen the door of your heart to-night, For

Je-sus now seeks you to win; He is wait-ing out-side, Swing the

door o-pen wide, And glad-ly He'll en-ter in.

244 Is there Any Sad Heart?

1. Is there a-ny sad heart that is hea-vy la-den—
2. Is there a-ny who thirsts for the liv-ing wa-ter?
3. Is there a-ny who longs to be own'd by Je-sus?

1. A-ny one here? A-ny one here? Is there a-ny poor soul who would
2. A-ny one here? A-ny one here? Is there a-ny who sighs for the
3. A-ny one here? A-ny one here? Is there a-ny will say "I be-

1. love the Sa-viour? Come and we will help you on your way!
2. crim-son foun-tain? Come and we will help you on your way!
3. lieve this mo-ment?" Come and we will help you on your way!

REFRAIN.

Just as you are, the Lord will save you, Come with-out de-lay! Is there

an-y poor soul who would fol-low Je-sus? Come, and we will help you on your way!

245 Into your Heart

LEILA NAYLOR MORRIS   LEILA NAYLOR MORRIS

1 If you are tir'd of the load of your sin, Let Je-sus come in-to your heart;
2 If 'tis for pur-i-ty now that you sigh, Let Je-sus come in-to your heart;
3 If there's a tem-pest your voice can-not still, Let Je-sus come in-to your heart;
4 If friends, once trust-ed, have pro-ven un-true, Let Je-sus come in-to your heart;
5 If you would join the glad songs of the blest, Let Je-sus come in-to your heart;

1 If you de-sire a new life to be-gin, Let Je-sus come in-to your heart.
2 Foun-tains for cleans-ing are flow-ing near by, Let Je-sus come in-to your heart.
3 If there's a void this world nev-er can fill, Let Je-sus come in-to your heart.
4 Find what a Friend He will be un-to you, Let Je-sus come in-to your heart.
5 If you would en-ter the man-sions of rest, Let Je-sus come in-to your heart.

REFRAIN

1-4 Just now, your doubt-ings give o'er; Just now, re-ject Him no more;
5 Just now, my doubt-ings are o'er; Just now, re-ject-ing no more;

1-4 Just now, throw o-pen the door; Let Je-sus come in-to your heart.
5 Just now, I o-pen the door, And Je-sus comes in-to my heart.

Drifting Away

246

J. A. GRIFFITH

P. P. BILHORN

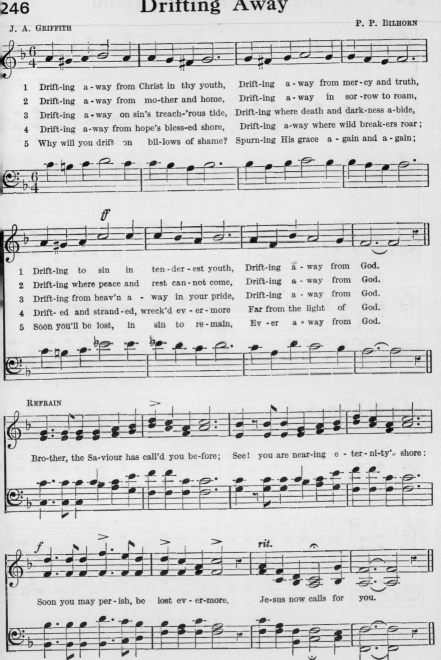

1 Drift-ing a-way from Christ in thy youth, Drift-ing a-way from mer-cy and truth,
2 Drift-ing a-way from mo-ther and home, Drift-ing a-way in sor-row to roam,
3 Drift-ing a-way on sin's treach-'rous tide, Drift-ing where death and dark-ness a-bide,
4 Drift-ing a-way from hope's bless-ed shore, Drift-ing a-way where wild break-ers roar;
5 Why will you drift on bil-lows of shame? Spurn-ing His grace a-gain and a-gain;

1 Drift-ing to sin in ten-der-est youth, Drift-ing a-way from God.
2 Drift-ing where peace and rest can-not come, Drift-ing a-way from God.
3 Drift-ing from heav'n a-way in your pride, Drift-ing a-way from God.
4 Drift-ed and strand-ed, wreck'd ev-er-more Far from the light of God.
5 Soon you'll be lost, in sin to re-main, Ev-er a-way from God.

REFRAIN

Bro-ther, the Sa-viour has call'd you be-fore; See! you are near-ing e-ter-ni-ty's shore:

Soon you may per-ish, be lost ev-er-more, Je-sus now calls for you.

247 The Nail=Pierced Hand

JOHN R. CLEMENTS

JOHN R. SWENEY

1 Dost thou know at thy bolt - ed.... heart's door to - night The Sa - viour in
2 You.... turn not a - way when a friend's at your door, Here's one there's none
3 All the pain and the shame of His death on the tree, A wel - come from

1 meekness doth stand, And.... longs for ad - mis - sion? Pray lis - ten.... now To the
2 like in the land, Who.... asks to come in and for ev - er a - bide, Heed the
3 you should command, Since the weight of your sins in His bo - dy He bore, Heed the

REFRAIN

knock of the nail-pier-ced hand. Heed the knock of the nail - pier - ced hand,........

Heed the knock, heed the knock of the nail-pier-ced hand

Heed the knock of the nail - pier - ced hand ;........ Swing the door op - en wide,

Heed the knock, heed the knock of the nail - pier - ced hand ;

Bid Him en - ter and a - bide, Heed the knock of the nail - pier - ced hand...........

Heed the knock, heed the knock of the nail-pier-ced hand.

248

Passing Onward

ALBERT MIDLANE DISMISSAL 8.7.8.7.8.7. W. L. VINER

1. Pass - ing on - ward, quick - ly pass - ing; But, I ask thee,
2. Pass - ing on - ward, quick - ly pass - ing; Nought the wheels of
3. Pass - ing on - ward, quick - ly pass - ing; Ma - ny on the
4. Pass - ing on - ward, quick - ly pass - ing; Time its course will

1. whi - ther bound? Is it to the ma - ny man - sions,
2. time can stay; Sweet the thought that some are go - ing
3. down - ward road; Care - less of their souls im - mor - tal,
4. quick - ly run; Still we hear the fond en - trea - ty

1. Where e - ter - nal rest is found? Pass - ing on - ward,
2. To the realms of per - fect day; Pass - ing on - ward,
3. Heed - ing not the call of God, Pass - ing on - ward,
4. Of the ev - er gra - cious One: Come and wel - come,

1. Pass - ing on - ward, Tell me, sin - ner, whi - ther bound?
2. Pass - ing on - ward, Christ their Lead - er, Christ their Way.
3. Pass - ing on - ward, Tramp - ling on the Sa - viour's blood.
4. Come and wel - come, 'Tis by Me that life is won.

Tune TYRE is on next page

248   Passing Onward

A. MIDLANE   TYRE 8.7. 8.7. 8.7.   H. J. GAUNTLETT

1 Pass - ing on - ward, quick - ly pass - ing; But, I ask thee,
2 Pass - ing on - ward, quick - ly pass - ing; Nought the wheels of
3 Pass - ing on - ward, quick - ly pass - ing; Man - y on the
4 Pass - ing on - ward, quick - ly pass - ing; Time its course will

1 whi - ther bound? Is it to the ma - ny man - sions,
2 time can stay; Sweet the thought that some are go - ing
3 down - ward road; Care - less of their souls im - mor - tal,
4 quick - ly run; Still we hear the fond en - trea - ty

1 Where e - ter - nal rest is found? Pass - ing on - ward,
2 To the realms of per - fect day; Pass - ing on - ward,
3 Heed - ing not the call of God, Pass - ing on - ward,
4 Of the ev - er gra - cious One: Come and wel - come,

1 Pass - ing on - ward, Tell me, sin - ner, whi - ther bound?
2 Pass - ing on - ward, Christ their Lead - er, Christ their Way.
3 Pass - ing on - ward, Tramp - ling on the Sa - viour's blood.
4 Come and wel - come, 'Tis by Me that life is won.

Tune DISMISSAL on previous page

249 The Harvest is Passing

JOHN B. HAGUE   PHILIP P. BLISS

1 Hark, sin-ner, while God from on high doth en-treat thee, And
2 How oft of thy dan-ger and guilt He hath told thee! How
3 Des-pis'd and re-ject-ed, at length He may leave thee; What
4 Ere long, and Je-ho-vah will come in His pow-er! Our
5 The Sa-viour will call thee in judg-ment be-fore Him, Oh,

1 warn-ing with lan-guage of mer-cy doth blend; At-tend to His
2 oft still the mes-sage of mer-cy doth send! Haste, haste, while He
3 an-guish and hor-ror thy bos-om will rend! Then haste thee, O
4 God will a-rise with His foe to con-tend: Haste, haste thee, O
5 let all thy sins go, and make Him thy friend; Now yield Him thy

1 voice, lest in judg-ment He meet thee. "The har-vest is pass-ing, the
2 waits in His arms to en-fold thee! "The har-vest is pass-ing, tho
3 sin-ner, while He will re-ceive thee; "The har-vest is pass-ing, tho
4 sin-ner! pre-pare for that ho-ur; "The har-vest is pass-ing, the
5 heart, and make haste to a-dore Him! "Thy har-vest is pass-ing, thy

REFRAIN. *cres.*

sum-mer will end." "The har-vest is pass-ing, the sum-mer will

end;" "The har-vest is pass-ing, the sum-mer will end."

250   Come Believing!

D. W. WHITTLE   ENTREATY 8.7. 8.7. D   JAS. M'GRANAHAN

1 Once a - gain the Gos - pel mes - sage From the Sa - viour you have heard;
2 Ma - ny sum - mers you have was - ted, Ri-pen'd har - vests you have seen;
3 Je - sus for your choice is wait - ing; Tar - ry not; at once de - cide!
4 Cease of fit - ness to be think - ing; Do not long - er try to feel!
5 Let your will to God be giv - en, Trust in Christ's a - ton - ing blood;

1 Will you heed the in - vi - ta - tion? Will you turn and seek the Lord?
2 Win - ter snows by spring have mel - ted, Yet you lin - ger in your sin.
3 While the Spi - rit now is striv - ing, Yield, and seek the Sa-viour's side.
4 It is trust - ing, and not feel - ing, That will give the Spi - rit's seal.
5 Look to Je - sus now in hea - ven, Rest on His un - chang-ing word.

REFRAIN

Come be - liev - ing! come be - liev - ing! Come to Je - sus! look and live! ......
come!   come!   look! oh, look and live!

Come be - liev - ing! come be - liev - ing! Come to Je - sus! look and live!
come!   come!

Almost Persuaded

251

PHILIPP BLISS   PHILIPP BLISS

1 "Al - most per - suad - ed" now to be - lieve;
2 "Al - most per - suad - ed:" come, come to - day!
3 "Al - most per - suad - ed:" har - vest is past!

1 "Al - most per - suad - ed" Christ to re - ceive;
2 "Al - most per - suad - ed:" turn not a - way!
3 "Al - most per - suad - ed:" doom comes at last!

1 Seems now some soul to say?—"Go, Spi - rit, go Thy way:
2 Je - sus in - vites you here, An - gels are ling - 'ring near,
3 "Al - most" can - not a - vail; "Al - most" is but to fail:

1 Some more con - ve - nient day On Thee I'll call."
2 Pray'rs rise from hearts so dear, O wand - 'rer come!
3 Sad, sad, that bit - ter wail— "Al - most"—*but lost!*

252 Sometime

L. H. EDMUNDS   WM. J. KIRKPATRICK

1 A voice is heard in the dew-y dawn, And the call is sweet and
2 The day is near-ing the noon-tide glow, And the voice is heard a-
3 The feet are tread-ing the west-ern slope, And the air is grow-ing
4 O soul, take heed, ere the sha-dows fall, And the day of grace is

1 low; Come now, my child, to the Shep-herd's fold, Where the
2 gain, It calls the soul to a no-bler life, 'Tis a
3 chill; O can it be God is wait-ing yet, That His
4 past, For how shall a tremb-ling sin-ner stand By the

1 liv-ing wa-ters flow; But the gay heart an-swers in
2 pa-tient, kind re-frain; En-ter now the Mas-ter's broad
3 voice is plead-ing still? That he'll flood with beau-ty the
4 gates of death at last? Hear the Sa-viour's call; at the

1 care-less tones, As light as the morn-ing chime,............ 'Let me
2 har-vest field In the strength of your ear-ly prime,............ Come and
3 sun-set sky, Bright rays from the Gold-en Clime?............ But the
4 Cross lay down Thy bur-den of guilt and crime,............ And the

Sometime—*Continued*

1 live for the world just a lit-tle while, I will turn to God—some-time,
2 bring to His work ser-vice good and true, Still the same re-ply—some-time!
3 sin-ner, long-hard-en'd, has turn'd a-way, With the fa-tal word—some-time!
4 an-gels shall sing thee a sweet-er song Than the sad re-frain—some-time.

REFRAIN

Be-ware! be-ware! At the pearl-y gate God may an-swer your

some-time—'Too late! too late!' Be-ware! be-ware! At the

ad lib.

pear-ly gate God may an-swer your some-time—'Too late! too late!'

253   After All, Eternity !

I. I. LESLIE   REPOSE L.M.D.   F. A. BLACKMER

1 Af - ter the storm that sweeps the sea ;   Af - ter the drift - ing
2 Af - ter the win - ter long and drear ;   Af - ter the snow clouds
3 Af - ter the long and toil - some day ;   Af - ter the sun's fierce
4 Af - ter the march of time shall cease ;   Af - ter earth-strife shall

1 to the lea ;   Af - ter the rocks and sands are pass'd,
2 dis - ap - pear ;   Af - ter the winds sweet o - dours bring,
3 burn - ing ray ;   Af - ter the toil - er home - ward goes,
4 end in peace :   Af - ter the change - ful dis - ap - pears,

REFRAIN

1 Com-eth the joy of home at last.
2 Com-eth the ev - er wel-come spring.
3 Com-eth the night and sweet re - pose.
4 Com-eth the long e - ter - nal years

Af - ter all that
here we see, What will there be, what will there be? Af - ter
all that here we see, Af - ter all— E - ter - ni - ty !

The tune MERTHYR TYDFIL is on the following page

After All, Eternity!

253

I. I. Leslie   Merthyr Tydfil L.M.D.   Joseph Parry

1 Af - ter the storm that sweeps the sea;   Af - ter the drift - ing to the lea;
2 Af - ter the win - ter long and drear;   Af - ter the snow clouds dis - ap - pear;
3 Af - ter the long and toil - some day;   Af - ter the sun's fierce burn - ing ray;
4 Af - ter the march of time shall cease;   Af - ter earth-strife shall end in peace;

1 Af - ter the rocks and sands are pass'd, Com-eth the joy of home at last.
2 Af - ter the winds sweet o - dours bring, Com-eth the ev - er wel-come spring.
3 Af - ter the toil - er home-ward goes, Com-eth the night and sweet re - pose.
4 Af - ter the change-ful dis - ap - pears, Com-eth the long e - ter - nal years.

REFRAIN

Af - ter all that here we see, What will there be, what will there

be? Af - ter all that here we see, Af - ter all— e - ter - ni - ty!

Music by permission of the Caniedydd Committee, Swansea

The tune Repose is on the preceding page

254   O Don't Stay Away!

JOHNSON OATMAN   ASHLAND 6.6.6.5.D.   W. J. STUART

1 Come, soul, and find thy rest, No lon - ger be dis - tress'd;
2 Dark is the world, and cold, Her cares can - not be told;
3 Come with thy load of sin, Christ died thy soul to win;
4 Time, here will soon be past, Mo - ments are fly - ing fast;
5 Come, O we pray thee, come! Come, and no lon - ger roam;

1 Come to thy Sa - viour's breast; O don't stay a - way!
2 Come to thy Sa - viour's fold; O don't stay a - way!
3 Now He will take thee in; O don't stay a - way!
4 Judg - ment will come at last; O don't stay a - way!
5 Come, now, and start for home; O don't stay a - way!

REFRAIN

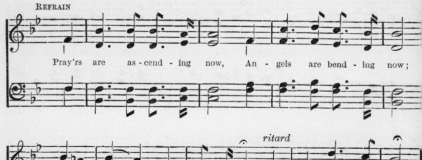

Pray'rs are as - cend - ing now, An - gels are bend - ing now;

ritard

Both worlds are blend - ing now; O don't stay a - way!

The tune BROUGHTON is on the following page

254 ## O Don't Stay Away!

JOHNSON OATMAN   BROUGHTON 6.6.6.5.D.   THOMAS HASTINGS

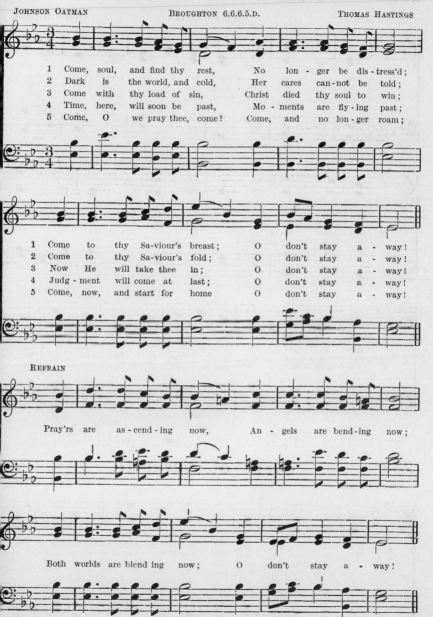

1 Come, soul, and find thy rest,   No lon - ger be dis - tress'd;
2 Dark is the world, and cold,   Her cares can - not be told;
3 Come with thy load of sin,   Christ died thy soul to win;
4 Time, here, will soon be past,   Mo - ments are fly - ing past;
5 Come, O we pray thee, come!   Come, and no lon - ger roam;

1 Come to thy Sa - viour's breast;   O don't stay a - way!
2 Come to thy Sa - viour's fold;   O don't stay a - way!
3 Now He will take thee in;   O don't stay a - way!
4 Judg - ment will come at last;   O don't stay a - way!
5 Come, now, and start for home   O don't stay a - way!

REFRAIN

Pray'rs are as - cend - ing now,   An - gels are bend - ing now;

Both worlds are blend ing now;   O don't stay a - way!

The tune ASHLAND is on the preceding page

255 Return, O Wanderer!

W. B. COLLYER   SHUBAH 8.6.8.6.4   THOMAS HASTINGS

1 Re- turn, O wan- d'rer, to thy home! Thy Fa-
2 Re- turn, O wan- d'rer, to thy home! 'Tis Je-
3 Re- turn, O wan- ·d'rer, to thy home! 'Tis mad-

1 ther calls for thee: No long- er now an ex - ile
2 sus calls for thee: The Spi - rit and the Bride say,
3 ness to de - lay: There are no par- dons in the

1 roam In guilt and mi - se - ry: Re- turn, re - turn!
2 'Come;' O now for re - fuge flee! Re- turn, re - turn!
3 tomb, And brief is mer - cy's day: Re- turn, re - turn!

256 Jesus of Nazareth

ETTA CAMPBELL   THEODORE E. PERKINS

1 What means this ea - ger, an - xious throng Which moves with bu - sy
2 Who is this Je - sus? Why should He The ci - ty move so
3 Je - sus! 'tis He who once be - low Man's path - way trod 'mid
4 A - gain He comes! From place to place His ho - ly foot - prints
5 Ho! all ye hea - vy la - den, come! Here's par - don, com - fort,
6 But if you still this call re - fuse, And all His won - drous

Jesus of Nazareth—*Continued*

1 haste a - long, These won - drous gath - 'rings day by day? What means this
2 might - i - ly? A pass - ing stran - ger, has He skill to move the
3 pain and woe; And bur - den'd ones, where - 'er He came, Brought out their
4 we can trace: He paus - eth at our thres - hold—nay, He en - ters -
5 rest and home; Ye wan - d'rers from a Fa - ther's face, Re - turn, ac -
6 love a - buse; Soon will He sad - ly from you turn; Your bit - ter

1 strange com - mo - tion, pray? In ac - cents hush'd the throng re - ply:
2 mul - ti - tude at will? A - gain the stir - ring notes re - ply:
3 sick, and deaf, and lame; The blind re - joic'd to hear the cry:
4 con - de - scends to stay: Shall we not glad - ly raise the cry:
5 cept His prof - fer'd grace: Ye temp - ted ones, there's re - fuge nigh,
6 pray'r for par - don spurn: 'Too late! too late!' will be the cry:

1 'Je - sus of Naz - a - reth pass - eth by.' In ac - cents hush'd
2 'Je - sus of Naz - a - reth pass - eth by.' A - gain the stir -
3 'Je - sus of Naz - a - reth pass - eth by.' The blind re - joic'd
4 'Je - sus of Naz - a - reth pass - eth by?' Shall we not glad -
5 'Je - sus of Naz - a - reth pass - eth by; Ye temp - ted ones,
6 'Je - sus of Naz - a - reth has pass'd by! 'Too late! too late!'

1 the throng re - ply: 'Je - sus of Naz - a - reth pass - eth by.'
2 ring notes re - ply: 'Je - sus of Naz - a - reth pass - eth by.'
3 to hear the cry: 'Je - sus of Naz - a - reth pass - eth by!'
4 ly raise the cry: 'Je - sus of Naz - a - reth pass - eth by!'
5 there's re - fuge nigh, 'Je - sus of Naz - a - reth pass - eth by!'
6 will be the cry: 'Je - sus of Naz - a - reth has pass'd by!'

257 Step Over the Line

S. C. KIRK

J. G. WILSON

1 Tho' on-ly a line, just a line in-ter-venes Be-
2 You may have gone far in the dark and the cold, Like
3 You may have been drift-ing the world's storm-y main, By
4 Has sin sown the seed of des-pair in your soul? O

1 tween your sal-va-tion and you, ... Your soul will be lost if the
2 one in the wil-der-ness lost; ...... But would you come back to the
3 bil-low and tem-pest been toss'd; .... But would you re-turn to the
4 come with-out mon-ey or cost! ..... The Sa-viour is wait-ing to

1 line is not cross'd, God's Word to the sin-ner is true. ......
2 true Shep-herd's fold, There's on-ly a line to be cross'd. ....
3 home port a-gain, There's on-ly a line to be cross'd. ....
4 say, 'Be thou whole;' There's on-ly a line to be cross'd. ....

REFRAIN

O won't you step o-ver, step o-ver it now! Be-

liev-ing His Word to be true; ..... Come then, at the foot of the

Step Over the Line—*Continued*

Cross hum-bly bow, And let the dear Sa - viour save you........

In the tune below the REFRAIN is sung as verse 5

S. C. KIRK

GREEK FOLK SONG

1 Though on - ly a line, just a line in - ter - venes Be -
2 You may have gone far in the dark and the cold, Like
3 You may have been drift - ing the world's storm - y main, By
4 Has sin sown the seed of des - pair in your soul? O
5 O won't you step o - ver, step o - ver it now! Be -

1 tween your sal - va - tion and you, Your soul will be lost if the
2 one in the wil - der - ness lost; But would you come back to the
3 bil - low and tem - pest been toss'd; But would you re - turn to the
4 come with-out mon - ey or cost! The Sa - viour is wait - ing to
5 liev - ing His Word to be true Come then, at the foot of the

1 line is not cross'd, God's Word to the sin - ner is true.
2 true Shep-herd's fold, There's on - ly a line to be cross'd.
3 home port a - gain, There's on - ly a line to be cross'd.
4 say, 'Be thou whole'; There's on - ly a line to be cross'd.
5 Cross hum - bly bow, And let the dear Sa - viour save you.

258 The Saviour is Bending

WM. LUFF

CHAS. REEVES

1. The Saviour is bend-ing a-bove thee, To hear what thy
2. Look up in the face of the Sa-viour, The thorn-crown'd yet
3. Thou hear-est His of-fers of mer-cy, The pro-mise of

1. spi-rit will say, To the ten-der em-brace Of His
2. beau-ti-ful brow, He waits the re-ply Of thy
3. par-don and peace, Come, wilt thou not say To His

1. mer-cy and grace Will the an-swer be "Yea, Lord," or "Nay."
2. tear-dim-ming eye, Oh, what wilt Thou an-swer Him now?
3. voice a glad "Yea," And bid all thy wa-ver-ings cease?

1. "I died for thee," sweet-ly He whis-pers, "See here are the
2. The Sa-viour is bend-ing a-bove thee, He asks for thy
3. The Sa-viour is bend-ing a-bove thee, His quick ear a-

The Saviour is Bending—*Continued.*

1. wounds in My hands," Thy fin - ger bring near And touch with - out
2. heart in re - turn For the heart that He gave, To ran - som and
3. waits the glad word, "Lord Je - sus, to - day, I whis - per my

1. fear The nail - prints as o'er thee He stands.
2. save, Oh, will not thy glad spi - rit burn?
3. 'Yea,' And know that my an - swer is heard."

CHORUS.

The Sa - viour is bend - ing a - bove thee, To hear what thy

spi - rit will say, To the ten - der em - brace Of His

mer - cy and grace, Will the an - swer be "Yea, Lord," or "Nay."

259 A Few More Years

H. BONAR   LEOMINSTER S.M.D.   G. W. MARTIN

1. A few more years shall roll, A few more sea-sons come,
2. A few more suns shall set O'er these dark hills of time,
3. A few more storms shall beat On this wild rock-y shore,

1. And we shall be with those that rest A - sleep with-in the tomb:
2. And we shall be where suns are not, A far se - ren - er clime:
3. And we shall be where tem - pests cease, And surg - es swell no more:

REFRAIN.

1. Then, oh, my Lord, pre - pare My soul for that great day;
2. Then, oh, my Lord, pre - pare My soul for that blest day;
3. Then, oh, my Lord, pre - pare My soul for that calm day;

1. Oh, wash me in Thy precious blood, And take my sins a - way.
2. Oh, wash me in Thy precious blood, And take my sins a - way.
3. Oh, wash me in Thy precious blood, And take my sins a - way.

260

Eternity !

E. A. HOFFMAN   OLAM 8.8.8.8.8.8   J. H. TENNEY

1 Where will you spend e - ter - ni - ty? This ques-tion comes to
2 Ma - ny are choos - ing Christ to - day, Turn - ing from all their
3 Leav - ing the strait and nar - row way, Go - ing the down - ward
4 Re - pent, be - lieve, this ve - ry hour, Trust in the Sa - viour's

1 you and me! Tell me, what shall your an - swer be?
2 sins a - way: Heav'n shall their hap - py por - tion be,
3 road to - day, Sad will their fi - nal end - ing be,—
4 grace and pow'r, Then will your joy - ous an - swer be,

1 Where will you spend e - ter - ni - ty? E - ter - ni - ty!
2 Where will you spend e - ter - ni - ty? E - ter - ni - ty!
3 Lost through a long e - ter - ni - ty! E - ter - ni - ty!
4 Saved through a long e - ter - ni - ty! E - ter - ni - ty!

1 e - ter - ni - ty! Where will you spend e - ter - ni - ty?
2 e - ter - ni - ty! Where will you spend e - ter - ni - ty?
3 e - ter - ni - ty! Lost through a long e - ter - ni - ty!
4 e - ter - ni - ty! Saved through a long e - ter - ni - ty!

261 Now He Will Save

F. TYLER   HARLESDEN 9.9.9.9   CHARLES REEVES

1 Now He will save you, now He will bless, If all your vile-ness
2 Now is God's mer-cy of-fer'd to thee; Now His sal - va - tion,
3 Now He be-seech-es you to be - lieve; Now He is long-ing

1 you but con - fess; He will re - ceive you home to His
2 pre-cious and free; Will you not take it? turn not a-
3 you to re - ceive; Now light and dark-ness, hea-ven and

1 breast, If you are wea-ry He'll give you rest.
2 side From the love of - fer'd and Him who died.
3 hell, Lie each be - fore you, now choose ye well.

F. TYLER   FFIGYSBREN 9.9.9.9   WELSH MELODY

1 Now He will save you, now He will bless, If all your vile - ness
2 Now is God's mer - cy of - fer'd to thee; Now His sal - va - tion,
3 Now He be - seech - es you to be - lieve; Now He is long - ing

Now He Will Save—*Continued*

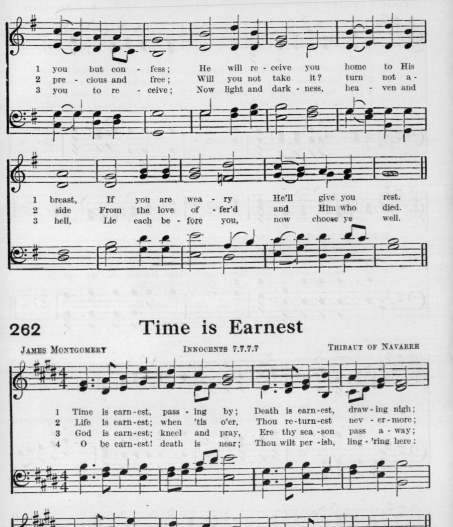

1 you but con - fess; He will re - ceive you home to His
2 pre - cious and free; Will you not take it? turn not a -
3 you to re - ceive; Now light and dark - ness, hea - ven and

1 breast, If you are wea - ry He'll give you rest.
2 side From the love of - fer'd and Him who died.
3 hell, Lie each be - fore you, now choose ye well.

262

Time is Earnest

JAMES MONTGOMERY   INNOCENTS 7.7.7.7   THIBAUT OF NAVARRE

1 Time is earn - est, pass - ing by; Death is earn - est, draw - ing nigh;
2 Life is earn - est; when 'tis o'er, Thou re - turn - est nev - er - more;
3 God is earn - est; kneel and pray, Ere thy sea - son pass a - way;
4 O be earn - est! death is near; Thou wilt per - ish, ling - 'ring here:

1 Sin - ner, wilt thou trif - ling be? Time and death ap - peal to thee.
2 Soon to meet e - ter - ni - ty; Wilt thou nev - er ser - ious be?
3 Ere be set His judg - ment throne— Ven - geance rea - dy, mer - cy gone.
4 Sleep no long - er, rise and flee; Lo, thy Sa - viour waits for thee!

263 Coming Home

Fanny J. Crosby

A. J. Showalter

1. Like a wayward child I wandered From my Father's house a-way.
2. I have wandered in the darkness, And my path was lone and drear,
3. O the rapture that a-waits me When I reach my Fa-ther's door!
4. I will ask Him to for-give me For the wrong that I have done.

1. But I hear His voice en-treat-ing, And I'm coming home to-day.
2. But my Father did not leave me, He was watching ev-er near.
3. Once with-in its blest en-clos-ure, I am safe for-ev-er-more.
4. To re-ceive, ac-cept, and bless me, Thro' His well-be-lov-ed Son.

REFRAIN.

Coming . . . . home, Coming . . . . home, For I can no longer roam;
Coming, coming, Coming, coming, no longer roam;

I am sad and broken heart-ed, And I'm com-ing, com-ing home!
I'm coming home.

Over the Line

264

Ellen K. Bradford   E. H. Phelps

1. Oh,   ten-der and sweet was the Mas-ter's voice As He lov-ing-ly call'd to
2. But my sins   are ma-ny, my faith   is small, Lo! the an-swer came quick and
3. But my flesh   is weak,   I   tear-ful-ly said, And the way   I   can-not
4. Ah, the world   is cold, and I   can-not go back, Press for-ward I   sure-ly

1. me,   "Come   o-ver the line, it is   on-ly a   step— I am
2. clear; . "Thou   need-est not trust in thy-self   at all,   Step
3. see; . I   fear if I try I may sad-ly fail,   And
4. must; . I will place   my hand in His woun-ded palm,   Step

REFRAIN.

1. wait-ing, my   child,   for   thee."
2. o-ver the   line, I   am   here,"
3. thus may dis-hon-our   Thee,
4. o-ver the   line, and   *trust.*   "O-ver the line," hear the

sweet re-frain,   An-gels are chant-ing the heav-en-ly strain:

"O-ver the line,"—Why should I re-main With a   step between me and Je sus.
4th v. "O-ver the line,"—I *will not* re-main, I'll   cross it and go   to Je-sus.

265 Come, Great Deliverer !

FANNY J. CROSBY

W. H. DOANE

1 O hear my cry, be grac-ious now to me, Come, Great De-liv - 'rer, come!
2 I have no place, nor shel-ter from the night, Come, Great De-liv - 'rer, come!
3 My path is lone, and wear-y are my feet, Come, Great De-liv - 'rer, come!
4 Thou wilt not spurn con-tri-tion's bro-ken sigh, Come, Great De-liv - 'rer, come!

1 My soul, bow'd down, is long-ing now for Thee, Come, Great De-liv - 'rer, come!
2 One look from Thee would give me life and light, Come, Great De-liv - 'rer, come!
3 Mine eyes look up Thy lov-ing smile to meet, Come, Great De-liv - 'rer, come!
4 Re - gard my pray'r, and hear my hum-ble cry, Come, Great De-liv - 'rer, come!

REFRAIN

I've wan-der'd far a-way o'er moun-tains cold, I've wan - der'd far a-way from home;

O take me now, and bring me to Thy fold! Come, Great De-liv - 'rer, come!

266

Trust!

Mrs. S. R. G. Clare.   L.M.   *Arr. by* Wm. J. Kirkpatrick.

1. He tells me to trust and not fear,   He bids me each pro-mise be-lieve:
2. My need He is pledged to sup-ply,   I trust for each breath that I breathe:
3. He of-fers me par-don and peace,   He of-fers me cleans-ing from sin;
4. Praise God, it is done— I am His!   The blood cov-ers bo-dy and soul;

1. His pre-sence and glo-ry seems near,   I o-pen my heart to re-ceive:
2. And since I take *life* at His hands,   Why not *all* He wish-es to give?
3. The foun-tain once o-pen'd I see,   Dear Je-sus, I dare to plunge in:
4. I am pardon'd and cleans'd,I am heal'd;   All glo-ry, I'm ev-'ry whit whole!

Refrain.

1. I am ran-som'd,I know, For His Word tells me so, So I trust, trust trust!
2. Lord, I yield ev-er-more, For Thy pro-mise is sure, So I trust, trust, trust!
3. Now I know I am free, For Thy blood cleanseth me, While I trust, trust, trust!
4. Praise His name,I be-lieve, And this mo-ment re-ceive,While I trust, trust, trust!

1. I am ransom'd, I know,For His Word tells me so, So I trust, trust, trust!
2. Lord,I yield ev-er-more, For Thy pro-mise is sure, So I trust, trust, trust!
3. Now I know I am free, For Thy blood cleanseth me,While I trust, trust, trust!
4. Praise His name,I be-lieve, And this mo-ment re-ceive,While I trust, trust, trust!

267　To Jesus I Will Go

FANNY J. CROSBY　　　(Ps. xxvii. 8.)　　　W. H. DOANE

1. There's a gen-tle voice with-in calls a-way (calls a-way), 'Tis a
warn-ing I have heard o'er and o'er (o'er and o'er), But my heart is melt-ed
now, I o-bey (I o-bey); From my Sa-viour I will wan-der no more.

2. He has pro-mised all my sins to for-give (to for-give), If I
ask in sim-ple faith for His love (for His love); In His ho-ly word I
learn how to live (how to live), And to la-bour for His king-dom a-bove.

3. I will try to bear the cross in my youth (in my youth), And be
faith-ful in its cause till I die (in the truth); If with cheer-ful step I
walk in the truth (in the truth), I shall wear a star-ry crown by-and-bye.

4. Still the gen-tle voice with-in calls a-way (calls a-way), And its
warn-ing I have heard o'er and o'er (o'er and o'er); But my heart is melt-ed
now, I o-bey (I o-bey): From my Sa-viour I will wan-der no more.

CHORUS.

Yes, I will go; Yes, I will go; To Je-sus I will go and be saved;
Yes, I will go; yes, I will go; To Je-sus I will go and be saved.

268 Lord, I'm Coming Home

WM. J. KIRKPATRICK

WM. J. KIRKPATRICK

1 I've wan-der'd far a - way from God, Now I'm com-ing home;
2 I've was - ted ma - ny pre - cious years, Now I'm com-ing home;
3 I'm tired of sin and stray - ing, Lord, Now I'm com-ing home;
4 My soul is sick, my heart is sore, Now I'm com-ing home:

1 The paths of sin too long I've trod, Lord, I'm com-ing home!
2 I now re-pent with bit - ter tears, Lord, I'm com-ing home!
3 I'll trust Thy love, be - lieve Thy word, Lord, I'm com-ing home!
4 My strength re-new, my hope re-store, Lord, I'm com-ing home!

REFRAIN

Com-ing home, com-ing home, Nev - er more to roam.

O - pen wide Thine arms of love Lord I'm com-ing home!

269   # Thy Welcome Voice

LEWIS HARTSOUGH   LEWIS HARTSOUGH

1 I hear Thy wel-come voice, That calls me, Lord, to Thee For
2 Tho' com - ing weak and vile, Thou dost my strength as - sure: Thou
3 All hail, a - ton- ing blood! All hail, re-deem-ing grace! All

1 cleans - ing in Thy pre-cious blood That flow'd on Cal - va - ry.
2 dost my vile - ness ful - ly cleanse, Till spot - less all and pure.
3 hail, the gift of Christ, our Lord, Our strength and right-eous - ness!

REFRAIN

I am com - ing, Lord, Com - ing now to Thee;

Trust - ing on - ly in the blood That flow'd on Cal - va - ry.

Angels Hovering 'Round

270

ANON.

OLD MELODY

1 There are an - gels hov-'ring 'round, There are an - gels hov-'ring 'round,
2 To   carry the tid - ings home, To   carry the tid - ings home,
3 To   the new Jer - u - sa - lem, To   the new Jer - u - sa - lem,
4 Poor   sinners are com - ing home, Poor   sinners are com - ing home,

1 There are an - gels, an - gels hov - 'ring   'round,
2 To   car - ry, car - ry the tid - ings   home,
3 To the new,   the new   Jer - u - sa - lem.
4 Poor   sin - ners, sin - ners are com - ing   home;

VERSES 5 to 8

5 And   Je - sus bids them come, And   Je - sus bids them come,
6 And   chil-dren, too, may come, And   chil-dren, too, may come,
7 For   Je - sus loves to save, For   Je - sus loves to save,
8 There's   glo - ry all a - round, There's   glo - ry all a - round,

5 And   Je - sus, Je - sus bids them come;
6 And   chil - dren, chil - dren, too, may come;
7 For   Je - sus, Je - sus loves to save.
8 There's   glo - ry, glo - ry all a - round.

271

Shall I Let Him In?

H. R. P.

H. R. PALMER

1. Christ is knocking at my sad heart, Shall I let Him in?
2. Shall I greet Him with lov-ing word, Shall I let Him in?
3. Yes, I'll o-pen this heart's proud door, Yes, I'll let Him in:

1. Pa-tient-ly plead-ing with my sad heart, Oh! shall I let Him in?
2. Meek-ly ac-cept-ing my gra-cious Lord, Oh! shall I let Him in?
3. Glad-ly I'll wel-come Him ev-er-more; Oh! yes, I'll let Him in!

1. Cold and proud is my heart with sin; Dark and cheer-less is all with-in;
2. He can in-fi-nite love im-part; He can par-don this re-bel heart;
3. Bless-ed Sa-viour, a-bide with me, Cares and tri-als will light-er be;

1. Christ is bid-ding me turn un-to Him, Oh! shall I let Him in?
2. Shall I bid Him for ev-er de-part, Or shall I let Him in?
3. I am safe if I'm on-ly with Thee, O! bless-ed Lord, come in!

272   # Shall I be Saved?

Fanny J. Crosby   M. Bliss Wilson

1 Je - sus is plead-ing with my poor soul, Shall I be saved to - night?
2 Je - sus was nail'd to the Cross for me, Shall I be saved to - night?
3 Je - sus is knock-ing at my poor heart, Shall I be saved to - night?
4 What if that voice I should hear no more, Shall I be saved to - night?

1 If I be-lieve, He will make me whole, Shall I be saved to - night?
2 How can my heart so un-grate - ful be? Shall I be saved to - night?
3 What if His Spi-rit should now de-part? Shall I be saved to - night?
4 Quick-ly I'll o-pen this bolt - ed door, Save me, O Lord, to - night!

1 Ten-der-ly, sad-ly, I hear Him say, How can you grieve Me from day to day?
2 Now He will save me by grace di-vine, Now, if I will, I may call Him mine,
3 O-ver and o-ver His voice I hear, Sweet-ly it falls on my list-'ning ear:
4 Bles-sed Re-deem-er, come in, come in, Pi - ty, my sor-row, for-give my sin!

1 Shall I go on in the old, old way, Or shall I be saved to - night?
2 Can I the pleas-ures of earth re - sign? O shall I be saved to - night!
3 Shall I re - ject Him, a Friend so dear? O shall I be saved to - night!
4 Now let Thy work in my soul be - gin, For I will be saved to - night!

273 Only a Step to Jesus

FANNY J. CROSBY

W. H. DOANE.

1. On - ly a step to Je - sus! Then why not take it now?
2. On - ly a step to Je - sus! Be - lieve, and thou shalt live;
3. On - ly a step to Je - sus! A step from sin to grace;
4. On - ly a step to Je - sus! O why not come, and say,

1. Come, and, thy sin con - fess - ing, To Him Thy Sa - viour bow.
2. Lov - ing - ly now He's wait - ing, And rea - dy to for - give.
3. What hast thy heart de - ci - ded? The mo - ments fly a - pace.
4. Glad - ly to Thee, my Sa - viour, I give my - self a - way.

REFRAIN.

On - ly a step, on - ly a step; Come, He waits for thee;

Come, and thy sin con - fess - ing, Thou shalt re - ceive a bless - ing;

Do not re - ject the mer - cy He free - ly of - fers thee.

274 Hallelujah! 'Tis Done

PHILIP P. BLISS

PHILIP P. BLISS

1 'Tis the pro-mise of God full sal - va - tion to give Un - to
2 Tho' the path-way be lone - ly and dan - ger - ous, too, Sure - ly
3 Ma - ny lov'd ones have I in yon hea - ven - ly throng; They are
4 There are pro - phets and kings in that throng I be - hold, And they
5 There's a part in that cho - rus for you and for me, And the

REFRAIN

1 him who on Je - sus, His Son, will be - lieve:
2 Je - sus is a - ble to car - ry me through;
3 safe now in glo - ry, and this is their song; } Hal - le - lu - jah! 'tis
4 sing while they march thro' the streets of pure gold:
5 theme of our prais - es for ev - er will be:

done, I be - lieve on the Son; I am saved by the blood of the

Cru - ci - fied One. Hal - le - lu - jah! 'tis done, I be - lieve on

the Son; I am saved by the blood of the Cru - ci - fied One.

275 One Sweetly Solemn Thought

PHŒBE CAREY

PHILIP PHILLIPS

1. One sweet-ly sol-emn thought Comes to me o'er and o'er; I'm near-er home to-day, to-day,
2. Near-er my Fa-ther's house, Where ma-ny man-sions be; Near-er the great white throne to-day,
3. Near-er the bound of life, Where bur-dens are laid down; Near-er to leave the cross to-day,
4. Be near me when my feet Are slip-ping o'er the brink; For I am near-er home to-day,

CHORUS.

1. Than I have been be-fore.
2. Near-er the crys-tal sea.
3. And near-er to the crown.
4. Per-haps, than now I think.

Near-er my home, Near er my home, Near-er my home to-day, to-day, Than I have been be-fore.

276 Cleansing for Me

HERBERT H. BOOTH

T. H. BAYLY

1 Lord, thro' the Blood of the Lamb that was slain, Cleans-ing for me,
2 From all the doubts that have fill'd me with gloom, Cleans-ing for me,
3 From all the care of what men think or say, Cleans-ing for me,

1 Cleans-ing for me: From all the guilt of my sins now I claim Cleans-ing
2 Cleans-ing for me: From all the fears that would point me to doom, Cleans-ing
3 Cleans-ing for me: From e-ver fear-ing to speak, sing, or pray, Cleans-ing

1 from Thee, Cleans-ing from Thee: Sin-ful and black tho' the past may have been,
2 for me, Cleans-ing for me: Je-sus, al-tho' I may not un-der-stand,
3 for me, Cleans-ing for me: Lord, in Thy love and Thy pow'r make me strong,

1 Man - y the crush - ing de - feats I have seen, Yet on Thy pro-
2 In child-like faith now I put forth my hand, And thro' Thy Word
3 That all may know that to Thee I be-long; When I am temp-

1 mise, O Lord, now I lean! Cleans-ing for me, Cleans-ing for me!
2 and Thy grace I shall stand, Cleans-ed by Thee, Cleans-ed by Thee.
3 ted let this be my song, Cleans-ing for me, Cleans-ing for me.

By permission of the INTERNATIONAL MUSIC BOARD OF THE SALVATION ARMY

277 Even Me

ELIZABETH CODNER GESHEM 8.7.8.7.6.7 WILLIAM B. BRADBURY

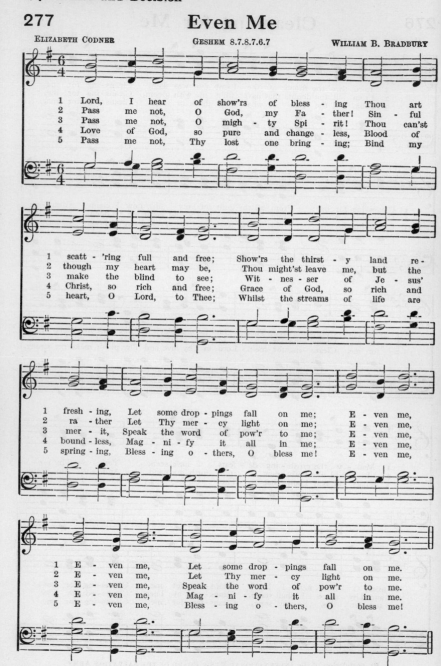

1 Lord, I hear of show'rs of bless - ing Thou art
2 Pass me not, O God, my Fa - ther! Sin - ful
3 Pass me not, O migh - ty Spi - rit! Thou can'st
4 Love of God, so pure and change - less, Blood of
5 Pass me not, Thy lost one bring - ing; Bind my

1 scatt - 'ring full and free; Show'rs the thirst - y land re -
2 though my heart may be, Thou might'st leave me, but the
3 make the blind to see; Wit - nes - ser of Je - sus'
4 Christ, so rich and free; Grace of God, so rich and
5 heart, O Lord, to Thee; Whilst the streams of life are

1 fresh - ing, Let some drop - pings fall on me; E - ven me,
2 ra - ther Let Thy mer - cy light on me; E - ven me,
3 mer - it, Speak the word of pow'r to me; E - ven me,
4 bound - less, Mag - ni - fy it all in me; E - ven me,
5 spring - ing, Bless - ing o - thers, O bless me! E - ven me,

1 E - ven me, Let some drop - pings fall on me.
2 E - ven me, Let Thy mer - cy light on me.
3 E - ven me, Speak the word of pow'r to me.
4 E - ven me, Mag - ni - fy it all in me.
5 E - ven me, Bless - ing o - thers, O bless me!

The tunes EVEN ME and SHOWERS OF BLESSING are on the following pages

277

Even Me

ELIZABETH CODNER   EVEN ME 8.7.8.7.9   MARY HORNABROOK

1. Lord, I hear of show'rs of bless-ing Thou art scat-t'ring full and free; Show'rs the thirst-y land re-fresh-ing, Let some drop-pings fall on me;
2. Pass me not, O God, my Fa-ther! Sin-ful though my heart may be, Thou might'st leave me, but the ra-ther Let Thy mer-cy light on me;
3. Pass me not, O migh-ty Spi-rit! Thou can'st make the blind to see; Wit-nes-ser of Je-sus' mer-it, Speak the word of pow'r to me;
4. Love of God, so pure and change-less, Blood of Christ, so rich and free; Grace of God, so rich and bound-less, Mag-ni-fy it all in me;
5. Pass me not, Thy lost one bring-ing; Bind my heart, O Lord, to Thee; Whilst the streams of life are spring-ing, Bless-ing o-thers, O bless me!

1-5 E-ven me, E-ven me, E-ven me.

Music by permission of the METHODIST CONFERENCE
The tunes GESHEM and SHOWERS OF BLESSING precede and follow this tune

Even Me

277

ELIZABETH CODNER

SHOWERS OF BLESSING 8.7.8.7.3

WILLIAM D. MACLAGAN

1 Lord, I hear of show'rs of bless - ing Thou art scatt - 'ring
2 Pass me not, O God, my Fa - ther! Sin - ful though my
3 Pass me not, O migh - ty Spi - rit! Thou can'st make the
4 Love of God, so pure and change - less, Blood of Christ, so
5 Pass me not, Thy lost one bring - ing; Bind my heart, O

1 full and free; . Show'rs the thirst - y land re - fresh - ing,
2 heart may be, . Thou might'st leave me, but the ra - ther
3 blind to see; . Wit - nes - ser of Je - sus' mer - it,
4 rich and free; . Grace of God, so rich and bound - less,
5 Lord, to Thee; . Whilst the streams of life are spring - ing,

1 Let some drop - pings fall on me; E - ven me.
2 Let Thy mer - cy light on me; E - ven me.
3 Speak the word of pow'r to me; E - ven me.
4 Mag - ni - fy it all in me, E - ven me.
5 Bless - ing o - thers, O bless me! E - ven me.

Music by permission of MICHAEL MACLAGAN
The tunes GESHEM and EVEN ME are on the preceding pages

278 Depth of Mercy

CHARLES WESLEY   WEBER 7.7.7.7   CARL M. VON WEBER

1 Depth of mer - cy! can there be   Mer - cy still re - serv'd for me?
2 I have long with - stood His grace,   Long pro - vok'd Him to His face;
3 Whence to me this waste of love?   Ask my Ad - vo - cate a - bove!
4 There for me the Sa - viour stands,   Shows His wounds, and spreads His hands:
5 If I right - ly read Thy heart,   If Thou all com - pas - sion art,

1 Can my God His wrath for - bear? Me, the chief of sin - ners, spare?
2 Would not heark - en to His calls, Griev'd Him by a thou - sand falls.
3 See the cause in Je - sus' face, Now be - fore the throne of grace.
4 God is love, I know, I feel; Je - sus lives and loves me still.
5 Bow Thine ear, in mer - cy bow, Par - don and ac - cept me now!

CHARLES WESLEY   WARFARE 7.7.7.7   GEORGE PRIOR

1 Depth of mer - cy! can there be   Mer - cy still re - serv'd for me?
2 I have long with - stood His grace,   Long pro - vok'd Him to His face;
3 Whence to me this waste of love?   Ask my Ad - vo - cate a - bove!
4 There for me the Sa - viour stands,   Shows His wounds, and spreads His hands:
5 If I right - ly read Thy heart,   If Thou all com - pas - sion art,

1 Can my God His wrath for - bear? Me, the chief of sin - ners, spare?
2 Would not heark - en to His calls, Griev'd Him by a thou - sand falls.
3 See the cause in Je - sus' face, Now be - fore the throne of grace.
4 God is love, I know, I feel; Je - sus lives and loves me still.
5 Bow Thine ear, in mer - cy bow, Par - don and ac - cept me now!

279 Thou Art Standing

W. W. How   Knecht 7.6.7.6   J. H. Knecht

1 O Je - sus, Thou art stand - ing Out - side the fast-clos'd door!
2 O Je - sus, Thou art knock - ing; And, lo! that hand is scarr'd,
3 O love that pass - eth know-ledge! So pa - tient - ly to wait;
4 O Je - sus, Thou art plead - ing In ac - cents meek and low,
5 O Lord, with shame and sor - row We o - pen now the door!

1 In low - ly pa - tience wait - ing To pass the thres - hold o'er.
2 And thorns Thy brow en - cir - cle, And tears Thy face have marr'd!
3 O sin that hath no e - qual! So fast to bar the gate.
4 'I died for you, My chil - dren, And will ye treat Me so?'
5 Dear Sa - viour, en - ter, en - ter! And leave us nev - er - more.

W. W. How   St. Victor 7.6.7.6   R. Redhead

1 O Je - sus, Thou art stand - ing Out - side the fast-clos'd door!
2 O Je - sus, Thou art knock - ing; And, lo! that hand is scarr'd,
3 O love that pass - eth know-ledge! So pa - tient - ly to wait;
4 O Je - sus, Thou art plead - ing In ac - cents meek and low,
5 O Lord, with shame and sor - row We o - pen now the door;

1 In low - ly pa - tience wait - ing To pass the thres - hold o'er.
2 And thorns Thy brow en - cir - cle, And tears Thy face have marr'd!
3 O sin that hath no e - qual! So fast to bar the gate.
4 'I died for you, My chil - dren, And will ye treat Me so?'
5 Dear Sa - viour, en - ter, en - ter! And leave us nev - er - more.

280   Pass Me Not

FANNY J. CROSBY   W. H. DOANE

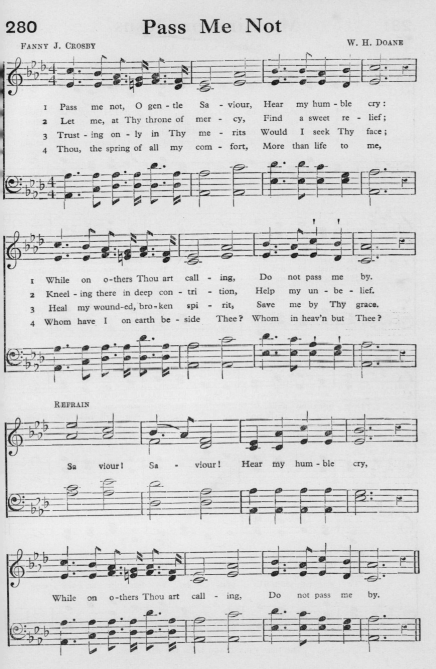

1 Pass   me not, O gen - tle   Sa - viour,   Hear my hum - ble   cry:
2 Let   me, at Thy throne of   mer - cy,   Find   a sweet   re - lief;
3 Trust - ing on - ly in Thy   me - rits   Would I seek Thy   face;
4 Thou, the spring of all my   com - fort,   More than life to   me,

1 While on o - thers Thou art call - ing,   Do   not pass me   by.
2 Kneel - ing there in deep con - tri - tion,   Help   my un - be - lief.
3 Heal my wound-ed, bro-ken   spi - rit,   Save   me by Thy   grace.
4 Whom have I on earth be - side   Thee? Whom in heav'n but   Thee?

REFRAIN

Sa - viour! Sa - viour!   Hear my hum - ble   cry,

While on o - thers Thou art call - ing,   Do   not pass me   by.

My Sins on Jesus

281

HORATIUS BONAR MISSIONARY 7.6.7.6.D LOWELL MASON

1 I lay my sins on Je - sus, The spot - less Lamb of God;
2 I lay my wants on Je - sus; All ful - ness dwells in Him;
3 I rest my soul on Je - sus, This wea - ry soul of mine:
4 I long to be like Je - sus, Meek, lov - ing, low - ly, mild;

1 He bears them all and frees us From the ac - curs - ed load.
2 He heals all my dis - eas - es, He doth my soul re - deem.
3 His right hand me em - brac - es, I on His breast re - cline.
4 I long to be like Je - sus, The Fa - ther's ho - ly child;

1 I bring my guilt to Je - sus, To wash my crim - son stains
2 I lay my griefs on Je - sus, My bur - dens and my cares:
3 I love the Name of Je - sus, Im - man - uel, Christ, the Lord;
4 I long to be with Je - sus A - mid the heav'n - ly throng,

1 White in His blood most pre - cious, Till not a spot re - mains.
2 He from them all re - leas - es, He all my sor - rows shares.
3 Like fra - grance on the breez - es His Name a - broad is poured.
4 To sing with saints His prais - es, To learn the an - gels' song.

The tune PILGRIMAGE is on the next page

281 My Sins on Jesus

Horatius Bonar   Pilgrimage 7.6.7.6.d   S. S. Wesley

1 I lay my sins on Je - sus, The spot - less Lamb of God;
2 I lay my wants on Je - sus: All ful - ness dwells in Him;
3 I rest my soul on Je - sus, This wea - ry soul of mine;
4 I long to be like Je - sus, Meek, lov - ing, low - ly, mild;

1 He bears them all and frees us From the ac - curs - ed load.
2 He heals all my dis - eas - es, He doth my soul re - deem.
3 His right hand me em - brac - es, I on His breast re - cline.
4 I long to be like Je - sus, The Fa - ther's ho - ly child;

1 I bring my guilt to Je - sus, To wash my crim - son stains
2 I lay my griefs on Je - sus, My bur - dens and my cares:
3 I love the Name of Je - sus, Im - man - uel, Christ, the Lord;
4 I long to be with Je - sus A - mid the heav'n - ly throng,

1 White in His blood most pre - cious, Till not a spot re - mains.
2 He from them all re - leas - es, He all my sor - rows shares.
3 Like fra - grance on the breez - es His Name a - broad is poured.
4 To sing with saints His prais - es, To learn the an - gels' song.

The tune Missionary is on the previous page

282 Trusting in His Word

J. C. MORGAN   FULLY TRUSTING 8.7.8.7.D   GEO. C. STEBBINS

1 All my doubts I give to Je - sus! I've His gra - cious prom - ise heard,
2 All my sins I lay on Je - sus! He doth wash me in His blood;
3 All my fears I give to Je - sus! Rests my wea - ry soul on Him;
4 All my joys I give to Je - sus! He is all I want of bliss;
5 All I am I give to Je - sus! All my bod - y, all my soul,

1 I shall ne - ver be con - found - ed, I am trust - ing in that Word.
2 He will keep me pure and ho - ly, He will bring me home to God.
3 Though my way be hid in dark - ness, Ne - ver can His light grow dim.
4 He of all the worlds is Mas - ter, He has all I need in this.
5 All I have, and all I hope for, While e - ter - nal a - ges roll.

REFRAIN

I am trust - ing, ful - ly trust - ing, Sweet - ly trust - ing in His Word.

I am trust - ing, ful - ly trust - ing, Sweet - ly trust - ing in His Word.

283 I Will Go

MARTHA J. LANKTON   RAWLINS 7.7. 7.5. D   WM. J. KIRKPATRICK

1 I will go, I can-not stay From the arms of love a-way;
2 Tho' I long have tried in vain, Tried to break the tem-pter's chain,
3 I am lost, and yet I know Earth can nev-er heal my woe;
4 Some-thing whis-pers in my soul, Tho' my sins like moun-tains roll,

1 O for strength of faith to say, Je - sus died for me.
2 Yet to - day I'll try a - gain, Je - sus, help Thou me.
3 I will rise at once and go, Je - sus died for me.
4 Je - sus' blood will make me whole, Je - sus died for me.

REFRAIN

Can it be, O can it be, There is hope for one like me?

I will go with this my plea, Je - sus died for me.

284 I'll Live for Thee

R. E. HUDSON   EAST LINTON 8.8.8.6   C. R. DUNBAR

1 My life, my love, I give to Thee, Thou Lamb of God, Who died for me;
2 I now be-lieve Thou dost re-ceive, For Thou hast died that I might live;
3 O Thou who died on Cal-va-ry, To save my soul, and make me free;

REF.—I'll live for Thee, I'll live for Thee, And O how glad my soul should be,

1 O may I ev - er faith - ful be, My Sa-viour and my God!
2 And now hence-forth I'll trust in Thee, My Sa-viour and my God!
3 I con - se-crate my life to Thee, My Sa-viour and my God!

That Thou didst give Thy - self for me, My Sa-viour and my God!

(In the tune below, the REFRAIN is sung as verse 4)

R. E HUDSON   HOWCROFT 8.8.8.6   G. TROTTER

1 My life, my love I give to Thee, Thou Lamb of God, Who died for
2 I now be-lieve Thou dost re - ceive For Thou hast died that I might
3 O Thou who died on Cal - va - ry To save my soul, and make me
4 I'll live for Thee, I'll live for Thee, And O how glad my soul should

1 me; O may I ev - er faith - ful be, My Sa-viour and my God!
2 live; And now hence-forth I'll trust in Thee, My Sa-viour and my God!
3 free; I con - se-crate my life to Thee, My Sa-viour and my God!
4 be, That Thou didst give Thy-self for me, My Sa-viour and my God!

285 Ring the Bells of Heaven!

W. O. Cushing

G. F. Root

1. Ring the bells of hea - ven! there is joy to - day, For a soul re -
2. Ring the bells of hea - ven! there is joy to - day, For the wan-d'rer
3. Ring the bells of hea - ven! spread the feast to - day! An - gels swell the

1. turn - ing from the wild; See! the Father meets him out up-on the way,
2. now is re - con - ciled; Yes, a soul is res - cued from his sin - ful way,
3. glad, tri-um-phant strain! Tell the joy - ful tid - ings! bear it far a - way!

CHORUS

1. Wel - com - ing His wea - ry, wan-d'ring child.
2. And is born a - new, a ran - som'd child.
3. For a pre - cious soul is born a - gain.

Glo - ry! glo - ry! how the

an - gels sing! Glo - ry! glo - ry! how the loud harps ring! 'Tis the ran-somed

ar - my, like a might - y sea, Peal - ing forth the an-them of the free!

286 The Penitent's Plea

H. H. BOOTH

H. H. BOOTH

1 Sa - viour, hear me, while be - fore Thy feet   I   the re - cord of my
2 Back, with all the guilt my spi - rit bears, Past   the haunt-ing mem-or-
3 Yet   why should I fear ? Hast Thou not died   That   no seek-ing soul should
4 All   the ri - vers of Thy grace I   claim, Ov - er ev - 'ry pro-mise

1 sins   re - peat, Stain'd with guilt, my-self ab - hor - ring,
2 ies   of years, Self   and shame and fear de - spis - ing,
3 be   de - nied ?   To   that heart, its sins con - fess - ing,
4 write   my name ;   As   I am I   come be - liev - ing,

1 Fill'd with grief, my soul out - pour - ing :   Canst Thou still in mer - cy
2 Foes   and taunt-ing fiends sur - pris - ing ;   Sav - iour, to Thy Cross I
3 Canst Thou fail to give a   bless - ing ?   By   the love and pi - ty
4 As   Thou art Thou dost, re - ceiv - ing,   Bid   me rise a freed and

1 think   of me, Stoop to set my shack - led spi - rit free,   Raise my
2 press   my way, And   a bro - ken heart be - fore   it lay ;   Ere   I
3 Thou hast shown, By   the blood that did for   me   a - tone,   Bold - ly
4 par - don'd slave ; Mas - ter o'er my sin, the world, the grave,   Charg - ing

The Penitent's Plea—*Continued*

1 sink-ing heart, and bid me be Thy child for - giv'n!
2 leave, O let me hear Thee say: I am for - giv'n!
3 will I kneel be - fore Thy throne, A plead - ing soul.
4 me to preach Thy pow'r to save To sin - bound souls.

REFRAIN *mp*

Grace there is my ev - 'ry debt to pay, Blood to

Grace there is my ev - 'ry debt to pay, Blood to wash my

wash my ev - 'ry sin a - way, Pow'r to keep me spot - less

ev - 'ry sin a - way, Pow'r to keep me spot - less

day by day, In Christ for me.

By permission of the INTERNATIONAL MUSIC BOARD OF THE SALVATION ARMY

287   Save Me at the Cross

FANNY J. CROSBY   HUBERT P. MAIN

1 Lov - ing Sa - viour, Hear my cry, Hear my cry, hear my cry; Trem-bling
2 Tho' I per - ish I will pray, I will pray, I will pray; Thou of
3 Wash me in Thy cleans-ing blood, Cleans-ing blood, cleans-ing blood; Plunge me

1 to Thine arms I fly: O save me at the Cross! I have sinn'd, but
2 life the Liv - ing Way: O save me at the Cross! Thou hast said Thy
3 now be - neath the flood : O save me at the Cross! On - ly faith will

1 Thou hast died, Thou hast died, Thou hast died; In Thy mer - cy let me hide,
2 grace is free, Grace is free, grace is free: Have com-pas - sion, Lord, on me:
3 par-don bring, Par - don bring, par - don bring: In that faith to Thee I cling:

REFRAIN

1-3 O save me at the Cross! Lord Je-sus, re-ceive me, No more would I

grieve Thee, Now, bless-ed Re - deem - er, O save me at the Cross!

288 Now I am Coming Home

Johnson Oatman

Geo. C. Hugg

1 Long I have wan-der'd a-far from my Lord, Now I am com-ing home;
2 Tired of the world with its fol-ly and sin, Now I am com-ing home;
3 Know-ing my Sa-viour can give me His rest, Now I am com-ing home;
4 Humb-ly I crave but a poor ser-vant's place, Now I am com-ing home;
5 O bless the Lord, my dear Sa-viour I see, Now I am com-ing home:

1 Long-ing to be to His fa-vour re-stor'd, Now I am com-ing home.
2 Be-lieving the Sa-viour will wel-come me in, Now I am com-ing home.
3 Long-ing to an-chor my soul on His breast, Now I am com-ing home.
4 On-ly de-sir-ing to taste of His grace, Now I am com-ing home.
5 Wait-ing to wel-come a sin-ner like me, Now I am com-ing home.

REFRAIN

Yes, I am com-ing, Dear Lord, I'm com-ing, Just now I'm com-ing home.

Yes, I am com-ing, Dear Lord, I'm com-ing, Just now I'm com-ing home.

289 Coming to the Cross

WILLIAM M'DONALD   SAMARIA 7.7.7.7. D   WILLIAM G. FISCHER

1 I am com - ing to the Cross, I am poor and weak and blind;
2 Long my heart has sigh'd for Thee, Long has e - vil reign'd with - in;
3 Here I give my all to Thee, Friends, and time, and earth - ly store;

1 I am count - ing all but dross, I shall full sal - va - tion find.
2 Je - sus sweet - ly speaks to me, 'I will cleanse you from all sin.'
3 Soul and bo - dy Thine to be, Whol - ly Thine for e - ver - more.

REFRAIN

I am trust - ing, Lord, in Thee, Blest Lamb of Cal - var - y;

Hum - bly at Thy Cross I bow; . Save me, Sa - viour, save me now.

The tune OAKLAND is on the following page

289 Coming to the Cross

WILLIAM M'DONALD   OAKLAND 7.7.7.7.D   LOWELL MASON
Arr. P. J. MANSFIELD

1 I am com - ing to the Cross, . I am poor and
2 Long my heart has sigh'd for Thee, . Long has e - vil
3 Here I give my all to Thee, . Friends, and time, and

1 weak and blind; . I am count - ing all but dross, . I shall
2 reign'd with - in; . Je - sus sweet - ly speaks to me, . 'I will
3 earth - ly store; . Soul and bo - dy Thine to be, . Whol - ly

REFRAIN

1 full sal - va - tion find.
2 cleanse you from all sin.'   I am trust - ing, Lord, in
3 Thine for e - ver - more.

Thee, . Blest . Lamb . of Cal - var - y; . Hum - bly

at Thy Cross I bow; . Save me, Sa - viour, save me now.

The tune SAMARIA is on the preceding page

290 Room for Jesus

E. W. CHAPMAN

J. H. TENNEY

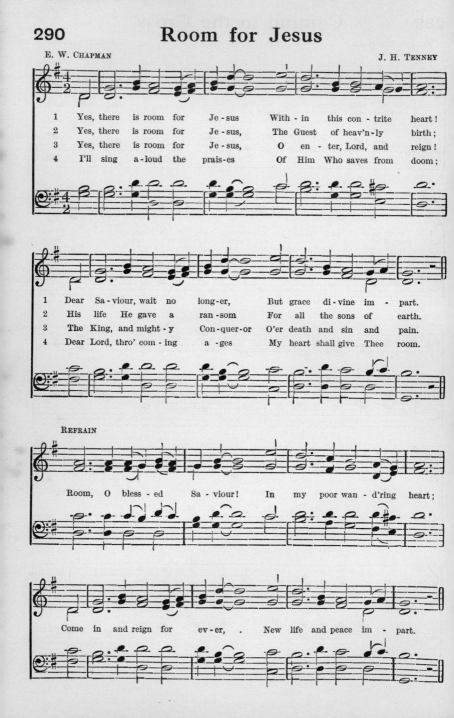

1 Yes, there is room for Je - sus With - in this con - trite heart!
2 Yes, there is room for Je - sus, The Guest of heav'n - ly birth;
3 Yes, there is room for Je - sus, O en - ter, Lord, and reign!
4 I'll sing a - loud the prais - es Of Him Who saves from doom;

1 Dear Sa - viour, wait no long - er, But grace di - vine im - part.
2 His life He gave a ran - som For all the sons of earth.
3 The King, and might - y Con - quer - or O'er death and sin and pain.
4 Dear Lord, thro' com - ing a - ges My heart shall give Thee room.

REFRAIN

Room, O bless - ed Sa - viour! In my poor wan - d'ring heart;

Come in and reign for ev - er, . New life and peace im - part.

291 ## The Great Physician

WM. HUNTER

J. H. STOCKTON

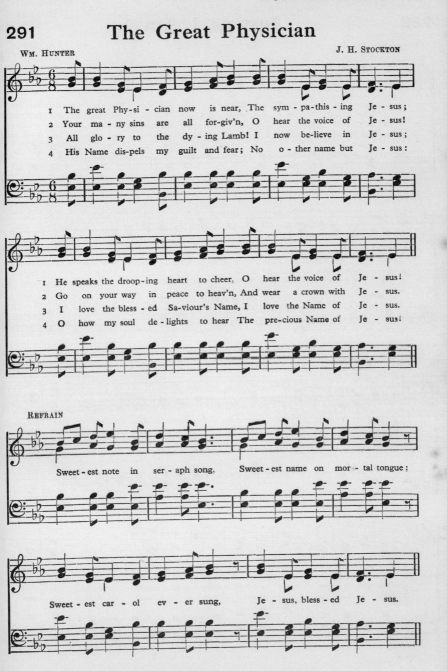

1 The great Phy-si - cian now is near, The sym - pa-this - ing Je - sus;
2 Your ma - ny sins are all for-giv'n, O hear the voice of Je - sus!
3 All glo - ry to the dy - ing Lamb! I now be-lieve in Je - sus;
4 His Name dis-pels my guilt and fear; No o - ther name but Je - sus:

1 He speaks the droop-ing heart to cheer, O hear the voice of Je - sus!
2 Go on your way in peace to heav'n, And wear a crown with Je - sus.
3 I love the bless - ed Sa-viour's Name, I love the Name of Je - sus.
4 O how my soul de - lights to hear The pre-cious Name of Je - sus!

REFRAIN

Sweet - est note in ser - aph song, Sweet - est name on mor - tal tongue;

Sweet - est car - ol ev - er sung, Je - sus, bless - ed Je - sus.

292
Just as I Am

CHARLOTTE ELLIOTT   WOODWORTH 8.8.8.8   WM. B. BRADBURY

1 Just as I am, with-out one plea, But that Thy blood was shed for me,
2 Just as I am, and wait - ing not To rid my soul of one dark blot,
3 Just as I am, Thou wilt re-ceive, Wilt wel - come, par-don, cleanse, re-lieve,
4 Just as I am, Thy love un-known Has bro - ken ev-'ry bar-rier down,

1 And that Thou bidst me come to Thee, O Lamb of God, I come, I come!
2 To Thee, whose blood can cleanse each spot, O Lamb of God, I come, I come!
3 Be - cause Thy pro - mise I be-lieve, O Lamb of God, I come, I come!
4 Now to be Thine, yea, Thine a-lone, O Lamb of God, I come, I come!

CHARLOTTE ELLIOTT   MISERICORDIA 8.8.8.6   HENRY SMART

1 Just as I am, with-out one plea, But that Thy blood was shed for me,
2 Just as I am, and wait-ing not To rid my soul of one dark blot,
3 Just as I am, Thou wilt re-ceive, Wilt wel-come, par-don, cleanse, re-lieve;
4 Just as I am, Thy love un-known Has bro-ken ev-'ry bar-rier down:

1 And that Thou bidst me come to Thee, O Lamb of God, I come!
2 To Thee, whose blood can cleanse each spot, O Lamb of God, I come!
3 Be-cause Thy pro - mise I be-lieve, O Lamb of God, I come!
4 Now to be Thine, yea, Thine a - lone, O Lamb of God, I come

293 Nothing but Thy Blood

RICHARD SLATER   RICHARD SLATER

1 Je - sus, see me at Thy feet, Noth-ing but Thy blood can save me;
2 See my heart, Lord, torn with grief, Noth-ing but Thy blood can save me;
3 Dark, in - deed, the past has been, Noth-ing but Thy blood can save me;
4 As I am, O hear me pray! Noth-ing but Thy blood can save me;
5 All that I can do is vain, Noth-ing but Thy blood can save me;
6 Lord, I cast my - self on Thee, Noth-ing but Thy blood can save me;

1 Thou a - lone my need canst meet, Noth-ing but Thy blood can save me.
2 Me un - par - don'd do not leave, Noth-ing but Thy blood can save me.
3 Yet in mer - cy take me in, Noth-ing but Thy blood can save me.
4 I can come no o - ther way, Noth-ing but Thy blood can save me.
5 I can ne'er re - move a stain, Noth-ing but Thy blood can save me.
6 From my guilt, O set me free! Noth-ing but Thy blood can save me.

REFRAIN

No! No! Noth-ing do I bring, But by faith I'm cling - ing

To Thy Cross, O Lamb of God! Noth-ing but Thy blood can save me.

By permission of the INTERNATIONAL MUSIC BOARD OF THE SALVATION ARMY

294 O Spotless Lamb!

C. BOOTH-CLIBBORN   C. BOOTH-CLIBBORN

1 O spot-less Lamb, I come to Thee! No long-er can I from Thee stay;
2 My hun-gry soul cries out for Thee, Come and for ev-er seal my breast;
3 I plunge be-neath Thy pre-cious blood, My hand in faith takes hold of Thee;

1 Break ev-'ry chain, now set me free, Take all my sins a-way.
2 To Thy dear arms at last I flee, There on-ly can I rest.
3 Thy prom-is-es just now I claim, Thou art e-nough for me.

REFRAIN

Take all my sins a-way! Take all my sins a-way!

O spot-less Lamb, I come to Thee; Take all my sins a-way!

295 The Steps of the Saviour

ELIZA E. HEWITT   WM. J. KIRKPATRICK

1 Try-ing to walk in the steps of the Sa-viour, Try-ing to
2 Press-ing more close-ly to Him who is lead-ing, When we are
3 Walk-ing in foot-steps of gen-tle for-bear-ance, Foot-steps of
4 Try-ing to walk in the steps of the Sa-viour, Up-ward, still

The Steps of the Saviour—*Continued*

1 fol - low our Sa - viour and King; Shap - ing our lives by His
2 temp - ted to turn from the way; Trust - ing the arm that is
3 faith - ful - ness, mer - cy, and love, Look - ing to Him for the
4 up - ward, we'll fol - low our Guide, When we shall see Him, 'the

1 bless - ed ex - am - ple, Hap - py, how hap - py, the songs that we bring.
2 strong to de - fend us, Hap - py, how hap - py our prais - es each day.
3 grace free - ly prom - is'd, Hap - py, how hap - py, our jour - ney a - bove.
4 King in His beau - ty,' Hap - py, how hap - py, our place at His side.

REFRAIN

How beau - ti - ful to walk in the steps of the Sa - viour!

Step-ping in the light, Step-ping in the light; How beau - ti - ful to

walk in the steps of the Sa - viour! Led in paths of light.

296

M. A. S.

Have Faith in God

MAY AGNEW STEPHENS

1. Do you ev-er feel down-heart-ed or dis-cour-aged? Do you
2. Dark-est night will al-ways come be-fore the dawn-ing, Sil-ver
3. God is might-y! He is a-ble to de-liv-er; Faith can

1. ev-er think your work is all in vain? Do the bur-dens thrust up-on you
2. lin-ings shine on God's side of the cloud; All your jour-ney He has promised
3. vic-tor be in ev-'ry try-ing hour; Fear, and care, and sin, and sor-row

1. make you trem-ble, And you fear that you shall ne'er the vic-t'ry gain? . . . vic-t'ry gain?
2. to be with you, Nought has come to you but what His love al-lowed. . . . His love al-lowed.
3. be de-feat-ed By our faith in God's al-might-y, conqu'ring pow'r. . . . conqu'ring pow'r.

CHORUS.

Have faith in God, ... the sun will shine, ...
Have faith in God, the sun will shine,

Tho' dark the cloud . . . . may be to-day; . . . .
Tho' dark the cloud may be to-day;

Have Faith in God—*Continued*

His heart hath plann'd .... your path and mine; ....
His heart hath plann'd   your path and mine;

Have faith in God, ... have faith al - way. ....
Have faith in God,   have faith al-way.

297

My Saviour Calling

E. W. BLANDLY   FOLLOW ME 8.8.8.9   J. S. NORRIS

1 I can hear my Sa-viour call-ing,   I can hear my Sa-viour call-ing,
2 I'll go with Him thro' the gar-den, I'll go with Him thro' the gar-den,
3 I'll go with Him thro' the judg-ment, I'll go with Him thro' the judg-ment,
4 He will give me grace and glo-ry,   He will give me grace and glo-ry,

REF.—Where He leads me I will fol-low,   Where He leads me I will fol-low,

1 I can hear my Sa-viour call-ing,   "Take thy cross and fol-low, fol-low Me."
2 I'll go with Him thro' the gar-den, I'll go with Him, with Him all the way.
3 I'll go with Him thro' the judg-ment, I'll go with Him, with Him all the way.
4 He will give me grace and glo-ry,   And go with me, with me all the way.

Where He leads me I will fol-low,   I'll go with Him, with Him all the way.

298 He Took My Place

E. E. HEWITT

JNO. R. SWENEY

1 A trem-bling soul, I sought the Lord, My sin con-fess'd, my guilt de-plor'd; How
2 Here rests my heart; as-sur-ance sweet His bless-ed work He will com-plete, Since
3 When sor-row veils the smil-ing day, When e-vil foes be-set my way, A-
4 No room for doubt, no room for fears, When to my view the Cross ap-pears, My

rit. REFRAIN

1 soft and sweet His word to me, 'I took thy place, and died for thee.'
2 in His love, so great and free, He took my place, and died for me.
3 bun-dant grace in Him I see, He took my place, and died for me.
4 joy-ful song shall ev-er be, He took my place, and died for me.

No

oth-er hope, ... no oth-er plea; . . . . He took my place,
No oth-er hope, no oth-er plea; He

. . . . and died for me; . . . O pre-cious Lamb . . . of Cal-va-
took my place, and died for me; pre-ci-ous Lamb

rit.

ry! . . . . He took my place, . . . and died for me.
of Cal-va-ry! He took my place, and died for me.

299   Soldiers of Zion, On we Go.

1. Sol - diers of Zi - on, on we go, Brave are the hearts that face the foe.
2. Hark to the trump that sounds for war, See how the flag goes on be - fore,
3. Sure as the Truth will dawn the day When gi - ant Wrong will end his sway,

CHORUS.—Sol - diers of Zi - on, on we go, Brave are the hearts that face the foe.

1. Vic - t'ry a-waits us, for we know We fol - low the Lord our King.
2. Look how the ranks swell more and more, As Je - sus the King leads on.
3. Bon - dagé and er - ror flee a - way, And earth to the Lord be - long.

Vic - t'ry a-waits us, for we know We fol - low the Lord our King.

1. Not by the might of hu - man arm, Not by the pow'r of earth to harm,
2. Strong are the hosts of Sin and Death, Strong - er the might of Him who saith,
3. Cour - age, ye souls who fight and plod, This is the path that wor - thies trod.

D.C. CHORUS.

1. But by the Spi - rit's ho - ly charm, Shall we the tri - umph sing.
2. "I will consume them with My breath!" Then will the field be won.
3. Gird up your loins, E - lect of God: Soon comes the vic - tor's song.

300 When Love Shines In

Mrs. Frank A. Breck

Wm. J. Kirkpatrick

1. Je - sus comes with pow'r to glad-den, When love shines in, Ev - 'ry life that
2. How the world will glow with beau-ty, When love shines in, And the heart re -
3. Dark - est sor - rows will grow brighter, When love shines in, And the heaviest
4. We may have un - fad - ing splendour, When love shines in, And a friendship

1. woe can sad-den, When love shines in. Love will teach us how to pray,
2. joice in du - ty, When love shines in. Tri - als may be sanc - ti - fied,
3. bur - den light-er, When love shines in. 'Tis the glo - ry that will throw
4. true and ten - der, When love shines in, When earth-vict'ries shall be won,

1. Love will drive the gloom a-way, Turn our darkness in - to day, When love shines in.
2. And the soul in peace a-bide, Life will all be glo - ri-fied, When love shines in.
3. Light to show us where to go; O the heart shall blessing know When love shines in.
4. And our life in heav'n be-gun, There will be no need of sun, For love shines in.

CHORUS.

When love shines in, . . . When love shines in, How the heart is
When love shines in, . .

When love shines in, When love shines in, When love shines in,

tuned to singing, When love shines in; . . When love shines in, . . When
When love shines in; . . When love shines in,

When Love Shines In—*Continued*

301 None but Christ can Satisfy

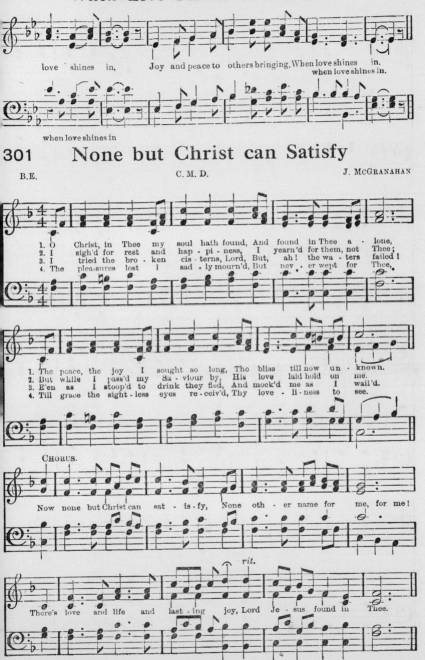

302 I Shall See Them Again

E. HUSBAND

E. HUSBAND

1. I shall see them again in the light of the morn-ing,
2. I shall know them again though ten thou-sand sur-round them,
3. 'Twas their lives in the past helped to fill me with glad-ness;
4. Would I wish for them back from their bright home in hea-ven?

1. When the night has pass'd by with its tears and its mourn-ing,
2. I shall hear their dear voice 'midst the bless-ed ones round them,
3. And the fu-ture is hea-ven, the home with no sad-ness,
4. No! in pa-tience I'll wait till the veil shall be ri-ven,

1. Where the light of God's love is the sun ev-er shin-ing,
2. And the love that was theirs on the earth shall de-tect them,
3. Where I see them to-day clad in bright robes of white-ness,
4. And the Sa-viour re-stores me the friends He has giv-en,

1. In the land where the wea-ry ones rest.
2. In the land where the wea-ry ones rest.
3. In the land where the wea-ry ones rest.
4. In the land where the wea-ry ones rest.

303 What a Reaping!

R. K. C.   R. KELSO CARTER

1. Oh! the sow - ing time seems wea - ry   And full oft the work - ers cry,
2. In the sor - row and the suff - 'ring,   When each breath is but a sigh;
3. When our hearts are strained to break-ing,   Comfort o - ther suff-'rers nigh;
4. For the love of Christ is flow - ing   In a stream that's nev - er dry;

1. To the Lord who rules the har - vest,   For the reap - ing by and by.
2. Tho' we sow in tears, re - mem - ber   There's a reap - ing by and by.
3 And our har - vest will be doub - led   In the reap - ing by and by.
4. He will wa - ter all our sow - ing,   For the reap - ing by and by.

CHORUS.

What a reap . . . ing,   reap . . . ing, What a
What a reap-ing, what a reap-ing, what a reap-ing that will be,

reaping it will be by and by (by and by),   Ev'ry sor-row we have known

Ev-'ry tear that we have sown, What a reap-ing it will be by and by!

304 The Same Old Way.

Johnson Oatman, Jr.

Geo. C. Hugg

1. The way our fa-thers travelled is good e-nough for me; They followed in the
2. The world may sneer and tell me I'll nev-er reach the goal, That good works are suf-
3. When bowers of sin en-tice me to rest my wea-ry feet, I find in Christ my
4. Mil-lions are now in glo-ry, in shin-ing white ar-rayed, Who travelled this same

1. foot-steps that led from Cal-'va-ry; It led them up to glo-ry, that
2. fi-cient to save a hu-man soul; But while the world is talk-ing, I
3. Sa-viour, a safe, a sure re-treat; He tells me to press on ward, and
4. path-way, and of-ten were dis-mayed; But hap-py now in glo-ry, they

D S.—My Sa-viour goes be-fore me, I

Fine.

1. land of end-less day; I ex-pect to get to hea-ven by the same old way.
2. still will watch and pray; I ex-pect to get to hea-ven by the same old way.
3. not look back, nor stay; I ex-pect to get to hea-ven by the same old way.
4. sing, both night and day; I ex-pect to get to hea-ven by the same old way.

fol-low Him each day; I ex-pect to get to hea-ven by the same old way.

Chorus.

O this bless-ed old way, it is good e-nough for me,

ritard.

D.S.

It is good e-nough for me, it is good e-nough for me;

305 The Sweet By-and-By

S. Fillmore Bennett

Jos. P. Webster

1. There's a land that is fair-er than day, And by faith we can see it a
2. We shall sing on that beau-ti-ful shore, The mel-o-di-ous songs of the
3. To our boun-ti-ful Fa-ther a-bove, We will of-fer our trib-ute of

1. far; For the Fa-ther waits o-ver the way, To pre-pare us a
2. blest, And our Spi-rits shall sor-row no more, Not a sigh for the
3. praise, For the glo-ri-ous gift of His love, And the bless-ings that

CHORUS.

1. dwelling place there. } In the sweet by-and-by, We shall
2. bless-ing of rest. } In the sweet by-and-by,
3. hal-low our days. }

meet on that beau-ti-ful shore, In the sweet by-and
by-and-by. by-and-by,

by, We shall meet on that beau-ti-ful shore.
by-and-by,

306 Onward and Upward

ELIZA E. HEWITT   JOHN R. SWENEY

1 On - ward still, and up - ward, Fol - low ev - er - more
2 On - ward, ev - er on - ward, Thro' the pas - tures green,
3 Up - ward, ev - er up - ward, T'ward the ra - diant glow,

1 Where our might - y Lead - er Goes in love be - fore;
2 Where the streams flow soft - ly Un - der skies se - rene;
3 Far a - bove the val - ley Where the mist hangs low;

1 Look - ing un - to Je - sus, Reach a help - ing hand
2 Or, if need be, up - ward O'er the rock - y steep,
3 On, with songs of glad - ness, Till the march shall end,

1 To a strug - gling neigh - bour, Help - ing him to stand.
2 Trust - ing Him to guide us, Strong to save and keep.
3 Where ten thou - sand, thou - sand Hal - le - lu - jahs blend.

Onward and Upward—*Continued*

REFRAIN

March-ing on - - - ward, Up -

March-ing on - ward, march-ing on - ward, on - ward, Up - ward

- - - - ward,

march-ing, up - ward, up - ward, March-ing stead - i - ly

March-ing on - - -

on - ward, Je - sus leads the way; March-ing on - ward, march-ing

- - ward, Up - - - - ward,

on - ward, on - ward, Up - ward march-ing, up - ward, up - ward,

On - ward un - to glo - ry to the per - fect day.

307 Good News for You

Old Revival Hymn   Redeemer's Song   *Arr.* R. F. Beveridge

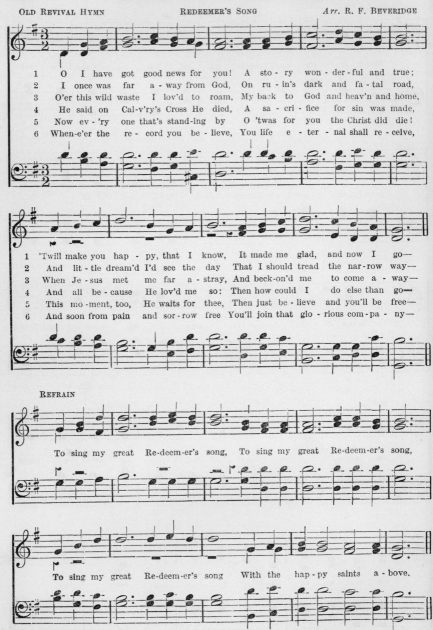

1. O I have got good news for you! A sto-ry won-der-ful and true;
2. I once was far a-way from God, On ru-in's dark and fa-tal road,
3. O'er this wild waste I lov'd to roam, My back to God and heav'n and home,
4. He said on Cal-v'ry's Cross He died, A sa-cri-fice for sin was made,
5. Now ev-'ry one that's stand-ing by O 'twas for you the Christ did die!
6. When-e'er the re-cord you be-lieve, You life e-ter-nal shall re-ceive,

1. 'Twill make you hap-py, that I know, It made me glad, and now I go—
2. And lit-tle dream'd I'd see the day That I should tread the nar-row way—
3. When Je-sus met me far a-stray, And beck-on'd me to come a-way—
4. And all be-cause He lov'd me so: Then how could I do else than go—
5. This mo-ment, too, He waits for thee, Then just be-lieve and you'll be free—
6. And soon from pain and sor-row free You'll join that glo-rious com-pa-ny—

REFRAIN

To sing my great Re-deem-er's song, To sing my great Re-deem-er's song,

To sing my great Re-deem-er's song With the hap-py saints a-bove.

The tune CAREY'S is on the following page

307 Good News for You

OLD REVIVAL HYMN   CAREY'S 8.8.8.8.8.8   HENRY CAREY

1 O I have got good news for you! A sto - ry
2 I once was far a - way from God, On ru - in's
3 O'er this wild waste I lov'd to roam, My back to
4 He said on Cal - v'ry's Cross He died, A sa - cri -
5 Now ev - 'ry one that's stand - ing by O 'twas for
6 When - e'er the re - cord you be - lieve, You life e -

1 won - der - ful and true; 'Twill make you hap - py that I
2 dark and fa - tal road, And lit - tle dream'd I'd see the
3 God and heav'n and home, When Je - sus met me far a -
4 fice for sin was made, And all be - cause He lov'd me
5 you the Christ did die! This mo - ment, too, He waits for
6 ter - nal shall re - ceive, And soon from pain and sor - row

REFRAIN

1 know, It made me glad and now I go
2 day That I should tread the nar - row way
3 stray, And beck - on'd me to come a - way
4 so: Then how could I do else than go   To sing my
5 thee, Then just be - lieve and you'll be free
6 free You'll join that glo - rious com - pa - ny

great Re - deem - er's song With the hap - py saints a - bove.

The tune REDEEMER'S SONG is on the preceding page

14

308 The Heavenly Pastures

M. A. WHITAKER

GEO. F. ROOT

1 In the heav'n-ly pas-tures fair, 'Neath the ten-der Shep-herd's
2 Far from all the noise and strife That dis-turb our dai-ly
3 O how good, and true, and kind Seek-ing His stray sheep to

1 care, Let us rest be-side the liv-ing stream to-day,
2 life, Let us pause a-while in si-lence and a-dore;
3 find, If they wan-der in-to dan-ger from His side!

1 Calm-ly there in peace re-cline, Drink-ing in the truth di-
2 Then the sound of His dear voice Will our wait-ing souls re-
3 Ev-er close-ly may we tread Where His ho-ly feet have

1 vine, As His lov-ing call we now with joy o-
2 joice, As He nam-eth us His own for ev-er-
3 led, So at last with Him in heav'n we may a-

The Heavenly Pastures—*Continued*

REFRAIN

1 bey.
2 more.
3 bide.

Glo - rious stream of life e - ter - nal,

Beau - teous fields of liv - ing green, liv - ing green,

Though re - veal'd with - in the word Of our Shep-herd and our Lord,

rit.

By the pure in heart a - lone can they be seen, ev - er seen.

309 Firmly Stand!

C. R. BLACKALL

W. H. DOANE

1 Firm-ly stand for God in the world's mad strife, Tho' the bleak winds roar, and the
2 Firm-ly stand for Right, with a mo-tive pure, With a true heart bold, and a
3 Firm-ly stand for Truth, it will serve you best; Tho' it wait-eth long, it is

1 waves beat high; 'Tis the Rock a-lone giv-eth strength and life, When the
2 faith e'er strong; 'Tis the Rock a-lone giv-eth tri-umph sure O'er the
3 sure at last; 'Tis the Rock a-lone giv-eth peace and rest When the

REFRAIN

1 hosts of sin are nigh.
2 world's ar-ray of wrong. } Let us stand on the Rock! Firm-ly
3 storms of life are past.

stand on the Rock; On the Rock of Christ a-lone: If the

strife we en-dure, We shall stand se-cure 'Mid the throng who sur-round the throne.

310 None Like Jesus

MAY MAURICE   WM. J. KIRKPATRICK

1 In the dew of ear-ly youth, None can help like Je-sus;
2 In the mid-day whirl of care, None can help like Je-sus;
3 In the twi-light's fad-ing glow, None can help like Je-sus;

1 Seek-ing af-ter pearls of truth, None can help like Je-sus;
2 When you heav-y bur-dens bear, None can help like Je-sus;
3 When your strength is ebb-ing slow, None can help like Je-sus:

1 He's the Source of liv-ing light, He will guide your steps a-right.
2 He will give you sweet-est rest, All who trust in Him are blest;
3 He will shield from death's a-larms, Fold you in His lov-ing arms.

1 None can help like Je-sus, No none like Je-sus.
2 None can help like Je-sus, No none like Je-sus.
3 None can help like Je-sus, No none like Je-sus.

311 It's Filling Me

JOHNSON OATMAN   HEAVENLY POWER 7.7.7.7. D   ADAM GEIBEL

1 All a - round this ver - y hour, Falls there streams of heav'n-ly pow'r;
2 Send us show'rs of heav'n-ly grace; Let Thy pres - ence fill this place;
3 Thou a - lone this pow'r canst give; With-out Thee I dare not live;

1 Fall - ing now so full and free; Praise the Lord, it's fill - ing me!
2 Speak the word and it shall be That Thy show - ers fall on me.
3 Give me pow'r to work for Thee; Let the stream reach e - ven me.

REFRAIN

Hal - le - lu - jah! feel the pow'r! Fall - ing like a might - y show'r,

Com - ing now so full and free; Praise the Lord, it's fill - ing me!

312 My Glorious Dress

N. L. Zinzendorf   Winchester New L.M.   *Musikalisches Handbuch*, 1690

1. Je - sus, Thy blood and right-eous-ness My beau - ty are, my glor-ious dress;
2. Bold shall I stand in Thy great day; For who aught to my charge shall lay?
3. When from the dust of death I rise To claim my man-sion in the skies,
4. Je - sus, be end-less praise to Thee Whose bound-less mer - cy hath for me,
5. O let the dead now hear Thy voice! Now bid Thy ban-ish'd ones re - joice;

1. 'Midst flam-ing worlds, in these ar - ray'd, With joy shall I lift up my head.
2. Ful - ly ab-solv'd through these I am From sin and fear, from guilt and shame.
3. Ev'n then, this shall be all my plea, Je - sus hath liv'd, hath died for me.
4. For me, a full a - tone - ment made, An ev - er-last-ing ran-som paid.
5. Their beau-ty this, their glo - rious dress, Je - sus, Thy blood and right-eous-ness.

N. L. Zinzendorf   Confidence L.M.   W. Moore

1. Je-sus, Thy blood and right - eous - ness My beau - ty are, my glor-ious dress;
2. Bold shall I stand in Thy great day; For who aught to my charge shall lay?
3. When from the dust of death I rise To claim my man - sion in the skies,
4. Je - sus, be end-less praise to Thee Whose bound-less mer - cy hath for me,
5. O let the dead now hear Thy voice! Now bid Thy ban - ish'd ones re - joice;

1. 'Midst flam-ing worlds, in these ar-ray'd, With joy shall I lift up my head.
2. Ful - ly ab-solv'd through these I am From sin and fear, from guilt and shame.
3. Ev'n then, this shall be all my plea, Je - sus hath lived, hath died for me.
4. For me, a full a-tone-ment made, An ev - er-last-ing ran - som paid.
5. Their beau - ty this, their glo-rious dress, Je - sus, Thy blood and right - eous - ness.

313 Jesus will Welcome Me There

F. J. Crosby   J. R. Sweney

1. O - ver the ri - ver they call me, Friends that are dear to my heart; . .
   heart, to my heart;
2. O - ver the ri - ver they call me; Hark! 'tis their voi - ces I hear, . . .
   voices I hear,
3. O - ver the ri - ver they call me, There, is no sor - row nor night; . .
   no sorrow nor night;
4. O - ver the ri - ver they call me, Watching with bright beaming eyes; . .
   beaming eyes;

1. Soon shall I meet them in glo - ry, Nev - er, no, nev - er to part . . .
2. Borne on the wings of the twi - light, Mur - mur - ing soft - ly and clear. .
3. There they are walking with Je - sus, Clothed in their garments of white. .
4. "O - ver the ri - ver, I'm com - ing," Glad - ly my spi - rit re - plies. .

CHORUS.

O - ver the ri - ver to E - den, Home to the mansions so fair;

An - gels will car - ry me safe - ly, Je - sus will welcome me there. .

314 We're Going Home

E. E. HEWITT   E. E. HEWITT

1 Let us sing a song that will cheer us by the way, In a lit-tle while we're
2 We will do the work that our hands may find to do, In a lit-tle while we're
3 We will smooth the path for some wea-ry, way-worn feet, In a lit-tle while we're
4 There's a rest be-yond, there's re-lief from ev-'ry care, In a lit-tle while we're

1 go-ing home; For the night will end in the ev-er-last-ing day, In a
2 go-ing home; And the grace of God will our dai-ly strength re-new, In a
3 go-ing home; O may lov-ing hearts spread a-round an in-flu'nce sweet In a
4 go-ing home; And no tears shall fall in that cit-y bright and fair, In a

REFRAIN

lit-tle while we're go-ing home. In a lit-tle while, In a
In a lit-tle while,

lit-tle while, We shall cross the bil-low's foam; We shall meet at last,
In a lit-tle while,

When the storm-y winds are past, In a lit-tle while we're go-ing home.

315 Count Your Mercies

FLORA KIRKLAND   CHARLES H. GABRIEL

1. Are you hea-vy la-den and with sor-row tried?
2. Think of hid-den dan-gers He has brought you through,
3. Does your path-way dark-en when the clouds draw near?
4. As He looks from hea-ven down on you and me,

1. Look in faith to Christ, your Help-er, Friend, and Guide;......
2. Of the cares and bur-dens He has borne for you,......
3. Count your ma-ny mer-cies, dry the flow-ing tear;......
4. Know you not He choos-eth what each day shall be?......

1. Think of all your mer-cies, such a bound-less store,
2. Of His words of com-fort in your deep-est need,
3. Trust Him in the sha-dows dim and have no fear;
4. Trust His lov-ing wis-dom, though the hot tears start,

1. Tears will change to prais-es as you count them o'er.
2. Count the times when Je-sus prov'd a Friend in-deed.
3. Heav'n will be the sweet-er for the dark down here.
4. Give to Him the in-cense of a grate-ful heart.

Count Your Mercies—*Continued*

REFRAIN

Count your mer - cies, such a bound - less store,
Count your man - y mer - cies, bound - less store,

Count your mer - cies, press'd and run - ning o'er,
Count your man - y mer - cies, run - ning o'er,

All your mer - cies, count them o'er and o'er;
All your mer - cies, count them o'er and o'er;

Lost in love and won - der at the bound - less store.

316

Give Him the Glory

ELISHA A. HOFFMAN

ELISHA A. HOFFMAN

1 It was down at the feet of Je - sus, O the hap - py, hap - py day!
2 It was down at the feet of Je - sus, Where I found such per - fect rest,
3 It was down at the feet of Je - sus, Where I bro't my guilt and sin,

1 That my soul found peace in be - liev - ing, And my sins were wash'd a - way.
2 Where the light first dawn'd on my spi - rit, And my soul was tru - ly blest.
3 That He can - cell'd all my trans - gres - sions, And sal - va - tion en - ter'd in.

REFRAIN

Let me tell the old, old sto - ry Of His grace so full and free,

For I feel like giv - ing Him the glo - ry For His won-drous love to me.

317

He that Winneth Souls

EMILY E. HEWITT.

J. M. HARRIS.

1 Bless - ed is the ser - vice of our Lord and King, Pre - cious
2 In the qui - et home- life, show - ing love's bright ray, More and
3 Out up - on the high- way, go - ing forth with pray'r, For the
4 Sow be - side all wa - ters, sow the Gos - pel seed, Here a

He that Winneth Souls—*Continued*

1 are the jew-els we may help to bring; Down the pass-ing
2 more like Je-sus, liv-ing ev-'ry day, We may guide a
3 lost and stray-ing, seek-ing ev-'ry-where, Close be-side the
4 word in sea-son, there a lov-ing deed, Sin-ners to the

rit. ad lib.

1 a-ges words of coun-sel ring, He that win-neth souls is wise.
2 dear one to the heav'n-ward way, He that win-neth souls is wise.
3 Shep-herd, we His joy may share, He that win-neth souls is wise.
4 Sav-iour be it ours to lead, He that win-neth souls is wise.

REFRAIN

He that win-neth souls is wise; In the
He that win-neth, win-neth souls is wise, In

home be-yond the skies, There's a crown of
the home be-yond, be-yond the skies,

rit. ad lib.

glo-ry, O the won-drous prize! He that win-neth souls is wise.

318 I'm a Pilgrim

MARY S. B. SHINDLER

J. LINCOLN HALL

1 I'm a pil - grim, and I'm a stran - ger;
2 Of that ci - ty to which I jour - ney,
3 There the sun - beams are ev - er shin - ing,

1 I can tar - ry, I can tar - ry but a night! ....
2 My Re - deem - er, my Re - deem - er is the light; ....
3 O my long - ing heart, my long - ing heart is there! ....

1 Do not de - tain me, For I am go - ing
2 There is no sor - row, nor a - ny sigh - ing
3 Here in this coun - try, so dark and drea - ry,

1 To where the foun - tains are ev - er flow - ing.
2 Nor a - ny tears there, nor a - ny dy - ing.
3 I long have wan - der'd for - lorn and wea - ry.

I'm a Pilgrim—*Continued*

319 Sweeter as the Days go By

EMILY E. HEWITT

JOHN R. SWENEY

1 The dear old sto-ry of a Sa-viour's love Is sweet-er as the days go by;
2 The sunbeams shining from the liv - ing Light Are bright-er as the days go by;
3 Hope's an-chor, hold-ing in the stor-my strife, Is strong-er as the days go by;
4 The peace that Je-sus gives to us a - new Is deep-er as the days go by;

1 The glad as - sur-ance of a home a - bove Is sweet-er as the days go by.
2 The stars of pro-mise cheering sor-row's night Are bright-er as the days go by.
3 We feel the throbbings of im-mor-tal life Grow strong-er as the days go by.
4 The prospects op'-ning to the Christian's view Are grand-er as the days go by.

REFRAIN

We'll fill the days with joy - ful praise, We'll sing as the hap-py mo-ments
We'll fill, we'll fill the days with joy-ful, joyful praise,

fly; The song of love to Him a-bove Grows sweeter as the days go by.
mo-ments fly;

320 His Love and Grace

E. C. GREEN E. A. HOFFMAN

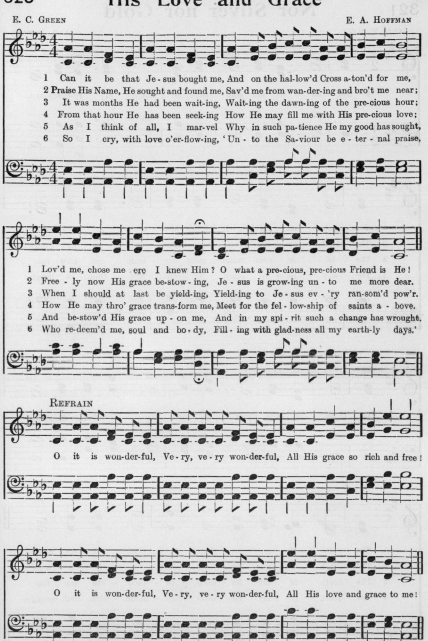

1 Can it be that Je-sus bought me, And on the hal-low'd Cross a-ton'd for me,
2 Praise His Name, He sought and found me, Sav'd me from wan-der-ing and bro't me near;
3 It was months He had been wait-ing, Wait-ing the dawn-ing of the pre-cious hour;
4 From that hour He has been seek-ing How He may fill me with His pre-cious love;
5 As I think of all, I mar-vel Why in such pa-tience He my good has sought,
6 So I cry, with love o'er-flow-ing, 'Un - to the Sa-viour be e - ter - nal praise,

1 Lov'd me, chose me ere I knew Him? O what a pre-cious, pre-cious Friend is He!
2 Free - ly now His grace be-stow - ing, Je - sus is grow-ing un - to me more dear.
3 When I should at last be yield-ing, Yield-ing to Je-sus ev - 'ry ran-som'd pow'r.
4 How He may thro' grace trans-form me, Meet for the fel - low-ship of saints a - bove.
5 And be-stow'd His grace up - on me, And in my spi - rit such a change has wrought.
6 Who re-deem'd me, soul and bo - dy, Fill - ing with glad-ness all my earth-ly days.'

REFRAIN

O it is won-der-ful, Ve - ry, ve - ry won-der-ful, All His grace so rich and free!

O it is won-der-ful, Ve - ry, ve - ry won-der-ful, All His love and grace to me!

321 Nor Silver nor Gold

JAMES M. GRAY

D. B. TOWNER

1-4 Nor sil - ver nor gold hath ob - tain'd my re-demp-tion.

1 No rich - es of earth could have sav'd my poor soul;
2 The guilt on my con - science too hea - vy had grown;
3 The ho - ly com - mand - ment for - bade me draw near;
4 The way in - to heav - en could not thus be bought;

1-4 The blood of the Cross is my on - ly foun - da - tion,

1 The death of my Sa - viour now mak - eth me whole.
2 The death of my Sa - viour could on - ly a - tone.
3 The death of my Sa - viour re - mov - eth my fear.
4 The death of my Sa - viour re - demp - tion hath wrought.

Nor Silver nor Gold—*Continued*

REFRAIN

I am re-deem'd, ... but not . with sil - -
I am re-deem'd, I am re-deem'd, but

ver, . . am bought, . . . but not with
not with sil - ver, ... I am bought, I am

gold; . . . . Bought with a price, ... the blood of
bought, but not with gold; . . . . . Bought with a price . . the

Je - sus, . . . Pre-cious price of love un - told.
pre-cious blood of Je-sus, Pre-cious price of love un - told.

322   How Sweet the Name!

JOHN NEWTON   ST. PETER C.M.   A. R. REINAGLE

1 How sweet the Name of Je-sus sounds In a be-liev-er's ear;
2 It makes the wound-ed spi-rit whole, And calms the trou-bled breast;
3 Dear Name! the rock on which I build, My shield, and hid-ing place,
4 Je-sus, my Shep-herd, Sa-viour, Friend, My Pro-phet, Priest, and King,
5 I would Thy bound-less love pro-claim With ev-'ry flee-ting breath;

1 It soothes his sor-rows, heals his wounds, And drives a-way his fears.
2 'Tis man-na to the hun-gry soul, And to the wea-ry rest.
3 My nev-er fail-ing treas-'ry fill'd With bound-less stores of grace.
4 My Lord, my Life, my Way, my End, Ac-cept the praise I bring.
5 So shall the mu-sic of Thy Name Re-fresh my soul in death.

JOHN NEWTON   LLOYD C.M.   CUTHBERT HOWARD

1 How sweet the Name of Je-sus sounds In a be-liev-er's ear;
2 It makes the wound-ed spi-rit whole, And calms the trou-bled breast;
3 Dear Name! the rock on which I build, My shield, and hid-ing place,
4 Je-sus, my Shep-herd, Sa-viour, Friend, My Pro-phet, Priest, and King,
5 I would Thy bound-less love pro-claim With ev-ry flee-ting breath;

1 It soothes his sor-rows, heals his wounds, And drives a-way his fears.
2 'Tis man-na to the hun-gry soul, And to the wea-ry rest.
3 My nev-er fail-ing treas-'ry fill'd With bound-less stores of grace.
4 My Lord, my Life, my Way, my End, Ac-cept the praise I bring.
5 So shall the mu-sic of Thy Name Re-fresh my soul in death.

By permission of JOHN T. PARK (Geo. Taylor), STAINLAND

323 The Good Old Way

Fanny J. Crosby
Jno. R. Sweney

1 We are trav'-ling on with our staff in hand, Walk-ing in the
2 We are trav'-ling on thro' a world of sin, Walk-ing in the
3 We are trav'-ling on in the Mas-ter's name, Walk-ing in the
4 We are trav'-ling on to the roll-ing tide, Walk-ing in the

1 good old way; We are pil-grims bound for the heav'n-ly land,
2 good old way; Tho' our foes are strong, we have peace with-in,
3 good old way; And we sing His praise with a loud ac-claim,
4 good old way; But we trust in Him who is still our Guide,

Refrain

1-4 Walk-ing in the good old way. Walk-ing in the bless-ed-ness of

love un-told, Trav'-ling to a coun-try that will ne'er grow old,

Je-sus, our Re-deem-er, we shall there be-hold, Home in the realms of day.

324   Keep Your Heart Singing

CHARLES H. GABRIEL   CHARLES H. GABRIEL

1. We may light-en toil and care, Or a heav-y bur-den share, With a word, a kind-ly deed, or sun-ny smile; We may gird le day and night With a ha-lo of de-light If we keep our hearts sing-ing all the while.

2. If His love is in the soul, And we yield to His con-trol, Sweet-est mu-sic will the lone-ly hours be-guile; We may drive the clouds a-way, Cheer and bless the dark-est day, If we keep our hearts sing-ing all the while.

3. How a word of love will cheer, Kin-dle hope and ban-ish fear, Soothe a pain, or take a-way the sting of guile! O how much we all may do In the world we tra-vel through! If we keep our hearts sing-ing all the while.

Keep Your Heart Singing—*Continued*

325   No, Never Alone

E. E. HEWITT   J. C. H. and V. A. WHITE

1 'Fear not, I am with thee'; Bless - ed gold - en ray,
2 Ros - es fade a - round me, Lil - ies bloom and die,
3 Steps un - seen be - fore me, Hid - den dan - gers near;

1 Like a star of glo - ry Light - ing up my way!
2 Earth - ly sun - beams van - ish, Ra - diant still the sky!
3 Near - er still my Sa - viour, Whis - p'ring, 'Be of cheer,'

1 Thro' the clouds of mid - night This bright prom - ise shone,
2 Je - sus, Rose of Shar - on, Bloom - ing for His own,
3 Joys, like birds of spring-time, To my heart have flown,

1 'I will nev - er leave thee, Nev - er will leave thee a - lone.'
2 Je - sus, hea-ven's sun - shine, Nev - er will leave me a - lone.
3 Sing-ing all so sweet - ly, 'He will not leave me a - lone.'

No, Never Alone—*Continued*

REFRAIN

No, nev-er a-lone,.................... No, nev-er a-

Nev-er a-lone, nev-er a-lone,

lone;............... He prom-ised nev-er to leave me,

Nev-er to leave me a-lone............ No, nev-er a-

Nev-er a-lone,

lone,.................... No, nev-er a-lone; He prom-ised

nev-er a-lone,

nev-er to leave me, Nev-er to leave me a-lone.

326 Glory to the Lamb!

L. M ROUSE   PRECIOUS SAVIOUR 8.7. 8.7. D   DORA BOOLE

1 Pre-cious Sa-viour, Thou hast sav'd me; Thine and on - ly Thine I am;
2 Long my yearn-ing heart was striv-ing To ob - tain this pre-cious rest;
3 Con - se - cra - ted to Thy ser - vice, I will live and die for Thee;
4 Glo - ry to the Lord who bought me! Glo - ry for His sav - ing pow'r!

1 O the cleans - ing blood has reach'd me! Glo - ry, glo - ry to the Lamb!
2 But when all my strug-gles end - ed, Sim - ply trust - ing, I was blest.
3 I will wit - ness to Thy glo - ry, Of sal - va - tion, full and free.
4 Glo - ry to the Lord who keeps me! Glo - ry, glo - ry, ev - er - more!

REFRAIN

Glo - ry, glo - ry, hal - le - lu - jah! Glo - ry, glo - ry to the Lamb!

O the cleans - ing blood has reach'd me! Glo - ry, glo - ry to the Lamb!

The tune ST. AMBROSE is on the next page

326 Glory to the Lamb!

L. M. ROUSE ST. AMBROSE 8. 7. 8. 7. D RICHARD CECIL

1 Pre - cious Sa - viour, Thou hast sav'd me; Thine and on - ly Thine I am;
2 Long my yearn - ing heart was striv - ing To ob - tain this pre - cious rest;
3 Con - se - cra - ted to Thy ser - vice, I will live and die for Thee;
4 Glo - ry to the Lord who bought me! Glo - ry for His sav - ing pow'r!

1 O the cleans - ing blood has reach'd me! Glo - ry, glo - ry to the Lamb!
2 But when all my strug - gles end - ed, Sim - ply trust - ing, I was blest.
3 I will wit - ness to Thy glo - ry, Of sal - va - tion, full and free.
4 Glo - ry to the Lord who keeps me! Glo - ry, glo - ry, ev - er - more!

REFRAIN

Glo - ry, glo - ry, hal - le - lu - jah! Glo - ry, glo - ry to the Lamb!

O the cleans - ing blood has reach'd me! Glo - ry, glo - ry to the Lamb!

The tune PRECIOUS SAVIOUR is on the previous page

327 Waiting for Me

W. C. MARTIN

EDWARD M. FULLER

1 Have you heard of that hea-ven-ly home, Just be-yond the rough wilds where we
2 How I long for that beau-ti-ful home, Just be-yond the dark vale and the
3 I will wel-come the dawn of the day, When the trum-pet shall call me a-

1 roam, Where the an-gels of light, And the saints rob'd in white, Lift their
2 tomb! For my lov'd ones are there, In those pal-a-ces fair, They are
3 way To my sweet peace-ful rest, In the home of the blest, In the

REFRAIN

1 voi-ces in song 'round the throne? Where Je-sus is
2 wait-ing for me by the throne. Where Je-sus is wait-ing, is
3 light of that ra-di-ant throne.

wait-ing for me, Where Je-sus is wait-ing for me, In those
Where Je-sus is wait-ing,

man-sions so fair, He has gone to pre-pare, Where Je-sus is wait-ing for me.......
is wait-ing for me.

328 Come, Ye that Fear the Lord

1. Come, ye that fear the Lord, Un-to Me, un-to Me; Come, ye that fear the Lord, Un-to Me! I've something good to say A-bout the nar-row way: For Christ the o-ther day Saved my soul, Saved my soul! For Christ the o-ther day saved my soul!

2. He gave me first to see What I was, what I was; He gave me first to see What I was! He gave me first to see My guilt and mis-e-ry, And then He set me free! Bless His Name! bless His Name! And then He set me free! Bless His Name!

3. My old com-pan-ions said, "He's un-done, he's un-done!" My old com-pan-ions said, "He's un-done!" My old com-pan-ions said, "He's sure-ly go-ing mad!" But Je-sus makes me glad! Bless His Name! bless His Name! But Je-sus makes me glad! Bless His Name!

4. Some said, "He'll soon give o'er, You shall see, you shall see!" Some said, "He'll soon give o'er, You shall see!" But time has passed a-way Since I be-gan to pray, And I feel His love to-day! Bless His Name! bless His Name! And I feel His love to-day! Bless His Name!

329 The Old-Fashioned Story

HARRIET E. JONES   D. B. TOWNER

1 There's an old-fash-ion'd sto-ry, And an old-fash-ion'd song,
2 There's a band of old sol-diers That to Je-sus be-long,
3 O the old-fash-ion'd sto-ry And the old-fash-ion'd song

1 That has glad-den'd the wea-ry Thro' the a-ges a-long,
2 Who have told this old sto-ry And have sung this old song,
3 O'er the broad earth are roll-ing! Win-ning souls all a-long;

1 In the old up-per cham-ber It was joy-ful-ly told,
2 In the heat of the bat-tle, In the face of the bold,
3 This sweet sto-ry of Je-sus And this glad song so old

1 O 'tis ver-y old-fash-ion'd! But as sweet as of old.
2 And to-day they will tell you, 'Tis as sweet as of old.
3 Shall be heard thro' the a-ges In that bright up-per fold.

The Old-Fashioned Story—*Continued*

O this old - fash - ion'd sto - ry And this old -

fash - ion'ed song Is a joy to the wea - ry

All life's jour - ney a - long; For they know, hal - le -

lu - jah! In the ci - ty of gold, They will

sing it for ev - er, This sweet sto - ry of old.

330   Jesus, Saviour, Pilot Me

EDWARD HOPPER   PILOT ME 7.7.7.7.7.7   J. E. GOULD

1   Je - sus, Sa - viour, pi - lot me   O - ver life's tem -
2   As a mo - ther stills her child   Thou canst hush the
3   When at last I reach the shore,   And the fear - ful

1   pes - tuous sea: Un - known waves be - fore me roll, . .
2   o - cean wild: Boist - 'rous waves o - bey Thy will . .
3   break - ers roar   'Twixt me and the peace - ful rest, . .

1   Hid - ing rock and treach - 'rous shoal: . . Chart and
2   When Thou sayst to them, 'Be still!' . . Won - drous
3   Then, while lean - ing on Thy breast, . . May I

1   com - pass come from Thee; Je - sus, Sa - viour, pi - lot me!
2   Sov - 'reign of the sea, Je - sus, Sa - viour, pi - lot me!
3   hear Thee say to me, 'Fear not, I will pi - lot thee!'

The tune TE LAUDANT OMNIA is on the following page

330   Jesus, Saviour, Pilot Me

EDWARD HOPPER   TE LAUDANT OMNIA 7.7.7.7.7.7.   JAMES F. SWIFT

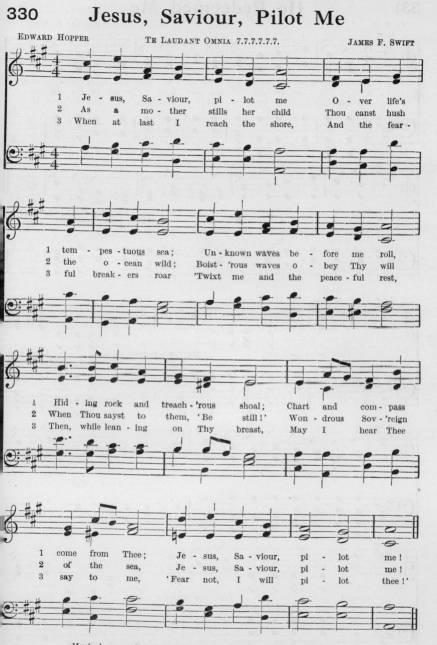

1 Je - sus, Sa - viour, pi - lot me   O - ver life's
2 As a mo - ther stills her child   Thou canst hush
3 When at last I reach the shore,   And the fear -

1 tem - pes - tuous sea;   Un - known waves be - fore me roll,
2 the o - cean wild;   Boist - 'rous waves o - bey Thy will
3 ful break - ers roar   'Twixt me and the peace - ful rest,

1 Hid - ing rock and treach - 'rous shoal;   Chart and com - pass
2 When Thou sayst to them, 'Be still!'   Won - drous Sov - 'reign
3 Then, while lean - ing on Thy breast,   May I hear Thee

1 come from Thee;   Je - sus, Sa - viour, pi - lot me!
2 of the sea,   Je - sus, Sa - viour, pi - lot me!
3 say to me,   'Fear not, I will pi - lot thee!'

Music by permission of JOHN T. PARK (Geo. Taylor), STAINLAND

The tune PILOT ME is on the preceding page

331 He Redeemed Me

G. F. R.

GEORGE F. ROOT

1. Would you know why Christ, my Saviour, Is my con-stant theme and song?
2. Oh, the days are full of gladness That I spend in His em-ploy!
3. Come, be-lov-ed, bow be-fore Him, Seek the par-don of your King,

1. Why to seek His lov-ing fa-vour Is my joy the whole day long?
2. I can ban-ish care and sadness In that song of heav'n-ly joy.
3. That on earth you may a-dore Him, And with saints in glo-ry sing.

CHORUS.

He re-deem'd me, He re-deem'd me, How the
He redeem'd me, He redeem'd me,

ransom'd choir re-peat it o'er and o'er; He re-
re-peat it o'er, He re-

deem'd me, He re-deem'd me, Glo-ry,
He redeem'd me, He redeem'd me,

He Redeemed Me—*Continued*

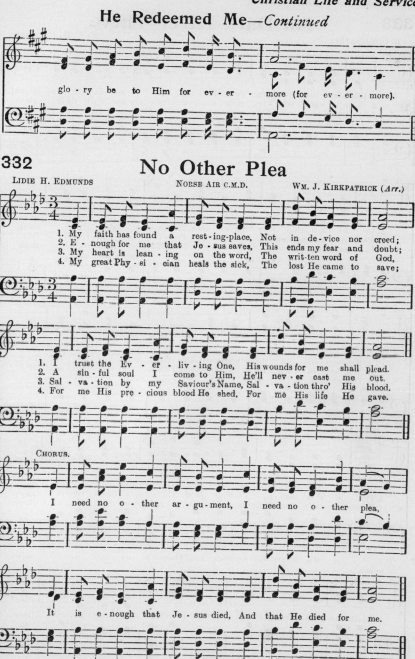

glo - ry be to Him for ev - er - more (for ev - er - more).

332

No Other Plea

LIDIE H. EDMUNDS

NORSE AIR C.M.D.

WM. J. KIRKPATRICK (*Arr.*)

1. My faith has found a rest - ing-place, Not in de - vice nor creed;
2. E - nough for me that Je - sus saves, This ends my fear and doubt;
3. My heart is lean - ing on the word, The writ - ten word of God,
4. My great Phy - si - cian heals the sick, The lost He came to save;

1. I trust the Ev - er - liv - ing One, His wounds for me shall plead.
2. A sin - ful soul I come to Him, He'll nev - er cast me out.
3. Sal - va - tion by my Saviour's Name, Sal - va - tion thro' His blood.
4. For me His pre - cious blood He shed, For me His life He gave.

CHORUS.

I need no o - ther ar - gu - ment, I need no o - ther plea,

It is e - nough that Je - sus died, And that He died for me.

333 No Dark River There

E. C. MACARTNEY

H. L. GILMOUR

1. When we have come to Jor-dan's tide, There'll be no dark riv-er there;
2. With an-gels bend-ing from a-bove, There'll be no dark riv-er there;
3. And when we've crossed the mys-tic tide, There'll be no dark riv-er there;
4. Let this blest thought fresh cour-age give, There'll be no dark riv-er there;

1. With Je-sus stand-ing close be-side, There'll be no dark riv-er there.
2. In fel-low-ship with Him we love, There'll be no dark riv-er there.
3. When we have reached the o-ther side, There'll be no dark riv-er there.
4. In that bright home of peace and love, There'll be no dark riv-er there.

1. His boundless grace shall light the place With beams of glo-ry fair,
2. His word di-vine shall bright-ly shine, His end-less life we'll share,
3. And hand in hand we'll walk the strand With loved ones bright and fair,
4. The gates a-jar, we see a-far, Be-yond this world of care;

FINE.

1. And in the sun-shine from His face, There'll be no dark riv-er there.
2. When all to Je-sus we re-sign, There'll be no dark riv-er there.
3. For in that hap-py heav'nly land, There'll be no dark riv-er there.
4. Though Jor-dan's stream may us di-vide, There'll be no dark riv-er there.

D.S. Up-on His breast we'll sweet-ly rest, There'll be no dark riv-er there.

CHORUS.

D.S.

There'll be no dark riv-er there, There'll be no dark riv-er there;

334 Seeds of Promise

JESSIE H. BROWN.

FRED. A. FILLMORE.

1. Oh, scat-ter seeds of lov-ing deeds, A-long the fer-tile field,
2. Tho' sown in tears thro' wea-ry years, The seed will sure-ly live;
3. The har-vest home of God will come, And af-ter toil and care;

1. For grain will grow from what you sow, And fruit-ful har-vest yield.
2. Tho' great the cost it is not lost, For God will fruit-age give.
3. With joy un-told your sheaves of gold, Will all be gar-ner'd there.

CHORUS.

Then day by day a-long your way, The seeds of
Then day by day a-long your way,

pro - - - mise cast, That ripen'd grain from hill and
The seeds of pro-mise cast, the seeds of promise cast, That ripen'd grain

plain, Be ga-ther'd home at last.
from hill and plain, Be gather'd home at last, be gather'd home at last.

335 The Christian's Rest

S. G. HARMER

W. McDonald

1 In the Christ-ian's home in glo-ry There re-mains a land of rest, Where the
2 He is fit-ting up my man-sion, Which e-ter-nal-ly shall stand, My
3 Pain nor sick-ness ne'er can en-ter, Grief nor woe my lot shall share; But in
4 Death it-self shall then be van-quish'd, And its sting shall be with-drawn; Shout with
5 Sing, O sing, ye heirs of glo-ry, Shout your tri-umphs as you go; Zi-on's

REFRAIN

1 Sa-viour's gone be-fore me To ful-fil my soul's re-quest.
2 stay shall not be trans-cient In that ho-ly, hap-py land.
3 that ce-les-tial cen-tre I a crown of life shall wear.
4 glad-ness, O ye ran-som'd Hail with joy the hap-py morn!
5 gates will o-pen to you, You shall find an en-trance through.

On the o-ther

side of Jor-dan, in the sweet fields of E-den, Where the Tree of Life is

bloom-ing, There is rest for you; There is rest for the wea-ry, There is

rest for the wea-ry, There is rest for the wea-ry, There is rest for you

336 I am His

G. WADE ROBINSON

I AM HIS 7.7.7.7.D

JAMES MOUNTAIN

1. Loved with ev - er - last-ing love, Led by grace that love to know;
2. Heaven a bove is soft - er blue, Earth a - round is sweeter green!
3. Things that once were wild a - larms Cannot now disturb my rest;
4. His for ev er, on - ly His; Who the Lord and me shall part?

1. Spir - it, breathing from a - bove, Thou hast taught me it is so!
2. Something lives in ev - 'ry hue, Christless eyes have ne - ver seen:
3. Closed in ev - er - last - ing arms, Pillowed on the lov - ing breast.
4. Ah, with what a rest of bliss, Christ can fill the lov - ing heart!

1. Oh this full and per - fect peace! Oh this trans - port all di - vine!
2. Birds with glad - der songs o'er - flow, Flowers with deep - er beau-ties shine,
3. Oh to lie for ev - er here, Doubt and care and self re - sign;
4. Heaven and earth may fade and flee, First-born light in gloom de - cline;

Repeat last two lines of each verse as CHORUS. p

1. In a love, which cannot cease, I am His, and He is mine.
2. Since I know, as now I know, I am His, and He is mine.
3. While He whis - pers in my ear— I am His, and He is mine!
4. But, while God and I shall be, I am His, and He is mine.

By permission of MARSHALL, MORGAN, and SCOTT, LTD.

337 He is Mine, I am His

GRACE ELIZABETH COBB   CHAS. H. GABRIEL

1. Bless-ed Lil-y of the Val-ley, oh, how fair is He! He is
2. Let me sing of all His mer-cies, of His kind-ness true, He is
3. Tho' He lead me thro' the val-ley of the shade of death, He is

1. mine, I am His; Sweeter than the an-gels' mu-sic is His
2. mine, I am His; Fresh at morn, and in the evening, comes a
3. mine, I am His; I am His; Should I fear, when oh, so ten-der-ly, He

He is mine,   D.S—Sweeter than the an-gels' mu-sic is His

FINE.

1. voice to me, He is mine, I am His! Where the lil-ies fair are
2. bless-ing new, He is mine, I am His! With the deep'ning shadows
3. whis-per-eth, He is mine, He is mine, I am His! For the sunshine of His

voice to me, He is mine, I am His!

1. blooming by the wa-ters calm, There He leads me, and up-holds me by His
2. comes a whis-per, "Safe-ly rest! Sleep in peace, for I am near thee, naught shall
3. presence doth il-lume the night, And He leads me thro' the val-ley to the

1. strong right arm; All the air is love a-round me, I can feel no harm,
2. thee mo-lest; I will lin-ger till the morn-ing, Keeper, Friend and Guest,"
3. moun-tain height: Out of bon-dage in-to freedom, in-to cloud-less light,

He is Mine, I am His—*Concluded.*

CHORUS.

He is mine, He is mine, I am His. Lil - y of the Val - ley, Bless-ed Lil - y of the Val - ley,

He is mine! Lil - y of the Val - ley, I am His!
Hal - le - lu - jah, He is mine! Bless-ed Lil - y of the Val - ley, I am His!

D.S.

---

338 Old Jordan's Waves

CHAS. J. BUTLER   JORDAN'S WAVES L.M.   CHAS. J. BUTLER

1. Some day, I know not when 'twill be, The an - gel death will come to me;
2. My sins He long a - go forgave, And still I feel His pow'r to save;
3. O'er me has sorrow's storm oft swept, Safe from the dan - ger me He's kept;
4. My lov'd ones they have cross'd the tide, But safe - ly cross'd with Christ their guide;
5. So when at death's cold brink I stand, My hand clasp'd in the Saviour's hand:

1. But this I know, if Christ be near, Old Jordan's waves I will not fear.
2. And if I keep the witness clear, Old Jordan's waves I will not fear.
3. If still I trust this friend so dear, Old Jordan's waves I will not fear.
4. They sweetly whispered in my ear, Old Jordan's waves I do not fear.
5. I too shall shout in tones so clear, Old Jordan's waves I do not fear.

True-Hearted

339

F. R. HAVERGAL   WATCHWORD   F. R. HAVERGAL

1 True-heart-ed, whole-heart-ed, faith-ful and loy-al, King of our lives
2 True-heart-ed, whole-heart-ed, full-est al-le-giance Yield-ing hence-forth
3 True-heart-ed, whole-heart-ed, Sa-viour all glo-rious! Take Thy great pow-

1 by Thy grace we will be! Un-der the stan-dard ex-alt-ed and roy-al,
2 to our glo-ri-ous King; Va-liant en-dea-vour and lov-ing o-be-dience
3 er and reign there a-lone; Ov-er our wills and af-fec-tions vic-to-rious,

REFRAIN *ff*

1 Strong in Thy strength we will bat-tle for Thee.
2 Free-ly and joy-ous-ly now would we bring. } Peal out the watch-word! si-lence
3 Free-ly sur-ren-der'd and whol-ly Thine own.

it nev-er! Song of our spi-rits re-joic-ing and free; Peal out the watch-

word! loy-al for ev-er, King of our lives, by Thy grace we will be!

The tune TRUE-HEARTED is on the next page

339 True-Hearted

F. R. HAVERGAL   TRUE-HEARTED 11.10.11.10. D   J. BOOTH

1 True-heart-ed, whole-heart-ed, faith-ful and loy-al, King of our lives,
2 True-heart-ed, whole-heart-ed! full-est al-le-giance yield-ing hence-forth
3 True-heart-ed, whole-heart-ed, Sa-viour all glo-rious! Take Thy great pow-

1 by Thy grace we will be: Un-der the stan-dard ex-alt-ed and roy-al,
2 to our glo-ri-ous King; Va-liant en-dea-vour and lov-ing o-be-dience
3 er and reign there a-lone: Ov-er our wills and af-fec-tions vic-to-rious.

REFRAIN

1 Strong in Thy strength we will bat-tle for Thee.
2 Free-ly and joy-ous-ly now would we bring.   Peal out the watch-word! si-lence
3 Free-ly sur-ren-der'd, and whol-ly Thine own.

it nev-er! Song of our spi-rits re-joic-ing and free; Peal out the watch-

word! loy-al for ev-er, King of our lives, by Thy grace we will be

By permission of CLIFFORD BOOTH   The tune WATCHWORD is on the previous page

340 God Helping Me, I'll Stand

W. C. MARTIN

EDWARD M. FULLER

1 A wor-thy sol-dier I would be Of Christ, who gave Him-self for me,
2 When o - ver me shall grand-ly wave The ban - ner of the mar-tyr'd brave,
3 Tho' I be wea-ry in the fight, And Sa - tan's le-gions, in their spite,

1 O - bey-ing His com - mand; And with the gos - pel shield and sword,
2 God's faith - ful, stead-fast band, Be - neath which none e'er fought in vain,
3 At - tack on ev - 'ry hand, I'll stand by Christ, my faith - ful Friend,

1 For truth and right, with Christ my Lord, God help - ing me, I'll stand!
2 All foes and dan - gers I'll dis - dain; God help - ing me, I'll stand!
3 And stead - i - ly un - to the end, God help - ing me, I'll stand!

REFRAIN

God help - ing me, I'll stand; With His un-yield-ing band;
I'll stand! With His un - yield-ing band;

All times and ev - 'ry - where for Christ, God help - ing me, I'll stand!

By permission of the CHARLES M. ALEXANDER COPYRIGHTS TRUST

341 Never Mind: Go On!

R. SLATER

HERBERT H. BOOTH

1 { In the fight, say, does your heart grow wea-ry? Do you find your path is rough and
 { Lay a - side all fear, and, on-ward press-ing, Brave - ly fight, and God will give His
2 { Faith-ful be, de - lay - ing not to fol - low Where Christ leads, tho' it may be thro'
 { Cheer-ful be, it will your bur-dens light-en, One glad heart will al-ways o - thers
3 { When down-heart-ed look a - way to Je - sus, Who for you did shed His blood most
 { Do your best in fight-ing for your Sa-viour, For His sake fear not to lose men's

cres. *f*

1 { thor - ny, And a - bove, the sky is dark and stor - my? Nev-er mind: go on!
 { bless - ing; Tho' the war at times may prove distress - ing, Nev-er mind: go on!
2 { sor - row; If the strife should fierc - er grow to-mor - row, Nev-er mind: go on!
 { bright-en, Tho' the strife the cow-ard's soul may fright-en, Nev-er mind: go on!
3 { prec-ious; Let us say, tho' all the world should hate us, Nev-er mind: go on!
 { fa - vour, If be - side you should a com - rade wa - ver, Nev-er mind: go on!

REFRAIN

When the road we tread is rough, Let us bear in mind, In our Sa-viour

cres.

strength e - nough We may al - ways find; Though the fight - ing may be tough,

ff Go on, go on, to vic - t'ry.

Let our mot-to be, Go on, go on to vic - t'ry!

By permission of the INTERNATIONAL MUSIC BOARD OF THE SALVATION ARMY

342 The Promised Home

J. LUTTON

JOHN R. SWENEY

1. There's a place in heav'n pre-pared for me, When the toils of this
2. In my Fa-ther's home are man-sions bright, Je-sus says it, and I
3. Ma-ny dear ones we lov'd are be-fore the throne, In that hap-py, hap-py
4. In that home a-bove, be-yond the skies, free from sickness, pain, and

1. life are o'er; Where the saints, rob'd in white, shall for ev-er be,
2. know 'tis true; There's a home for me in that land of light,
3. home on high; I shall walk with them thro' the streets of gold,
4. death I'll be, There with Je-sus to reign for ev-er-more,

CHORUS.

1. Sing-ing prais-es for ev-er-more.
2. Bro-ther, sis-ter, there is one for you.
3. I shall wear a star-ry crown by-and-by.
4. Through-out all e-ter-ni-ty.

Je-sus promised me a

home o-ver there, Je-sus promised me a home o-ver there; No more

sick-ness, sor-row, pain or death, Je-sus promis'd me a home o-ver there.

343 Tell It to Jesus

HERBERT H. BOOTH   HERBERT H. BOOTH

1. Tell it to Jesus, He understands thee, Reads all the secret in tents of thy heart; Foes may misjudge and friends may mistake thee, He will not deal with thee but as thou art.

2. Tell it to Jesus, He understands thee, Knows all thy sorrows, and sees all thy tears; Knows all the hidden pow'rs that withstand thee, Knows all thy tremblings, thy doubts and thy fears.

3. Tell it to Jesus, He understands thee, He can explain ev'ry mys't'ry of life; He can unravel tangles that try thee, He can speak peace 'midst thy turmoil and strife.

4. Tell it to Jesus, He understands thee, Seeks by His spirit to perfect thy soul; Sorrows and trials He sends to refine thee, Tell Him thy case, not in part, but in whole.

5. Tell it to Jesus, He understands thee, Hide not thy faults, and excuse not thy sin; For in the day of account He will greet thee, Not as thou art from without, but within.

mf CHORUS. *Allegretto.*

Tell it to Jesus, He understands thee, What is thy gain, and what is thy loss; While thou art His no harm can befall thee, Tell out thy heart at the foot of His cross.

344 A Channel of Blessing

H. G. Smyth   H. G. Smyth

1 Is your life a chan-nel of bless-ing? Is the love of God flow-ing
2 Is your life a chan-nel of bless-ing? Are you bur-den'd for those that
3 Is your life a chan-nel of bless-ing? Is it dai - ly tell-ing
4 We can-not be chan-nels of bless-ing If our lives are not free from

1 thro' you? Are you tell-ing the lost of the Sa-viour? Are you rea-dy
2 are lost? Have you urged up-on those who are stray-ing, The Sa-viour
3 for Him? Have you spo-ken the word of sal-va-tion To those who
4 all sin; We will bar-ri-ers be and a hin-drance To those we

REFRAIN

1 His ser-vice to do?
2 who died on the Cross?
3 are dy-ing in sin?
4 are try-ing to win.

Make me a chan-nel of bless-ing to-day!

Make me a chan-nel of bless-ing, I pray! My life pos-sess-ing,

rit.

my ser-vice bless-ing, Make me a chan-nel of bless-ing to-day!

345 The Precious Blood

MACLEOD WYLIE   CRIMSON TIDE C.M.D.   GEO. C. STEBBINS

1. The blood has al-ways pre-cious been, 'Tis pre-cious now to me;
2. I will re-mem-ber now no more, God's faith-ful Word has said,
3. Not all my well-re-membered sins Can star-tle or dis-may;
4. Per-haps this fee-ble frame of mine Will soon in sick-ness lie,

1. Through it a-lone my soul has rest, From fear and doubt set free.
2. The fol-lies and the sins of him For whom My Son has bled.
3. The pre-cious blood a-tones for all And bears my guilt a-way.
4. But rest-ing on the prec-ious blood How peace-ful-ly I'll die.

CHORUS.

Oh, won-drous is the crim-son tide Which from my Sa-viour flowed;

And still in heav'n my song shall be, The pre-cious, precious blood.

346 Sowing and Reaping

ELLA LAUDER

D. B. TOWNER

1. Sow flow-ers and flow-ers will blos-som A - round you wher-
2. Sow bless-ings, and bless-ings will rip - en, Sow ha - tred, and
3. Sow love, and its sweet-ness up - ris - ing Shall fill all your
4. In faith sow the word of the Mas - ter, A bless-ing He'll
5. Preach Christ in His won - der - ful full - ness, That all His sal-

1. ev - er you go; Sow weeds, and of weeds reap the har - vest,
2. ha - tred will grow; Sow mer - cy, and reap sweet com-pas - sion,
3. heart with its glow; Sow hope, and re - ceive its fru - i - tion,
4. sure - ly be - stow; And souls shine like stars for your crown-ing,
5. va - tion may know; Reap life thro' the a - ges e - ter - nal,

REFRAIN

You'll reap what-so - ev - er you sow. You'll reap what-so - ev - er you
You'll reap, sure-ly reap what-so-

sow, ... You'll reap what - so - ev - er you sow, ... The
ev - er you sow, You'll reap, sure-ly reap what - so - ev - er you sow,

har - vest is cer-tain-ly com-ing, You'll reap what-so-ev-er you sow.

347   O how He Loves Me!

JOHNSON OATMAN   H. L. GILMOUR

1 I have a Friend, a pre-cious Friend,   O   how He loves me!
2 Why He should come, I can-not tell,   O   how He loves me!
3 He died to save my soul from death,   O   how He loves me!
4 He walks with me a-long life's road,   O   how He loves me!
5 He has a home pre-par'd for me,   O   how He loves me!

1 He says His love will nev-er end,   O   how He loves me!
2 In my poor brok-en heart to dwell,   O   how He loves me!
3 I'll praise Him while He gives me breath,   O   how He loves me!
4 He car-ries ev-'ry heav-y load,   O   how He loves me!
5 With Him I'll spend e-ter-ni-ty,   O   how He loves me!

REFRAIN

O how He loves me!   O how He loves me!

I know not why, I on-ly cry,   O how He loves me!

348 For Ever with the Lord

JAMES MONTGOMERY   NEARER HOME   I. B. WOODBURY, *Arr.* SULLIVAN

1 For ev - er with the Lord! A - men, so let it be!
2 My Fa-ther's house on high, Home of my soul, how near
3 For ev - er with the Lord! Fa - ther, if 'tis Thy will,
4 So when my la - test breath Shall rend the veil in twain,

1 Life from the dead is in that word; 'Tis im - mor - tal - i - ty,
2 At times to faith's fore - see - ing eye Thy gol - den gates ap - pear!
3 The pro - mise of that faith - ful word, E'en here to me ful - fil.
4 By death I shall es - cape from death, And life e - ter - nal gain.

1 Here in the bo - dy pent, Ab - sent from Him I roam;
2 My thirst - y spi - rit faints To reach the land I love,
3 Be Thou at my right hand, Then can I nev - er fail;
4 Know - ing as I am known, How shall I love that word!

1 Yet night - ly pitch my mov - ing tent A day's march near - er home.
2 The bright in - her - it - ance of saints— Je - ru - sa - lem a - bove.
3 Up - hold Thou me, so I shall stand, Fight, and I must pre - vail.
4 And oft re - peat be - fore the throne, For ev - er with the Lord!

REFRAIN

Near - er home, near - er home, A day's march near - er home.

The tune ISHMAEL is on the following page

348 ## For Ever with the Lord!

JAMES MONTGOMERY   ISHMAEL S.M.D.   CHARLES VINCENT

Unison

1 For ev-er with the Lord!   A-men, so let it be!
2 My Fa-ther's house on high,   Home of my soul, how near
3 For ev-er with the Lord!   Fa-ther, if 'tis Thy will,
4 So, when my la-test breath   Shall rend the veil in twain,

Harmony

1 Life from the dead is in that word; 'Tis im-mor-tal-i-ty.
2 At times to faith's fore-see-ing eye Thy gold-en gates ap-pear!
3 The pro-mise of that faith-ful word, E'en here to me ful-fil.
4 By death I shall es-cape from death, And life e-ter-nal gain.

1 Here in the bo-dy pent, Ab-sent from Him I roam;
2 My thirst-y spi-rit faints To reach the land I love,
3 Be Thou at my right hand, Then can I nev-er fail;
4 Know-ing as I am known, How shall I love that word!

1 Yet night-ly pitch my mov-ing tent A day's march near-er home.
2 The bright in-her-it-ance of saints—Je-ru-sa-lem a-bove.
3 Up-hold Thou me, so I shall stand, Fight, and I must pre-vail.
4 And oft re-peat be-fore the throne, For ev-er with the Lord!

The tune NEARER HOME is on the previous page

349 The Healing Waters

INA DULEY OGDON

P. P. BILHORN

1 I've cast my heav-y bur-dens down on Ca-naan's hap-py shore,
2 With Is-rael's trust-ing chil-dren I'm re - joic-ing on my way,
3 My hun-g'ring soul is sa - tis-fied with man-na from a-bove,
4 I'm sing-ing 'Hal - le - lu - jah,' safe - ly an-chor'd is my soul,

1-4 I'm liv-ing where the heal-ing wa-ters flow;

1 I'll wan-der in the wil-der-ness of doubt and sin no more;
2 The cloud-y, fier-y pil-lar is my guid-ing light to-day;
3 No more I thirst, the Rock I've found, that fount of end-less love;
4 I'm rest-ing on His pro-mis-es; the blood has made me whole;

1-4 I'm liv-ing where the heal-ing wa-ters flow, wa-ters flow.

REFRAIN

Liv-ing on the shore, I'm liv-ing on the shore, I'm liv-ing where

The Healing Waters—*Continued*

the heal-ing wa-ters flow; Liv-ing on the shore, I'm liv-ing

on the shore, I'm liv-ing where the heal-ing wa-ters flow (wa-ters flow).

Alternative tune when the REFRAIN is used alone

I. D. OGDON GEORGE ALLEN

Liv-ing on the shore, I'm liv-ing on the shore, I'm liv-ing where the heal-

ing wa-ters flow, I'm liv-ing on the shore, I'm liv-

heal-ing wa-ters flow,

ing on the shore, I'm liv-ing where the heal-ing wa-ters, flow.

heal-ing wa-ters flow.

flow.

350 Roll the Sea Away

H. J. Zelley

H. L. Gilmour

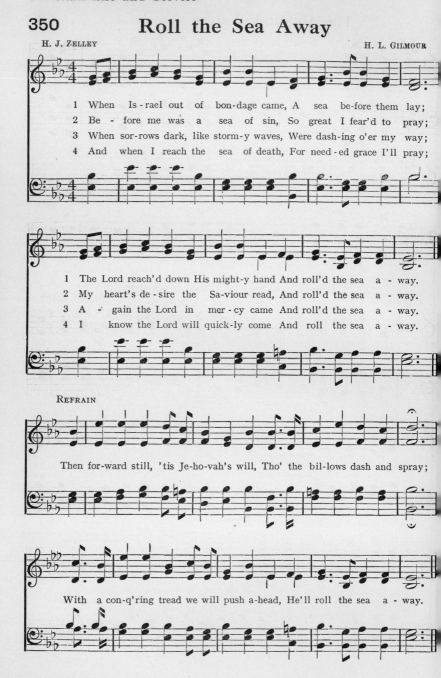

1 When Is-rael out of bon-dage came, A sea be-fore them lay;
2 Be - fore me was a sea of sin, So great I fear'd to pray;
3 When sor-rows dark, like storm-y waves, Were dash-ing o'er my way;
4 And when I reach the sea of death, For need-ed grace I'll pray;

1 The Lord reach'd down His might-y hand And roll'd the sea a - way.
2 My heart's de-sire the Sa-viour read, And roll'd the sea a - way.
3 A - gain the Lord in mer-cy came And roll'd the sea a - way.
4 I know the Lord will quick-ly come And roll the sea a - way.

REFRAIN

Then for-ward still, 'tis Je-ho-vah's will, Tho' the bil-lows dash and spray;

With a con-q'ring tread we will push a-head, He'll roll the sea a - way.

351 Jehovah Tsidkenu

R. M. M'CHEYNE CLARENDON STREET 11.11.11.11 A. J. GORDON

1. I once was a stranger To grace and to God,
I knew not my danger And felt not my load;
Tho' friends spoke in rapture Of Christ on the tree,
Jehovah Tsidkenu Was nothing to me.

2. Like tears from the daughters Of Zion that roll,
I wept when the waters Went over His soul;
Yet thought not that my sins Had nail'd to the tree
Jehovah Tsidkenu: 'Twas nothing to me.

3. When free grace awoke me By light from on high,
Then legal fears shook me, I trembled to die;
No refuge, no safety, In self could I see,
Jehovah Tsidkenu My Saviour must be.

4. My terrors all vanish'd Before the sweet Name;
My guilty fears banish'd, With boldness I came
To drink at the fountain, Life-giving and free,
Jehovah Tsidkenu Is all things to me.

5. E'en treading the valley, The shadow of death,
This watch-word shall rally My faltering breath;
For when from life's fever My God sets me free,
Jehovah Tsidkenu My death song shall be.

352 Christ Arose!

ROBERT LOWRY

ROBERT LOWRY

1 Low in the grave He lay— Je - sus, my Sav - iour! Wait - ing the
2 Vain - ly they watch His bed— Je - sus, my Sav - iour! Vain - ly they
3 Death can - not keep His prey— Je - sus, my Sav - iour! He tore the

REFRAIN *Faster*

1 com-ing day— Je - sus, my Lord! Up from the grave He a - rose!
2 seal the dead— Je - sus, my Lord!
3 bars a - way— Je - sus, my Lord!
He a - rose!

With a might - y tri - umph o'er His foes; He a - rose a
He a - rose!

Vic - tor from the dark do-main, And He lives for - ev - er with His saints to reign;

He a - rose! He a - rose! Hal - le - lu - jah! Christ a - rose!
He a - rose! He a - rose!

353 No one like the Saviour

JOHNSON OATMAN

JOHN R. SWENEY

1 Who can wash a sin-ner's guilt a-way? There is no one like the
2 When we're low-ly bent with grief and care, There is no one like the
3 When we're tem-pest toss'd up-on life's deep, There is no one like the
4 When we feel the i-cy touch of death, There is no one like the
5 O-ver in that blest home of the soul, There is no one like the

1 Saviour, hal-le-lu-jah! Who can turn his dark-ness in-to day? There is
2 Saviour, hal-le-lu-jah! He speaks and the sun-beams lin-ger there, There is
3 Saviour, hal-le-lu-jah! He speaks and the wild waves hush to sleep, There is
4 Saviour, hal-le-lu-jah! He will take us at our clos-ing breath, There is
5 Saviour, hal-le-lu-jah! This shall be our song while a-ges roll, There is

REFRAIN

no one like the Sav-iour, hal-le-lu-jah! Oh glo-ry, glo-ry, hal-le-

lu-jah! There is no one like the Saviour, hal-le-lu-jah! While we live or

die, in the earth or sky, There is no one like the Saviour, hal-le-lu-jah!

354 I'm Going Home at Last

JOHNSON OATMAN   ADAM GEIBEL.

1. When I see life's gold-en sun-set light-ing up the ro-sy west,
2. Tho' the road at times was wea-ry o-ver which my feet have trod,
3. When I pass down thro' the val-ley and the sha-dow of the dead,

1. When the sha-dows back-ward o'er my way are cast, I shall look up-on that
2. Tho' thro' ma-ny trib-u-la-tions I have passed, Yet I soon will reach my
3. To my bless-ed Sa-viour's hand I will hold fast; He has pro-mised to go

1. mo-ment as the one su-preme-ly blest; I'm go-ing home at last.
2. man-sion in the ci-ty of our God; I'm go-ing home at last.
3. with me, so my soul will have no dread; I'm go-ing home at last.

CHORUS.

I'm go-ing home at last, I'm go-ing home at last; When my
       at last,   at last:

work on earth is end-ed and my race be-low is run I'm go-ing home at last.

355

Beyond the Shadows

Irvin H. Mack   J. Lincoln Hall

1. When the trou-bles ga - ther And the bil - lows roll, Dark the way be -
2. Tho' you can - not fa-thom Why you're called to bear All the hea - vy
3. Go, with faith, to con-quer Tri - als that ap - pear: Know that Christ your
4. Tho' se - vere the con-flict And the an - guish deep; Tho' the tri - al's
5. Tried and found not want-ing Will the Mas - ter say; Tried yet ev - er

1. fore you Cares op - press the soul, There is bless-ed sunshine Just be-yond your view;
2. burdens That you can-not share, Keep the cross be-fore you in the dark-est day;
3. Saviour With His help is near. Ne'er give up the bat-tle, Hard though it may be,
4. hea - vy That may o'er you sweep; God is al - ways near you, Giving strength to bear,
5. faithful, All a - long life's way; Tried as in the fur-nace Of re - fin - ing fire,

CHORUS.

1. Oft 'tis but a tri - al You are go - ing thro'.
2. Put your trust in Je - sus All a - long the way.
3. For your Lord has pro-mised You the vic - to - ry.   See the sun-light,
4. All the hea - vy bur-dens When they shall ap - pear.
5. You shall see the tri - umph of your heart's de - sire.

shining bright and clear; Bless-ed sunlight drives a - way all fear; Look a - bove you,

clouds will dis - ap - pear; Put your trust in Je - sus, He is ev - er near.

356 Jesus Leads My Footsteps

1. They tell me there are dan-gers In the path my feet must
2. They tell me life has tri - als, And the fair - est hopes will
3. I know my heart is sin - ful, And my love is all too

1. tread, But they can-not see the glo-ry That is shin-ing round my head.
2. flee, But I trust my all to Je - sus, For I know He cares for me.
3. small, But with Je - sus' arms a - round me, I shall win and con-quer all.

CHORUS.

Oh! 'tis Je - sus leads my foot-steps, He has made my heart His

own, For I would not dare to jour-ney Thro' the wide, wide world a - lone.

357   We're Marching to Zion.

I. WATTS.

R. LOWRY.

1. Come, ye that love the Lord, And let your joys be known; Join
2. Let those re - fuse to sing Who nev - er knew our God: But
3. The hill of Zi - on yields A thou - sand sa - cred sweets; Be -
4. Then let our songs abound, And ev - 'ry tear be dry; We're

1. in a song with sweet ac - cord, Join in a song with sweet ac - cord, And
2. chil - dren of the heav'n - ly King, But chil - dren of the heav'n - ly King Shall
3. fore we reach the heav'n - ly fields, Be - fore we reach the heav'n - ly fields, Or
4. march - ing thro' Im - man - uel's ground, We're marching thro' Im - man-uel's ground To

And

1. thus sur - round the throne, And thus sur - round the throne.
2. speak their joys a - broad, Shall speak their joys a - broad.
3. walk the gold - en streets, Or walk the gold - en streets.
4. fair - er worlds on high, To fair - er worlds on high.

thus surround the throne, And thus sur - round the throne.

CHORUS.

We're march - ing to Zi - on, Beau - ti - ful, beau - ti - ful, Zi - on: We're
We're march - ing on to Zi - on,

march-ing upward to Zi - on, The beau - ti - ful cit - y of God.
Zi - on, Zi - on,

358 # The Gospel Light

JOHNSON OATMAN

ADAM GEIBEL

1. Standing like a light-house on the shores of time, Look-ing o'er the waves of
2. There are hu-man shipwrecks ly-ing all around! O what mo-ral darkness
3. Do not let the bush-el co-ver up your light, Keep your lamp in or-der,
4. Try to live for Je-sus till this life is o'er, For a-long this pathway

darkness, sin and crime, O-pen up your windows, there's a work sub-lime:
ev-'ry-where is found! Warn some o-ther ves-sels off from dang'rous ground:
trimmed and burning bright; Try to be a blessing, bright-en up the night:
you will pass no more; Till He bids you wel-come on the o ther shore,

CHORUS.

Let the gos-pel light shine out........ Let the gos-pel light shine

out, shine out, Let the gos-pel light shine out, shine out, While your lamp is

burn-ing, keep the win-dows clean, Let the gos-pel light shine out.

359 The Blessed Sunlight

A. F. MYERS

A. F. MYERS

1. Would you al - ways cheer - ful be? Let the blessed sun - light in;
2. Would you bright - en drea - ry days? Let the blessed sun - light in;
3. Would you ease a bur - den'd heart? Let the blessed sun - light in;
4. Would you speed the truth a - broad? Let the blessed sun - light in;

Would you bid the dark - ness flee? Let the blessed sun - light in.
Would you fill your heart with praise? Let the blessed sun - light in.
Would you joy and strength im - part? Let the blessed sun - light in.
Would you bring the world to God? Let the blessed sun - light in.

CHORUS.

Let the bless - ed sun - light, sun - light in, Let the bless - ed
Let the bless - ed sun - light in, Let the bless - ed

sun - light in; Would you nev - er wea - ry When the days are
sun - light, sun - light in;

Repeat softly.

drear - y? Let the bless - ed sun - light in.
sun - light in.

16

360 The Lily of the Valley

C. W. FRY   *Arr.* JOSHUA GILL

1 I've found a Friend in Je - sus, He's ev - 'ry-thing to me,
2 He all my grief has tak - en and all my sor - rows borne;
3 He'll nev - er, nev - er leave me, nor yet for - sake me here,

1 He's the Fair - est of Ten Thous-and to my soul; The Li - ly
2 In temp - ta - tion He's my strong and migh - ty tow'r; I've all for
3 While I live by faith and do His bless - ed will; A wall of

1 of the Val - ley, in Him a - lone I see All I need to cleanse and
2 Him for - sak - en, I've all my i - dols torn From my heart, and now He
3 fire a - bout me, I've noth-ing now to fear; With His man - na He my

1 make me full - y whole; In sor - row He's my com-fort, in trou - ble
2 keeps me by His pow'r. Tho' all the world for - sake me, and Sa - tan
3 hun - gry soul shall fill; Then sweep-ing up to glo - ry I'll see His

1 He's my stay, He tells me ev - 'ry care on Him to roll.
2 tempt me sore, Through Je - sus I shall safe - ly reach the goal.
3 bless - ed face, Where riv - ers of de - light shall ev - er flow.

The Lily of the Valley—*Continued*

1-3 He's the Li - ly of the Val - ley, the Bright and Morn - ing Star,

REFRAIN

1-3 He's the Fair - est of Ten Thous - and to my soul. In sor - row He's

my com - fort, in trou - ble He's my stay, He tells me ev - 'ry

care on Him to roll; He's the Li - ly of the Val - ley, the Bright

and Morn - ing Star, He's the Fair - est of Ten Thous - and to my soul.

361 Can Ye Not Watch ?

JESSIE H. BROWN   GEO. C. STEBBINS

1 One lit-tle hour for watch-ing with the Mas-ter, E-ter-nal years to
2 One lit-tle hour to suf-fer scorn and loss-es, E-ter-nal years be-
3 One lit-tle hour for wea-ry toils and tri-als, E-ter-nal years for

1 walk with Him in white; One lit-tle hour to brave-ly meet dis-as-ter,
2 yond earth's cru-el frowns; One lit-tle hour to car-ry heav-y cross-es,
3 calm and peace-ful rest; One lit-tle hour for pa-tient self-de-ni-als,

REFRAIN

1 E-ter-nal years to reign with Him in light.
2 E-ter-nal years to wear un-fad-ing crowns. } Then souls, be brave, and watch un-til the
3 E-ter-nal years of life where life is blest.

mor-row! A-wake! a-rise! your lamps of pur-pose trim; Your Sa-viour speaks a-

cross the night of sor-row; Can ye not watch one lit-tle hour with Him?

362 Glory All the Way!

J. H. SAMMIS

D. B. TOWNER

1. Saved by grace a - lone, God's own Word be - liev-ing; It is glo - ry
2. Not a care have I since my Sa - viour car - eth: It is glo - ry
3. Se - ver'd from the world His dear name con - fess-ing; It is glo - ry
4. Sin - ner, put your trust in this lov - ing Sa-viour: It is glo - ry

1. all the way! Walk-ing in the light, dai - ly grace re - ceiv-ing: It is
2. all the way! Guid - ed by His eye, while with me He far - eth, It is
3. all the way! Tak - ing up the cross, shar - ing in the bless - ing: It is
4. all the way! Free - ly He for - gives all our past be - ha - viour: It is

CHORUS.

glo - ry all the way! Glo - - - ry! Glo - - - ry!
Glo - ry all the way! yes, Glo - ry all the way!

It is glo - ry all the way! Glo - - - ry!
It is glo - - ry, glo - ry all the way! Glo - ry all the way! yes,

glo - - - ry? It is glo - ry all the way! . . . .
glo - ry all the way! It is glo - ry, glo - ry, glo - ry all the way?

363 I Know I Love Thee

F. R. HAVERGAL　　　THE HALF NOT TOLD C.M.D　　　R. E. HUDSON

1. I know I love Thee bet-ter, Lord, Than an-y earth-ly joy, For
2. I know that Thou art near-er still Than an-y earth-ly throng, And
3. Thou hast put glad-ness in my heart; Then well may I be glad; With-
4. O Sa-viour, pre-cious Sa-viour mine! What will Thy pre-sence be If

1. Thou hast giv-en me the peace Which noth-ing can de-stroy.
2. sweet-er is the thought of Thee Than an-y love-ly song.
3. out the se-cret of Thy love I could not but be sad.
4. such a life of joy can crown Our walk on earth with Thee?

REFRAIN

The half has ne-ver yet been told　　Of
　　　　　　　yet been told

love so full and free: The half has nev-er yet been

rit.

told,　　　　The blood it cleans-eth me.
　　yet been told,　　　　　　cleans-eth me.

364 I Shall Know Him

FANNY J. CROSBY   JNO. R. SWENEY

1. When my life-work is end-ed, and I cross the swell-ing tide, When the bright and glo-rious morn-ing I shall see; I shall know my Re-deem-er when I reach the oth-er side, And His smile will be the first to wel-come me.

2. O the soul-thrill-ing rap-ture when I view His bless-ed face! And the lus-tre of His kind-ly beam-ing eye; How my full heart will praise Him for the mer-cy, love, and grace That pre-pares for me a man-sion in the sky.

3. O the dear ones in glo-ry, how they beck-on me to come! And our part-ing at the riv-er I re-call; To the sweet vales of E-den they will sing my wel-come home, But I long to meet my Sa-viour first of all.

4. Thro' the gates to the cit-y in a robe of spot-less white, He will lead me where no tears shall ev-er fall; In the glad song of a-ges I shall min-gle with de-light; But I long to meet my Sa-viour first of all.

REFRAIN

I shall know . . Him, I shall know Him, As re-deem'd by His side I shall stand,
I shall know
I shall know . . Him, I shall know Him, By the print of the nails in His hand.
I shall know

365 The Prize is Set

C. R. BLACKALL

H. R. PALMER

1 The prize is set be-fore us To win, His words im-plore us; The eye of
2 We'll fol-low where He lead-eth, We'll pas-ture where He feed-eth, We'll yield to
3 Our home is bright a-bove us, No tri-als dark to move us, But Je-sus

1 God is o'er us, From on high, from on high! His lov-ing tones are call-ing, While
2 Him who plead-eth From on high, from on high! Then nought from Him shall sev-er, Our
3 dear to love us, There on high, there on high! We'll give Him best en-deav-our, And

1 sin is dark, ap-pall-ing; 'Tis Je-sus gent-ly call-ing— He is nigh, He is nigh.
2 hope shall bright-en ev-er, And faith shall fail us nev-er— He is nigh, He is nigh.
3 praise His Name for ev-er, His pre-cious ones can nev-er, Nev-er die, nev-er die.

REFRAIN

1st time

By-and-by we shall meet Him, By-and-by we shall greet Him, And with Je-sus reign

2nd time

in glo-ry, By-and-by, by-and-by; Je-sus reign in glo-ry, By-and-by.

366 The Glory Song

CHARLES H. GABRIEL

Arr. CHARLES H. GABRIEL

1 When all my la-bours and tri-als are o'er, And I am safe on that
2 When by the gift of His in-fin-ite grace I am ac-cord-ed in
3 Friends will be there I have lov'd long a-go; Joy like a riv-er a-

1 beau-ti-ful shore, Just to be near the dear Lord I a-dore
2 heav-en a place, Just to be there and to look on His face
3 round me will flow; Yet, just a smile from my Sa-viour, I know,

REFRAIN

O that will be . .

1-3 Will thro' the a-ges be glo-ry for me. . . . O . . . that will

O that will be . .

glo-ry for me! . . glo-ry for me, . . glo-ry for me, . . When by His grace

be . . glo-ry for me, . . glo-ry for me, . . glo-ry for me; . . When

glo-ry for me! . . glo-ry for me, . . glo-ry for me, . . When by His grace

I shall look on His face, That will be glo-ry, be glo-ry for me.

367 Close to Thee

FANNY J. CROSBY

SILAS J. VAIL

1 Thou, my ev - er - last - ing Por - tion, More than friend or life to me;
2 Not for ease or world - ly pleas - ure; Nor for fame my pray'r shall be;
3 Lead me thro' this vale of sha - dows; Bear me o'er life's fit - ful sea;

1 All a - long my pil - grim jour - ney, Sa - viour, let me walk with Thee.
2 Glad - ly will I toil and suf - fer, On - ly let me walk with Thee.
3 Then the gate of life e - ter - nal May I en - ter, Lord, with Thee.

REFRAIN

1-3 Close to Thee, close to Thee, Close to Thee, close to Thee,

1 All a - long my pil - grim jour - ney, Sa - viour, let me walk with Thee.
2 Glad - ly will I toil and suf - fer, On - ly let me walk with Thee.
3 Then the gate of life e - ter - nal May I en - ter, Lord, with Thee.

368   'Tis Heaven There

C. J Butler   J. M. Clark

1 Since Christ my soul from sin set free This world has been a heav'n to me;
2 Once heav-en seem'd a far-off place, Till Je-sus show'd His smil-ing face;
3 What mat-ters where on earth we dwell? On moun-tain top or in the dell?

1 And, 'mid earth's sor-rows and its woe, 'Tis heav'n my Je - sus here to know.
2 Now it's be - gun with-in my soul 'Twill last while end - less a - ges roll.
3 In cot-tage or a man-sion fair? Where Je-sus is 'tis heav - en there!

REFRAIN

O hal - le - lu - jah, yes, 'tis heav'n! 'Tis heav'n to know my sins for-giv'n;

On land or sea, what mat-ters where, Where Je-sus is 'tis heav - en there.

369

Give Me Jesus

FANNY J. CROSBY   LIFE ABOVE 8.7.8.7.D   JOHN R. SWENEY

1. Take the world, but give me Je-sus, All its joys are but a name;
2. Take the world, but give me Je-sus, Sweet-est com-fort of my soul;
3. Take the world, but give me Je-sus, Let me view His con-stant smile;
4. Take the world, but give me Je-sus, In His cross my trust shall be,

1. But His love a-bid-eth e-ver, Thro' e-ter-nal years the same.
2. With my Sa-viour watching o'er me I can sing, tho' bil-lows roll.
3. Then throughout my pil-grim jour-ney Light will cheer me all the while.
4. Till, with clear-er, bright-er vis-ion, Face to face my Lord I see.

CHORUS.

Oh, the height and depth of mer-cy! Oh, the length and breadth of love!

Oh, the ful-ness of re-demp-tion, Pledge of end-less life a-bove.

370 Lead Me, Saviour

F. M. D.

FRANK M. DAVIS

1. Sa-viour, lead me, lest I stray, Gen-tly lead me all the
2. Thou, the re-fuge of my soul When life's stormy billows
3. Sa-viour, lead me, then at last, When the storm of life is

1. Sa - iour, lead me, lest I stray, Gent - ly

1. way; I am safe when by Thy side,
2. roll, I am safe when Thou art nigh,
3. past, To the land of end-less day,

1. lead me all the way; I am safe when by Thy side,

CHORUS.

1. I would in Thy love a - bide.
2. All my hopes on Thee re - ly,
3. Where all tears are wip'd a-way.

Lead me, Lead me,

1. I would in Thy love a - bide.

Sa - viour, lead me, lest I stray; Gen - tly down the stream of
lest I stray;

rit e dim.

time, Lead me, Sa-viour, all the way.
stream of time, all the way.

371 He Hideth My Soul

FANNY J. CROSBY

WM. J. KIRKPATRICK

1. A won-der-ful Sa-viour is Je-sus my Lord, A won-der-ful Sa-viour to
2. A won-der-ful Sa-viour is Je-sus my Lord, He tak-eth my bur-den a-
3. With num-ber-less blessings each mo-ment He crowns, And fill'd with His fulness di-
4. When cloth'd in His brightness trans-port-ed I rise, To meet Him in clouds of the

1. me, He hid-eth my soul in the cleft of the rock, Where
2. way, He hold-eth me up, and I shall not be mov'd, He
3. vine, I sing in my rap-ture, oh, glo-ry to God For
4. sky, His per-fect sal-va-tion, His won-der-ful love, I'll

CHORUS.

1. ri-vers of pleasure I see.
2. giveth me strength as my day.
3. such a Redeem-er as mine!
4. shout with the millions on high.

He hid-eth my soul in the cleft of the rock, That

shadows a dry thirsty land; He hid-eth my life in the depths of His love, And

cov-ers me there with His hand. And cov-ers me there with His hand.

372   ## Jerusalem, the Golden

BERNARD OF CLUNY   EWING 7.6.7.6.D   ALEX. EWING

1. Je - ru - sa - lem the gold - en, With milk and ho - ney blest,
2. They stand, those halls of Zi - on, All ju - bi - lant with song;
3. There is the throne of Da - vid: And there from care re - leas'd;
4. Oh, sweet and bless - ed coun - try, The home of God's e - lect!

1. Be - neath thy con - tem - pla - tion Sink heart and voice op - prest:
2. And bright with many an an - gel, And all the mar - tyr throng:
3. The shout of them that tri - umph, The song of them that feast:
4. Oh, sweet and bless - ed coun - try That ea - ger hearts ex - pect!

1. I know not oh! I know not, What joys a - wait us there,
2. The Prince is ev - er in them, The day - light is se - rene,
3. And they who with their Lead - er, Have conquer'd in the fight,
4. Je - sus, in mer - cy bring us To that dear land of rest,

1. What ra - dian - cy of glo - ry, What bliss be - yond com - pare.
2. The pas - tures of the bless - ed Are deck'd in glo - rious sheen.
3. For ev - er and for ev - er Are cloth'd in robes of white.
4. Who art, with God the Fa - ther, And Spi - rit, ev - er blest.

373 There's Grace and Glory

T. M. EASTWOOD

MARY HUBBERT MUNFORD

1. O the grace of God is bound-less, It is like a mighty sea,
2. There is grace for each temp-ta-tion, There is strength for ev-'ry day,
3. For the grace that God has giv-en I will praise Him in my song,

1. And it rolls on thro' the a-ges, Bear-ing love to you and me;
2. There's a lift for ev-'ry bur-den That we car-ry on the way;
3. I will love Him and will serve Him While my days of life pro-long;

1. But the Lord's so great in good-ness, That He o-pens heav'n to view,
2. There's a ref-uge from the tem-pest, There is help for all we do,
3. And when I shall get to hea-ven, And my jour-ney I re-view,

1. And not on-ly gives us mer-cy, But He gives us glo-ry too.
2. And when we shall end the jour-ney, We will find there's glo-ry too.
3. Then I'll bless His name for ev-er, That there's grace and glo-ry too.

CHORUS.

There's grace . . . and glo-ry too, There's grace . . . and glo-ry
There's grace and glo-ry too, There's grace

There's Grace and Glory—*Continued*

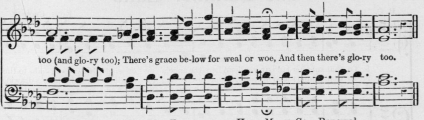

too (and glo-ry too); There's grace be-low for weal or woe, And then there's glo-ry too.

374 The Shadow of His Wings

J. B. ATCHINSON

E. O. EXCELL

1 In the sha-dow of His wings There is rest, sweet rest; There is rest from care and la-bour,
2 In the sha-dow of His wings There is peace, sweet peace, Peace that pass-eth un-der-stand-ing,
3 In the sha-dow of His wings There is joy, glad joy; There is joy to tell the sto-ry,

1 There is rest for friend and neighbour: In the sha-dow of His wings There is rest, sweet rest,
2 Peace, sweet peace, that knows no ending: In the sha-dow of His wings There is peace, sweet peace,
3 Joy ex-ceed-ing, full of glo-ry: In the sha-dow of His wings There is joy, glad joy,

rit. REFRAIN

1 In the sha-dow of His wings There is rest, sweet rest.
2 In the sha-dow of His wings There is peace, sweet peace.
3 In the sha-dow of His wings There is joy, glad joy.
There is rest! sweet rest! There is

1st time *2nd time*

peace! sweet peace! There is joy, glad joy, In the sha-dow of His wings! sha-dow of His wings.

375 The Summer Land

R. C.

ROBT. CROSBIE.

1. To that summer land up yonder Where the angels ev-er sing Hal-le-lu-jahs to the
2. To that summer land up yonder Some are go-ing ev-'ry day, And the time is drawing
3. In that summer land up yonder There's a place prepared for all Who are trusting in the

1. Saviour, Sweet hosannahs to the King: We are marching swiftly onward Guided by a Father's hand,
2. nearer When we too, shall go away; We are going straight to Jesus, There to join the ransom'd band,
3. Saviour, Who will lis-ten to His call; And the happy time is coming When the Lord shall give command,

CHORUS.

1. Thro' this world of sin and sorrow To that happy summer land.
2. We will praise His name for ever In that happy summer land. Oh, the joy when we get
3. And we'll leave this world for ever For that happy summer land.

Oh, the joy, the joy, when we get

there, Gold - en crowns of life to wear,
to wear, of life to wear,

there, when we get there, Golden, golden crowns of life to wear, of life to wear; yes, o - ver

In that hap-py land so fair, In that summer land up yon - der.

in that happy land so fair, that land so fair, In that summer land up yon - der.

376

Keep Close to Jesus

J. L.

JOHN LANE.

1. When you start for the land of hea-ven-ly rest, Keep close to Je-sus all the
2. Nev - er mind the storms or tri - als as you go, Keep close to Je-sus all the
3. To be safe from the darts of the e - vil one, Keep close to Je-sus all the
4. We shall reach our home in hea-ven by and by, Keep close to Je-sus all the

1. way; For He is the Guide, and He knows the way best,
2. way; 'Tis a com - fort and joy His fa - vour to know,
3. way; Take the shield of faith till the vic - t'ry is won,
4. way; Where to those we love we'll ne - ver say "good-bye,"

CHORUS.

1-4. Keep close to Je - sus all the way. Keep close to Je sus,

Keep close to Je - sus, Keep close to Je - sus all the way; By

day or by night ne-ver turn from the right, Keep close to Je-sus all the way.

377 The Everlasting Arms

E. A. HOFFMAN

A. J. SHOWALTER

1 What a fel-low-ship, what a joy di-vine! Lean-ing on the ev - er-
2 O how sweet to walk in this pil-grim way! Lean-ing on the ev - er-
3 What have I to dread, what have I to fear? Lean-ing on the ev - er-

1 last - ing arms; What a bless-ed-ness, what a peace is mine!
2 last - ing arms; O how bright the path grows from day to day!
3 last - ing arms; I have bless-ed peace with my Lord so near,

REFRAIN

1-3 Lean-ing on the ev - er - last-ing arms. Lean - ing,
Lean-ing on Je - sus,

lean - ing, Safe and se-cure from all a - larms;
Lean - ing on Je - sus,

Lean - ing, lean - ing, Lean-ing on the ev - er - last -ing arms.
Lean-ing on Je - sus, Lean-ing on Je - sus,

378 Peace, Sweet Peace

P. P. BILHORN — P. P. BILHORN

1. There comes to my heart one sweet strain (sweet strain), A glad and a joy-ous re-frain (re-frain), I sing it a-gain and a-gain, Sweet
2. By Christ on the Cross peace was made (was made), My debt by His death was all paid (all paid), No o-ther foun-da-tion is laid, For
3. When Je-sus, as Lord I had crown'd (had crown'd), My heart with this peace did a-bound (a-bound), In Him the rich bless-ing I found, Sweet
4. In Je-sus for peace I a-bide (a-bide), And as I keep close to His side (His side), There's no-thing but peace doth be-tide, Sweet

REFRAIN

1-4 peace, the gift of God's love. Peace, peace, sweet peace,

Won-der-ful gift from a-bove (a-bove); O won-der-ful,

rit.

won-der-ful peace! Sweet peace, the gift of God's love.

379 Since I have been Redeemed.

E. O. E.

E. O. Excell.

1. I have a song I love to sing, Since I have been re-deemed, Of
2. I have a Christ that sat-is-fies, Since I have been re-deemed, To
3. I have a wit-ness bright and clear, Since I have been re-deemed, Dis-
4. I have a joy I can't ex-press, Since I have been re-deemed, All
5. I have a home pre-pared for me. Since I have been re-deemed, Where

1. my Re-deem-er, Sa-viour, King, Since I have been re-deemed.
2. do His will my high-est prize, Since I have been re-deemed.
3. pel-ling ev-'ry doubt and fear, Since I have been re-deemed.
4. thro' His blood and right-eous-ness, Since I have been re-deemed.
5. I shall dwell e-ter-nal-ly, Since I have been re-deemed.

REFRAIN. I . . . . have been redeemed,
Since I have been redeemed, Since I have been redeemed, Since
I have been redeemed, I will glo-ry in His name, Since I have been redeemed, Since
I . . . . have been re-deemed,
I have been redeemed, I will glo-ry in the Sa-viour's name.

380 From Death Unto Life

ALICE CARY SALVATION'S STORY 7.6.7.6.D WM. J. KIRKPATRICK

1. Till I learned to love Thy name, Lord, Thy grace de-ny-ing,
2. Noth-ing could the world im-part, Dark-ness held no mor-row;
3. When I learned to love Thy name, O Thou meek and low-ly;
4. Henceforth shall cre-a-tion ring With sal-va-tion's sto-ry,

1. I was lost in sin and shame, Dy-ing, dy-ing, dy-ing!
2. In my soul and in my heart, Sor-row, sor-row, sor-row!
3. Rap-ture kin-dled to a flame, Ho-ly, ho-ly, ho-ly!
4. Till I rise with Thee to sing, Glo-ry, glo-ry, glo-ry!

REFRAIN.

1, 2, & 3, This is now my con-stant theme, This my fav-'rite sto-ry,
4. Hal-le-lu-jah! grace is free, I will tell the sto-ry,

1, 2, & 3. Je-sus' blood a-vails for me, Glo-ry, glo-ry, glo-ry!
4. Je-sus' blood hath made me free, Glo-ry, glo-ry, glo-ry!

381 Sunshine in My Soul

E. E. HEWITT

JOHN R. SWENEY

1. There is sunshine in my soul to-day, More glo-ri-ous and bright,
2. There is mu-sic in my soul to-day, A ca-rol to my King,
3. There is springtime in my soul to-day, For when the Lord is near
4. There is gladness in my soul to-day, And hope, and praise, and love,

1. Than glows in a-ny earth-ly sky, For Je-sus is my light.
2. And Je-sus, list-en-ing, can hear The song I can-not sing.
3. The dove of peace sings in my heart, The flow'rs of grace ap-pear.
4. For bless-ings which He gives me now, For joys "laid up" a-bove.

REFRAIN.

Oh, there's sun - - - - - shine, Bless-ed sun - - - - - - - shine,
Oh, there's sun-shine in my soul, Bless-ed sun-shine in my soul,

While the peace-ful, hap-py moments roll; When
hap-py moments roll,

Je-sus shows His smil-ing face There is sunshine in my soul.

382 The Valley of Blessing

A. WITTENMEYER · W. G. FISCHER

1 I have en-ter'd the val-ley of bless-ing so sweet, And Je-sus a-
2 There is peace in the val-ley of bless-ing so sweet, And plent-y the
3 There is love in the val-ley of bless-ing so sweet, Such as none but the
4 There's a song in the val-ley of bless-ing so sweet, And an-gels would

1 bides with me there; And His Spi-rit and blood make my cleans-ing com-plete,
2 land doth im-part; There is rest for the wea-ry worn tra-vel-ler's feet,
3 blood-wash'd may feel, When hea-ven comes down re-deem'd spi-rits to greet,
4 fain join the strain, As with rap-tu-rous prais-es we bow at His feet,

REFRAIN

1 And His per-fect love cast-eth out fear.
2 And joy for the sor-row-ing heart.
3 And Christ sets His cov-e-nant seal.
4 Cry-ing, 'Wor-thy the Lamb that was slain!'

O come to this val-ley of bless-ing
so sweet, Where Je-sus will ful-ness be-stow, O be-lieve and re-
ceive and con-fess Him! That all His sal-va-tion may know.

383 To the Work!

FANNY J. CROSBY

W. H. DOANE

1. To the work! to the work! we are ser-vants of God, Let us
2. To the work! to the work! let the hun-gry be fed; To the
3. To the work! to the work! there is la-bour for all, For the
4. To the work! to the work! press-ing on to the end, For the

1. fol - low the path that our Mas - ter has trod; With the
2. foun - tain of Life let the wea - ry be led; In the
3. king - dom of dark - ness and er - ror shall fall, And the
4. har - vest will come, and the reap - ers des - cend; And the

1. balm of His coun - sel our strength to re - new, Let us
2. cross and its ban - ner our glo - ry shall be, While we
3. name of Je - ho - vah ex - alt - ed shall be In the
4. home of the ran - somed our dwell - ing will be, And our

1. do with our might what our hands find to do.
2. her - ald the tid - ings, "Sal - va - tion is free!"
3. loud swell - ing cho - rus, "Sal - va - tion is free!"
4. cho - rus for ev - er, "Sal - va - tion is free!"

CHORUS.

Toil - ing on, toil - ing on, Toil - ing
Toil - ing on, toil - ing on, Toil - ing on,

To the Work !—*Continued*.

on, toil - ing on, toil - ing on, toil - ing on, Let us

hope, and trust, let us watch, and pray, And la - bour till the Mas - ter comes.

384

Follow Me

FINE.

{ 1. I hear my dy - ing Sa - viour say: Fol - low Me! come, fol - low Me! }
{ For thee I gave my life a - way, Fol - low Me! come, fol - low Me! }

Do thou, my child, o'er hill and dale, Fol - low Me! come, fol - low Me!

D.C.

I know how heart and flesh may fail, I've borne the fu ry of the gale;

2. Tho' thou hadst sinned I pardoned thee;
   Follow Me! come, follow Me!
   From inbred sin I'll set thee free;
   Follow Me! come, follow Me!
   Oh, look to Me, dismiss thy fears,
   And trust Me thro' all coming years !
   My hand shall wipe away thy tears,
   Follow Me! come, follow Me !

3. Come, cast upon Me all thy cares !
   Follow Me! come, follow Me !
   Thy heavy load Mine arm upbears.
   Follow Me! come, follow Me !
   In all thy changeful life I'll be
   Thy God and Guide, o'er land and sea
   Thy bliss through all eternity,
   Follow Me! come, follow Me !

385 Yesterday, To=day, Forever

A. B. SIMPSON.   J. H. BURKE.

1. O, how sweet the glorious message, Simple faith may claim;
2. He who was the Friend of Sinners, Seeks thee, lost one, now;
3. Him who pardoned erring Peter, Never need'st thou fear;
4. He who 'mid the raging billows, Walk'd upon the sea;
5. As of old He walk'd to Emmaus, With them to abide;

1. Yesterday, to-day, forever, Jesus is the same.
2. Sinner, come, and at His footstool, Penitently bow.
3. He that came to faithless Thomas, All thy doubt will clear.
4. Still can hush our wildest tempest, As on Galilee.
5. So thro' all life's way He walketh, Ever near our side.

1. Still He loves to save the sinful, Heal the sick and lame;
2. He who said, "I'll not condemn thee, Go, and sin no more,"
3. He who let the loved disciple On His bosom rest,
4. He who wept and prayed in anguish, In Gethsemane,
5. Soon again shall we behold Him, Hasten, Lord, the day!

1. Cheer the mourner, still the tempest, Glory to His name!
2. Speaks to thee that word of pardon, As in days of yore.
3. Bids thee still, with love as tender, Lean upon His breast,
4. Drinks with us each cup of trembling, In our agony.
5. But 'twill still be "this same Jesus," As He went away.

CHORUS.

Yesterday, to-day, forever, Jesus is the same, All may change, but

Yesterday, To-day, Forever—*Continued*

Je - sus nev - er! Glo - ry to His name, Glo - ry to His name,

Glo - ry to His name, All may change, but Je-sus nev-er! Glo - ry to His name.

386 Thou Thinkest of Me

EDWARD MUND

E. S LORENZ

1 A - mid the tri - als which I meet, A - mid the thorns that pierce my feet,
2 The cares of life come thronging fast, Up - on my soul their sha-dow cast;
3 Let sha-dows come, let sha-dows go, Let life be bright or dark with woe,

FINE.

1 One thought re-mains su - preme-ly sweet, Thou think-est, Lord, of me!
2 Their gloom re-minds my heart at last, Thou think-est, Lord, of me!
3 I am con-tent, for this I know, Thou think-est, Lord, of me!

D.S.—*What need I fear since Thou art near, And think - est, Lord, of me!*

REFRAIN

D.S.

Thou think-est, Lord, of me, (of me,) Thou think - est, Lord, of me, (of me,)

387 Enthroned is Jesus Now

T. J. JUDKIN

T. C. O'KANE

1 En-thron'd is Je-sus now, Up-on His heav'n-ly seat; The
2 In shin-ing white they stand, That great and count-less throng; A
3 They sing, the Lamb of God, Once slain on earth for them: The
4 Thy grace, O Ho-ly Ghost! Thy bless-ed help sup-ply, That

1 king-ly crown is on His brow, The saints are at His feet.
2 palm-y scep-tre in each hand, On ev-'ry lip a song.
3 Lamb, thro' whose a-ton-ing blood Each wears his di-a-dem.
4 we may join that ra-diant host, Tri-um-phant in the sky.

REFRAIN

There with the glo-ri-fied, Safe by our Sa-viour's side, We shall be

sat-is-fied, By and by; By . . . and by, . .

There, there with the glo-ri-fied,

By . . and by, . . We shall be sat-is-fied, By and by.

Safe, safe, by our Saviour's side.

388

Sound the Battle=Cry

W. F. S.

W. F. Sherwin.

1. Sound the bat-tle cry! See! the foe is nigh; Raise the stan-dard high
2. Strong to meet the foe, March-ing on we go, While our cause we know
3. Oh! Thou God of all, Hear us when we call; Help us one and all,

For the Lord; Gird your ar-mour on, Stand firm, ev-'ry one;
Must pre - vail; Shield and ban-ner bright Gleam-ing in the light;
By Thy grace; When the bat-tle's done, And the vic-t'ry won,

CHORUS. *ff*

Rest your cause up-on His ho - ly word.
Bat - tling for the right, We ne'er can fail.   Rouse, then, sol - diers!
May we wear the crown Be - fore Thy face.

ral - ly round the ban - ner! Read-y, stead-y, pass the word a-long;

On-ward, for-ward, shout aloud Ho-san-nah! Christ is Cap-tain of the mighty throng.

389 Beulah Land

EDGAR PAGE STITES

JOHN R. SWENEY

1 I've reach'd the land of corn and wine, And all its rich-es free-ly mine;
2 My Sa-viour comes and walks with me, And sweet com-mun-ion here have we;
3 A sweet per-fume up-on the breeze Is borne from ev-er-ver-nal trees,
4 The zeph-yrs seem to float to me Sweet sounds of heav-en's mel-o-dy,

1 Here shines un-dimm'd one bliss-ful day, For all my night has pass'd a-way.
2 He gent-ly leads me by His hand, For this is heav-en's bor-der-land.
3 And flow'rs that nev-er fad-ing grow Where streams of life for ev-er flow.
4 As an-gels with the white-rob'd throng Join in the sweet re-demp-tion song.

REFRAIN

O Beu-lah Land! sweet Beu-lah Land! As on thy high-est mount I stand

I look a-way a-cross the sea, Where man-sions are pre-par'd for me,

And view the shin-ing glo-ry shore, My heav'n, my home for ev-er more.

390   Near the Cross

FANNY J. CROSBY   NEAR THE CROSS 7.6.7.6.6.6.7.6   W. H. DOANE

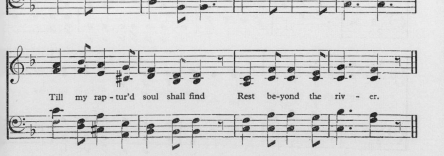

1 Je - sus, keep me near the Cross;   There a pre - cious foun - tain,
2 Near the Cross, a tremb - ling soul,   Love and mer - cy found me;
3 Near the Cross, O Lamb of God!   Bring its scenes be - fore me;
4 Near the Cross I'll watch and wait,   Hop - ing, trust - ing, ev - er,

1 Free to all, a heal - ing stream,   Flows from Cal - v'ry's moun - tain.
2 There the bright and morn - ing star   Shed its beams a - round me.
3 Help me walk from day to day   With its sha - dow o'er me.
4 Till I reach the gol - den strand   Just be - yond the riv - er.

REFRAIN

In the Cross, in the Cross   Be my glo - ry ev - er,

Till my rap - tur'd soul shall find   Rest be - yond the riv - er.

17

391 His Grace is Sufficient

R. M'Naughton

D. B. Towner

1. His grace was suf-fi-cient for me! When in trembling and fear, To His side I drew near, And He cleansed me from sin, Made my heart pure with-in, His grace was suf-fi-cient for me.
2. His grace is suf-fi-cient for me! And what-ev-er my lot, I can hear His "Fear not!" I am safe in His care, Who can guard from each snare, His grace is suf-fi-cient for me.
3. His grace is suf-fi-cient for me! All my need He'll pro-vide, And my steps homeward guide; And in death I shall sing, As I rest 'neath His wing, His grace is suf-fi-cient for me.
4. His grace is suf-fi-cient for me! When in mansions of bliss, Still my theme shall be this; And for aye I shall sing, To the praise of my King, Whose grace is suf-fi-cient for me.

REFRAIN.

For me, for me. His grace is suf-fi-cient for me; ....
For me, for me, is suf-fi-cient for me;

For me, for me, His grace is suf-fi-cient for me.
For me, for me,

392 Over Jordan

M. B. C. SLADE

J. R. MURRAY

1. With His dear and lov-ing care, Will the Sa-viour lead us on To the
2. Through the rock-y wil-der-ness, Will the Sa-viour lead us on To the
3. With His strong and might-y hand, Will the Sa-viour lead us on To that
4. In the Pro-mised Land to be, Will the Sa-viour lead us on, Till fair

1. hills and val-leys fair, O - ver Jor - dan? Yes, we'll rest our wea-ry feet
2. land we shall possess, O - ver Jor - dan? Yes, by night the wondrous ray,
3. good and pleasant land, O - ver Jor - dan? Yes, where vine and o - live grow,
4. Ca-naan's shore we see, O - ver Jor - dan? Yes, to dwell with Thee at last,

1. By the crys-tal wa-ters sweet, When the peaceful shore we greet, O - ver Jor - dan.
2. Cloud-y pil - lar by the day, They shall guide us on our way, O - ver Jor - dan.
3. And the brooks and fountains flow, Thirst nor hunger shall we know, O - ver Jor - dan.
4. Guide and lead us, as Thou hast, Till the part-ed wave be passed, O - ver Jor - dan.

CHORUS.

O - ver Jor - dan! O - ver Jor-dan! Yes, we'll rest our weary feet, By the crystal waters sweet,

O - ver Jor - dan! O - ver Jordan! When the peaceful shore we'll greet, Over Jor-dan!

393   Himself Alone

A. B. SIMPSON   HIMSELF ALONE 6.5. 6.5. 8   A. B. SIMPSON

1 Once it was the bless - ing, Now it is the Lord; Once it was the
2 Once 'twas pain - ful try - ing, Now 'tis per - fect trust; Once a half sal-
3 Once 'twas bu - sy plan - ning, Now 'tis trust - ful pray'r; Once 'twas anx - ious
4 Once it was my work - ing, His it hence shall be; Once I tried to
5 Once I hoped in Je - sus, Now I know He's mine; Once my lamps were

1 feel - ing, Now it is His Word; Once His gifts I want - ed,
2 va - tion, Now the ut - ter - most; Once 'twas cease - less hold - ing,
3 car - ing, Now He has the care; Once 'twas what I want - ed,
4 use Him, Now He us - es me: Once the pow'r I want - ed,
5 dy - ing, Now they bright - ly shine; Once for death I wait - ed,

1 Now the Giv - er own; Once I sought for heal - ing, Now Him-self a - lone.
2 Now He holds me fast; Once 'twas con-stant drift - ing, Now my an-chor's cast.
3 Now what Je - sus says; Once 'twas con-stant ask - ing, Now 'tis cease-less praise.
4 Now the Might-y One; Once for self I la - bour'd, Now for Him a - lone.
5 Now His com-ing hail; And my hopes are an - chor'd Safe with - in the veil.

REFRAIN

All in all for - ev - er, Je - sus will I sing;

Ev - 'ry - thing in Je - sus, And Je - sus ev - 'ry - thing.

The tune ANYTHING FOR JESUS is on the next page

393   Himself Alone

A. B. SIMPSON   ANYTHING FOR JESUS 6.5.6.5.8   R. LOWRY

1 Once it was the bless-ing, Now it is the Lord; Once it was the
2 Once 'twas pain-ful try-ing, Now 'tis per-fect trust; Once a half sal-
3 Once 'twas bu-sy plan-ning, Now 'tis trust-ful pray'r; Once 'twas anx-ious
4 Once it was my work-ing, His it hence shall be; Once I tried to
5 Once I hoped in Je-sus, Now I know He's mine; Once my lamps were

1 feel-ing, Now it is His Word; Once His gifts I want-ed,
2 va-tion, Now the ut-ter-most; Once 'twas cease-less hold-ing,
3 car-ing, Now He has the care; Once 'twas what I want-ed,
4 use Him, Now He us-es me: Once the pow'r I want-ed,
5 dy-ing, Now they bright-ly shine; Once for death I wait-ed,

1 Now the Giv-er own; Once I sought for heal-ing, Now Him-self a-lone.
2 Now He holds me fast; Once 'twas con-stant drift-ing, Now my an-chor's cast.
3 Now what Je-sus says: Once 'twas con-stant ask-ing, Now 'tis cease-less praise.
4 Now the Might-y One; Once for self I la-bour'd, Now for Him a-lone.
5 Now His com-ing hail; And my hopes are an-chor'd Safe with-in the veil.

REFRAIN

All in all for-ev-er, Je-sus will I sing;

Ev-'ry-thing in Je-sus, And Je-sus ev-'ry-thing.

The tune HIMSELF ALONE is on the previous page

394 The King of Love

H. W. Baker   Dominus Regit Me 8.7. 8.7   J. B. Dykes

1 The King of love my Shep-herd is, Whose good-ness fail-eth nev - er;
2 Where streams of liv - ing wa - ter flow My ran-som'd soul He lead - eth,
3 Per - verse and fool - ish oft I stray'd, But yet in love He sought me,
4 In death's dark vale I fear no ill With Thee, dear Lord, be - side me;
5 And so thro' all the length of days Thy good - ness fail - eth nev - er;

1 I noth - ing lack if I am His, And He is mine for - ev - er.
2 And, where the ver - dant pas-tures grow, With food ce - les - tial feed - eth.
3 And on His should-er gen - tly laid, And home re - joic - ing brought me.
4 Thy rod and staff my com-fort still, Thy Cross be - fore to guide me.
5 Good Shep-herd, may I sing Thy praise With - in Thy house for - ev - er.

H. W. Baker   St. Columba 8. 7. 8. 7   Irish Melody
Arr. C. V. Stanford

1 The King of love my Shep-herd is, Whose good-ness fail-eth nev - er;
2 Where streams of liv - ing wa - ter flow My ran-som'd soul He lead - eth,
3 Per - verse and fool - ish oft I stray'd, But yet in love He sought me,
4 In death's dark vale I fear no ill With Thee, dear Lord, be - side me;
5 And so thro' all the length of days Thy good - ness fail - eth nev - er;

1 I noth - ing lack if I am His, And He is mine for - ev - er.
2 And, where the ver - dant pas-tures grow, With food ce - les - tial feed - eth.
3 And on His should-er gen - tly laid, And home re - joic - ing brought me.
4 Thy rod and staff my com - fort still, Thy Cross be - fore to guide me.
5 Good Shep-herd, may I sing Thy praise With-in Thy house for - ev - er.

By permission of Stainer & Bell, Ltd.

395 My Saviour

DORA GREENWELL   CARRADALE 8.8.8.7   WM. J. KIRKPATRICK

1 I am not skill'd to un-der-stand What God hath will'd, what God hath plann'd ;
2 I take Him at His word in-deed : 'Christ died for sin - ners,' this I read ;
3 That He should leave His place on high, And come for sin - ful man to die,
4 And O that He ful - fill'd may see The tra - vail of His soul in me,
5 Yea, liv-ing, dy-ing, let me bring My strength, my so - lace from this spring,

1 I on - ly know at His right hand Stands One who is my Sa - viour.
2 For in my heart I find a need Of Him to be my Sa - viour.
3 You count it strange ? so once did I, Be - fore I knew my Sa - viour.
4 And with His work con - tent - ed be, As I with my dear Sa - viour.
5 That He who lives to be my King Once died to be my Sa - viour.

DORA GREENWELL   GREENWELL 8.8.8.7   ERNEST B. LESLIE

1 I am not skill'd to un - der - stand What God hath will'd, what God hath plann'd ;
2 I take Him at His word in - deed : 'Christ died for sin - ners,' this I read ;
3 That He should leave His place on high, And come for sin - ful man to die,
4 And O that He ful - fill'd may see The tra - vail of His soul in me,
5 Yea, liv - ing, dy - ing, let me bring My strengh, my so - lace from this spring,

1 I on - ly know at His right hand Stands One who is my Sa - viour.
2 For in my heart I find a need Of Him to be my Sa - viour.
3 You count it strange ? so once did I, Be - fore I knew my Sa - viour.
4 And with His work con - tent - ed be, As I with my dear Sa - viour.
5 That He who lives to be my King Once died to be my Sa - viour.

By permission of THE NATIONAL SUNDAY SCHOOL UNION

396   The Land of Beulah

HARRIET W. RE QUA   LAND OF BEULAH 8.7.8.7. D   J. W. DADMUN

1 I am dwell-ing on the moun-tain Where the gold-en sun-light gleams
2 I am drink-ing at the foun-tain Where I ev-er would a-bide:
3 O the Cross has won-drous glo-ry, Oft I've prov'd this to be true;

1 O'er a land whose won-drous beau-ty Far ex-ceeds my fond-est dreams,
2 For I've tast-ed life's pure riv-er, And my soul is sat-is-fied;
3 When I'm in the way so nar-row I can see a path-way through.

1 Where the air is pure, e-ther-eal, La-den with the breath of flow'rs,
2 There's no thirst-ing for life's pleas-ures, Nor a-dorn-ing, rich and gay,
3 And how sweet-ly Je-sus whis-pers: Take the cross, thou need'st not fear,

FINE

1 That are bloom-ing by the foun-tain, 'Neath the nev-er-fad-ing bow'rs.
2 For I've found a rich-er treas-ure, One that fad-eth not a-way.
3 For I've tried the way be-fore thee, And the glo-ry lin-gers near.

D.S.—Where the flow-ers bloom for ev-er, And the sun is al-ways bright.

D.S. al Fine

REFRAIN

Is not this the land of Beu-lah? Bless-ed, bless-ed land of light,

397 My Times

W. F. LLOYD   DENNIS S.M.   JOHANN G. NAGELI

1 My times are in Thy hand; My God, I wish them there; My
2 My times are in Thy hand, What-ev - er they may be, Pleas-
3 My times are in Thy hand; Why should I doubt or fear? My
4 My times are in Thy hand, Je - sus, the cru - ci - fied! Those
5 My times are in Thy hand; I'll al - ways trust in Thee; And,

1 life, my friends, my soul I leave En - tire - ly to Thy care.
2 ing or pain - ful, dark or bright, As best may seem to Thee.
3 Fa - ther's hand will ne - ver cause His child a need - less tear.
4 hands my cru - el sins had pierc'd Are now my guard and guide.
5 af - ter death, at Thy right hand I shall for ev - er be.

For a lower setting see No. 538

W. F. LLOYD   FRANCONIA S.M.   *Konig's Choralbuch*, 1738

1 My times are in Thy hand; My God, I wish them there;
2 My times are in Thy hand, What - ev - er they may be,
3 My times are in Thy hand; Why should I doubt or fear?
4 My times are in Thy hand, Je - sus, the cru - ci - fied!
5 My times are in Thy hand; I'll al - ways trust in Thee;

1 My life, my friends, my soul I leave En - tire - ly to Thy care.
2 Pleas - ing or pain - ful, dark or bright, As best may seem to Thee.
3 My Fa - ther's hand will ne - ver cause His child a need - less tear.
4 Those hands my cru - el sins had pierc'd Are now my guard and guide.
5 And, af - ter death, at Thy right hand I shall for ev - er be.

398 Thy Way, not Mine

HORATIUS BONAR   WESTENHANGER S.M.   C. W. POOLE

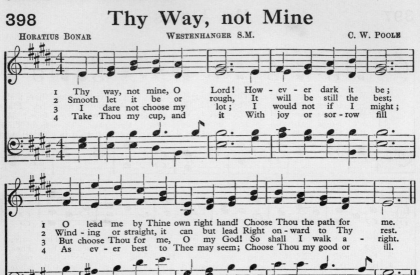

1 Thy way, not mine, O Lord! How-ev-er dark it be;
2 Smooth let it be or rough, It will be still the best;
3 I dare not choose my lot; I would not if I might;
4 Take Thou my cup, and it With joy or sor-row fill

1 O lead me by Thine own right hand! Choose Thou the path for me.
2 Wind-ing or straight, it can but lead Right on-ward to Thy rest.
3 But choose Thou for me, O my God! So shall I walk a-right.
4 As ev-er best to Thee may seem; Choose Thou my good or ill.

By permission of CONSTANCE MORELY HORDER

5 Choose Thou for me my friends,
  My sickness or my health ;
Choose Thou my every care for me,
  My poverty or wealth.

6 Not mine, not mine the choice
  In things or great or small ;
Be Thou to me my Guide, my Strength,
  My Wisdom, and my All.

HORATIUS BONAR   VIGIL S.M.   T. BAIRSTOW

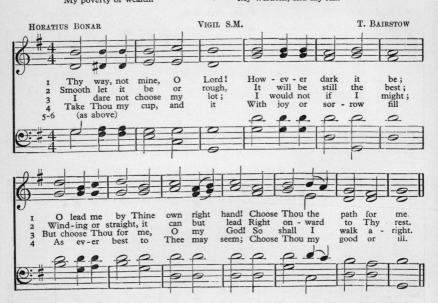

1 Thy way, not mine, O Lord! How-ev-er dark it be ;
2 Smooth let it be or rough, It will be still the best ;
3 I dare not choose my lot ; I would not if I might ;
4 Take Thou my cup, and it With joy or sor-row fill
5-6 (as above)

1 O lead me by Thine own right hand! Choose Thou the path for me.
2 Wind-ing or straight, it can but lead Right on-ward to Thy rest.
3 But choose Thou for me, O my God! So shall I walk a-right.
4 As ev-er best to Thee may seem; Choose Thou my good or ill.

399   I am Trusting Thee

F. R. Havergal   Bullinger 8.5. 8.3   E. W. Bullinger

1 I am trust-ing Thee, Lord Je-sus, Trust-ing on-ly Thee!
2 I am trust-ing Thee for par-don, At Thy feet I bow;
3 I am trust-ing Thee for cleans-ing In the crim-son flood;
4 I am trust-ing Thee to guide me, Thou a-lone shalt lead,

1 Trust-ing Thee for full sal-va-tion, Great and free.
2 For Thy grace and ten-der mer-cy, Trust-ing now.
3 Trust-ing Thee to make me ho-ly By Thy blood.
4 Ev-'ry day and hour sup-ply-ing All my need.

Music by permission of the Bullinger Publications Trust

5 I am trusting Thee for power,
    Thine can never fail ;
Words which Thou thyself shalt give me,
    Must prevail.

6 I am trusting Thee, Lord Jesus,
    Never let me fall !
I am trusting Thee for ever,
    And for all.

F. R. Havergal   St. Helen's 8.5. 8.3   R. P. Stewart

1 I am trust-ing Thee, Lord Je-sus, Trust-ing on-ly Thee !
2 I am trust-ing Thee for par-don, At Thy feet I bow;
3 I am trust-ing Thee for cleans-ing In the crim-son flood;
4 I am trust-ing Thee to guide me, Thou a-lone shalt lead,
5-6 (as above)

1 Trust-ing Thee for full sal-va-tion, Great and free.
2 For Thy grace and ten-der mer-cy, Trust-ing now.
3 Trust-ing Thee to make me ho-ly By Thy blood.
4 Ev-'ry day and hour sup-ply-ing All my need.

400 When We All Get to Heaven

E. E. HEWITT

J. G. WILSON

1. Sing the won-drous, love of Je - sus, Sing His mer - cy and His grace;
2. While we walk the pil - grim pathway, Clouds will o - ver-spread the sky;
3. Let us, then, be true and faithful, Trust - ing, serv - ing ev - 'ry day;
4. On - ward to the prize be - fore us! Soon His beau - ty we'll be - hold:

1. In the man - sions, bright and bless - ed, He'll pre - pare for us a place.
2. But when trav - 'ling days are o - ver, Not a shad - ow, not a sigh.
3. Just one glimpse of Him in glo - ry, Will the toils of life re - pay.
4. Soon the pear - ly gates will o - pen, We shall tread the streets of gold.

for us a place.

CHORUS.

When we all When we all get to hea - ven, What a day of re -
What a

joic - ing that will be! When we all see
day of re - joic - ing that will be! When we all

Je - sus, We'll sing and shout the vic - to - ry.
and shout the vic - to - ry

401 Does Jesus Care?

Frank E. Graeff

J. Lincoln Hall

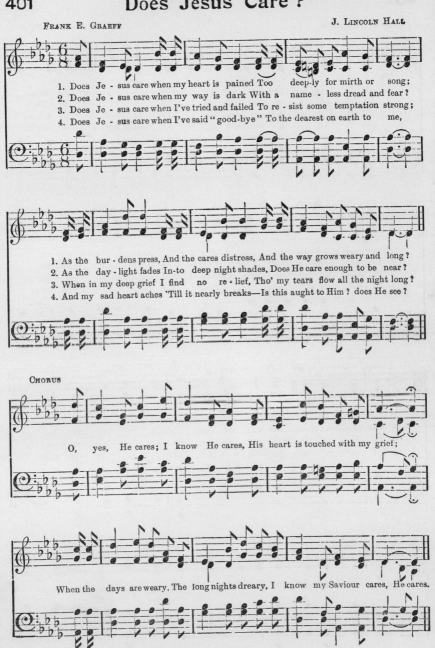

1. Does Je - sus care when my heart is pained Too deep-ly for mirth or song;
2. Does Je - sus care when my way is dark With a name - less dread and fear?
3. Does Je - sus care when I've tried and failed To re - sist some temptation strong;
4. Does Je - sus care when I've said "good-bye" To the dearest on earth to me,

1. As the bur - dens press, And the cares distress, And the way grows weary and long?
2. As the day - light fades In-to deep night shades, Does He care enough to be near?
3. When in my deep grief I find no re - lief, Tho' my tears flow all the night long?
4. And my sad heart aches 'Till it nearly breaks—Is this aught to Him? does He see?

Chorus

O, yes, He cares; I know He cares, His heart is touched with my grief;

When the days are weary, The long nights dreary, I know my Saviour cares, He cares.

402   He Knows

Mary G. Brainard.

P. P. Bliss.

1. I know not what a-waits me, God kind-ly veils mine eyes,
2. One step I see be-fore me, 'Tis all I need to see,
3. O bliss-ful lack of wis-dom, 'Tis bles-sed not to know;
4. So on I go not know-ing, I would not if I might;

1. And o'er each step of my on-ward way He makes new scenes to rise;
2. The light of heav'n more bright-ly shines, When earth's il-lu-sions flee;
3. He holds me with His own right hand, And will not let me go,
4. I'd rath-er walk in the dark with God Than go a-lone in the light;

1. And ev-'ry joy He sends me, comes A sweet and glad sur-prise.
2. And sweet-ly through the si-lence came His lov-ing "Fol-low Me."
3. And lulls my trou-bled soul to rest In Him who loves me so.
4. I'd rath-er walk by faith with Him Than go a-lone by sight.

CHORUS.

Where He may lead I'll fol-low, My trust in Him re-pose;

He Knows—*Continued*

And ev-'ry hour in per-fect peace I'll sing, He knows, He knows;

And ev-'ry hour in per-fect peace I'll sing, He knows, He knows.

403

Loved !

GRACE PENNELL

MEMORIAL 8.8.8.4.

H. ROSS PHILLIPS

1. Loved! then the way will not be drear; For One we know is
2. Loved with an e - ver - last - ing love By Him who left His
3. Loved, when our sky is cloud - ed o'er, And days of sor - row

1. e - ver near, Prov-ing it to our hearts so clear That we are loved.
2. home a - bove, To bring us life, and light, and love, Be - cause He loved.
3. press us sore; Still will we trust Him e - ver - more, For we are loved.

By permission of RANDLE & SON, Hastings

4. Loved, when we leave our native soil,
   In heathen lands to live and toil;
   Under His shadow nought can foil—
   Still we are loved.

5. Time, that affects all things below,
   Can never change the love He'll show;
   The heart of Christ with love will flow,
   And we are loved.

6. Loved in the past of yesterday,
   And all along our future way,
   And in the present of to-day—
   For ever loved.

7. Loved when we sing the glad new song
   To Christ, for whom we've waited long,
   With all the happy, ransomed throng—
   For ever loved.

404   Loyalty to Christ

E. TAYLOR CASSEL

FLORA H. CASSEL

1. Up - on the wes - tern plain There comes the sig - nal strain,
2. O hear, ye brave, the sound That moves the earth a - round!
3. Come, join our loy - al throng, We'll rout the gi - ant wrong,
4. The strength of youth we lay At Je - sus' feet to - day.

1-4 'Tis loy - al - ty, loy - al - ty, loy - al - ty to Christ!

1. Its mus - ic rolls a - long, The hills take up the song
2. A - rise to dare and do, Ring out the watch-word true
3. Where Sa - tan's ban - ners float We'll send the bu - gle note
4. His Gos - pel we'll pro - claim Through - out the world's do - main

1-4 Of loy - al - ty, loy - al - ty, Yes, loy - al - ty to Christ!

Loyalty to Christ—*Continued*

REFRAIN

On to vic - tor - y! On to vic - tor - y!

Cries our great Com - man - der; 'On!' . . . . We'll
Cries our great Com - man - der, great Com - man - der; 'On!' We'll

move at His com - mand, We'll soon pos - sess the land, Through

loy - al - ty, loy - al - ty Yes, loy - al - ty to Christ!

405 Stars in My Crown

ELIZA E. HEWITT

JOHN R. SWENEY

1 I am think-ing to-day of that beau-ti-ful land I shall
2 In the strength of the Lord let me la-bour and pray, Let me
3 O what joy will it be when His face I be-hold! Liv-ing

1 reach when the sun go-eth down; When thro' won-der-ful grace by my
2 watch as a win-ner of souls: That bright stars may be mine in the
3 gems at His feet to lay down; It would sweet-en my bliss in the

1 Sa-viour I stand, Will there be an-y stars in my crown?
2 glo-ri-ous day When His praise like the sea-bil-low rolls.
3 ci-ty of gold Should there be an-y stars in my crown.

Stars in My Crown—*Continued*

REFRAIN

Will there be an-y stars, an-y stars in my crown,

When at ev-'ning the sun go-eth down? . . .

go-eth down?

When I wake with the blest In the man-sions of rest,

Will there be an-y stars in my crown? . . .

an-y stars in my crown?

406 We Would See Jesus

ANNA B. WARNER RAYNOLDS 11.10.11.10 FELIX MENDELSSOHN

1 We would see Je - sus, for the sha-dows length-en A - cross this
2 We would see Je - sus, the great Rock Foun-da - tion Where-on our
3 We would see Je - sus; o-ther lights are pal - ing Which for long
4 We would see Je - sus; this is all we're need-ing, Strength, joy, and

1 lit - tle land-scape of our life; We would see Je - sus, our weak
2 feet were set with sov-'reign grace; Not life, nor death, with all their
3 years we have re-joic'd to see; The bless-ings of our pil-grim-
4 will - ing-ness come with the sight; We would see Je - sus, dy - ing,

1 faith to strength-en For the last wea - ri - ness—the fi - nal strife.
2 a - gi - ta - tion, Can thence re - move us if we see His face.
3 age are fail - ing, We would not mourn them for we go to Thee.
4 ri - sen, plead - ing, Then wel-come day, and fare-well mor - tal night!

ANNA B. WARNER STRENGTH AND STAY 11.10.11.10 J. B. DYKES

1 We would see Je - sus, for the sha-dows length - en A - cross this
2 We would see Je - sus, the great Rock Foun - da - tion Where-on our
3 We would see Je - sus; o-ther lights are pal - ing Which for long
4 We would see Je - sus; this is all we're need - ing, Strength, joy, and

We Would See Jesus—*Continued*

1 lit - tle land-scape of our life; We would see Je - sus, our weak
2 feet were set with sov-'reign grace; Not life, nor death, with all their
3 years we have re-joic'd to see; The bless-ings of our pil-grim-
4 will - ing-ness come with the sight; We would see Je - sus, dy-ing,

1 faith to strength-en For the last wea-ri-ness—the fi - nal strife.
2 a-gi-ta - tion, Can thence re-move us if we see His face.
3 age are fail - ing, We would not mourn them for we go to Thee.
4 ri-sen, plead - ing, Then wel-come day, and fare-well mor - tal night!

ANNA B. WARNER ZU MEINEM HERRN 11.10.11.10 J. G. SCHICHT

1 We would see Je - sus, for the sha-dows length-en A - cross this
2 We would see Je - sus, the great Rock Foun-da - tion Where-on our
3 We would see Je - sus; o-ther lights are pal - ing Which for long
4 We would see Je - sus; this is all we're need - ing, Strength, joy, and

1 lit - tle land-scape of our life; We would see Je - sus, our weak
2 feet were set with sov - 'reign grace; Not life, nor death, with all their
3 years we have re - joic'd to see; The bless-ings of our pil-grim-
4 will-ing - ness come with the sight; We would see Je - sus, dy-ing,

1 faith to strength - en For the last wea - ri-ness—the fi - nal strife.
2 a-gi-ta - tion, Can thence re-move us if we see His Thee.
3 age are fail - ing, We would not mourn them for we go to Thee.
4 ri-sen, plead - ing, Then wel-come day, and fare-well mor - tal night!

407 Every Day and Hour

FANNY J. CROSBY

W. H. DOANE

1 Sa - viour, more than life to me, I am cling-ing cling-
2 Thro' this chang - ing world be - low Lead me gent-ly, gent-
3 Let me love Thee more and more Till this fleet-ing, fleet-

1 ing close to Thee; Let Thy pre - cious blood ap - plied Keep me
2 ly as I go; Trust-ing Thee I can - not stray, I can
3 ing life is o'er; Till my soul is lost in love; In a

REFRAIN

1 ev - er, ev - er near Thy side. } Ev - 'ry day,
2 nev - er, nev - er lose my way. } Ev - 'ry day and hour,
3 fair - er, bright-er world a - bove. }

ev - 'ry hour, Let me feel Thy cleans-ing pow'r; May Thy
ev - 'ry day and hour, Let me feel Thy cleans-ing pow'r; May Thy

ten - der love to me Bind me clos-er, clos-er, Lord, to Thee!

408 Power in Jesus' Blood

HOPE TRYAWAY

WM. J. KIRKPATRICK

1 My hap-py soul re-joic-es, The sky is bright a-bove;
2 I heard the bless-ed sto-ry Of Him who died to save;
3 His gra-cious words of par-don Were mu-sic to my heart;
4 I plunge be-neath this foun-tain That cleans-eth white as snow;
5 O crown Him King for e-ver! My Sa-viour and my Friend!

1 I'll join the heav'n-ly voi-ces, And sing re-deem-ing love.
2 The love of Christ swept o'er me, My all to Him I gave.
3 He took a-way my bur-den, And bade my fears de-part.
4 It pours from Cal-v'ry's moun-tain With bless-ings in its flow.
5 By Zi-on's crys-tal ri-ver His praise shall ne-ver end.

REFRAIN

For there's pow'r in Je-sus' blood, Pow'r in Je-sus' blood;

There's pow'r in Je-sus' blood To wash me white as snow.

409 As the Day Breaks

A. A. Payn

C. Austin Miles

1. As the sha-dows of the night round are fall - ing, I am thinking of that
2. When we ga - ther home at last there'll be sing - ing, Such as an - gels round the
3. I shall rise to be with Je - sus for - ev - er, I shall meet the ones who

1. day by and by; When the trumpet of the Lord shall be call - ing,
2. throne nev - er heard; For the song of souls re-deemed shall go ring - ing,
3. passed on be - fore; We shall meet to part no more, nev - er, nev - er,

CHORUS

1. As the day breaks o'er the hills.
2. As the day breaks o'er the hills. } I'll go singing, I'll go shouting on my
3. When the day breaks o'er the hills.

jour - ney home, Till the day breaks, till the day breaks, There'll be singing, there'll be

shouting, when we all get home, When the day breaks o'er the hills (the heav'nly hills).

410 Labour On

C. R. BLACKALL   W. H. DOANE

1. In the harvest field there is work to do, For the grain is ripe, and the reapers few;
2. Crowd the garner well with its sheaves all bright, Let the song be glad, and the heart be light;
3. In the gleaner's path may be rich reward, Tho' the time seems long, and the labour hard;
4. Lo! the Harvest Home in the realms above Shall be gained by each who has toil'd and strove,

1. And the Master's voice bids the workers true Heed the call that He gives to-day.
2. Fill the precious hours, ere the shades of night Take the place of the golden day.
3. For the Master's joy, with His chosen shared Drives the gloom from the darkest day.
4. When the Master's voice, in its tones of love, Calls a-way to e-ter-nal day.

CHORUS

Labour on! Labour on! labour on! labour on! Keep the bright reward in view;

For the Master has said, He will strength renew; Labour on till the close of day!

411 # The Sands of Time

ANNE ROSS COUSIN   RUTHERFORD 7.6.7.6.7.6.7.5   CHRETIEN URHAN

1 The sands of time are sink - ing; The dawn of hea - ven breaks :
2 O Christ! He is the foun - tain, The deep, sweet well of love;
3 With mer - cy and with judg - ment My web of time He wove,
4 The bride eyes not her gar - ment, But her dear bride-groom's face :
5 I've wrest - l'd on to - wards heav'n, 'Gainst storm, and wind, and tide :

1 The sum - mer morn I've sigh'd for, The fair, sweet morn, a - wakes :
2 The streams on earth I've tast - ed More deep I'll drink a - bove :
3 And aye the dews of sor - row Were lus - tred by His love :
4 I will not gaze at glo - ry, But on my King of grace,
5 Now, like a wea - ry trav - 'ler That lean - eth on his guide,

1 Dark, dark hath been the mid - night, But day - spring is at hand,
2 There to an o - cean ful - ness His mer - cy doth ex - pand,
3 I'll bless the hand that guid - ed, I'll bless the heart that plann'd,
4 Not at the crown He gift - eth, But on His pierc - ed hand :
5 A - mid the shades of ev' - ning, While sinks life's ling - 'ring sand,

1 And glo - ry, glo - ry dwell - eth In Im - man - uel's land.
2 And glo - ry, glo - ry dwell - eth In Im - man - uel's land.
3 When thron'd where glo - ry dwell - eth. In Im - man - uel's land.
4 The Lamb is all the glo - ry Of Im - man - uel's land.
5 I hail the glo - ry dawn - ing In Im - man - uel's land.

412 Trusting More

F. A. BLACKMER

F. A. BLACKMER

1 Once I thought I walk'd with Je-sus, Yet such change-ful
2 For He call'd me clos-er to Him, Bade my doubt-ing
3 Now I'm trust-ing ev-'ry mo-ment, Less than this is
4 Bless-ed Sa-viour, Thou dost keep me By Thy pow'r from

1 moods I had; .. Some-times trust-ing, some-times doubt-ing;
2 trem-ors cease; .. And, when I had ful-ly trust-ed,
3 not e-nough; .. And my Sa-viour bears me gent-ly
4 day to day, .. And my heart is full of glad-ness,

REFRAIN

1 Some-times joy-ful, some-times sad.
2 Fill'd my soul with per-fect peace.
3 O'er the pla-ces once so rough.
4 For Thou'lt keep me all the way.

O the peace my

Sa-viour gives! Peace I nev-er knew be-fore; .. For my

way has bright-er grown Since I learn'd to trust Him more. ..

413 It is Well

HORATIO G. SPAFFORD

PHILIP P. BLISS

1 When peace like a riv-er at-tend-eth my way, When sor-
2 If Sa-tan should buf-fet, if tri-als should come, Let this
3 My sin, O the bliss of this glo-ri-ous thought! My sin,
4 For me be it Christ, be it Christ hence to live! If Jor-
5 But Lord, 'tis for Thee, for Thy com-ing we wait, The sky,

1 rows like sea bil-lows roll; What-ev-er my lot, Thou hast taught me to
2 blest as-sur-ance con-trol, That Christ hath re-gard-ed my help-less es-
3 not in part but the whole, Is nail'd to His cross; and I bear it no
4 dan a-bove me shall roll No pang shall be mine, for in death as in
5 not the grave, is our goal: O trump of the an-gel! O voice of the

REFRAIN

It is well . . .

1 know It is well, it is well with my soul.
2 tate, And hath shed His own blood for my soul.
3 more: Praise the Lord, praise the Lord, O my soul!
4 life Thou wilt whis-per Thy peace to my soul.
5 Lord! Bless-ed hope! bless-ed rest of my soul!

. . . It is well

with my soul, . . . It is well, it is well with my soul.

with my soul, It is well, it is well with my soul.

414

Let the Sunshine In

ADA BLENKHORN   CHARLES H. GABRIEL

1   Do you fear the foe will in   the   con - flict   win?   Is   it dark with-
2   Does your faith grow faint - er in   the   cause you   love?   Are your pray'rs un -
3   Would you go   re - joic - ing on   the   up - ward   way,   Know-ing naught of

1   out you, dark - er   still   with - in?   Clear the dark - en'd win - dows, o - pen
2   an - sw'red by your   God   a - bove?   Clear the dark - en'd win - dows, o - pen
3   dark - ness, dwell - ing   in   the   day?   Clear the dark - en'd win - dows, o - pen

REFRAIN

wide the door,   Let a lit - tle sun - shine in. . Let the bless - ed

sun - shine in, . . . Let the bless - ed sun - shine .   in; . . .

sun-shine, the sun-shine in, . Let the bless - ed sun - shine, the sun-shine in; .

Clear the dark-en'd win-dows, o - pen wide the door,   Let a lit - tle sun-shine in.

415

He Saves Me

J. W. VAN DE VENTER   WINFIELD S. WEEDEN

1 The dear lov-ing Sav-iour hath found me, And shat-ter'd the
2 He sought me so long ere I knew Him, But fi-nal-ly
3 I nev-er, no nev-er will leave Him! Grow wea-ry of

1 fet-ters that bound me, Though all was con-fu-sion a-round me He
2 win-ning me to Him, I yield-ed my all to pur-sue Him, And
3 ser-vice and grieve Him, I'll con-stant-ly trust and be-lieve Him, Re-

1 came and spake peace to my soul: . The bless-ed Re-deem-er that
2 asked to be fill'd with His grace: . Al-though a vile sin-ner be-
3 main in His pres-ence di-vine: . A-bid-ing in love ev-er

1 bought me In ten-der-ness con-stant-ly sought me, The way of Sal-
2 fore Him, Thro' faith I was led to im-plore Him, And now I re-
3 flow-ing, In know-ledge and grace ev-er grow-ing, Con-fid-ing im-

He Saves Me—*Continued*

1 va-tion He taught me, And made my heart per-fect-ly whole. .
2 joice and a-dore Him, Re-stor'd to His lov-ing em-brace. .
3 pli-cit-ly, know-ing That Je-sus the Sav-iour is mine. .

REFRAIN

He saves me, He saves me, His love fills my soul, hal-le-lu-jah!

O glo-ry! O glo-ry! His Spi-rit a-bid-eth with-in; .

He saves me, He saves me, His love fills my soul, hal-le-lu-jah!

rit.

O glo-ry! O glo-ry! His blood cleans-eth me from all sin. .

416   # Lead, kindly Light

J. H. NEWMAN   SANDON 10.4. 10.4. 10.10.   C. H. PURDAY

1 Lead, kind - ly Light, a - mid th' en-cir-cling gloom; Lead Thou me on;
2 I was not e - ver thus, nor pray'd that Thou Shouldst lead me on;
3 So long Thy pow'r hath blest me, sure it still Will lead me on

1 The night is dark, and I am far from home; Lead Thou me on.
2 I lov'd to choose and see my path; but now Lead Thou me on;
3 O'er moor and fen, o'er crag and torr - ent, till The night is gone;

1 Keep Thou my feet; I do not ask to see
2 I loved the gar - ish day, and, spite of fears,
3 And with the morn those an - gel fa - ces smile,

1 The dis - tant scene;— one step e nough for me.
2 Pride ruled my will: re - mem - ber not past years.
3 Which I have lov'd long since, and lost a - while.

The tune LUX BENIGNA is on the next page

416   Lead, kindly Light

J. H. Newman   Lux Benigna 10.4. 10.4. 10.10.   J. B. Dykes

1 Lead, kindly Light, a-mid th' en-cir-cling gloom;   Lead Thou me on;
2   I was not e - ver thus, nor pray'd that Thou   Shouldst lead me on;
3   So long Thy pow'r hath blest me, sure it still   Will lead me on

1 The night is dark, and I   am far from home;   — Lead Thou me   on.
2   I lov'd to choose and see my path; but now   Lead Thou me   on;
3 O'er moor and fen, o'er crag and tor-rent, till   The night is   gone:

1 Keep Thou my   feet;   I   do not ask   to   see...............
2   I   loved the   gar - ish day, and, spite of   fears,...........
3 And with the   morn   those an - gel fa - ces   smile,.... ......

1 The dis - tant   scene;—one step e - nough   for   me.
2 Pride ruled my   will: re - mem-ber not   past years.
3 Which I   have   lov'd long since, and lost   a - while.

The tune Sandon is on the previous page

417 ## Blessed Assurance

FANNY J. CROSBY

JOSEPH F. KNAPP

1 Bless-ed as-sur-ance, Je-sus is mine! . O what a fore-taste of
2 Per-fect sub-mis-sion, per-fect de-light, . Vis-ions of rap-ture now
3 Per-fect sub-mis-sion, all is at rest, . I in my Sav-iour am

1 glo-ry di-vine! . Heir of sal-va-tion, pur-chase of God;
2 burst on my sight; . An-gels de-scend-ing, bring from a-bove .
3 hap-py and blest; . Watch-ing and wait-ing, look-ing a-bove, .

REFRAIN

1 Born of His Spir-it, wash'd in His blood. .
2 Ech-oes of mer-cy, whis-pers of love. . } This is my sto-ry,
3 Fill'd with His good-ness, lost in His love. .

this is my song, . Prais-ing my Sav-iour all the day long; . This is my

sto-ry, this is my song, . Prais-ing my Sav-iour all the day long. .

418 A River Glorious

FRANCES R. HAVERGAL   WYE VALLEY 6.5.6.5.6.5.D   JAMES MOUNTAIN

1 Like a ri - ver glo - rious Is God's per-fect peace, O - ver all vic -
2 Hid-den in the hol - low Of His bless-ed hand, Ne - ver foe can
3 Ev'- ry joy or tri - al Fall-eth from a - bove, Trac'd up - on our

1 to - rious In its bright in - crease; Per-fect, yet it flow - eth
2 fol - low, Ne - ver trai - tor stand; Not a surge of wor - ry,
3 di - al By the Sun of Love; We may trust Him ful - ly,

1 Full - er ev'- ry day, Per-fect, yet it grow - eth Deep - er all the way.
2 Not a shade of care, Not a blast of hur - ry Touch the spi - rit there.
3 All for us to do, They who trust Him whol - ly Find Him whol - ly true.

REFRAIN

Stay'd up - on Je - ho - vah, Hearts are ful - ly blest;

Find - ing, as He pro - mis'd, Per - fect peace and rest.

By permission of MARSHALL, MORGAN AND SCOTT, LTD.

419 ## Elijah's God

WILLIAM GRUM

WILLIAM GRUM

1 E - li - jah made a sac - ri - fice To of - fer
2 E - li - jah's God still lives to - day And an - swers
3 E - li - jah's God still lives to - day And an - swers

1 to Je - ho - vah; It had been wet with wa - ter thrice,
2 still by fi - re; My friend, just let Him have His way;
3 still in pow - er, As when E - li - jah pray'd for rain,

1 Baal's sac - ri - fice was o - ver: E - li - jah pray'd: the
2 He'll grant your heart's de - si - re: Con - sume the sac - ri -
3 God ans - w'red with a show - er: If you would have your

1 fire came down And lick'd the wa - ter all a - round; So doubt - ing
2 fice you make, and bid your slumb - 'ring soul a - wake; The chains of
3 soul re - fresh'd With rain that falls from heav - en, You must pray

Elijah's God—*Continued*

1 ones be - liev'd, and found E - li - jah's God was liv - ing.
2 in - bred sin will break; E - li - jah's God is liv - ing.
3 through like all the rest, And show-ers shall be giv - en.

REFRAIN

E - li - jah's God still lives to - day To take the

guilt of sin a - way; And when I pray my

heart's de - sire, Up - on my soul He sends the fire.

420   The Solid Rock

EDWARD MOTE   SOLID ROCK 8.8.8.8.8.8.8.8   WILLIAM B. BRADBURY

1 My hope is built on no-thing less Than
2 When dark-ness seems to veil His face I
3 His oath, His co-ve-nant, and blood, Sup-

1 Je-sus' blood and right-eous-ness; I dare not trust the
2 rest on His un-chang-ing grace; In ev-'ry high and
3 port me in the whelm-ing flood; When all a-round my

1 sweet-est frame, But whol-ly lean on Je-sus' name.
2 stor-my gale My an-chor holds with-in the veil.
3 soul gives way He then is all my hope and stay.

REFRAIN

On Christ, the sol-id rock, I stand; All o-ther ground is

sink-ing sand, All o-ther ground is sink-ing sand.

The tune ST. CATHERINE is on the following page

The Solid Rock

420

EDWARD MOTE   ST. CATHERINE 8.8.8.8.8.8   H. F. HEMY; J. G. WALTON

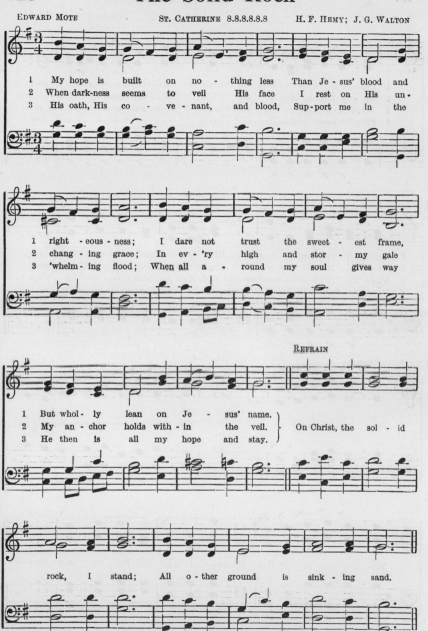

1 My hope is built on no - thing less Than Je - sus' blood and
2 When dark-ness seems to veil His face I rest on His un -
3 His oath, His co - ve - nant, and blood, Sup-port me in the

1 right - eous - ness; I dare not trust the sweet - est frame,
2 chang - ing grace; In ev - 'ry high and stor - my gale
3 'whelm - ing flood; When all a - round my soul gives way

REFRAIN

1 But whol - ly lean on Je - sus' name.
2 My an - chor holds with - in the veil.   On Christ, the sol - id
3 He then is all my hope and stay.

rock, I stand; All o - ther ground is sink - ing sand.

The tune SOLID ROCK is on the preceding page

421   Face to Face

F. A. BRECK   VISION 8.7. 8.7. D   GRANT COLFAX TULLAR

1 Face to face with Christ my Sa - viour, Face to face—what will it be?
2 On - ly faint-ly now I see Him, With the dark-ling veil be - tween,
3 What re - joic-ing in His pres - ence, When are ban-ish'd grief and pain;
4 Face to face! O bliss-ful mo - ment! Face to face—to see and know!

1 When with rap-ture I be - hold Him, Je - sus Christ who died for me.
2 But a bless-ed day is com - ing, When His glo - ry shall be seen.
3 When the crook-ed ways are straight-en'd, And the dark things shall be plain!
4 Face to face with my Re - deem - er, Je - sus Christ who loves me so.

REFRAIN

Face to face shall I be - hold Him, Far be-yond the star-ry sky;

Face to face in all His glo - ry, I shall see Him by and by!

422 Safe in the Glory Land

JAMES L. BLACK.

JNO. R. SWENEY

1. In the good old way where the saints have gone, And the
2. In the good old way like the ran-somed throng, Un-to
3. In the good old way with a stead-fast faith, In the
4. Tho' our feet must stand on the cold, cold brink Of the

1 King leads on be-fore us, We are travelling home to the
2. Zi-on now re-turn-ing, We are travelling home at the
3. bonds of love and un-ion, What a joy is ours for the
4. Jor-dan's storm-y riv-er, With the King we'll cross to the

CHORUS.

1. heavenly hills, With the day-star shining o'er us.
2. King's command, And our lamps are trimm'd and burn-ing.
3. King we see, And with Him we hold com-mun-ion.
4. oth-er side, And we'll sing His praise for ev-er.

Travelling home to the

man-sions fair, Crowns of re-joic-ing and life to wear;

O what a shout when we all get there, Safe in the glo-ry land!

423 Anywhere with Jesus

JESSIE H. BROWN   11.11. 11.11. 11.11.   D. B. TOWNER

1 An-y-where with Je-sus I can safe-ly go, An-y-where He
2 An-y-where with Je-sus I am not a-lone, O-ther friends may
3 An-y-where with Je-sus I can go to sleep, When the dark-'ning

1 leads me in this world be-low. An-y-where with-out Him, dear-est
2 fail me, He is still my own. Tho' His hand may lead me o-ver
3 sha-dows round a-bout me creep; Know-ing I shall wak-en, nev-er

1 joys would fade, An-y-where with Je-sus I am not a-fraid.
2 drear-est ways, An-y-where with Je-sus is a house of praise.
3 more to roam, An-y-where with Je-sus will be home, sweet home.

REFRAIN

An-y-where! an-y-where! Fear I can-not know.

An-y-where with Je-sus I can safe-ly go.

424 ## The Cross is not Greater

BALLINGTON BOOTH   BALLINGTON BOOTH

1 The cross that He gave may be hea-vy,   But it ne'er out-weighs His grace,
2 The thorns in my path are not sharp-er   Than com-pos'd His crown for me,
3 The light of His love shin-eth bright-er   As it falls on paths of   woe,
4 His will I have joy in ful-fill-ing   As I'm walk-ing in His sight,

1 The storm that I fear'd may sur-round me,   But it ne'er ex-cludes His face.
2 The cup that I drink not more bit-ter   Than He drank in Geth-sem-an-e.
3 The toil of my work grow-eth light-er   As I stoop to raise the low.
4 My all to the blood I am bring-ing,   It a-lone can keep me right.

REFRAIN

The cross is not great-er than His grace,   The

storm can-not hide His bless-ed face;   I am sat-is-fied to

know That with Je-sus here be-low I can con-quer ev-'ry foe.

425
He will Hide Me

M. E. Servoss

James M'Granahan

1. When the storms of life are ra-ging, Tempests wild on sea and land,
2. Tho' He may send some af-flic-tion, 'Twill but make me long for home;
3. En-e-mies may strive to in-jure, Sa-tan all His arts em-ploy;
4. So, while here the cross I'm bear-ing, Meet-ing storms and bil-lows wild,

1. I will seek a place of re-fuge In the sha-dow of God's hand.
2. For in love and not in an-ger, All His chast-en-ings will come.
3. He will turn what seems to harm me In-to ev-er-last-ing joy.
4. Je-sus, for my soul is car-ing, Naught can harm His Fa-ther's child.

Chorus

He will hide me, He will hide me, Where no

He will hide me. He will hide me,

harm can e'er be-tide me; He will hide me, safe-ly

Where no harm can e'er be-tide me; He will hide me,

He will Hide Me—*Continued*

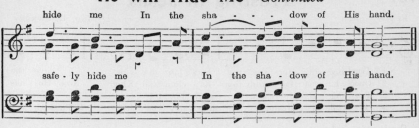

hide   me   In   the   sha - - - dow   of   His   hand.

safe - ly hide me   In   the   sha - dow   of   His   hand.

426   'Tis so Sweet to Trust

LOUISA M. R. STEAD   FALL RIVER   8.7. 8.7. D   WM. J. KIRKPATRICK

1 'Tis so sweet to trust in Je - sus, Just to take Him at His word;
2 Oh, how sweet to trust in Je - sus! Just to trust His cleans-ing blood;
3 Yes, 'tis sweet to trust in Je - sus! Just from sin and self to cease;
4 I'm so glad I learn'd to trust Thee, Pre-cious Je - sus, Sa-viour, Friend;

1 Just to rest up - on His prom-ise; Just to know, "Thus saith the Lord."
2 Just in sim - ple faith to plunge me 'Neath the heal - ing, cleans-ing flood.
3 Just from Je - sus sim - ply tak - ing Life and rest, and joy and peace.
4 And I know that Thou art with me, Wilt be with me to the end.

REFRAIN

Je - sus, Je - sus, how I trust Him! How I've prov'd Him o'er and o'er!

p

Je - sus, Je - sus, pre - cious Je - sus! Oh, for grace to trust Him more!

427 Trusting in Jesus

FRANK GOULD

JNO. R. SWENEY

1 Trust-ing in Je - sus, my Sa - viour di - vine, I have the
2 Once I was far from my Sa - viour and King, Now He has
3 Trust-ing in Je - sus, O what should I fear! No - thing can
4 If while a stran-ger I jour - ney be - low, Fill'd with His

1 wit - ness that still He is mine; Great are the bless-ings He
2 taught me His mer - cy to sing: Peace in be - liev - ing He
3 harm me when He is so near; Sweet is the pro - mise He
4 ful - ness such rap - ture I know, What will the bliss of e -

1-3 giv - eth to me: O I am hap - py as mor - tal can be!
4 ter - ni - ty be When in His beau - ty the King I shall see?

Trusting in Jesus—*Continued*

REFRAIN

I am re-deem'd, . . . and I know it full well, . . .

I am re-deem'd, and I know it full well, full well,

Sav'd by His grace, . . . I with Him shall dwell; . . .

Sav'd by His grace, I with Him shall dwell, shall dwell;

I am re-deem'd, . . . and the child of His love, . . .

I am re-deem'd, and the child of His love, His love,

Heir to a glo - - ri - ous crown a - bove. . . .

Heir to a glo - ri - ous crown a - bove, a - bove.

428   Jesus, Lover of My Soul

CHARLES WESLEY   HOLLINGSIDE 7.7.7.7. D   J. B. DYKES

1 Je - sus, Lov - er of my soul, Let me to Thy bo - som fly,
2 O - ther re - fuge have I none; Hangs my help - less soul on Thee;
3 Thou, O Christ! art all I want; More than all in Thee I find:
4 Plen-teous grace with Thee is found, Grace to co - ver all my sin;

1 While the near - er wa - ters roll, While the tem - pest still is high:
2 Leave, ah! leave me not a - lone, Still sup - port and com - fort me.
3 Raise the fall - en, cheer the faint, Heal the sick, and lead the blind.
4 Let the heal - ing streams a - bound, Make and keep me pure with - in:

1 Hide me, O my Sa - viour, hide! Till the storm of life is past;
2 All my trust on Thee is stay'd, All my help from Thee I bring;
3 Just and ho - ly is Thy Name, I am all un - right - eous-ness;
4 Thou of life the foun - tain art, Free - ly let me take of Thee;

1 Safe in - to the ha - ven guide; O re - ceive my soul at last!
2 Cov - er my de - fence-less head With the sha - dow of Thy wing.
3 Vile and full of sin I am, Thou art full of truth and grace.
4 Spring Thou up with - in my heart, Rise to all e - ter - ni - ty.

The tunes ABERYSTWYTH and JUDD STREET are on the following pages

428 Jesus, Lover of My Soul

CHARLES WESLEY   ABERYSTWYTH 7.7.7.7.D   JOSEPH PARRY

1 Jesus, Lover of my soul, Let me to Thy bosom fly,
2 Other refuge have I none; Hangs my helpless soul on Thee;
3 Thou, O Christ! art all I want; More than all in Thee I find;
4 Plenteous grace with Thee is found, Grace to cover all my sin;

1 While the nearer waters roll, While the tempest still is high:
2 Leave, ah! leave me not alone, Still support and comfort me.
3 Raise the fallen, cheer the faint, Heal the sick, and lead the blind.
4 Let the healing streams abound, Make and keep me pure within:

1 Hide me, O my Saviour, hide, Till the storm of life is past;
2 All my trust on Thee is stay'd, All my help from Thee I bring;
3 Just and holy is Thy name, I am all unrighteousness;
4 Thou of life the fountain art, Freely let me take of Thee;

1 Safe into the haven guide; O receive my soul at last.
2 Cover my defence-less head With the shadow of Thy wing.
3 Vile and full of sin I am, Thou art full of truth and grace.
4 Spring Thou up within my heart, Rise to all eternity.

Music by permission of HUGHES A'I FAB PUBLISHERS LTD.

The tune HOLLINGSIDE comes before, while JUDD STREET follows this one

428   # Jesus, Lover of My Soul

CHARLES WESLEY   JUDD STREET 7.7.7.7. D   ANON

1 Je - sus, Lov - er of my soul, Let me
2 O - ther re - fuge have I none ; Hangs my
3 Thou, O Christ, art all I want ; More than
4 Plen - teous grace with Thee is found, Grace to

1 to Thy bo - som fly, While the near - er wa -
2 help - less soul on Thee ; Leave, ah ! leave me not
3 all in Thee I find ; Raise the fall - en, cheer
4 cov - er all my sin ; Let the heal - ing streams

1 ters roll, While the tem - pest still is high ;
2 a - lone ; Still sup - port and com - fort me.
3 the faint, Heal the sick, and lead the blind.
4 a - bound ; Make and keep me pure with - in.

Jesus, Lover of My Soul—*Continued*

1 Hide me, O my Sa - viour! hide,
2 All my trust on Thee is stay'd,
3 Just and ho - ly is Thy Name,
4 Thou of life the foun - tain art,

1 Hide me, O my Sa - viour! hide, Till the
2 All my trust on Thee is stay'd; All my
3 Just and ho - ly is Thy Name, I am
4 Thou of life the foun - tain art, Free - ly

cres.   *mf*

1 Till the storm of life is past; Safe in - to the
2 All my help from Thee I bring; Cov - er my de -
3 I am all un - right - eous - ness; Vile and full of
4 Free - ly let me take of Thee; Spring Thou up with

1 storm of life is past; Safe in -
2 help from Thee I bring; Cov - er
3 all un - right - eous - ness; Vile and
4 let me take of Thee; Spring Thou

cres.   *f*

1 ha - ven guide; O re - ceive my soul at last!
2 fence - less head With the sha - dow of Thy wing.
3 sin I am, Thou art full of truth and grace.
4 in my heart, Rise to all e - ter - ni - ty.

1 to the ha - ven guide; O re - ceive my soul at last!
2 my de - fence - less head With the sha - dow of Thy wing.
3 full of sin I am, Thou art full of truth and grace.
4 up with - in my heart, Rise to all e - ter - ni - ty.

The tunes HOLLINGSIDE and ABERYSTWYTH precede this one

429 The Night is Coming

A. L. COGHILL. DILIGENCE 7.6.7.5. D LOWELL MASON

1 Work, for the night is com - ing! Work thro' the morn-ing hours;
2 Work, for the night is com - ing! Work thro' the sun - ny noon;
3 Work, for the night is com - ing! Un - der the sun - set skies,

1 Work while the dew is spark - ling; Work 'mid spring-ing flow'rs;
2 Fill the bright hours with la - bour; Rest comes sure and soon.
3 While their bright tints are glow - ing, Work, for day - light flies.

1 Work while the day grows bright - er, Un - der the glow - ing sun;
2 Give to each fly - ing min - ute Some-thing to keep in store;
3 Work till the last beam fad - eth, Fad - eth to shine no more;

1 Work, for the night is com - ing, When man's work is done.
2 Work, for the night is com - ing, When man works no more.
3 Work, while the night is dark - 'ning, When man's work is o'er.

430 Ashamed of Jesus

JOSEPH GRIGG   BOSTON L.M.   LOWELL MASON

1 Je - sus, and shall it ev - er be A mor-tal man a-sham'd of Thee?
2 A-sham'd of Je - sus! soon-er far Let ev'n-ing blush to own a star;
3 A-sham'd of Je - sus! just as soon Let mid-night be a-sham'd of noon:
4 A-sham'd of Je - sus! that dear Friend On whom my hopes of heav'n de - pend!

1 A-sham'd of Thee whom an - gels praise, Whose glo-ries shine thro' end - less days!
2 He shed the beams of light di - vine O'er this be - night - ed soul of mine.
3 'Twas mid-night with my soul till He, Bright morn-ing star, bade dark - ness flee.
4 No! when I blush be this my shame That I no more re - vere His Name.

JOSEPH GRIGG   FEDERAL STREET L.M.   HENRY K. OLIVER

1 Je - sus, and shall it ev - er be A mor-tal man a-sham'd of Thee?
2 A-sham'd of Je - sus! soon-er far Let ev'n-ing blush to own a star;
3 A-sham'd of Je - sus! just as soon Let mid-night be a-sham'd of noon:
4 A-sham'd of Je - sus! that dear Friend On whom my hopes of heav'n de - pend!

1 A-sham'd of Thee whom an - gels praise, Whose glo-ries shine thro' end - less days!
2 He shed the beams of light di - vine O'er this be - night - ed soul of mine.
3 'Twas mid-night with my soul till He, Bright morn-ing star, bade dark-ness flee.
4 No! when I blush be this my shame That I no more re - vere His Name.

431 Soldiers of Immanuel

J. J. SIMS

J. J. SIMS
Arr. P. J. MANSFIELD

1 Sol - diers of Je - sus! sol - diers of the Cross!
2 Sol - diers of Je - sus! gird ye to the fray,
3 Sol - diers of Je - sus! lift your stan - dard high;
4 Sol - diers of Je - sus! when the bat - tle's done,
5 Sol - diers of Je - sus! of the Lamb once slain,

1 Fol - low your Cap - tain, count - ing all but loss;
2 Stand in your ar - mour in this e - vil day;
3 Write on your ban - ners: Je - sus came to die;
4 Foes all are van - quish'd, and the vic - t'ry won;
5 Know ye that Je - sus soon will come to reign;

1 If you fight the bat - tle you shall gain re - nown,
2 Where the bat - tle rag - es there may ye be found,
3 By the Cross of Je - sus we the vic - t'ry win,
4 Then with shouts of tri - umph we shall hail the King,
5 Lift your heads in glad - ness, vic - tor - y is nigh,

1 And if you are faith - ful you shall wear a crown.
2 Where the need is great - est that is ho - ly ground.
3 For the blood of Je - sus cleans - eth from all sin.
4 When the vaults of hea - ven with His prais - es ring.
5 Send a shout of wel - come through the earth and sky.

Soldiers of Immanuel—*Continued*

REFRAIN

1-4 March on! March on! sol - diers of Im - man - u - el;
5 Come, Lord, Je - sus! come and take Thy peo - ple home;

1-4 March on! March on! sing - ing as we go: . . .
5 Come, O come! we long Thy face to see; . . .

1-4 Glo - ry! glo - ry to the Lamb of Cal - va - ry!
5 Come, Lord Je - sus! claim the king - dom and the pow'r,

1-4 In His might we con - quer ev - 'ry foe.
5 Set the earth from all its bon - dage free.

432 More about Jesus

E. E. HEWITT

JNO. R. SWENEY

1 More a-bout Je-sus would I know, More of His grace to o-thers show;
2 More a-bout Je-sus let me learn, More of His ho-ly will dis-cern;
3 More a-bout Je-sus, in His Word, Hold-ing com-mun-ion with my Lord;
4 More a-bout Je-sus, on His throne, Rich-es in glo-ry all His own;

1 More of His sav-ing full-ness see, More of His love who died for me.
2 Spi-rit of God, my Teach-er be, Show-ing the things of Christ to me.
3 Hear-ing His voice in ev-'ry line, Mak-ing each faith-ful say-ing mine.
4 More of His king-dom's sure in-crease; More of His com-ing, Prince of Peace.

REFRAIN

More, more a-bout Je-sus, More, more a-bout Je-sus;

More of His sav-ing full-ness see, More of His love who died for me.

433 My Heart is Resting

ANNA L. WARING   BERNE C.M.   SWISS MELODY

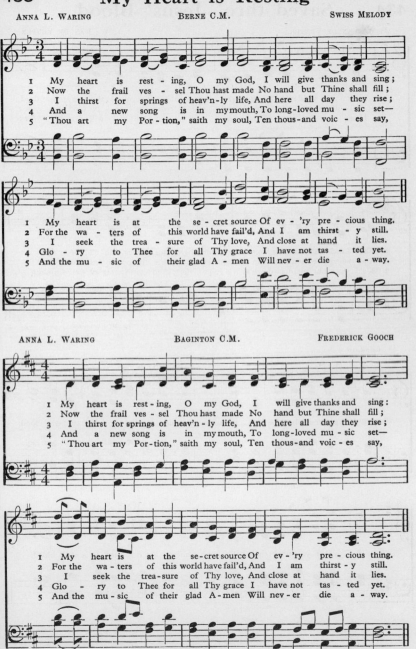

1 My heart is rest - ing, O my God, I will give thanks and sing;
2 Now the frail ves - sel Thou hast made No hand but Thine shall fill;
3 I thirst for springs of heav'n-ly life, And here all day they rise;
4 And a new song is in my mouth, To long-loved mu - sic set—
5 "Thou art my Por - tion," saith my soul, Ten thous-and voic - es say,

1 My heart is at the se - cret source Of ev - 'ry pre - cious thing.
2 For the wa - ters of this world have fail'd, And I am thirst - y still.
3 I seek the trea - sure of Thy love, And close at hand it lies.
4 Glo - ry to Thee for all Thy grace I have not tas - ted yet.
5 And the mu - sic of their glad A - men Will nev - er die a - way.

ANNA L. WARING   BAGINTON C.M.   FREDERICK GOOCH

1 My heart is rest - ing, O my God, I will give thanks and sing:
2 Now the frail ves - sel Thou hast made No hand but Thine shall fill;
3 I thirst for springs of heav'n - ly life, And here all day they rise;
4 And a new song is in my mouth, To long-loved mu - sic set—
5 "Thou art my Por - tion," saith my soul, Ten thous-and voic - es say,

1 My heart is at the se - cret source Of ev - 'ry pre - cious thing.
2 For the wa - ters of this world have fail'd, And I am thirst - y still.
3 I seek the trea - sure of Thy love, And close at hand it lies.
4 Glo - ry to Thee for all Thy grace I have not tas - ted yet.
5 And the mu - sic of their glad A - men Will nev - er die a - way.

434   Saved thro' Jesus' Blood

J. W. Van de Venter

J. W. Van de Venter

1 Some - time we'll stand be - fore the judg-ment bar, The quick, the ris - en dead;
2 I'll then re - ceive a bright and star - ry crown, As on - ly God can give;
3 Then we shall meet to nev - er part a - gain, Our toil will then be o'er;

1 The Lord will then make known the re - cord there; Our names will all be read.
2 And when I've been with Him ten thous-and years, I'll have no less to live.
3 We'll lay our bur-dens down at Je - sus' feet, And rest for ev - er - more.

REFRAIN

I'll be pre-sent when the roll is call'd, Pure and spot-less thro' the crim-son flood;

I will an-swer when they call my name; Sav'd thro' Je - sus' blood.

435 Rescue the Perishing

FANNY J. CROSBY

W. H. DOANE

1 Res - cue the per - ish - ing, Care for the dy - ing, Snatch them in
2 Tho' they are slight - ing Him, Still He is wait - ing, Wait - ing the
3 Down in the hu - man heart, Crush'd by the temp - ter, Feel - ings lie
4 Res - cue the per - ish - ing, Du - ty de - mands it; Strength for thy

1 Pit - y from sin and the grave; Weep o'er the err - ing one, Lift
2 Pen - i - tent child to re - ceive. Plead with them earn - est - ly, Plead
3 Bur - ied that grace can re - store; Touch'd by a lov - ing heart, Wak -
4 La - bour the Lord will pro - vide. Back to the nar - row way Pa -

1 up the fall - en, Tell them of Je - sus, the might - y to save.
2 with them gent - ly; He will for - give if they on - ly be - lieve.
3 en'd by kind - ness, Cords that were bro - ken will vi - brate once more.
4 tient - ly win them; Tell the poor wan - d'rer a Sav - iour has died.

REFRAIN

Res - cue the per - ish - ing, Care for the dy - ing;

Je - sus is mer - ci - ful, Je - sus will save!

436 Behold, what Love!

ROBERT BOSWELL, Alt. M. S. SULLIVAN

JAMES McGRANAHAN

1 Be - hold, what love, what bound-less love, The Fa - ther hath be - stow'd
2 No long - er far from Him, but now By pre - cious blood made nigh;
3 What we in glo - ry soon shall be It doth not yet ap - pear;
4 With such a bless - ed hope in view, We would more ho - ly be,

1 On sin - ners lost, that we should be Now call'd the sons of God!
2 Ac - cept - ed in the Well-belov'd, Near to God's heart we lie.
3 But when our pre - cious Lord we see, We shall His im - age bear.
4 More like our ris - en, glo - rious Lord, Whose face we soon shall see.

REFRAIN

Be - hold, ... what man-ner of love! . . . . . What man-ner of
Be-hold, what man-ner of love! . be - hold, what man-ner of love! What man-ner of

love the Fa-ther hath be-stow'd up - on us, That we, . . . that we should be
love the Fa-ther hath be-stow'd up - on us; That we should be call'd, . we should be

call'd, ... Should be call'd the sons of God!
call'd the sons of God, Should be call'd the sons of God!

437 Peace, Perfect Peace

E. H. BICKERSTETH   PAX TECUM 10.10.   G. T. CALDBECK

1 Peace, per - fect peace, in this dark world of sin?
2 Peace, per - fect peace, by throng - ing du - ties press'd?
3 Peace, per - fect peace, with sor - rows surg - ing round?
4 Peace, per - fect peace, with lov'd ones far a - way?
5 Peace, per - fect peace, our fu - ture all un - known?
6 Peace, per - fect peace, death shad - 'owing us and ours?
7 It is e - nough; earth's strug - gles soon shall cease,

1 The blood of Je - sus whis - pers peace with - in.
2 To do the will of Je - sus, this is rest.
3 On Je - sus' bo - som naught but calm is found.
4 In Je - sus' keep - ing we are safe, and they.
5 Je - sus we know, and He is on the throne.
6 Je - sus has van - quish'd death and all its pow'rs.
7 And Je - sus call us to heav'n's per - fect peace.

E. H. BICKERSTETH   SONG 46 10.10.   ORLANDO GIBBONS

1 Peace, per - fect peace, in this dark world of sin?
2 Peace, per - fect peace, by throng - ing du - ties press'd?
3 Peace, per - fect peace, with sor - rows surg - ing round?
4 Peace, per - fect peace, with lov'd ones far a - way?
5 Peace, per - fect peace, our fu - ture all un - known?
6 Peace, per - fect peace, death shad - 'owing us and ours?
7 It is e - nough; earth's strug - gles soon shall cease,

1 The blood of Je - sus whis - pers peace with - in.
2 To do the will of Je - sus, this is rest.
3 On Je - sus' bo - som naught but calm is found.
4 In Je - sus' keep - ing we are safe, and they.
5 Je - sus we know, and He is on the throne.
6 Je - sus has van - quish'd death and all its pow'rs.
7 And Je - sus call us to heav'n's per - fect peace.

Music by permission of the CHURCH BOOK ROOM PRESS LTD.

438 I've Seen the Face of Jesus

W. SPENCER WALTON   WONDROUS SIGHT 7.6.7.6.7.6.D.   D. B. TOWNER

1 I've seen the face of Je - sus, He smil'd in love on me; It
2 And since I've seen His beau - ty, All else I count but loss; The
3 I've heard the voice of Je - sus, He told me of His love, And
4 I felt the hand of Je - sus,— My brow, it throbb'd with care,— He
5 I know He's com - ing short - ly To take us all a - bove; We'll

1 fill'd my heart with rap - ture, My soul with ec - sta - sy. The scars of deep - est
2 world, its fame and pleas - ure, Is now to me but dross. His light dis-pell'd my
3 call'd me His own trea - ure, His un - de - fil'd, His dove. It came like soft - est
4 plac'd it there so soft - ly, And whis-per'd, "Do not fear." Like clouds be - fore the
5 sing re-demp-tion's sto - ry, The sto - ry of His love; We'll hear His voice of

1 an - guish Were lost in glo - ry bright; I've seen the face of Je - sus, It
2 dark - ness, His smile was, oh! so sweet; I've seen the face of Je - sus, I
3 mu - sic A - cross an o - cean calm, And seem'd to play so sweet - ly Some
4 sun - shine, My cares have roll'd a - way; I'm sit - ting in His pres - ence, It
5 mu - sic, We'll feel His hand of care; He'll nev - er rest, He says so, Un -

REFRAIN

1 was a won-drous sight!
2 can but kiss His feet.
3 won-drous ho - ly psalm.   Oh! glo - rious face of beau - ty, Oh! gen - tle touch of
4 is a cloud-less day.
5 til He has us there.

The Face of Jesus—*Continued*

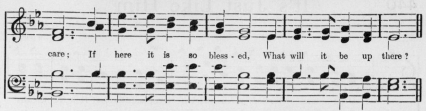

care; If here it is so bless-ed, What will it be up there?

By permission of THE CHARLES M. ALEXANDER COPYRIGHTS TRUST

439

My Jesus, I Love Thee

W. R. FEATHERSTONE   AFFECTION 12.12.12.12   ANON

1 My Je-sus, I love Thee, I know Thou art mine, For Thee all the
2 I love Thee be-cause Thou hast first lov-ed me And pur-chas'd my
3 I will love Thee in life, I will love Thee in death, And praise Thee as

1 plea-sures of sin I re-sign; My gra-cious Re-deem-er, my
2 par-don when nail'd to the Tree; I love Thee for wear-ing the
3 long as Thou lend-est me breath, And say, when the death-dew lies

mp   *cres.*

1 Sa-viour art Thou, If ev-er I lov'd Thee, if ev-er I
2 thorns on Thy brow, If ev-er I lov'd Thee, if ev-er I
3 cold on my brow, If ev-er I lov'd Thee, if ev-er I

f

lov'd Thee, if ev-er I lov'd Thee, my Je-sus, 'tis now!

440 It's Just Like Him

W. L. STONE

W. L. STONE, *Arr.* G. ALLAN

1 O I love to read of Je-sus and His love; and His love! How He left His
2 O I love to read of Je-sus as He went as He went Ev-'ry-where to
3 O I love to read of Je-sus on the tree! on the tree! For it shows how
4 O my dear and pre-cious Sa-viour, at Thy feet! at Thy feet. Here I give my-

1 Fa-ther's man-sion far a - bove, far a-bove; How He came on earth to live, How He
2 do His Fa-ther's will in - tent, will in-tent; How He gave the blind their sight, How He
3 great the love that died for me, died for me; And the blood that from His side Flow'd, when
4 self, and all I have com-plete, have com-plete; I will serve Thee all my days With a

1 came His life to give: O I love to read of Je-sus and His love, and His love!
2 gave the wrong'd ones right, How He swift de-liv-'rance to the cap-tive sent, cap-tive sent.
3 on the Cross He died, Paid my debt and ev-er-more doth make me free, make me free.
4 heart all fill'd with praise, And I'll thank Thee face to face when we shall meet, we shall meet.

REFRAIN

It's just like Him to take my sins a-way, To make me glad and free,

It's Just Like Him—*Continued*

To keep me day by day It's just like Him to give His life for me,

rall.

That I might go to hea-ven, and ev-er with Him be.

441 Old Time Religion

ANON

OLD TIME RELIGION 7.7.7.6

Arr. G. ALLAN

1 'Tis the old time re-lig-ion, 'Tis the old time re-lig-ion,
2 It was good for our mo-thers, It was good for our mo-thers,
3 Makes me love ev-'ry-bod-y, Makes me love ev-'ry-bod-y,
4 It has sav-ed our fa-thers, It has sav-ed our fa-thers,

FINE

1 'Tis the old time re-lig-ion, It's good e-nough for me.
2 It was good for our mo-thers, It's good e-nough for me.
3 Makes me love ev-'ry-bod-y, It's good e-nough for me.
4 It has sav-ed our fa-thers, It's good e-nough for me.

D.S. — 'Tis the old time re-lig-ion, It's good e-nough for me.

REFRAIN

D.S.

'Tis the old time re-lig-ion, 'Tis the old time re-lig-ion.

5 It was good for the Prophet Daniel,
6 It was good for the Hebrew Children,
7 It was tried in the fiery furnace,

8 It was good for Paul and Silas,
9 It will do when I am dying,
10 It will take us all to heaven,

442 Just the Same

S. Z. KAUFMAN

W. A. OGDEN

1 Have you ev - er heard the sto - ry Of the Babe of Beth - le - hem,
2 Have you ev - er heard the sto - ty How He walked up - on the sea
3 Have you ev - er heard of Je - sus Pray - ing in Geth - sem - an - e,

1 Who was wor-shipp'd by the an - gels And the wise and ho - ly men,
2 To His dear dis - ci - ples toss - ing On the waves of Gal - i - lee?
3 And the ev - er thrill-ing sto - ry How He died up - on the tree,

1 How He taught the learn-ed doc - tors In the tem - ple far a - way?
2 How the waves in an - gry mo - tion Quick-ly would His will o - bey?
3 Cru - el thorns His fore-head pierc-ing, As His spi - rit pass'd a - way?

1 O I'm glad, so glad to tell you, He is just the same to-day!
2 O I'm glad, so glad to tell you, He is just the same to-day!
3 This He did for you, my bro-ther, And He's just the same to-day!

REFRAIN

He is just . . . . . the same to - day, He is
just the same to - day, He is just the same to-day,

Just the Same—*Continued*

just . . . . the same to-day,   Seek-ing those who are a-stray,

just the same to-day,   He   is   just the   same to-day,

Sav-ing souls a-long the way; Thank God! He is just the same to - day.

An alternative tune when the REFRAIN is used alone

S. Z. KAUFMAN   GEORGE ALLAN

He is just the same to-day,   He is just the same to-day,   He is

just, He is just,   just the same to - day, Seek-ing those who are   a-stray,

Sav-ing souls a-long the way, Thank God! Thank God! He is just the same to-day.

443 More to Follow

PHILIPP BLISS

PHILIPP BLISS

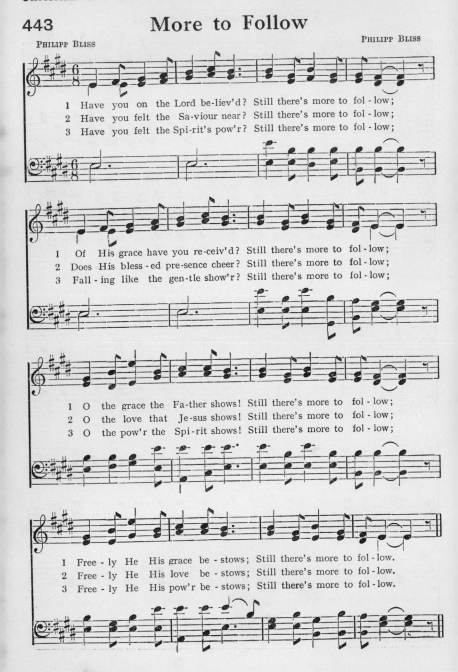

1 Have you on the Lord be-liev'd? Still there's more to fol-low;
2 Have you felt the Sa-viour near? Still there's more to fol-low;
3 Have you felt the Spi-rit's pow'r? Still there's more to fol-low;

1 Of His grace have you re-ceiv'd? Still there's more to fol-low;
2 Does His bless-ed pre-sence cheer? Still there's more to fol-low;
3 Fall-ing like the gen-tle show'r? Still there's more to fol-low;

1 O the grace the Fa-ther shows! Still there's more to fol-low;
2 O the love that Je-sus shows! Still there's more to fol-low;
3 O the pow'r the Spi-rit shows! Still there's more to fol-low;

1 Free-ly He His grace be-stows; Still there's more to fol-low.
2 Free-ly He His love be-stows; Still there's more to fol-low.
3 Free-ly He His pow'r be-stows; Still there's more to fol-low.

More to Follow—*Continued*

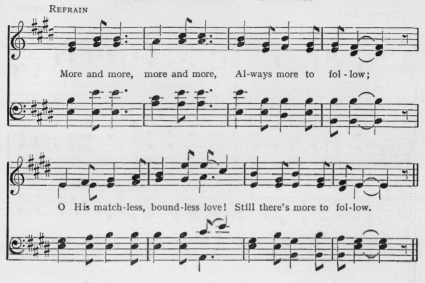

More and more, more and more, Al-ways more to fol-low;

O His match-less, bound-less love! Still there's more to fol-low.

Alternative tune when the REFRAIN is used alone

PHILIPP BLISS   E. H. SWINSTEAD

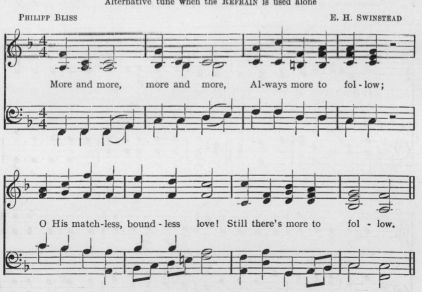

More and more, more and more, Al-ways more to fol-low;

O His match-less, bound-less love! Still there's more to fol-low.

By permission of the COMPOSER

444   The New, New Song

FLORA L. BEST   JOHN R. SWENEY

1. There are songs of joy that I loved to sing, When my heart was blithe as a
2. There are strains of home that are dear as life, And I list to them oft 'mid the
3. Can my lips be mute, or my heart be sad, When the gra-cious Mas-ter hath
4. I shall catch the gleam of its jas-per wall When I come to the gloom of the

1. bird in spring, But the song I have learn'd is so full of cheer, That the
2. din of strife; But I know of a home that is won-drous fair, And I
3. made me glad? When He points where the ma - ny man-sions be, And
4. e - ven-fall, For I know that the sha - dows, drea-ry and dim, Have a

Vivace.
REFRAIN.

1. dawn shines out in the darkness drear.   O, the new,   new song!   O the
2. sing the psalm they are sing-ing there.
3. sweet-ly says "There is one for thee?"
4. path of light that will lead to Him.   O, the new,   new song!

new,   new song,   I can sing   it   now   With the
O, the new,   new song,   I can sing   just now

The New, New Song—*Continued*

ran - som'd throng:
ransom'd, the ransom'd throng:
Pow-er and do - min - ion to Him that shall

reign,
that shall reign;
Glo - ry and praise to the Lamb that was slain.

445 My Saviour Leads Me

FANNY J. CROSBY DIJON 8.7.8.7. GERMAN MELODY

1. All the way my Sa-viour leads me: What have I to ask be - side?
2. Heav'n-ly peace, div-in - est com - fort, Here by faith in Him to dwell!
3. All the way my Sa-viour leads me: Cheers each wind-ing path I tread;
4. Tho' my wea - ry steps may fal - ter, And my soul a-thirst may be,

p rit.

1. Can I doubt His ten - der mer - cy, Who thro' life has been my Guide?
2. For I know what e'er be - fall me, Je - sus do - eth all things well.
3. Gives me grace for ev'ry tri - al, Feeds me with the liv - ing bread.
4. Gush - ing from the rock be - fore me, Lo! a spring of joy I see.

5. All the way my Saviour leads me:
   Oh, the fulness of His love!
   Perfect rest to me is promis'd
   In my Father's house above.

6. When my spirit, cloth'd immortal,
   Wings its flight to realms of day,
   This, my song through endless ages—
   Jesus led me all the way.

446   On for Jesus!

J. HOWARD ENTWISLE   J. HOWARD ENTWISLE

1. On for Je-sus! stead-y be your arm and brave; On-ward, on-ward,
2. On for Je-sus! tiresome tho' the con-flict be, Tho' the hosts of
3. On for Je-sus! till the sound of strife is o'er! When the great Com

D.C.—"On for Je-sus!" this shall be the bat-tle cry, Ne'er re-treat-ing,

1. take the shield and sword; On for Je-sus! stand-ard of your
2. sin are press-ing hard; On for Je-sus! striv-ing for the
3. mand-er calls for thee, Thou shalt wear a crown of life for-

ev-er press-ing on; On for Je-sus! march-ing on to

1. Cap-tain wave, Press-ing on-ward, trust-ing in His word.
2. vic-to-ry, End-less life will soon be your re-ward.
3. ev-er-more, And with Je-sus reign e-ter-nal-ly.

FINE.

vic-to-ry, As we shout the glad re-demp-tion song.

March-ing, marching on, We're marching on-ward still for Je-sus;
Marching on, marching on,

D.C.

March-ing, marching on, Beneath the ban-ner of the free;
Marching on, marching on,

447 **I have a Friend**

FANNY J. CROSBY

JNO. R. SWENEY

1. I have a Friend and He came to seek me, I was a - far on the
2. O how my heart with its joy is bound - ing, O what a Sa - viour and
3. I have a Friend that will ne'er for - sake me, I shall be kept by His
4. I have a hope that is sure and stead - fast,— Firm as the rock where by

1. o - cean wave, In - to the fold of His love He brought me, Peace to my
2. Friend is He, Full of com - pas - sion and rich in bless - ing, O how He
3. might - y pow'r, Safe in the arms of His love that folds me, Moment by
4. faith I stand; I have the pledge of a rest e - ter - nal Waiting for

CHORUS.

1. soul from that hour He gave.
2. loves and He cares for me.
3. mo - ment and hour by hour.
4. me in the soul's bright land.

Glo - ry, glo - ry, Je - sus is my Sa - viour,

I will sing and praise Him in the glad, new song; Glo - ry, glo - ry,

I will give Him glo - ry, When mine eyes be - hold Him, in the blood-wash'd throng.

448 Abiding in Him.

CHAS. B. J. ROOT   D. C. WRIGHT

1. A - bid - ing, oh, so wondrous sweet! I'm rest - ing at the Saviour's feet,
2. He speaks, and by His word is giv'n His peace, a rich fore - taste of heav'n!
3. I live; not I; thro' Him a - lone By Whom the might-y work is done,
4. Now rest, my heart, the work is done, I'm saved thro' the E - ter - nal Son!

1. I trust in Him I'm sa - tis - fied, I'm rest - ing in the Cru - ci - fied!
2. Not as the world He peace doth give, 'Tis thro' this hope my soul shall live.
3. Dead to my-self, a - live to Him, I count all loss His rest to gain.
4. Let all my pow'rs my soul em - ploy, To tell the world my peace and joy.

CHORUS.

A - bid - ing, a - bid - ing, Oh! so won - drous sweet!
A - bid - ing in Him, I'm rest - ing in Him, Oh! so wondrous sweet, wondrous sweet!

I'm rest - ing, rest - ing At the Sa - viour's feet.
I'm rest - ing in Him, rest - ing in Him, At the Sa - viour's feet, at His feet.

449 The Sure Foundation

T. C. O'KANE

1. There stands a Rock on shores of time That rears to heav'n its head sublime;
2. That Rock's a cross, its arms out-spread, Ce-les-tial glo-ry bathes its head;
3. That Rock's a tower, whose lof-ty height, Il-lum'd with heav'n's unclouded light,

1. That Rock is cleft, and they are blest Who find within this cleft a rest.
2. To its firm base my all I bring, And to the rock of a-ges cling.
3. Opes wide its gate be-neath the dome Where saints find rest with Christ at home.

CHORUS.

Some build their hopes on the ev-er drift-ing sand, Some on their fame, or their trea-sure, or their land; Mine's on a Rock that for-ev-er will stand, Je-sus, the "Rock of A-ges."

450 No Stranger There

E. E. Hewitt

A. F. Bourne

1. When the pearl-y gates are o-pen'd To a sin-ner sav'd by grace, When thro'
2. Thro' time's ev-er-chang-ing sea-sons, I am press-ing t'ward the goal; 'Tis my
3. There my dear Re-deem-er liv-eth, Bless-ed Lamb up-on the throne; By the

1. ev-er-last-ing mer-cy, I be-hold my Sa-viour's face, When I en-ter in the
2. heart's sweet na-tive coun-try, 'Tis the home-land of my soul; Many lov'd ones, cloth'd with
3. crim-son marks up-on them, He will sure-ly claim His own. So, when-ev-er sad or

1. man-sions Of the cit-y bright and fair, I shall have a roy-al wel-come, For I'll
2. beau-ty, In those won-drous glo-ries share; When I rise, re-deemed, for-giv-en, I shall
3. lone-ly, Look be-yond the earth-ly care; Wea-ry child of God, re-mem-ber, You will

REFRAIN

be no stran-ger there. I shall be no stran-ger there, Je-sus will my place pre-

I shall be no stran-ger there, Jesus will my place pre-

pare; He will meet me, He will greet me, I shall be no stran-ger there.

pare; He will meet me, He will greet me, I shall be no stran-ger there.

Sunlight

451

J. W. Van De Venter

W. S. Weeden

1 I wan-dered in the shades of night, Till Je - sus came to me,
2 Tho' clouds may ga - ther in the sky, And bil - lows round me roll,
3 While walk-ing in the light of God, I, sweet com-mun - ion find;
4 I cross the wide ex - tend - ed fields, I jour - ney o'er the plain,
5 Soon I shall see Him as He is, The Light that came to me;

1 And with the sun - light of His love Bade all my dark - ness flee.
2 How - ev - er dark the world may be, I've sun - light in my soul.
3 I press with ho - ly vig - our on And leave the world be - hind.
4 And in the sun - light of His love I reap the gold - en grain.
5 Be - hold the bright-ness of His face, Through-out e - ter - ni - ty.

REFRAIN

Sun - light, sun - light in my soul to - day,
to - day, yes,
Sun - light, sun - light

all a - long the way,
nar - row way,
Since the Sav - iour found me,

took a - way my sin,
load of sin,
I have had the sun-light of His love with-in.

452 Homeward Bound

R. F. Beveridge

Arr. R. F. Beveridge

1 Trav-'ling on the sea of life we're home-ward bound, Drift-ing
2 Je - sus guides our storm-toss'd barque a - cross the seas, He will
3 Come on board the Gos - pel ves - sel, do not stay, And we'll

1 wrecks and strug-gling souls are all a - round; But we do not fear the
2 bring us safe - ly to the port of peace; He's the Pi - lot; He is
3 help you as we jour - ney on the way; Soon to har - bour at our

1 voy-age, for we know That the Sa-viour steers us as we on-ward go.
2 stand-ing at the helm, And no an-gry winds or waves can ov-er-whelm.
3 Fa-ther's blest a-bode, We will wor-ship in the ci-ty of our God.

REFRAIN

We're home-ward bound for glo-ry, Home-ward bound for glo-ry;

Yes, we're glo-ry;

There we'll meet with lov'd ones gone be-fore,............We're homeward bound for glo-ry,........

Yes, we're

Homeward Bound—*Continued*

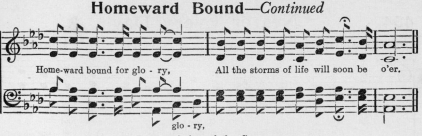

Home-ward bound for glo - ry,　All the storms of life will soon be　o'er.

glo - ry,

By permission of the COMPOSER

453　One More Day's Work

ANNA B. WARNER　　　　　　　　　ROBERT LOWRY

1 One more day's work for Je - sus; One less of life for me! But heav'n is
2 One more day's work for Je - sus; How glo - rious is my King! 'Tis joy, not
3 One more day's work for Je - sus; How sweet the work has been To tell the
4 One more day's work for Je - sus— O, yes, a wea - ry day; But heav'n shines
5 O bless - ed work for Je - sus! O rest at Je - sus' feet! There toil seems

1 near - er, And Christ is dear - er, Than yes - ter - day to me; His love and light Fill
2 du - ty, To speak His beau - ty, My soul mounts on the wing At the mere thought How
3 sto - ry, To show the glo - ry, When Christ's flock en - ter in! How it did shine In
4 clear - er, And rest comes near - er, At each step of the way; And Christ in all— Be -
5 pleas - ure, My wants are treas - ure, And pain for Him is sweet: Lord, if I may, I'll

REFRAIN

1 all my soul to - night.
2 Christ my life has bought.
3 this poor heart of mine.
4 fore His face I fall.
5 serve an - oth - er day.

One more day's work for Je - sus,　　One more day's work

for Je - sus,　One more day's work for Je - sus,　One less of life for me.

454 Nearer Every Day

Johnson Oatman   Adam Geibel, *Arr.* P. J. Mansfield

1 To my bless - ed Lord and Sa - viour, as He walks be - fore me
2 To the pure and per - fect sta - ture of our great and liv - ing
3 To the time when I shall glad - ly lay my cross and bur - dens
4 To that blest e - ter - nal cit - y that lies just a - cross the

1 here, I am get - ting near - er, near - er ev - 'ry day; . . .
2 Head I am get - ting near - er, near - er ev - 'ry day; . . .
3 down I am get - ting near - er, near - er ev - 'ry day; . . .
4 foam I am get - ting near - er, near - er ev - 'ry day; . . .

ev - 'ry day;

1 And He says I shall be like Him when be - fore Him I ap -
2 To the per - fect will of Je - sus in the way that I am
3 To the time when from my Sa - viour I'll re - ceive a robe and
4 Of - ten thro' faith's o - pen vis - ion I can see the spires of

1 pear, And I'm get - ting near - er, near - er ev - 'ry day.
2 led I am get - ting near - er, near - er ev - 'ry day.
3 crown I am get - ting near - er, near - er ev - 'ry day.
4 home, And I'm get - ting near - er, near - er ev - 'ry day.

Nearer Every Day—*Continued*

REFRAIN

Ev-'ry day, praise the Lord, I'm get-ting near-er,

And the way, praise the Lord, is get-ting clear-er;

From my Lord no more I'll roam, For I see the lights of home,

And I'm get-ting near-er, near-er ev-'ry day.

ev-'ry day.

455 The Lower Lights

PHILIP P. BLISS   LOWER LIGHTS 8.7.8.7. D   PHILIP P. BLISS

1 Bright-ly beams our Fa-ther's mer-cy From His light-house ev-er-more,
2 Dark the night of sin has set-tled, Loud the an-gry bil-lows roar;
3 Trim your fee-ble lamp, my bro-ther: Some poor sail-or tem-pest-toss'd,

1 But to us He gives the keep-ing Of the lights a-long the shore.
2 Ea-ger eyes are watch-ing, long-ing, For the lights a-long the shore.
3 Try-ing now to make the har-bour, In the dark-ness may be lost.

REFRAIN

Let the low-er lights be burn-ing! Send a gleam a-cross the wave!

Some poor faint-ing, strug-gling sea-man You may res-cue, you may save!

The tune HARBOUR is on the following page

455 The Lower Lights

PHILIP P. BLISS HARBOUR 8.7.8.7. D DAVID CARYLL

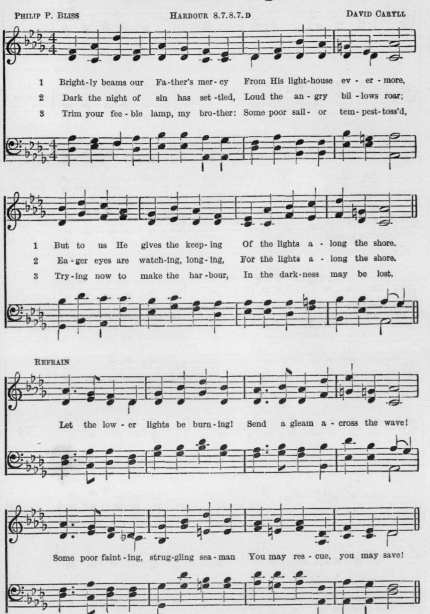

1 Bright-ly beams our Fa-ther's mer-cy From His light-house ev-er-more,
2 Dark the night of sin has set-tled, Loud the an-gry bil-lows roar;
3 Trim your fee-ble lamp, my bro-ther: Some poor sail-or tem-pest-toss'd,

1 But to us He gives the keep-ing Of the lights a-long the shore.
2 Ea-ger eyes are watch-ing, long-ing, For the lights a-long the shore.
3 Try-ing now to make the har-bour, In the dark-ness may be lost,

REFRAIN

Let the low-er lights be burn-ing! Send a gleam a-cross the wave!

Some poor faint-ing, strug-gling sea-man You may res-cue, you may save!

The tune LOWER LIGHTS is on the preceding page

456 # The Precious Story

FANNY J. CROSBY

JNO. R. SWENEY

1 Tell me the sto - ry of Je - sus, Write on my heart ev - 'ry word,
2 Fast-ing, a - lone in the des - ert, Tell of the days that He pass'd,
3 Tell of the Cross where they nail'd Him, Writh-ing in an - guish and pain ;

FINE

1 Tell me the sto - ry most pre - cious, Sweet-est that ev - er was heard ;
2 How for our sins He was temp - ted, Yet was tri-umph-ant at last ;
3 Tell of the grave where they laid Him, Tell how He liv - eth a - gain ;

D.S.—Tell me the sto - ry most pre - cious, Sweet-est that ev - er was heard.

1 Tell how the an - gels in cho - rus Sang as they wel-com'd His birth,
2 Tell of the years of His la - bour, Tell of the sor - row He bore,
3 Love in that sto - ry so ten - der Clear-er than ev - er I see ;

1 Glo - ry to God in the high - est ! Peace and good tid - ings to earth.
2 He was des-pis'd and af - flict - ed, Home-less, re - ject - ed and poor.
3 Stay, let me weep while you whis - per, Love paid the ran - som for me.

REFRAIN

D.S.

Tell me the sto - ry of Je - sus, Write on my heart ev - 'ry word,

457 # Serving Him Truly

Eli G. Christy

Eli G. Christy

1 It pays to serve Je - sus, I speak from my heart; He'll al - ways be
2 And oft when I'm temp-ted to turn from the track, I think of my
3 A place I re - mem-ber where I was set free, 'Twas where I found
4 How rich is the bless-ing the world can - not give, I'm sat - is - fied
5 There's no one like Je - sus can cheer me to - day, His love and His
6 Will you have this bless-ing that Je - sus be - stows? A free, full sal -

1 with us if we do our part; There's naught in this wide world can
2 Sa - viour,— my mind wan-ders back To the place where they nail'd Him on
3 par - don, a hea - ven to me; There Je - sus spoke sweet - ly to
4 ful - ly for Je - sus to live, Tho' friends may for - sake me and
5 kind-ness can ne'er fade a - way; In win - ter, in sum - mer, in
6 va - tion for sin's bit - ter throes, O come to the Sa - viour, to

Fine

1 pleas-ure af - ford, There's peace and con-tent-ment 'in serv-ing the Lord.'
2 Cal - va - ry's tree— I hear a voice say - ing: I suf-fer'd for thee.
3 my wea - ry soul, My sins were for - giv - en, He made my heart whole.
4 tri - als a - rise, I'm trust-ing in Je - sus, His love nev - er dies.
5 sun-shine and rain, His love and af - fec - tion are al - ways the same.
6 Cal - va - ry's tree! The foun - tain is o - pen'd, is flow - ing for thee.

D.S.—ev - er the cost, I'll be a true sol - dier, I'll die at my post.

D.S.

{ I love Him far bet-ter than in days of yore, } I'll do as He bids me what-
{ I'll serve Him more tru - ly than ev - er be-fore. }

458 Still Sweeter Every Day

W. C. MARTIN

C. AUSTIN MILES

1. To Je - sus ev - 'ry day I find my heart is closer drawn; He's fair - er than the
2. His glo - ry broke up-on me when I saw Him from a-far; He's fair - er than the
3. My heart is sometimes heavy, but He comes with sweet relief; He folds me to His

1. glo - ry of the gold and pur-ple dawn; He's all my fan - cy pictured in its
2. lil - y, brighter than the morning star; He fills and sat - is - fies my long - ing
3. bosom when I droop with blighting grief; I love the Christ who all my bur - dens

1. fairest dreams and more; Each day He grows still sweeter than He was the day be-fore.
2. spi - rit o'er and o'er; Each day He grows still sweeter than He was the day be-fore.
3. in His bod - y bore; Each day He grows still sweeter than He was the day be-fore.

CHORUS.

The half . . . . can - not be fan - cied, this
The half can - not be fan - cied on this side the gold - en shore, The

side . . . the gold - en shore; O
half can - not be fan - cied on this side the gold - en shore; O

Still Sweeter Every Day—*Continued*

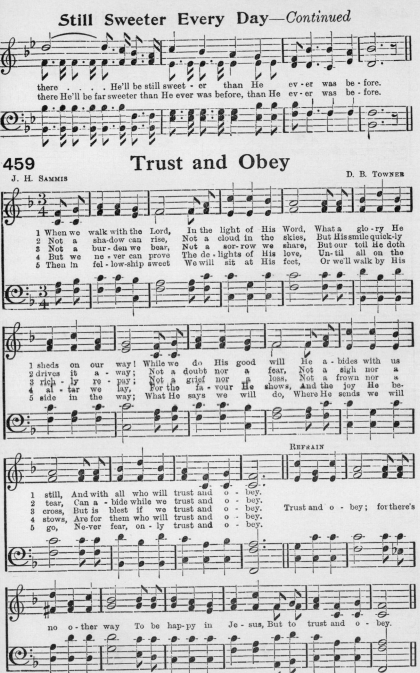

there . . . He'll be still sweet - er than He ev - er was be - fore.
there He'll be far sweeter than He ever was before, than He ev - er was be - fore.

459   Trust and Obey

J. H. SAMMIS   D. B. TOWNER

1 When we walk with the Lord, In the light of His Word, What a glo-ry He
2 Not a sha-dow can rise, Not a cloud in the skies, But His smile quick-ly
3 Not a bur-den we bear, Not a sor-row we share, But our toil He doth
4 But we ne-ver can prove The de-lights of His love, Un-til all on the
5 Then In fel-low-ship sweet We will sit at His feet, Or we'll walk by His

1 sheds on our way! While we do His good will He a-bides with us
2 drives it a-way; Not a doubt nor a fear, Not a sigh nor a
3 rich-ly re-pay; Not a grief nor a loss, Not a frown nor a
4 al-tar we lay, For the fa-vour He shows, And the joy He be-
5 side in the way; What He says we will do, Where He sends we will

REFRAIN

1 still, And with all who will trust and o-bey.
2 tear, Can a-bide while we trust and o-bey.
3 cross, But is blest if we trust and o-bey.   Trust and o-bey; for there's
4 stows, Are for them who will trust and o-bey.
5 go, Ne-ver fear, on-ly trust and o-bey.

no o-ther way To be hap-py in Je-sus, But to trust and o-bey.

460 Onward! Christian Soldiers

S. BARING-GOULD   ST. GERTRUDE 6.5.6.5.6.5. D   A. S. SULLIVAN

1 On-ward! Christ-ian sol - diers, march-ing as to war, Look-ing un - to
2 At the Name of Je - sus Sa-tan's host doth flee; On then, Christ-ian
3 Like a might-y arm - y moves the Church of God: Bro-thers, we are
4 Crowns and thrones may per - ish, king-doms rise and wane; But the Church of
5 On-ward! then, ye peo - ple, join our hap-py throng; Blend with ours your

1 Je - sus, who is gone be-fore; Christ, the Roy-al Mas - ter, leads
2 sol - diers, on to vic-to-ry! Hell's found-a-tions quiv - er at
3 tread - ing where the saints have trod; We are not di - vi - ded, all
4 Je - sus con-stant will re-main: Gates of hell can nev - er 'gainst
5 voic - es in the tri-umph song: Glo-ry, praise, and hon - our un-

1 a-gainst the foe; For-ward in - to bat - tle, see! His ban-ners go.
2 the shout of praise: Bro-thers, lift your voi - ces, loud your an-thems raise.
3 one bo - dy we, One in hope and doc - trine, one in cha - ri - ty.
4 that church pre-vail; We have Christ's own pro - mise—and that can-not fail.
5 to Christ the King,—This, thro' count-less a - ges men and an-gels sing.

REFRAIN

On - ward! Christ-ian sol - diers, march - ing as to

war, Look - ing un - to Je - sus, Who is gone be - fore.

Words by permission of J. CURWEN & SONS LTD.

The tune ARMAGEDDON is on the next page

460 Onward! Christian Soldiers

S. BARING-GOULD   ARMAGEDDON 6.5.6.5.6.5.D   L. REICHARDT (*Arr.* GOSS)

1. On-ward! Christ-ian sol - diers, march-ing as to war, Look-ing un-to
2. At the Name of Je - sus Sa-tan's host doth flee; On then, Christ-ian
3. Like a might-y arm - y moves the Church of God: Bro-thers, we are
4. Crowns and thrones may per - ish, king-doms rise and wane; But the Church of
5. On-ward! then, ye peo - ple, join our hap - py throng; Blend with ours your

1. Je - sus, who is gone be - fore; Christ, the Roy - al Mas - ter,
2. sol - diers, on to vic - to - ry! Hell's found-a-tions quiv - er
3. tread - ing where the saints have trod: We are not di - vid - ed,
4. Je - sus con-stant will re - main: Gates of hell can nev - er
5. voi - ces in the tri-umph song: 'Glo-ry, praise and hon - our,

1. leads a - gainst the foe; For-ward in - to bat - tle, see! His
2. at the shout of praise: Bro-thers, lift your voi - ces, loud your
3. all one bo - dy we; One in hope and doc - trine, one in
4. 'gainst that Church pre - vail; We have Christ's own pro-mise—and that
5. un - to Christ the King'— This, thro' count-less a - ges, men and

REFRAIN

1. ban - ners go.
2. an - thems raise.
3. cha - ri - ty. } On-ward! Christ-ian sol - diers, march-ing as to
4. can - not fail.
5. an - gels sing.

war, Look - ing un - to Je - sus, Who is gone be - fore.

Words by permission of J. CURWEN & SONS LTD.   Tune ST. GERTRUDE is on previous page

461 There is Joy

MARGARET MOODY

W. A. OGDEN

1 When a sin - ner comes as a sin - ner may There is
2 When a soul is born in the king - dom bright There is
3 When a pil - grim comes to the riv - er wide There is

1 joy,................ there is joy ;................ When he turns to God in the
2 joy,................ there is joy ;................ When it walks by faith in the
3 joy,................ there is joy ;................ When he dwells se - cure on the

There is joy,   there is joy ;

1 Gos - pel way There is joy,................ there is joy.
2 Gos - pel light There is joy,................ there is joy.
3 oth - er side There is joy,................ there is joy.

There is joy,

REFRAIN

There is joy a - mong the an - gels, And their harps with mu - sic ring;
mu - sic ring;

When a sin - ner comes re - pent - ing, Bend-ing low be - fore our King.

An Alternative Tune is given on the next page

461 There is Joy

MARGARET MOODY

E. H. SWINSTEAD

1 When a sin-ner comes, as a sin-ner may, There is
2 When a soul is born in the king-dom bright, There is
3 When a pil-grim comes to the ri-ver wide, There is

1 joy, there is joy; When he turns to God in the
2 joy, there is joy; When it walks by faith in the
3 joy, there is joy; When he dwells se-cure on the

Animato

REFRAIN

1 Gos-pel way, There is joy, there is joy.
2 Gos-pel light, There is joy, there is joy. } There is
3 oth-er side, There is joy, there is joy.

joy a-mong the an-gels, And their harps with mu-sic ring;

rall.

When a sin-ner comes re-pent-ing, Bend-ing low be-fore our King.

By permission of the COMPOSER   An alternative Tune is on the previous page

462   A Light along the Way

E. E. HEWITT   J. LINCOLN HALL

1 The Lord hath made this world of ours Most beau - ti - ful and bright,
2 So man - y need a help - ing hand, A kind - ly word of cheer,
3 Some lives shine out like bea - cons grand, Some seem but can - dles small,

1 The gold - en sun to rule by day, The moon and stars by night;
2 To tell them of the might - y Friend Whose grace is al - ways near.
3 But if we tru - ly shine for Him, The Lord hath need of all.

1 But souls are wan - d'ring far from Him, In dark - en'd paths a - stray;
2 O make me prompt to hear Thy voice, And rea - dy to o - bey!
3 O may His Spi - rit fill my soul And lead me day by day!

1 So make me, Sa - viour, more and more A light a - long the way.
2 That I may be to sad - den'd hearts A light a - long the way.
3 That, tho' un - worth - y, I shall be A light a - long the way.

A Light along the Way—*Continued*

Refrain

A light a-long the way, Make me, dear Lord, I pray;

Love's hap-py rays show forth Thy praise, A light a-long the way;

A light a-long the way, Make me, dear Lord, I pray;

Love's hap-py rays show forth Thy praise, A light a-long the way.

463   Bringing in the Sheaves

KNOWLES SHAW

GEORGE A. MINOR

1 Sow - ing in the morn - ing, sow - ing seeds of kind - ness,
2 Sow - ing in the sun - shine, sow - ing in the shad - ows,
3 Go then, ev - er weep - ing, sow - ing for the Mas - ter,

1 Sow - ing in the noon - tide, and the dew - y eve;
2 Fear - ing neith - er clouds nor win - ter's chill - ing breeze;
3 Tho' the loss sus - tain'd our spir - it oft - en grieves;

1 Wait - ing for the har - vest, and the time of reap - ing,
2 By and by the har - vest, and the la - bour end - ed,
3 When our weep ing's o - ver, He will bid us wel - come,

1-3 We shall come, re - joic - ing, bring - ing in the sheaves.

Bringing in the Sheaves—*Continued*

REFRAIN

Bring - ing in the sheaves, bring - ing in the sheaves,

We shall come, re - joic - ing, bring ing in the sheaves,

Bring - ing in the sheaves, bring - ing in the sheaves,

We shall come, re - joic - ing, bring - ing in the sheaves.

464 There'll be No Shadows

EDGAR LEWIS

L. E. JONES

1. Tho' dark the path my feet may tread, it is a joy to know There'll
2. Life's brightest day may have its clouds, but still our heart should sing, There'll
3. We're marching homeward to a land where weary feet may rest; There'll

1. be no sha-dows on the o-ther side; We should not fear the
2. be no sha-dows on the o-ther side; 'Twill not be long till
3. be no sha-dows on the o-ther side; No pain or sor-row

1. wild-est storm, but sing as on we go, There'll be no sha-dows
2. cares are o'er and we are with the King; There'll be no sha-dows
3. e'er can touch the re-gions of the blest; There'll be no sha-dows

CHORUS.

on the o-ther side. There'll be no shadows, no shadows,
there will be no shadows,

Je-sus is the sunshine of that land so fair; There'll be no shadows

There'll be No Shadows—*Continued.*

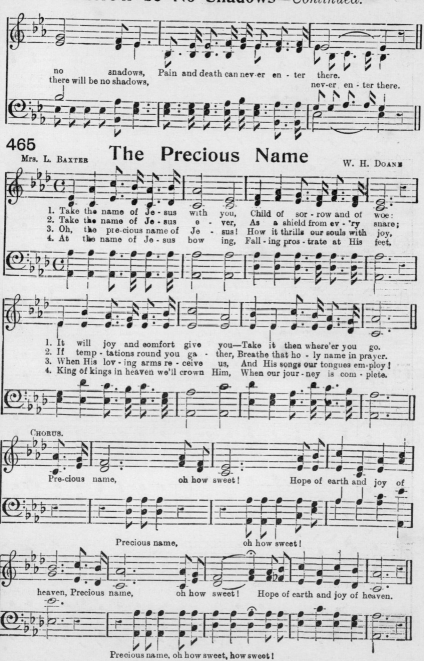

no   snadows,   Pain and death can nev-er en-ter   there.
there will be no shadows,   nev-er en-ter there.

465

Mrs. L. Baxter   The Precious Name   W. H. Doane

1. Take the name of Je-sus   with   you,   Child of sor-row and of   woe:
2. Take the name of Je-sus   e - ver,   As   a shield from ev-'ry   snare;
3. Oh, the pre-cious name of   Je -   sus! How it thrills our souls with joy,
4. At the name of Je - sus   bow   ing, Fall-ing pros-trate at His   feet.

1. It   will joy and comfort give   you—Take it then where'er you   go.
2. If   temp-tations round you ga -   ther, Breathe that ho - ly name in prayer.
3. When His lov-ing arms re-ceive   us, And His songs our tongues em-ploy!
4. King of kings in heaven we'll crown Him, When our jour-ney is com-plete.

Chorus.

Pre-cious name,   oh how sweet!   Hope of earth and joy of

Precious name,   oh how sweet!

heaven, Precious name,   oh how sweet! Hope of earth and joy of heaven.

Precious name, oh how sweet, how sweet!

466 When I get Home

C. AUSTIN MILES

C. AUSTIN MILES

1. I shall wear a gold-en crown. When I get home; I shall lay my
2. All the dark-ness will be past, When I get home; I shall see the
3. I shall see my Saviour's face, When I get home; Sing a-gain of

1. bur-dens down, When I get home; Clad in robes of glo-ry,
2. light at last, When I get home; Light from heav-en streaming,
3. sav-ing grace, When I get home; I shall stand be-fore Him;

1. I shall sing the sto-ry Ot the Lord who bought me, When I get home.
2. O'er my pathway beaming, Ev-er guides me on-ward Till I get home.
3. Gladly I'll a-dore Him; Ev-er to be with Him, When I get home.

CHORUS.

When I get home, When I get home, All
When I get home, when I get home, When I get home, when I get home,

sor-row will be o-ver when I get home; When I get home, When
When I get home, when I get home, When

When I get Home—*Concluded*

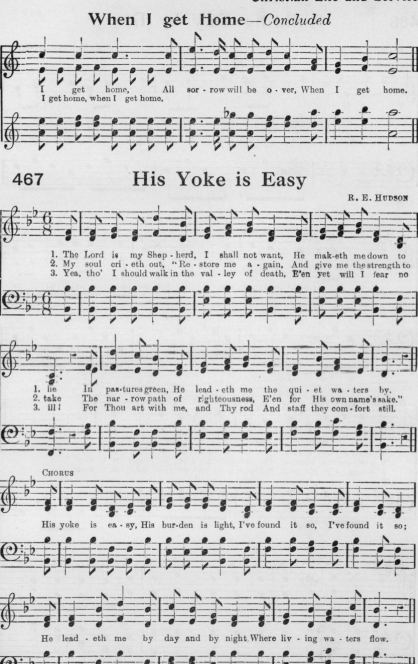

I get home, All sor-row will be o-ver, When I get home.
I get home, when I get home,

467 His Yoke is Easy

R. E. HUDSON

1. The Lord is my Shep-herd, I shall not want, He mak-eth me down to
2. My soul cri-eth out, "Re-store me a-gain, And give me the strength to
3. Yea, tho' I should walk in the val-ley of death, E'en yet will I fear no

1. lie   In pas-tures green, He lead-eth me the qui-et wa-ters by.
2. take The nar-row path of righteousness, E'en for His own name's sake."
3. ill!   For Thou art with me, and Thy rod And staff they com-fort still.

CHORUS

His yoke is ea-sy, His bur-den is light, I've found it so, I've found it so;

He lead-eth me by day and by night, Where liv-ing wa-ters flow.

468 Building Day by Day

Henrietta E. Blair

Herbert D. Lothrop

1. We are build - ing in sor - row and build - ing in joy, A
2. Ev - 'ry deed forms a part in this build - ing of ours, That is
3. Then be watch - ful and wise, let the tem - ple we rear Be

1. tem - ple the world can - not see; But we know it will stand if we
2. done in the name of the Lord; For the love that we show and the
3. one that no tem - pest can shock; For the Mas - ter has said and He

1. found it on a rock, Thro' the a - ges of e - ter - ni - ty.
2. kind-ness we be-stow, He has pro - mis'd us a bright re - ward.
3. taught us in His word, We must build up - on the sol - id rock.

CHORUS.

We are build - ing day by day as the mo - ments glide a - way,

Building Day by Day—*Continued*

Our temple which the world may not see;
which the world may not see;
Ev-'ry vic-t'ry won by grace

Will be sure to find its place In our building for e-ter-ni - ty, e-ter-ni-ty.
for e - ter - ni - ty.

ad lib.

469 Happy in the Love

Jennie Wilson

J. Lincoln Hall

1st time. *2nd time.*

1. Home to Zi-on we are bound, Hap-py in the love of Je-sus,
   Peace a-biding we have found, Hap-py in the love of Je-sus.

CHORUS.

1st time. *2nd time.*

Hap-py, hap-py, Singing all the way, Happy all the day;
Hap-py, hap-py, Hap-py in the love of Je-sus.

2. Trusting, we will forward go,
   Happy in the love of Jesus,
   Treading changeful paths below,
   Happy in the love of Jesus.

3. Soon we'll reach the homeland fair,
   Happy in the love of Jesus,
   And shall dwell for ever there,
   Happy in the love of Jesus

470 The Mist will Roll Away

GEORGE COOPER

H.M.

1. Yon- der's the land where the lov'd ones are, Soon will the mist roll a - way!
2. Dark looms the path, but the pro- mise heed, Soon will the mist roll a - way!
3. Bear thou the Cross till the Crown is won, Soon will the mist roll a - way!

1. Joy soon to rest in that realm a - far, Soon will the mist roll a - way!
2. Je - sus a - lone can re - lieve thy need, Soon will the mist roll a - way!
3. Work till the will of the Lord be done, Soon will the mist roll a - way!

1. There in the loving smile of Christ to a-bide, Vis- ions of glo- ry day by day!
2. Clear will the purpose of the Lord be to thee, Hast-en the Mas-ter to o- bey;
3. All will be re-con-ciled to thee by-and-bye, Faith guideth on to per- fect day;

1. Faith fond-ly whispers while in sha-dows we hide, Soon will the mist roll a - way!
2. Bliss - ful the vis -ion that be- yond we shall see, Soon will the mist roll a - way!
3. Soon shall the glo- ry dawn up- on ev -'ry eye, Soon will the mist roll a - way!

Yon-der's the land where the lov'd ones are, Soon will the mist roll a - way!

The Mist will Roll Away—*Continued*

Joy soon to rest in that realm a - far, Soon will the mist roll a - way!

471 On the Victory Side

James L. Black   Jno. R. Sweney

1 Our souls cry out, Hal - le - lu - jah! And our faith en - rap - tur'd sings,
2 Our souls cry out, Hal - le - lu - jah! For the Lord Him - self comes near,
3 Our souls cry out, Hal - le - lu - jah! For the temp - ter flies a - pace,
4 Our souls cry out, Hal - le - lu - jah! And our hearts beat high with praise,

1 While we throw to the breeze the stan - dard Of the might - y King of kings.
2 And the shout of a roy - al ar - my On the bat - tle - field we hear.
3 And the chains he has forg'd are break-ing, Thro' the pow'r of re - deem - ing grace.
4 Un - to Him, in whose Name we'll con - quer, And our song of tri - umph raise.

REFRAIN

On the vic - t'ry side, on the vic - t'ry side, In the ranks of the Lord are we ;

On the vic - t'ry side we will bold - ly stand, Till the glo - ry land we see.

472   Saved by Believing

J. A. Brown   J. A. Brown

1 I be-lieve in the sto-ry nev-er old, I be-lieve it!
2 I be-lieve in the ti-dings of His birth, I be-lieve it!
3 I be-lieve that the shep-herds heard the song, I be-lieve it!
4 I be-lieve that the wise men saw His star, I be-lieve it!
5 I be-lieve that He came to seek and save, I be-lieve it!

1 I be-lieve in the Sav-iour long fore-told, I be-lieve it!
2 I be-lieve in the song of peace on earth, I be-lieve it!
3 I be-lieve that they saw the heav'n-ly throng, I be-lieve it!
4 I be-lieve that they fol-low'd from a-far, I be-lieve it!
5 I be-lieve that e-ter-nal life He gave, I be-lieve it!

1 I be-lieve He's more pre-cious far than gold, I be-lieve it! I am
2 I be-lieve 'twas a time of joy and mirth, I be-lieve it! I am
3 I be-lieve that the glo-ry shone a-round, I be-lieve it! I am
4 I be-lieve that they found the Sav-iour there, I be-lieve it! I am
5 I be-lieve I shall live be-yond the grave, I be-lieve it! I am

REFRAIN

sav'd by be-liev-ing on His Name. I am sav'd by be-liev-ing on His
by be-

Saved by Believing—*Continued*

Name, I am sav'd, for His Word is just the
liev-ing on His Name,

same, 'Tis the same "who-so-ev-er," For His
just the same,

love chang-eth nev-er, I am sav'd by be-liev-ing on His Name.

473 Sufficient for Me

Suf-fi-cient for me, suf-fi-cient for me, His grace so a-bun-dant and free; In

sor-row or pain this joy shall re-main—His grace is suf-fi-cient for me! (for me!)

474 Never Thirst Again

Isaac Watts (*Verses*) Arr. George Allan

1 There is a land of pure de-light Where saints im-mor-tal reign,
2 There ev-er-last-ing spring a-bides, And nev-er-with-'ring flow'rs:
3 O could we make our doubts re-move Those gloom-y thoughts that rise,
4 Could we but climb where Mos-es stood And view the land-scape o'er!

1 In-fi-nite day ex-cludes the night, And plea-sures ban-ish pain.
2 Death, like a nar-row sea, di-vides This heav'n-ly land from ours.
3 And see the Ca-naan that we love With un-be-cloud-ed eyes!
4 Not Jor-dan's stream, nor death's cold flood, Should fright us from the shore.

REFRAIN

We're feed-ing on the liv-ing Bread, We're drink-ing at the

Alternative Refrain

We're march-ing thro' Im-man-uel's ground, And soon shall hear the

foun-tain-head; And who-so drink-eth, Je-sus said, Shall nev-er, nev-er,
trum-pet sound, And then we shall with Je-sus reign, And nev-er, nev-er,

thirst a-gain. What! nev-er thirst a-gain? No, nev-er thirst a-gain!
part a-gain. What! nev-er part a-gain? No, nev-er part a-gain!

Never Thirst Again—*Continued*

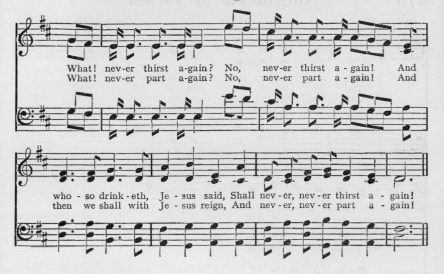

What! nev-er thirst a-gain? No, nev-er thirst a-gain! And
What! nev-er part a-gain? No, nev-er part a-gain! And

who - so drink-eth, Je - sus said, Shall nev-er, nev-er thirst a - gain!
then we shall with Je - sus reign, And nev-er, nev-er part a - gain!

Alternative Tune when the Verses are used alone

ISAAC WATTS   SALISBURY C.M.   *Ravencroft's Psalter*, 1621
                                        Arr. C. E. HORSLEY

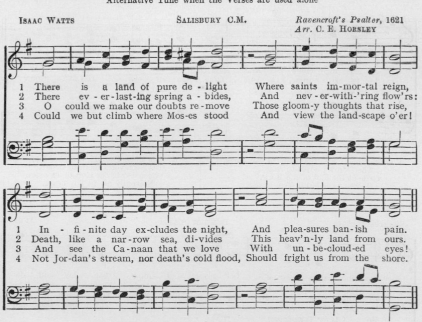

1 There   is a land of pure de - light   Where saints im-mor-tal reign,
2 There   ev - er-last-ing spring a - bides,   And   nev - er-with-'ring flow'rs:
3 O   could we make our doubts re-move   Those gloom-y thoughts that rise,
4 Could   we but climb where Mos-es stood   And   view the land-scape o'er!

1 In - fi - nite day ex-cludes the night,   And   plea-sures ban-ish   pain.
2 Death, like a nar-row sea, di-vides   This heav'n-ly land from   ours.
3 And   see the Ca-naan that we love   With   un - be-cloud-ed   eyes!
4 Not Jor-dan's stream, nor death's cold flood, Should fright us from the   shore.

May also be sung to BEATITUDO, No. 509

475 Shepherd of Israel

CHARLES WESLEY   CELESTE 8.8.8.8   *Lancashire S.S. Songs, 1857*

1 Thou Shep-herd of Is-rael, and mine, The joy
2 The pas-ture I lan-guish to find, Where all
3 Ah! show me that hap-pi-est place, That place
4 Thy love for a sin-ner de-clare, Thy pas-

1 and de-sire of my heart, For clo-ser com-mun-
2 who their Shep-herd o-bey Are fed on His bos-
3 of Thy peo-ple's a-bode, Where saints in an ecs-
4 sion and death on the tree: My spi-rit to Cal-

1 ion I pine; I long to re-side where Thou art.
2 om re-clin'd, And screen'd from the heat of the day.
3 ta-sy gaze, And hang on a cru-ci-fied God.
4 va-ry bear To suf-fer and tri-umph with Thee.

5 'Tis there, with the lambs of Thy flock,
    There only I covet to rest;
To lie at the foot of the Rock,
    Or rise to be hid in Thy breast.

6 'Tis there I would always abide,
    And never a moment depart,
Concealed in the cleft of Thy side,
    Eternally hid in Thy heart.

CHARLES WESLEY   DURSLEY 8.8.8.8.   ANON.

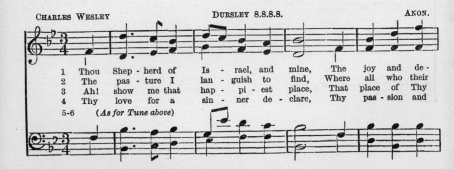

1 Thou Shep-herd of Is-rael, and mine, The joy and de-
2 The pas-ture I lan-guish to find, Where all who their
3 Ah! show me that hap-pi-est place, That place of Thy
4 Thy love for a sin-ner de-clare, Thy pas-sion and
5-6 *(As for Tune above)*

Shepherd of Israel—*Continued*

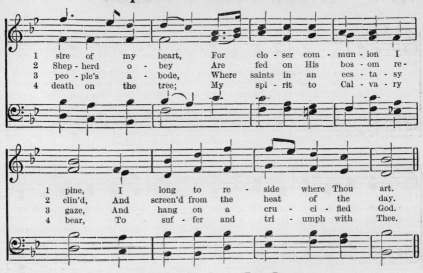

1 sire of my heart, For clo-ser com-mun-ion I
2 Shep-herd o-bey, Are fed on His bos-om re-
3 peo-ple's a-bode, Where saints in an ecs-ta-sy
4 death on the tree; My spi-rit to Cal-va-ry

1 pine, I long to re-side where Thou art.
2 clin'd, And screen'd from the heat of the day.
3 gaze, And hang on a cru-ci-fied God.
4 bear, To suf-fer and tri-umph with Thee.

Music from THE BOTLEY TUNE BOOK

476   # The God We Adore

JOSEPH HART   CELESTE 8.8.8.8   *Lancashire S.S. Songs, 1857*

1 How good is the God we a-dore, Our faith-
2 'Tis Je-sus, the First and the Last, Whose Spir-

1 ful, un-change-a-ble Friend: Whose love is as great
2 it shall guide us safe home; We'll praise Him for all

1 as His pow'r, And knows nei-ther mea-sure nor end.
2 that is past, And trust Him for all that's to come.

477 A Few More Marchings

FANNY J. CROSBY

W. H. DOANE

1 A few more march-ings wea-ry, Then we'll ga-ther home; A few more
2 A few more nights of weep-ing, Then we'll ga-ther home; A few more
3 A few more sweet links bro-ken, Then we'll ga-ther home; A few more

1 storm-clouds drear-y, Then we'll ga-ther home: A few more days the cross to
2 watch-es keep-ing, Then we'll ga-ther home: A few more vic-t'ries o-ver
3 kind words spo-ken, Then we'll ga-ther home: A few more part-ings on the

1 bear, And then with Christ a crown to wear; A few more march-ings wea-ry,
2 sin, A few more sheaves to ga-ther in; A few more march-ings wea-ry,
3 strand, And then a-way to Ca-naan's land; A few more march-ings wea-ry,

REFRAIN

1-3 Then we'll ga-ther home. { O'er time's ra-pid riv-er Soon we'll
O'er time's ra-pid, Soon we'll rest, we'll

rest for ev-er, No more march-ings wea-ry When we ga-ther home.

478 Canaan's Land

H. G. JACKSON

CANAAN'S LAND L.M.D.

W. S. NICKLE

1 From E - gypt's cru - el bond - age fled, O - be - dient to our
2 Thro' wil - der - ness - es wide and drear Our Lord will guide our
3 His pow'r the smit - ten rock con - trols, A cry - stal stream our
4 In hos - tile lands we feel no fear; No foe our on - ward
5 Ere long, the riv - er cross'd, we'll meet The ransom'd host at

1 Lord's com - mand, And by His word and Spir - it led, We're
2 steps a - right, Be - hold, to prove His pres - ence here, The
3 need sup - plies, He feeds our hun - gry, faint - ing souls With
4 march can stay; In ev - 'ry con - flict He is near, Whose
5 His right hand; And there re - ceive a wel - come sweet, From

REFRAIN

1 on the way to Ca - naan's Land,
2 cloud by day, the fire by night!
3 dai - ly man - na from the skies.   We're on the way, A
4 pres - ence cheers us on the way.
5 our dear Lord, to Ca - naan's Land!

pil - grim band; We're on the way to Ca - naan's land; Di -

vine - ly guid - ed day by day, We're on the way, we're on the way.

479 **Sunshine**

C. AUSTIN MILES

C. AUSTIN MILES

1 The sun-shine I have found will fill each day with
2 Look up and praise the Lord! the flow-ers need the
3 But for the child of God there al-ways is a
4 It is the light that shines when Je-sus speaks to

1 joy, And ev-'ry mo-ment sweet-ly bless; The
2 rain That falls up-on them day by day, Just
3 ray That strug-gles thro' the clouds a-bove; That
4 me And tells me I am sav'd by grace; The

1 rays that gent-ly fall up-on my dai-ly
2 as our thirs-ty souls would seek the cool-ing
3 shines a-cross his path and helps his wav-'ring
4 sun-shine I have found is free to all who

1 path Are giv-en by the Sun of Right-eous-ness.
2 springs If we were walk-ing in a des-ert way.
3 faith To rest se-cure-ly in a Fa-ther's love.
4 seek The sun-shine of my bless-ed Sa-viour's face.

Sunshine—*Continued*

REFRAIN

So if the sky is dark, and if the day is drear - y, The sun is shin - ing some - where, this I know, I know; And so to keep my heart from ev - er grow - ing wea - ry, I'll car ry my sun - shine with me ev - 'ry - where I go

480 A Soldier of the Cross

ISAAC WATTS, *Refrain by* T. C. O'KANE

Arr. CAROLINE WICHERN

1 Am I a sol-dier of the Cross, of the Cross, A fol-low'r
2 Must I be car-ried to the skies, to the skies On flow-'ry
3 Are there no foes for me to face? me to face? Must I not
4 Since I must fight if I would reign, I would reign, In-crease my

1 of the Lamb? of the Lamb? And shall I fear to
2 beds of ease? beds of ease? While o-thers fought to
3 stem the flood? stem the flood? Is this vile world a
4 cou-rage, Lord! cou-rage, Lord! I'll bear the toil, en-

1 own His cause, Or blush to speak His name? . . .
2 win the prize, And sail'd thro' blood-y seas. . . .
3 friend to grace To help me on to God? . . .
4 dure the pain, Sup-port-ed by Thy word. . . .

REFRAIN

We will stand . . the . storm, . . . We will

We will stand the storm, We will stand, the storm, We will
We will stand the storm, the . storm, . . We will

We will stand the storm, We will stand, stand the storm, We will

A Soldier of the Cross—*Continued*

an - chor by - and - bye, . . We will stand . . the

an - chor by - - and - bye, We will stand the storm, We will
an - chor by - and - bye, We will stand the storm, We will

an - chor by - and - bye, . . We will stand the storm, the

storm, . . . We will an - chor by - and - bye.. . .

stand, stand the storm, We will an - chor by - and - bye by -and-bye.
stand the . storm, We will an - chor by - and - bye, by - and - bye.

storm, ... We will an - chor by - and - bye. . . .

Alternative tune when the Refrain is not used

ISAAC WATTS   HEATHSIDE C.M.   E. BUNNETT

1 Am   I   a   sol - dier of the Cross, A fol -low'r of the Lamb?
2 Must   I   be car - ried   to the skies On flow- 'ry beds of ease?
3 Are there no foes for   me to face? Must I not stem the flood?
4 Since I must fight if   I would reign, In - crease my cou - rage, Lord !

1 And shall I fear to   own His cause, Or blush to speak His name?
2 While o - thers fought to   win the prize, And sail'd thro' blood - y seas.
3 Is   this vile world a friend to grace To help me on to God?
4 I'll bear the toil, en - dure the pain, Sup - port - ed by Thy word.

Music by permission of E. BUNNETT

481   Jesus, My All

JOHN CENNICK   WALTON L.M.   GARDINER'S SACRED MELODIES

1 Je - sus, my all, to heav'n is gone, He whom I
2 The way the ho - ly pro - phets went, The road that
3 This is the way I long have sought, And mourn'd be -

1 fix my hopes . up - on; His track I see, and
2 leads from ban - ish - ment, The King's high - way of
3 cause I found . it not, Till late I heard my

1 I'll pur - sue . The nar - row way . till Him . I view.
2 ho - li - ness . I'll go; for all . His paths are peace.
3 Sa - viour say, 'Come hith - er, child; I am . the way.'

482   Soldiers of Christ! Arise

CHARLES WESLEY   SILCHESTER S.M.   HENRI A. C. MALAN

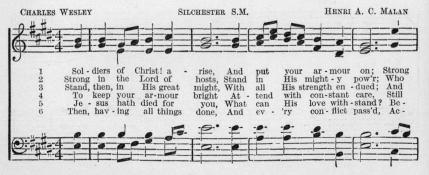

1 Sol - diers of Christ! a - rise, And put your ar - mour on; Strong
2 Strong in the Lord of hosts, Stand in His might - y pow'r; Who
3 Stand, then, in His great might, With all His strength en - dued; And
4 To keep your ar - mour bright At - tend with con - stant care, Still
5 Je - sus hath died for you, What can His love with - stand? Be -
6 Then, hav - ing all things done, And ev - 'ry con - flict pass'd, Ac -

Soldiers of Christ! Arise—*Continued*

CHARLES WESLEY   ST. ETHELWALD S.M.   WILLIAM H. MONK

1. in the strength which God sup-plies Thro' His e-ter-nal Son;
2. in the strength of Je-sus trusts Is more than con-quer-or.
3. take, to arm you for the fight, The pan-op-ly of God.
4. march-ing in your Cap-tain's sight, And watch-ing un-to pray'r.
5. lieve, hold fast your shield, and who Shall pluck you from His hand?
6. cep-ted each through Christ a-lone, You shall be crown'd at last.

1. Sol-diers of Christ! a-rise, And put your
2. Strong in the Lord of hosts, Stand in His
3. Stand, then, in His great might, With all His
4. To keep your ar-mour bright, At-tend with
5. Je-sus hath died for you, What can His
6. Then, hav-ing all things done, And ev-'ry

1. ar-mour on; Strong in the strength which God sup-
2. might-y pow'r; Who in the strength of Je-sus
3. strength en-dued; And take, to arm you for the
4. con-stant care; Still march-ing in your Cap-tain's
5. love with-stand? Be-lieve, hold fast your shield, and
6. con-flict pass'd, Ac-cep-ted each through Christ a-

1. plies Through His e-ter-nal Son;
2. trusts Is more than con-quer-or.
3. fight, The pan-op-ly of God.
4. sight, And watch-ing un-to pray'r.
5. who Shall pluck you from His hand?
6. lone, You shall be crown'd at last.

The tune FROM STRENGTH TO STRENGTH is on the following page

482 Soldiers of Christ! Arise

CHARLES WESLEY   FROM STRENGTH TO STRENGTH S.M.D.   EDWARD W. NAYLOR

UNISON

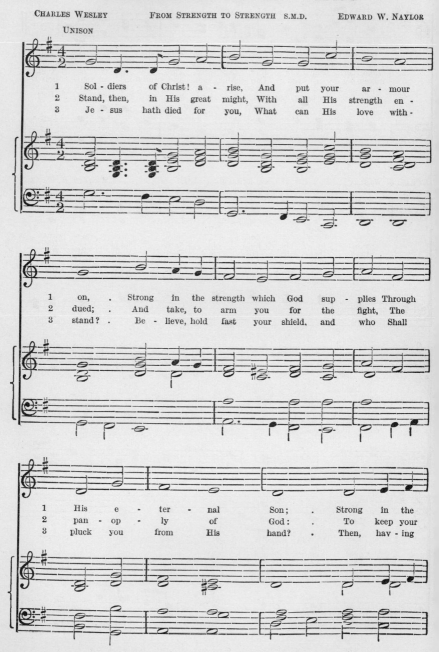

1 Sol - diers of Christ! a - rise, And put your ar - mour
2 Stand, then, in His great might, With all His strength en -
3 Je - sus hath died for you, What can His love with -

1 on, . Strong in the strength which God sup - plies Through
2 dued; . And take, to arm you for the fight, The
3 stand? . Be - lieve, hold fast your shield, and who Shall

1 His e - ter - nal Son; . Strong in the
2 pan - op - ly of God: . To keep your
3 pluck you from His hand? . Then, hav - ing

Soldiers of Christ! Arise—*Continued*

1 Lord . of . hosts Stand in His migh - .
2 ar - mour . bright At - tend with con - .
3 all . things . done, And ev - 'ry con - .

1 ty . . pow'r; . Who in the strength of
2 stant . . care, . Still march-ing in your
3 flict . . pass'd . Ac - cep -ted each through

1 Je - sus trusts Is more than con - - quer - or.
2 Cap - tain's sight, And watch - ing un - - to pray'r.
3 Christ a - lone, You shall be crown'd . at last.

Music by permission of EDWARD W. NAYLOR
The tunes SILCHESTER and ST. ETHELWALD precede this one

483 I Waited for the Lord

JOHN HOPKINS   BALLERMA C.M.   ROBERT SIMPSON

1 I wait- ed for the Lord my God, And
2 He took me from a fear- ful pit And
3 He put a new song in my mouth Our
4 O bless- ed is the man whose trust Up-
5 In Thee let all be glad, and joy, Who

1 pa- tient- ly did bear: At length to me He
2 from the mi- ry clay, And on a rock He
3 God to mag- ni- fy: Man- y sha see it
4 on the Lord re- lies; Res- pect- ing not the
5 seek- ing Thee a- bide; Who Thy sal- va- tion

1 did in- cline My voice and cry to hear.
2 set my feet, Es- tab- lish- ing my way.
3 and shall fear, And on the Lord re- ly.
4 proud, nor such As turn a- side to lies.
5 love, say still, 'The Lord be mag- ni- fy'd!'

484 Watch and Pray

CHARLOTTE ELLIOTT   VIGILATE 7.7.7.3   WILLIAM H. MONK

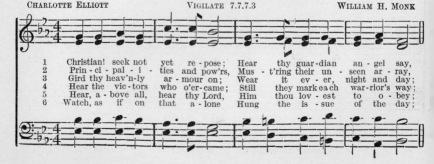

1 Christian! seek not yet re- pose; Hear thy guar- dian an- gel say,
2 Prin- ci- pal- i- ties and pow'rs, Mus- t'ring their un- seen ar- ray,
3 Gird thy heav'n- ly ar- mour on; Wear it ev- er, night and day;
4 Hear the vic- tors who o'er- came; Still they mark each war- rior's way;
5 Hear, a- bove all, hear thy Lord, Him thou lov- est to o- bey;
6 Watch, as if on that a- lone Hung the is- sue of the day;

Watch and Pray—*Continued*

1 'Thou art in the midst of foes: Watch . . and pray.'
2 Wait for thy un-guard-ed hours: Watch . . and pray.
3 Am-bush'd lies the e-vil one: Watch . . and pray.
4 All with one sweet voice ex-claim, 'Watch . . and pray.'
5 Hide with-in thy heart His word, Watch . . and pray.
6 Pray that help may be sent down: Watch . . and pray.

CHARLOTTE ELLIOTT — 7.7.7.3 — F. H. COWEN

1 Christ-ian! seek . not yet re-pose; Hear thy
2 Prin-ci-pal-i-ties and pow'rs, Mus-t'ring
3 Gird Thy heav'n-ly ar-mour on; Wear it
4 Hear the vic-tors who o'er-came! Still they
5 Hear, a-bove . all, hear thy Lord, Him thou
6 Watch, as if . on that a-lone Hung the

1 guar-dian an-gel say, 'Thou . art in the
2 their un-seen ar-ray, Wait . for thy un-
3 ev-er, night and day: Am . bush'd lies the
4 mark each war-rior's way; All . with one sweet
5 lov-est to . o-bey; Hide with-in thy
6 is-sue of . the day; Pray . that help may

1 midst of foes; . Watch and pray, . watch and pray.'
2 guard-ed hours: . Watch and pray, . watch and pray.
3 e-vil one: . Watch and pray, . watch and pray.
4 voice ex-claim, . 'Watch and pray, . watch and pray.'
5 heart His word, . Watch and pray, . watch and pray.
6 be sent down: . Watch and pray, . watch and pray.

Music by permission of NOVELLO & CO., LTD.

485 The Name I Love

FREDERICK WHITFIELD · BELMONT C.M. · GARDINER'S SACRED MELODIES

1 There is a name I love to hear, I love to sing its worth, It sounds like mu-sic in mine ear, The sweet-est name on earth.
2 It tells me of a Sa-viour's love, Who died to set me free, It tells me of His pre-cious blood, The sin-ner's per-fect plea.
3 It bids my trem-bling soul re-joice, And dries each ris-ing tear; It tells me in a still, small voice, To trust and nev-er fear.
4 Je-sus, the name I love so well, The name I love to hear, No saint on earth its worth can tell, No heart con-ceive how dear.
5 This name shall shed its fra-grance still A-long this thorn-y road, Shall sweet-ly smooth the rug-ged hill That leads me up to God.
6 And there with all the blood-bought throng, From sin and sor-row free, I'll sing the new e-ter-nal song Of Je-sus' love to me.

FREDERICK WHITFIELD · FAUX BOURDON SETTING · PURCELL J. MANSFIELD

3 It bids my trem-bling soul re-joice, And
5 This name shall shed its fra-grance still A-

The Name I Love—*Continued*

3 dries each ris - ing tear; It tells me in a
5 long this thorn - y road, Shall sweet - ly smooth the

3 still, small voice, To trust and nev - er fear.
5 rug - ged hill That leads me up to God.

FREDERICK WHITFIELD   EDGEWARE C.M.   UNKNOWN

1 There is a name I love to hear, I love to sing its worth,
2 It tells me of a Sa - viour's love, Who died to set me free,
3 It bids my trem - bling soul re - joice, And dries each ris - ing tear;
4 Je - sus, the name I love so well, The name I love to hear,
5 This name shall shed its fra - grance still A - long this thorn - y road,
6 And there with all the blood-bought throng, From sin and sor - row free,

1 It sounds like mu - sic in mine ear, the sweet - est name on earth.
2 It tells me of His pre - cious blood, The sin - ner's per - fect plea.
3 It tells me in a still, small voice, To trust and nev - er fear,
4 No saint on earth its worth can tell, No heart con - ceive how dear.
5 Shall sweet - ly smooth the rug - ged hill That leads me up to God.
6 I'll sing the new e - ter - nal song Of Je - sus' love to me.

486 The Lord's My Shepherd

WHITTINGHAM and ROUS   WILTSHIRE C.M.   GEORGE T. SMART

1 The Lord's my Shep - herd, I'll not want, He makes me
2 My soul He doth re - store a - gain; And me to
3 Yea, though I walk in death's dark vale, Yet will I
4 My ta - ble Thou hast fur - nish - ed In pres - ence
5 Good - ness and mer - cy all my life Shall sure - ly

1 down to lie . In pas - tures green; . He
2 walk doth make . With - in the paths . of
3 fear none ill; . For Thou art with . me;
4 of . my foes; . My head Thou dost . with
5 fol - low me; . And in God's house for

1 lead - eth me The qui - et wa - ters by.
2 right - eous - ness, Ev'n for His own name's sake.
3 and Thy rod And staff me com - fort still.
4 oil a - noint, And my cup o - ver - flows.
5 ev - er - more My dwell - ing - place shall be.

WHITTINGHAM and ROUS   CRIMOND C.M.   JESSIE S. IRVINE

1 The Lord's my Shep - herd, I'll not want, He
2 My soul He doth re - store a - gain; And
3 Yea, though I walk in death's dark vale, Yet
4 My ta - ble Thou hast fur - nish - ed In
5 Good - ness and mer - cy all my life Shall

The Lord's My Shepherd—*Continued*

1 makes me down to lie In pas - tures green: He
2 me to walk doth make With - in the paths of
3 will I fear none ill: For Thou art with me;
4 pres - ence of my foes; My head Thou dost with
5 sure - ly fol - low me: And in God's house for

1 lead - eth me The qui - et wa - ters by.
2 right - ous - ness, Ev'n for His own name's sake.
3 and Thy rod And staff me com - fort still.
4 oil a - noint, And my cup o - ver flows.
5 ev - er - more My dwell - ing place shall be.

WHITTINGHAM AND ROUS   CRIMOND—FAUX BOURDON SETTING   PURCELL J. MANSFIELD

2 My soul He doth re - store a - gain; And me to walk doth make
5 Good - ness and mer - cy all my life Shall sure - ly fol - low me;

2 With - in the paths of right - eous - ness, Ev'n for His own name's sake.
5 And in God's house for ev - er - more My dwell - ing place shall be.

487   To Calvary, Lord

EDWARD DENNY   ST. PAUL C.M.   CHALMER'S COLLECTION, 1749

1 To Cal-v'ry, Lord, in spi-rit now Our weary souls repair; To dwell upon Thy dying love, And taste its sweetness there.
2 Sweet rest-ing place of ev-ry heart That feels the plague of sin; Yet knows that deep, mysterious joy, The peace of God within.
3 There thro' Thine hour of deep-est woe, Thy suff-'ring Spirit pass'd; Grace there its won-drous vic-t'ry gain'd, And love en-dur'd its last.
4 Dear suff-'ring Lamb! Thy bleeding wounds, With cords of love di-vine, Have drawn our willing hearts to Thee, And link'd our life with Thine.
5 Our long-ing eyes would fain be-hold That bright and bless-ed brow, Once wrung with bit-t'rest anguish, wear Its crown of glo-ry now.

A HIGHER SETTING

1 To Cal-v'ry, Lord, in spi-rit now Our wear-y souls re-pair,
2 Sweet rest-ing place of ev-ry heart That feels the plague of sin;
3 There thro' Thine hour of deep-est woe, Thy suff-'ring Spi-rit pass'd;
4 Dear suff-'ring Lamb! Thy bleed-ing wounds, With cords of love di-vine,
5 Our long-ing eyes would fain be-hold That bright and bless-ed brow,

To Calvary, Lord—*Continued*

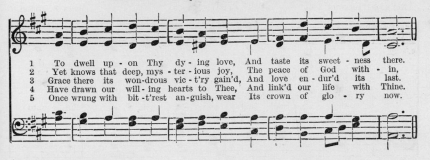

1. To dwell up - on Thy dy - ing love, And taste its sweet - ness there.
2. Yet knows that deep, mys - ter - ious joy, The peace of God with - in,
3. Grace there its won-drous vic - t'ry gain'd, And love en - dur'd its last.
4. Have drawn our will - ing hearts to Thee, And link'd our life with Thine.
5. Once wrung with bit - t'rest an-guish, wear Its crown of glo - ry now.

FAUX BOURDON SETTING BY P. J. MANSFIELD

1. To Cal - v'ry, Lord, in spi - rit now Our wear - y souls re - pair, . To dwell up - on Thy dy - ing love, And taste its sweet - ness there.
2. Sweet rest - ing place of ev - ry heart That feels the plague of sin; . Yet knows that deep, mys - ter - ious joy, The peace of God with - in,
3. There thro' Thine hour of deep - est woe, Thy suff - 'ring Spi - rit pass'd; . Grace there its won-drous vic - t'ry gain'd, And love en - dur'd its last.
4. Dear suff - 'ring Lamb! Thy bleed - ing wounds, With cords of love di - vine, . Have drawn our will - ing hearts to Thee, And link'd our life with Thine.
5. Our long - ing eyes would fain be - hold That bright and bless - ed brow, . Once wrung with bit - t'rest an - guish, wear Its crown of glo - ry now.

488   Courage, Brother!

NORMAN MACLEOD   ST. OSWALD 8.7.8.7   JOHN B. DYKES

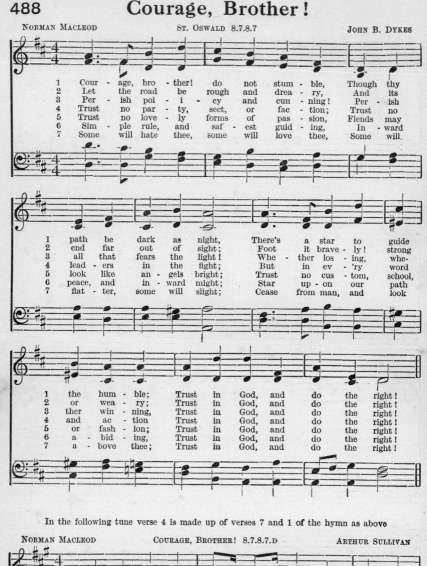

1 Cour - age, bro - ther! do not stum - ble, Though thy
2 Let the road be rough and drea - ry, And its
3 Per - ish pol - i - cy and cun - ning! Per - ish
4 Trust no par - ty, sect, or fac - tion; Trust no
5 Trust no love - ly forms of pas - sion, Fiends may
6 Sim - ple rule, and saf - est guid - ing, In - ward
7 Some will hate thee, some will love thee, Some will

1 path be dark as night, There's a star to guide
2 end far out of sight; Foot it brave - ly! strong
3 all that fears the light! Whe - ther los - ing, whe-
4 lead - ers in the fight; But in ev - 'ry word
5 look like an - gels bright; Trust no cus - tom, school,
6 peace, and in - ward might; Star up - on our path
7 flat - ter, some will slight; Cease from man, and look

1 the hum - ble; Trust in God, and do the right!
2 or wea - ry; Trust in God, and do the right!
3 ther win - ning; Trust in God, and do the right!
4 and ac - tion Trust in God, and do the right!
5 or fash - ion; Trust in God, and do the right!
6 a - bid - ing, Trust in God, and do the right!
7 a - bove thee; Trust in God, and do the right!

In the following tune verse 4 is made up of verses 7 and 1 of the hymn as above

NORMAN MACLEOD   COURAGE, BROTHER! 8.7.8.7.D   ARTHUR SULLIVAN

1 Cour - age, bro - ther! do not stum - ble, Though thy
2 Per - ish pol - i - cy and cun - ning! Per - ish
3 Trust no love - ly forms of pas - sion, Fiends may
4 Some will hate thee, some will love thee, Some will

Courage, Brother!—*Continued*

1 path be dark as night, There's a star to guide the hum - ble;
2 all that fears the light! Whe - ther los - ing, whe - ther win - ning,
3 look like an - gels bright; Trust no cus - tom, school, or fash - ion,
4 flat - ter, some will slight; Cease from man, and look a - bove thee;

1 Trust in God, and do the right! Let the road be
2 Trust in God, and do the right! Trust no par - ty,
3 Trust in God, and do the right! Sim - ple rule, and
4 Trust in God, and do the right! Cour - age, bro - ther!

1 rough and drea - ry, And its end far out of sight;
2 sect, or fac - tion; Trust no lead - ers in the fight;
3 saf - est guid - ing, In - ward peace, and in - ward might;
4 do not stum - ble, Though thy path be dark as night,

1 Foot it brave - ly! strong or wea - ry; Trust in God,
2 But in ev - 'ry word and ac - tion; Trust in God,
3 Star up - on our path a - bid - ing, Trust in God,
4 There's a star to guide the hum - ble; Trust in God,

1-4 trust in God, trust in God, and do the right!

489   Jesus Calls Us

C. FRANCES ALEXANDER   ST. ANDREW 8.7.8.7   EDWARD H. THORNE

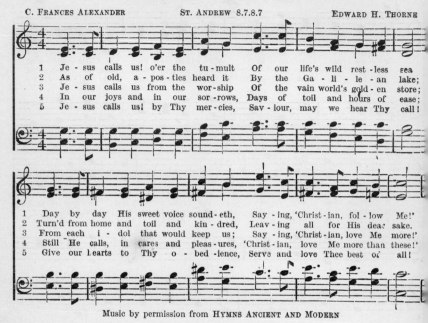

1 Je - sus calls us! o'er the tu - mult Of our life's wild rest - less sea
2 As of old, a - pos - tles heard it By the Ga - li - le - an lake:
3 Je - sus calls us from the wor - ship Of the vain world's gold - en store;
4 In our joys and in our sor - rows, Days of toil and hours of ease,
5 Je - sus calls us! by Thy mer - cies, Sav - iour, may we hear Thy call!

1 Day by day His sweet voice sound - eth, Say - ing, 'Christ - ian, fol - low Me!'
2 Turn'd from home and toil and kin - dred, Leav - ing all for His dear sake.
3 From each i - dol that would keep us; Say - ing, 'Christ - ian, love Me more!'
4 Still He calls, in cares and pleas - ures, 'Christ - ian, love Me more than these!'
5 Give our hearts to Thy o - bed - ience, Serve and love Thee best of all!

Music by permission from HYMNS ANCIENT AND MODERN

C. FRANCES ALEXANDER   ST. CATHERINE 8.7.8.7   S. FLOOD JONES

1 Je - sus calls us! o'er the tu - mult Of our life's wild rest - less sea
2 As of old, a - pos - tles heard it By the Ga - li - le - an lake;
3 Je - sus calls us from the wor - ship Of the vain world's gold - en store;
4 In our joys and in our sor - rows, Days of toil and hours of ease,
5 Je - sus calls us! by Thy mer - cies, Sa - viour, may we hear Thy call!

1 Day by day His sweet voice sound - eth, Say - ing, 'Christ - ian, fol - low Me!'
2 Turn'd from home and toil and kin - dred, Leav - ing all for His dear sake.
3 From each i - dol that would keep us; Say - ing, 'Christ - ian, love Me more!'
4 Still He calls, in cares and plea - sures, 'Christ - ian, love Me more than these!'
5 Give our hearts to Thy o - bed - ience, Serve and love Thee best of all!

490

The Cross of Christ

JOHN BOWRING   STUTTGART 8.7.8.7.   CHRISTIAN F. WITT

1 In the Cross of Christ I glo-ry, Tow-'ring o'er the wrecks of time;
2 When the woes of life o'er-take me, Hopes de-ceive and fears an-noy,
3 When the sun of bliss is beam-ing Light and love up-on my way,
4 Bane and bless-ing, pain and pleas-ure, By the Cross are sanc-ti-fied;

1 All the light of sa-cred sto-ry Ga-thers round its head su-blime.
2 Nev-er shall the Cross for-sake me; Lo! it glows with peace and joy.
3 From the Cross the ra-diance stream-ing Adds new lus-tre to the day.
4 Peace is there that knows no meas-ure, Joys that through all time a-bide.

JOHN BOWRING   CHAPEL BRAE 8.7.8.7.   E. F. ABBOTT

1 In the Cross of Christ I glo-ry, Tow-'ring o'er the wrecks of time;
2 When the woes of life o'er-take me, Hopes de-ceive and fears an-noy,
3 When the sun of bliss is beam-ing Light and love up-on my way,
4 Bane and bless-ing, pain and pleas-ure, By the Cross are sanc-ti-fied;

1 All the light of sa-cred sto-ry Ga-thers round its head su-blime
2 Nev-er shall the Cross for-sake me; Lo! it glows with peace and joy.
3 From the Cross the ra-diance stream-ing, Adds new lus-tre to the day.
4 Peace is there that knows no meas-ure, Joys that through all time a-bide

491 Glorious Things

JOHN NEWTON   IL BUON PASTOR 8.7.8.7.7   Canzuns Spirituaelas, 1765

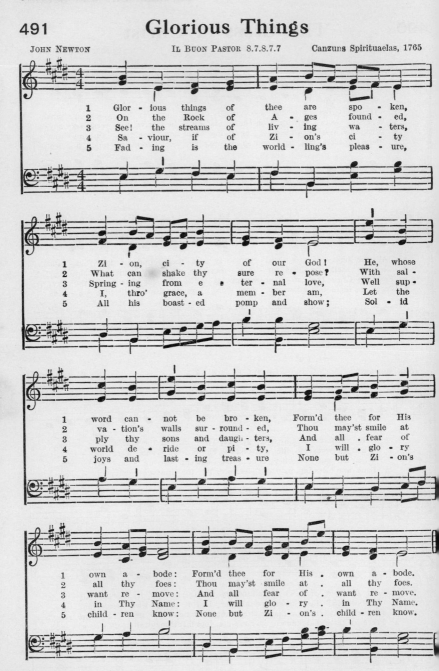

1 Glor - ious things of thee are spo - ken,
2 On the Rock of A - ges found - ed,
3 See! the streams of liv - ing wa - ters,
4 Sa - viour, if of Zi - on's ci - ty
5 Fad - ing is the world - ling's pleas - ure,

1 Zi - on, ci - ty of our God! He, whose
2 What can shake thy sure re - pose? With sal -
3 Spring - ing from e - ter - nal love, Well sup -
4 I, thro' grace, a mem - ber am, Let the
5 All his boast - ed pomp and show; Sol - id

1 word can - not be bro - ken, Form'd thee for His
2 va - tion's walls sur - round - ed, Thou may'st smile at
3 ply thy sons and daugh - ters, And all fear of
4 world de - ride or pi - ty, I will glo - ry
5 joys and last - ing treas - ure None but Zi - on's

1 own a - bode: Form'd thee for His own a - bode.
2 all thy foes: Thou may'st smile at all thy foes.
3 want re - move: And all fear of want re - move.
4 in Thy Name: I will glo - ry in Thy Name.
5 child - ren know: None but Zi - on's child - ren know.

From SONGS OF PRAISE by permission of OXFORD UNIVERSITY PRESS

492 The Pilgrim Band

SABINE BARING-GOULD (Trs.)   MARCHING 8.7.8.7   MARTIN SHAW

1 Thro' the night of doubt and sor-row On-ward goes the pil-grim band,
2 Clear be-fore us through the dark-ness Gleams and burns the guid-ing Light;
3 One the strain that lips of thou-sands Lift as from the heart of one;
4 One the glad-ness of re-joic-ing On the far e-ter-nal shore
5 On-ward, there-fore, pil-grim bro-thers, On-ward with the Cross our aid!
6 Soon shall come the great a-wak-ing, Soon the rend-ing of the tomb;

1 Sing-ing songs of ex-pec-ta-tion, March-ing to the Prom-is'd Land.
2 Bro-ther clasps the hand of bro-ther, Step-ping fear-less through the night.
3 One the con-flict, one the per-il, One the march in God be-gun;
4 Where the one Al-migh-ty Fa-ther Reigns in love for ev-er-more.
5 Bear its shame, and fight its bat-tle, Till we rest be-neath its shade.
6 Then the scat-t'ring of all sha-dows, And the end of toil and gloom.

Music and words by permission of J. CURWEN & SONS, LTD.

SABINE BARING-GOULD (Trs.)   ST. OSWALD 8.7.8.7   JOHN B. DYKES

1 Through the night of doubt and sor-row On-ward goes the pil-grim band,
2 Clear be-fore us through the dark-ness Gleams and burns the guid-ing Light;
3 One the strain that lips of thou-sands Lift as from the heart of one;
4 One the glad-ness of re-joic-ing On the far e-ter-nal shore
5 On-ward, there-fore, pil-grim bro-thers, On-ward with the Cross our aid!
6 Soon shall come the great a-wak-ing, Soon the rend-ing of the tomb;

1 Sing-ing songs of ex-pec-ta-tion, March-ing to the Prom-is'd Land.
2 Bro-ther clasps the hand of bro-ther, Step-ping fear-less through the night.
3 One the con-flict, one the per-il, One the march in God be-gun;
4 Where the one Al-migh-ty Fa-ther Reigns in love for ev-er-more.
5 Bear its shame, and fight its bat-tle, Till we rest be-neath its shade.
6 Then the scat-t'ring of all sha-dows, And the end of toil and gloom.

Words by permission of J. CURWEN & SONS, LTD.

The tunes AUSTRIAN HYMN and ST. ASAPH are on the following pages

492 The Pilgrim Band

BERNHARDT S. INGEMANN   AUSTRIAN HYMN 8.7.8.7.D   FRANZ JOSEPH HAYDN

1 Through the night of doubt and sor-row On-ward goes the
2 One the strain that lips of thou-sands Lift as from the
3 On-ward, there-fore, pil-grim bro-thers, On-ward with the

1 pil-grim band, Sing-ing songs of ex-pec-ta-tion,
2 heart of one; One the con-flict, one the per-il,
3 Cross our aid! Bear its shame, and fight its bat-tle,

1 March-ing to the Prom-is'd Land: Clear be-fore us through the
2 One the march in God be-gun: One the glad-ness of re-
3 Till we rest be-neath its shade: Soon shall come the great a-

1 dark-ness Gleams and burns the guid-ing Light; Bro-ther clasps the
2 joic-ing On the far e-ter-nal shore, Where the one Al-
3 wak-ing, Soon the rend-ing of the tomb; Then the scat-t'ring

1 hand of bro-ther, Step-ping fear-less through the night.
2 migh-ty Fa-ther Reigns in love for ev-er-more.
3 of all sha-dows, And the end of toil and gloom.

The tunes MARCHING and ST. OSWALD are on the preceding page

492 # The Pilgrim Band

BERNHARDT S. INGEMANN   ST. ASAPH 8.7.8.7.D   WILLIAM S. BAMBRIDGE

1 Thro' the night of doubt and sor - row On - ward goes the
2 One the strain that lips of thou - sands Lift as from the
3 On - ward, there - fore, pil - grim bro - thers, On - ward with the

1 pil - grim band, Sing - ing songs of ex - pec - ta - tion, March - ing
2 heart of one; One the con - flict, one the per - il, One the
3 Cross our aid! Bear its shame, and fight its bat - tle, Till we

1 to the Prom - is'd Land: Clear be - fore us through the
2 march in God be - gun: One the glad - ness of re -
3 rest be - neath its shade: Soon shall come the great a -

1 dark - ness Gleams and burns the guid - ing Light, Bro - ther clasps the
2 joic - ing On the far e - ter - nal shore, Where the one Al -
3 wak - ing, Soon the rend - ing of the tomb, Then the scat - t'ring

1 hand of bro - ther, Step - ping fear - less through the night.
2 migh - ty Fa - ther Reigns in love for ev - er - more.
3 of all sha - dows, And the end of toil and gloom.

The tunes MARCHING, ST. OSWALD, and AUSTRIAN HYMN are on the preceding pages

493 Go, Labour On

HORATIUS BONAR   DUKE STREET L.M.   JOHN HATTON

1 Go, la-bour on, spend, and be spent, Thy joy to
2 Go, la-bour on: 'tis not for nought, Thy earth-ly
3 Men die in dark-ness at your side With-out a
4 Toil on, and in thy toil re-joice, For toil comes

1 do the Fa-ther's will; It is the way the
2 loss is heav'n-ly gain; Men heed thee, love thee,
3 hope to cheer the tomb: Take up the torch and
4 rest, for ex-ile home; Soon shalt thou hear the

1 Mas-ter went, Should not the ser-vant tread it still?
2 praise thee not, The Mas-ter prais-es—what are men!
3 wave it wide, The torch that lights time's thick-est gloom.
4 Bride-groom's voice, The mid-night peal, 'Be-hold, I come!'

HORATIUS BONAR   GRENOBLE L.M.   GRENOBLE CHURCH MELODY

1 Go, la-bour on, spend, and be spent, Thy joy to do the Fa-ther's will;
2 Go, la-bour on: 'tis not for nought, Thy earth-ly loss is heav'n-ly gain;
3 Men die in dark-ness at your side With-out a hope to cheer the tomb:
4 Toil on, and in thy toil re-joice, For toil comes rest, for ex-ile home;

Go, Labour On—*Continued*

1 It is the way the Mas - ter went, Should not the ser - vant tread it still?
2 Men heed thee, love thee, praise thee not, The Mas - ter prais - es— what are men!
3 Take up the torch and wave it wide, The torch that lights time's thick - est gloom.
4 Soon shalt thou hear the Bridegroom's voice, The mid - night peal, 'Be - hold, I come!

HORATIUS BONAR   HOPE L.M.   H. S. IRONS

1 Go, la - bour on, spend and be spent, Thy joy to
2 Go, la - bour on: 'tis not for nought, Thy earth - ly
3 Men die in dark - ness at your side With - out a
4 Toil on, and in thy toil re - joice, For toil comes

1 do the Fa - ther's will; It is the way the
2 loss is heav'n - ly gain; Men heed thee, love thee,
3 hope to cheer the tomb: Take up the torch and
4 rest, for ex - ile home; Soon shalt thou hear the

1 Mas - ter went, Should not the ser - vant tread it still?
2 praise thee not, The Mas - ter prais - es— what are men!
3 wave it wide, The torch that lights time's thick - est gloom.
4 Bride-groom's voice, The mid - night peal, 'Be - hold, I come!'

494 Lo! Round the Throne

ROWLAND HILL   CYPRUS L.M.   LOWELL MASON

1 Lo! round the throne at God's right hand The saints in count-less my-riads stand;
2 Thro' tri - bu - la-tion great they came, They bore the cross, des-pis'd the shame;
3 Hun-ger and thirst they feel no more, Nor sin, nor pain, or death de - plore;
4 They see their Sa-viour face to face, And sing the tri-umphs of His grace;
5 O may we tread the sa-cred road That ho - ly saints and mar-tyrs trod!

1 Of ev - 'ry tongue re-deem'd to God, Ar-ray'd in gar-ments wash'd in blood.
2 From all their la - bours now they rest, In God's e - ter - nal glo - ry blest.
3 The tears are wip'd from ev - 'ry eye, And sor - row yields to end - less joy.
4 Him day and night they cease-less praise, To Him their loud ho - san - nas raise.
5 Wage to the end the glo - rious strife, And win, like them, the crown of life.

ROWLAND HILL   ONTARIO L.M.   AMERICAN MELODY

1 Lo! round the throne of God's right hand The saints in count - less
2 Thro' tri - bu - la - tion great they came, They bore the cross, des -
3 Hun - ger and thirst they feel no more, Nor sin, nor pain, or
4 They see their Sa - viour face to face, And sing the tri - umphs
5 O may we tread the sa - cred road That ho - ly saints and

1 my - riads stand; Of ev - 'ry tongue re - deem'd to
2 pis'd the shame; From all their la - bours now they
3 death de - plore; The tears are wip'd from ev - 'ry
4 of His grace; Him day and night they cease - less
5 mar - tyrs trod! Wage to the end the glo - rious

Lo! Round the Throne—*Continued*

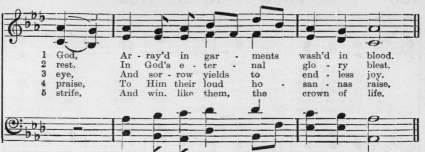

1 God,   Ar - ray'd in gar - ments wash'd in blood.
2 rest,   In God's e - ter - nal   glo - ry   blest.
3 eye,   And sor - row yields to   end - less joy.
4 praise, To Him their loud ho - san - nas raise.
5 strife, And win. like them, the   crown of life.

495

Thou Wounded Lamb

DESSLER   PLAISTOW L.M.   *Magdalen Chapel*
                                                Hymns, 1760

1 I   thirst, Thou wound - ed   Lamb of God,   To   wash me
2 Take my   poor heart and   let   it   be   For   ev - er
3 How can it   be,   Thou   heav'n - ly King, That Thou shouldst
4 Hence our hearts melt, our   eyes o'er - flow, Our   words are

1 in   Thy   cleans - ing blood, To   dwell with - in Thy
2 clos'd to   all   but Thee! Seal Thou my   breast, and
3 us   to   glo - ry   bring? Make slaves the   part - ners
4 lost: nor   will we   know, Nor   will we   think of

1 wounds, then pain Is   sweet, and life or   death is   gain.
2 let   me   wear That pledge of   love for   ev - er there.
3 of   Thy throne, Deck'd with a   nev - er - fad - ing crown?
4 aught be - side, 'My Lord, my   Love is   cru - ci - fied!'

496 Thou Will of God

GERHARD TERSTEEGEN   RIVAULX L.M.   J. B. DYKES

1 Thou sweet be - lov - ed will of God! My an - chor
2 O Will! that wil - lest good a - lone, Lead Thou the
3 O light - est bur - den, sweet - est yoke! It lifts, it
4 Up - on God's will I lay me down, As child up -
5 Thy won - der - ful grand will, my God, With tri - umph

1 ground, my for - tress hill, My spi - rit's si - lent,
2 way, Thou gui - dest best; A lit - tle child, I
3 bears my hap - py soul, It giv - eth wings to
4 on its mo - ther's breast; No sil - ken couch, nor
5 now I make it mine; And faith shall cry a

1 fair a - bode, In Thee I hide me, and am still.
2 fol - low on, And trust-ing, lean up - on Thy breast.
3 this poor heart; My free - dom is Thy grand con - trol.
4 soft - est bed, Could ev - er give me such deep rest.
5 joy - ous, Yes! To ev - 'ry dear com - mand of Thine.

497 Brethren in Christ

CHARLES WESLEY   HOLLEY L.M.   GEORGE HEWS

1 Breth - ren in Christ, and well be - lov'd, To Je - sus
2 Wel - come from earth: lo, the right hand Of fol - low -
3 Say, are your hearts re - solv'd as ours? Then let them
4 Thou God that an - swer - est by fire, The Spirit of
5 In part we on - ly know Thee here, But wait Thy

Brethren in Christ—*Continued*

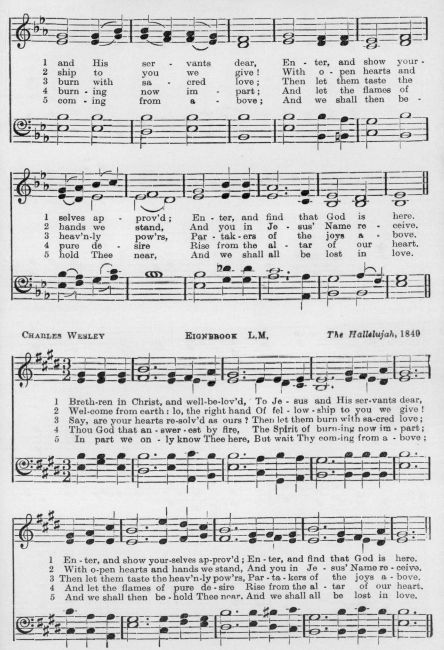

1 and His ser - vants dear, En - ter, and show your -
2 ship to you we give! With o - pen hearts and
3 burn with sa - cred love; Then let them taste the
4 burn - ing now im - part; And let the flames of
5 com - ing from a - bove; And we shall then be -

1 selves ap - prov'd; En - ter, and find that God is here.
2 hands we stand, And you in Je - sus' Name re - ceive.
3 heav'n-ly pow'rs, Par - tak - ers of the joys a - bove.
4 pure de - sire Rise from the al - tar of our heart.
5 hold Thee near, And we shall all be lost in love.

CHARLES WESLEY   EIGNBROOK L.M.   *The Hallelujah, 1840*

1 Breth-ren in Christ, and well-be-lov'd, To Je - sus and His ser-vants dear,
2 Wel-come from earth: lo, the right hand Of fel - low-ship to you we give!
3 Say, are your hearts re-solv'd as ours? Then let them burn with sa-cred love;
4 Thou God that an - swer - est by fire, The Spirit of burn-ing now im - part;
5 In part we on - ly know Thee here, But wait Thy com-ing from a - bove;

1 En - ter, and show your-selves ap-prov'd; En - ter, and find that God is here.
2 With o-pen hearts and hands we stand, And you in Je - sus' Name re - ceive.
3 Then let them taste the heav'n-ly pow'rs, Par - ta-kers of the joys a - bove.
4 And let the flames of pure de - sire Rise from the al - tar of our heart.
5 And we shall then be - hold Thee near, And we shall all be lost in love.

498 We Sing the Praise

THOMAS KELLY   MAINZER L.M.   JOSEPH MAINZER

1 We sing the praise of Him who died, Of Him who died up-on the Cross;
2 In-scrib'd up-on the Cross we see In shin-ing let-ters, 'God is Love;'
3 The Cross! it takes our guilt a - way; It holds the faint-ing spi-rit up;
4 It makes the cow-ard spi-rit brave, And nerves the fee-ble arm for fight;
5 The balm of life, the cure of woe, The mea-sure and the pledge of love,

1 The sin-ner's hope let men de-ride, For this we count the world but loss.
2 He bears our sins up-on the tree, He brings us mer-cy from a-bove.
3 It cheers with hope the gloom-y day, And sweet-ens ev-'ry bit-ter cup.
4 It takes its ter-ror from the grave, And gilds the bed of death with light.
5 The sin-ner's re-fuge here be-low, The an-gels' theme in heav'n a-bove.

THOMAS KELLY   HALIFAX L.M.   *Greenwood's Psalmody, 1838*

1 We sing the praise of Him who died, Of
2 In - scrib'd up - on the Cross we see In
3 The Cross! it takes our guilt a - way; It
4 It makes the cow - ard spi - rit brave, And
5 The balm of life, the cure of woe, The

1 Him who died up - on the Cross; The sin - ner's hope let
2 shin - ing let - ters, 'God is Love'; He bears our sins up -
3 holds the faint - ing spi - rit up; It cheers with hope the
4 nerves the fee - ble arm for fight; It takes its ter - ror
5 mea - sure and the pledge of love, The sin - ner's re - fuge

We Sing the Praise—*Continued*

1 men de - ride, For this we count the world but loss.
2 on the tree, He brings us mer - cy from a - bove.
3 gloom - y day, And sweet - ens ev - 'ry bit - ter cup.
4 from the grave, And gilds the bed of death with light.
5 here be - low, The an - gels' theme in heav'n a - bove.

THOMAS KELLY   MELROSE L.M.   F. C. MAKER

1 We sing the praise of Him who died, Of Him who
2 In-scrib'd up - on the Cross we see In shi - ning
3 The Cross! it takes our guilt a - way; It holds the
4 It makes the cow - ard spi - rit brave, And nerves the
5 The balm of life, the cure of woe, The mea - sure

1 died up - on the Cross; The sin - ner's hope let
2 let - ters, 'God is Love'; He bears our sins up -
3 faint - ing spi - rit up; It cheers with hope the
4 fee - ble arm for fight; It takes its ter - ror
5 and the pledge of love, The sin - ner's re - fuge

1 men de - ride, For this we count the world but loss.
2 on the tree, He brings us mer - cy from a - bove.
3 gloom - y day, And sweet-ens ev - 'ry bit - ter cup.
4 from the grave, And gilds the bed of death with light.
5 here be - low, The an - gels' theme in heav'n a - bove.

Copyright by F. C. MAKER

499 The Creator's Praise

ISAAC WATTS WAREHAM L.M. WILLIAM KNAPP

1 From all that dwell be - low the skies Let the Cre -
2 E - ter - nal are Thy mer - cies, Lord; E - ter - nal

1 a - tor's praise a - rise; Let the Re - deem - er's
2 truth at - tends Thy word; Thy praise shall sound from

1 Name be sung Thro' ev - 'ry land, by ev - 'ry tongue.
2 shore to shore Till suns shall rise and set no more.

ISAAC WATTS ST. FRANCIS *Geistliche Kirchengesang, 1623*

Unison

1 From all that dwell be - low the skies Let
2 E - ter - nal are Thy mer - cies, Lord; E -

The Creator's Praise—*Continued*

Harmony

1 the Cre - a - tor's praise a - rise; Hal - le - lu - jah!
2 ter - nal truth at - tends Thy word; Hal - le - lu - jah!

Unison

1 Hal - le - lu - jah! Let the Re - deem - er's Name be
2 Hal - le - lu - jah! Thy praise shall sound from shore to

1 sung Thro' ev - 'ry land, by ev - 'ry tongue,
2 shore Till suns shall rise and set no more,

Harmony

1-2 Hal - le - lu - jah! Hal - le - lu - jah! Hal - le - lu - jah!

Unison

1-2 Hal - le - lu - jah! Hal - le - lu - jah!

500 Come, Holy Spirit

JOHN STEWART   ST. PETROX L.M.   R. F. DALE

1 Come, Ho - ly Spi - rit, calm our minds, And fit
2 Hast Thou im - par - ted to our souls A liv -
3 Im - press up - on our wan - 'dring hearts The love
4 A bright - er faith and hope im - part, And let

1 us to ap - proach our God; Re - move each vain, each
2 ing spark of heav'n - ly fire? O kin - dle now the
3 that Christ to sin - ners bore; Help us to look on
4 us now Thy glo - ry see; O soothe and cheer each

1 world - ly thought, And lead us to Thy blest a - bode.
2 sa - cred flame! And make us burn with pure de - sire.
3 Him we pierc'd, And our re - deem - ing God a - dore.
4 bur - den'd heart! And bid our spi - rits rest in Thee.

By permission of Miss MILICENT PICKERSGILL - CUNLIFFE

JOHN STEWART   GRACE L.M.   FRED. BEVAN

1 Come, Ho - ly Spi - rit, calm our minds, And fit us to ap - proach our God;
2 Hast Thou im - par - ted to our souls A liv - ing spark of heav'n - ly fire?
3 Im - press up - on our wan - 'dring hearts The love that Christ to sin - ners bore;
4 A bright - er faith and hope im - part, And let us now Thy glo - ry see;

Come, Holy Spirit—*Continued*

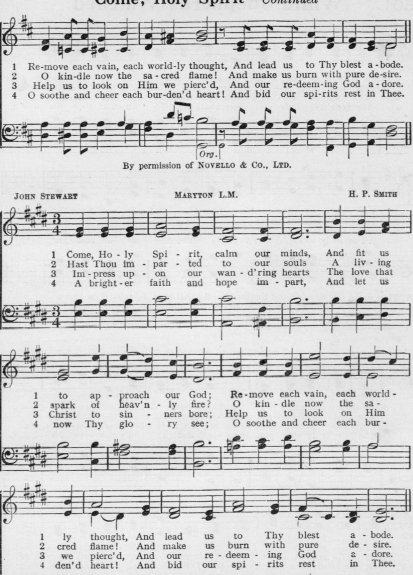

1 Re-move each vain, each world-ly thought, And lead us to Thy blest a-bode.
2 O kin-dle now the sa-cred flame! And make us burn with pure de-sire.
3 Help us to look on Him we pierc'd, And our re-deem-ing God a-dore.
4 O soothe and cheer each bur-den'd heart! And bid our spi-rits rest in Thee.

By permission of Novello & Co., Ltd.

JOHN STEWART   MARYTON L.M.   H. P. SMITH

1 Come, Ho-ly Spi-rit, calm our minds, And fit us
2 Hast Thou im-par-ted to our souls A liv-ing
3 Im-press up-on our wan-d'ring hearts The love that
4 A bright-er faith and hope im-part, And let us

1 to ap-proach our God; Re-move each vain, each world-
2 spark of heav'n-ly fire? O kin-dle now the sa-
3 Christ to sin-ners bore; Help us to look on Him
4 now Thy glo-ry see; O soothe and cheer each bur-

1 ly thought, And lead us to Thy blest a-bode.
2 cred flame! And make us burn with pure de-sire.
3 we pierc'd, And our re-deem-ing God a-dore.
4 den'd heart! And bid our spi-rits rest in Thee.

501 While Shepherds Watched

NAHUM TATE   WINCHESTER OLD C.M.   *Este's Psalter*, 1592

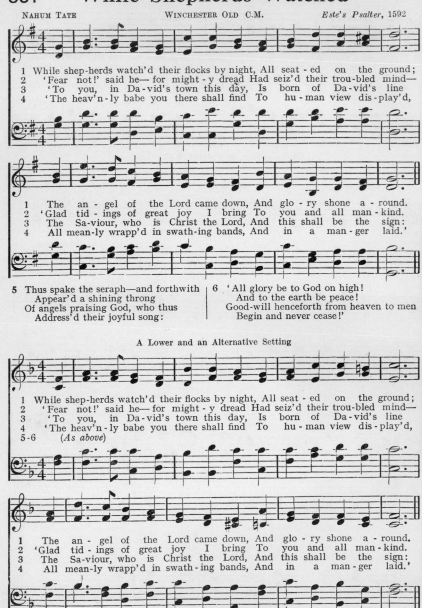

1 While shep-herds watch'd their flocks by night, All seat-ed on the ground;
2 'Fear not!' said he— for might-y dread Had seiz'd their trou-bled mind—
3 'To you, in Da-vid's town this day, Is born of Da-vid's line
4 'The heav'n-ly babe you there shall find To hu-man view dis-play'd,

1 The an-gel of the Lord came down, And glo-ry shone a-round.
2 'Glad tid-ings of great joy I bring To you and all man-kind.
3 The Sa-viour, who is Christ the Lord, And this shall be the sign:
4 All mean-ly wrapp'd in swath-ing bands, And in a man-ger laid.'

5 Thus spake the seraph—and forthwith
  Appear'd a shining throng
Of angels praising God, who thus
  Address'd their joyful song:

6 'All glory be to God on high!
  And to the earth be peace!
Good-will henceforth from heaven to men
  Begin and never cease!'

A Lower and an Alternative Setting

1 While shep-herds watch'd their flocks by night, All seat-ed on the ground;
2 'Fear not!' said he— for might-y dread Had seiz'd their trou-bled mind—
3 'To you, in Da-vid's town this day, Is born of Da-vid's line
4 'The heav'n-ly babe you there shall find To hu-man view dis-play'd,
5-6   (*As above*)

1 The an-gel of the Lord came down, And glo-ry shone a-round.
2 'Glad tid-ings of great joy I bring To you and all man-kind.
3 The Sa-viour, who is Christ the Lord, And this shall be the sign:
4 All mean-ly wrapp'd in swath-ing bands, And in a man-ger laid.'

The tune EVANGEL is on the next page

501 While Shepherds Watched

NAHUM TATE   EVANGEL C.M.D.   G. W. FINK

1 While shep-herds watch'd their flocks by night, All seat-ed on the ground;
2 'To you, in Dav-id's town this day, Is born of Da-vid's line
3 Thus spake the ser-aph, and forth-with Ap-pear'd a shin-ing throng

1 The an-gel of the Lord came down, And glo-ry shone a-round.
2 The Sa-viour, who is Christ the Lord; And this shall be the sign:
3 Of an-gels prais-ing God, who thus Ad-dress'd their joy-ful song:

1 'Fear not!' said he, for might-y dread Had seized their trou-bled mind;
2 'The heav'n-ly babe you there shall find To hu-man view dis-play'd,
3 'All glo-ry be to God on high! And to the earth be peace!

1 'Glad tid-ings of great joy I bring To you and all man-kind.'
2 All mean-ly wrapp'd in swath-ing bands, And in a man-ger laid.'
3 Good-will hence-forth from heav'n to men Be-gin and ne-ver cease!'

The tune WINCHESTER OLD is on the previous page

502 Beneath that Cross

HORATIUS BONAR   ABRIDGE C.M.   ISAAC SMITH

1 Op-press'd by noon-day's scorch-ing heat, To
2 Be-neath that Cross clear wa-ters burst, A
3 For bur-den'd ones, a rest-ing place Be-
4 A stran-ger here, I pitch my tent Be-

1 yon-der Cross I flee. Be-neath its shel-ter
2 foun-tain spark-ling free, And there I quench my
3 neath that Cross I see; Here I cast off my
4 neath this spread-ing tree; Here shall my pil-grim

1 take my seat: No shade like this to me!
2 des-ert thirst: No spring like this to me!
3 wea-ri-ness: No rest like this for me!
4 life be spent: No home like this for me!

HORATIUS BONAR   SWANSIDE C.M.   FRANCIS DUCKWORTH

1 Op-press'd by noon-day's scorch-ing heat, To yon-der Cross I flee,
2 Be-neath that Cross clear wa-ters burst, A foun-tain spark-ling free,
3 For bur-den'd ones, a rest-ing place Be-neath that Cross I see;
4 A stran-ger here, I pitch my tent Be-neath this spread-ing tree;

Beneath that Cross—*Continued*

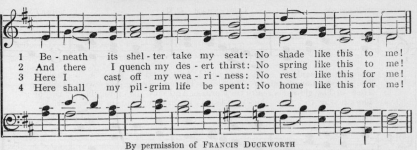

```
1  Be - neath   its shel - ter  take my  seat:  No  shade  like this  to  me!
2  And  there   I quench my des - ert thirst:  No  spring like this  to  me!
3  Here I       cast off  my wea - ri - ness:  No  rest   like this  for me!
4  Here shall   my pil - grim life be spent:   No  home   like this  for me!
```

By permission of FRANCIS DUCKWORTH

503

Thy Word My Choice

ISAAC WATTS   ST. STEPHEN C.M.   WILLIAM JONES

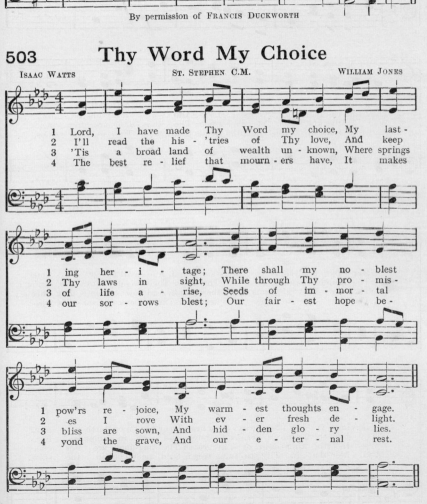

```
1  Lord,   I    have made   Thy   Word    my  choice,  My   last -
2  I'll    read the    his - 'tries   of    Thy  love,    And  keep
3  'Tis    a    broad land  of    wealth un - known, Where springs
4  The     best re - lief   that  mourn - ers have,   It   makes
```

```
1  ing   her - i -   tage;  There  shall  my    no - blest
2  Thy   laws  in    sight;  While through Thy  pro - mis -
3  of    life  a -   rise,  Seeds  of    im -  mor - tal
4  our   sor - rows  blest;  Our   fair - est  hope  be -
```

```
1  pow'rs re - joice,  My   warm - est  thoughts en -  gage.
2  es    I   rove   With  ev - er  fresh  de -   light.
3  bliss are  sown,  And   hid - den glo - ry   lies.
4  yond  the grave,  And   our   e - ter - nal   rest.
```

504 Happy the Souls

CHARLES WESLEY   TOTTENHAM C.M.   T. GREATOREX

1 Hap-py the souls to Je-sus join'd, And sav'd by grace a - lone;
2 The Church tri-umph-ant in Thy love, Their might-y joys we know;
3 Thee in Thy glo-rious realm they praise, And bow be - fore Thy throne;
4 The ho - ly to the ho - liest leads; From thence our spi - rits rise:

1 Walk-ing in all His ways they find Their heav'n on earth be - gun.
2 They sing the Lamb in hymns a - bove, And we in hymns be - low.
3 We in the king-dom of Thy grace: The king-doms are but one.
4 And he that in Thy sta-tutes treads Shall meet Thee in the skies.

CHARLES WESLEY   GORDON C.M.   HENRY SMART

1 Hap-py the souls to Je-sus join'd, And sav'd by grace a - lone;
2 The Church tri-umph-ant in Thy love, Their might-y joys we know;
3 Thee in Thy glo-rious realm they praise, And bow be - fore Thy throne;
4 The ho - ly to the ho - liest leads; From thence our spi - rits rise:

1 Walk-ing in all His ways they find Their heav'n on earth be - gun.
2 They sing the Lamb in hymns a - bove, And we in hymns be - low.
3 We in the king-dom of Thy grace: The king-doms are but one.
4 And he that in Thy sta-tutes treads Shall meet Thee in the skies.

505 Father of Mercies

ANNE STEELE   FRENCH C.M.   *Scottish Psalter, 1615*

1 Fa-ther of mer-cies! in Thy Word What end-less glo-ry shines!
2 Here may the wretch-ed sons of want Ex-haust-less rich-es find;
3 Here the Re-deem-er's wel-come voice Spreads heav'n-ly peace a-round;
4 O may these heav'n-ly pa-ges be My ev-er dear de-light,
5 Di-vine In-struc-tor, gra-cious Lord! Be Thou for ev-er near;

1 For ev-er be Thy Name a-dor'd For these ce-les-tial lines.
2 Rich-es a-bove what earth can grant, And last-ing as the mind.
3 And life and ev-er-last-ing joys At-tend the bliss-ful sound.
4 And still new beau-ties may I see, And still in-creas-ing light.
5 Teach me to love Thy sa-cred Word, And view my Sa-viour there.

ANNE STEELE   TILTEY ABBEY C.M.   A. H. BROWN

1 Fa-ther of mer-cies! in Thy Word What end-less glo-ry shines!
2 Here may the wretch-ed sons of want Ex-haust-less rich-es find;
3 Here the Re-deem-er's wel-come voice Spreads heav'n-ly peace a-round;
4 O may these heav'n-ly pa-ges be My ev-er dear de-light,
5 Di-vine In-struc-tor, gra-cious Lord! Be Thou for ev-er near;

1 For ev-er be Thy Name a-dor'd For these ce-les-tial lines.
2 Rich-es a-bove what earth can grant, And last-ing as the mind.
3 And life and ev-er-last-ing joys At-tend the bliss-ful sound.
4 And still new beau-ties may I see, And still in-creas-ing light.
5 Teach me to love Thy sa-cred Word, And view my Sa-viour there.

By permission of the OXFORD UNIVERSITY PRESS

506 God is Our Refuge

JOHN HOPKINS   STROUDWATER C.M.   *Wilkins' Psalmody*, 1750

1 God is our re - fuge and our strength, In straits a pre - sent aid;
2 Tho' hills a - midst the seas be cast; Tho' wa - ters roar - ing make,
3 A riv - er is, whose streams do glad The ci - ty of our God;
4 God in the midst of her doth dwell; No - thing shall her re - move;
5 Be still, and know that I am God; A - mong the hea - then I

1 There - fore, al - though the earth re - move, We will not be a - fraid;
2 And trou - bled be; yea, though the hills By swell - ing seas do shake.
3 The ho - ly place, where - in the Lord Most High hath His a - bode.
4 The Lord to her an help - er will, And that right ear - ly, prove.
5 Will be ex - al - ted; I on earth Will be ex - al - ted high.

507 O Sing a New Song

JOHN HOPKINS   SOUTHWARK C.M.   CHRISTOPHER TYE

1 O sing a new song to the Lord For won - ders He hath done:
2 The Lord God His sal - va - tion Hath caus - ed to be known;
3 He mind - ful of His grace and truth To Is - rael's house hath been;
4 Let all the earth un - to the Lord Send forth a joy - ful noise;
5 With harp, with harp, and voice of psalms, Un - to Je - ho - vah sing!

1 His right hand and His ho - ly arm Him vic - tor - y hath won.
2 His jus - tice in the hea - then's sight He o - pen - ly hath shown.
3 And the sal - va - tion of our God All ends of th' earth have seen.
4 Lift up your voice a - loud to Him, Sing prais - es, and re - joice.
5 With trum - pets, cor - nets, glad - ly sound Be - fore the Lord the King.

508 All Thy Mercies

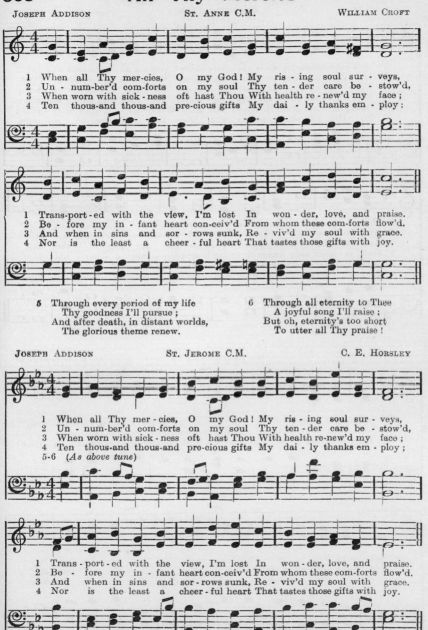

JOSEPH ADDISON   ST. ANNE C.M.   WILLIAM CROFT

1 When all Thy mer-cies, O my God! My ris-ing soul sur-veys,
2 Un-num-ber'd com-forts on my soul Thy ten-der care be-stow'd,
3 When worn with sick-ness oft hast Thou With health re-new'd my face;
4 Ten thous-and thous-and pre-cious gifts My dai-ly thanks em-ploy:

1 Trans-port-ed with the view, I'm lost In won-der, love, and praise.
2 Be-fore my in-fant heart con-ceiv'd From whom these com-forts flow'd.
3 And when in sins and sor-rows sunk, Re-viv'd my soul with grace.
4 Nor is the least a cheer-ful heart That tastes those gifts with joy.

5 Through every period of my life
  Thy goodness I'll pursue;
And after death, in distant worlds,
  The glorious theme renew.

6 Through all eternity to Thee
  A joyful song I'll raise;
But oh, eternity's too short
  To utter all Thy praise!

JOSEPH ADDISON   ST. JEROME C.M.   C. E. HORSLEY

1 When all Thy mer-cies, O my God! My ris-ing soul sur-veys,
2 Un-num-ber'd com-forts on my soul Thy ten-der care be-stow'd,
3 When worn with sick-ness oft hast Thou With health re-new'd my face;
4 Ten thous-and thous-and pre-cious gifts My dai-ly thanks em-ploy;
5-6 (*As above tune*)

1 Trans-port-ed with the view, I'm lost In won-der, love, and praise.
2 Be-fore my in-fant heart con-ceiv'd From whom these com-forts flow'd.
3 And when in sins and sor-rows sunk, Re-viv'd my soul with grace.
4 Nor is the least a cheer-ful heart That tastes those gifts with joy.

509 These Glorious Spirits

ISAAC WATTS BEATITUDO C.M. J. B. DYKES

1 How bright these glo-rious spi - rits shine ! Whence all their white ar - ray ?
2 Lo ! these are they from suf-'frings great Who came to realms of light,
3 Now, with tri - um - phal palms they stand Be - fore the throne on high,
4 Hun - ger and thirst are felt no more, Nor suns with scorch-ing ray ;
5 'Mong pas-tures green He'll lead His flock, Where liv - ing streams ap - pear ;
6 To Him who sits up - on the throne, The God whom we a - dore,

1 How came they to the bliss - ful seats Of ev - er - last - ing day ?
2 And in the blood of Christ have wash'd Those robes which shine so bright.
3 And serve the God they love, a - midst The glo - ries of the sky.
4 God is their sun, whose cheer-ing beams Dif - fuse e - ter - nal day.
5 And God the Lord from ev - 'ry eye Shall wipe off ev - 'ry tear.
6 And to the Lamb that once was slain, Be glo - ry ev - er - more !

ISAAC WATTS ST. ASAPH C.M.D. G. M. GIORNIVICHI

1 How bright these glo-rious spi - rits shine ! Whence all their white ar - ray ?
2 Now, with tri - um - phal palms they stand Be - fore the throne on high,
3 'Mong pas-tures green He'll lead His flock, Where liv - ing streams ap - pear ;

1 How came they to the bliss - ful seats Of ev - er - last - ing day ?
2 And serve the God they love, a - midst The glo - ries of the sky.
3 And God the Lord from ev - 'ry eye Shall wipe off ev - 'ry tear.

These Glorious Spirits—*Continued*

1 Lo! these are they from suf-f'rings great, Who came to realms of light,
2 Hun-ger and thirst are felt no more, Nor suns with scorch-ing ray;
3 To Him who sits up-on the throne, The God whom we a-dore,

1 And in the blood of Christ have wash'd Those robes which shine so bright.
2 God is their sun, whose cheer-ing beams Dif-fuse e-ter-nal day.
3 And to the Lamb that once was slain, Be glo-ry ev-er-more!

510   A Mysterious Way

WILLIAM COWPER   LONDON NEW C.M.   *Scottish Psalter, 1635*

1 God moves in a mys-te-rious way   His won-ders to per-form;
2 Deep in un-fath-om-a-ble mines   Of ne-ver-fail-ing skill
3 Ye fear-ful saints, fresh cour-age take; The clouds ye so much dread
4 Judge not the Lord by fee-ble sense, But trust Him for His grace.
5 His pur-pos-es will ri-pen fast,   Un-fold-ing ev-'ry hour;
6 Blind un-be-lief is sure to err,   And scan His work in vain;

1 He plants His foot-steps in the sea,   And rides up-on the storm.
2 He treas-ures up His bright de-signs, And works His sov-'reign will.
3 Are big with mer-cy, and shall break   In bless-ings on your head.
4 Be-hind a frown-ing pro-vi-dence He hides a smi-ling face.
5 The bud may have a bit-ter taste,   But sweet will be the flow'r.
6 God is His own in-ter-pre-ter,   And He will make it plain.

511 The Thought of Thee

BERNARD OF CLAIRVAUX   ST. AGNES, DURHAM C.M.   J. B. DYKES

1 Je-sus, the ve - ry thought of Thee With sweet-ness fills my breast;
2 Nor voice can sing, nor heart can frame, Nor can the mem-'ry find
3 O Hope of ev -'ry con - trite heart! O Joy of all the meek!
4 But what to those who find? Ah! this Nor tongue nor pen can show;
5 Je-sus, our on - ly joy be Thou, As Thou our prize wilt be;

1 But sweet-er far Thy face to see, And in Thy pre - sence rest.
2 A sweet-er sound than Thy blest Name, O Sa-viour of man-kind!
3 To those who fall, how kind Thou art! How good to those who seek!
4 The love of Je - sus, what it is None but His lov'd ones know.
5 Je-sus, be Thou our glo - ry now, And thro' e - ter - ni - ty.

512 John Three Sixteen

THOMAS DENNIS   *Arr.* W. H. HARPER

1 I love to tell the sto - ry, How Christ the King of Glo - ry
2 So now I'll try to please Him, My life I'll give to serve Him;
3 Then, bro-ther, won't you love Him? And, sis - ter, won't you trust Him?

1 Left heav'n a - bove to come and res - cue me; For sin - ners
2 His true and faith - ful ser - vant I will be: And when call'd
3 I know He died for you as well as me: We need our

John Three Sixteen—*Continued*

1 He re-ceives them, His blood was shed to save them, So Je - sus
2 home to glo - ry, I'll sing the good old sto - ry That Je - sus
3 sins for - giv - en That we may go to hea - ven, To live with

REFRAIN

1 died for sin - ners just like me.
2 died for sin - ners just like me.
3 Christ, who died for you and me.

Yes, yes, yes!

O yes! Je - sus died to set poor sin - ners free.

You say: 'How do I know it?' John three six - teen will show it;

That big word 'who - so - ev - er' just means me.

513 The Rock Stands Fast

E. S. LORENZ

E. S. LORENZ

1 In my soul oft ri-ses, bring-ing pain and woe, The a-
2 When, be-fore me mar-shall'd, all my sins a-rise, Swords of
3 While life's storm is rag-ing, heap-ing up hope's wrecks, While de-

1 larm-ing ques-tion, Am I saved or no? Then the Word brings com-
2 flame that bar the gates of par-a-dise, Tho' op-press'd with doubt-
3 lights al-lure and sore temp-ta-tions vex, I will cry, tho' fears

1 fort, it doth ful-ly show, Tho' my faith may wa-ver, Christ, the
2 ings, still my soul re-plies, Tho' my faith may wa-ver, Christ, the
3 and doubts my soul per-plex, Tho' my faith may wa-ver, Christ, the

REFRAIN

1-3 Rock, stands fast. The Rock stands fast, the Rock stands fast, Tho' my

The Rock Stands Fast—*Continued*

faith may wa-ver, Christ, the Rock, stands fast. The Rock stands fast, the

Rock stands fast ; Glo - ry be to God! Christ, the Rock, stands fast.

An Alternative Tune when the REFRAIN is used alone

E. S. LORENZ   E. H. SWINSTEAD

The Rock stands fast, The Rock stands fast, Though my faith

may wa-ver, Christ, the Rock, stands fast : The Rock stands fast, The

Rock stands fast ; Glo - ry be to God! Christ, the Rock, stands fast.

By permission of E. H. SWINSTEAD

514 **Coming To-Night?**

HARRIET E. JONES   J. HOWARD ENTWISLE

1 If our Lord should come to - night With the bright an - gel - ic host,
2 If our Lord should come to - night, Come as King and Judge of all,
3 Christ as King and Judge will come, 'Tis re - cord - ed in His book;

1 Would He find us in His vine - yard, Ev - 'ry ser - vant at His post?
2 Are there a - ny here as - sem - bled who would trem - ble at His call?
3 He will bid us stand be - fore Him, Not a soul will He o'er - look!

1 Thro' the pre-cious, cleans-ing blood Are our gar-ments clean and white? Are we
2 Is there one, O is there one! Far from Je - sus and the light, Un - re -
3 Are we read - y, ev - 'ry one? Are we in the rai - ment white. If the

1 dwell - ing in the light Should our Lord ap-pear to - night?
2 pent - ant, lost, un - done, If the Judge should come to - night?
3 Judge of all man - kind Should ap-pear this ve - ry night?

Coming To-Night?—*Continued*

REFRAIN

Are we watch-ing, are we wait-ing In the rai-ment pure and white?
watch-ing, watch-ing, wait-ing, wait-ing, In the rai-ment pure and white?

Should we joy at His ap-pear-ing If our Lord should come to-night?
to-night?

An Alternative Tune when the REFRAIN is used alone

HARRIET E. JONES   TAMWORTH 8.7.8.7.8.7   LOCKHART

Are we watch-ing, are we wait-ing In the rai-ment pure and white?

Should we joy at His ap-pear-ing If our Lord should come to-night?

Are we watch-ing, are we wait-ing, If our Lord should come to-night?

515   The Breaking of the Day

G. W. SEDERQUIST   G. W. SEDERQUIST

1 'Tis al - most time for the Lord to come, I hear the
2 The signs fore - told in the sun and moon, In earth and
3 It must be time for the wait - ing Church To cast her
4 Go quick - ly out in the streets and lanes, And in the

1 peo - ple . say; The stars of heav'n are grow - ing
2 sea . and . sky, A - loud pro - claim to all man -
3 pride a - way, With gird - ed loins and burn - ing
4 broad high - way, And call the maim'd, the halt, and

1 dim, It . must be the break - ing of the day.
2 kind, The . com - ing of the Mas - ter draw - eth nigh.
3 lamps, To . look . for the break - ing of the day.
4 blind, To be read - y for the break - ing of the day.

The Breaking of the Day—*Continued*

REFRAIN

O it must be the break-ing of the day! O it must be the break-ing of the day! , The night is al-most gone, The day is com-ing on; O it must be the break-ing of the day!

516   O Be Ready!

J. G. B.

M. A. CLIFTON, *Arr.* P. J. MANSFIELD

1-6 When the Bride-groom com-eth by and by (by and by), When the Bride-groom

1-6 com-eth by and by, (by and by,)

Will your lamps be burn-ing bright? Will your
O   be rea - dy for that day! With your
Will your wear-ied heart re - joice At the
Will the sor-rows of the past All be
When the Lord shall call His own, Can you
Will you join the ran-som'd host, Or be

1   robes be pure and white?
2   sins   all wash'd a - way,
3   sound of Je - sus' voice?
4   chang'd to joy at last?
5   stand be-fore the throne?
6   found a-mong the lost?

When the Bride - groom com - eth by and by.

REFRAIN

O be rea - dy! O be rea - dy! Rea-dy when the Bride-groom comes;

Are you rea-dy?

O be rea - dy! O be rea - dy! Rea-dy when the Bride-groom comes.

517 # When Jesus Comes

FANNY J. CROSBY

WILLIAM H. DOANE, *Arr.* P. J. MANSFIELD

1 When Je - sus comes to re - ward His ser-vants, . Whe-ther it be
2 If at the dawn of the ear - ly morn-ing . He shall call us
3 Have we been true to the trust He left us? Do we seek to
4 Bless - ed are those whom the Lord finds watch-ing, In His glo - ry

1 noon or night, Faith - ful to Him will He find us watch-ing,
2 one by one, When to the Lord we re - store our ta-lents,
3 do our best? If in our hearts there is nought con-demns us,
4 they shall share; If He should come at the dawn or mid-night,

REFRAIN

1 With our lamps all trimm'd and bright?
2 Will He an - swer thee—'Well done!'?
3 We shall have a glo - rious rest.
4 Will He find us watch - ing there?

O can we say we are

rea - dy, bro-ther! Rea-dy for the soul's bright home? . Say, will He

find you and me still watch-ing, Wait-ing, wait-ing, when the Lord shall come?

518 ## The Bridegroom Comes

E. R. LATTA

WM. J. KIRKPATRICK, *Arr.* P. J. MANSFIELD

1 Will our lamps be fill'd and rea - dy When the
2 Shall we hear a wel - come sound - ing When the
3 Don't de - lay our pre - par - a - tion Till the
4 It may be a time of sor - row When the
5 O there'll be a glo - rious meet - ing When the

1 Bride - groom comes? And our lights be clear and stead - y
2 Bride - groom comes? And a shout of joy re - sound - ing
3 Bride - groom comes; Lest there be a se - par - a - tion
4 Bride - groom comes; if our oil we hope to bor - row
5 Bride - groom comes! And a hal - le - lu - jah greet - ing

1-5 When the Bride - groom comes In the night, . . .
In the night,

1-4 that sol - emn night? . . . . Will our
5 that joy - ful night! . . . . With our

1-4 that sol - emn night?
5 that joy - ful night!

The Bridegroom Comes—*Continued*

1-4 lamps be burn - ing bright when the Bride - groom comes?
5 lamps all burn - ing bright when the Bride - groom comes!

REFRAIN

O be read - y! O be read - y! O be read - y

when the Bride - groom comes! O be read - y! O be

read - y! O be read - y when the Bride - groom comes!

519   The Lord is Coming!

E. A. HOFFMANN   E. A. HOFFMANN

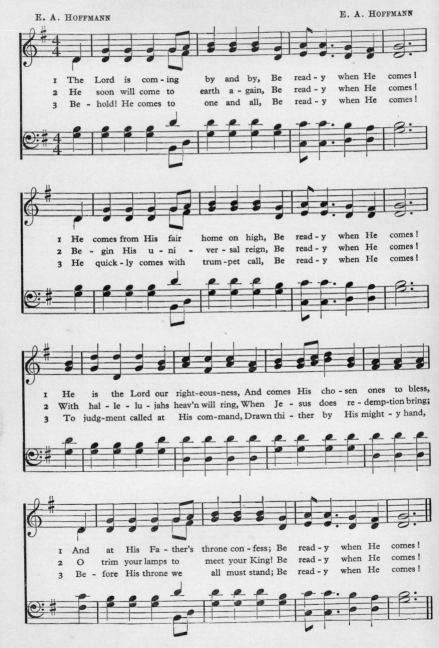

1 The Lord is com-ing by and by, Be read-y when He comes!
2 He soon will come to earth a-gain, Be read-y when He comes!
3 Be-hold! He comes to one and all, Be read-y when He comes!

1 He comes from His fair home on high, Be read-y when He comes!
2 Be-gin His u-ni-ver-sal reign, Be read-y when He comes!
3 He quick-ly comes with trum-pet call, Be read-y when He comes!

1 He is the Lord our right-eous-ness, And comes His cho-sen ones to bless,
2 With hal-le-lu-jahs heav'n will ring, When Je-sus does re-demp-tion bring;
3 To judg-ment called at His com-mand, Drawn thi-ther by His might-y hand,

1 And at His Fa-ther's throne con-fess; Be read-y when He comes!
2 O trim your lamps to meet your King! Be read-y when He comes!
3 Be-fore His throne we all must stand; Be read-y when He comes!

The Lord is Coming!—*Continued*

REFRAIN

Will you be read - y when the Bride - groom comes?

When He comes?

Will you be read - y when the Bride - groom comes?

When He comes?

Will your lamps be trimm'd and bright, Be it morn-ing, noon, or night?

Will you be read - y when the Bride - groom comes?

520   Christ Returneth!

H. L. TURNER   JAS. McGRANAHAN

1 It may be at morn, when the day is a - wak-ing, When sun-light thro'
2 It may be at mid-day, it may be at twi - light, It may be, per-
3 While hosts cry "Ho-san - na!" from hea - v'n de-scend-ing, With glo - ri - fied
4 Oh, joy! oh, de-light! should we go with-out dy-ing; No sick-ness, no

1 dark-ness and sha-dow is break-ing, That Je - sus will come in the ful-
2 chance, that the black-ness of mid-night Will burst in - to light in the blaze
3 saints and the an-gels at-tend-ing, With grace on His brow, like a ha-
4 sad-ness, no dread, and no cry-ing; Caught up thro' the clouds with our Lord

REFRAIN

1 ness of glo - ry, To re - ceive from the world "His own."
2 of His glo - ry, When Je - sus re - ceives "His own."
3 lo of glo - ry, Will Je - sus re - ceive "His own."
4 in-to glo - ry, When Je - sus re - ceives "His own."

O Lord Je - sus,

how long? How long ere we shout the glad song?—Christ re - turn-eth,

rit.

Hal - le - lu-jah! hal - le - lu-jah! A - men, Hal - le - lu-jah! A - men.

521   ANON

Trim Your Lamps!

OLD MELODY

1 Re - joice, ye saints! the   time draws near   When Christ will   in   the
2 The trum - pet sounds, the   thun-ders roll ;   The hea - vens   pass - ing
3 Poor sin - ners then on   earth will cry,   While light-nings flash from
4 Come, breth - ren all, and   let us try   To warn poor   sin - ners,

REFRAIN

1 clouds ap - pear, And for His peo - ple   call.
2 as a scroll; The earth will burn with   fire.
3 out the sky, "O moun-tains, on us   fall !"   } Trim your lamps, and be rea-dy !
4 and to cry, "Be-hold, the Bride-groom comes !"

Trim your lamps, and be rea - dy ! Trim your lamps, and be rea - dy

for the mid - night cry ! For the mid - night cry, For the mid - night

cry, Trim your lamps, and be rea - dy for the mid - night cry !

522   Jesus is Coming!

D. W. WHITTLE   JAMES McGRANAHAN

1 Je - sus is com - ing!   sing the glad word,
2 Je - sus is com - ing! the dead shall a - rise,
3 Je - sus is com - ing! His saints to re - lease;
4 Je - sus is com - ing! the pro - mise is true;

1 Com - ing for those He re - deem'd by His blood,
2 Lov'd ones shall meet in a joy - ful sur - prise,
3 Com - ing to give to the war - ring earth peace:
4 Who are the cho - sen, the faith - ful, the few,

1 Com - ing to reign as the glo - ri - fied
2 Caught up to - geth - er to Him in the
3 Sin - ning and sigh - ing and sor - row shall
4 Wait - ing and watch - ing, pre - par'd for re -

Jesus is Coming!—*Continued*

1 Lord;
2 skies;
3 cease;
4 view?

Je - sus is com - ing a - gain!

REFRAIN

Je - sus is com - ing, is com - ing a - gain! Je - sus is

com - ing a - gain!   Shout the glad tid -
Yes, Je - sus is com - ing! O shout the glad tid -

ings o'er moun - tain and plain! Je - sus is com - ing a - gain!

523   I'm Waiting for Thee

H. K. Burlingham   Jewels 6.6.11.D   G. F. Root

1. I'm wait-ing for Thee, Lord, Thy beau-ty to see, Lord,
2. 'Mid dan-ger and fear, Lord, I'm oft wea-ry here, Lord,
3. Whilst Thou art a-way, Lord, I stum-ble and stray, Lord,
4. Our lov'd ones be-fore, Lord, Their trou-bles are o'er, Lord,
5. E'en now let my ways, Lord, Be bright with Thy praise, Lord,

1. I'm wait-ing for Thee, for Thy com-ing a-gain,
2. The day must be near of Thy com-ing a-gain.
3. Oh, has-ten the day of Thy com-ing a-gain!
4. I'll meet them once more at Thy com-ing a-gain.
5. For brief are the days ere Thy com-ing a-gain.

1. Thou art gone o-ver there, Lord, A place to pre-pare, Lord,
2. 'Tis all sun-shine there, Lord, No sigh-ing nor care, Lord,
3. This is not my rest, Lord; A pil-grim con-fest, Lord,
4. The blood was the sign, Lord, That mark'd them as Thine, Lord,
5. I'm wait-ing for Thee, Lord, Thy beau-ty to see, Lord,

1. Thy home I shall share at Thy com-ing a-gain.
2. But glo-ry so fair at Thy com-ing a-gain.
3. I wait to be blest at Thy com-ing a-gain.
4. And bright-ly they'll shine at Thy com-ing a-gain.
5. No tri-umph for me like Thy com-ing a-gain.

524   A Little While

JANE CREWDSON   EMILIA 11.10.11.10   F. L. BENJAMIN

1 O for the peace which flow - eth like a riv - er,
2 A lit - tle while for pa - tient vi - gil - keep - ing,
3 A lit - tle while to keep the oil from fail - ing,
4 And He who is Him - self the gift and giv - er,

1 Mak - ing life's des - ert pla - ces bloom and smile!
2 To face the storm, to bat - tle with the strong;
3 A lit - tle while faith's flick - 'ring lamp to trim;
4 The fu - ture glo - ry and the pre - sent smile,

1 O for the faith to grasp heav'n bright for - ev - er
2 A lit - tle while to sow the seed with weep - ing,
3 And then the Bride - groom's com - ing foot - steps hail - ing,
4 With the bright pro - mise of the glad for - ev - er,

1 A - mid the sha - dows of earth's lit - tle while!
2 Then bind the sheaves and sing the har - vest song.
3 To haste to meet Him with the bri - dal hymn.
4 Will light the sha - dows of the lit - tle while.

525   # Till He Come!

E. H. BICKERSTETH   WELLS 7.7.7.7.7.7.   D. S. BORTNIANSKI

1 Till He come! O let the words Lin - ger on the
2 When the wea - ry ones we love En - ter on their
3 Clouds and con - flicts round us press, Would we have one
4 See, the feast of love is spread! Drink the wine and

1 trem - bling chords! Let the lit - tle while be - tween
2 rest a - bove, Seems the earth so poor and vast?
3 sor - row less? All the sharp - ness of the cross,
4 break the bread— Sweet me - mo - rials— till the Lord

1 In their gol - den light be seen; Let us think how
2 All our life - joy o - ver - cast? Hush! be ev - 'ry
3 All that tells the world is loss— Death and dark - ness,
4 Call us round His heav'n - ly board; Some from earth, from

1 hea - ven and home Lie be - yond that Till He come!
2 mur - mur dumb; It is on - ly Till He come!
3 and the tomb— On - ly whis - per: Till He come!
4 glo - ry some, Se - ver'd on - ly Till He come!

The tune CROMER is on the following page

525   Till He Come!

E. H. BICKERSTETH   CROMER 7.7.7.7.7.7.   ANON

1 Till He come! O let the words Ling - er on the
2 When the wea - ry ones we love En - ter on their
3 Clouds and con - flicts rounds us press; Would we have one
4 See, the feast of love is spread! Drink the wine and

1 trem - bling chords! Let the lit - tle while be - tween
2 rest a - bove, Seems the earth so poor and vast?
3 sor - row less? All the sharp - ness of the cross,
4 break the bread— Sweet me - mo - rials— till the Lord

1 In their gold - en light be seen; Let us think how
2 All our life - joy o - ver - cast? Hush! be ev - 'ry
3 All that tells the world is loss— Death and dark - ness,
4 Call us round His heav'n - ly board; Some from earth, from

1 heav'n and home Lie be - yond that Till He come!
2 mur - mur dumb; It is on - ly Till He come!
3 and the tomb— On - ly whis - per: Till He come!
4 glo - ry some, Se - ver'd on - ly Till He come!

The tune WELLS is on the preceding page

526   Thou Art Coming

FRANCES R. HAVERGAL   JAMES McGRANAHAN, *Arr.* P. J. MANSFIELD

1 Thou art coming, O my Saviour! Thou art coming, O my King!
2 Thou art coming, not a shadow, Not a mist, and not a tear,
3 Thou art coming! we are waiting With a hope that cannot fail;

1 Ev-'ry tongue Thy Name confessing, Well may we rejoice and sing;
2 Not a sin, and not a sorrow On that sunrise, grand and clear;
3 Asking not the day or hour, . Anchor'd safe within the vail:

1 Thou art coming! rays of glory, Thro' the vail Thy death has rent,
2 Thou art coming! Jesus, Saviour, Nothing else seems worth a thought;
3 Thou art coming! at Thy table We are witnesses for this,

1 Gladden now our pilgrim pathway, Glory from Thy presence sent.
2 O how marvellous the glory, And the bliss Thy pain hath bought,
3 As we meet Thee in communion, Earnest of our coming bliss.

Thou Art Coming !—*Continued*

REFRAIN

Thou art com-ing! Thou art com-ing! We shall meet Thee

on Thy way; Thou art com-ing! we shall see Thee, And be

like Thee on that day; Thou art com-ing! Thou art com-ing!

Je-sus, our be-lov-ed Lord! O the joy to

see Thee reign-ing! Wor-shipp'd, glo-ri-fied, a-dor'd.

527   # Lord of the Harvest

JENNIE JOHNSON   JOHN R. SWENEY

1 Have ye heard the song from the gold - en land? Have ye
2 They are look - ing down from the gold - en land, Our be -
3 O the song rolls on from the gold - en land! And our
4 O the song rolls on from the gold - en land! From its

1 heard the glad new song? . Let us bind our sheaves
2 lov'd are look - ing down; . They have done their work,
3 hearts are strong to - day; . For it nerves our souls
4 vales o joy and flow'rs; . And we feel and know

1 with a will - ing hand For the time will not be long.
2 they have borne their cross, And re - ceiv'd their pro - mis'd crown.
3 with its mu - sic sweet As we toil in the noon - tide ray.
4 by a liv - ing faith That its tones will soon be ours.

Lord of the Harvest—*Continued*

The Lord of the har - vest will soon ap -
pear; His smile, His . voice, we shall see and
hear; The Lord of the har vest wll
soon ap - pear, And ga - ther the reap - ers home.

528 # When the Roll is Called

JAMES M. BLACK

J. M. BLACK, *Arr.* P. J. MANSFIELD

1 When the trum - pet of the Lord shall sound and time shall be
2 On that bright and cloud - less morn - ing when the dead in Christ
3 Let us la - bour for the Mas - ter from the dawn till set -

1 no more, And the morn - ing breaks e - ter - nal, bright, and
2 shall rise, And the glo - ry of His re - sur - rec - tion
3 ting sun, Let us talk of all His won - drous love and

1 fair; . . . . . When the sav'd of earth shall gath - er o - ver on
2 share: . . . . . When His chos - en ones shall gath - er to their home
3 care, ... Then, when all of life is o - ver, and our work

When the sav'd . . . . . . of
When His chos - - en
Then, when all . . . . . . of

1 the oth - er shore, }
2 be - yond the skies, } And the roll is call'd up yon - der, I'll be there !
3 on earth is done, }

When the Roll is Called—*Continued*

529 Are You Ready?

E. E. HEWITT

W. J. KIRKPATRICK

1 There's an hour which no man know-eth, Nor the an-gels round the
2 What a bless-ed trans-form-a-tion! In the twink-ling of an
3 Though our sins have been as scar-let, Let us seek the streams that

1 throne, When the Lord shall come in glo-ry from the sky;
2 eye, When the mor-tal shall im-mor-tal life put on;
3 flow From the Cross that rose on Cal-v'ry's rug-ged height;

1 All the saints shall rise to meet Him, For He call-eth for His
2 Those who love Him shall be like Him When He com-eth from on
3 He is a-ble still to keep us, And pre-sent us white as

1 own; They shall hear the trum-pet sound-ing by-and-bye.
2 high, At the noon-tide, at the mid-night, or at dawn.
3 snow, When He comes a-gain as clouds of dazz-ling light.

REFRAIN Faster

Are you read-y? read-y? look-ing for the King?
are you are you

Are You Ready?—*Continued*

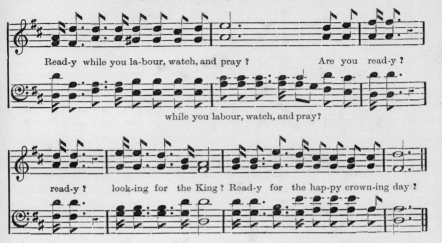

Read-y while you la-bour, watch, and pray ? Are you read-y ?

while you labour, watch, and pray?

read-y ? look-ing for the King ? Read-y for the hap-py crown-ing day ?

Alternative Tune when the Refrain is used alone

E. E. HEWITT   FARLEY CASTLE 10. 10. 10. 10   HENRY LAWES

Are you read-y, look-ing for the King ? Read-y

while you la-bour, watch, and pray ? Are you read-y, look-ing

for the King ? Read-y for the hap-py crown-ing day ?

530 The King's Coming

THOMAS GRAHAM   THOMAS GRAHAM

1 When the King comes back from the far - off land, And the trum - pet
2 When the morn - ing breaks on the hills of time And the sha - dows
3 When the fight is o'er, and the vict - 'ry won, And the van-quish'd
4 O to share the grace of the ho - ly place Where the an - gel -
5 Speed,.... speed that hour when Thy blood-bought pow'r Shall re - veal Thy

1 sounds to meet Him; O the joy that thrills thro' the rap - tur'd band
2 all are flee - ing; When the Bride a - wakes to the mar - riage chime,
3 foe is fly - ing; When the Cap - tain calls with His own 'Well done!'
4 hosts a - dore Him; Where our eyes shall gaze on the Bride-groom's face
5 full sal - va - tion; And the world re - sound to her ut - most bound

REFRAIN

1 Of the saints as they rise to greet Him!
2 And her faith is........ lost in see - ing.
3 To the crown of the life un - dy - ing.
4 As we stand all........ fair be - fore Him.
5 With the song of the new cre - a - tion.

1-4 O has - ten, Lord, that
5 All bless-ing, glo - ry,

1-4 hap - py day, The King-dom of Thy glo - ry! For our spi - rits
5 hon - our be, And praise that ceas - eth ne - ver, For........ Him that

1-4 yearn for Thy blest re - turn, As we muse on the Gos - pel sto - ry.
5 sits up........ - on the throne, And........ to the........ Lamb for ev - er!

531   Happy Home Coming

George C. Hugg

George C. Hugg

1 Hap - py home com - ing of our King ;........ We'll meet our
2 Bless - ed home com - ing of our King ;........ We'll join the
3 Glo - rious home com - ing of our King ;........ With Je - sus

1 lov'd ones gone be - fore; And sweet the greet-ing they will bring
2 ev - er - last - ing psalm Of joy that an - gel voi - ces sing:
3 we will live for aye Where songs of love and glad - ness ring

REFRAIN

1 To us up - on the gold - en shore.
2 The song of Mo - ses and the Lamb. } Hap - py home com-ing, Bless-ed
3 In tune thro' heav'n's e - ter - nal day.

home com-ing, Glor-ious home com-ing of our Sa-viour, King ! Hap-py, glad

meet-ing On that great morn-ing At the home com-ing of our Sa-viour, King !

532 # He'll Come Again

Johnson Oatman   Wm. J. Kirkpatrick

1 As once to earth the Sa-viour came, Some-time He'll come a-gain;
2 Tell ev-'ry-where with great de-light, Some-time He'll come a-gain;
3 O'er all the earth the ti-dings ring, Some-time He'll come a-gain;
4 When dawns that bless-ed morn-ing fair, Some-time He'll come a-gain;
5 O let us live and do our best, Some-time He'll come a-gain;

1 The sky with heav'n-ly light a-flame, Some-time He'll come a-gain.
2 Up-on the clouds of glo-ry bright, Some-time He'll come a-gain.
3 Not as a babe, but as a King, Some-time He'll come a-gain.
4 His saints will meet Him in the air, Some-time He'll come a-gain.
5 Then He will take us home to rest, Some-time He'll come a-gain.

REFRAIN

Some-time, some-time, Christ shall come to reign;
Some-time, some-time,

Repeat pp at close

Pre-pare my soul to meet Him, Some-time He'll come a-gain.

The tune WESTGATE is on the next page

532

He'll Come Again

JOHNSON OATMAN   WESTGATE C.M.D.   J. M. GIBSON

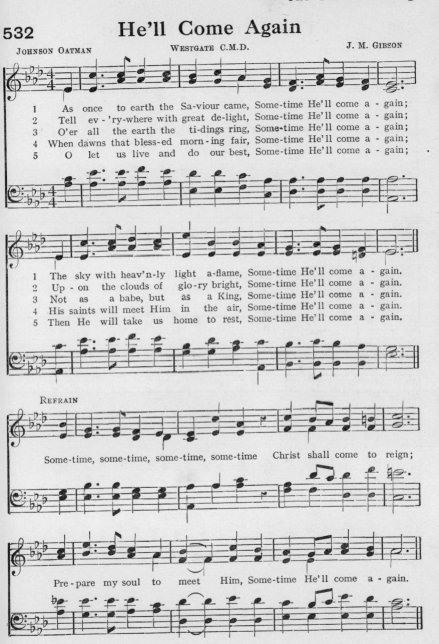

1 As once to earth the Sa-viour came, Some-time He'll come a - gain;
2 Tell ev - 'ry-where with great de-light, Some-time He'll come a - gain;
3 O'er all the earth the ti-dings ring, Some-time He'll come a - gain;
4 When dawns that bless-ed morn-ing fair, Some-time He'll come a - gain;
5 O let us live and do our best, Some-time He'll come a - gain;

1 The sky with heav'n-ly light a-flame, Some-time He'll come a - gain.
2 Up - on the clouds of glo-ry bright, Some-time He'll come a - gain.
3 Not as a babe, but as a King, Some-time He'll come a - gain.
4 His saints will meet Him in the air, Some-time He'll come a - gain.
5 Then He will take us home to rest, Some-time He'll come a - gain.

REFRAIN

Some-time, some-time, some-time, some-time Christ shall come to reign;

Pre - pare my soul to meet Him, Some-time He'll come a - gain.

Copyright by W. REEVES. An alternative Tune is on the previous page

533   The Lord's Anointed

JAMES MONTGOMERY   ELLACOMBE 7.6.7.6.D   *Mainz Gesangbuch,* 1833

1 Hail to the Lord's A - noint - ed, Great Da - vid's great-er Son;
2 He shall come down like show - ers Up - on the fruit-ful earth:
3 Kings shall fall down be - fore Him, And gold and in-cense bring;

1 Hail in the time ap - point - ed, His reign on earth be - gun!
2 And love, joy, hope, like flow - ers, Spring in His path to birth:
3 All na - tions shall a - dore Him, His praise all peo - ple sing;

1 He comes to break op - pres - sion, To set the cap-tive free;
2 Be - fore Him on the moun - tains Shall Peace, the her - ald, go;
3 For He shall have do - min - ion O'er ri - ver, sea, and shore,

1 To take a - way trans-gres - sion, And rule in e - qui - ty.
2 And right-eous - ness in foun - tains From hill to val - ley flow.
3 Far as the ea - gle's pin - ion Or dove's light wing can soar.

The tune CRUGER is on the next page

533 The Lord's Anointed

JAMES MONTGOMERY   CRÜGER 7.6.7.6.D   JOHANN CRÜGER

1 Hail to the Lord's A - noint - ed, Great Da-vid's great - er Son;
2 He shall come down like show - ers Up - on the fruit-ful earth:
3 King's shall fall down be - fore Him, And gold and in - cense bring;

1 Hail in the time ap - point - ed, His reign on earth be - gun!
2 And love, joy, hope, like flow - ers, Spring in His path to birth:
3 All na - tions shall a - dore Him, His praise all peo - ple sing;

1 He comes to break op - pres - sion, To set the cap - tive free;
2 Be - fore Him on the moun - tains Shall Peace, the her - ald, go;
3 For He shall have do - min - ion O'er ri - ver, sea, and shore,

1 To take a - way trans - gres - sion, And rule in e - qui - ty.
2 And right-eous-ness in foun - tains From hill to val - ley flow.
3 Far as the ea - gle's pin - ion or dove's light wing can soar.

The tune ELLACOMBE is on the previous page

23

534 The Glad Tidings

ANON.   OLD REVIVAL MELODY

1 Hark! hark! hear the glad tid - ings; Soon, soon Je - sus will come, Rob'd,
2 Joy! joy! sound it more loud - ly; Sing, sing glo - ry to God; Soon,
3 Bright, bright ser - aphs at - tend - ing; Shouts, shouts fill - ing the air; Down,
4 Still, still rest on the pro - mise; Cling, cling fast to His word; Wait,

1 rob'd in hon - our and glo - ry, To gath - er His ran - som'd ones home; .
2 soon Je - sus is com - ing, Pub - lish the tid - ings a - broad; .
3 down swift - ly from hea - ven Je - sus our Lord will ap - pear: .
4 wait if He should tar - ry, We'll pa - tient - ly wait for the Lord: .

1 Yes, yes, O yes! To gath - er His ran - som'd ones home: .
2 Yes, yes, O yes! Pub - lish the tid - ings a - broad: .
3 Yes, yes, O yes! Je - sus our Lord will ap - pear: .
4 Yes, yes, O yes! Pa - tient - ly wait for the Lord: .

1 Yes, yes, O yes! To gath - er His ran - som'd ones home. .
2 Yes, yes, O yes! Pub - lish the tid - ings a - broad. .
3 Yes, yes, O yes! Je - sus our Lord will ap - pear. .
4 Yes, yes, O yes! Pa - tient - ly wait for the Lord. .

An Alternative Tune is on the following page

534 The Glad Tidings

ANON.

DAVID CARYLL

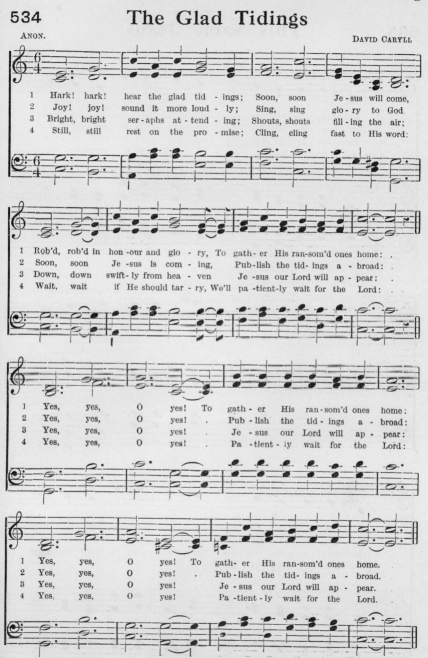

1 Hark! hark! hear the glad tid - ings; Soon, soon Je - sus will come,
2 Joy! joy! sound it more loud - ly; Sing, sing glo - ry to God
3 Bright, bright ser - aphs at - tend - ing; Shouts, shouts fill - ing the air;
4 Still, still rest on the pro - mise; Cling, cling fast to His word:

1 Rob'd, rob'd in hon - our and glo - ry, To gath - er His ran - som'd ones home: .
2 Soon, soon Je - sus is com - ing, Pub - lish the tid - ings a - broad: .
3 Down, down swift - ly from hea - ven Je - sus our Lord will ap - pear: .
4 Wait, wait if He should tar - ry, We'll pa - tient - ly wait for the Lord: .

1 Yes, yes, O yes! To gath - er His ran - som'd ones home:
2 Yes, yes, O yes! . Pub - lish the tid - ings a - broad:
3 Yes, yes, O yes! . Je - sus our Lord will ap - pear:
4 Yes, yes, O yes! . Pa - tient - ly wait for the Lord:

1 Yes, yes, O yes! To gath - er His ran - som'd ones home.
2 Yes, yes, O yes! . Pub - lish the tid - ings a - broad.
3 Yes, yes, O yes! . Je - sus our Lord will ap - pear.
4 Yes, yes, O yes! . Pa - tient - ly wait for the Lord.

An Alternative Tune is on the preceding page

535 # This Same Jesus

ELIZA E. HEWITT

W. A. POST

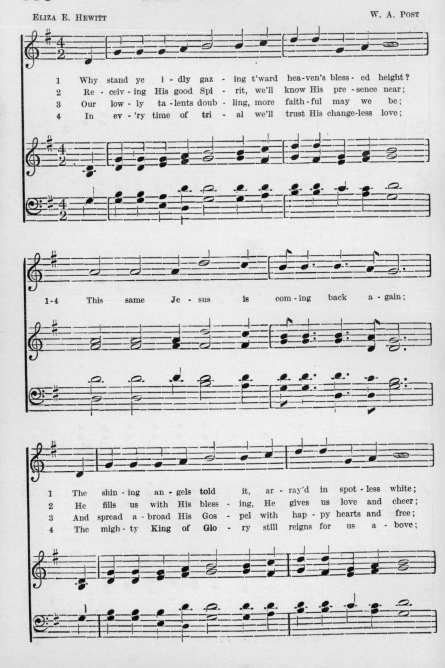

1 Why stand ye i - dly gaz - ing t'ward hea-ven's bless - ed height?
2 Re - ceiv-ing His good Spi - rit, we'll know His pre - sence near;
3 Our low - ly ta - lents doub - ling, more faith - ful may we be;
4 In ev - 'ry time of tri - al we'll trust His change-less love;

1-4 This same Je - sus is com - ing back a - gain;

1 The shin - ing an - gels told it, ar - ray'd in spot - less white;
2 He fills us with His bless - ing, He gives us love and cheer;
3 And spread a - broad His Gos - pel with hap - py hearts and free;
4 The migh - ty King of Glo - ry still reigns for us a - bove;

This Same Jesus—*Continued*

1-4 This same Je - sus is com - ing back a - gain.

REFRAIN

This same Je - sus, this same Je - sus; O tell the joy - ful

ti - dings to all the sons of men; O let us work and pray, re-

joic - ing ev - 'ry day; This same Je - sus is com - ing back a - gain.

536 The Comforter has Come

F. BOTTOME   COMFORTER 12.12.12.6.D   WM. J. KIRKPATRICK

1. O spread the ti-dings round, wher-ev-er man is found, Wher-ev-
2. The long, long night is past, the morn-ing breaks at last; And hush'd
3. Lo, the great King of kings, with heal-ing in His wings, To ev-
4. O bound-less Love di-vine! how shall this tongue of mine To won-
5. Sing till the ech-oes fly a-bove the vault-ed sky, And all

1. er hu-man hearts and hu-man woes a-bound; Let ev-'ry Christ-ian
2. the dread-ful wail and fu-ry of the blast, As o'er the gold-en
3. 'ry cap-tive soul a full de-liv-'rance brings; And thro' the va-cant
4. d'ring mor-tals tell the match-less grace di-vine— That I, a child of
5. the saints a-bove to all be-low re-ply, In strains of end-less

1. tongue pro-claim the joy-ful sound: The Com-for-ter has come!
2. hills the day ad-van-ces fast; The Com-for-ter has come!
3. cells the song of tri-umph rings: The Com-for-ter has come!
4. hell, should in His im-age shine? The Com-for-ter has come!
5. love, the song that ne'er will die: The Com-for-ter has come!

D.S.—round, Wher-ev-er man is found—The Com-for-ter has come!

REFRAIN

The Com-for-ter has come, The Com-for-ter has come! The
Ho-ly Ghost from heav'n, The Fa-ther's pro-mise giv'n; O spread the tid-ings

537 Open my Eyes

CLARA H. SCOTT

CLARA H. SCOTT

1 O - pen my eyes that I may see Glimp-ses of truth Thou
2 O - pen my ears that I may hear Voi - ces of truth Thou
3 O - pen my mouth and let me bear Glad - ly the warm truth

1 hast for me; Place in my hands the won - der - ful key
2 send - est clear; And while the wave - notes fall on my ear,
3 ev - 'ry - where; Op - en my heart and let me pre - pare

1 That shall un - clasp and set me free. Si - lent - ly now I
2 Ev - 'ry - thing false will dis - ap - pear. Si - lent - ly now I
3 Love with Thy chil - dren thus to share. Si - lent - ly now I

1-3 wait for Thee, Rea - dy, my God, Thy will to see;

1 O - pen my eyes, il - lum - ine me, Spi - rit di - vine!
2 O - pen my ears, il - lum - ine me, Spi - rit di - vine!
3 O - pen my heart, il - lum - ine me, Spi - rit di - vine!

538 The Spirit's Presence

F. BOTTOME DENNIS S.M. JOHANN G. NAGELI

1 The Ho - ly Ghost is come, We feel His pre - sence here,
2 This ten - der - ness of love, The hush of so - lemn pow'r,
3 Earth's dark - ness all has fled, Heav'ns light ser - ene - ly shines;
4 No more let sin de - ceive, Nor earth - ly cares be - tray:

1 Our hearts would now no long - er roam, But bow in fi - lial fear.
2 'Tis heav'n de - scend - ing from a - bove To fill this fa - vour'd hour.
3 And ev - 'ry heart di - vine - ly led To ho - ly thought in - clines.
4 O let us nev - er, nev - er grieve The Com - fort - er a - way!

F. BOTTOME NEWLAND S.M. H. J. GAUNTLETT

1 The Ho - ly Ghost is come, We feel His pre - sence here,
2 This ten - der - ness of love, The hush of so - lemn pow'r,
3 Earth's dark - ness all has fled, Heav'ns light ser - ene - ly shines;
4 No more let sin de - ceive, Nor earth - ly cares be - tray:

1 Our hearts would now no long - er roam, But bow in fi - lial fear.
2 'Tis heav'n de - scend - ing from a - bove To fill this fa - vour'd hour.
3 And ev - 'ry heart di - vine - ly led To ho - ly thought in - clines.
4 O let us nev - er, nev - er grieve The Com - fort - er a - way!

539 Our Blest Redeemer

HARRIET AUBER   ST. CUTHBERT 8.6.8.4   J. B. DYKES

1 Our blest Re-deem-er, ere He breath'd His ten-der last fare-well,
2 He came sweet in-flu'nce to im-part, A gra-cious will-ing Guest,
3 And His that gen-tle voice we hear, Soft as the breath of ev'n,
4 And ev-'ry vir-tue we poss-ess, And ev-'ry con-quest won,
5 Spi-rit of pur-i-ty and grace, Our weak-ness pity-ing see:
6 O praise the Fa-ther, praise the Son; Blest Spi-rit, praise to Thee;

1 A Guide, A Com-fort-er be-queath'd With us to dwell.
2 Where He can find one hum-ble heart Where-in to rest.
3 That checks each thought, that calms each fear, And speaks of heav'n.
4 And ev-'ry thought of ho-li-ness Are His a-lone.
5 O make our heart Thy dwell-ing place, And wor-thier Thee!
6 All praise to God, the Three in One, The One in Three!

HARRIET AUBER   WREFORD 8.6.8.4   E. S. CARTER

1 Our blest Re-deem-er, ere He breath'd His ten-der last fare-well,
2 He came sweet in-flu-'nce to im-part, A gra-cious, will-ing Guest,
3 And His that gen-tle voice we hear, Soft as the breath of ev'n,
4 And ev-'ry vir-tue we poss-ess, And ev-'ry con-quest won,
5 Spi-rit of pur-i-ty and grace, Our weak-ness pity-ing see:
6 O praise the Fa-ther, praise the Son; Blest Spi-rit, praise to Thee;

1 A Guide, A Com-fort-er be-queath'd With us to dwell.
2 Where He can find one hum-ble heart Where-in to rest.
3 That checks each thought, that calms each fear, And speaks of heav'n.
4 And ev-'ry thought of ho-li-ness Are His a-lone.
5 O make our heart Thy dwell-ing place, And wor-thier Thee!
6 All praise to God, the Three in One, The One in Three!

540 Come, Gracious Spirit

SIMON BROWNE WALTON L.M. *Gardiner's Sacred Melodies, 1815*

1 Come, gra-cious Spi - rit, heav'n - ly Dove, With light and
2 The light of truth to us dis - play, That we may
3 Con - duct us safe, con - duct us far From ev - 'ry
4 Lead us to ho - li - ness, the road That we must

1 com - fort from a - bove: Be Thou our Guard - ian, Thou our
2 know and choose Thy way; Plant ho - ly fear in ev - 'ry
3 sin and hurt - ful snare: Lead us to Christ, the liv - ing
4 take to dwell with God; Lead us to God, our fin - al

1 Guide, O'er ev - 'ry thought and step pre - side.
2 heart, That we from God may ne'er de - part.
3 way, Nor let us from His pas - tures stray.
4 rest, To be with Him for ev - er bless'd.

SIMON BROWNE LUDBOROUGH L.M. T. R. MATTHEWS

1 Come, gra-cious Spi - rit, heav'n-ly Dove, With light and com-fort from a - bove
2 The light of truth to us dis - play, That we may know and choose Thy way
3 Con - duct us safe, con - duct us far From ev - 'ry sin and hurt-ful snare
4 Lead us to ho - li - ness, the road That we must take to dwell with God

Come, Gracious Spirit—*Continued*

1 Be Thou our Guard-ian, Thou our Guide, O'er ev-'ry thought and step pre-side.
2 Plant ho-ly fear in ev-'ry heart, That we from God may ne'er de-part.
3 Lead us to Christ, the liv-ing way, Nor let us from His pas-tures stray.
4 Lead us to God, our fin-al rest, To be with Him for ev-er bless'd.

By permission of NOVELLO & Co., LTD.

SIMON BROWNE   STAINCLIFFE L.M.   R. W. DIXON

1 Come, gra-cious Spi-rit, heav'n-ly Dove, With light and
2 The light of truth to us dis-play, That we may
3 Con-duct us safe, con-duct us far From ev-'ry
4 Lead us to ho-li-ness, the road That we must

1 com-fort from a-bove: Be Thou our Guard-ian,
2 know and choose Thy way; Plant ho-ly fear in
3 sin and hurt-ful snare: Lead us to Christ, the
4 take to dwell with God; Lead us to God, our

1 Thou our Guide, O'er ev-'ry thought and step pre-side.
2 ev-'ry heart, That we from God may ne'er de-part.
3 liv-ing way, Nor let us from His pas-tures stray.
4 fin-al rest, To be with Him for ev-er bless'd.

541 Faithful Guide

MARCUS M. WELLS   FAITHFUL GUIDE 7.7.7.7. D   MARCUS M. WELLS

1 Ho - ly Spi - rit, faith - ful Guide, Ev - er near the Chris - tian's side,
2 Ev - er pre - sent, tru - est Friend, Ev - er near Thine aid to lend,
3 When our days of toil shall cease, May our hearts be fill'd with peace;

1 Gent - ly lead us by the hand, Pil-grims in a des - ert land;
2 Leave us not to doubt and fear, Grop-ing on in dark - ness here;
3 Draw-ing near in praise and pray'r, Know-ing that our names are there;

1 Wea - ry souls for - e'er re - joice While they hear that sweet-est voice
2 When the storms are rag - ing sore, Hearts grow faint, and hopes give o'er,
3 Plead-ing naught but Je - sus' blood, He'll be with us in the flood,

1-3 Whis - per soft - ly: 'Wan - d'rer, come, Fol - low Me, I'll guide thee home.'

The tune TICHFIELD is on the next page

541 Faithful Guide

Marcus M. Wells   Tichfield 7.7.7.7 d   R. W. Beaty

1 Ho - ly Spi - rit, faith - ful Guide, Ev - er near the Christ-ian's side,
2 Ev - er pre - sent, tru - est Friend, Ev - er near Thine aid to lend,
3 When our days of toil shall cease, May our hearts be fill'd with peace;

1 Gent - ly lead us by the hand, Pil - grims in a des - ert land;
2 Leave us not to doubt and fear, Grop - ing on in dark - ness here;
3 Draw - ing near in praise and pray'r, Know-ing that our names are there;

1 Wea - ry souls for - e'er re - joice While they hear that sweet-est voice
2 When the storms are rag - ing sore, Hearts grow faint, and hopes give o'er,
3 Plead-ing naught but Je - sus' blood, He'll be with us in the flood,

1-3 Whis - per soft - ly: 'Wan-d'rer, come, Fol - low Me, I'll guide thee home.'

The tune Faithful Guide is on the previous page

542 # Come, Holy Ghost

CHARLES WESLEY WINCHESTER OLD C.M. *Este's Psalter, 1592*

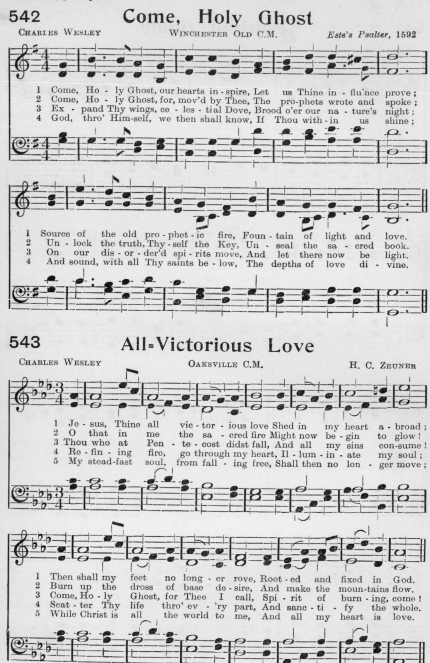

1 Come, Ho - ly Ghost, our hearts in - spire, Let us Thine in - flu'nce prove;
2 Come, Ho - ly Ghost, for, mov'd by Thee, The pro-phets wrote and spoke;
3 Ex - pand Thy wings, ce - les - tial Dove, Brood o'er our na - ture's night;
4 God, thro' Him-self, we then shall know, If Thou with - in us shine;

1 Source of the old pro - phet - ic fire, Foun - tain of light and love.
2 Un - lock the truth, Thy - self the Key, Un - seal the sa - cred book.
3 On our dis - or - der'd spi - rits move, And let there now be light.
4 And sound, with all Thy saints be - low, The depths of love di - vine.

543 ## All=Victorious Love

CHARLES WESLEY OAKSVILLE C.M. H. C. ZEUNER

1 Je - sus, Thine all vic - tor - ious love Shed in my heart a - broad;
2 O that in me the sa - cred fire Might now be - gin to glow!
3 Thou who at Pen - te - cost didst fall, And all my sins con-sume!
4 Re - fin - ing fire, go through my heart, Il - lum - in - ate my soul;
5 My stead-fast soul, from fall - ing free, Shall then no lon - ger move;

1 Then shall my feet no long - er rove, Root - ed and fixed in God.
2 Burn up the dross of base de - sire, And make the moun-tains flow.
3 Come, Ho - ly Ghost, for Thee I call, Spi - rit of burn - ing, come!
4 Scat - ter Thy life thro' ev - 'ry part, And sanc - ti - fy the whole.
5 While Christ is all the world to me, And all my heart is love.

544

Spirit Divine

ANDREW REED

PRIEER D'ESPRIT C.M.

W. C. FOSTER

1 Spi - rit di - vine! at - tend our pray'rs, And make our hearts Thy home;
2 Come as the light: to us re - veal Our need of Thee be - low;
3 Come as the fire, and purge our hearts With sac - ri - fic - ial flame;
4 Come as the dew, and sweet - ly bless This con - se - cra - ted hour;
5 Come as the dove, and spread Thy wings, The wings of peace - ful love;
6 Come as the wind, with rush - ing sound And pen - te - cos - tal grace;

1 De-scend with all Thy gra - cious pow'rs; O come, great Spi - rit, come!
2 And lead us in those paths of life Where all the right - eous go.
3 Let our whole self an off - 'ring be To our Re - deem - er's Name.
4 May bar - ren - ness re - joice to own Thy fer - ti - lis - ing pow'r.
5 And let Thy Church on earth be - come Blest as the Church a - bove.
6 That all of wo - man born may see The glo - ry of Thy face.

545

Gracious Spirit

JOHN STOCKER

WEBER 7.7.7.7

CARL VON WEBER

1 Gra - cious Spi - rit, Love di - vine, Let Thy light with - in me shine;
2 Speak Thy match - less grace to me, From my sin, O set me free!
3 Faith, and hope, and cha - ri - ty, Com - fort - er! de - scend from Thee:
4 Life and peace to me im - part, Seal sal - va - tion on my heart;

1 All my sin and fear re - move, Fill me with Thy heav'n - ly love.
2 Lead me to the Lamb of God, Wash me in His pre - cious blood.
3 Thou th'a - noint - ing Spi - rit art; These Thy gifts to me im - part.
4 Breathe Thy - self in - to my breast Ear - nest of im - mor - tal rest.

546 Dwell with Me

T. T. Lynch   Dix 7.7.7.7.7.7   Conrad Kocher

1 Gra - cious Spi - rit, dwell with me: I my - self would
2 Ten - der Spi - rit, dwell with me: I my - self would
3 Might - y Spi - rit, dwell with me: I my - self would
4 Ho - ly Spi - rit, dwell with me: I my - self would

1 gra - cious be; And, with words that help and heal,
2 ten - der be; Shut my heart up like a flow'r
3 might - y be; Might - y so as to pre - vail,
4 ho - ly be; Se - par - ate from sin, I would

1 Would Thy life in mine re - veal; And, with ac - tions
2 At temp - ta - tion's dark - some hour; O - pen it when
3 Where un - aid - ed man must fail; Ev - er by a
4 Choose and cher - ish all things good; And, what - ev - er

1 bold and meek; Would for Christ my Sa - viour speak.
2 shines the sun, And His love by fra - grance own.
3 might - y hope Press - ing on and bear - ing up.
4 I can be, Give to Him who gave me Thee.

547 Blessed Quietness

Manie Payne Ferguson

W. S. Marshall
Arr. J. M. Kirk

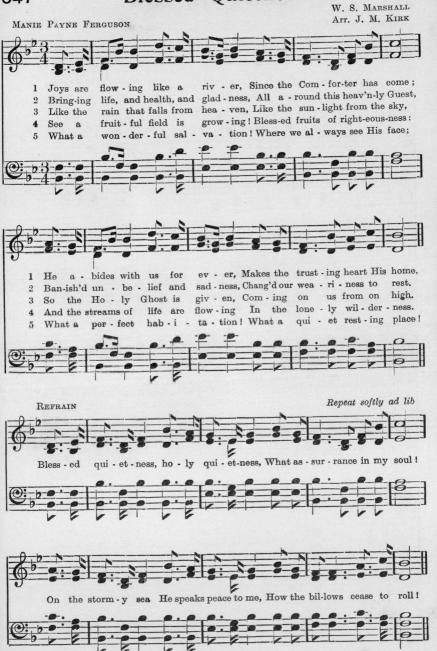

1 Joys are flow - ing like a riv - er, Since the Com - for-ter has come;
2 Bring-ing life, and health, and glad - ness, All a - round this heav'n-ly Guest,
3 Like the rain that falls from hea - ven, Like the sun - light from the sky,
4 See a fruit - ful field is grow - ing! Bless-ed fruits of right-eous-ness:
5 What a won - der - ful sal - va - tion! Where we al - ways see His face;

1 He a - bides with us for ev - er, Makes the trust - ing heart His home.
2 Ban-ish'd un - be - lief and sad - ness, Chang'd our wea - ri - ness to rest.
3 So the Ho - ly Ghost is giv - en, Com - ing on us from on high.
4 And the streams of life are flow - ing In the lone - ly wil - der - ness.
5 What a per - fect hab - i - ta - tion! What a qui - et rest - ing place!

Refrain

Repeat softly ad lib

Bless - ed qui - et - ness, ho - ly qui - et - ness, What as - sur - ance in my soul!

On the storm - y sea He speaks peace to me, How the bil - lows cease to roll!

548 Jesus We Seek

FANNY J. CROSBY   TRYST 6.4.6.4.6.6.6.4   W. H. DOANE

1 Here from the world we turn, Je - sus to seek;
2 Come, Ho - ly Com - fort - er, Pre - sence di - vine,
3 Sa - viour, Thy work re - vive! Here may we see

1 Here may His lov - ing voice Gra - cious - ly speak:
2 Now in our long - ing hearts Gra - cious - ly shine:
3 Those who are dead in sin Quick - en'd by Thee:

1 Je - sus, our dear - est Friend, While at Thy feet we bend,
2 O for Thy might - y pow'r! O for a bless - ed show'r
3 Come to our hearts to - night, Make ev - 'ry bur - den light,

1 O let Thy smile de - scend! 'Tis Thee we seek.
2 Fill - ing this hal - low'd hour With joy di - vine!
3 Cheer Thou our wait - ing sight; We long for Thee.

The tune ST. NICHOLAS is on the next page

Jesus We Seek

548

FANNY J. CROSBY · ST. NICHOLAS 6.4.6.4.6.6.6.4 · C. W. PEARCE

1 Here from the world we turn, Je - sus to seek;
2 Come, Ho - ly Com - fort - er, Pre - sence di - vine,
3 Sa - viour, Thy work re - vive! Here may we see

1 Here may His lov - ing voice Gra - cious - ly speak :
2 Now in our long - ing hearts Gra - cious - ly shine :
3 Those who are dead in sin Quick - en'd by Thee :

1 Je - sus, our dear - est Friend, While at Thy feet we bend,
2 O for Thy might - y pow'r ! O for a bless - ed show'r
3 Come to our hearts to-night, Make ev - 'ry bur - den light,

1 O let Thy smile de - scend ! 'Tis Thee we seek.
2 Fill - ing this hal - low'd hour With joy di - vine !
3 Cheer Thou our wait - ing sight ; We long for Thee.

The tune TRYST is on the previous page

549

Power from God

CHARLIE D. TILLMAN

CHARLIE D. TILLMAN

1 They were in an up-per cham-ber, They were all with one ac-cord,
2 Yes, this pow'r from heav'n de-scend-ed With the sound of rush-ing wind;
3 Yes, this old-time pow'r was giv-en To our fa-thers who were true;

1 When the Ho-ly Ghost de-scend-ed, As was pro-mised by our Lord.
2 Tongues of fire came down up-on them, As the Lord said He would send.
3 This is pro-mis'd to be-liev-ers, And we all may have it too.

REFRAIN

O Lord, send the pow'r just now! O Lord, send the pow'r just now!

O Lord, send the pow'r just now! And bap-tize ev-'ry one.

550

Jesus for Me

Je-sus for me, Je-sus for me, All the time, ev-'ry-where, Je-sus for me.

551 ## O Spirit of Faith!

Henrietta E. Blair   Wm. J. Kirkpatrick

1 Thy Ho - ly Spi - rit, Lord, a - lone Can turn our hearts from sin;
2 Thy Ho - ly Spi - rit, Lord, a - lone Can deep - er love in - spire;
3 Thy Ho - ly Spi - rit, Lord, can bring The gifts we seek in pray'r;
4 Thy Ho - ly Spi - rit, Lord, can give The grace we need this hour;

1 His pow'r a - lone can sanc - ti - fy And keep us pure with - in.
2 His pow'r a - lone with - in our souls Can light the sa - cred fire.
3 His voice can words of com - fort speak, And still each wave of care.
4 And while we wait, O Spi - rit, come In sanc - ti - fy - ing power!

1-3 O Spi - rit of Faith and Love! Come in our midst, we pray,
4 O Spi - rit of Love! de - scend, Come in our midst, we pray,

1-3 And pur - i - fy each wait - ing heart; Bap - tize us with pow'r to - day!
4 And, like a rush - ing, might - y wind, Sweep o - ver our souls to - day!

552 Thou Art Enough

W. Elwin Oliphant

Richard Slater

Thou art e-nough for me; .... Thou art e-nough for me; .... O for me;

for me;

pre - cious, liv - ing, lov-ing Lord, Yes, Thou art e-nough for me!

By permission of the International Music Board of the Salvation Army

553 Remember Me

Isaac Watts

Abney C.M.

Asa Hull

1 A - las! and did my Sa-viour bleed? And did my Sov-'reign die?
2 Was it for crimes that I had done He groan'd up - on the tree?
3 Well might the sun in dark-ness hide, And shut his glo - ries in,
4 Thus might I hide my blush-ing face While His dear Cross ap - pears,
5 But drops of grief can ne'er re - pay The debt of love I owe;

Ref.—Help me, dear Sa - viour, Thee to own, And ev - er faith-ful be:

1 Would He de - vote that sa - cred head For such a worm as I?
2 A - maz - ing pi - ty! grace un-known! And love be-yond de - gree!
3 When Christ, the might - y Ma - ker, died For man, the crea-ture's sin.
4 Dis - solve my heart in thank - ful - ness, And melt mine eyes to tears.
5 Here, Lord, I give my - self a - way; 'Tis all that I can do.

And when Thou sit - test on Thy throne, O Lord, re - mem - ber me.

554 Search Me, O God!

F. BOTTOME
ST. FLAVIAN C.M.
Day's Psalter, 1563

1 Search me, O God! my ac - tions try, And let my life ap - pear
2 Search all my sense and know my heart, Who on - ly canst make known,
3 Throw light in - to the dark - en'd cells Where pas - sion reigns with - in;
4 Search all my thoughts, the se - cret springs, The mo - tives that con - trol;
5 Search, till Thy fier - y glance hast cast Its ho - ly light thro' all,
6 Thus pros - trate, I shall learn of Thee What now I fee - bly prove,

1 As seen by Thine all - search - ing eye— To mine my ways make clear.
2 And let the deep, the hid - den part, To me be ful - ly shown.
3 Quick - en my con - science till it feels The loath - some - ness of sin.
4 The cham - bers where pol - lu - ted things Hold em - pire o'er the soul.
5 And I by grace am brought at last Be - fore Thy face to fall.
6 That God a - lone in Christ can be Un - ut - ter - a - ble love.

F. BOTTOME
CROWLE C.M.
Green's Psalm Tunes, 1724
Harmonized by E. J. HOPKINS

1 Search me, O God! my ac - tions try, And let my life ap - pear
2 Search all my sense and know my heart, Who on - ly canst make known,
3 Throw light in - to the dark - en'd cells Where pass - ion reigns with - in;
4 Search all my thoughts, the se - cret springs, The mo - tives that con - trol;
5 Search, till the fier - y glance hast cast Its ho - ly light thro' all,
6 Thus pros - trate, I shall learn of Thee What now I fee - bly prove,

1 As seen by Thine all - search - ing eye— To mine my ways make clear.
2 And let the deep, the hid - den part, To me be ful - ly shown.
3 Quick - en my con - science till it feels The loath - some - ness of sin.
4 The cham - bers where pol - lu - ted things Hold em - pire o'er the soul.
5 And I by grace am brought at last Be - fore Thy face to fall.
6 That God a - lone in Christ can be Un - ut - ter - a - ble love.

555   The Mercy-Seat

HUGH STOWELL   PASCAL L.M.   *Katholisches Gesangbuch,* 1774

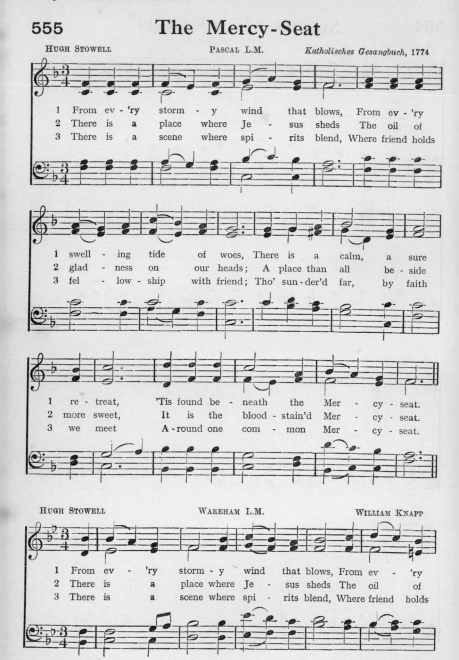

1 From ev - 'ry storm - y wind that blows, From ev - 'ry
2 There is a place where Je - sus sheds The oil of
3 There is a scene where spi - rits blend, Where friend holds

1 swell - ing tide of woes, There is a calm, a sure
2 glad - ness on our heads; A place than all be - side
3 fel - low - ship with friend; Tho' sun - der'd far, by faith

1 re - treat, 'Tis found be - neath the Mer - cy - seat.
2 more sweet, It is the blood - stain'd Mer - cy - seat.
3 we meet A - round one com - mon Mer - cy - seat.

HUGH STOWELL   WAREHAM L.M.   WILLIAM KNAPP

1 From ev - 'ry storm - y wind that blows, From ev - 'ry
2 There is a place where Je - sus sheds The oil of
3 There is a scene where spi - rits blend, Where friend holds

The Mercy-Seat—*Continued*

1 swell - ing tide of woes, There is a calm, a
2 glad - ness on our heads; A place than all be -
3 fel - low - ship with friend; Tho' sun - der'd far, by

1 sure re - treat, 'Tis found be - neath the Mer - cy - seat.
2 side more sweet, It is the blood-stain'd Mer - cy - seat.
3 faith we meet A - round one com - mon Mer - cy - seat.

HUGH STOWELL   TOTLAND L.M.   JOHN STAINER

1 From ev - 'ry storm - y wind that blows, From ev - 'ry swell - ing tide of woes,
2 There is a place where Je - sus sheds The oil of glad - ness on our heads;
3 There is a scene where spi - rits blend, Where friend holds fel - low - ship with friend;

1 There is a calm, a sure re - treat; 'Tis found be - neath the Mer - cy - seat.
2 A place than all be - side more sweet, It is the blood - stain'd Mer - cy - seat.
3 Tho' sun - der'd far, by faith we meet A - round one com - mon Mer - cy - seat.

556 Yes, Dear Lord

C. H. MORRIS

C. H. MORRIS

1 Long my wil - ful heart said 'No' To Je - sus' ten - der plead - ing;
2 Bring-ing all I am and have In hum - ble con - se - cra - tion,
3 Giv-ing o'er my doubts and fears And all my use - less try - ing,
4 Yes, dear Lord, in life or death, With Thee all good pos - sess - ing,

1 Now I long His love to know, My stub - born will is yield - ing.
2 Trust-ing in the blood I claim This ut - ter - most sal - va - tion.
3 Trust-ing not my pray'rs or tears, But on Thy word re - ly - ing.
4 Not by feel - ing, but by faith I take the pro-mis'd bless - ing.

REFRAIN

Yes, dear Lord, Yes, dear Lord, Here I give my all to Thee;

I be - lieve, I be - lieve The blood a - vails for me.

557 Follow all the Way

Geo. W. Collins   Akolo 8.8. 8.9. D   *Arr.* Wm. J. Kirkpatrick

1 I have heard my Sa-viour call-ing, I have heard my Sa-viour call-ing,
2 Tho' He leads me thro' the val - ley, Tho' He leads me thro' the val - ley,
3 Tho' He leads me thro' the gar - den, Tho' He leads me thro' the gar - den,
4 Tho' He leads me to the con - flict, Tho' He leads me to the con - flict,
5 Tho' He leads thro' fie - ry tri - als, Tho' He leads thro' fie - ry tri - als,

1 I have heard my Sa-viour call-ing, Take thy cross and fol - low, fol - low Me.'
2 Tho' He leads me thro' the val - ley, I'll go with Him, with Him all the way.
3 Tho' He leads me thro' the gar - den, I'll go with Him, with Him all the way.
4 Tho' He leads me to the con - flict, I'll go with Him, with Him all the way.
5 Tho' He leads thro' fie - ry tri - als, I'll go with Him, with Him all the way.

Refrain

Where He leads me I will fol - low, Where He leads me I will fol - low,

Where He leads me I will fol - low, I'll go with Him, with Him all the way.

558   Following Thee

HENRY F. LYTE   FREETOWN 8.7.8.7. D   ANON.

1 Je - sus, I my cross have ta - ken, All to leave and fol - low Thee;
2 Per - ish ev - 'ry fond am - bi - tion, All I've sought, and hop'd, and known;
3 Let the world de - spise and leave me: They have left my Sa - viour, too;
4 And whilst Thou shalt smile up - on me, God of wis - dom, love, and might,
5 Man may trou - ble and dis - tress me, 'Twill but drive me to Thy breast;
6 O 'tis not in grief to harm me While Thy love is left to me!

1 Des - ti - tute, de - spis'd, for - sa - ken, Thou from hence my all shalt be.
2 Yet how rich is my con - di - tion! God and heav'n are still mine own.
3 Hu - man hearts and looks de - ceive me: Thou art not, like them, un - true.
4 Foes may hate, and friends dis - own me: Show Thy face, and all is bright.
5 Life with tri - als hard may press me, Heav'n will bring me sweet - er rest.
6 O 'twere not in joy to charm me Were that joy un - mix'd with Thee!

REFRAIN

I will fol - low Thee, my Sa - viour, Thou didst shed Thy blood for me,

And tho' all the world for - sake Thee, By Thy grace I'll fol - low Thee.

The tune ELLESDIE (without Refrain) is on the next page

Following Thee

558

HENRY F. LYTE

ELLESDIE 8.7. 8.7. D

From MOZART

1 Je - sus, I my cross have ta - ken, All to leave and fol - low Thee;
2 Let the world de - spise and leave me: They have left my Sa - viour, too;
3 Man may trou - ble and dis - tress me, 'Twill but drive me to Thy breast;

1 Des - ti - tute, de - spis'd, for - sa - ken, Thou from hence my all shalt be:
2 Hu - man hearts and looks de - ceive me; Thou art not, like them, un - true:
3 Life with tri - als hard may press me, Heav'n will bring me sweet - er rest:

1 Per - ish ev - 'ry fond am - bi - tion, All I've sought, and hop'd, and known;
2 And whilst Thou shalt smile up - on me, God of wis - dom, love, and might,
3 O 'tis not in grief to harm me While Thy love is left to me!

1 Yet how rich is my con - di - tion! God and heav'n are still mine own.
2 Foes may hate, and friends dis - own me: Show Thy face, and all is bright.
3 O 'twere not in joy to charm me Were that joy un - mix'd with Thee!

The tune FREETOWN (with Refrain) is on the previous page

559 What a Friend!

JOSEPH SCRIVEN   CONVERSE 8.7.8.7.D.   CHARLES C. CONVERSE

1 What a Friend we have in Je - sus,   All our sins and griefs to bear!
2 Have we tri - als and temp - ta - tions?   Is there trou-ble an - y - where?
3 Are we weak and hea - vy la - den,   Cum-ber'd with a load of care?

1 What a priv - i - lege to car - ry   Ev - 'ry-thing to God in pray'r!
2 We should nev - er be dis - cou - rag'd: Take it to the Lord in pray'r!
3 Pre - cious Sa - viour, still our ref - uge: Take it to the Lord in pray'r!

1 O what peace we oft en for - feit!   O what need-less pain we bear!
2 Can we find a friend so faith - ful   Who will all our sor-rows share?
3 Do thy friends de-spise, for - sake thee?   Take it to the Lord in pray'r!

1 All be-cause we do not car - ry   Ev - 'ry-thing to God in pray'r.
2 Je - sus knows our ev - 'ry weak - ness: Take it to the Lord in pray'r!
3 In His arms He'll take and shield thee,   Thou wilt find a sol - ace there.

The tune CONQUEROR is on the following page

What a Friend!

59

JOSEPH SCRIVEN   CONQUEROR 8.7.8.7.D.   JOHN S. WISEMAN

1 What a Friend we have in Je-sus, All our sins and griefs to bear! What a
2 Have we tri-als and temp-ta-tions? Is there trou-ble an-y-where? We should
3 Are we weak and hea-vy la-den, Cumber'd with a load of care? Pre-cious

1 priv-i- lege to car-ry Ev-'ry-thing to God in pray'r!
2 nev-er be dis-cou-rag'd: Take it to the Lord in pray'r!
3 Sa-viour, still our ref-uge: Take it to the Lord in pray'r!

1 O what peace we oft-en tor-feit! O what need-less pain we bear!
2 Can we find a friend so faith-ful Who will all our sor-rows share?
3 Do thy friends de-spise, for-sake thee? Take it to the Lord in pray'r!

1 All be-cause we do not car-ry Ev-'ry-thing to God in pray'r.
2 Je-sus knows our ev-'ry weak-ness: Take it to the Lord in pray'r!
3 In His arms He'll take and shield thee, Thou wilt find a sol-ace there.

The tune CONVERSE is on the preceding page

560   Sweet Hour of Prayer

W. W. WALFORD   HOUR OF PRAYER L.M. D.   WM. B. BRADBURY

1 Sweet hour of pray'r, sweet hour of pray'r, That calls me from a world of care,
2 Sweet hour of pray'r, sweet hour of pray'r, The joy I feel, the bliss I share
3 Sweet hour of pray'r, sweet hour of pray'r, Thy wings shall my pe - ti - tion bear

1 And bids me at my Father's throne Make all my wants and wish-es known;
2 Of those whose anx-ious spi - rits burn With strong de-sires for thy re - turn!
3 To Him whose truth and faith - ful - ness En - gage the wait - ing soul to bless;

1 In sea - sons of dis - tress and grief My soul has oft - en found re - lief,
2 With such I has - ten to the place, Where God, my Sa-viour, shows His face,
3 And since He bids me seek His face, Be - lieve His word, and trust His grace,

1 And oft es-caped the temp-ter's snare, By thy re-turn, sweet hour of pray'r.
2 And glad - ly take my sta - tion there, And wait for thee, sweet hour of pray'r.
3 I'll cast on Him my ev - 'ry care, And wait for thee, sweet hour of pray'r.

561 Draw Me Nearer

FANNY J. CROSBY

W. H. DOANE

1 I am Thine, O Lord, I have heard Thy voice, And it told Thy
2 Con - se - crate me now to Thy ser - vice, Lord, By the pow'r of
3 Oh, the pure de - light of a sin - gle hour That be - fore Thy
4 There are depths of love that I can - not know Till I cross the

1 love to me; But I long to rise in the arms of faith, And be
2 grace di - vine; Let my soul look up with a stead-fast hope, And my
3 throne I spend! When I kneel in pray'r, and with Thee, my God, I com-
4 nar - row sea, There are heights of joy that I may not reach Till I

REFRAIN

1 clo - ser drawn to Thee.
2 will be lost in Thine.
3 mune as friend with friend.
4 rest in peace with Thee.

Draw me near - er, near-er, bless-ed

near-er, near-er,

Lord, To the Cross where Thou hast died; Draw me near - er, near - er,

near - er, bless - ed Lord, To Thy pre - cious, bleed - ing side.

562   Jesus Only

HATTIE M. CONREY   JESUS ONLY 8.7.8.7. D.   ROBERT LOWRY

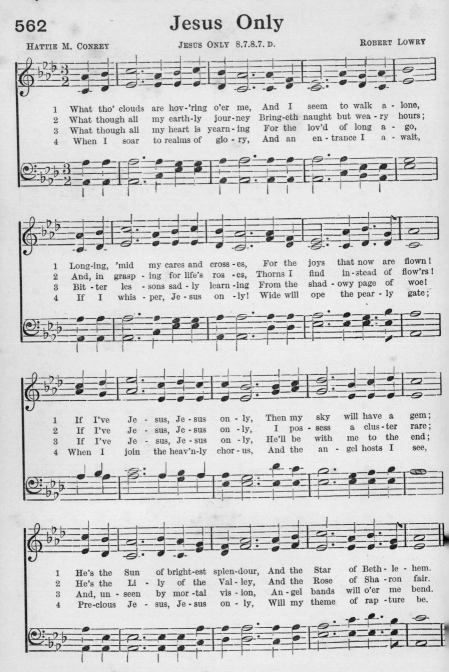

1 What tho' clouds are hov-'ring o'er me, And I seem to walk a - lone,
2 What though all my earth-ly jour-ney Bring-eth naught but wea-ry hours;
3 What though all my heart is yearn-ing For the lov'd of long a - go,
4 When I soar to realms of glo-ry, And an en-trance I a - wait,

1 Long-ing, 'mid my cares and cross-es, For the joys that now are flown!
2 And, in grasp-ing for life's ros-es, Thorns I find in-stead of flow'rs!
3 Bit-ter les-sons sad-ly learn-ing From the shad-owy page of woe!
4 If I whis-per, Je-sus on-ly! Wide will ope the pear-ly gate;

1 If I've Je-sus, Je-sus on-ly, Then my sky will have a gem;
2 If I've Je-sus, Je-sus on-ly, I pos-sess a clus-ter rare;
3 If I've Je-sus, Je-sus on-ly, He'll be with me to the end;
4 When I join the heav'n-ly chor-us, And the an-gel hosts I see,

1 He's the Sun of bright-est splen-dour, And the Star of Beth-le-hem.
2 He's the Li-ly of the Val-ley, And the Rose of Sha-ron fair.
3 And, un-seen by mor-tal vis-ion, An-gel bands will o'er me bend.
4 Pre-cious Je-sus, Je-sus on-ly, Will my theme of rap-ture be.

The tune ELLAN VANNIN is on the following page

562   **Jesus Only**

HATTIE M. CONREY   ELLAN VANNIN 8.7.8.7.D.   MANX MELODY
Arr. M. L. WOOD

1 What tho' clouds are hov-'ring o'er me, And I seem to walk a - lone,
2 What though all my earth-ly jour-ney Bring-eth naught but wea-ry hours;
3 What though all my heart is yearn-ing For the lov'd of long a - go,
4 When I soar to realms of glo - ry, And an en-trance I a - wait,

1 Long-ing, 'mid my cares and cross-es, For the joys that now are flown!
2 And, in grasp - ing for life's ros - es, Thorns I find in - stead of flow'rs!
3 Bit - ter les - sons sad - ly learn-ing From the shad-ow-y page of woe!
4 If I whis - per, Je - sus on - ly! Wide will ope the pear - ly gate;

1 If I've Je - sus, Je - sus on - ly, Then my sky will have a gem;
2 If I've Je - sus, Je - sus on - ly, I pos-sess a clus-ter rare;
3 If I've Je - sus, Je - sus on - ly, He'll be with me to the end;
4 When I join the heav'n-ly chor-us, And the an - gel hosts I see,

1 He's the Sun of bright-est splen-dour, And the Star of Beth - le - hem.
2 He's the Li - ly of the Val - ley, And the Rose of Sha - ron fair.
3 And, un - seen by mor - tal vis - ion, An - gel bands will o'er me bend.
4 Pre-cious Je - sus, Je - sus on - ly, Will my theme of rap - ture be.

Music by permission of J. BLAKEMORE & SONS, Douglas
The tune JESUS ONLY is on the preceding page

563   Come Ye Apart

E. H. BICKERSTETH   EVENTIDE 10.10.10.10   W. H. MONK

1 Come ye your-selves a - part and rest a - while,
2 Come ye a - side from all the world holds dear,
3 Come, tell Me all that ye have said and done,
4 Come ye and rest; the jour - ney is too great,
5 Then, fresh from con - verse with your Lord, re - turn

1 Wear - y, I know it, of the press and throng,
2 For con - verse which the world has nev - er known,
3 Your vic - tor - ies and fail - ures, hopes and fears,
4 And ye will faint be - side the way and sink:
5 And work till day - light soft - ens in - to ev'n:

1 Wipe from your brow the sweat and dust of toil,
2 A - lone with Me and with My Fa - ther here,
3 I know how hard - ly souls are wooed and won:
4 The bread of life is here for you to eat,
5 The brief hours are not lost in which ye learn

1 And in My qui - et strength a - gain be strong.
2 With Me and with My Fa - ther not a - lone.
3 My choi - cest wreaths are al - ways wet with tears.
4 And here for you the wine of love to drink.
5 More of your Mas - ter and His rest in heav'n.

The tune GLASTON is on the following page

Come Ye Apart

563

E. H. BICKERSTETH

GLASTON 10.10. 10.10

MRS. EVANS

1 Come ye your - selves a - part and rest a - while,
2 Come ye a - side from all the world holds dear;
3 Come, tell Me all that ye have said and done,
4 Come ye and rest: the jour - ney is too great,
5 Then, fresh from con - verse with your Lord, re - turn

1 Wear - y, I know it, of the press and throng,
2 For con - verse which the world has nev - er known,
3 Your vic - tor - ies and fail - ures, hopes and fears:
4 And ye will faint be - side the way and sink:
5 And work till day - light soft - ens in - to ev'n:

1 Wipe from your brow the sweat and dust of toil,
2 A - lone with Me and with My Fa - ther here,
3 I know how hard - ly souls are wooed and won:
4 The bread of life is here for you to eat,
5 The brief hours are not lost in which ye learn

1 And in My qui - et strength a - gain be strong.
2 With Me and with My Fa - ther not a - lone.
3 My choi - cest wreaths are al - ways wet with tears.
4 And here for you the wine of love to drink.
5 More of your Mas - ter and His rest in heav'n.

By permission of MRS. EVANS   The tune EVENTIDE is on the previous page

564   Go Bury Thy Sorrow

MARY A. BACHELOR   MAMRE 6.5.6.5.D   PHILIPP BLISS

1 Go bu-ry thy sor - row, The world hath its share;
2 Go tell it to Je - sus. He know-eth thy grief;
3 Hearts grow-ing a-wea - ry With hea-vi-er woe

1 Go bu-ry it deep-ly, Go hide it with care,
2 Go tell it to Je - sus, He'll send thee re - lief,
3 Now droop 'mid the dark - ness— Go, com-fort them, go!

1 Go think of it calm - ly, When cur-tain'd by night,
2 Go ga-ther the sun - shine He sheds on the way;
3 Go bu-ry thy sor - rows, Let o-thers be blest;

rit.

1 Go tell it to Je - sus, And all will be right.
2 He'll light-en thy bur - den, Go, wea-ry one, pray.
3 Go give them the sun - shine; Tell Je-sus the rest.

565   Hark, My Soul!

WM. COWPER   ST. BEES 7.7.7.7   J. B. DYKES

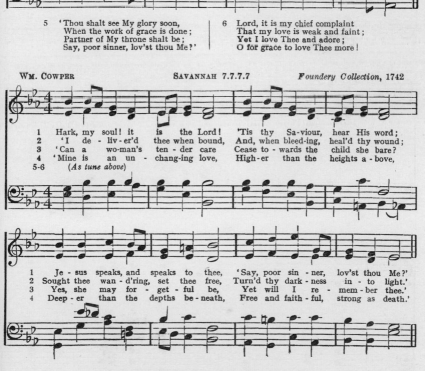

1 Hark, my soul! it is the Lord! 'Tis thy Sa-viour, hear His word;
2 'I   de - liv - er'd thee when bound, And, when bleed-ing, heal'd thy wound;
3 'Can a wo-man's ten - der care Cease to - wards the child she bare?
4 'Mine is an un - chang-ing love, High - er than the heights a - bove,

1 Je - sus speaks, and speaks to thee, 'Say, poor sin - ner, lov'st thou Me?'
2 Sought thee wan - d'ring, set thee right, Turn'd thy dark-ness in - to light.'
3 Yes, she may for - get - ful be, Yet will I re - mem - ber thee.'
4 Deep - er than the depths be - neath, Free and faith - ful, strong as death.'

5 'Thou shalt see My glory soon,
   When the work of grace is done;
   Partner of My throne shalt be;
   Say, poor sinner, lov'st thou Me?'

6 Lord, it is my chief complaint
   That my love is weak and faint;
   Yet I love Thee and adore;
   O for grace to love Thee more!

WM. COWPER   SAVANNAH 7.7.7.7   *Foundery Collection*, 1742

1 Hark, my soul! it is the Lord! 'Tis thy Sa-viour, hear His word;
2 'I   de - liv - er'd thee when bound, And, when bleed-ing, heal'd thy wound;
3 'Can a wo-man's ten - der care Cease to - wards the child she bare?
4 'Mine is an un - chang-ing love, High-er than the heights a - bove,
5-6 (*As tune above*)

1 Je - sus speaks, and speaks to thee, 'Say, poor sin - ner, lov'st thou Me?'
2 Sought thee wan - d'ring, set thee free, Turn'd thy dark - ness in - to light.'
3 Yes, she may for - get - ful be, Yet will I re - mem - ber thee.'
4 Deep - er than the depths be - neath, Free and faith - ful, strong as death.'

566 Sweet the Moments

WILLIAM SHIRLEY   SICILIAN MARINERS 8.7.8.7   SICILIAN MELODY

1 Sweet the mo - ments, rich in bless - ing, Which be
2 Here I rest, for ev - er view - ing Mer - cy
3 Tru - ly bless - ed is this sta - tion, Low be -
4 Here it is I find my hea - ven, While up -
5 Love and grief my heart a - bid - ing, With my

1 fore the Cross I spend; Life, and health, and peace
2 pour'd in streams of blood; Pre - cious drops, my soul
3 fore His Cross to lie, While I see di - vine
4 on the Lamb I gaze; Love I much? I've much
5 tears His feet I'll bathe; Con - stant still in faith

1 pos - sess - ing From the sin - ner's dy - ing Friend.
2 be - dew - ing, Plead and claim my peace with God.
3 com - pas - sion Beam - ing in His lan - guid eye.
4 for - giv - en— I'm a mir - a - cle of grace!
5 a - bid - ing, Life de - riv - ing from His death.

WILLIAM SHIRLEY   SHARON 8.7.8.7   WILLIAM BOYCE

1 Sweet the mo - ments, rich in bless - ing, Which be
2 Here I rest, for ev - er view - ing Mer - cy
3 Tru - ly bless - ed is this sta - tion, Low be -
4 Here it is I find my hea - ven, While up -
5 Love and grief my heart a - bid - ing, With my

Sweet the Moments—*Continued*

1 fore the Cross I spend; Life, and health, and
2 pour'd in streams of blood; Pre - cious drops, my
3 fore His Cross I lie, While I see di -
4 on the Lamb I gaze; Love I much? I've
5 tears His feet I'll bathe; Con - stant still in

1 peace pos - sess - ing From the sin - ner's dy - ing Friend.
2 soul be - dew - ing, Plead and claim my peace with God.
3 vine com - pas - sion Beam - ing in His lan - guid eye.
4 much for - giv - en— I'm a mir - a - cle of grace!
5 faith a - bid - ing, Life de - riv - ing from His death.

W. SHIRLEY   SUNNYSIDE 8.7. 8.7   R. BROWN-BORTHWICK

1 Sweet the mo - ments, rich in bless-ing, Which be - fore the Cross I spend;
2 Here I rest, for ev - er view - ing Mer - cy pour'd in streams of blood;
3 Tru - ly bless - ed is this sta - tion, Low be - fore His Cross I lie,
4 Here it is I find my hea - ven, While up - on the Lamb I gaze;
5 Love and grief my heart a - bid - ing, With my tears His feet I'll bathe;

1 Life, and health, and peace pos - sess - ing From the sin - ner's dy - ing Friend.
2 Pre - cious drops, my soul be - dew - ing, Plead and claim my peace with God.
3 While I see di - vine com - pas - sion Beam-ing in His lan - guid eye.
4 Love I much? I've much for - giv - en— I'm a mir - a - cle of grace!
5 Con - stant still in faith a - bid - ing, Life de - riv - ing from His death.

567 Speak to My Soul

L. L. Pickett

Arr. L. L. Pickett

1 Speak to my soul, Lord Jesus, Speak now in tenderest tone;
2 Speak to Thy children ever, Lead in the holy way;
3 Speak now as in the old time Thou didst reveal Thy will;

1 Whisper in loving kindness: 'Thou art not left alone.'
2 Fill them with joy and gladness, Teach them to watch and pray,
3 Let me know all my duty, Let me Thy law fulfil:

1 Open my heart to hear Thee, Quickly to hear Thy voice;
2 May they in consecration Yield their whole lives to Thee;
3 Lead me to glorify Thee, Help me to show Thy praise,

1 Fill Thou my soul with praises, Let me in Thee rejoice.
2 Hasten Thy coming kingdom, Till our dear Lord we see.
3 Gladly to do Thy bidding, Honour Thee all my days.

Speak to My Soul—*Continued*

Refrain

Speak Thou in soft-est whis-pers, Whis-pers of love to

me ;............ 'Thou shalt be al-ways con-q'ror,

Thou shalt be al-ways free':............ Speak Thou to me each

day, Lord, Al-ways in tend-'rest tone ;........ Let me now

hear Thy whis-per, 'Thou art not left a-lone.'........

568   # I Need Thee

ANNIE S. HAWKS   ROBERT LOWRY

1 I need Thee ev-'ry hour, Most gra - cious Lord;
2 I need Thee ev-'ry hour, Stay Thou near by;
3 I need Thee ev-'ry hour In joy or pain;
4 I need Thee ev-'ry hour; Teach me Thy will,
5 I need Thee ev-'ry hour, Most Ho - ly One:

1 No ten - der voice like Thine Can peace af - ford.
2 Temp - ta - tions lose their pow'r When Thou art nigh.
3 Come quick - ly and a - bide, Or life is vain.
4 And Thy rich pro - mis - es In me ful - fil.
5 O make me Thine in - deed, Thou bless - ed Son!

REFRAIN

I need Thee, O I need Thee! Ev - 'ry hour I need Thee,

O bless me now my Sa - viour, I come to Thee!

569 Nearer to Thee

SARAH F. ADAMS EXCELSIOR 6.4.6.4.6.6.4 LOWELL MASON

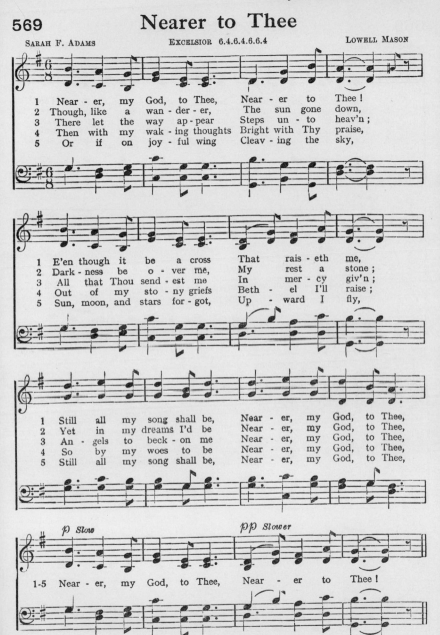

1 Near - er, my God, to Thee, Near - er to Thee !
2 Though, like a wan - der - er, The sun gone down,
3 There let the way ap - pear Steps un - to heav'n ;
4 Then with my wak - ing thoughts Bright with Thy praise,
5 Or if on joy - ful wing Cleav - ing the sky,

1 E'en though it be a cross That rais - eth me,
2 Dark - ness be o - ver me, My rest a stone ;
3 All that Thou send - est me In mer - cy giv'n ;
4 Out of my sto - ny griefs Beth - el I'll raise ;
5 Sun, moon, and stars for - got, Up - ward I fly,

1 Still all my song shall be, Near - er, my God, to Thee,
2 Yet in my dreams I'd be Near - er, my God, to Thee,
3 An - gels to beck - on me Near - er, my God, to Thee,
4 So by my woes to be Near - er, my God, to Thee,
5 Still all my song shall be, Near - er, my God, to Thee,

p Slow *pp Slower*

1-5 Near - er, my God, to Thee, Near - er to Thee !

The tunes HORBURY and NENTHORN are on the following pages

569 Nearer to Thee

SARAH F. ADAMS HORBURY 6.4.6.4.6.6.6.4 J. B. DYKES

1 Near - er, my God, to Thee, Near - er to Thee!
2 Though, like a wan - der - er, The sun gone down,
3 There let the way ap - pear Steps un - to heav'n;
4 Then with my wak - ing thoughts Bright with Thy praise,
5 Or if on joy - ful wing Cleav - ing the sky,

1 E'en though it be a cross That rais - eth
2 Dark - ness be o - ver me, My rest a
3 All that Thou send - est me In mer - cy
4 Out of my sto - ny griefs Beth - el I'll
5 Sun, moon, and stars for - got, Up - ward I

Rall.   *a tempo*

1 me, Still all my song shall be, Near - er,
2 stone; Yet in my dreams I'd be Near - er,
3 giv'n; An - gels to beck - on me Near - er,
4 raise; So by my woes to be Near - er,
5 fly, Still all my song shall be, Near - er,

1-5 my God, to Thee, Near - er to Thee!

The tunes EXCELSIOR and NENTHORN precede and follow this tune

569 Nearer to Thee

SARAH F. ADAMS NENTHORN 6.4.6.4.6.6.4 THOMAS L. HATELY

1 Near - er, my God, to Thee, Near - er to Thee !
2 Though like the wan - der - er, The sun gone down,
3 There let the way ap - pear Steps un - to heav'n ;
4 Then with my wak - ing thoughts Bright with Thy praise,
5 Or if on joy - ful wing Cleav - ing the sky,

1 E'en though it be a cross That rais - eth me,
2 Dark - ness be o - ver me, My rest a stone ;
3 All that Thou send - est me In mer - cy giv'n ;
4 Out of my sto - ny griefs Beth - el I'll raise ;
5 Sun, moon, and stars for - got, Up - ward I fly,

1 Still all my song shall be, Near - er,
2 Yet in my dreams I'd be Near - er,
3 An - gels to beck - on me Near - er,
4 So by my woes to be Near - er,
5 Still all my song shall be, Near - er,

1-5 my God, to Thee, Near - er to Thee !

The tunes EXCELSIOR and HORBURY are on the preceding pages

570 Thy Life for Me!

FRANCES R. HAVERGAL   BACA 6.6. 6.6. 6.6.   WILLIAM H. HAVERGAL

1 Thy life was giv'n for me! Thy blood, O Lord, was shed
2 Long years were spent for me In wea-ri-ness and woe,
3 Thy Fa-ther's home of light, Thy rain-bow cir-cled throne,
4 Thou, Lord, hast borne for me More than my tongue can tell

1 That I might ran-som'd be, And quick-en'd from the dead.
2 That through e-ter-ni-ty Thy glo-ry I might know.
3 Were left for earth-ly night For wan-d'rings sad and lone.
4 Of bit-t'rest a-gon-y, To res-cue me from hell.

Slower

1 Thy life was giv'n for me: What have I giv'n for Thee?
2 Long years were spent for me: Have I spent one for Thee?
3 Yea, all was left for me! Have I left aught for Thee?
4 Thou suf-fredst all for me: What have I borne for Thee?

571 Himself for Me!

ARTHUR T. PIERSON   WATER STREET 6.6. 6.6. 8.6.   PHILIP P. BLISS

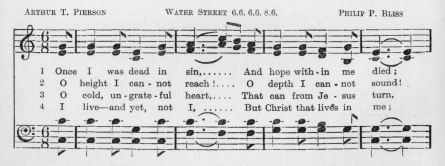

1 Once I was dead in sin,...... And hope with-in me died;
2 O height I can-not reach!.... O depth I can-not sound!
3 O cold, un-grate-ful heart,.... That can from Je-sus turn,
4 I live—and yet, not I, ... But Christ that lives in me;

Himself for Me!—*Continued*

1 But now I'm dead to sin,...... With Je - sus cru - ci - fied.
2 O love, O bound-less love,..... In my Re - deem - er found!
3 When liv - ing fires of love...... Should on His al - tar burn!
4 Who from the law of sin...... And death hath made me free.

REFRAIN

And can it be that "He lov'd me, And gave Him-self for me"?

572 The Golden Key

GOLDEN KEY 5.5.7. 5.5.7.

JNO. R. SWENEY

1 Pray·er is the key, With the bend-ing knee, To o - pen the morn's first hours;
2 Not a soul so sad, Nor a heart so glad, When com-eth the shades of night,
3 Take the gold-en key In your hand and see, As the night tide drifts a - way,
4 When the sha-dows fall, And the ves - per call Is sob - bing its low re - frain,
5 Soon the year's dark door Shall be shut no more: Life's tears shall be wip'd a - way,

1 See the in - cense rise To the star - ry skies, Like per - fume from the flow'rs.
2 But the day-break song Will the joy pro - long, And some dark-ness turn to light.
3 How its bless - ed hold Is a crown of gold, Thro' the wea - ry hours of day.
4 'Tis a gar - land sweet To the toil - worn feet, And an an - ti - dote for pain.
5 As the pearl gates swing, And the gold harps ring, And the sun un - sheathes for aye.

573 When I Survey

ISAAC WATTS   BOSTON L.M.   LOWELL MASON

1 When I sur - vey the won - drous Cross On which the Prince of Glo - ry died,
2 For - bid it, Lord, that I should boast, Save in the death of Christ, my God;
3 See! from His head, His hands, His feet, Sor - row and love flow min - gled down;
4 Were the whole realm of na - ture mine, That were an off - 'ring far too small;

1 My rich-est gain I count but loss, And pour con-tempt on all my pride.
2 All the vain things that charm me most I sac - ri - fice them to His blood.
3 Did e'er such love and sor - row meet, Or thorns com-pose so rich a crown?
4 Love so a - maz - ing, so di - vine, De-mands my soul, my life, my all.

ISAAC WATTS   ROCKINGHAM L.M.   EDWARD MILLER

1 When I sur - vey the won - drous Cross On which the Prince of Glo - ry died,
2 For - bid it, Lord, that I should boast, Save in the death of Christ, my God;
3 See! from His head, His hands, His feet, Sor - row and love flow min - gled down,
4 Were the whole realm of na - ture mine, That were an off - 'ring far too small;

1 My rich-est gain I count but loss, And pour con-tempt on all my pride.
2 All the vain things that charm me most I sac - ri - fice them to His blood.
3 Did e'er such love and sor - row meet, Or thorns com-pose so rich a crown?
4 Love so a - maz - ing, so di - vine, De-mands my soul, my life, my all.

The tune LACRIMA is on the following page

573

When I Survey

ISAAC WATTS   LACRIMA L.M.D.   ALEX. LEE.   *Arr.* G. ALLAN

1 When I sur-vey the won-drous Cross, On which the Prince of Glo-ry
2 See! from His head, His hands, His feet, Sor-row and love flow min-gled

1 died, My rich-est gain I count but loss, And pour con-
2 down; Did e'er such love and sor-row meet, Or thorns com-

1 tempt on all my pride: For-bid it, Lord, that I should
2 pose so rich a crown? Were the whole realm of na-ture

1 boast, Save in the death of Christ my God; All the vain
2 mine, That were an off-'ring far too small; Love so a-

1 things that charm me most I sac-ri-fice them to His blood.
2 maz-ing, so di-vine, De-mands my soul, my life, my all.

TUNES BOSTON and ROCKINGHAM are on previous page.   FOR SOLO SETTING see No. 812

574 His Way with Thee

CYRUS S. NUSBAUM

CYRUS S. NUSBAUM

1 Would you live for Je - sus, and be al-ways pure and good? Would you walk with
2 Would you have him make you free, and fol - low at His call? Would you know the
3 Would you in His king-dom find a place of con-stant rest? Would you prove Him

1 Him with - in the nar - row road? Would you have Him bear your bur - den,
2 peace that comes by giv - ing all? Would you have Him save you, so that
3 true each prov - i - den - tial test? Would you in His ser - vice la - bour

REFRAIN

1 car - ry all your load?
2 you need ne - ver fall? } Let Him have His way with thee. His pow'r can
3 al - ways at your best?

make you what you ought to be; His blood can cleanse your heart and make you free; His

love can fill your soul, and you will see 'Twas best for Him to have His way with thee.

575 My Portion for Ever

J. Wakefield MacGill

OLD MELODY

1 All, all to Je-sus, I con-se-crate a-new: He is my
2 All, all to Je-sus, my trust-ing heart can say: He is my
3 Tho' He may try me, this bless-ed truth I know: He is my
4 All, all to Je-sus, I cheer-ful-ly re-sign: He is my

1 por-tion for ev-er. On-ly His glo-ry hence-forth will I pur-sue:
2 por-tion for ev-er. Led by His mer-cy I'm walk-ing ev-'ry day:
3 por-tion for ev-er. He will not leave me, His pro-mise tells me so:
4 por-tion for ev-er. I have the wit-ness that He, my Lord, is mine:

REFRAIN

He is my por-tion for ev-er. Take, take the world with
Alternative refrain—Make Je-sus Christ the

all its gild-ed toys, Take, take the world, I cov-et not its joys,
cen-tre of your life, He'll reign su-preme, where on-ly sin was rife;

Mine is a wealth no moth nor rust de-stroys; Je-sus, my por-tion for ev-er.
He'll speak the word and end the dead-ly strife, Make Him the cen-tre for ev-er.

Words and Arrangement copyright by PICKERING & INGLIS, LTD.

576

On the Altar

MARY D. JAMES

ARIEL 7.6.7.6. D.

J. F. KNAPP

1 My spi - rit, soul, and bo - dy, Je - sus, I give to Thee,
2 O Je - sus, might-y Sa - viour, I trust in Thy great Name;
3 Now, Lord, I yield my mem - bers, From sin's do - min - ion free,
4 I'm Thine, O bless - ed Je - sus, Wash'd in Thy pre - cious blood,

1 A con - se - cra - ted off - 'ring, Thine ev - er - more to be.
2 I look for Thy sal - va - tion, Thy pro - mise now I claim.
3 For war - fare and for tri - umph, As wea - pons un - to Thee.
4 Seal'd by Thy Ho - ly Spi - rit, A sac - ri - fice to God.

REFRAIN

My all is on the al - tar, Lord, I am all Thine own;

rit.

O may my faith ne'er fal - ter; Lord, keep me Thine a - lone. . .

The tune MEIRIONYDD is on the following page

576   # On the Altar

MARY D. JAMES   MEIRIONYDD 7.6. 7.6. D   WILLIAM LLOYD

1 My spi - rit, soul, and bo - dy, Je - sus, I give to Thee,
2 O Je - sus, might - y Sa - viour, I trust in Thy great Name;
3 Now, Lord, I yield my mem - bers, From sin's do - min - ion free,
4 I'm Thine, O bless - ed Je - sus! Wash'd in Thy pre - cious blood,

1 A con - se - cra - ted off - 'ring, Thine ev - er - more to be.
2 I look for Thy sal - va - tion, Thy pro - mise now I claim.
3 For war - fare and for tri - umph, As wea - pons un - to Thee.
4 Seal'd by Thy Ho - ly Spi - rit, A sac - ri - fice to God.

REFRAIN

My all is on the al - tar, Lord, I am all Thine own;

O may my faith ne'er fal - ter; Lord, keep me Thine, a - lone!

The tune ARIEL is on the previous page

577 Pray, Always Pray

E. H. BICKERSTETH PAX TECUM 10.10. G. T. CALDBECK

1 Pray, al - ways pray; the Ho - ly Spi - rit pleads
2 Pray, al - ways pray; be - neath sin's hea - viest load,
3 Pray, al - ways pray; though wea - ry, faint, and lone,
4 Pray, al - ways pray; a - mid the world's tur - moil,
5 Pray, al - ways pray; if joys thy path - way throng,
6 Pray, al - ways pray; if lov'd ones pass the veil,
7 All earth - ly things with earth shall pass a - way;

1 With - in thee all thy dai - ly, hour - ly needs.
2 Pray'r sees the blood from Je - sus' side that flowed.
3 Pray'r nest - les by the Fa - ther's shel - t'ring throne.
4 Pray'r keeps the heart at rest, and nerves for toil.
5 Pray'r strikes the harp, and sings the an - gels' song.
6 Pray'r drinks with them of springs that can - not fail.
7 Pray'r grasps e - ter - ni - ty; pray, al - ways pray.

By permission of the CHURCH BOOK ROOM PRESS LTD.

E. H. BICKERSTETH HISPANIA 10.10. ANON

1 Pray, al - ways pray; the Ho - ly Spi - rit pleads
2 Pray, al - ways pray; be - neath sin's hea - viest load,
3 Pray, al - ways pray; though wea - ry, faint, and lone,
4 Pray, al - ways pray; a - mid the world's tur - moil,
5 Pray, al - ways pray; if joys thy path - way throng,
6 Pray, al - ways pray; if lov'd ones pass the veil,
7 All earth - ly things with earth shall pass a - way;

1 With - in thee all thy dai - ly, hour - ly needs.
2 Pray'r sees the blood from Je - sus' side that flowed.
3 Pray'r nest - les by the Fa - ther's shel - t'ring throne.
4 Pray'r keeps the heart at rest, and nerves for toil.
5 Pray'r strikes the harp, and sings the an - gels' song.
6 Pray'r drinks with them of springs that can - not fail.
7 Pray'r grasps e - ter - ni - ty; pray, al - ways pray.

Music from THE CHURCH HYMNAL FOR THE CHRISTIAN YEAR

578 Something for Thee

S. D. Phelps   Fenwick 6.4. 6.4. 6.4. 6.6. 6.4.   R. Lowry

1 Sa - viour! Thy dy - ing love Thou ga - vest me,
2 At the blest mer - cy seat, Plead - ing for me,
3 Give me a faith - ful heart, Like - ness to Thee,
4 All that I am and have, Thy gifts so free;

1 Nor should I aught with - hold, My Lord, from Thee;
2 My fee - ble faith looks up, Je - sus, to Thee:
3 That each de - part - ing day Hence - forth may see
4 In joy, in grief, through life, O Lord, for Thee!

1 In love my soul would bow, My heart ful - fil its vow,
2 Help me the cross to bear. Thy won - drous love de - clare,
3 Some work of love be - gun, Some deed of kind - ness done,
4 And when Thy face I see, My ran - som'd soul shall be,

1 Some of - f'ring bring Thee now, Some - thing for Thee.
2 Some song to raise, or pray'r, Some - thing for Thee.
3 Some wan - d'rer sought and won, Some - thing for Thee.
4 Through all e - ter - ni - ty, Some - thing for Thee.

579 Come, Ye Disconsolate

THOMAS MOORE ALMA REDEMPTORIS 11.10.11.10 SAMUEL WEBBE

1 Come, ye dis - con - so-late! wher - e'er ye lan - guish,
2 Joy of the des - o - late, light of the stray - ing,
3 Here see the Bread of Life; see wa - ters flow - ing

1 Come to the mer - cy - seat, fer - vent - ly kneel;
2 Hope of the pen - i - tent, fade - less and pure!
3 Forth from the throne of God, pure from a - bove;

1 Here bring your wound - ed hearts, Here tell your
2 Here speaks the Com - for - ter, Ten - der - ly
3 Come to the feast of love: Come, ev - er

1 an - guish; Earth has no sor - row that heav'n can - not heal.
2 say - ing, Earth has no sor - row that heav'n can - not cure.
3 know - ing Earth has no sor - row but heav'n can re - move.

The tune TAVY CLEAVE is on the following page

579 Come, Ye Disconsolate

THOS. MOORE TAVY CLEAVE 11.10.11.10 FERRIS TOZER

1 Come, ye dis - con - so - late! wher - e'er ye lan - guish,
2 Joy of the des - o - late, light of the stray - ing,
3 Here see the Bread of Life; see wa - ters flow - ing

1 Come to the mer - cy - seat, fer - vent - ly kneel;
2 Hope of the pen - i - tent, fade - less and pure!
3 Forth from the throne of God, pure from a - bove;

1 Here bring your wound - ed hearts, Here tell your an - guish;
2 Here speaks the Com - for - ter, Ten - der - ly say - ing,
3 Come to the feast of love; Come, ev - er know - ing

1 Earth has no sor - row that heav'n can - not heal.
2 Earth has no sor - row that heav'n can - not cure.
3 Earth has no sor - row but heav'n can re - move.

Music by permission of CONSTANCE MORLEY HORDER

The tune ALMA REDEMPTORIS is on the preceding page

580 My Faith Looks Up

RAY PALMER   OLIVET 6.6.4.6.6.6.4   LOWELL MASON

1 My faith looks up to Thee, Thou Lamb of Cal-
2 May Thy rich grace im-part Strength to my faint-
3 While life's dark maze I tread, And griefs a-round
4 When ends life's trans-ient dream, When death's cold sul-

1 va-ry, Sa-viour di-vine; Now hear me while
2 ing heart, My zeal in-spire; As Thou hast died
3 me spread, Be Thou my Guide; Bid dark-ness turn
4 len stream Shall o'er me roll, Blest Sa-viour then

1 I pray: Take all my guilt a-way; O
2 for me, O may my love to Thee. Pure,
3 to day, Wipe sor-row's tears a-way; Nor
4 in love. Fear and dis-trust re-move O

1 let me from this day Be whol-ly Thine!
2 warm, and change-less, be A liv-ing fire.
3 let me ev-er stray From Thee a-side.
4 bear me safe a-bove A ran-som'd soul!

The tune GREENWOOD is on the following page

580   My Faith Looks Up

RAY PALMER   GREENWOOD 6.6.4.6.6.6.4.   EBENEZER PROUT

1 My faith looks up to Thee, Thou Lamb of
2 May Thy rich grace im - part Strength to my
3 While life's dark maze I tread, And griefs a -
4 When ends life's tran - sient dream, When death's cold

1 Cal - va - ry, Sa - viour di - vine; . . Now hear me
2 faint - ing heart, My zeal in - spire; . . As Thou hast
3 round me spread, Be Thou my Guide; . . Bid dark - ness
4 sul - len stream Shall o'er me roll, . . . Blest Sa - viour,

1 while I pray: Take all my guilt a - way;
2 died for me, O may my love to Thee
3 turn to day, Wipe sor - row's tears a - way;
4 then in love, Fear and dis - trust re - move;

1 O let me from this day Be whol - ly Thine!
2 Pure, warm, and change - less, be A liv - ing fire!
3 Nor let me ev - er stray From Thee a - side.
4 O bear me safe a - bove, A ran - somed soul!

Music by permission of the CONGREGATIONAL UNION OF ENGLAND AND WALES

The tune OLIVET is on the preceding page

581 I Surrender All

JUDSON W. VAN DE VENTER

WINFIELD S. WEEDEN

1 All to Je-sus I sur-ren-der, All to Him I free-ly give;
2 All to Je-sus I sur-ren-der, Hum-bly at His feet I bow;
3 All to Je-sus I sur-ren-der, Make me, Sa-viour, whol-ly Thine;
4 All to Je-sus I sur-ren-der, Lord, I give my-self to Thee!
5 All to Je-sus I sur-ren-der, Now I feel the sac-red flame,

1 I will ev-er love and trust Him, In His pres-ence dai-ly live.
2 World-ly pleas-ures all for-sak-en, Take me, Je-sus, take me now,
3 Let me feel the Ho-ly Spi-rit, Tru-ly know that Thou art mine.
4 Fill me with Thy love and pow-er, Let Thy bless-ing fall on me.
5 O the joy of full sal-va-tion! Glo-ry, glo-ry to His name.

REFRAIN

I sur-ren-der all, ... I sur-ren-der all; . . . . .
. . . . . I sur-ren-der all, ... I sur-ren-der all,

All to Thee, my bless-ed Sa-viour, I sur-ren-der all.

582 The Hour of Prayer

FANNY J. CROSBY

W. H. DOANE

1. 'Tis the bless-ed hour of pray'r, when our hearts low-ly bend, And we
2. 'Tis the bless-ed hour of pray'r, when the Sa-viour draws near, With a
3. 'Tis the bless-ed hour of pray'r, when the tempt-ed and tried To the
4. At the bless-ed hour of pray'r, trust-ing Him we be-lieve That the

1. gath-er to Je-sus, our Sa-viour and Friend; If we come to Him in
2. ten-der com-pas-sion His child-ren to hear; When He tells us we may
3. Sa-viour who loves them their sor-row con-fide; With a sym-pa-thiz-ing
4. bless-ings we're need-ing we'll sure-ly re-ceive, In the ful-ness of this

1. faith, His pro-tec-tion to share; What a balm for the wea-ry! O how
2. cast at His feet ev-'ry care; What a balm for the wea-ry! O how
3. heart He re-moves ev-'ry care; What a balm for the wea-ry! O how
4. trust we shall lose ev-'ry care; What a balm for the wea-ry! O how

REFRAIN

1-4 sweet to be there! Bless-ed hour of pray'r, Bless-ed hour of

pray'r; What a balm for the wea-ry! O how sweet to be there!

583 Teach Us to Pray

DOOR OF HOPE 4.8.8.4.4.

J. H. TENNEY

1 Teach us to pray! O Fa - ther, we look up to Thee! And this our
2 Teach us to pray! A form of words will not suf - fice; The heart must
3 Teach us to pray! To whom shall we, Thy chil-dren, turn? Teach us the
4 Teach us to pray! To Thee a - lone our hearts look up; Pray'r is our

mf   *<>*   *pp*   *<>*

1 one re - quest shall be, Teach us to pray, Teach us to pray.
2 bring its sac - ri - fice; Teach us to pray, Teach us to pray.
3 les - son we should learn: Teach us to pray, Teach us to pray.
4 on - ly door of hope; Teach us to pray, Teach us to pray.

584 Nearer, still Nearer

LEILA N. MORRIS

NEARER 9.10.9.10.10.

LEILA N. MORRIS

1 Near - er, still near - er, close to Thy heart, Draw me, my
2 Near - er, still near - er, no - thing I bring, Naught as an
3 Near - er, still near - er, Lord, to be Thine! Sin with its
4 Near - er, still near - er, while life shall last, Till all its

1 Sa - viour, so pre - cious Thou art; Fold me, O fold me
2 of - f'ring to Je - sus, my King; On - ly my sin - ful,
3 fol - lies I glad - ly re - sign, All of its plea - sures,
4 strug-gles and tri - als are past; Then thro' e - ter - ni - ty,

Nearer, still Nearer—*Continued*

1 close to Thy breast, Shel - ter me safe in that "Ha - ven of
2 now con-trite heart; Grant me the cleans-ing Thy blood doth im-
3 pomp, and its pride: Give me but Je - sus, my Lord cru-ci-
4 ev - er I'll be, Near - er, my Sa-viour, still near - er to

1 Rest," Shel - ter me safe in that "Ha - ven of Rest!"
2 part, Grant me the cleans - ing Thy blood doth im - part.
3 fied, Give me but Je - sus, my Lord cru - ci - fied.
4 Thee! Near - er, my Sa - viour, still near - er to Thee!

585   **The Light of Day**

GEO. W. DOANE   WEBER 7.7.7.7.   C. M. VON WEBER

1 Soft - ly now the light of day Fades up - on our sight a - way;
2 Thou whose all - per - vad - ing eye Naught es - capes, without, with - in,
3 Soon for us the light of day Shall for ev - er pass a - way;

1 Free from care, from la - bour free, Lord, we would com - mune with Thee.
2 Par - don each in - firm - i - ty, O - pen fault and se - cret sin.
3 Then, from sin and sor - row free, Take us, Lord, to dwell with Thee.

586 Hear and Answer Prayer

FANNY J. CROSBY   RIVERSIDE 8.7. 8.7. D.   WM. J. KIRKPATRICK

1 I am pray-ing, bless-ed Sa-viour, To be more and more like Thee;
2 I am pray-ing, bless-ed Sa-viour, For a faith so clear and bright
3 I am pray-ing to be hum-bled By the pow'r of grace di-vine,
4 I am pray-ing, bless-ed Sa-viour, And my con-stant pray'r shall be,

1 I am pray-ing that Thy Spi-rit Like a dove may rest on me.
2 That its eye will see Thy glo-ry Thro' the deep-est, dark-est night.
3 To be cloth'd up-on with meek-ness, And to have no will but Thine.
4 For a per-fect con-se-cra-tion, That shall make me more like Thee.

REFRAIN

Thou who know-est all my weak-ness, Thou who know-est all my care,

While I plead each pre-cious pro-mise, Hear, oh, hear and an-swer pray'r!

587 Take My Life

F. R. HAVERGAL   KYRIE 7.7.7.7   From MOZART

1 Take my life, and let it be   Con - se - cra - ted, Lord, to Thee;
2 Take my hands, and let them move   At the im - pulse of Thy love;
3 Take my voice, and let me sing   Al - ways, on - ly, for my King;
4 Take my sil - ver and my gold;   Not a mite would I with - hold;
5 Take my will, and make it Thine,   It shall be no long - er mine:
6 Take my love; my Lord, I pour   At Thy feet its treas - ure - store!

1 Take my mo - ments and my days,   Let them flow in cease-less praise.
2 Take my feet, and let them be   Swift and beau - ti - ful for Thee.
3 Take my lips, and let them be   Fill'd with mes - sa - ges from Thee.
4 Take my in - tel - lect, and use   Ev - 'ry pow'r as Thou shalt choose.
5 Take my heart— it is Thine own;   It shall be Thy roy - al throne.
6 Take my - self, and I will be   Ev - er, on - ly, ALL for Thee !

F. R. HAVERGAL   PATMOS 7.7.7.7   W. H. HAVERGAL

1 Take my life, and let it be   Con - se - cra - ted,   Lord, to   Thee ;
2 Take my hands, and let them move   At the im - pulse   of Thy   love ;
3 Take my voice, and let me sing   Al - ways, on - ly,   for my   King ;
4 Take my sil - ver and my gold;   Not a mite would   I with - hold ;
5 Take my will, and make it Thine,   It shall be no   long - er   mine :
6 Take my love; my Lord, I pour   At Thy feet its   treas - ure - store !

1 Take my mo - ments and my days,   Let them flow in   cease - less praise.
2 Take my feet, and let them be   Swift and beau - ti -   ful for Thee.
3 Take my lips, and let them be   Fill'd with mes - sa -   ges from Thee.
4 Take my in - tel - lect, and use   Ev - 'ry pow'r as   Thou shalt choose.
5 Take my heart— it is Thine own;   It shall be Thy   roy - al throne.
6 Take my - self, and I will be   Ev - er, on - ly,   ALL for Thee !

588 We Seek Thy Face

ALEX. STEWART   WALTON L.M.   GARDINER'S SACRED MELODIES

1 Lord Jesus Christ, we seek Thy face; Within the
2 We thank Thee for the precious blood That purg'd our
3 Shut in with Thee far, far above The restless
4 The brow that once with thorns was bound, Thy hands, Thy

1 veil we bow the knee; O let Thy glory
2 sins and brought us nigh, All cleans'd and sancti-
3 world that wars below; We seek to learn and
4 side, we fain would see; Draw near, Lord Jesus,

1 fill the place! And bless us while we wait on Thee.
2 fied to God, Thy holy Name to magnify.
3 prove Thy love, Thy wisdom and Thy grace to know.
4 glory crown'd, And bless us while we wait on Thee.

ALEX. STEWART   RETREAT L.M.   THOMAS HASTINGS

1 Lord Jesus Christ, we seek Thy face; Within the
2 We thank Thee for the precious blood That purg'd our
3 Shut in with Thee far, far above The restless
4 The brow that once with thorns was bound, Thy hands, Thy

We Seek Thy Face—*Continued*

1 vail we bow the knee; O let Thy glo - ry fill the
2 sins and brought us nigh, All cleans'd and sanc - ti - fied to
3 world that wars be - low; We seek to learn and prove Thy
4 side, we fain would see; Draw near, Lord Je - sus, glo - ry

1 place! And bless us while we wait on Thee.
2 God, Thy ho - ly Name to mag - ni - fy.
3 love, Thy wis - dom and Thy grace to know.
4 crown'd, And bless us while we wait on Thee.

ALEXANDER STEWART   UNDERSHAFT L.M.   JOHN GOSS

1 Lord Je - sus Christ, we seek Thy face; With - in the vail we bow the knee,
2 We thank Thee for the pre-cious blood That purg'd our sins and brought us nigh,
3 Shut in with Thee far, far a - bove The rest-less world that wars be - low;
4 The brow that once with thorns was bound, Thy hands, Thy side, we fain would see;

1 O let Thy glo - ry fill the place! And bless us while we wait on Thee.
2 All cleans'd and sanc-ti - fied to God, Thy ho - ly Name to mag - ni - fy.
3 We seek to learn and prove Thy love, Thy wis-dom and Thy grace to know.
4 Draw near, Lord Je - sus, glo - ry crown'd, And bless us while we wait on Thee.

589 Keep on Praying

R. O. SMITH   J. LINCOLN HALL

1 Tho' the foes of right op-press, Keep on pray-ing; Christ, the Lord, is near to bless,
2 Christian, has your faith grown weak? Keep on pray-ing; Do the tears roll down your cheek?
3 Pil-grim, have you wea-ry grown? Keep on pray-ing; God is yet up-on His throne,
4 Prais-es shall with pray'rs as-cend, Keep on pray-ing; Pray and praise till life shall end,

1 All pre-vail-ing. Let not fear your heart ap-pal, Naught of e-vil can be-fall,
2 Keep on pray-ing, Soon you nev-er more will sigh, Tears no more shall dim your eye,
3 Keep on pray-ing. He will hear your faith-ful cry, He to help is ev-er nigh,
4 Keep on pray-ing. Till you reach the gold-en gate Where the ran-som'd souls a-wait,

REFRAIN

1 Strong-er is your God than all, Keep on pray-ing.
2 Pray to Him who's al-ways nigh, Nev-er fail-ing.
3 You shall con-quer by-and-bye, Keep on pray-ing.
4 Claim-ing there your tri-umph great, Keep on pray-ing.

Keep on pray-ing,

Keep on pray-ing, Thro' the Sav-iour's bless-ed Name, all pre-vail-ing.

My Prayer

590

PHILIP P. BLISS   ASPIRATION   6.5. 6.5. D   PHILIP P. BLISS

1 More ho - li - ness give me, More striv-ings with - in;
2 More gra - ti - tude give me, More trust in the Lord;
3 More pur - i - ty give me, More strength to o'er - come;

1 More pa - tience in suff - 'ring, More sor - row for sin;
2 More pride in His glo - ry, More hope in His word;
3 More free - dom from earth - stains, More long - ings for home;

1 More faith in my Sa - viour, More sense of His care;
2 More tears for His sor - rows, More pain at His grief;
3 More fit for the king - dom, More used would I be;

1 More joy in His ser - vice, More pur - pose in pray'r;
2 More meek-ness in tri - al, More praise for re - lief.
3 More bless - ed and ho - ly, More, Sa - viour, like Thee.

591 The Victory Side

Leila N. Morris

Leila N. Morris

1 I'm o-ver in Ca-naan where rich-es a-bound, Liv-ing on the
2 No long-er by fears am I fet-ter'd and bound, Liv-ing on the
3 I walk in the sun-shine of God's ho-ly light, Liv-ing on the
4 The Lord, whom I trust, is my strength and my song, Liv-ing on the

1 vic-t'ry side; Each day go-ing on to pos-sess high-er ground,
2 vic-t'ry side; Sweet free-dom in ser-vice for Christ I have found,
3 vic-t'ry side; The will of my Lord is my joy and de-light,
4 vic-t'ry side; No foes can a-larm since to Him I be-long,

Liv-ing on the vic-t'ry side;

REFRAIN

1-4 Liv-ing on the vic-t'ry side. Sing glo - ry, hal-le-
Sing glo-ry, hal-le-

lu-jah! I'm liv-ing on the vic-t'ry side; Since
lu-jah, praise the Lord!

Christ my soul hath sanc-ti-fied, I'm liv-ing on the vic-t'ry side.

592 Tell It to Jesus

J. E. RANKIN   E. S. LORENZ

1 Are you wea - ry, are you hea - vy - heart-ed? Tell it to Je - sus,
2 Do the tears flow down your cheeks un-bid - den? Tell it to Je - sus,
3 Do you fear the gath - 'ring clouds of sor - row? Tell it to Je - sus,
4 Are you trou-bled with the thought of dy - ing? Tell it to Je - sus,

1 Tell it to Je - sus; Are you griev - ing o - ver joys de - part - ed?
2 Tell it to Je - sus; Have you sins that to man's eyes are hid - den?
3 Tell it to Je - sus; Are you an - xious what shall be to - mor - row?
4 Tell it to Je - sus; For Christ's com - ing king-dom are you sigh-ing?

REFRAIN

1-4 Tell it to Je - sus a - lone. Tell it to Je - sus, Tell it to

Je - sus, He is a friend that's well known; You have no oth - er

such a friend or bro - ther, Tell it to Je - sus a - lone.

593   Ever Thine

RICHARD SLATER   EVER THINE 6.7. 8.7   RICHARD SLATER

Ev - er Thine, Thine a - lone, Hence-forth, Sa - viour, I will be;

This my joy, my life's am - bi - tion, Day by day to grow like Thee.

By permission of the INTERNATIONAL MUSIC BOARD OF THE SALVATION ARMY

594   The Soul's Desire

JAMES MONTGOMERY   FRENCH C.M.   *Scottish Psalter*, 1615

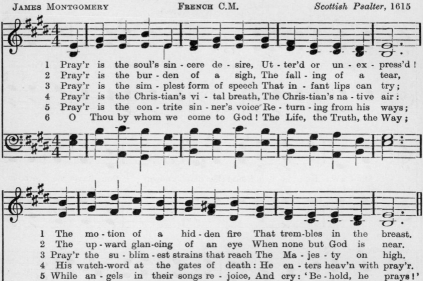

1 Pray'r is the soul's sin - cere de - sire, Ut - ter'd or un - ex - press'd !
2 Pray'r is the bur - den of a sigh, The fall - ing of a tear,
3 Pray'r is the sim - plest form of speech That in - fant lips can try;
4 Pray'r is the Chris-tian's vi - tal breath, The Chris-tian's na - tive air:
5 Pray'r is the con - trite sin - ner's voice Re - turn - ing from his ways;
6 O Thou by whom we come to God ! The Life, the Truth, the Way;

1 The mo - tion of a hid - den fire That trem-bles in the breast.
2 The up - ward glan-cing of an eye When none but God is near.
3 Pray'r the su - blim - est strains that reach The Ma - jes - ty on high.
4 His watch-word at the gates of death: He en - ters heav'n with pray'r.
5 While an - gels in their songs re - joice, And cry: 'Be - hold, he prays !'
6 The path of pray'r Thy - self hast trod: Lord ! teach us how to pray.

The tunes HOLY TRINITY and ILFRACOMBE are on the following page

594 The Soul's Desire

JAMES MONTGOMERY HOLY TRINITY C.M. J. BARNBY

1 Pray'r is the soul's sin - cere de - sire, Ut - ter'd or un - ex - press'd!
2 Pray'r is the bur - den of a sigh, The fall - ing of a tear,
3 Pray'r is the sim - plest form of speech That in - fant lips can try;
4 Pray'r is the Chris-tian's vi - tal breath, The Chris-tian's na - tive air:
5 Pray'r is the con - trite sin - ner's voice Re - turn - ing from his ways;
6 O Thou by whom we come to God! The Life, the Truth, the Way;

1 The mo - tion of a hid - den fire That trem - bles in the breast.
2 The up - ward glan-cing of an eye When none but God is near.
3 Pray'r the su - blim-est strains that reach The Ma - jes - ty on high.
4 His watch-word at the gates of death: He en - ters heav'n with pray'r.
5 While an - gels in their songs re - joice, And cry: 'Be - hold, he prays!'
6 The path of pray'r Thy - self hast trod: Lord! teach us how to pray.

JAMES MONTGOMERY ILFRACOMBE C.M. W. A. F. SCHULTHES

1 Pray'r is the soul's sin - cere de - sire, Ut-ter'd or un - ex - press'd!
2 Pray'r is the bur - den of a sigh, The fall-ing of a tear,
3 Pray'r is the sim - plest form of speech That in-fant lips can try;
4 Pray'r is the Chris-tian's vi - tal breath, The Chris-tian's na - tive air:
5 Pray'r is the con - trite sin - ner's voice Re - turn-ing from his ways;
6 O Thou by whom we come to God! The Life, the Truth, the Way;

1 The mo - tion of a hid - den fire That trem-bles in the breast.
2 The up - ward glan - cing of an eye When none but God is near.
3 Pray'r the su - blim - est strains that reach The Ma - jes - ty on high.
4 His watch-word at the gates of death: He en - ters heav'n with pray'r.
5 While an - gels in their songs re - joice, And cry: 'Be - hold, he prays!'
6 The path of pray'r Thy - self hast trod: Lord! teach us how to pray.

The tune FRENCH is on the previous page

595 More Love to Thee

ELIZABETH PRENTISS

W. H. DOANE

1 More love to Thee, O Christ, More love to Thee!
2 Once earth-ly joy I crav'd, Sought peace and rest;
3 Let sor - row do its work, Come grief or pain;
4 Then shall my la - test breath Whis - per Thy praise;

1 Hear Thou the pray'r I make On bend - ed knee;
2 Now Thee a - lone I seek, Give what is best;
3 Sweet are Thy mes - sen - gers, Sweet their re - frain,
4 This be the part - ing cry My heart shall raise;

1 This is my ear - nest plea, More love, O Christ, to Thee,
2 This all my pray'r shall be, More love, O Christ, to Thee,
3 When they can sing with me, More love, O Christ, to Thee,
4 This still its pray'r shall be, More love, O Christ, to Thee,

1-4 More love to Thee! More love to Thee!

596   O Teach Me More!

JAMES HUTTON   SAWLEY C.M.   JAMES WALCH

1 O teach me more of Thy blest ways! Thou ho-ly Lamb of God,
2 O tell me of-ten of Thy love, Of all Thy grief and pain!
3 For this, O may I free-ly count What-e'er I have but loss,
4 En-grave this deep-ly on my heart With an e-ter-nal pen,

1 And fix and root me in Thy grace, As one re-deem'd by blood.
2 And let my heart with joy con-fess That thence comes all my gain.
3 The dear-est ob-ject of my love, Com-par'd with Thee, but dross.
4 That I may, in some small de-gree, Re-turn Thy love a-gain.

JAMES HUTTON   FINGAL C.M.   J. S. ANDERSON

1 O teach me more of Thy blest ways! Thou ho-ly Lamb of God,
2 O tell me of-ten of Thy love, Of all Thy grief and pain!
3 For this, O may I free-ly count What-e'er I have but loss,
4 En-grave this deep-ly on my heart With an e-ter-nal pen,

1 And fix and root me in Thy grace, As one re-deem'd by blood.
2 And let my heart with joy con-fess That thence comes all my gain.
3 The dear-est ob-ject of my love, Com-par'd with Thee, but dross,
4 That I may, in some small de-gree, Re-turn Thy love a-gain.

By permission of the OXFORD UNIVERSITY PRESS

597 Approach, My Soul

JOHN NEWTON

ST. CYRIL C.M.

ARTHUR PATTON

1 Ap - proach, my soul, the mer - cy seat, Where Je - sus an - swers pray'r;
2 Thy pro - mise is my on - ly plea, With this I ven - ture nigh;
3 Bow'd down be - neath a load of sin, By Sa - tan sore - ly press'd;
4 Be Thou my shield and hid - ing place; That, shel - ter'd near Thy side,
5 O won - drous love! to bleed and die, To bear the Cross and shame,

1 There hum - bly fall be - fore His feet, For none can per - ish there.
2 Thou call - est bur - den'd souls to Thee, And such, O Lord, am I!
3 By wars with - out, and fears with - in— I come to Thee for rest.
4 I may my fierce ac - cu - ser face, And tell him Thou hast died.
5 That guilt - y sin - ners such as I Might plead Thy gra - cious Name.

JOHN NEWTON

GLASGOW C.M.

Moore's Psalm-Singer's Pocket Companion, 1756

1 Ap - proach, my soul, the mer - cy seat, Where
2 Thy pro - mise is my on - ly plea, With
3 Bow'd down be - neath a load of sin, By
4 Be Thou my shield and hid - ing place; That,
5 O won - drous love! to bleed and die, To

1 Je - sus an - swers pray'r; There hum - by fall be -
2 this I ven - ture nigh; Thou call - est bur - den'd
3 Sa - tan sore - ly press'd; By wars with - out, and
4 shel - ter'd near Thy side, I may my fierce ac -
5 bear the Cross and shame, That guilt - y sin - ners

Approach, My Soul—*Continued*

1 fore His feet, For none can per - ish there.
2 souls to Thee, And such, O Lord, am I!
3 fears with - in— I come to Thee for rest.
4 cu - ser face, And tell him Thou hast died.
5 such as I Might plead Thy gra - cious Name.

JOHN NEWTON   CONTEMPLATION C.M.   F. A. G. OUSELEY

1 Ap - proach, my soul, the mer - cy seat, Where Je - sus
2 Thy pro - mise is my on - ly plea, With this I
3 Bow'd down be - neath a load of sin, By Sa - tan
4 Be Thou my shield and hid - ing place ; That, shel - ter'd
5 O won - drous love ! to bleed and die, To bear the

1 an - swers pray'r ;............ There hum - bly fall be -
2 ven - ture nigh ;............ Thou call - est bur - den'd
3 sore - ly press'd ;............ By wars with - out, and
4 near Thy side,............ I may my fierce ac -
5 Cross and shame,............ That guilt - y sin - ners

1 fore His feet, For none can per - ish there............
2 souls to Thee, And such, O Lord, am I !............
3 fears with - in— I come to Thee for rest. ....
4 cu - ser face, And tell him Thou hast died. ....
5 such as I Might plead Thy gra - cious Name. ....

598 I've Found the Pearl

JOHN MASON CARTON C.M. T. A. GEARY

JOHN MASON UNIVERSITY C.M. JOHN RANDALL

1 I've found the Pearl of great-est price, My
2 My Christ, He is the Lord of lords, The
3 My Christ, He is the Tree of Life That
4 Christ is my meat, Christ is my drink, My

1 heart doth sing for joy; And sing I must, for
2 sov-'reign King of kings, The ris-en Sun of
3 in God's E-den grows, The liv-ing, clear as
4 med-'cine, and my health; My por-tion, mine in-

1 Christ I have— O what a Christ have I !
2 Right-eous-ness, With heal-ing in His wings !
3 crys-tal stream Whence life for ev-er flows !
4 her-i-tance, Yea, all my bound-less wealth !

I've Found the Pearl—*Continued*

1 heart doth sing for joy; And sing I must, for
2 sov - 'reign King of kings, The ris - en Sun of
3 in God's E - den grows, The liv - ing, clear as
4 med - 'cine, and my health; My por - tion, mine in -

1 Christ I have— O what a Christ have I !
2 Right - eous - ness, With heal - ing in His wings !
3 crys - tal stream Whence life for ev - er flows !
4 her - i - tance, Yea, all my bound - less wealth !

JOHN MASON   CASTLEFORD C.M.   *Sacred Harmony, Leeds, 1720*

1 I've found the Pearl of great - est price, My heart doth sing for joy;
2 My Christ, He is the Lord of lords, The sov - 'reign King of kings,
3 My Christ, He is the Tree of Life That in God's E - den grows,
4 Christ is my meat, Christ is my drink, My med - 'cine, and my health;

1 And sing I must, for Christ I have— O what a Christ have I !
2 The ris - en Sun of Right - eous - ness, With heal - ing in His wings !
3 The liv - ing, clear as crys - tal stream Whence life for ev - er flows !
4 My por - tion, mine in - her - i - tance, Yea, all my bound - less wealth !

599   O for a Heart !

CHARLES WESLEY   ST. ETHELDREDA C.M.   THOMAS TURTON

1 O for a heart to praise my God! A heart from sin set free ;
2 A heart re-sign'd, sub - miss - ive, meek, My great Re - deem-er's throne,
3 A hum - ble, ho - ly, con - trite heart, Be - liev - ing, true, and clean,
4 A heart in ev - 'ry thought re-new'd, And full of love di - vine,
5 Thy na - ture, gra - cious Lord, im-part; Come quick-ly from a - bove;

1 A heart that al - ways feels the blood So free - ly shed for me ;
2 Where on - ly Christ is heard to speak, Where Je - sus reigns a - lone ;
3 Which nei - ther life nor death can part From Him that dwells with - in ;
4 Per - fect and right and pure and good, A co - py, Lord, of Thine !
5 Write Thy new Name up - on my heart, Thy new, best Name of Love.

CHARLES WESLEY   RICHMOND C.M.   SAMUEL WEBBE

1 O for a heart to praise my God ! A
2 A heart re - sign'd, sub - miss - ive, meek, My
3 A hum - ble, ho - ly, con - trite heart, Be -
4 A heart in ev - 'ry thought re - new'd, And
5 Thy na - ture, gra - cious Lord, im - part ; Come

1 heart from sin set free ; A heart that al - ways
2 great Re - deem - er's throne, Where on - ly Christ is
3 liev - ing, true, and clean, Which nei - ther life nor
4 full of love di - vine, Per - fect and right and
5 quick - ly from a - bove ; Write Thy new Name up -

O for a Heart !—*Continued*

1 feels the blood So free - ly shed for me ;
2 heard to speak, Where Je - sus reigns a - lone ;
3 death can part From Him that dwells with - in ;
4 pure and good, A co - py, Lord, of Thine !
5 on my heart, Thy new, best Name of Love.

CHARLES WESLEY   BUDE C.M.   S. S. WESLEY

1 O for a heart to praise my God ! A
2 A heart re - sign'd, sub - miss - ive, meek, My
3 A hum - ble, ho - ly, con - trite heart, Be -
4 A heart in ev - 'ry thought re - new'd, And
5 Thy na - ture, gra - cious Lord, im - part ; Come

1 heart from sin set free ; A heart that al - ways
2 great Re - deem - er's throne, Where on - ly Christ is
3 liev - ing, true, and clean, Which nei - ther life nor
4 full of love di - vine ; Per - fect and right and
5 quick - ly from a - bove ; Write Thy new Name up -

1 feels the blood So free - ly shed for me ;
2 heard to speak, Where Je - sus reigns a - lone ;
3 death can part From Him that dwells with - in ;
4 pure and good, A co - py, Lord, of Thine !
5 on my heart, Thy new, best Name of Love.

600 The Worth of Prayer

WILLIAM COWPER   MAINZER, L.M.   JOSEPH MAINZER

1 What various hindrances we meet In coming
2 Pray'r makes the darken'd cloud withdraw, Pray'r climbs the
3 Re - straining pray'r, we cease to fight; Pray'r makes the
4 While Mo - ses stood with arms spread wide, Suc - cess was
5 Have you no words? ah! think a - gain, Words flow a -
6 Were half the breath thus vain - ly spent, To heav'n in

1 to the mer - cy seat! Yet who that knows the
2 lad - der Ja - cob saw, Gives ex - er - cise to
3 Chris - tian's ar - mour bright: And Sa - tan trem - bles
4 found on Is - rael's side; But when through wear - i -
5 pace when you com - plain, And fill your fel - low -
6 sup - pli - ca - tion sent, Your cheer - ful song would

1 worth of pray'r But wish - es to be of - ten there?
2 faith and love, Brings ev - 'ry bless - ing from a - bove.
3 when he sees The weak - est saint up - on his knees.
4 ness they fail'd, That mo - ment A - ma - lek pre - vail'd.
5 crea - ture's ear With the sad tale of all your care.
6 oft - 'ner be: 'Hear what the Lord has done for me!'

WILLIAM COWPER   ROWLAND L.M.   S. B. TUCKERMAN

1 What various hindrances we meet In coming
2 Pray'r makes the darken'd cloud with - draw, Pray'r climbs the
3 Re - straining pray'r, we cease to fight; Pray'r makes the
4 While Mo - ses stood with arms spread wide, Suc - cess was
5 Have you no words? ah! think a - gain, Words flow a -
6 Were half the breath thus vain - ly spent, To heav'n in

The Worth of Prayer—*Continued*

1 to the mer - cy seat! Yet who that knows the
2 lad - der Ja - cob saw, Gives ex - er - cise to
3 Chris - tian's ar - mour bright: And Sa - tan trem - bles
4 found on Is - rael's side; But when thro' wear - i -
5 pace when you com - plain, And fill your fel - low -
6 sup - pli - ca - tion sent, Your cheer - ful song would

1 worth of pray'r But wish - es to be of - ten there?
2 faith and love, Brings ev - 'ry bless - ing from a - bove.
3 when he sees The weak - est saint up - on his knees.
4 ness they fail'd, That mo - ment A - ma - lek pre - vail'd.
5 crea - ture's ear With the sad tale of all your care.
6 oft - 'ner be: 'Hear what the Lord has done for me!'

WILLIAM COWPER

ROCHESTER L.M.

Day's Psalter, 1562
Harm. by E. J. HOPKINS

1 What va - rious hin - dran - ces we meet In com - ing to the mer - cy seat!
2 Pray'r makes the dar - ken'd cloud with-draw, Pray'r climbs the lad - der Ja - cob saw,
3 Re - strain-ing pray'r, we cease to fight; Pray'r makes the Chris-tian's ar-mour bright:
4 While Mo - ses stood with arms spread wide, Suc - cess was found on Is-rael's side;
5 Have you no words? ah! think a - gain, Words flow a - pace when you com-plain,
6 Were half the breath thus vain - ly spent, To heav'n in sup - pli - ca - tion sent,

1 Yet who that knows the worth of pray'r But wish - es to be of - ten there?
2 Gives ex - er - cise to faith and love, Brings ev - 'ry bless-ing from a - bove.
3 And Sa - tan trem - bles when he sees The weak-est saint up - on his knees.
4 But when thro' wear - i - ness they fail'd, That mo - ment A - ma - lek pre-vail'd.
5 And fill your fel - low-crea-ture's ear With the sad tale of all your care.
6 Your cheer-ful song would oft - 'ner be: 'Hear what the Lord has done for me!'

601 Jesus, Thou Joy

BERNARD OF CLAIRVAUX   HEIRAPOLIS L.M.   SAMUEL WESLEY

1 Je - sus, Thou Joy of lov - ing hearts, Thou Fount of life, Thou Light of men !
2 Thy truth un-chang'd hath ev - er stood; Thou sa-vest those that on Thee call;
3 We taste Thee, O Thou liv - ing Bread ! And long to feast up - on Thee still;
4 Our rest - less spi - rits yearn for Thee Where-'er our change-ful lot is cast,
5 O Je - sus, ev - er with us stay ! Make all our mo-ments calm and bright;

1 From the best bliss that earth im - parts We turn un - fill'd to Thee a - gain.
2 To them that seek Thee Thou art good, To them that find Thee, all in all.
3 We drink of Thee, the Foun-tain-head, And thirst our souls from Thee to fill.
4 Glad when Thy gra-cious smile we see, Blest when our faith can hold Thee fast.
5 Chase the dark night of sin a - way; Shed o'er the world Thy ho - ly light.

BERNARD OF CLAIRVAUX   CROMER L.M.   J. A. LLOYD

1 Je - sus, Thou Joy of lov - ing hearts, Thou Fount of
2 Thy truth un - chang'd hath ev - er stood; Thou sa - vest
3 We taste Thee, O Thou liv - ing Bread ! And long to
4 Our rest - less spi - rits yearn for Thee Where - e'er our
5 O Je - sus, ev - er with us stay ! Make all our

1 life, Thou Light of men ! From the best bliss that
2 those that on Thee call; To them that seek Thee
3 feast up - on Thee still; We drink of Thee, the
4 change - ful lot is cast, Glad when Thy gra - cious
5 mo - ments calm and bright; Chase the dark night of

Jesus, Thou Joy—*Continued*

1 earth im - parts We turn un - fill'd to Thee a - gain.
2 Thou art good, To them that find Thee, all in all.
3 Foun - tain - head, And thirst our souls from Thee to fill.
4 smile we see, Blest when our faith can hold Thee fast.
5 sin a - way; Shed o'er the world Thy ho - ly light.

Bernard of Clairvaux   Hampstead L.M.   W. Smallwood

1 Je - sus, Thou joy of lov - ing hearts, Thou Fount of
2 Thy truth un - chang'd hath ev - er stood; Thou sa - vest
3 We taste Thee, O Thou liv - ing Bread! And long to
4 Our rest - less spi - rits yearn for Thee Where - 'er our
5 O Je - sus, ev - er with us stay! Make all our

1 life, Thou Light of men! From the best bliss that
2 those that on Thee call; To them that seek Thee
3 feast up - on Thee still; We drink of Thee, the
4 change - ful lot is cast, Glad when Thy gra - cious
5 mo - ments calm and bright; Chase the dark night of

1 earth im - parts We turn un - fill'd to Thee a - gain.
2 Thou art good, To them that find Thee, all in all.
3 Foun - tain - head, And thirst our souls from Thee to fill.
4 smile we see, Blest when our faith can hold Thee fast.
5 sin a - way; Shed o'er the world Thy ho - ly light.

602

Lord, Speak to Me

F. R. HAVERGAL   WINSCOTT L.M.   S. S. WESLEY

1 Lord, speak to me that I may speak In living
2 O lead me, Lord, that I may lead The wan-d'ring
3 O teach me, Lord, that I may teach The pre-cious
4 O give Thine own sweet rest to me! That I may
5 O fill me with Thy ful - ness, Lord! Un - til my
6 O use me, Lord; use ev - en me! Just as Thou

1 e - choes of Thy tone; As Thou hast sought, so
2 and the wav - 'ring feet! O feed me, Lord, that
3 things Thou dost im - part! And wing my words that
4 speak with sooth - ing pow'r A word in sea - son,
5 ve - ry heart o'er - flow In kind - ling thought and
6 wilt, and how, and where, Un - til Thy bless - ed

1 let me seek Thy err - ing chil - dren lost and lone.
2 I may feed Thy hun - g'ring ones with man - na sweet!
3 they may reach The hid - den depths of many a heart.
4 as from Thee, To wea - ry ones in need - ful hour.
5 glow - ing word, Thy love to tell, Thy praise to show.
6 face I see, Thy rest, Thy joy, Thy glo - ry share.

F. R. HAVERGAL   NE DERELINQUAS ME L.M.   CHARLES H. LLOYD

1 Lord, speak to me that I may speak In liv - ing
2 O lead me, Lord, that I may lead The wan - d'ring
3 O teach me, Lord, that I may teach The pre - cious
4 O give Thine own sweet rest to me! That I may
5 O fill me with Thy ful - ness, Lord! Un - til my
6 O use me, Lord; use ev - en me! Just as Thou

Lord, Speak to Me—*Continued*

1 e - choes of Thy tone; As Thou hast sought, so
2 and the wav - 'ring feet! O feed me, Lord, that
3 things Thou dost im - part! And wing my words that
4 speak with sooth - ing pow'r A word in sea - son,
5 ve - ry heart o'er - flow In kind - ling thought and
6 wilt, and how, and where, Un - til Thy bless - ed

1 let me seek Thy err - ing chil - dren lost and lone.
2 I may feed Thy hun - g'ring ones with man - na sweet!
3 they may reach The hid - den depths of many a heart.
4 as from Thee, To wea - ry ones in need - ful hour.
5 glow - ing word, Thy love to tell, Thy praise to show.
6 face I see, Thy rest, Thy joy, Thy glo - ry share.

Music by permission of SEELEY, SERVICE & CO., LTD.

F. R. HAVERGAL   LLEF L.M.   GRIFFITH H. JONES

1 Lord, speak to me that I may speak In liv - ing e - choes of Thy tone;
2 O lead me, Lord, that I may lead The wan-d'ring and the wav-'ring feet!
3 O teach me, Lord, that I may teach The pre-cious things Thou dost im - part!
4 O give Thine own sweet rest to me! That I may speak with sooth-ing pow'r
5 O fill me with Thy ful - ness, Lord! Un - til my ve - ry heart o'er - flow
6 O use me, Lord; use ev - en me! Just as Thou wilt, and how, and where,

1 As Thou hast sought, so let me seek Thy err - ing chil - dren lost and lone.
2 O feed me, Lord, that I may feed Thy hun-g'ring ones with man-na sweet!
3 And wing my words that they may reach The hid - den depths of many a heart.
4 A word in sea - son, as from Thee, To wea - ry ones in need - ful hour.
5 In kind-ling thought and glow-ing word, Thy love to tell, Thy praise to show.
6 Un - til Thy bless - ed face I see, Thy rest, Thy joy, Thy glo - ry share.

Music by permission of ALEX. MORRIS

603 Roll the Stone Away

E. E. PICKARD

E. E. PICKARD

1. Who shall roll the stone a-way? Who shall break the seal?
2. Who can lead the wea-ry soul To the Sa-viour's cross?
3. Who can ban-ish un-be-lief, As in prayer we bow?
4. Who can cleanse our sins a-way, By His pre-cious blood?
5. Who will come to Je-sus now? Now, this ver-y hour?

Who can drive the clouds a-way, Wound-ed hearts to heal?
Who can make us joy-ful-ly Count all else but loss?
Who can ope the si-lent lips? God can—here and now!
On-ly one can these things do— Christ, the son of God!
He will save you will-ing-ly, Keep you by His pow'r!

CHORUS. *Allegro.* *f*

On-ly God can lift the weight That keeps fast the glo-ry gate!

ff

Ev-en now, Lord, while we pray, Thou can'st roll the stones a-way!

604 Is your Name There?

M. A. K.

F. M. DAVIS

Is your name written there, On the page white and fair? In the book of His kingdom, Is your name written there?

605

Only a Sinner

JAMES M. GRAY

D. B. TOWNER

1. Naught have I got-ten but what I re-ceived; Grace hath bestow'd it since
2. Once, I was fool-ish, and sin ruled my heart, Caus-ing my foot-steps from
3. Tears un-a-vail-ing, no mer-it had I; Mer-cy had saved me, or
4. Suf-fer a sin-ner whose heart o-ver-flows, Lov-ing his Sa-viour, to

1. I have be-lieved; Boast-ing ex-clud-ed, pride I a-base; I'm
2. God to de-part; Je-sus hath found me, hap-py my case— I
3. else I must die; Sin had a-larm'd me, fear-ing God's face; But
4. tell what he knows; Once more to tell it, would I em-brace— I'm

CHORUS.

1. on-ly a sin-ner saved by grace!
2. now am a sin-ner saved by grace! } On-ly a sin-ner saved by grace!
3. now I'm a sin-ner saved by grace!
4. on-ly a sin-ner saved by grace!

On-ly a sin-ner saved by grace! This is my sto-ry— to

God be the glo-ry— I'm on-ly a sin-ner saved by grace!

606   I Love to Tell the Story

KATHERINE HANKEY   W. G. FISCHER

1. I love to tell the Sto - ry Of unseen things a - bove, Of Je - sus and His
2. I love to tell the Sto - ry! More won-der-ful it seems, Than all the gold-en
3. I love to tell the Sto - ry! 'Tis pleasant to re - peat What seems, each time I
4. I love to tell the Sto - ry! For those who know it best Seem hun-ger-ing and

1. glo - ry, Of Je - sus and His love! I love to tell the Sto - ry! Be-
2. fan - cies Of all our gold - en dreams, I love to tell the Sto - ry! It
3. tell it More won - der - ful - ly sweet. I love to tell the Sto - ry! For
4. thirsting To hear it, like the rest. And when, in scenes of glo - ry, I

1. cause I know it's true! It sat - is-fies my longings, As nothing else would do.
2. did so much for me! And that is just the rea-son I tell it now to thee.
3. some have nev-er heard The mes-sage of sal - va-tion From God's own Ho-ly Word.
4. sing the NEW, NEW SONG, 'Twill be—the OLD, OLD STORY That I have loved so long.

CHORUS.

I love to tell the Sto - ry! 'Twill be my theme in glo - ry,

To tell the Old, Old Sto - ry Of Je - sus and His love.

Words by permission of Dr. SYBIL TREMELLEN

607 He Rescued Me

L. S. L.

LIDA SHIVERS LEECH

1. I was a sin-ner, but now I'm free, His wondrous grace has res-cued me;
2. Once I was wayward, a-far would stray, His wondrous grace has res-cued me;
3. Once e-vil led me, but now God reigns, His wondrous grace has res-cued me;

1. Once I was blind, but now I see, A brand from the burning, He res-cued me.
2. Now I am on the "King's Highway," A brand from the burning, He set me free.
3. Bro-ken for e'er are sin's dark chains, A brand from the burning, He set me free.

CHORUS.

He res-cued me His own to be, A brand from the burning, He set me free;

Oh, how I'll praise Him thro' e-ter-ni-ty, A brand from the burning, He res-cued me.

608 Let us Hear you Tell it

J. M. W.

J. M. WHITE. *Arr.*

1. O, brother, have you told how the Lord for-gave? Let us hear you tell it o-ver once a-gain; Thy com-ing to the cross, where He died to save, Let us hear you tell it o-ver once a-gain. Are you walk-ing now in His bless-ed light? Are you cleansed from ev-'ry guilt-y stain? Is He your joy by day and your

2. When toil-ing up the way was the Sa-viour there? Let us hear you tell it o-ver once a-gain; Did Je-sus bear you up in His ten-der care? Let us hear you tell it o-ver once a-gain. Nev-er have you found such a friend as He Who can help you 'midst the toil and pain; O all the world should hear what He's

3. Was ev-er on your tongue such a bless-ed theme? Let us hear you tell it o-ver once a-gain; 'Tis ev-er sweeter far than the sweet-est dream, Let us hear you tell it o-ver once a-gain. There are ach-ing hearts in the world's great throng, Who have sought for rest, and all in vain; Hold Je-sus up to them by your

4. The bat-tles you have fought, and the vict-'ries won, Let us hear you tell it o-ver once a-gain; 'Twill help them on the way who have just be-gun, Let us hear you tell it o-ver once a-gain. We are striv-ing now with the hosts of sin, Soon with Christ our Sa-viour we shall reign; Ye ransomed of the Lord, try a

Let us Hear you Tell it —*Continued*.

1. song by night? Let us hear you tell it o - ver once a - gain.
2. done for thee? Let us hear you tell it o - ver once a - gain.
3. word and song; Let us hear you tell it o - ver once a - gain.
4. soul to win; Let us hear you tell it o - ver once a - gain.

CHORUS.

Let us hear you tell it o - ver,
Let us hear you tell it o - ver once a - gain.

tell it o - ver once a - gain,
tell it o - ver, tell it o - ver once a - gain,

Tell the sweet and bless - ed sto - ry, It will help you on to

glo - ry, Let us hear you tell it o - ver once a - gain.

609 Just a Word for Jesus

FANNY J. CROSBY   JUST A WORD   7.6.7.6.D   W. H. DOANE

1. Now just a word for Je - sus, Your dear - est friend so true; Come cheer our hearts and tell us What He has done for you.
2. Now just a word for Je - sus, You feel your sins for-giv'n, And by His grace are striv - ing To reach a home in heav'n.
3. Now just a word for Je - sus, A cross it can - not be To say I love my Sa - viour Who gave His life for me.
4. Now just a word for Je - sus, Let not the time be lost; The heart's ne - glect - ed du - ty Brings sor - row to its cost.
5. Now just a word for Je - sus, And if your faith be dim, A - rise in all your weak - ness, And leave the rest to Him.

REFRAIN.

Now just a word for Je - sus—'Twill help us on our way; One lit - tle word for Je - sus, O speak, or sing, or pray.

610 Jesus, the Shepherd

Leonard Weaver

M. E. Upham

1. I have a Shep-herd, One I love so well; How He has blessed me
2. Pas-tures a-bun-dant doth His hand pro-vide, Still wa-ters flow-ing
3. When I would wan-der from the path a-stray, Then He will draw me
4. When la-bour's end-ed and the jour-ney done, Then He will lead me

1. tongue can nev-er tell; On the cross He suf-fered, shed His blood and died,
2. ev-er at my side, Good-ness and mer-cy fol-low on my track,
3. back in-to the way; In the dark-est val-ley I need fear no ill,
4. safe-ly to my home; There I shall dwell in rap-ture sure and sweet,

CHORUS.

1. That I might ev-er in His love con-fide.
2. With such a Shep-herd nothing can I lack.
3. For He, my Shep-herd, will be with me still.
4. With all the loved ones gathered round His feet.

Fol-low-ing Je-sus, ev-er day by

day, Noth-ing can harm me when He leads the way; Dark-ness or

sun-shine, what-e'er be-fall, Je-sus, the Shepherd, is my All in All.

611 I'm Not Ashamed

ISAAC WATTS

R. E. HUDSON

1. I'm not ashamed to own my Lord, Or to defend His cause;
2. Jesus, my Lord! I know His name—His name is all my trust,
3. Firm as His throne His promise stands, And He can well secure
4. Then will He own my worth-less name Before His Father's face;

1. Maintain the honour of His Word, The glory of His cross.
2. Nor will He put my soul to shame, Nor let my hope be lost.
3. What I've committed to His hands, Till the decisive hour.
4. And, in the new Jerusalem, Appoint my soul a place.

CHORUS.

At the cross At the cross, where I first saw the light, And the burden of my heart roll'd away, roll'd away, It was there by faith I received my sight, And now I am happy all the day.

612   He threw out the Life=Line

J. E. F.   J. E. FRENCH

1. I was wrecked on a rock-y and des-o-late shore, Sinking
2. The bil-lows were dash-ing, the waves roll-ing high, No
3. When all was con-fus-ion 'midst dark bil-lows' roll, No
4. And now as I wan-der I sing as I go, His
5. Your sins like the bil-lows a-round you may rise, And

1. slow-ly be-neath the wild sea; When all of my struggles and
2. help from the land could I see, When hope had all vanished and
3. light thro' the gloom could I see, By trust-ing Him ful-ly He
4. mer-cy is bound-less and free, And tell the glad sto-ry, that
5. dan-gers your frail bark pur-sue, There's One who will heed you and

CHORUS.

1. ef-forts were o'er, Christ threw out the life-line to me.
2. dan-ger was nigh, Christ threw out the life-line to me.
3. res-cued my soul, Christ threw out the life-line to me.
4. others may know, Christ threw out the life-line to me.
5. hear your faint cries, He'll throw out the life-line to you.

He threw out the life-

line to me (to me), He threw out the life-line to me (to me). From

Cal-va-ry's tree, Far o-ver the sea, Christ threw out the life-line to me.

613   It was Jesus

JAMES ROWE   F. S. SHEPARD

1 My path was al-ways rough and drear, My soul was al-ways sad;
2 My soul was stain'd with ma-ny sins, I lived in fear and dread;
3 O wan-d'ring one in paths of sin, The Sa-viour calls to thee;

1 But now my path is smooth and bright, My soul for ev-er glad.
2 But now my soul is free from stain, And all my tears have fled.
3 He longs to give you peace and rest, From sin to set you free.

REFRAIN

It was Je - sus, my Sa - viour, Who wrought this change in me.
It was Je - sus Christ, my Sa - viour,

It was Je - sus my Sa - viour, Blest Lamb of Cal - va - ry.
It was Je - sus Christ, my Sa - viour.

I came to Him just as I was, From sin He set me free;

It was Jesus—*Continued*

It was Je - sus, my Sa - viour, Who wrought this change in me.
It was Je - sus Christ, my Sa - viour.

614   ## A Sinner Like Me!

C. J. BUTLER   BUTLER 10.8. 10.8   C. J. BUTLER

1 I was once far a - way from the Sa - viour, And as
2 I wan - der'd on in the dark - ness, Not a
3 And then, in that dark lone - ly hour, A
4 I list - en'd: and lo! 'twas the Sa - viour, That was
5 I then ful - ly trust - ed in Je - sus; And,

1 vile as a sin - ner could be; And I won - der'd f Christ the Re -
2 ray of light could I see; And the thought fill'd my heart with
3 voice sweet - ly whis - per'd to me, Say - ing, "Christ the Re - deem - er has
4 speak - ing so kind - ly to me; I cried: "I'm the chi - ef of
5 oh, what a joy came to me! My heart was fill'd with His

1 deem - er Could save a poor sin - ner like me.
2 sad - ness, There's no hope for a sin - ner like me.
3 pow - er To save a poor sin - ner like thee."
4 sin - ners, Thou canst save a poor sin - ner like me!"
5 prais - es For sav - ing a sin - ner like me.

615   He is so Precious to Me.

C. H. G.

CHAS. H. GABRIEL.

1. I'm hap-py in Je-sus, my Sa-viour, my King, And all the day
2. He stood at the door a-mid sun-shine and rain, So pa-tient-ly
3. I stand on the moun-tain of sun-shine at last, No cloud in the
4. I praise Him be-cause He ap-point-ed a place Where, some day, thro'

1. long of His good-ness I sing; To Him in my weak-ness I lov-ing-ly
2. wait-ing an en-trance to gain; What shame that so long He en-treat-ed in
3. hea-vens a sha-dow to cast; His smile is up-on me, the val-ley is
4. faith in His mar-vel-lous grace, My eyes shall be-hold Him, shall look on His

CHORUS.

1. cling, For He is so precious to me. . . . so
2. vain, For He is so precious to me. . . . } For He is so precious to
3. past, For He is so precious to me. . . .
4. face, For He is so precious to me. . . .

precious to me. so precious to me,
me, ... For He is so precious to me. . . . . 'Tis hea-ven be-

low My Re-deem-er to know, For He is so precious to me. . . .

616 O What a Change!

C. D. MARTIN

CHAS. H. GABRIEL

1 O what a change! From the dark-ness of night In - to the blaze of the
2 O what a change! From my hun-ger for bread In - to the place where God's
3 O what a change! From my bur-den of care In - to the love He in -
4 O what a change! In the flash of an eye, When we shall meet with our

1 clear shin-ing light; Out of my weak-ness to pow-er and might,
2 chil-dren are fed; In - to the bless-ing of life from the dead,
3 vites me to share In - to His joy from the sor-row I bear,
4 Lord by and by; In - to a realm where we nev-er shall die,

REFRAIN

1-4 O what a change! O what a change! O what a change in my

heart there has been, O what a change since the Sa-viour came in, O what a

change to be free from all sin, O what a change! O what a change!

617   Whom I have Believed

D. W. WHITTLE   JAMES McGRANAHAN

1 I know not why God's won-drous grace To me He hath made known,
2 I know not how this sav - ing faith To me He did im - part,
3 I know not how the Spi - rit moves, Con-vinc-ing men of sin,
4 I know not what of good or ill May be re-serv'd for me,
5 I know not when my Lord may come, At night or noon-day fair,

1 Nor why, un-worth-y of such love, He bought me for His own :
2 Nor how be-liev-ing in His word Wrought peace with-in my heart :
3 Re-veal-ing Je - sus through the Word, Cre-a-ting faith in Him :
4 Of wea-ry ways or gold-en days Be-fore His face I see :
5 Nor when I'll walk the vale with Him, Or meet Him in the air :

REFRAIN—*Fervente*

But 'I know whom I have be-liev-ed, And am per-suad-ed that He is a - ble

To keep that which I've com-mit-ted Un-to Him a-gainst that day.'

618

THOMAS SULLIVAN

He Made Me Whole

THOMAS SULLIVAN

1 To the feet of my Sa-viour in trem-bling, and fear, A pen-i-tent
2 I knew not the ten-der com-pas-sion and love That Je-sus, my
3 'My grace is suf-fi-cient,' I heard His dear voice, 'O come and find
4 O Je-sus, dear Je-sus, Thy Name I a-dore! For sav-ing and
5 O come, my dear bro-ther, He's wait-ing for you! Your sin-bur-den'd

1 sin-ner I came; He saw, and in mer-cy He bade me draw near; All
2 Sa-viour, had shown; Tho' bur-den'd with grief, His dear hand brought re-lief; He
3 rest for your soul! From sin you to save My life free-ly I gave; I
4 keep-ing my soul; Thy prais-es I'll sing, my Re-deem-er and King, Thy
5 heart to con-sole; Your wea-ry head rest on His dear, lov-ing breast; He

REFRAIN

1 glo-ry and praise to His Name.
2 heal'd me and call'd me His own.
3 died that you might be made whole.'
4 dear, lov-ing hand made me whole.
5 suf-fer'd and died for your soul.

He touch'd me and thus made me whole,
He touch'd me, He touch'd me and thus made me whole,

Bring-ing com-fort and rest to my soul; .... O glad hap-py day,
bring-ing rest to my soul:

all my sins roll'd a-way! For He touch'd me and thus made me whole.

made me whole.

619 The Promised Land

JOSHUA GILL   WM. J. KIRKPATRICK

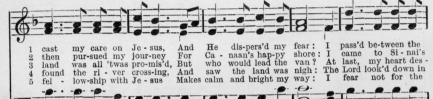

1 I fied from E - gypt's bond-age, I heard that help was near; I
2 I sang a song of tri - umph, I shout - ed o'er and o'er, And
3 The spies brought back their mess-age, Some wept, some said, 'We can'; The
4 Then, af - ter wear - y march-es, And many a long - ing sigh, I
5 And now my song of glad-ness I'm sing - ing day by day, For

1 cast my care on Je - sus, And He dis-pers'd my fear: I pass'd be-tween the
2 then pur-sued my jour-ney For Ca - naan's hap-py shore: I came to Si - nai's
3 land was all 'twas pro-mis'd, But who would lead the van? At last, my heart des-
4 found the ri - ver cross-ing, And saw the land was nigh: The Lord look'd down in
5 fel - low-ship with Je - sus Makes calm and bright my way: I fear not for the

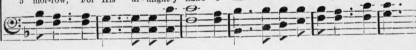

1 bil-lows, Wall'd up on ev - 'ry hand, I trust - ed to my Cap-tain, And sought
2 moun-tain, I trod the de - sert sand, I drank at Ho-reb's foun-tain, Seek - ing
3 pair-ing Of en - t'ring with this band, I cried a - loud to Je - sus, To show
4 mer - cy, By faith I touch'd His hand, I fol - low'd close be - side Him, And found
5 mor-row, For His al - might-y hand I know shall lead and keep me In this

REFRAIN

1-5 the pro-mis'd land. I am o - ver, yes o - ver On Ca-naan's shore I

stand; I am o - ver, yes, o - ver.... In the pro-mis'd land.

620   A Sinner Made Whole

W. M. Lighthall   Chas. H. Gabriel

1. There's a song in my heart that my lips can-not sing, 'Tis praise in the
2. I shall stand one day fault-less and pure by His throne, Transformed from my
3. All the mu-sic of hea-ven, so per-fect and sweet, Will blend with my

1. high-est to Je-sus my King; Its mu-sic each mo-ment is thrill-ing my soul,
2. im-age, conformed to His own; Then I shall find words for the song in my soul.
3. song, and will make it complete; Thro' a-ges un-end-ing the e-choes will roll.

CHORUS.

1. For I was a sin-ner, but Christ made me whole.
2. For I was a sin-ner, but Christ made me whole.
3. For I was a sin-ner, but Christ made me whole.

A sin-ner made whole! a

rit.

sinner made whole! The Saviour hath bought me and ransomed my soul! My heart it is

rit.

singing, the an-them is ringing, For I was a sinner, but Christ made me whole.

621 Speak Just a Word

E. C. Avis.

E. C. Avis.

1. Tell what the Lord has done for you, Speak just a word, speak just a word;
2. Ear - ly be - gin to bear the cross, Speak just a word, speak just a word;
3. Tell if the Lord has cleansed your sin, Speak just a word, speak just a word;
4. Fear not the world, nor heed its frown, Speak just a word, speak just a word;

1. Stand for the right, be brave and true, Speak just a word for Je - sus.
2. They who de - ny Him suf - fer loss, Speak just a word for Je - sus.
3. It may to Him some o - thers win, Speak just a word for Je - sus.
4. They who en - dure shall wear the crown, Speak just a word for Je - sus.

Refrain.

Speak just a word, speak just a word, Glad - ly His love pro - claim;

Tell what the Lord has done for you, Speak just a word for Je - sus.

622

O Happy Day!

P. DODDRIDGE

ENGLISH MELODY

1 O hap-py day that fix'd my choice On Thee, my Sa-viour and my God!
2 'Tis done, the great trans-ac-tion's done! I am my Lord's, and He is mine;
3 Now rest, my long di - vi-ded heart; Fix'd on this bliss - ful cen-tre, rest:
4 High heav'n that heard the sol-emn vow, That vow re-new'd shall dail - y hear

1 Well may this glow-ing heart re - joice, And tell its rap - tures all a - broad.
2 He drew me, and I fol-low'd on, Charm'd to con - fess the voice di - vine.
3 Nor ev - er from the Lord de - part, With Him of ev - 'ry good pos-sess'd.
4 Till in life's la - test hour I bow, And bless in death a bond so dear.

REFRAIN

Hap - py day! Hap - py day! When Je - sus wash'd my sins a - way;

He taught me how to watch and pray, And live re - joic - ing ev - 'ry day;

Hap - py day Hap - py day! When Je - sus wash'd my sins a - way.

623 The Miry Clay

H. L. GILMOUR

MIRY CLAY 9.9.9.8

H. L. GILMOUR

He brought me out of the mir - y clay, He set my
teet on the Rock to stay; He puts a song in my
soul to - day, A song of praise, Hal - le - lu - jah!

624 He Took My Sins Away

M. J. HARRIS

M. J. HARRIS

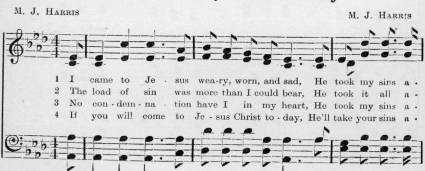

1 I came to Je - sus wea-ry, worn, and sad, He took my sins a -
2 The load of sin was more than I could bear, He took it all a -
3 No con - dem - na - tion have I in my heart, He took my sins a -
4 If you will come to Je - sus Christ to - day, He'll take your sins a -

He Took My Sins Away—*Continued*

1 way, He took my sins away; His wondrous love has
2 way, He took it all away; And now on Him I
3 way, And keeps me day by day; His perfect peace He
4 way, He'll take your sins away; And keep you happy

1 made my heart so glad, He took my sins away.
2 roll my ev'ry care, He took my sins away.
3 did to me impart, He took my sins away.
4 in the narrow way, He'll take your sins away.

REFRAIN

He took my sins away, He took my sins away, And

keeps my foot-steps day by day; I'm so glad He

sav'd my guilty soul, And took my sins away.

625 Ten Thousand Voices

H. W. Fox

JUBILEE 9.8.9.8.D

J. H. MAUNDER

1 I hear ten thous-and voi-ces sing-ing Their prais-es to the Lord on high;
2 On China's shores I hear His prais-es From lips that once kiss'd i-dol stones;
3 The song has soun-ded o'er the wa-ters, And In-dia's plains re-e-cho joy;

1 Far dis-tant shores and hills are ring-ing With an-thems of their na-tions' joy:
2 Soon as His ban-ner He up-rais-es, The Spi-rit moves the breath-less bones;
3 Be-neath the moon sit In-dia's daughters, Soft sing-ing, as the wheel they ply,

1 'Praise ye the Lord! for He has giv-en To lands in dark-ness hid His light;
2 'Speed, speed Thy word o'er land and o-cean; The Lord in tri-umph has gone forth:
3 'Thanks to Thee, Lord! for hopes of glo-ry, For peace on earth to us re-veal'd;

ORG.

1 As morn-ing rays light up the hea-ven, His word has chas'd a-way our night.'
2 The na-tions hear with strange e-mo-tion, From East to West, from South to North.'
3 Our cher-ish'd i-dols fell be-fore Thee, Thy Spi-rit has our par-don seal'd.'

By permission of the LONDON MISSIONARY SOCIETY

626

From Pole to Pole

REGINALD HEBER MISSIONARY 7.6.7.6.D LOWELL MASON

1 From Green-land's i - cy moun-tains, From In - dia's cor - al strand,
2 What though the spi - cy breez - es Blow soft o'er Cey-lon's isle,
3 Can we, whose souls are ligh - ted With wis - dom from on high,
4 Waft, waft, ye winds, His sto - ry, And you, ye wa - ters, roll,

1 Where A - fric's sun - ny foun - tains Roll down their gold - en sand,
2 Though ev - 'ry pros - pect pleas - es, And on - ly man is vile;
3 Can we to men be - nigh - ted The lamp of life de - ny?
4 Till, like a sea of glo - ry, It spreads from pole to pole;

1 From many an an - cient ri - ver, From many a pal - my plain,
2 In vain with lav - ish kind - ness The gifts of God are strewn,
3 Sal - va - tion! O Sal - va - tion! The joy - ful sound pro - claim,
4 Till o'er our ran-som'd na - ture The Lamb for sin - ners slain,

1 They call us to de - li - ver Their land from er - ror's chain.
2 The hea - then, in his blind - ness, Bows down to wood and stone.
3 Till each re - mo - test na - tion Has learnt Mes - si - ah's Name.
4 Re - deem - er, King, Cre - a - tor, In bliss re - turns to reign.

The tune GREENLAND is on the following page

626 From Pole to Pole

Reginald Heber   GREENLAND 7.6.7.6.D   J. M. Haydn

1 From Green-land's i - cy moun-tains, From In - dia's cor - al strand,
2 What though the spi - cy breez - es Blow soft o'er Cey - lon's isle,
3 Can we, whose souls are ligh - ted With wis - dom from on high,
4 Waft, waft, ye winds, His sto - ry, And you, ye wa - ters, roll,

1 Where A - fric's sun - ny foun - tains Roll down their gold - en sand,
2 Though ev - 'ry pros-pect pleas - es, And on - ly man is vile;
3 Can we to men be - nigh - ted The lamp of life de - ny?
4 Till, like a sea of glo - ry, It spreads from pole to pole;

1 From many an an - cient ri - ver, From many a pal - my plain,
2 In vain with lav - ish kind - ness The gifts of God are strewn,
3 Sal - va - tion! O Sal - va - tion! The joy - ful sound pro - claim,
4 Till o'er our ran - som'd na - ture The Lamb for sin - ners slain,

1 They call us to de - li - ver Their land from er - ror's chain.
2 The hea - then, in his blind - ness, Bows down to wood and stone.
3 Till each re - mo - test na - tion Has learnt Mes - si - ah's Name.
4 Re - deem - er, King, Cre - a - tor, In bliss re - turns to reign.

The tune MISSIONARY is on the previous page

627

Tell Them the Story

W. C. POOLE   ANNA G. LAMBERT

1 Ov - er the moun-tains so bleak and so cold, Far from the
2 Lost ones are grop - ing in sin's aw - ful night, Fall - ing and
3 Speed with the mess - age, O speed in His Name! Hast - en the

1 beau - ti - ful cit - y of gold; Lost ones are stray - ing be -
2 dy - ing a - way from the right; Man - y the mes - sage of
3 sto - ry of Christ to pro - claim! Hast - en to bring back the

1 cause you and I Nev - er have told them a Sa - viour stood nigh.
2 Christ nev - er heard, Lost ones for whom no one ev - er has cared.
3 fall - en and lost! Speed with the mes - sage, what-ev - er the cost!

REFRAIN

O wont some-bod - y tell them! Tell them of Cal - va - ry's tree;

Tell them the sto - ry of Je - sus, What a great Sa - viour is He.

628 Send the Light!

CHARLES H. GABRIEL

CHARLES H. GABRIEL

1 There's a call comes ring - ing o'er the rest - less wave,
2 We have heard the Ma - ce - do - nian call to - day,
3 Let us pray that grace may ev - 'ry - where a - bound,
4 Let us not grow wea - ry in the work of love,

1 Send the light! . . . Send the light!
2 Send the light! . . . Send the light! . . .
3 Send the light! . . . Send the light!
4 Send the light! . . . Send the light!

. . . Send the light! . . . Send the light!

1 There are souls to res - cue, there are souls to save,
2 And a gold - en off - 'ring at the Cross we lay,
3 And a Christ - like spi - rit ev - 'ry - where be found,
4 Let us ga - ther jew - els for a crown a - bove,

1-4 Send the light! . . . Send the light! . . .

. . . Send the light! . . . Send the light!

Send the Light!—*Continued*

Send the light, . . the bless - ed gos . pel . light!
. . . . Send the light, . the . bless - ed gos - pel light!

Let it shine . . . from shore to shore! . . . .
. . Let it shine . . . . . from shore to shore!

Send the light! . . . and let its ra - diant beams
. , . Send the light! and . let its ra - diant beams

Light the world . . . for ev - er - more. . . . .
. . Light the world . . . . . for ev - er - more.

629 Blow Ye the Trumpet

CHARLES WESLEY   LENOX 6.6.6.6.8.8.8   LEWIS EDSON

1 Blow ye the trum - pet, blow The glad - ly sol - emn sound;
2 Je - sus, our great high priest, Has full a - tone - ment made,
3 Ex - alt the Lamb of God, The sin a - ton - ing Lamb,

1 Let all the na - tions know, To earth's re - mot - est bound;
2 Ye wea - ry spi - rits rest, Ye mourn - ing souls be glad;
3 Re - demp - tion by His blood Through all the world pro - claim;

1 The year of ju - bi - lee is come, The year of ju -
2 The year of ju - bi - lee is come, The year of ju -
3 The year of ju - bi - lee is come The year of ju -

1 bi - lee is come, Re turn, ye ran - som'd sin - ners, home.
2 bi - lee is come, Re - turn, ye ran - som'd sin - ners, home.
3 bi - lee is come, Re - turn ye ran - som'd sin - ners, home.

The tune WARSAW is on the following page

629
Blow Ye the Trumpet

CHARLES WESLEY   WARSAW 6.6.6.6.8.8   THOMAS CLARK

1 Blow ye the trum - pet, blow The glad - ly sol - emn
2 Je - sus, our great high priest, Has full a - tone - ment
3 Ex - alt the Lamb of God, The sin a - ton - ing

1 sound; Let all the na - tions know, To earth's
2 made, Ye wea - ry spi - rits rest, Ye mourn -
3 Lamb, Re - demp - tion by His blood Through all

1 re - mot - est bound; The year of ju - bi - lee is
2 ing souls be glad; The year of ju - bi - lee is
3 the world pro - claim; The year of ju - bi - lee is

1 come, Re - turn, ye ran - som'd sin - ners, home.
2 come, Re - turn, ye ran - som'd sin - ners, home.
3 come, Re - turn, ye ran - som'd sin - ners, home.

The tune LENOX is on the preceding page

630
Coming, Coming!

J Wakefield Macgill   Lucknow 7. 7. 8. 7. 8. 7   E. Husband

1-6 Com-ing, com-ing, yes, they are! Com-ing, com-ing from a - far,

1 From the wild and scorch-ing des - ert Af - ric's sons of col - our deep;
2 From the fields and crowd - ed cit - ies Chi - na ga - thers to His feet;
3 From the In - dus and the Gan - ges Stea - dy flows the liv - ing stream,
4 From the steppes of Rus - sia drear - y, From Sla - von - ia's scat-ter'd lands,
5 From the fro - zen realms of mid-night, O - ver many a wear - y mile
6 All to meet in plains of glo - ry, All to sing His prais - es sweet;

1 Je - su's love has drawn and won them, At His Cross they bow and weep.
2 In His love Shem's gen - tle chil - dren Now have found a safe re - treat.
3 To love's o - cean, to His bos - om, Cal - va - ry their won-d'ring theme.
4 They are yield - ing soul and spir - it In - to Je - su's lov - ing hands.
5 To ex-change their soul's long-win-ter For the sum-mer of His smile.
6 What a cho - rus! what a meet-ing With the fam - i - ly com - plete!

631
The Straying Sheep

E. M. H. Gates   Robert Lowry

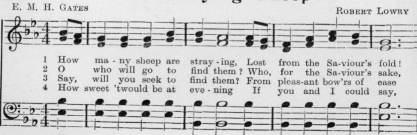

1 How ma - ny sheep are stray - ing, Lost from the Sa-viour's fold!
2 O who will go to find them? Who, for the Sa-viour's sake,
3 Say, will you seek to find them? From pleas-ant bow'rs of ease
4 How sweet 'twould be at eve - ning If you and I could say,

The Straying Sheep—*Continued*

632 Some One Shall Go

SARAH G. STOCK   SARAH G. STOCK

1 Some one shall go at the Mas-ter's word   O-ver the seas to the
2 Some one shall ga-ther the sheaves for Him,   Some one shall bind them with
3 Some one shall tra-vel with ea-ger feet   O-ver the moun-tain and
4 Some one shall car-ry His ban-ner high,   Wav-ing it out where the

1 lands a-far,   Tell-ing to those who have   nev-er heard What His
2 joy-ful hand: Some one shall toil through the   sha-dows dim, For the
3 through the wild,   Bring-ing the news of re-   demp-tion sweet To each
4 foe holds sway,   Some in His ser-vice shall   live and die, And with

1 won-der-ful mer-cies   are.   Shall it be you— Shall it be I—Who shall
2 morn in the heav'n-ly   land.   Shall it be you— Shall it be I—Who shall
3 wan-der-ing sin-ful   child.   Shall it be you— Shall it be I—Who shall
4 Je-sus shall win the   day!   Shall it be you— Shall it be I—Who His

1 haste to tell what we   know so well? Shall you?   Shall   I?
2 bind the corn for the   gol-den morn? Shall you?   Shall   I?
3 sound the tale o-ver   hill and dale? Shall you?   Shall   I?
4 Name shall bear, and His   tri-umph share? Shall you?   Shall   I?

Speed Away!

633

JULIA STERLING   L. B. WOODBURY (*Arr.*)

1 Speed a - way! speed a - way on your mis - sion of light,
2 Speed a - way! speed a - way with the life - giv - ing Word,
3 Speed a - way! speed a - way with the mes - sage of rest,

1 To the lands that are ly - ing in dark - ness and night; 'Tis the
2 To the na - tions that know not the voice of the Lord; Take the
3 To the souls by the temp - ter in bon - dage op - prest; For the

1 Mas - ter's com-mand: go ye forth in His Name, The won - der - ful
2 wings of the morn - ing and fly o'er the wave, In the strength of your
3 Sa - viour has pur-chas'd their ran - som from sin. And the ban - quet is

1 Gos - pel of Je - sus pro - claim. Take your lives in your hand, to the
2 Mas - ter the lost ones to save. He is call - ing once more— not a
3 rea - dy: O ga - ther them in! To the res - cue make haste, there's no

1 work while 'tis day, ⎫
2 mo - ment's de - lay! ⎬ Speed a - way! speed a - way! speed a - way!
3 time for de - lay, ⎭

634   # Far, Far Away

JAMES McGRANAHAN   FAR AWAY   JAMES McGRANAHAN

1 Far, far a-way, in hea-then dark-ness dwell-ing,
2 See o'er the world wide o-pen doors in-vit-ing:
3 Why will ye die? the voice of God is call-ing,
4 God speed the day when those of ev-'ry na-tion

1 Mill-ions of souls for ev-er may be lost;
2 Sol-diers of Christ, a-rise and en-ter in;
3 Why will ye die? re-ech-o in His name;
4 Glo-ry to God tri-umph-ant-ly shall sing;

1 Who, who will go? sal-va-tion's sto-ry tell-ing,
2 Christ-ians, a-wake! your for-ces all u-nit-ing,
3 Je-sus hath died to save from death ap-pall-ing;
4 Ran-somed, re-deemed, re-joic-ing in sal-va-tion,

Far, Far Away—*Continued*

1 Look - ing to Je - sus, count - ing not the cost.
2 Send forth the gos - pel, break the chains of sin.
3 Life and sal - va - tion there - fore go pro - claim.
4 Shout Hal - le - lu - jah, for the Lord is King!

REFRAIN

All power is giv - en un - to Me; All power is

giv - en un - to Me; Go ye in - to all the world and

preach the gos - pel; And lo, am with you al - way.

635 Where You want Me to Go

MARY BROWN

CARRIE E. ROUNSEFELL

1 It may not be on the moun-tain's height, Or o - ver the storm - y sea; .
2 Per - haps to - day there are lov - ing words Which Je - sus would have me speak; .
3 There's sure - ly some-where a low - ly place In earth's har-vest fields so wide; .

1 It may not be at the bat - tle's front My Lord will have need of me; . But
2 There may be now in the paths of sin Some wan-d'rer whom I should seek; . O
3 Where I may la-bour thro' life's short day For Je - sus the cru - ci - fied; . So

1 if by a still, small voice He calls To paths that I do not know, . I'll
2 Sa - viour, if Thou wilt be my guide, Tho' dark and rug-ged . the way, . My
3 trust - ing my all to Thy ten - der care, And know-ing Thou lov - est me. . I'll

Where You want Me to Go—*Continued*

1 an-swer, dear Lord, with my hand . in Thine, I'll go where you want me to go. .
2 voice . shall ech - o the mes - sage sweet, I'll say what you want me to say. .
3 do Thy will with a heart . sin - cere, I'll be what you want me to be. .

REFRAIN

I'll go where you want me to go, dear Lord, O - ver moun - tain or

plain . or sea: . I'll say what you want me to

say, . dear Lord, I'll be what you want me to be. .

636 A Story for the Nations

Colin Sterne   H. Ernest Nichol

Unison

1 We've a sto - ry to tell to the na - tions That shall turn their
2 We've a song to be sung to the na - tions That shall lift their
3 We've a mes - sage to give to the na - tions That the Lord who
4 We've a Sa - viour to show to the na - tions, Who the path of

1 hearts to the right; . . A sto - ry of truth and sweet - ness, A
2 hearts to the Lord; . A song that shall con - quer e - vil, And
3 reign - eth a - bove . . Hath sent us His Son to save us, And
4 sor - row has trod, . . That all of the world's great peo - ples Might

1 sto - ry of peace and light, . A sto - ry of peace and light:
2 shat - ter the spear and sword, . And shat - ter the spear and sword:
3 show us that God is love, . And show us that God is love:
4 come to the truth of God, . Might come to the truth of God:

A Story for the Nations—*Continued*

REFRAIN

Harmony

For the dark-ness shall turn **to** dawn-ing, And the dawn-ing to

noon-day bright, . And Christ's great king-dom shall come on earth, The

Unison

king-dom of Love and Light; **For** the dark-ness shall turn to

Harmony

dawn-ing, And the dawn-ing to noon-day bright, . And

rall.

Christ's great king-dom shall come on earth, The king-dom of Love and Light.

By permission of H. E. NICHOL & SONS

637 Hear the Wail

J. WAKEFIELD MACGILL   LAMENT—7.7.7.8   *Arr.* ELLA MACGILL

1 Hear the wail a-cross the sea, Comes from mil-lions
2 Wail-ing of the pro-phet cursed, Of fan-a-tics,
3 Wail-ings reach this fav-oured shore, Wail-ings ceas-ing

1 un-to thee— Wea-ry ones who might be free Did they but
2 wild-est, worst, Help us, Lord, their chains to burst, And set them
3 nev-er-more; Men are dy-ing ev-er-more; Go, tell them

REFRAIN

1 know of Cal-va-ry.
2 free by Cal-va-ry. } Wail-ing, wail-ing o'er the sea;
3 all of Cal-va-ry!

Wail-ing, wail-ing un-to thee; Wail-ing, wail-ing

to be free; Go, tell them all of Cal-va-ry!

638 The Call for Reapers

J. O. Thompson REAPERS 8.7.8.7. D J. B. O. Clemm

1 Far and near the fields are teem-ing With the waves of
2 Send them forth with morn's first beam-ing, Send them in the
3 O thou, whom thy Lord is send-ing, Gath-er now the

1 ri-pen'd grain; Far and near their gold is gleam-ing O'er the
2 noon-tide's glare; When the sun's last rays are gleam-ing Bid them
3 sheaves of gold! Heav'n-ward then at ev-'ning wend-ing Thou shalt

REFRAIN

1 sun-ny slope and plain.
2 gath-er ev-'ry-where. } Lord of har-vest, send forth
3 come with joy un-told.

reap-ers! Hear us, Lord, to Thee we cry! Send them now the

sheaves to gath-er, Ere the har-vest time pass by!

The tunes ST. AMBROSE and SALVATOR are overleaf

638 The Call for Reapers

J. O. THOMPSON   ST. AMBROSE (CECIL) 8.7.8.7. D.   RICHARD CECIL

1 Far and near the fields are teem-ing With the waves of
2 Send them forth with morn's first beam-ing, Send them in the
3 O thou, whom thy Lord is send-ing, Gath-er now the

1 ri-pen'd grain; Far and near their gold is gleam-ing O'er the
2 noon-tide's glare; When the sun's last rays are gleam-ing Bid them
3 sheaves of gold! Heav'n-ward then at ev-'ning wend-ing Thou shalt

REFRAIN

1 sun-ny slope and plain.
2 gath-er ev-'ry-where. } Lord of har-vest, send forth
3 come with joy un-told,

reap-ers! Hear us, Lord, to Thee we cry! Send them now the

sheaves to gath-er, Ere the har-vest time pass by!

The tune REAPERS is on the preceding page and SALVATOR on the following page

638 The Call for Reapers

J. O. THOMPSON   SALVATOR 8.7.8.7.D.   JAMES P. JEWSON

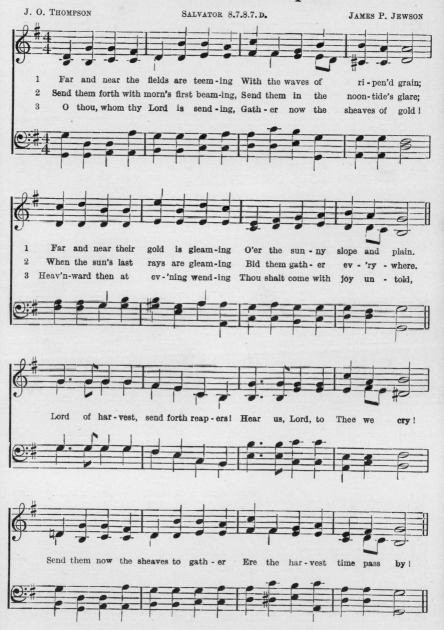

1 Far and near the fields are teem-ing With the waves of ri-pen'd grain;
2 Send them forth with morn's first beam-ing, Send them in the noon-tide's glare;
3 O thou, whom thy Lord is send-ing, Gath-er now the sheaves of gold!

1 Far and near their gold is gleam-ing O'er the sun-ny slope and plain.
2 When the sun's last rays are gleam-ing Bid them gath-er ev-'ry-where.
3 Heav'n-ward then at ev-'ning wend-ing Thou shalt come with joy un-told,

Lord of har-vest, send forth reap-ers! Hear us, Lord, to Thee we cry!

Send them now the sheaves to gath-er Ere the har-vest time pass by!

The tunes REAPERS and ST. AMBROSE are on the preceding pages

639 Where are the Reapers?

EBENEZER E. REXFORD   HARVEST HOME P.M.   GEORGE F. ROOT

1. O where are the reap-ers that gar-ner in The sheaves of the good from the fields of sin! With sic-kles of truth must the work be done, And no one may rest till the har-vest home.

2. Go out in the bye-ways and search them all; The wheat may be there, though the weeds are tall; Then search in the high-way and pass none by, But ga-ther from all for the home on high.

3. The fields are all rip'n-ing, and far and wide The world is a-wait-ing the har-vest tide; But reap-ers are few and the work is great, And much will be lost should the har-vest wait.

4. So come with your sic-kles, ye sons of men, And ga-ther to-geth-er the gold-en grain; Toil on till the Lord of the har-vest come, Then share in the joy of the har-vest home.

REFRAIN

Where are the reap-ers? O who will come And share in the glo-ry of the har-vest home! O who will help us to

Where are the Reapers ?—*Continued*

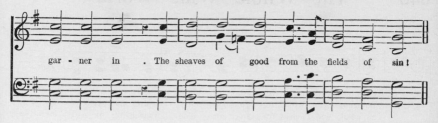

gar-ner in . The sheaves of good from the fields of sin!

In the following tune the REFRAIN appears as verse 5

EBENEZER E. REXFORD   DATCHET 11.11.11.11.   GEORGE J. ELVEY

1 O where are the reap-ers that gar-ner in The sheaves of the
2 Go out in the bye-ways and search them all; The wheat may be
3 The fields are all rip'n-ing, and far and wide The world is a-
4 So come with your sic-kles, ye sons of men, And ga-ther to-
5 O where are the reap-ers! O who will come and share in the

1 good from the fields of sin! With sic-kles of truth must the
2 there, tho' the weeds are tall; Then search in the high-way and
3 wait-ing the har-vest tide; But reap-ers are few and the
4 geth-er the gold-en grain; Toil on till the Lord of the
5 glo-ry of the har-vest home! O who will help us to

1 work be done, And no one may rest till the har-vest home.
2 pass none by, But ga-ther from all for the home on high.
3 work is great, And much will be lost should the har-vest wait.
4 har-vest come, Then share in the joy of the har-vest home.
5 gar-ner in The sheaves of good from the fields of sin!

640   The Whole Wide World

Cath. Johnson   J. H. Maunder

1 The whole wide world for Je - sus— This shall our watch-word be
2 The whole wide world for Je - sus, In - spires us with the thought
3 The whole wide world for Je - sus— The march-ing or - der sound—
4 The whole wide world for Je - sus— In the Fa - ther's house a - bove

1 Up - on the high - est moun-tain, Down by the wi - dest sea—
2 That ev - 'ry son of A - dam Should by His blood be bought;
3 Go ye and preach the Gos - pel Wher - e - ver man is found,
4 Are ma - ny won - drous man-sions— Man - sions of light and love;

1 The whole wide world for Je - sus! To Him all men shall bow,
2 The whole wide world for Je - sus! O faint not by the way!
3 The whole wide world for Je - sus! Our ban - ner is un - furl'd—
4 The whole wide world for Je - sus! Ride forth, O conq-'ring King!

1 In ci - ty or in prai - rie— The world for Je - sus now!
2 The Cross shall sure - ly con - quer In this our glo - rious day.
3 We bat - tle now for Je - sus, And faith de-mands the world!
4 Thro' all the migh-ty na - tions The world to glo - ry bring.

The Whole Wide World—*Continued*

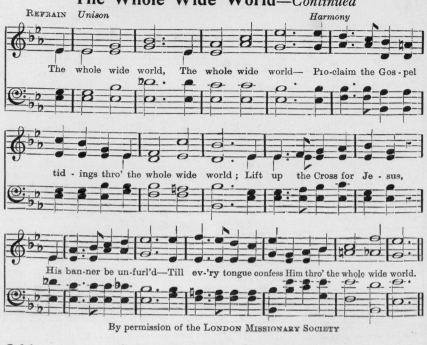

The whole wide world, The whole wide world— Pro-claim the Gos-pel tid-ings thro' the whole wide world; Lift up the Cross for Je-sus, His ban-ner be un-furl'd—Till ev-'ry tongue confess Him thro' the whole wide world.

By permission of the LONDON MISSIONARY SOCIETY

641 Our Saviour's Voice

E. PARSON   EVAN C.M.   W. H. HAVERGAL

1 Our Sa-viour's voice is soft and sweet When, bend-ing from a-bove, He bids us ga-ther round His feet, And calls us by His love,
2 But while our thank-ful hearts re-joice That thus He bids us come, "Je-sus!" we cry with plead-ing voice, "Bring hea-then wan-d'rers home."
3 They ne-ver heard the Sa-viour's Name, They have not learn'd His way; They do not know His grace who came To take their sins a-way.
4 Dear Sa-viour, let the joy-ful sound In dis-tant lands be heard; And, oh! wher-e-ver sin is found, Send forth Thy pard-'ning word.
5 And if our lips may breathe a pray'r, Tho' rais'd in trem-bling fear, O let Thy grace our hearts pre-pare! And choose some her-alds here.

Tell it Out!

F. R. HAVERGAL   F. R. HAVERGAL

1 Tell it out a-mong the hea-then that the Lord is King! Tell it
2 Tell it out a-mong the hea-then that the Sa - viour reigns! Tell it
3 Tell it out a-mong the hea-then, Je - sus reigns a - bove! Tell it

Tell it out!   Tell it out!   Tell it

1 out!   Tell it out!   Tell it out a-mong the nations, bid them
2 out!   Tell it out!   Tell it out a-mong the nations, bid them
3 out!   Tell it out!   Tell it out a-mong the nations that He

Tell it out! . . .

out! . . . . . . Tell it out! Tell it out! Tell it out!

1 shout and sing! Tell it out!   Tell it out! Tell it
2 burst their chains! Tell it out!   Tell it out! Tell it
3 reigns in love! Tell it out!   Tell it out! Tell it

Tell it out!

Tell . . . . it out! Tell it

1 out with a - do - ra - tion that He shall in - crease, That the migh-ty King of
2 out a-mong the weep-ing ones that Je - sus lives; Tell it out a - mong the
3 out a-mong the high-ways and the lanes at home; Let it ring a - cross the

out! . . . .

out! . . . .

Tell it Out!—*Continued*

1 Glo - ry is the King of Peace; Tell it out with ju - bi - la - tion, tho' the
2 wea - ry ones what rest He gives; Tell it out a - mong the sin - ners that He
3 moun - tains and the o - cean foam! Like the sound of ma - ny wa - ters let our

1 waves may roar, That He sit - teth on the wa - ter-floods, our King for e - ver-more!
2 came to save; Tell it out a - mong the dy - ing that He triumph'd o'er the grave!
3 glad shout be, Till it e - cho and re - e - cho from the is - lands of the sea!

REFRAIN

Tell it out a - mong the hea-then that the Lord is King! Tell it

Tell it out! Tell it out! Tell it

out! Tell it out! Tell it out a - mong the

Tell it out! . . . . Tell it out!

out! . . . . Tell it out! Tell it out! Tell it

na - tions, bid them shout and sing! Tell it out! Tell it out!

Tell it out!

out! Tell . . . it out!

643 Harvest-Fields

BIRDIE BELL

WILLIAM J. KIRKPATRICK

1 Har-vest-fields are wait-ing, White the wav-ing grain; Christ the Mas-ter
2 Har-vest-fields are wait-ing, Do not lin-ger long; Borne up-on the
3 Har-vest-fields are wait-ing, Who will come to-day, Join the band of

1 call-eth, Soon the day will wane: Hast-en at His bid-ding,
2 bree-zes Comes the rea-per's song: Pa-tient-ly, O toil-er,
3 rea-pers, Bear the sheaves a-way? Soon the day of toil-ing

1 Join the rea-per band; Help them at their la-bour, Work with will-ing hand.
2 Pluck the gold-en grain Ere the shades of ev-'ning Fall o'er hill and plain.
3 Will be ev-er past; May the Mas-ter's greet-ing Be, Well done! at last.

REFRAIN

Har . . . . vest fields are wait . . . ing, . .
Har-vest-fields are wait-ing, . . Har-vest-fields are wait-ing,

La . . . . bour while you may; . . . . Time . . .
La-bour while you may, . La-bour while you may: Time is swift-ly

Harvest Fields—*Continued*

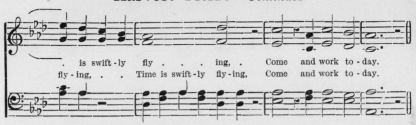

. is swift-ly fly . . . ing, . Come and work to - day.
fly-ing, . . Time is swift-ly fly-ing, Come and work to - day.

644   Let the Song

SARAH G. STOCK   MOEL LLYS 7.5.7.5.7.7.   SARAH G. STOCK

1 Let the song go round the earth,   Je - sus Christ is   Lord!
2 Let the song go round the earth   From the east - ern   sea,
3 Let the song go round the earth;   Lands, where Is - lam's sway
4 Let the song go round the earth   Where the sum - mer smiles;
5 Let the song go round the earth,   Je - sus Christ is   King!

1 Sound His prais - es, tell His worth,   Be His name a - dored; .
2 Where the day - light has its birth,   Glad and bright and   free; .
3 Dark - ly broods o'er home and hearth,   Cast their bonds a - way: .
4 Let the notes of ho - ly mirth   Break from dis - tant   isles; .
5 With the sto - ry of His worth   Let the whole world   ring

1 Ev - 'ry clime and ev - 'ry tongue   Join the grand, the glo - rious song.
2 Chi - na's mill - ions join the strains, Waft them on to In - dia's plains.
3 Let His praise from Af - ric's shore Rise and swell her wide lands o'er.
4 In - land for - ests dark and dim, Snow-bound coasts give back the hymn.
5 Him cre - a - tion all a - dore Ev - er - more and ev - er - more,

645

The Golden Fields

Fanny J. Crosby

Wm. J. Kirkpatrick

1 Lo ! the gol - den fields are smil - ing, Where - fore
2 Take the balm of con - so - la - tion That so
3 Go and ga - ther souls for Je - sus ! Pre - cious
4 Go, then, work, the Mas - ter call - eth ! Go, no

1 i - dle shouldst thou be ? Great the har-vest, few the wor - kers,
2 oft has cheer'd thy heart ; Let some wea - ry bro - ther toil - er
3 souls thy love may win ; Lead them to the door of mer - cy ;
4 long - er i - dle be ! Waste no more thy pre-cious mo - ments,

1 And the Lord hath need of thee ; Go and
2 In thy com - fort share a part : Go and
3 Tell them how to en - ter in : Go and
4 For the Lord hath need of thee : Once He

1 work, the time is wan - ing, Let thy ear-nest heart re - ply
2 lift the hea-vy bur - den He has strug-gled long to bear,
3 ga - ther souls for Je - sus, Work while strength and breath re - main ;
4 gave His life thy ran - som, That thy soul with Him might live :

The Golden Fields—*Continued*

ad lib.

1 To the call so oft re-peat-ed, 'Bless-ed
2 Go, and kneel-ing down be-side Him, Blend thy
3 What are years of con-stant la-bour To the
4 Now the ser-vice He de-man-deth Can thy

REFRAIN

1 Mas-ter, here am I.'
2 faith with his in pray'r.
3 joy thou yet shalt gain?
4 heart re-fuse to give?

Hark! the song, the song of bus-y

wor-kers In the fields so fair to see; Go and fill thy place a-

mong them, For the Lord hath need of thee.

646   Jesus Shall Reign

ISAAC WATTS   DUKE STREET L.M.   JOHN HATTON

1 Jesus shall reign wher-e'er the sun Does his suc-ces-sive jour-neys run; His king-dom spread from shore to shore, Till moons shall wax and wane no more.

2 To Him shall end-less pray'r be made, And end-less prais-es crown His head; His Name like sweet per-fume shall rise With ev-'ry morn-ing sac-ri-fice.

3 Peo-ple and realms of ev-'ry tongue Dwell on His love with sweet-est song; And in-fant voi-ces shall pro-claim Their ear-ly bless-ings on His Name.

4 Bless-ings a-bound wher-e'er He reigns; The pris-'ner leaps to lose his chains; The wea-ry find e-ter-nal rest, And all the sons of want are blest.

5 Let ev-'ry crea-ture rise and bring Pe-cu-liar hon-ours to our King; An-gels de-scend with songs a-gain, And earth re-peat the loud A-men!

ISAAC WATTS   RIMINGTON L.M.   FRANCIS DUCKWORTH

1 Je-sus shall reign wher-e'er the sun Does his suc-ces-sive jour-neys run;

2 To Him shall end-less pray'r be made, And end-less prais-es crown His head;

3 Peo-ple and realms of ev-'ry tongue Dwell on His love with sweet-est song;

4 Bless-ings a-bound wher-e'er He reigns; The pris-'ner leaps to lose his chains;

5 Let ev-'ry crea-ture rise and bring Pe-cu-liar hon-ours to our King;

Jesus Shall Reign—*Continued*

1 His king-dom spread from shore to shore, Till moons shall wax and wane no more.
2 His Name like sweet per-fume shall rise With ev-'ry morn-ing sac-ri-fice.
3 And in-fant voi-ces shall pro-claim Their ear-ly bless-ings on His Name.
4 The wea-ry find e-ter-nal rest, And all the sons of want are blest.
5 An-gels de-scend with songs a-gain, And earth re-peat the loud A-men!

Music by permission of FRANCIS DUCKWORTH

ISAAC WATTS　　　　REGNABIT L.M.　　　　ALFRED BEER

1 Je-sus shall reign wher-e'er the sun Does his suc-
2 To Him shall end-less pray'r be made, And end-less
3 Peo-ple and realms of ev-'ry tongue Dwell on His
4 Bless-ings a-bound wher-e'er He reigns; The pris-'ner
5 Let ev-'ry crea-ture rise and bring Pe-cu-liar

1 ces-sive jour-neys run; His king-dom spread from shore to
2 prais-es crown His head; His Name like sweet per-fume shall
3 love with sweet-est song; And in-fant voi-ces shall pro-
4 leaps to lose his chains; The wea-ry find e-ter-nal
5 hon-ours to our King; An-gels de-scend with songs a-

1 shore, Till moons shall wax and wane no more.
2 rise With ev-'ry morn-ing sac-ri-fice.
3 claim Their ear-ly bless-ings on His Name.
4 rest, And all the sons of want are blest.
5 gain, And earth re-peat the loud A-men!

Music by permission of A. WEEKES & CO., LTD.

647
He Expecteth

ALICE J. JANVRIN   BULLINGER 8.5.8.3   E. W. BULLINGER

1 He ex-pec-teth, He ex-pec-teth! Down the stream of time,
2 Oft-times faint, now wax-ing loud-er As the hour draws near,
3 He is wait-ing with long pa-tience For His crown-ing day,
4 And till ev-'ry tribe and na-tion Bow be-fore His throne,
5 He ex-pec-teth, but He hear-eth Still the bit-ter cry
6 He ex-pec-teth; doth He see us Bus-y here and there,

1 Still the words come soft-ly ring-ing Like a chime.
2 When the King in all His glo-ry Shall ap-pear.
3 For that king-dom which shall nev-er Pass a-way.
4 He ex-pec-teth loy-al ser-vice From His own.
5 From earth's mill-ions, 'Come and help us, For we die!'
6 Heed-less of those plead-ing ac-cents Of des-pair?

By permission of (Words) Miss M. E. JANVRIN, and (Music) BULLINGER PUBLICATIONS TRUST

7 Shall we, dare we disappoint Him?
   Brethren, let us rise!
He who died for us is watching
   From the skies;

8 Watching till His royal banner
   Floateth far and wide,
Till He seeth of His travail
   Satisfied.

648
He Was Not Willing

LUCY R. MEYER   AKON 11.10.11.10.D   LUCY R. MEYER

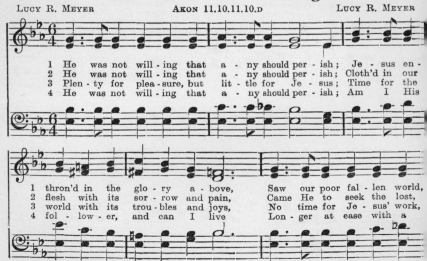

1 He was not will-ing that a-ny should per-ish; Je-sus en-
2 He was not will-ing that a-ny should per-ish; Cloth'd in our
3 Plen-ty for plea-sure, but lit-tle for Je-sus; Time for the
4 He was not will-ing that a-ny should per-ish; Am I His

1 thron'd in the glo-ry a-bove, Saw our poor fal-len world,
2 flesh with its sor-row and pain, Came He to seek the lost,
3 world with its trou-bles and joys, No time for Je-sus' work,
4 fol-low-er, and can I live Lon-ger at ease with a

He Was Not Willing—*Continued*

1 pit - ied our sor - rows, Pour'd out His life for us—won - der - ful love!
2 com - fort the mourn - er, Heal the heart brok-en by sor - row and shame.
3 feed - ing the hun - gry, Lift - ing lost souls to e - ter - ni - ty's joys.
4 soul go - ing down-ward, Lost for the lack of the help I might give?

1 Per - ish - ing, per - ish - ing! Throng-ing our path - way, Hearts break with
2 Per - ish - ing, per - ish - ing! Har - vest is pass - ing, Reap - ers are
3 Per - ish - ing, per - ish - ing! Hark, how they call us; Bring us your
4 Per - ish - ing, per - ish - ing! Thou wast not will - ing; Mas - ter, for -

1 bur - dens too hea - vy to bear; Je - sus would save, but there's
2 few and the night draw-eth near; Je - sus is call - ing thee,
3 Sa - viour, O tell us of Him! We are so wea - ry, so
4 give, and in - spire us a - new; Ban - ish our world - li - ness,

1 no one to tell them, No one to lift them from sin and des - pair.
2 haste to the reap - ing, Thou shalt have souls, pre-cious souls for thy hire.
3 hea - vi - ly la - den, And with long weep-ing our eyes have grown dim.
4 help us to ev - er Live with e - ter - ni - ty's val - ues in view.

649   O'er those Gloomy Hills

W. Williams   Triumph 8.7.8.7.8.7   H. J. Gauntlett

1 O'er those gloom-y   hills of darkness, Look, my soul; be   still, and gaze;
2 Let the In - dian, let the Ne - gro, Let the rude bar - bar - ian see
3 King-doms wide that sit in darkness, Let them have the glo - rious light;
4 Fly a - broad, e - ter - nal Gos - pel! Win and con - quer, nev - er cease;

1 All the pro - mis - es do tra - vail With a glo - rious day of grace;
2 That di - vine and glo - rious con-quest Once ob - tain'd on Cal - va - ry;
3 And from east - ern coast to west - ern May the morn - ing chase the night,
4 May thy last - ing wide do - min - ions Mul - ti - ply and still in - crease;

1 Bless - ed ju - bilee! bless - ed ju - bilee! Let thy glo - rious morn - ing dawn.
2 Let the Gos - pel, let the Gos - pel Loud re - sound from pole to pole.
3 And re - demp-tion, and re - demp-tion, Free - ly pur-chas'd, win the day.
4 May thy scep - tre, may thy scep - tre Sway th'en-light-en'd world a - round.

W. Williams   Blaencefn 8.7.8.7.8.7   John Thomas

1 O'er those gloom-y hills of darkness, Look, my soul; be still and gaze;
2 Let the In - dian, let the Ne - gro, Let the rude bar - bar - ian see
3 King-doms wide that sit in darkness, Let them have the glo - rious light;
4 Fly a - broad, e - ter - nal Gos - pel! Win and con - quer, nev - er cease;

O'er those Gloomy Hills—*Continued*

1 All the pro-mis-es do tra-vail With a glo-rious day of grace:
2 That di-vine and glo-rious con-quest Once ob-tain'd on Cal-va-ry;
3 And from east-ern coast to west-ern May the morn-ing chase the night,
4 May thy last-ing, wide do-min-ions Mul-ti-ply and still in-crease;

1 Bless-ed ju-bilee! bless-ed ju-bilee! Let thy glo-rious morn-ing dawn.
2 Let the Gos-pel, let the Gos-pel Loud re-sound from pole to pole.
3 And re-demp-tion, and re-demp-tion, Free-ly pur-chas'd, win the day.
4 May thy scep-tre, may thy scep-tre Sway th' en-light-en'd world a-round,

Music by permission of G. T. LEWIS

650 Thou Shepherd Divine

ANON   *Arr.* P. J. MANSFIELD

O Je-sus, Thou Shep-herd di-vine! Keep us in the safe, nar-row way;

And out of the cold lead in-to Thy fold Some poor wan-d'ring soul, we pray.

651 Send Them, O Lord

J. W. MacGill

J. E. Stewart, *Arr.* C. W. MacGill

1 Lord, Thou hast gone two thou-sand years, Yet they have nev - er heard
2 Once o'er this bright and fa-vour'd land Lay there the pall of night;
3 So would we do for o - ther lands Ly - ing in deep - est death,

1 Ti - dings of Thy re-deem - ing love, Or seen Thy ho - ly Word:
2 Gloom of a sa - vage hea - then-dom, With foul and blood - y rite:
3 Sink - ing to meet their aw - ful doom With ev - 'ry pass - ing breath:

1 Sleep-ing and still Thy Church has lain, Heed-less of the high com- mand;
2 Brave ones a-rose and came to us, Bring-ing o'er the tid-ings sweet,
3 Hear, Je-sus, hear our fer - vent pray'r! Wake Thy sleeping Church to know

Send Them, O Lord—*Continued*

1 Go forth to ev - 'ry   tribe and tongue, To ev - 'ry dis - tant land.
2 Then cru - el men bent   low to Thee, And wor-shipp'd at   Thy feet.
3. Her hour of pri - vil - ege and pow'r, And bid her rise   and go.

REFRAIN

Send   them,   O   Lord, .. to   speak   of   Thee,   Tell - ing

of   Thy   love   and   grace; ..   Send   them,   O   Lord,   to

tell   of   Thee   To   ev - 'ry   tribe   and   race.

652 Let there be Light!

JOHN MARRIOTT   MOSCOW 6.6.4.6.6.6.4   FELICE DE GIARDINI

1 Thou whose al - migh - ty word   Cha - os and dark - ness heard,
2 Thou who didst come to bring   On Thy re - deem - ing wing
3 Spi - rit of truth and love,   Life - giv - ing, ho - ly Dove,
4 Bless - ed and ho - ly Three,   Glo - ri - ous Trin - i - ty,

1 And took their flight,   Hear us, we   hum - bly pray, And, where the
2 Heal - ing and sight,   Health to the   sick in mind, Sight to the
3 Speed forth Thy flight!   Move on the   wa - ter's face, Spread - ing the
4 Wis - dom, Love, Might;   Bound - less as   o - cean's tide, Roll - ing in

1 Gos - pel day Sheds not its glo - rious ray, Let there be light!
2 in - ly blind, O now to all man - kind Let there be light!
3 beams of grace, And in earth's dark - est place Let there be light!
4 full - est pride, Thro' the earth far and wide Let there be light!

JOHN MARRIOTT   MALVERN 6.6.4.6.6.6.4   *The Hallelujah,* 1849
Arr. JOHN ROBERTS

1 Thou whose al - migh - ty word   Cha - os and dark - ness heard,
2 Thou who didst come to bring   On Thy re - deem - ing wing
3 Spi - rit of truth and love,   Life - giv - ing, ho - ly Dove,
4 Bless - ed and ho - ly Three,   Glo - ri - ous Trin - i - ty,

Let there be Light !—*Continued*

1 And took their flight, Hear us, we hum-bly pray, And, where the
2 Heal-ing and sight, Health to the sick in mind, Sight to the
3 Speed forth Thy flight! Move on the wa-ter's face, Spread-ing the
4 Wis-dom, Love, Might; Bound-less as o-cean's tide, Roll-ing in

1 Gos-pel day Sheds not its glo-rious ray, Let there be light !
2 in-ly blind, O now to all man-kind Let there be light !
3 beams of grace, And in earth's dark-est place Let there be light !
4 full-est pride, Thro' the earth far and wide Let there be light !

JOHN MARRIOTT　　　　LIGHT 6.6.4.·6,6,6,4　　　　H. FORD BENSON

1 Thou whose al-migh-ty word Cha-os and darkness heard, And took their flight, Hear us, we
2 Thou who didst come to bring On Thy re-deem-ing wing Heal-ing and sight, Health to the
3 Spi-rit of truth and love, Life-giv-ing, ho-ly Dove, Speed forth Thy flight! Move on the
4 Bless-ed and ho-ly Three, Glo-ri-ous Trin-i-ty, Wis-dom, Love, Might; Bound-less as

1 hum-bly pray, And, where the Gos-pel day Sheds not its glo-rious ray, Let there be light !
2 sick in mind, Sight to the in-ly blind, O now to all man-kind Let there be light !
3 wa-ter's face, Spreading the beams of grace, And in earth's darkest place Let there be light !
4 o-cean's tide, Roll-ing in full-est pride, Thro' the earth far and wide Let there be light !

Music copyright by H. FORD BENSON

653 The Only Way

ADA ROSE

Je - sus is the way— the on - ly way, Lov - ing - ly He
call - eth, thus the Scrip-tures say, Who - so - ev - er will let him
come to - day— The bless - ed Je - sus is the on - ly way.

654 I'll be a Sunbeam

NELLIE TALBOT

E. O. EXCELL

1 Je - sus wants me for a sun - beam, To shine for
2 Je - sus wants me to be lov - ing, And kind to
3 I will ask Je - sus to help me, To keep my
4 I'll be a sun - beam for Je - sus; I can if

I 'll be a Sunbeam—*Continued*

1 Him each day;.................... In ev-'ry way try to
2 all I see, ... Show-ing how pleas-ant and
3 heart from sin; .... Ev-er re-flect-ing His
4 I but try;....................... Ser-ving Him mo-ment by

1 please Him— At home, at school, at play................
2 hap - py His lit - tle one may be.................
3 good - ness, And al - ways shine for Him............
4 mo - ment, Then live with Him on high.............

REFRAIN

A sun - beam, a sun - beam, Je-sus wants

me for a sun - beam; A sun - beam, a

sun - beam, I'll be a sun-beam for Him !..............

655 Scatter Sunshine

LANTA WILSON SMITH

E. O. EXCELL

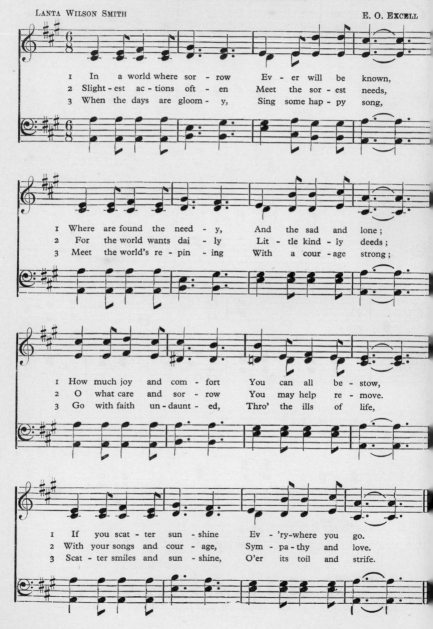

1 In a world where sor - row Ev - er will be known,
2 Slight - est ac - tions oft - en Meet the sor - est needs,
3 When the days are gloom - y, Sing some hap - py song,

1 Where are found the need - y, And the sad and lone;
2 For the world wants dai - ly Lit - tle kind - ly deeds;
3 Meet the world's re - pin - ing With a cour - age strong;

1 How much joy and com - fort You can all be - stow,
2 O what care and sor - row You may help re - move.
3 Go with faith un - daunt - ed, Thro' the ills of life,

1 If you scat - ter sun - shine Ev - 'ry-where you go.
2 With your songs and cour - age, Sym - pa - thy and love.
3 Scat - ter smiles and sun - shine, O'er its toil and strife.

Scatter Sunshine—*Continued*

Scat - ter sun - shine all a - long your
Scat-ter the smiles and sun - shine all a - long

way,...... Cheer and bless and bright - en
o - ver the way, Cheer and bless and bright - en

Ev - 'ry pass - ing day, Scat - ter
Ev - 'ry pass - ing day, Scat-ter the smiles and

sun - shine all a - long your way,......
sun - shine all a - long o - ver the way,

Cheer and bless and bright - en Ev - 'ry pass - ing day.
Cheer and bless and bright - en Ev - 'ry pass - ing day.

656 The Angels' Story

Emily H. Miller   Ellon 7.6.7.6. d   George F. Root

1 I love to hear the sto - ry Which an - gel voi - ces tell,
2 I'm glad my bless - ed Sa - viour Was once a child like me,
3 To sing His love and mer - cy My sweet-est songs I'll raise,

1 How once the King of Glo - ry Came down on earth to dwell:
2 To show how pure and ho - ly His lit - tle ones might be;
3 And though I can - not see Him, I know He hears my praise;

1 I am both weak and sin - ful, But this I sure - ly know,
2 And if I try to fol - low His foot - steps here be - low,
3 For He has kind - ly prom - is'd That I shall sure - ly go

1 The Lord came down to save me, Be - cause He loved me so.
2 He ne - ver will for - get me, Be - cause He loved me so.
3 To sing a - mong His an - gels, Be - cause He loved me so.

The tune Angels' Story is on the following page

The Angels' Story

656

EMILY H. MILLER · ANGELS' STORY 7.6.7.6. D. · ARTHUR H. MANN

1 I love to hear the sto - ry Which an - gel voi - ces tell,
2 I'm glad my bless - ed Sa - viour Was once a child like me,
3 To sing His love and mer - cy My sweet-est songs I'll raise,

1 How once the King of Glo - ry Came down on earth to dwell;
2 To show how pure and ho - ly His lit - tle ones might be:
3 And, though I can - not see Him, I know He hears my praise;

1 I am both weak and sin - ful, But this I sure - ly know,
2 And if I try to fol - low His foot-steps here be - low,
3 For He has kind - ly prom - is'd That I shall sure - ly go

1 The Lord came down to save me, Be - cause He lov'd me so.
2 He nev - er will for - get me, Be - cause He lov'd me so.
3 To sing a - mong His an - gels, Be - cause He lov'd me so.

By permission of BAYFORD STONE   The tune ELLON precedes this one

657 A Friend for Children

Albert Midlane   Morning Light 8.6.7.6.7.6.7.6   G. J. Webb

1 There's a Friend for lit-tle chil-dren A-bove the bright blue sky,
2 There's a rest for lit-tle chil-dren A-bove the bright blue sky,
3 There's a home for lit-tle chil-dren A-bove the bright blue sky,
4 There's a crown for lit-tle chil-dren A-bove the bright blue sky,
5 There's a song for lit-tle chil-dren A-bove the bright blue sky,

1 A Friend that nev-er chang-es, Whose love will nev-er die:
2 Who love the bless-ed Sa-viour, And to His Fa-ther cry:
3 Where Je-sus reigns in glo-ry, A home of peace and joy:
4 And all who look to Je-sus Shall wear it by-and-by;
5 And a harp of sweet-est mu-sic For their hymn of vic-tor-y:

1 Un-like our friends by na-ture, Who change with chang-ing years,
2 A rest from ev-'ry trou-ble, From sin and dan-ger free;
3 No home on earth is like it, Nor can with it com-pare,
4 A crown of bright-est glo-ry, Which He shall sure be-stow
5 And all a-bove is pleas-ure, And found in Christ a-lone;

1 This Friend is al-ways wor-thy The pre-cious name He bears.
2 There ev-'ry lit-tle pil-grim Shall rest e-ter-nal-ly.
3 For ev-'ry one is hap-py, Nor can be hap-pier there.
4 On all who love the Sa-viour, And walk with Him be-low.
5 O come, dear lit-tle chil-dren, That all may be your own!

The tune In Memoriam is on the following page

657 A Friend for Children

ALBERT MIDLANE   In Memoriam 8.6.7.6.7.6.7.6   JOHN STAINER

1 There's a Friend for lit - tle chil - dren A - bove the bright blue sky,
2 There's a rest for lit - tle chil - dren A - bove the bright blue sky,
3 There's a home for lit - tle chil - dren A - bove the bright blue sky,
4 There's a crown for lit - tle chil - dren A - bove the bright blue sky,
5 There's a song for lit - tle chil - dren A - bove the bright blue sky,

1 A Friend that nev - er chan - ges, Whose love will nev - er die:
2 Who love the bless - ed Sa - viour, And to His Fa - ther cry:
3 Where Je - sus reigns in glo - ry, A home of peace and joy:
4 And all who look to Je - sus Shall wear it by - and - by:
5 And a harp of sweet - est mu - sic For their hymn of vic - tor - y:

1 Un - like our friends by na - ture, Who change with chang-ing years,
2 A rest from ev - 'ry tur - moil, From sin and sor - row free,
3 No home on earth is like it, Nor can with it com - pare;
4 A crown of bright - est glo - ry, Which He shall sure be - stow
5 And all a - bove is pleas - ure, And found in Christ a - lone;

1 This Friend is al - ways wor - thy The pre - cious name He bears.
2 Where ev - 'ry lit - tle pil - grim Shall rest e - ter - nal - ly.
3 For ev - 'ry one is hap - py, Nor can be hap - pier there.
4 On all who love the Sav - iour, And walk with Him be - low.
5 O come, dear lit - tle chil - dren, That all may be your own!

The tune MORNING LIGHT is on the previous page

I Will Follow Jesus

Anna B. Warner   *Arr.* Purcell J. Mansfield

1 The world looks ve - ry beau - ti - ful, And full of joy to me;
2 I'm but a youth-ful pil - grim, My jour-ney's just be - gun;
3 Then, like a lit - tle pil - grim, What - ev - er I may meet,
4 Then tri - als can - not vex me, And pain I need not fear,

1 The sun shines out in glo - ry On ev - 'ry-thing I see: I
2 They say I'll meet with sor - row Be - fore my jour-ney's done: The
3 I'll take it, joy or sor - row, And lay at Je - sus' feet: He'll
4 For when I'm close by Je - sus, Grief can - not come too near: Not

1 know I shall be hap - py While in the world I stay, For I will fol - low
2 world is full of trou - ble, And tri - als, too, they say; But I will fol - low
3 com-fort me in trou - ble, He'll wipe my tears a - way; With joy I'll fol - low
4 e - ven death can harm me, When death I meet one day; To heav'n I'll fol - low

Refrain

1-4 Je - sus All the way. For I will fol - low Je - sus, For

I will fol - low Je - sus, For I will fol - low Je - sus All the way.

The tune Cliftonville is on the following page

658   I Will Follow Jesus

ANNA B. WARNER   CLIFTONVILLE P.M.   F. C. MAKER

1 The world looks ve - ry beau - ti - ful And full of joy to me;
2 I'm but a youth-ful pil - grim, My jour-ney's just be - gun;
3 Then, like a lit - tle pil - grim, What-ev - er I may meet,
4 Then tri - als can - not vex me, And pain I need not fear,

1 The sun shines out in glo - ry On ev - 'ry-thing I see:
2 They say I'll meet with sor - row Be - fore my jour - ney's done:
3 I'll take it, joy or sor - row, And lay at Je - sus' feet:
4 For when I'm close by Je - sus, Grief can - not come too near:

1 I know I shall be hap - py While in the world I stay,
2 The world is full of trou - ble, And tri - als, too, they say;
3 He'll com - fort me in trou - ble, He'll wipe my tears a - way;
4 Not e - ven death can harm me When death I meet one day;

1 For I will fol - low Je - sus All the way.
2 But I will fol - low Je - sus All the way.
3 With joy I'll fol - low Je - sus All the way.
4 To heav'n I'll fol - low Je - sus All the way.

Music by permission of the METHODIST YOUTH DEPARTMENT

An Alternative Tune is on the preceding page

659 When He Cometh

WILLIAM O. CUSHING   JEWELS P.M.   GEORGE F. ROOT, *Arr.* D. CARYLL

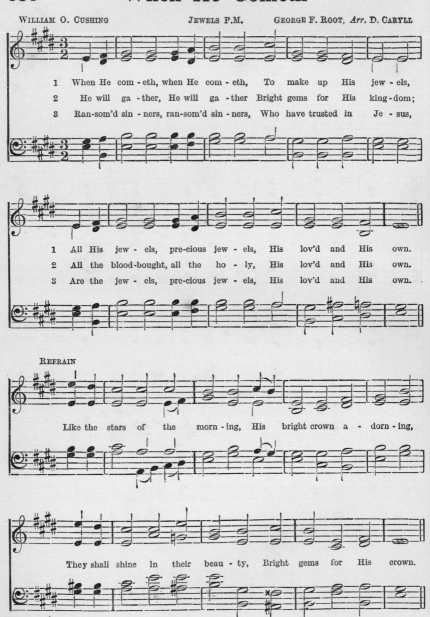

1 When He com - eth, when He com - eth, To make up His jew - els,
2 He will ga - ther, He will ga - ther Bright gems for His king - dom;
3 Ran-som'd sin - ners, ran-som'd sin - ners, Who have trusted in Je - sus,

1 All His jew - els, pre-cious jew - els, His lov'd and His own.
2 All the blood-bought, all the ho - ly, His lov'd and His own.
3 Are the jew - els, pre-cious jew - els, His lov'd and His own.

REFRAIN

Like the stars of the morn - ing, His bright crown a - dorn - ing,

They shall shine In their beau - ty, Bright gems for His crown.

The tune BRIGHT GEMS is on the following page

659   When He Cometh

WILLIAM O. CUSHING   BRIGHT GEMS P.M.   DAVID CARYLL

1 When He com - eth, when He com - eth, To make up His jew - els,
2 He will ga - ther, He will ga - ther Bright gems for His king - dom;
3 Ran-som'd sin - ners, ran-som'd sin - ners, Who have trusted in Je - sus,

1 All His jew - els, pre-cious jew - els, His lov'd and His own.
2 All the blood-bought, all the ho - ly, His lov'd and His own.
3 Are the jew - els, pre-cious jew - els, His lov'd, and His own.

REFRAIN

Like the stars of the morn - ing, His bright crown a - dorn - ing,

They shall shine in their beau - ty, Bright gems for His crown.

The tune JEWELS is on the preceding page

660 Jesus Bids Us Shine

SUSAN WARNER   LITTLE CANDLE 5.5. 6.5. 6.4. 6.4.   E. O. EXCELL
Arr. P. J. MANSFIELD

1 Je - sus bids us shine With a clear, pure light, Like a lit - tle
2 Je - sus bids us shine, First of all for Him; Well He sees and
3 Je - sus bids us shine, Then for all a - round, Man - y kinds of

1 can - dle Burn - ing in the night: In this world is dark - ness,
2 knows it If our light is dim; He looks down from hea - ven
3 dark - ness In this world a - bound— Sin and want and sor - row—

1 So we must shine, You in your small cor - ner, And I in mine.
2 To see us shine, You in your small cor - ner, And I in mine.
3 So we must shine, You in your small cor - ner, And I in mine.

SUSAN WARNER   GLENIFFER 5.5. 6.5. 6.4. 6.4.   JAMES MERRYLEES

1 Je - sus bids us shine With a clear, pure light, Like a lit - tle
2 Je - sus bids us shine, First of all for Him; Well He sees and
3 Je - sus bids us shine, Then for all a - round, Man - y kinds of

Jesus Bids Us Shine—*Continued*

1 can - dle Burn - ing in the night: In this world is dark - ness,
2 knows it If our light is dim; He looks down from hea - ven
3 dark - ness In this world a - bound— Sin and want and sor - row—

1 So we must shine, You in your small cor - ner, And I in mine.
2 To see us shine, You in your small cor - ner, And I in mine.
3 So we must shine, You in your small cor - ner, And I in mine.

661 God Make My Life

M. BETHAM-EDWARDS   SAWLEY C.M.   JAMES WALCH

1 God make my life a lit - tle light With-in the world to glow,
2 God make my life a lit - tle flower That giv-eth joy to all,
3 God make my life a lit - tle song That com-for-teth the sad,
4 God make my life a lit - tle staff Where-on the weak may rest,
5 God make my life a lit - tle hymn Of ten - der - ness and praise,

1 A lit - tle flame that burn - eth bright Wher - ev - er I may go.
2 Con-tent to bloom in na - tive bower, Al - tho' the place be small.
3 That help-eth o - thers to be strong, And makes the sing - er glad.
4 That so what health and strength I have May serve my neigh-bours best.
5 Of faith that nev - er wax - eth dim In all His won - drous ways.

Words by permission of Miss CONSTANCE MORLEY HORDER

662 Whispering in My Heart

J. B. MACKAY   J. B. MACKAY

1 Je - sus found me wand'ring, Far from Him a - stray, Ten - der - ly He led me
2 I can hear Him whis - per, When my soul is tried, 'Fear not, I am with thee;
3 Would you hear the Sa - viour's gen - tle voice with - in? Now, while He is call - ing,

1 To the shin - ing way; Words of peace He whis - per'd, Bade my fears de - part;
2 I am at thy side.' When the foe as - sails me Je - sus takes my part;
3 Leave the path of sin. Peace that pas - seth know - ledge Free - ly He'll im - part;

REFRAIN

1 O 'twas sweet to hear Him Whis-p'ring in my heart!
2 I re - joice to hear Him Whis-p'ring in my heart. } Whis-p'ring, whis-p'ring,
3 You to - day may hear Him Whis-p'ring in your heart.

O what joy is mine! Whisp'ring, whisp'ring, Words of love di - vine: No strain of earth - ly

mu - sic Such rap-ture can impart; I'm glad I ev - er heard Him Whisp'ring in my heart.

663 The Arms of Jesus

Fanny J. Crosby   Refuge 7.6.7.6 d   W. H. Doane

1 Safe in the arms of Je - sus, Safe on His gen - tle breast,
2 Safe in the arms of Je - sus, Safe from cor - rod - ing care,
3 Je - sus, my heart's dear re - fuge, Je - sus has died for me ;

Refrain—Safe in the arms of Je - sus, Safe on His gen - tle breast,

1 There, by His love o'er - shad - ed, Sweet - ly my soul shall rest.
2 Safe from the world's temp - ta - tions, Sin can - not harm me there.
3 Firm on the Rock of A - ges Ev - er my trust shall be.

There, by His love o'er - shad - ed, Sweet - ly my soul shall rest.

1 Hark ! 'tis the voice of an - gels Borne in a song to me,
2 Free from the blight of sor - row, Free from my doubts and fears ;
3 Here let me wait with pa - tience, Wait till the night is o'er ;

1 O - ver the fields of glo - ry, O - ver the jas - per sea.............
2 On - ly a few more tri - als, On - ly a few more tears.............
3 Wait till I see the morn - ing Break on the gold - en shore.............

664   The Beautiful River

Robert Lowry   Robert Lowry

1 Shall we ga - ther at the ri - ver, Where bright an - gel feet have trod,
2 On the mar - gin of the ri - ver, Wash - ing up its sil - ver spray,
3 Ere we reach the shin - ing ri - ver, Lay we ev - 'ry bur - den down;
4 At the smil - ing of the ri - ver, Mir - ror of the Sa - viour's face,
5 Soon we'll reach the shin - ing ri - ver, Soon our pil - grim - age will cease;

1 With its crys - tal tide for ev - er Flow - ing from the throne of God?
2 We will walk and wor - ship ev - er, All the hap - py gol - den day.
3 Grace our spi - rits will de - li - ver, And pro - vide a robe and crown.
4 Saints whom death will nev - er se - ver Lift their songs of sav - ing grace.
5 Soon our hap - py hearts will qui - ver With the mel - o - dy of peace.

REFRAIN

Yes, we'll ga - ther at the ri - ver, The beau - ti - ful, the beau - ti - ful ri - ver,

Ga - ther with the saints at the ri - ver That flows from the throne of God.

665

Shining for Jesus

Charles Inglis

Arr. Purcell J. Mansfield

1 Shin-ing for Je-sus ev-'ry-where I go; Shin-ing for Je-sus
2 Shin-ing for Je-sus when the way is bright; Shin-ing for Je-sus
3 Shin-ing for Je-sus in a world of sin; Shin-ing for Je-sus
4 Shin-ing for Je-sus while He gives me grace; Shin-ing for Je-sus

1 in this world of woe; Shin-ing for Je-sus, more like Him I grow;
2 in the dark-est night; Shin-ing for Je-sus, mak-ing bur-dens light;
3 bring-ing lost ones in; Shin-ing for Je-sus, glo-ri-fy-ing Him;
4 while I run the race; Shin-ing for Je-sus till I see His face;

REFRAIN

1-4 Shin-ing all the time for Je - sus. Shin-ing all the time,

shin-ing all the time, Shin-ing for Je-sus, beams of love di-vine;

Glo-ri-fy-ing Him ev-'ry day and hour, Shin-ing all the time for Je - sus.

Jesus Lives!

666

JOHN R. COLGAN

A. F. MYERS

1 Migh - ty ar - my of the young Lift the voice of cheer-ful song,
2 Tongues of chil-dren light and free, Tongues of youth all full of glee,
3 Je - sus lives, O bless - ed words! King of kings, and Lord of lords;

1 Send the wel - come word a - long, Je - sus lives!
2 Sing to all on land and sea, Je - sus lives!
3 Lift the Cross and sheathe the swords, Je - sus lives!

1 Once He died for you and me, Bore our sins up - on the tree,
2 Light for you and all man - kind, Sight for all by sin made blind,
3 See, He breaks the pris - on wall, Throws a - side the dread-ful pall,

1 Now He lives to make us free, Je - sus lives!
2 Life in Je - sus all may find, Je - sus lives!
3 Con - quers death at once for all, Je - sus lives!

Jesus Lives!—*Continued*

REFRAIN

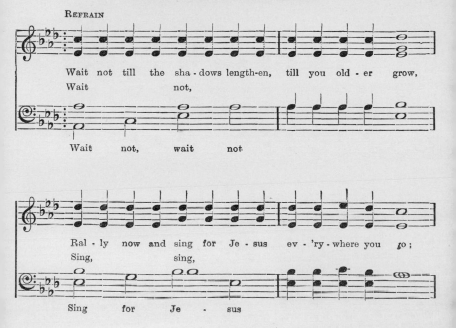

Wait not till the sha - dows length-en, till you old - er grow,
Wait not,

Wait not, wait not

Ral - ly now and sing for Je - sus ev - 'ry - where you go;
Sing, sing,

Sing for Je - sus

Lift your joy - ful voi - ces high, Ring-ing clear thro' earth and sky,

f rit. Repeat Refrain *pp*

Let the bless - ed tid - ings fly, Je - sus lives!

An Alternative Setting follows this one

Jesus Lives!

John R. Colgan   An Alternative Setting   A. F. Myers
Arr. P. J. Mansfield

1 Migh - ty ar - my of the young   Lift the voice of cheer-ful song,
2 Tongues of chil - dren light and free, Tongues of youth all full of glee,
3 Je - sus lives, O bless - ed words! King of kings, and Lord of lords!

1 Send the wel - come word a - long,   Je - sus   lives!
2 Sing to all on land and sea,   Je - sus   lives!
3 Lift the Cross and sheathe the swords, Je - sus   lives!

1 Once He died for you and me,   Bore our sins up - on the tree,
2 Light for you and all man-kind, Sight for all by sin made blind,
3 See, He breaks the pris - on wall, Throws a - side the dread-ful pall,

1 Now He lives to make us free,   Je - sus   lives!
2 Life in Je - sus all may find, Je - sus   lives!
3 Con - quers death at once for all, Je - sus   lives!

Jesus Lives !—*Continued*

Wait not till the sha-dows length-en, Till you old-er grow,

Wait not Till you old-er grow,

Ral-ly now and sing for Je-sus Ev-'ry-where you go;

Sing, sing Ev-'ry-where you go;

Lift your joy-ful voi-ces high, Ring-ing clear thro'

Repeat Refrain pp
rit.

earth and sky, Let the bless-ed tid-ings fly, ƒ Je-sus lives !

The usual Arrangement of the tune precedes this one

667 Jesus is Our Shepherd

HUGH STOWELL   GOSHEN 6.5. 6.5. D   MARCHEL DAVIS

1 Je - sus is our Shep - herd, Wip - ing ev - 'ry tear;
2 Je - sus is our Shep - herd: Well we know His voice;
3 Je - sus is our Shep - herd: For the sheep He bled;
4 Je - sus is our Shep - herd; Guard - ed by His arm,

1 Fold - ed in His bo - som, What have we to fear?
2 How its gen - tle whis - per Makes our heart re - joice!
3 Ev - 'ry lamb is sprin - kled With the blood He shed:
4 Tho' the wolves may rav - en, None can do us harm:

1 On - ly let us fol - low Whi - ther He doth lead,
2 E - ven when He chid - eth, Ten - der is His tone;
3 Then on each He set - teth His own se - cret sign;
4 When we tread death's val - ley, Dark with fear - ful gloom,

1 To the thirs - ty des - ert Or the dew - y mead.
2 None but He shall guide us; We are His a - lone.
3 'They that have My Spi - rit, These,' saith He, 'are Mine.'
4 We will fear no e - vil, Vic - tors o'er the tomb.

The tune KIRKBRADDAN is on the following page

667 **Jesus is Our Shepherd**

HUGH STOWELL KIRKBRADDAN 6.5. 6.5. D E. C. WALKER

1 Je-sus is our Shep-herd, Wip-ing ev-'ry tear;
2 Je-sus is our Shep-herd: Well we know His voice;
3 Je-sus is our Shep-herd: For the sheep He bled;
4 Je-sus is our Shep-herd: Guard-ed by His arm,

1 Fold-ed in His bo-som, What have we to fear?
2 How its gen-tle whis-per Makes our heart re-joice!
3 Ev-'ry lamb is sprin-kled With the blood He shed!
4 Tho' the wolves may rav-en, None can do us harm:

1 On-ly let us fol-low Whi-ther He doth lead,
2 E-ven when He chid-eth, Ten-der is His tone;
3 Then on each He set-teth His own se-cret sign;
4 When we tread death's val-ley, Dark with fear-ful gloom,

1 To the thirs-ty des-ert Or the dew-y mead.
2 None but He shall guide us; We are His a-lone.
3 'They that have My Spi-rit, These,' saith He, 'are Mine.'
4 We will fear no e-vil, Vic-tors o'er the tomb.

The tune GOSHEN is on the previous page

668 Golden Harps

F. R. HAVERGAL   HERMAS 6.5. 6.5. 6.5 D   F. R. HAVERGAL

1 Gold-en harps are sound-ing, An-gel voi-ces ring, Pear-ly gates are
2 He who came to save us, He who bled and died, Now is crown'd with
3 Pray-ing for His chil-dren In that bless-ed place, Call-ing them to

1 o-pen'd, O-pen'd for the King: Christ, the King of Glo-ry,
2 glo-ry At His Fa-ther's side: Ne-ver-more to suf-fer,
3 glo-ry, Send-ing them His grace; His bright home pre-par-ing,

1 Je-sus, King of Love, Is gone up in tri-umph To His home a-bove.
2 Ne-ver-more to die, Je-sus, King of Glo-ry, Is gone up on high.
3 Lit-tle ones, for you, Je-sus ev-er liv-eth, Ev-er lov-eth too.

REFRAIN

All His work is end-ed, Joy-ful-ly we sing,

Je-sus has as-cend-ed! Glo-ry to our King!

The tune RACHIE is on the following page

668 Golden Harps

F. R. HAVERGAL   RACHIE 6.5. 6.5. 6.5. 6.5. D   CARADOG ROBERTS

1 Gold-en harps are sound-ing, An-gel voi-ces ring, Pear-ly gates are
2 He who came to save us, He who bled and died, Now is crown'd with
3 Pray-ing for His chil-dren In that bless-ed place, Call-ing them to

1 o-pen'd, O-pen'd for the King; Christ, the King of Glo-ry,
2 glo-ry At His Fa-ther's side; Ne-ver more to suf-fer,
3 glo-ry, Send-ing them His grace, His bright home pre-par-ing,

1 Je-sus, King of Love, Is gone up in tri-umph To His home a-bove.
2 Ne-ver more to die, Je-sus, King of Glo-ry Is gone up on high.
3 Lit-tle ones, for you, Je-sus ev-er liv-eth, Ev-er lov-eth too.

REFRAIN

All His work is end-ed, Joy-ful-ly we sing,
All His work is end-ed, Joy-ful-ly we sing,

Je-sus has as-cend-ed! Glo-ry to our King!

Music by permission of the CANIEDYDD COMMITTEE, SWANSEA
The tune HERMAS is on the preceeding page

Looking unto Jesus

GODFREY THRING   OUR WATCHWORD 6.5. 6.5. 6.5. D   HENRY ALFORD

1 Sa - viour, bless-ed Sa - viour, List-en while we sing, Hearts and voi-ces rais - ing
2 Near-er, ev - er near - er, Christ, we draw to Thee, Deep in a - dor - a - tion
3 Great, and ev - er great - er, Are Thy mer-cies here; True and ev - er - last - ing
4 On-ward, ev - er on - ward, Journeying o'er the road Worn by saints be - fore us,
5 High-er then and high - er Bear the ran-som'd soul, Earth-ly toils for - got - ten,

1 Prais-es to our King: All we have to of - fer, All we hope to be,
2 Bend-ing low the knee: Thou, for our re - demp-tion, Cam'st on earth to die;
3 Are the glo - ries there: Where no pain or sor - row, Toil or care is known;
4 Journeying on to God: Leav - ing all be - hind us, May we has - ten on;
5 Sa - viour, to its goal; Where, in joys un-thought of, Saints with an - gels sing,

REFRAIN

1 Bo - dy, soul, and spi - rit, All we yield to Thee.
2 Thou, that we might fol - low, Hast gone up on high.
3 Where the an - gel le - gions Cir - cle round Thy throne. } Looking un - to Je - sus,
4 Back-ward nev - er look - ing Till the prize is won.
5 Nev - er wear - y rais - ing Prais - es to their King.

Nev - er need we yield, O - ver all the ar - mour, Faith, the bat - tle shield.

The tune FORWARD is on the following page

Looking unto Jesus

669

1 Sa-viour, bless-ed Sa-viour, List-en while we sing, Hearts and voi-ces rais-ing
2 Near-er, ev-er near-er, Christ, we draw to Thee, Deep in a-do-ra-tion
3 Great, and ev-er great-er, Are Thy mer-cies here; True and ev-er-last-ing
4 On-ward, ev-er on-ward, Journeying o'er the road Worn by saints be-fore us,
5 High-er then and high-er Bear the ran-som'd soul, Earth-ly toils for-got-ten,

1 Prais-es to our King: All we have to of-fer, All we hope to be,
2 Bend-ing low the knee: Thou, for our re-demp-tion, Cam'st on earth to die,
3 Are the glo-ries there: Where no pain or sor-row, Toil or care is known;
4 Journeying on to God: Leav-ing all be-hind us, May we hast-en on;
5 Sa-viour, to its goal; Where, in joys un-thought of, Saints with an-gels sing,

REFRAIN

1 Bo-dy, soul, and spi-rit, All we yield to Thee.
2 Thou, that we might fol-low, Hast gone up on high.
3 Where the an-gel le-gions Cir-cle round Thy throne.   Look-ing un-to Je-sus,
4 Back-ward nev-er look-ing Till the prize is won.
5 Nev-er wear-y rais-ing Prais-es to their King.

Nev-er need we yield,   O-ver all the ar-mour, Faith, the bat-tle shield.

The tune OUR WATCHWORD precedes this one

Jesus Loves Me

ANNA B. WARNER

WM. B. BRADBURY

1 Je-sus loves me! this I know, For the Bi-ble tells me so;
2 Je-sus loves me! He who died Hea-ven's gate to o-pen wide;
3 Je-sus loves me! He will stay Close be-side me all the way:

1 Lit-tle ones to Him be-long; They are weak, but He is strong.
2 He will wash a-way my sin, Let His lit-tle child come in.
3 If I love Him, when I die He will take me home on high.

REFRAIN

Yes! Je-sus loves me! Yes! Je-sus loves me!

Yes! Je-sus loves me! The Bi-ble tells me so.

671

I Am So Glad

PHILIP P. BLISS   TRINITY CHAPEL P.M.   P. P. BLISS, *Arr.* G. ALLAN

1 I am so glad that our Fa-ther in heav'n Tells of His
2 Je-sus loves me and I know I love Him; Love bro't Him
3 In this as-sur-ance I find sweet-est rest, Trust-ing in
4 O if there's on-ly one song I can sing! When in His

1 love in the Book He has giv'n; Won-der-ful things in the
2 down my lost soul to re-deem; Yes, it was love made Him
3 Je-sus I know I am blest; Sa-tan dis-may'd from my
4 beau-ty I see the great king, This shall my song in e-

1 Bi-ble I see; This is the dear-est that Je-sus loves me.
2 die on the tree: O I am cer-tain that Je-sus loves me!
3 soul now doth flee When I just tell him that Je-sus loves me.
4 ter-ni-ty be, O what a won-der that Je-sus loves me!

REFRAIN

I am so glad that Je-sus loves me, Je-sus loves me, Je-sus loves me;

I am so glad that Je-sus loves me, Je-sus loves e-ven me. . . .

The tune THE GLORY SONG is on the following page

672 ## I am So Glad

PHILIP P. BLISS THE GLORY SONG 10.10.10.10 *Arr.* CHARLES H. GABRIEL

1 I am so glad that our Fa - ther in heav'n
2 Je - sus loves me and I know I love Him;
3 In this as - sur - ance I find sweet - est rest,
4 O if there's on - ly one song I can sing!

1 Tells of His love in the Book He has giv'n:
2 Love brought Him down my lost soul to re - deem;
3 Trust - ing in Je - sus I know I am blest;
4 When in His beau - ty I see the great King,

1 Won - der - ful things in the Bi - ble I see;
2 Yes, it was love made Him die on the tree:
3 Sa - tan dis - may'd from my soul now doth flee,
4 This shall my song in e - ter - ni - ty be,

1 This is the dear - est, that Je - sus loves me.
2 O I am cer - tain that Je - sus loves me!
3 When I just tell Him that Je - sus loves me.
4 O what a won - der that Je - sus loves me!

I am So Glad—*Continued*

REFRAIN

1-4 I am so glad Je-sus loves me, Je-sus loves me,

1-4 I . . . am so glad Je-sus loves me, Je-sus loves

1-4 I am so glad Je-sus loves me, Je-sus loves me,

1 Je-sus loves me; Won-der-ful things in the Bi-ble I see,
2 Je-sus loves me; Yes, it was love made Him die on the tree;
3 Je-sus loves me; Sa-tan dis-may'd from my soul now doth flee,
4 Je-sus loves me; This shall my song in e-ter-ni-ty be,

1 me, Je-sus loves me; Won-der-ful things I can see,
2 me, Je-sus loves me; Yes, it was love made Him die;
3 me, Je-sus loves me; Sa-tan dis-may'd now doth flee,
4 me, Je-sus loves me; This shall my song ev-er be.

1 Je-sus loves me; Won-der-ful things in the Bi-ble I see,
2 Je-sus loves me; Yes, it was love made Him die on the tree;
3 Je-sus loves me; Sa-tan dis-may'd from my soul now doth flee,
4 Je-sus loves me; This shall my song in e-ter-ni-ty be,

1 This is the dear-est, that Je-sus loves me.
2 O I am cer-tain that Je-sus loves me!
3 When I just tell Him that Je-sus loves me.
4 O what a won-der that Je-sus loves me!

Music by permission of the CHARLES M. ALEXANDER COPYRIGHTS TRUST
The tune TRINITY CHAPEL precedes this one

673 All the World for Jesus!

F. A. BRECK

GRANT C. TULLAR, *Arr.* P. J. MANSFIELD

1 Take up the bat-tle-cry all a-long the line, Vic-tor-y
2 Truth's ar-mour you may claim, faith will be your shield, . Fight-ing on in
3 Sol-diers, with cour-age go, go for-sak-ing all, . On-ward, then, to

1 by and by, vic-tor-y di-vine; With your Com-man-der nigh,
2 Je-sus' Name, might-y pow'r you wield; Glo-ry for God your aim,
3 meet the foe, soon the foe shall fall; Send might-y blow on blow,

1 foes in vain com-bine, . . Raise a-loft the ban-ner, let it bear the sign:
2 naught can make you yield, . . Shout a-loud the tri-umph, sure to be re-veal'd.
3 let no fear ap-pall, . . In the Name of Je-sus sound a-far the call.

REFRAIN

All the world for Je-sus! let the chor-us ring; All the world for

Je-sus! crown Him King: All the world for Je-sus! Let the

All the World for Jesus—*Continued*

watch-word be: For-ward go in Je-sus' name to vic-tor-y.

574 # Around the Throne

ANNE SHEPHERD GLORY 8.6.8.6.8.8 CURWEN'S TUNE BOOK, 1842

1 A - round the throne of   God in heav'n Thou-sands of chil-dren stand,
2 What brought them to that world a-bove? That heav'n so bright and fair,
3 Be - cause the Sa-viour shed His blood To wash a-way their sin;
4 On earth they sought the Sa-viour's grace, On earth they loved His name:

1 Chil-dren whose sins are all for-giv'n, A ho-ly, hap-py band
2 Where all is peace, and joy, and love; How came those chil-dren there?
3 Bathed in that pure and pre-cious flood, Be-hold them white and clean
4 So now they see His bless-ed face, And stand be-fore the Lamb

REFRAIN   *ff molto rall.*

Sing-ing: Glo-ry, glo-ry, glo-ry! Sing-ing: Glo-ry, glo-ry, glo-ry!

675 The Sweet Story of Old

Jemima Luke

Salamis P.M.

Greek Air
Arr. P, J. Mansfield

1 I think when I read that sweet sto-ry of old, When
2 Yet still to His foot-stool in pray'r I may go And
3 But thous-ands and thous-ands who wan-der and fall Nev-er

1 Je-sus was here a-mong men, How He call'd lit-tle chil-dren as
2 ask for a share in His love; And if I thus earn-est-ly
3 heard of that hea-ven-ly home: I should like them to know there is

1 lambs to His fold; I should like to have been with Him then: I
2 seek Him be-low, I shall see Him and hear Him a-bove; In that
3 room for them all, And that Je-sus has bid them to come, I

The Sweet Story of Old—*Continued*

1 wish that His hands had been plac'd on my head; That His arms had been
2 beau - ti - ful place He has gone to pre - pare For all who are
3 long for that bless - ed and glo - ri - ous time, The fair - est and

1 thrown a - round me, And that I might have seen His kind
2 wash'd and for - giv'n; And man - y dear chil - dren are
3 bright - est and best, When the dear lit - tle chil - dren of

1 look when He said, 'Let the lit - tle ones come un - to Me.'
2 ga - ther - ing there, 'For of such is the king - dom of heaven.'
3 e - ver - y clime Shall crowd to His arms and be blest.

676 A Message of Love

ANON

GREEK FOLK SONG

1 There's a mes - sage of love Come down from a -
2 For there they may read How Je - sus did
3 And then, when they die, He takes them on
4 And O what de - light In hea - ven so

1 bove To in - vite lit - tle chil - dren to heav'n;
2 bleed, His life ev - er - last - ing to give;
3 high To be with Him in hea - ven a - bove;
4 bright When they see the dear Sa - viour's face;

1 In God's bless - ed book Poor sin - ners may
2 He cleans - eth the soul, He mak - eth us
3 For so kind is His heart That He nev - er will
4 On His beau - ty to gaze, And sing to His

1 look, And see how all sin is for - giv'n.
2 whole, That with Him in heav'n we may live.
3 part From a child that has tas - ted His love.
4 praise, And re - joice in His own bound - less grace.

677 Little Friends of Jesus

Fanny J. Crosby   Portrush 11.11. 11.12   Hubert P. Main

1 We are lit - tle chil - dren, ver - y young in - deed,
2 Lit - tle friends of Je - sus, what a hap - py thought!
3 Lit - tle friends of Je - sus, walk - ing by His side,
4 We must love Him dear - ly with a con - stant love,

1 But the Sa-viour's pro - mise each of us may plead.
2 What a pre - cious pro - mise in the Bi - ble taught!
3 With His arm a - round us ev - 'ry step to guide.
4 Then we'll go and see Him in our home a - bove.

Refrain

If we seek Him ear - ly, if we come to - day,

We can be His lit - tle friends, He has said we may.

678 Little Children Weak

C. F. ALEXANDER   ALSTONE L.M.   C. E. WILLING

1 We are but lit - tle chil - dren weak, Nor born in
2 O day by day each Chris - tian child Has much to
3 When deep with - in our swell - ing hearts The thoughts of
4 Then we may stay the an - gry blow, Then we may
5 With smiles of peace and looks of love, Light in our
6 There's not a child so small and weak But has his

1 a - ny high es - tate; What can we do for
2 do with - out, with - in; A death to die for
3 pride and an - ger rise, When bit - ter words are
4 check the has - ty word, Give gen - tle an - swers
5 dwell - ings we may make; Bid kind good hu - mour
6 lit - tle cross to take, His lit - tle work of

1 Je - sus' sake, Who is so high and good and great?
2 Je - sus' sake, A wea - ry war to wage with sin.
3 on our tongues, And tears of pas - sion in our eyes.
4 back a - gain, And fight a bat - tle for our Lord.
5 bright - en there, And still do all for Je - sus' sake.
6 love and praise That he may do for Je - sus' sake.

The tune CONSORT is on the following page

378 Little Children Weak

C. F. ALEXANDER   CONSORT L.M.   J. C. BEAZLEY

1 We are but lit - tle chil - dren weak, Nor
2 O day by day each Chris - tian child Has
3 When deep with - in our swell - ing hearts The
4 Then we may stay the an - gry blow, Then
5 With smiles of peace and looks of love, Light
6 There's not a child so small and weak But

1 born in a - ny high es - tate; What can we do for
2 much to do, with - out, with - in; A death to die for
3 thoughts of pride and an - ger rise, When bit - ter words are
4 we may check the has - ty word, Give gen - tle an - swers
5 in our dwell - ings we may make; Bid kind good hu - mour
6 has his lit - tle cross to take, His lit - tle work of

1 Je - sus' sake, Who is so high and good and great?
2 Je - sus' sake, A wea - ry war to wage with sin.
3 on our tongues, And tears of pas - sion in our eyes,
4 back a - gain, And fight a bat - tle for our Lord.
5 bright - en there, And still do all for Je - sus' sake.
6 love and praise That he may do for Je - sus' sake.

Music by permission of WILLIAM NICHOLSON & SONS
The tune ALSTONE is on the preceding page

29

679 Yield not to Temptation

H. R. PALMER

H. R. PALMER

1 Yield not to tempt - a - tion, For yield - ing is sin, . . .
2 Shun e - vil com - pan - ions, Bad lan-guage dis - dain, . .
3 To him that o'er - com - eth God giv - eth a crown; . .

1 Each vic-t'ry will help you Some o - ther to win; . . Fight man-ful-ly
2 God's Name hold in rev - 'rence, Nor take it in vain; . . Be thought-ful an
3 Thro' faith we shall con - quer, Though oft - en cast down; . He who is our

1 on - ward, Dark pas-sions sub - due, . . Look ev - er to Je - sus,
2 ear - nest, Kind heart-ed and true, . . Look ev - er to Je - sus,
3 Sa - viour Our strength will re - new, . . Look ev - er to Je - sus,

REFRAIN

1-3 He'll car-ry you through. Ask the Saviour to help you, Com-fort, strengthen an

keep you, He is will-ing to aid you, He will car-ry you through.

An alternative and lower Setting is on the following page

679 Yield not to Temptation

H. R. PALMER   H. R. PALMER

1 Yield not to tempt - a - tion, For yield-ing is sin,
2 Shun e - vil com - pan - ions, Bad lan-guage dis - dain,
3 To him that o'er - com - eth God giv - eth a crown;

1 Each vic-t'ry will help you Some o - ther to win; Fight man-ful-ly
2 God's Name hold in rev - 'rence, Nor take it in vain; Be thoughtful and
3 Thro' faith we shall con - quer, Tho' oft - en cast down; He who is our

1 on - ward, Dark pas-sions sub - due, Look ev - er to Je - sus,
2 ear - nest, Kind heart-ed and true, Look ev - er to Je - sus,
3 Sa - viour, Our strength will re - new, Look ev - er to Je - sus,

REFRAIN

1-3 He'll car-ry you through. Ask the Saviour to help you, Comfort, strengthen and

keep you, He is will-ing to aid you, He will car-ry you through.

An alternative and higher Setting is on the preceding page

680 There is a Happy Land

ANDREW YOUNG   HAPPY LAND 6.4.6.4.6.7.6.4.   TELUGU MELODY

1 There is a hap-py land, Far, far a-way, Where saints in glo-ry stand,
2 Come to this hap-py land, Come, come a-way; Why will ye doubting stand?
3 Bright in that hap-py land Beams ev-'ry eye; Kept by a Fa-ther's hand,

1 Bright, bright as day: O how they sweet-ly sing, 'Wor-thy is our
2 Why still de-lay? O we shall hap-py be When, from sin and
3 Love can-not die: On then to glo-ry run; Be a crown and

1 Sa-viour King!' Loud let His prai-ses ring, Praise, praise for aye.
2 sor-row free, Lord, we shall live with Thee, Blest, blest for aye.
3 king-dom won; And, bright a-bove the sun, Reign, reign for aye.

An alternative and lower Setting is on the following page

680 There is a Happy Land

ANDREW YOUNG   HAPPY LAND 6.4.6.4.6.7.6.4.   TELUGU MELODY

1 There is a hap-py land, Far, far a - way, Where saints in glo - ry stand,
2 Come to this hap-py land, Come, come a - way; Why will ye doubting stand?
3 Bright in that hap-py land Beams ev - 'ry eye; Kept by a Fa-ther's hand,

1 Bright, bright as day: O how they sweet-ly sing, 'Wor - thy is our
2 Why still de - lay? O we shall hap - py be When, from sin and
3 Love can - not die: On then to glo - ry run; Be a crown and

1 Sa-viour King!' Loud let His prais - es ring, Praise, praise for aye.
2 sor - row free, Lord, we shall live with Thee, Blest, blest for aye.
3 king-dom won; And, bright a - bove the sun, Reign, reign for aye.

An alternative and higher Setting is on the preceding page

681 Whither, Pilgrims?

ANON

WM. B. BRADBURY

1. { Whither, pil-grims, are you go - ing, Go-ing each with staff in hand?
   { We are go - ing on a jour-ney, Go-ing at our King's com-mand.

2. { Tell us, pil-grims, what you hope for, In that far off, bet-ter land?
   { Spot-less robes and crowns of glo - ry, From a Sa - viour's lov-ing hand.

3. { Pil-grims, may we tra-vel with you To that bright and bet-ter land?
   { Come and wel - come, come and wel - come, Welcome to our pil-grim band.

1. O - ver hills, and plains, and val - leys, We are go - ing to His pal - ace,
2. We shall drink of life's clear ri - ver, We shall dwell with God for ev - er,
3. Come, oh! come, and do not leave us; Christ is wait - ing to re - ceive us,

1. We are go - ing to His pal - ace, Go-ing to the bet - ter land;
2. We shall dwell with God for ev - er In that bright, that bet - ter land;
3. Christ is wait - ing to re - ceive us In that bright, that bet - ter land;

1. We are go - ing to His pal - ace, Go-ing to the bet - ter land.
2. We shall dwell with God for ev - er In that bright, that bet - ter land.
3. Christ is wait - ing to re - ceive us In that bright, that bet - ter land.

682 The King's Highway

ANON
AMERICAN AIR

1. Our God will guide us right, and, walk-ing in the light, We shall
2. Wher-ev-er you may be, what-ev-er you may see That would
3. The mea-dows may be green where "bye-path stile" is seen: "Turn a-
4. For, on en-chant-ed ground, there's dan-ger all a-round And a

:S:

1. win a crown of glo-ry on that day (on that day), When Je-sus calls His own, to-
2. lead you in-to e-vil, say you "Nay!" (say you "Nay"): I will not turn a-side, what-
3. side!" the lit-tle flowers seem to say (seem to say), Be sure you give no heed, they're
4. thousand pleasant voices bid you stay (bid you stay), With fingers stop your ears, and

D.S.—Our God will guide us right, and

FINE.

1. ge-ther round the throne, Who keep a-long the middle of the King's high-way.
2. ev-er may be-tide: I'll keep a-long the middle of the King's high-way.
3. try-ing to mislead; Just keep a-long the middle of the King's high-way.
4. ne-ver mind their jeers; Just keep a-long the middle of the King's high-way.

walking in the light, We'll keep a-long the middle of the King's high-way.

REFRAIN.   D.S.

The King's highway! the king's highway! Oh, turn a-side from ev'rything that leads a-stray!

683 # Mothers of Salem

WILLIAM M. HUTCHINGS

SALEM

GERMAN MELODY,
Arr. A. RHODES

1 When mo - thers of Sal - em Their chil - dren brought to Je - sus,
2 'For I will re - ceive them, And fold them in My bo - som:
3 How kind was our Sa - viour To bid those chil - dren wel - come!
4 O soon may the hea - then Of ev - 'ry tribe and na - tion

1 The stern dis - ci - ples drove them back And bade them de - part;
2 I'll be a Shep - herd to those lambs, O drive them not a - way!
3 But there are ma - ny thou - sands who Have ne - ver heard His Name;
4 Ful - fil Thy bless - ed word, and cast Their i - dols all a - way:

1 But Je - sus saw them ere they fled, And sweet - ly smil'd, and
2 For, if their hearts to Me they give, They shall with Me in
3 The Bi - ble they have nev - er read; They know not that the
4 O shine up - on them from a - bove, And show Thy - self a

1 kind - ly said, 'Suf - fer lit - tle chil - dren to come un - to Me;'
2 glo - ry live; Suf - fer lit - tle chil - dren to come un - to Me.'
3 Sa - viour said, 'Suf - fer lit - tle chil - dren to come un - to Me.'
4 God of love; Teach the lit - tle chil - dren to come un - to Thee.

The tune ATHLONE is on the following page

683

Mothers of Salem

WILLIAM M. HUTCHINGS   ATHLONE   R. N. QUAILE

1 When mo-thers of Sal-em Their chil-dren brought to Je - sus,
2 'For I will re-ceive them, And fold them in My bo - som;
3 How kind was our Sa-viour To bid those chil-dren wel-come!
4 O soon may the hea-then Of ev-'ry tribe and na-tion

1 The stern dis-ci-ples drove them back And bade them de-part;
2 I'll be a Shep-herd to those lambs, O drive them not a-way!
3 But there are ma-ny thou-sands who have ne-ver heard His Name;
4 Ful-fil Thy bless-ed word, and cast their i-dols all a-way:

1 But Je-sus saw them ere they fled, And sweet-ly smil'd, and
2 For, if their hearts to Me they give, They shall with Me in
2 The Bi-ble they have nev-er read; They know not that the
4 O shine up-on them from a-bove, And show Thy-self a

1 kind-ly said, 'Suf-fer lit-tle chil-dren to come un-to Me;'
2 glo-ry live; Suf-fer lit-tle chil-dren to come un-to Me.'
3 Sa-viour said, 'Suf-fer lit-tle chil-dren to come un-to Me.'
4 God of love; Teach the lit-tle chil-dren to come un-to Thee.

Music by permission of METHODIST YOUTH DEPARTMENT. The tune SALEM precedes this one

684 That Sweet Story

JAMES ROWE

E. O. EXCELL

1 I once heard a sweet sto - ry of won - der - ful love
2 Though a - far I had wan - der'd in dark - ness and sin,
3 That sweet sto - ry of Je - sus who died on the tree

1 And it lift - ed the cross that I bore, . . .
2 And though help - less, and wea - ry, and poor, . . .
3 Will be told on e - ter - ni - ty's shore; . .

1 Made me think of the home and the dear ones a - bove;
2 This sweet sto - ry left light, hope, and glad - ness with - in;
3 How He came as a ran - som for you and for me;

1-3 I am long - ing to hear it once more. . . .

That Sweet Story—*Continued*

REFRAIN

I am long-ing to hear it once more; . . once more;

The sto-ry re-peat o'er and o'er; . . . . I am sure;

It is rap-ture di-vine to know He is mine;

I am long-ing to hear it once more. . .

685 Open Wide the Door

FANNY J. CROSBY   DUET   JNO. R. SWENEY

1 Wea - ry child, thy sin for - sak - ing, Close thy heart no more;
2 To the Sa - viour's ten - der plead - ing, Close thy heart no more;
3 To the Gos - pel in - vi - ta - tion Close thy heart no more;
4 To the joy that fad - eth nev - er Close thy heart no more;

1 From thy dream of pleas - ure wak - ing, O - pen wide the door.
2 Now the call of mer - cy heed - ing, O - pen wide the door.
3 To re - ceive a full sal - va - tion O - pen wide the door.
4 To the peace a - bid - ing ev - er O - pen wide the door.

REFRAIN

While the lamp of life is burn - ing, And the heart of God is

yearn - ing, To His lov - ing arms re - turn - ing, Give thy wan - d'ring o'er.

686

He's My Friend

WILL L. THOMPSON

WILL L. THOMPSON

1. Je - sus is all the world to me, My life, my joy, my all;
2. Je - sus is all the world to me, My friend in tri - als sore;
3. Je - sus is all the world to me, And true to Him I'll be;
4. Je - sus is all the world to me, I want no bet - ter friend;

1. He is my strength from day to day, With - out Him I would fall.
2. I go to Him for bless-ings and He gives them o'er and o'er.
3. O, how could I this friend de - ny, When He's so true to me?
4. I trust Him now, I'll trust Him when Life's fleet - ing days shall end;

1. When I am sad, to Him I go, No oth - er one can cheer me so;
2. He sends the sun-shine and the rain, He sends the harvest's gold - en grain;
3. Fol-low - ing Him I know I'm right, He watch-es o'er me day and night;
4. Beau-ti - ful life with such a friend; Beau-ti - ful life that has no end;

1. When I am sad He makes me glad, He's my friend.
2. Sun-shine and rain, har - vest of grain, He's my friend.
3. Fol - low - ing Him, by day and night, He's my friend.
4. E - ter - nal life, e - ter - nal joy, He's my friend.

687   The Story of His Love

JAMES ROWE   DUET—SOPRANO AND ALTO   IRA B. WILSON

1 There's a sweet old sto - ry which I long
2 There's a sweet old sto - ry that I love
3 There's a sweet old sto - ry that I love

1 to . hear When the night is long and drear - y;
2 to . read When my spi - rit dreads the mor - row;
3 to . tell To the heart by grief o'er - tak - en,

1 When I feel the pow - er of the tempt - er
2 When, to help me on - ward, strength or cheer I
3 To the friend - less bro - thers who in dark - ness

1 near, And my soul is sad and wea - ry.
2 need; Or when com - fort I would bor - row.
3 dwell, And to those by hope for - sak - en.

The Story of His Love—*Continued*

'Tis the old, old sto-ry of His love, ...
'Tis the old, old sto-ry, . the sto-ry of His love,

'Tis the sweet, old mess-age from a - bove; . . . .
'Tis the sweet, old mess-age, . the mess-age from a - bove;

For no o-ther I can find that can calm a trou-bled mind.

Like the sweet old sto-ry of His love! . . .
Like the sweet old sto-ry, . the sto-ry of His love!

688 What Shall I Bring?

LIZZIE DE ARMOND

W. A. POST

1 What shall I bring to the Sa - viour . . . What shall I lay at His feet? . . I have no glit - ter - ing jew - els, . . Gold, or frank-in-cense so sweet (so sweet).

2 What shall I bring to the Sa - viour . . praiz - es to sing, . . Feet that will walk in the path - way . . Lead - ing to Je - sus, our King (our King).

3 What shall I bring to the Sa - viour . . Lips His dear prais - es to sing, . . Life in its sweet - ness and beau - ty . . All for His ser - vice so blest (so blest).

REFRAIN

Gifts to the Sa - viour I'm bring-ing, Love's rich-est trea-sures to lay Low at His feet with re - joic - ing, Ere yon-der sun set to - day (to - day).

rit.

The tune TANTUM ERGO is on the following page

688 What Shall I Bring?

LIZZIE DE ARMOND TANTUM ERGO 8.7.8.7. D VINCENT NOVELLO

1 What shall I bring to the Sa - viour? What shall I lay at
2 What shall I bring to the Sa - viour? Lips His dear prais - es
3 What shall I bring to the Sa - viour? Love that is pur - est

1 His feet? I have no glit - ter-ing jew - els, Gold, or
2 to sing, Feet that will walk in the path - way Lead - ing
3 and best, Life in its sweet-ness and beau - ty, All for

REFRAIN

1 frank - in - cense so sweet.
2 to Je - sus, our King.   Gifts to the Sa - viour I'm
3 His ser - vice so blest.

bring - ing, Love's rich-est trea - sures to lay Low at His

feet with re - joic - ing, Ere yon-der sun set to - day.

An Alternative Tune is on the preceding page

Now He Uses Me

C. D. MARTIN   W. STILLMAN MARTIN

1. How oft I prayed for pow - er, And tar - ried by the way,
2. I did not get the bless - ing Un - til the Bless - er came,
3. To - day my rich - est bless - ing Is do - ing His sweet word,

1. I want - ed some great bless - ing To use each bus - y day.
2. Nor was I fit for ser - vice, Till filled with love's warm flame.
3. My high - est joy each mo - ment, Is to be used of God.

CHORUS.

But now He us - es me, Praise God, He us - es me, The
     ev - en me,   ev - en me,

bless - ed Ho - ly Spi - rit us - es me, But now He us - es me, Praise
                   ev - en me,

God, He us - es me, The bless - ed Ho - ly Spi - rit us - es me.
     ev - en me,

690

Love So Mighty

Frank. E. Graeff

C. Harold Lowden

1. Be - fore a cross up - lift - ed high, I stood a - lone one day;
2. In grief and pain I wept a - loud In help - less a - go - ny;
3. That voice, so sweet, entranced my soul, It gave me hope and cheer;
4. And there up - on that cru - el cross My Sa - viour died that day;

1. My soul was bur - dened with a guilt No tears could wash a - way.
2. When from the cross I heard One speak, "I gave my life for thee."
3. Tho' tremb-ling, I drew near the cross, For I had naught to fear,
4. I looked, believed, and from my soul The bur - den roll'd a - way.

CHORUS.

Love mighty and won-der-ful, Love boundless and free !

Love, love so mighty and won-der-ful ! Love, the love so boundless and free !

yes

so free and

Love that suf-fered up - on the cross,

Love, the love that suf-fered up - on the cross, The love that died for me.

691

Best of All

C. W. Ray

Wm. J. Kirkpatrick

1. Je - sus all my grief is shar - ing, He my man - sion is pre - par - ing;
2. Je - sus loves and watch - es o'er me, With His grace He will re - store me;
3. Je - sus loves and He will guide me, All I need He will pro - vide me;

1. When I'm trem - bling and des - pair - ing, He will sure - ly hear my call;
2. An - gel guards He sends be - fore me, Lest in fa - tal snares I fall;
3. In His bo - som He will hide me When the woes of life ap - pal;

1. When the storms a - round me sweep - ing, Tho' in help - less - ness I'm sleep - ing,
2. With His friends He hath en - rolled me, By His might He will up - hold me,
3. He will hear my fee - blest sigh - ing, Need - ful grace to me sup - ply - ing,

1. I am safe in His own keep - ing, This to me is best of all, Best of
2. In His arms He will en - fold me, This to me is best of all, Best of
3. He'll be with me when I'm dy - ing, This to me is best of all, Best of

ad lib.

1. all, best of all; I am safe in His own keep - ing, This to me is best of all.
2. all, best of all: In His arms He will en - fold me, This to me is best of all.
3. all, best of all; He'll be with me when I'm dy - ing, This to me is best of all.

The Golden City

692

H. H. Booth

1. I've a home fair and bright in yonder City, To its gates I am marching a-long; When my
2. It is true on the way to yonder City, I've to cross o'er a cold rolling flood; But I
3. Do you know there's no place in yonder City For a soul that is burdened with guilt? Do you

1. fight-ing for Je-sus here is o-ver, I shall then take my place with the throng That
2. trust Him to guide me by whose pi-ty I've been led to the sin-cleansing blood; As
3. know that no sin can ev-er en-ter? Has-ten then to the blood that was spilt To

1. face to face be-holds the Sa-viour, In whose praise is raised its song.
2. He has said He'll nev-er leave me, I will trust my Friend, my God,
3. cleanse from sin, and with me jour-ney To the Ci-ty God has built.

f CHORUS.

Up in the gold-en Ci-ty There's a man-sion to me will be giv'n; I have

rich-es I know That the world can't bestow, I'm an heir of the wealth of heav'n.

693   Anon.

Not a Disappointment

H. Green

1. He is not a dis-ap-point-ment! Je-sus is far more to me
2. He is not a dis-ap-point-ment! He has saved my soul from sin:
3. He is not a dis-ap-point-ment! He is com-ing by and by,
4. He is not a dis-ap-point-ment! He is all in all to me—

1. Than in all my glow-ing day-dreams I had fancied He could be;
2. All the guilt, and all the an-guish, which oppressed my heart with-in.
3. In my heart I have the wit-ness that His com-ing draw-eth nigh.
4. Bles-sed Sa-viour, Sanc-ti-fi-er; the un-changing Christ is He!

1. And the more I get to know Him, so the more I find Him true,
2. He has ban-ished by His pre-sence, and His bles-sed kiss of peace
3. All the scof-fers may des-pise me, and no change a-round may see,
4. He has won my heart's af-fec-tions, and He meets my ev-'ry need;

1. And the more I long that o-thers should be led to know Him too,
2. Has as-sured my heart for-ev-er that His love will nev-er cease.
3. But He tells me He is com-ing, and that's quite e-nough for me,
4. He is not a dis-ap-point-ment, for He sa-tis-fies in-deed,

1. And the more I long that o-thers should be led to know Him too.
2. Has as-sured my heart for ev-er that His love will nev-er cease.
3. But He tells me He is com-ing, and that's quite e-nough for me.
4. He is not a dis-ap-point-ment, for He sa-tis-fies in-deed.

By permission of the SOUTH AFRICA GENERAL MISSION

An Atoning Death

694

THOMAS DENNIS

THOMAS DENNIS

1 Have you read the sto - ry of the Cross, Where Je - sus
2 Have you read how they placed the crown of thorns Up - on His
3 Have you read how He saved the dy - ing thief When hang-ing
4 Have you read that He looked to heav'n and said, 'Tis fin-ish'd—

1 bled and died: Where your debt was paid by His pre - cious blood That
2 love - ly brow? When He pray'd, for - give them, oh! for - give, They
3 on the tree? Who looked with pi - ty - ing eyes and said, Dear
4 'twas for thee? Have you ev - er said, I thank Thee, Lord, For

REFRAIN

1 flow'd from His wound - ed side? ⎫
2 know not what they do. ⎬ He died an a - ton - ing
3 Lord, re - mem - ber me. ⎪
4 giv - ing Thy life for me? ⎭

death for thee, He died an a - ton - ing death; Oh, wondrous

love! it was for thee, He died an a - ton - ing death!

695 A Sinner Saved by Grace

A. B. S.

A. B. SIMPSON

1. When I shall reach my home in glo - ry, And see my Sa - viour face to face,
2. I'll tell how by His blood He bought me, With all our lost and ransomed race;
3. I'll tell them how His Spi - rit sealed me, And cleansed me from each sin-ful trace;
4. I'll sing how lov - ing-ly He led me At last to yon - der heavenly place;
5. Yes, when I reach my home in glo - ry, And see my Sa - viour face to face;

1. This shall be all my song and sto - ry, A sin - ner saved by grace.
2. And how so ten - der-ly He sought me, And saved me by His grace.
3. And how when sick and worn He healed me, And saved me by His grace.
4. And how He shep - herd-ed and fed me, And kept me by His grace.
5. This shall be all my song and sto - ry, A sin - ner saved by grace.

CHORUS.

Saved by grace, saved by grace, For ev - er I'll tell the sto - ry,
Saved by grace, saved by grace, sto - ry of love,

How Je-sus saved me by His grace, And brought me to His glo - ry.
How Je-sus saved me by His grace,

696 ## I Know

S. C. Kirk

J. Lincoln Hall

1 The works and ways of God on high I can-not solve, I do not try;
2 I know that my Re-deem-er lives, I know, I know that He for-gives;
3 How at His word the dark-ness flies, And beams of sun-light flood my eyes,
4 Be-yond this mor-tal vale there stands A house for me not made with hands;

1 But tho' I can-not these un-fold, One thing I know, to this I'll hold
2 I know that I who once was dead Am now a-live in Christ, my head;
3 I do not know; e-nough for me That I who once was blind now see!
4 E'en now I see be-yond the dome, And oc-cu-py my heav'n-ly home;

1 Tho' all the world be-sides de-ny, A sin-ner saved by grace am I.
2 Let all the world be-sides de-ny, 'I know I live!' shall be my cry.
3 Let all the world be-sides de-ny, 'I know I see!' shall be my cry.
4 Let all the world be-sides de-ny, I know I have a home on high.

REFRAIN

I can-not tell you why, nor how, For O I do not un-der-stand;

I on-ly say, 'I know! I know!' On this un-shak-en ground I stand.

Copyright by the Rodeheaver Hall-Mack Co.

697 I have Christ!

M. J. W.

LETHA H. SIMS

1. In the heart of Lon-don ci-ty, 'Mid the dwell-ings of the poor,
2. Spo-ken by a lone-ly wo-man, Dy-ing on a gar-ret floor,
3. Oh, her words will live for ev-er, I re-peat them o'er and o'er,
4. Oh, my dear, my fel-low sin-ners, High and low, and rich and poor,
5. Look a-way from earth's at-tractions, All its joys will soon be o'er;

1. These bright gold-en words were ut-tered: I have Christ! what want I more?
2. Hav-ing not one earth-ly com-fort: I have Christ! what want I more?
3. God de-lights to hear me say-ing: I have Christ! what want I more?
4. Can you say with deep thanks-giv-ing: I have Christ! what want I more?
5. Trust Him now and say with glad-ness: I have Christ! what want I more?

REFRAIN.

1. I have Christ! what want I more?
2. I have Christ! what want I more?
3. I have Christ! what want I more?
4. I have Christ! what want I more?
5. I have Christ! what want I more?

I have Christ! what want I more?

I have Christ! What want I more?

I have Christ! what want I more? I have Christ! what want I more?

I have Christ! what want I more? I have Christ!

698 The Child of a King

HATTIE E. BUELL   JOHN CORBETT, *Arr.* P. J. MANSFIELD

1 My Fa-ther is rich in hous-es and lands, He hold-eth the wealth
2 My Fa-ther's own Son, the Sa-viour of men, Once wan-der'd o'er earth
3 I once was an out-cast stran-ger on earth, A sin-ner by choice,
4 A tent or a cot-tage, why should I care? They're build-ing a pal-

1 of the world in His hands; Of ru-bies and dia-monds of sil-ver and
2 as the poor-est of them; But now He is reign-ing for ev-er on
3 an a-lien by birth; But I've been a-dopt-ed, my name's writ-ten
4 ace for me o-ver there! Tho' ex-iled from home, yet still I may

REFRAIN

1 gold, His cof-fers are full, He has rich-es un-told...
2 high, And will give me a home in heav'n by and by. I'm the
3 down, An heir to a man-sion, a robe, and a crown.
4 sing: All glo-ry to God, I'm the child of a King!

child of a King, ... I'm the child of a King; With

rall.

Je-sus my Sa-viour, I'm the child, I'm the child of a King.

699 Just as He Promised

W. M. LIGHTHALL

CHAS. H. GABRIEL

1 My Fa-ther will not let me fall, His strong and lov-ing arms en - fold me;
2 My Sa-viour will not let me stray, The path He trod is plain be - fore me;
3 I trust Him as a lit-tle child, Con - tent be-neath His wings to hide me;
4 His love will still re-mem-ber me, In life, in death, in joy, in sor - row;

1 To Him I trust my life, my all, And know that He will safe-ly hold me.
2 And He who said, 'I am the Way' Is watch - ing, ev - er watch-ing o'er me.
3 Tho' all a-round is rough and wild, He walks the path of peace be-side me.
4 What-e'er be - tide, He still will be My Guide to-day, My Hope to-mor-row.

REFRAIN

Just as He pro-mis'd, pro-mis'd to do, When first to Him I trem-bling came;

Now I have trust-ed, pro-ven Him true, Hal - le - lu - jah to His Name!

700 Waiting, Knocking

C. Austin Miles

C. Austin Miles

1 Who is this that's wait-ing, wait-ing, Just out - side the door ? Who is He that's
2 Don't you hear Him say-ing, say - ing, 'Come, O come to Me; 'Twas for you that,
3 Still His voice is call-ing, call - ing, Sweet the tones and low; Bid Him en - ter
4 Some-time you'll be wait-ing, wait - ing, Just out - side the gate; Some-time you'll be

1 knock-ing, knock-ing, Has He knock'd be - fore ? Rise and bid Him en - ter in ! Peace and
2 dy - ing, dy - ing, I hung on the tree; Come and see My hands, My side ; Look on
3 quick-ly, quick-ly, Ere He turns to go ! Must His plead-ing be in vain ? Must He,
4 plead-ing, plead-ing, Then 'twill be too late ; Now ac-cept your heav'nly Guest ! He'll for-

1 hope He'll bring ; 'Tis thy Sa-viour knock-ing, knock-ing, 'Tis thy Lord and King.
2 Me and live ; Tho' your sins be ma-ny, ma-ny, Par-don I can give.'
3 then, de - part, All be-cause His plead-ing, plead-ing, Reaches not your heart ?
4 give your sin ! While He still is wait-ing, wait-ing, Rise and let Him in ;

REFRAIN

Let Him in ! Let Him in ! He waits out - side the door ;

Let Him in ere He de - parts To re - turn no more !

701 What will You Do?

A. B. SIMPSON   A. B. SIMPSON

1 Je-sus is stand-ing in Pi-late's hall, Friend-less, for-sak-en, be-tray'd by all;
2 Je-sus is stand-ing on tri-al still; You can be false to Him if you will;
3 Will you e-vade Him as Pi-late tried? Or shall you choose Him what-e'er be-tide?
4 Shall you, like Pe-ter, your Lord de-ny? Or shall you scorn from His foes to fly?
5 Je-sus, I give Thee my heart to-day; Je-sus, I'll fol-low Thee all the way;

1 Heark-en, what mean-eth the sud-den call! What will you do with Je-sus?
2 You can be faith-ful thro' good or ill: What will you do with Je-sus?
3 Vain-ly you strug-gle from Him to hide: What will you do with Je-sus?
4 Dar-ing for Je-sus to live or die: What will you do with Je-sus?
5 Glad-ly o-bey-ing Him, will you say: 'This will I do with Je-sus.'

REFRAIN

What will you do with Je sus? Neu-tral you can-not be,

What will you do? What will you do? Neu-tral you can-not, can-not be,

Some day your heart will be ask-ing: What will He do with me?

ritard

Some day your heart will be ask-ing: What will He do? What will He do?

ritardando

An Alternative Tune is on the following page

701 What will You Do?

A. B. SIMPSON   DUET   M. W. STUBBS

1 Je-sus is stand-ing in Pi-late's hall, Friend-less, for-sa-ken, be-
2 Je-sus is stand-ing on tri-al still, You can be false to Him
3 Will you e-vade Him as Pi-late tried? Or shall you choose Him what-
4 Shall you, like Pe-ter, your Lord de-ny? Or shall you scorn from His
5 Je-sus, I give Thee my heart to-day; Je-sus, I'll fol-low Thee

1 tray'd by all; . Heark-en! what mean-eth the sud-den call? . .
2 if you will; . You can be faith-ful thro' good or ill: . .
3 e'er be-tide? . Vain-ly you strug-gle from Him to hide: . .
4 foes to fly? . Dar-ing for Je-sus to live or die: . .
5 all the way; . Glad-ly o-bey-ing Him, will you say: . .

UNISON or DUET   REFRAIN

What will you do with Je - sus?
Verse 5 This will I do with Je - sus.   What will you do? . .

what will you do? Neu-tral you can-not be; . . .

Some day your heart will be ask-ing, What will He do with me? . . .

An Alternative Tune is on the preceding page

702   I Know it is True

S. C. KIRK

J. G. WILSON

1. So strange it seemed and wondrous, When first it came to me, The sto-ry of my
2. And when I heard the sto-ry Told o'er and o'er a-gain, How Je-sus, now in
3. Then soft-ly was it spo-ken, "Come, lean up-on My breast, Ye weary ones, heart-
4. A voice came sweet and ten-der! It seemed to touch my woe; I felt my heart sur-

1. Sa-viour; I asked, "Can such things be?" I felt my heart re-ply-ing, "O
2. glo-ry, Was walk-ing still with men, Was fill-ing hearts with gladness, And
3. bro-ken, And I will give you rest." My heart, so sad and lone-ly, A
4. ren-der— I cried, "O Lord, I know!" My Sa-viour, Thou hast spo-ken! The

1. if I on-ly knew! The cross, the thorns, the dy-ing! O is it, is it true?
2. scatt'ring sunshine thro'; My own heart longed in sadness To know if it were true!
3. lit-tle clos-er drew; I cried, "O Lord, if on-ly I felt and knew it true!"
4. old, old story's new! And Thou dost give the to-ken! I know, I know it's true!

CHORUS.

1, 2, 3. I love to hear it spo-ken, I love to read it through;
4. My Sa-viour, O my Sa-viour! The old, old sto-ry's new!

1, 2, 3. But O for word or to-ken To tell me it is true!
4. My strength, my joy for-ev-er. I know, I know it's true.

703

All for Me

C. A. M.

C. AUSTIN MILES.

1. Wea - ry and wan-d'ring and sunk - en in sin, Vile as a
2. Foot - sore and wea - ry He toil'd all the way, E - ven to
3. Still I re - ject - ed your Sa - viour and mine, Till I be -

1. sin - ner could be, Je - sus be - held and to Beth - le - hem came,
2. Geth-sem - a - ne, Oft I have met Him and heard His sweet voice,
3. held on the tree, Suf - fer - ing, dy - ing, my Sa - viour and yours,

1. Left His bright throne for me, . Left His bright throne for me, for me.
2. Pray-ing for me, for me, . Pray-ing for me, for me, for me.
3. Dy - ing for you and me, . Dy - ing for you and me, for me.

CHORUS.

All for me, (was it) All for me? Lord was it all for me? . From the

all for me,

throne to the manger, From there to the cross, Yes, it was all for me.

704 This Man of Sorrows

LEILA N. MORRIS   LEILA N. MORRIS

1. Who is this that com-eth from E - dom, Crim-son-red His gar-ments dyed,
2. Who is this, despised and re-ject-ed, Who the wine-press trod a - lone?
3. Who is this with bear-ing so king-ly, And a crown His brow a - dorns,
4. Who is this on Cal-va-ry's moun-tain, Dy-ing there such shameful death?

In His hands are cru-el nail-prints, And a spear-wound in His side?
Who is this by all for-sak-en, Left to com-fort there are none?
Not of gold and gems be-fit-ting, But of mock-ing, cru-el thorns?
Who for His tor-men-tors pray-ing, With His last ex-pir-ing breath?

Say, who is this "Man of Sor-rows?" Why is He thus pierced and scarred?
Who is this oppressed, af-flic-ted, Yet no mur-mur ev-er heard;
Why with ma - ny stripes thus beat-en? Why thus scourged and spit up-on?
Who is this that earth should trem-ble And the sun in darkness hide,

Who with face and form so king-ly! Why His beau-teous vis-age marred?
As a Lamb led to the slaugh-ter, Yet He an-swers not a word!
Why His an-guish in the gar-den, Kneel-ing, pray-ing all a - lone?
Rocks be rent and graves be o-pened, When He bowed His head and died?

This Man of Sorrows—*Continued*

CHORUS

It is Christ, the King of glo - ry, Who His life a ran - som gave,

It is Christ, the King, the King of glory, Who His life, His life a ransom gave,

Bow be-fore Him, and a - dore Him, Jesus Christ the mighty . . . . . to save. . .

the mighty, the mighty to save.

705

Seek Ye First

GEORGINA M. TAYLOR   PITCAIRN 8.8.8.6   THOS. CAIRNS

1. Seek ye first, not earth - ly pleasure, Fad - ing joy and fail - ing trea-sure,
2. Seek ye first, not earth's as - pi - rings, Cease-less long - ings, vain de - sir - ings,
3. Seek ye first, God's peace and bless-ing; Ye have all if this pos-sess-ing:
4. Seek Him first; then when for-giv - en, Pardon'd, made an heir of hea-ven,
5. Seek the com - ing of his king-dom; Seek the souls a - round to win them,

1. But the love that knows no mea-sure Seek ye first, Seek ye first.
2. But your pre - cious soul's re - quir-ings Seek ye first, Seek ye first.
3. Come, your need and sin con - fess-ing, Seek Him first, Seek Him first.
4. Let your life to Him be giv - en: Seek this first, Seek this first.
5. Seek to Je sus Christ to bring them: Seek this first, Seek this first.

706   O Wandering Souls!

F. W. FABER

J. JEFFERYS

1. I was wan-der-ing and wea-ry When my Saviour came un-to me;
2. At first I would not heark-en And put off un-til the mor-row;
3. At last I stopp'd to list-en— His voice could not de-ceive me;
4. I thought His love would weak-en, As more and more He knew me;

1. For the ways of sin grew drea-ry, And the world had ceased to woo me
2. But life be-gan to dark-en, And I was sick with sor-row;
3. I saw His kind eyes glist-en, So anx-ious to re-lieve me;
4. But it burneth like a bea-con, And its light and heat go thro' me;

1. And I thought I heard Him say, As He came a-long His way:
2. And I thought I heard Him say, As He came a-long His way:
3. And I thought I heard Him say, As He came a-long His way:
4. And I ev-er hear Him say, As He goes a-long His way:

CHORUS.

"O wand'ring souls, come near Me, My sheep should never fear Me—I am the Shepherd true!

An Alternative Tune is on the following page

706 O Wandering Souls!

F. W. FABER SECOND TUNE M. W. STUBBS

UNISON or SOLO.

1. I was wan-der-ing and wea-ry When my Saviour came un-to me;
2. At first I would not heark-en, And put off un-til the mor-row;
3. At last I stopped to lis-ten, His voice could not de-ceive me;
4. I thought His love would weak-en, As more and more He knew me;

ACCOMPT. pizz.

rall.

1. For the ways of sin grew drea-ry, And the world had ceased to woo me:
2. But life be-gan to dark-en, And I was sick with sor-row;
3. I saw His kind eyes glist-en, So anx-ious to re-lieve me;
4. But it burn-eth like a bea-con, And its light and heat go through me:

f Harmony.

1, 2, 3. And I thought I heard Him say, As He came a-long His way,—
4. And I ev-er hear Him say, As He goes a-long His way,—

REFRAIN. Unison.

"O wand'ring souls, come near Me, My sheep should nev-er

rall.

fear Me—I am the Shep-herd true, I am the Shep-herd true!"

An Alternative Tune is on the preceding page

707 The Door of God's Mercy

ELLEN OLIVER

E. B. SMITH.

1. The door of God's mer-cy is o-pen To all who are wea-ry of sin,
2. The world is e'er wan-ton-ly woo-ing Your soul from the ways of the blest,
3. So ma-ny who hear the glad message Will nev-er its mandates o-bey,
4. Sad hearts there will sure-ly be moan-ing Out-side of the gate-way of life,
5. The door of God's mer-cy is o-pen, In-vit-ing-ly o-pen to all,

1. And Je-sus is pa-tient-ly wait-ing, Still wait-ing to welcome you in.
2. But Je-sus is ten-der-ly bid ding You turn to His hea-ven-ly rest.
3. But turn from the precious, dear pleadings, And wil-ful-ly wan-der a-way.
4. And pray ing to Him they re-ject-ed When earth with gay pleasure was rife.
5. Who list to the voice of the Mas-ter, And hear-ing shall heed His sweet call.

CHORUS.

Come, says the Sa-viour, come en-ter the gate; I watch by the por-tals both

ear-ly and late, Lest some pre cious soul, not far from the goal, Should

wan-der a-way in-to darkness and hate, And miss it for ev-er, the pear-ly gate.

708 Roll the Stone Away

ORA SAMUEL GRAY   CHARLES H. MARCH

1 Je-sus was stand-ing be-side a grave,   Weep-ing, but know-ing His pow'r to save;
2 Je-sus is speak-ing to you in song,   Ask-ing why have you de-lay'd so long?
3 Je-sus is stand-ing by hearts of sin,   Knock-ing and say-ing, 'Let Me come in.'

1 'Take ye a-way now the stone from the door,' And Christ will His pow-er dis-play. . .
2 While men are ly-ing in grave-clothes of sin, For whom Je-sus died on the Cross. . .
3 Rouse, then, ye sleep-er, and o-pen the door, For Je-sus has pow-er to save. . .

REFRAIN

They roll'd the stone a-way, . . For Christ was there that day, . . And call'd up-

on a man to leave the dark-en'd grave. We'll roll the stone a-way. . . For

rit.

He is here to-day, . . And waits to show His might-y pow'r, His pow'r to save. . .

709 He Did Not Die in Vain

DUET FOR MEZZO-SOPRANO AND TENOR, OR UNISON CHORUS THROUGHOUT

F. A. BRECK

GRANT COLFAX TULLAR

1 My bless-ed Lord was cru-ci-fied, The day was dark and grief was
2 He brings His great sal-va-tion nigh, And on His love bids us re-
3 O won-drous news of life and love! That Je-sus lives and reigns a-

1 wide, For hope was crush'd and all seem'd vain, Un-
2 ly; He bought our peace through grief and pain; But
3 bove, He made the path to glo-ry plain; Ah,

REFRAIN

1 til that Sa-viour rose a-gain.
2 Oh, He did not die in vain! Ring out the bless-ed news a-
3 no! He did not die in vain.

He Did Not Die in Vain—*Continued*

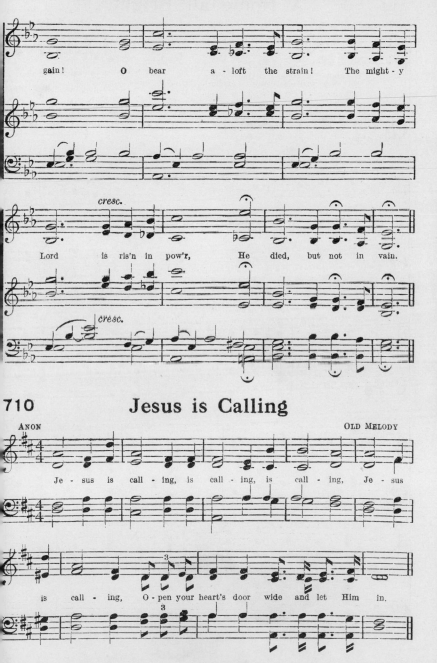

gain! O bear a - loft the strain! The might - y

cresc.

Lord is ris'n in pow'r, He died, but not in vain.

cresc.

710

Jesus is Calling

ANON

OLD MELODY

Je - sus is call - ing, is call - ing, is call - ing, Je - sus

is call - ing, O - pen your heart's door wide and let Him in.

711 A Home all Bright

Maggie E. Gregory   Duet.   Chas. H. Gabriel

1. Above this earth - ly home of ours, Of chill - ing winds, and fad-ing flow'rs, There
2. There we shall meet the lov'd and lost, Who o - ver death's dark riv - er cross'd; There
3. Here we may suf - fer grief and pain, And tears may flow like fall - ing rain; But

1. is a home all bright and fair, And all our hopes are cen - tered there.
2. we shall see our Saviour's face, And praise the wonders of His grace.
3. there where shines e - ter - nal day, God's hand shall wipe all tears a - way.

CHORUS.

Oh hap - py home, Oh man - sions blest, Where all God's
hap - py home, Oh man - sions blest, Where

wea - ry ones may rest; For in that bright un - cloud - ed
all God's wea - ry ones may rest; For in that bright, glad day, that un-

day, Our God shall wipe all tears a - way.
cloud - ed day,

712 An Everlasting Friend

ROBERT CROSBIE

1 I have a Friend, an ev-er-last-ing Friend, He is so kind, He
2 This Friend of mine, O how He longs to give The help you need in
3 Thro' a-ges past He's prov'd a glo-rious Friend, None ev-er ask'd and

1 is so good to me, He bore my sins, He suf-fer'd to the end That
2 this dark world of sin! He bids you come, no long-er sin-ful live, And
3 were by Him de-nied, His blood was shed that you and I might spend E-

REFRAIN

1 I might win a glo-rious vic-to-ry.
2 thro' His Name a crown of glo-ry win. } Come to this Friend, He's waiting
3 ter-ni-ty at His, our Sa-viour's side.

now for thee, He'll be so kind, so lov-ing, warm, and true, He'll break your

bands, from sin He'll set you free, He'll be an ev-er-last-ing Friend to you.

By permission of R. F. BEVERIDGE

713

Saved by His Grace

Geo. O. Webster.
QUARTETTE.

Grant Colfax Tullar

1. When in His beauty my Sa-viour I see, When I shall look on His face,
2. Long I had wan-der'd in pathways of sin, Of-ten His grace had I spurn'd;
3. How I re-joice that sal-va-tion is free, That I was not turn'd a-way;

1. Tongue cannot tell of the joy it will be, Sav'd by His won-der-ful grace (His grace).
2. Of-ten re-sis-ted His striving with-in, Ere to the Sa-viour I turn'd (I turn'd).
3. How I re-joice that my Sa-viour I'll see, Where I may praise Him for aye (for aye).

CHORUS.
DUET.

QUARTETTE.

Saved, . . . ; saved, . . . Sav'd by His won-der-ful grace ! . . .
Glo-ry, I'm sav'd by won-der-ful grace, won-der-ful grace !

DUET.

QUARTETTE.

Saved, . . . saved, . . . Granted in heaven a place; . . .
Glo-ry, I'm saved by won-der-ful grace, beau-ti-ful place;

Saved by His Grace—*Continued.*

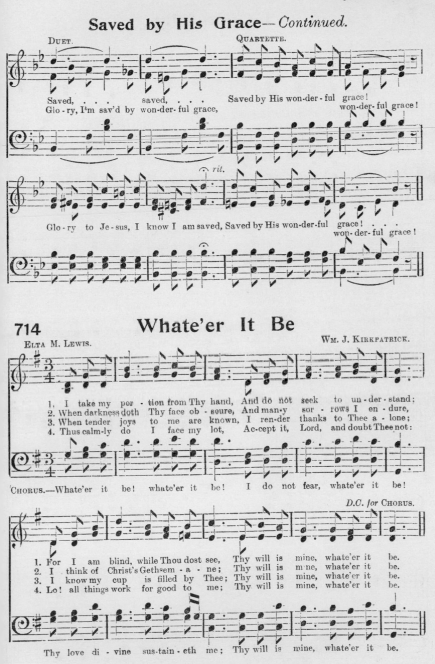

DUET.

QUARTETTE.

Saved, . . . saved, . . . Saved by His won-der-ful grace!

Glo-ry, I'm sav'd by won-der-ful grace, won-der-ful grace!

rit.

Glo-ry to Je-sus, I know I am saved, Saved by His won-der-ful grace! . . .

won-der-ful grace!

714

Whate'er It Be

ELTA M. LEWIS.

WM. J. KIRKPATRICK.

1, I take my por-tion from Thy hand, And do not seek to un-der-stand;
2. When darkness doth Thy face ob-scure, And man-y sor-rows I en-dure,
3. When tender joys to me are known, I ren-der thanks to Thee a-lone;
4. Thus calm-ly do I face my lot, Ac-cept it, Lord, and doubt Thee not:

CHORUS.—Whate'er it be! whate'er it be! I do not fear, whate'er it be!

D.C. for CHORUS.

1. For I am blind, while Thou dost see, Thy will is mine, whate'er it be.
2. I think of Christ's Gethsem-a-ne; Thy will is mine, whate'er it be.
3. I know my cup is filled by Thee; Thy will is mine, whate'er it be.
4. Lo! all things work for good to me; Thy will is mine, whate'er it be.

Thy love di-vine sus-tain-eth me; Thy will is mine, whate'er it be.

715   I Love Him

C. F. O.

S. C. FOSTER. *Arr. by* A. S. M.

1. Gone from my heart the world with all its charm, Now thro' the blood I'm
2. Once I was far a - way, deep down in sin, Once was a slave to
3. Once I was bound, but now I am set free, Once I was blind, but

1. saved from sin's a - larm; Down at the cross my heart is bend-ing low, The
2. pas - sions fierce with-in; Once was a - fraid to meet an an - gry God, But
3. now the light I see; Once I was dead, but now in God I live, And

mp CHORUS.   *pp*

1. pre - cious blood of Je - sus wash - es white as snow.
2. now I'm cleans'd from ev - 'ry stain thro' Je - sus' blood. } I love Him, I love Him,
3. tell the world a - round the peace that He doth give.

Be - cause He first loved me, And purchased my sal - va - tion on Mount Cal - va - ry.

716 My Mother's Bible

M. B. WILLIAMS   DUET   C. D. TILLMAN

1 There's a dear and pre-cious Book, Though it's worn and fa-ded now, Which re-
2 There she read of Je-sus' love, As He blest the chil-dren dear, How He
3 Well, those days are past and gone, But their mem-'ry lin-gers still, And the

1 calls the hap-py days of long a-go; When I stood at moth-er's knee,
2 suf-fer'd, bled, and died up-on the tree; Of His hea-vy load of care;
3 dear old Book each day has been my guide; And I seek to do His will,

1 With her hand up-on my brow, And I heard her voice in gen-tle tones and low.
2 Then she dried my flow-ing tear With her kiss-es as she said it was for me.
3 As my mo-ther taught me then, And ev-er in my heart His words a-bide.
D.S.—As I walk the nar-row way That leads at last to that bright home a-bove.

FINE

REFRAIN

Bles-sed Book, . . pre-cious Book, . .
bles-sed Book, pre-cious Book, On thy dear old tear-stained

leaves I love to look; love to look; Thou art sweet-er day by day,

D.S.

717 My Saviour is Precious

J. Wakefield MacGill

Arr. E. W. MacGill

1 My . . heart was op-press'd with the load of my sin, And it
2 Then He fill'd me with peace that the world know-eth not, That is
3 Then He shel-ters, and bless-es, and watch-es o'er me, Be my
4 O . . will you not love Him who first lov-ed you! Just re-

1 bent with the weight of its woe; . . At a touch of His hand all the
2 with me wher-ev-er I go; . . 'Tis the ver-y same calm that is
3 path-way the high or the low; . . I am safe, for His arm is pro-
4 spond and His sweet-ness you'll know, . . And . . nev-er a-gain will you

rit.

1 bur-den fell off, Do you won-der my lov-ing Him so? . .
2 fill-ing His heart, Do you won-der my lov-ing Him so? . .
3 tect-ing His child, Do you won-der my lov-ing Him so? . .
4 want o-ther love, Nor will won-der my lov-ing Him so. . .

REFRAIN

My Sa-viour is pre-cious to me, My Sa-viour is pre-cious to me, . .

And the more He is known by His lov'd and His own, More pre-cious He's cer-tain to be.

718 Thy Lord is Near

EMMA G. DIETRICK   EDWARD M. FULLER

1 Oh, ach-ing heart, with sor-row torn! Thy Lord is near and knows; He
2 Oh, faint-ing soul, with doubts oppress'd! Thy Lord is near and knows; He
3 Oh, wea-ry head, that fain would rest! Thy Lord is near and knows; He
4 Oh, lone-ly one, live thou thy best! Thy Lord is near and knows; He

1 knows it all— the feet way-worn, The wea-ry cares and woes,   The
2 knows it all— how thou art press'd On ev'-ry side with foes;   He
3 knows it all, and on His breast, Thou may-st now re-pose;   Drop
4 knows it all, sees ev'-ry test, Yes, ev'-ry tear that flows!   Re-

1 load of grief in an-guish borne, Thy Lord is near.............. He knows.
2 waits to be the cher-ish'd Guest;
3 ev'-ry care at His be-hest;
4 joice, faint heart, His way is best;   Thy Lord is near, He knows.

REFRAIN   rall.

He knows,   He knows,   Thy Lord is near, ... He knows.
He knows,   He knows,

My Lord and I

L. SHOREY

K. F. GARRARD

1 I have a Friend so pre-cious, So ve-ry dear to me.
2 He knows how much I love Him, He knows I love Him well;
3 He knows how I am long-ing Some wea-ry soul to win.
4 So up in-to the moun-tains Of hea-ven's cloud-less light,
5 And when the jour-ney's end-ed In rest and peace at last,

1 He loves me with such ten-der love, He loves so faith-ful-ly:
2 But with what love He lov-eth me My tongue can nev-er tell;
3 And so He bids me go and speak The lov-ing word for Him;
4 Or a-way in-to the val-leys .. Of dark-ness or of night,
5 When ev-'ry thought of dan-ger .. And wear-i-ness is past,

1 I could not live a-part from Him, I love to feel Him nigh,
2 It is an ev-er-last-ing love In ev-er rich sup-ply,
3 He bids me tell His won-drous love, And why He came to die,
4 Tho' round us tem-pests ga-ther .. And storms are rag-ing high,
5 In the king-dom of the fu-ture, .. In the glo-ry by and by,

1 And so we dwell to-ge-ther, My Lord and .. I.
2 And so we love each o-ther, My Lord and .. I.
3 And so we work to-ge-ther, My Lord and .. I.
4 We'll tra-vel on to-ge-ther, My Lord and .. I.
5 We'll live and reign to-ge-ther, My Lord and .. I.

720 Just One Touch

BIRDIE BELL

J. HOWARD ENTWISLE

1 Just one touch as He moves a-long, Push'd and press'd by the jost-ling throng,
2 Just one touch! and He makes me whole, Speaks sweet peace to my sin-sick soul,
3 Just one touch! and the work is done, I am saved by the bless-ed Son,
4 Just one touch! and He turns to me, O the love in His eyes I see!
5 Just one touch! by His might-y pow'r He can heal thee this ve-ry hour,

1 Just one touch and the weak was strong, Cured by the Heal-er di-vine.
2 At His feet all my bur-dens roll, Cured by the Heal-er di-vine.
3 I will sing while the a-ges run, Cured by the Heal-er di-vine.
4 I am His for He hears my plea, Cured by the Heal-er di-vine.
5 Thou canst hear tho' the tem-pests low'r, Cured by the Heal-er di-vine.

REFRAIN

Just one touch as He pass-es by, He will list to the faint-est cry.

Come and be sav'd while the Lord is nigh, Christ is the Heal-er di-vine.

di-vine.

Pilot Me

721

LEILA N. MORRIS

LEILA N. MORRIS

1 On the o - cean of life we are sail - ing, For the Ca - naan a -
2 For He knows where the dan - gers are lurk - ing, Where the rocks and the
3 Soon the ha - ven our barques will be near - ing, The Je - ru - sa - lem

1 bove we are bound; We are cer - tain the port to be gain - ing, Since the
2 hid - den reefs lie; We are safe tho' the bil - lows are break - ing, And the
3 gol - den and fair; Soon the lights of the ci - ty ap - pear - ing, Soon the

REFRAIN

1 hea - ven - ly Pi - lot we've found. } Pi - lot me, pi - lot me;
2 hun - gry waves dash mountain high. }
3 home of the ran - som'd we'll share. } O Sa - viour, pi - lot, pi - lot me!

Take the helm in Thine own hand, Bring my sink - ing barque to land; Pi - lot
Pi - lot me,

me, . . . pi - lot me, . . . Pi - - - lot me. . . . . .
pi - lot me, Sa - viour, pi - lot me, Je - sus, Sa - viour, pi - lot e - ven me.

722 O to be Like Him

E. C. ELLSWORTH — DUET — JNO. R. SWENEY

1 O! to be like Him, ten-der and kind, Gen-tle in
2 O! to be like Him, Quick to o-bey Child-like and
3 O! to be like Him, Tempt-ed in vain, Dwell-ing with

1 spi-rit, Low-ly in mind; More like to Je-sus
2 truth-ful, Rea-dy to say; 'I and my Fa-ther
3 sin-ners, Yet with-out stain; Giv-ing our life-work

1 Day af-ter day, Fill'd with His Spi-rit Now and al-way.
2 Pur-pose have one, Thine, not my will, Ev-er be done.'
3 Sin-ners to save, Tri-umph-ing o-ver Death and the grave.

REFRAIN

Yes, to be like Him, We must a-bide
Near to our Sa-viour, Close to His side.

Jesus Alone can Save

KATE ULMER SHELTERED 7.6.7.6.D WM. J. KIRKPATRICK

1 Where shall I flee for re - fuge, Hid - ing when storms are near?
2 Soft - ly I hear Him call - ing, 'Come un - to Me, and rest;
3 Bur - dens oft-times op - press me, Bur - dens so hard to bear;
4 Thus would I ev - er jour - ney On tow'rd my home a - bove,

1 Where find a place of safe - ty, Dwell - ing with-out a fear?
2 Here in My arms find shel - ter, Close to My lov - ing breast.
3 O, then, how sweet His whis - per, 'Cast up - on Me thy care.'
4 Rest - ing a - lone on Je - sus, Whom, tho' un - seen, I love.

REFRAIN

Je - sus a - lone can save me, All of my joys in - crease;

From ev - 'ry storm He'll shield me, Giv - ing my soul sweet peace.

724

Christ is All

ANON

W. A. WILLIAMS

1 I en - ter'd once a home of care, Old age and pen - u - ry were there,
2 I stood be - side a dy - ing bed Where lay a child with ach - ing head,
3 I saw the mar - tyr at the stake, The flames could not his cour - age shake,
4 I saw the Gos - pel her - ald go To Af - ric's sand and Greenland's snow,
5 I dream'd that hoar - y time had fled, And earth and sea gave up their dead,
6 Then come to Christ, O come to - day! The Fa - ther, Son, and Spir - it say,

1 Yet peace and joy with - al; ask'd the lone - ly mo - ther whence Her help - less
2 Wait - ing for Je - sus' call; I mark'd his smile, 'twas sweet as May, And as his
3 Nor death his soul ap - pal, I ask'd him whence his strength was giv'n, He look'd tri -
4 To save from Sa - tan's thrall. No home nor life he count - ed dear, 'Midst wants and
5 A fire dis - solv'd this ball: I saw the Church 's ran - som'd throng, I heard the
6 The Bride re - peats the call, For He will cleanse your guil - ty stains, His love will

REFRAIN

1 wi - dow - hood's de - fence: She told me, 'Christ was all.'
2 spi - rit pass'd a - way, He whis - per'd, 'Christ is all.'
3 um - phant - ly to heav'n, And an - swer'd, 'Christ is all.'
4 per - ils own'd no fear, He felt that 'Christ is all.'
5 bur - den of their song, 'Twas Christ is all in all.
6 soothe your wear - y pains, For Christ is all in all.

Christ is all, all in

1st time

all, Yes, Christ is all in all:

2nd time

Yes, Christ is all in all.

725
No Love like His

JOHN L. NEWKIRK   SOLO OR DUET   POWELL G. FITHIAN

1 There's no love to me like the love of Je - sus, Ev - er, al - ways
2 When far, far a - way, and in con - dem - na - tion, Feel - ing no one
3 O won - der - ful love is the love of Je - sus, Who on Cal - v'ry's

1 just the same; E'en tho' of this world you may be most low - ly,
2 car'd for me, There came a sweet voice, I shall ne'er for - get it,
3 cru - el tree Was wound - ed and died to make full a - tone - ment

REFRAIN

1 Je - sus still loves you, bless His Name.
2 'Je - sus, thy Sa - viour, still loves thee.'
3 For a poor sin - ner, lost, like me.
There ne - ver was

one like Je - sus, Ev - er, al - ways true is He; There ne - ver was

one like Je - sus, There's no love like His love to me. . . .

726 By Grace Alone

IDA SCOTT TAYLOR   SOLO OR DUET   J. HOWARD ENTWHISTLE

1 A mes-sage sweet is borne to me On wings of joy .. di - vine,
2 I'm sav'd by grace, by grace a - lone, Thro' Christ whose love .. I claim,
3 I hear the mes - sage that I love When morn-ing dawns a - new,
4 I hear it in the twi - light still, And at the sun - set hour;
5 O won-drous grace for all man - kind That spreads from sea .. to sea!
6 The soul that seeks it can - not fail to see the Sa - viour's face,

1 A won-drous mes - sage, glad and free, That thrills this heart .. of mine.
2 No oth - er could for sin a - tone, Ho - san - na to .. His Name!
3 I read it in the sun a - bove, That shines a - cross .. the blue.
4 I'm sav'd by grace! what words can thrill With such a ma - gic pow'r?
5 It heals the sick and leads the blind, And sets the pris - 'ner free.
6 And Sa-tan's pow'r can - not pre - vail If we are sav'd .. by grace.

REFRAIN

O glo-rious song, .. that all day long, With tune-ful note .. is ring - ing!
O glo-rious, glo-rious song, that all day, all day long, With tune-ful note .. is ring - ing!

I'm sav'd by grace, a - maz-ing grace, And that is why .. I'm sing - ing.
I'm sav'd, I'm sav'd by grace, a - maz-ing grace, And that is why .. I'm sing - ing.

727 On Calvary

J. WAKEFIELD MACGILL   J. W. MACGILL

SOLO   *pp* QUARTET

1 It pleas'd the Lord to bruise His on - ly Son on Cal - va - ry,
2 Al - tho' the pierc-ing wail went up on high from Cal - va - ry,
3 And canst thou, sin - ner, stand be-neath the Cross of Cal - va - ry,
4 The Cross un-folds the won-drous love di - vine on Cal - va - ry,

SOLO   *pp* QUARTET

1 That He might ran-som sin-ners such as you, and set you free:
2 'My God, O why hast Thou for - sak - en me on Cal - va - ry?'
3 To see His life's blood drop-ping sure-ly down un - heed-ing - ly;
4 And shows in woe love's ma - jes - ty su-preme on Cal - va - ry;

SOLO   *pp* QUARTET

1 He hid His face from Je - sus, whom He lov'd so ten - der - ly,
2 The heav'ns return'd nor ech - o groan nor sigh on that dark day,
3 And treat His cru - el suf - fer - ing as dross on Cal - va - ry,
4 Then yield to Him that bur-den'd heart of thine at Cal - va - ry,

SOLO   *pp* QUARTET

1 With all His heart in yearn-ings deep and true on Cal - va - ry.
2 And all that He might free - ly par - don me on Cal - va - ry.
3 While He is wear-ing sor-row's hea - vy crown in ag - o - ny?
4 And then the Cross will be thy theme through-out e - ter - ni - ty.

728

Sweet Will of God

LEILA N. MORRIS

DUET

LEILA N. MORRIS

1 My stub-born will at last hath yield-ed; I would be
2 I'm tired of sin, foot-sore and wea-ry, The dark-some
3 Thy pre-cious will, O con-qu'ring Sa-viour, Doth now em-
4 Shut in with Thee, O Lord, for ev-er, My way-ward

1 Thine, and Thine a - lone; And this the pray'r . . my lips are
2 path hath drear-y grown, But now a light . . has ris'n to
3 brace and com-pass me; All dis-cords hush'd, . . my peace a
4 feet no more to roam; What pow'r from Thee . . my soul can

rit.

REFRAIN

1 bring-ing, Lord, let in me Thy will be done.
2 cheer me; I find in Thee my Star, my Sun.
3 riv - er, My soul a pris-on'd bird set free.
4 sev - er? The cen-tre of God's will my home.

Sweet will of God, still

fold me clos-er, Till I am whol-ly lost in Thee; Sweet will of

God, still fold me clos-er, Till I . . am whol-ly lost in Thee.

729 Saving Grace

Julia H. Johnston

D. B. Towner

1 O gold-en day, when light shall break And dawn's bright glories shall un - fold,
2 Life's up-ward way, a nar - row path, Leads on to that fair dwelling-place
3 I dim - ly see my jour-ney's end, But well I know who guideth me.

1 When He who knows the path I take Shall ope for me the gates of gold.
2 Where, safe from sin, and storm, and wrath, They live who trust re-deem-ing grace.
3 I fol-low Him, that won-drous Friend Whose matchless love is full and free.

1 Earth's lit - tle while will soon be past, My pil - grim song will
2 Sing, sing, my heart a - long the way, The grace that saves will
3 And when with Him I en - ter in, And all the way look

rall. *a tempo*

1 soon be o'er, The grace that saves shall time out - last, And
2 keep and guide Till breaks the glo - rious crown - ing day, And
3 back to trace, The conq - 'ror's palm I then shall win Thro'

Refrain

1 be my theme on yon - der shore.
2 I shall cross to yon - der side.
3 Christ, and His re - deem ing grace.

Then I shall know, as

Saving Grace—*Continued*

I am known, and stand com - plete be - fore the throne; Then

I shall see my Sa - viour's face, And all my song be, "Sa - ving grace."

730 Gentle Shepherd

HENRIETTA E. BLAIR

WM. J. KIRKPATRICK

1 Far a - way my steps have wan-der'd, On the rug-ged moun-tain's brow;
2 Thou has borne my weight of sor - row, At Thy feet I hum-bly bow;
3 Though Thy love I long have slight-ed, Though un - grate-ful I have been,
4 Though Thy love I long have slight-ed, O'er my was-ted years I weep:

FINE

1 But to Thee my heart is cry - ing, Gen - tle Shep-herd, save me now!
2 And my heart with Thee is plead-ing, Gen - tle Shep-herd, save me now!
3 To Thy fold my faith has brought me; Let my wea - ry soul come in.
4 In Thy bless-ed arms of mer - cy, Shield and save Thy wan-d'ring sheep.

D.S.—Un - to Thee my heart is cry - ing, Gen - tle Shep-herd, save me now!

REFRAIN

D.S.

Save me now! save me now! Gen - tle Shep-herd, save me now!

731 My Anchor Holds

W. C. Martin

D. B. Towner

1 Tho' the an-gry surg-es roll On my tem-pest driv-en soul,
2 Might-y tides a-bout me sweep, Per-ils lurk with-in the deep;
3 Troubles al-most whelm the soul; Griefs like bil-lows o'er me roll;

1 I am peace-ful, for I know, Wild-ly tho' the winds may blow,
2 An-gry clouds o'er-shade the sky, And the tem-pest ris-es high;
3 Temp-ters seek to lure a-stray; Storms ob-scure the light of day;

1 I've an an-chor safe and sure, That can ev-er-more en-dure.
2 Still I stand the tem-pest's shock, For my an-chor grips the rock.
3 I can face them and be bold, I've an an-chor that shall hold.

REFRAIN

And it holds, my an-chor holds;.... Blow your wild-est, then, O
And it holds,.... my an-chor holds; Blow your wild - - est,

gale! On my bark so small and frail; I shall nev-er, nev-er
then, O gale!

My Anchor Holds—Continued

fail, For my an - chor holds, my an - chor holds.
For my an - chor holds, it firm - ly holds.

732   Wondrous Love

FLORA KIRKLAND   DUET   H. W. PORTER

1 O con-de-scen - sion won-der-ful ! O bound-less love, sur-pass-ing thought ! That
2 O joy to know that He is mine! This wondrous Friend beyond com-pare ! O
3 O peace that pass-eth hu-man thought ! The peace of God so free-ly giv'n ! The

1 Christ, the might - y Coun-sel-lor, From heav'n to earth Sal-va - tion brought !
2 joy a - bove all hu-man joy, He will a place for me pre-pare !
3 world can - not this peace de - stroy, This peace that fills the soul with heav'n !

REFRAIN f   cres.

O love di-vine ! O match-less grace ! O mer - cy flow-ing full and free !

p   pp

With won-drous love and win-ning voice, We hear Him whis-per, "Come to Me."

733 That Beautiful City

Lanta Wilson Smith

G. W. Elderkin

1 I know that a - far in God's bound-less realm, Per - haps 'mid the star - ry
2 That beau - ti - ful ci - ty with jas - per walls Ne'er clo - ses its pearl - ly
3 The long-ings of life shall be sat - is - fied, The fet - ters of earth be

1 spa - - ces, Lies the prom - is'd home of the saints re - deem'd, Re -
2 por - - tals, And the heal - ing pow'r of its ho - ly light Sweeps
3 bro - - ken, And the words im - pris-on'd with - in the soul With

1 plete with ce - les - tial gra - - ces; In dreams I have walk'd on the
2 o - ver the blest im - mor - tals; There sor - row and tears shall be
3 rap - ture shall then be spo - ken; The mu - sic that sor - row hath

That Beautiful City—*Continued*

1 streets of gold, As I sought for my own fair dwell - ing, And
2 wip'd a - way In the dawn of an end - less morn - ing, Our
3 hush'd a - while, And the si - lence of life's sad sto - ry, Shall

cres.   *f rit.*

1 voi - ces I knew and lov'd of old I've heard in the mu - sic swell - ing.
2 tri - umphs of faith like stars shall shine, Bright crowns for the soul's a - dorn - ing.
3 leap in - to songs of per - fect joy At - tun'd to e - ter - nal glo - ry.

cres.   *f rit.*

f REFRAIN

That beau-ti-ful ci - ty is home to me, Each day it is grow - ing dear - er; And

voi-ces that call from be - yond the sea Are draw-ing me near-er and near - er.

734 The Better Land

Gurdon Robins (arr.)

D. B. Towner

1 There is a land mine eye hath seen In vi-sions of en-rap-tur'd thought,
2 A land up-on whose bliss-ful shore There rests no shad-ow, falls no stain;
3 Its skies are not like earth-ly skies, With vary-ing hues of shade and light!
4 There sweeps no des-o-la-ting wind A-cross the calm, se-rene a-bode;

1 So bright that all which spreads be-tween Is with its ra-diant glo-ries fraught.
2 There those who meet shall part no more, And those long part-ed meet a-gain.
3 It hath no need of suns to rise To dis-si-pate the gloom of night.
4 The wan-d'rer there a home may find With-in the par-a-dise of God.

REFRAIN

O land of love, . . . of joy and light, . . . Thy glo-ries
O land of love, of joy and light,

gild . . . . earth's dark-est night; . . . Thy tran-quil shore . . .
Thy glo-ries gild earth's dark-est night (earth's dark-est night); Thy tran-quil shore

we, too, shall see . . . When day shall break . . . and sha-dows flee.
(we, too, shall see) When day shall break

735 Jesus Leads

John R. Clements

John R. Sweney

1 Like a shep-herd, ten-der, true, Je-sus leads, Je-sus leads,
2 All a-long life's rug-ged road Je-sus leads, Je-sus leads,
3 Thro' the sun-lit ways of life Je-sus leads, Je-sus leads,
Je-sus leads, Je-sus leads.

1 Dai-ly finds us pas-tures new, Je-sus leads, Je-sus leads;
2 Till we reach yon blest a-bode, Je-sus leads, Je-sus leads;
3 Thro' the war-rings and the strife Je-sus leads, Je-sus leads;
Je-sus leads, Je-sus leads;

1 If thick mists are o'er the way, Or the flock 'mid dan-ger feeds,
2 All the way be-fore He's trod, And He now the flock pre-cedes,
3 When we reach the Jor-dan's tide Where life's bound-'ry line re-cedes,

1 If thick mists are o'er the way, Or the flock 'mid dan-ger feeds,
2 All the way be-fore He's trod, And He now the flock pre-cedes,
3 When we reach the Jor-dan's tide Where life's bound-'ry line re-cedes,

rit.

1 He will watch them lest they stray, Je-sus leads, Je-sus leads.
2 Safe in-to the folds of God Je-sus leads, Je-sus leads.
3 He will spread the waves a-side, Je-sus leads, Je-sus leads.
Je-sus leads,

736 I Know Who Pilots Me

JAMES ROWE

HOWARD E. SMITH

1 When an - gry waves a - bout me roll And hide my path a - cross life's sea,
2 Day af - ter day, tho' toss'd a - bout, And of - ten dang - 'rous rocks I see,
3 Tho' each new day brings tri - als sore, Tho' rough - er still the o - cean be,
4 My Sa - viour's love still guides me on, My on - ly chart and com - pass He;

1 No fear a - larms my trust - ing soul, For well I know who pi - lots me.
2 There comes to me no fear nor doubt, For well I know who pi - lots me.
3 I know that I shall reach the shore, For well I know who pi - lots me.
4 I'll trust Him till the jour - ney's done, For well I know who pi - lots me.

REFRAIN

Yes, well I know . . . . . who pi - lots me . . . . . A - cross life's
Yes, well I know who pi - lots me

ev - - - er troub - led sea; . . . . The winds may rave . . . and waves may
A - cross life's ev - er troub - led, ev - er troub - led sea; The winds may rave

swell, ... While Je - sus pi - lots, all is well. . . . .
and waves may swell, While Je - sus pi - lots, all is well, yes, all is well.

737 Nailed to the Cross

F. A. BRECK   DUET   GRANT COLFAX TULLAR

1 There was One who was will-ing to die in my stead That a
2 He is ten-der and lov-ing and pa-tient with me, While He
3 I will cling to my Sa-viour and nev-er de-part, I will

1 soul so un-wor-thy might live, And the path to the Cross He was
2 cleans-es my heart of its dross, But there's no con-dem-na-tion, I
3 joy-ful-ly jour-ney each day, With a song on my lips and a

REFRAIN

1 will-ing to tread, All the sins of my life to for-give.
2 know I am free, For my sins are all nail'd to the Cross.
3 song in my heart, That my sins have been ta-ken a-way.

They are nail'd to the

Cross, they are nail'd to the Cross, O how much He was will-ing to bear! With what

rit.

an-guish and loss Je-sus went to the Cross! And He car-ried my sins with Him there.

738 Beyond the Sea

FRANK H. MASHAW J. LINCOLN HALL

1 Be-yond the sea . . . . . . that rolls be - tween . . . . . This world of
2 Be-yond the sea . . . . . . lies heav'n's fair shore, ... Where all of
3 No more shall beat . . . . . . the flood of years . . . . . A-cross these
4 Be-yond the sea . . . . . . there's rest and peace, ... There Je-sus

1 Be-yond the sea . . . . that rolls be-tween
2 Be-yond the sea . . . . . . lies heav'n's fair shore,
3 No more shall beat . . . . the flood of years
4 Be-yond the sea . . . . . . there's rest and peace,

1 care . . . . . . and things un-seen, ... There is a land
2 sin . . . . . . and earth are o'er; . . . . . . Where care and toil
3 forms . . . . . . so frail and worn; . . . . . No more shall roll
4 bids . . . . . . His chil-dren come; . . . . . Be-yond the sea

1 This world of care . . . . . and things un-seen, ... There is a land
2 Where all of sin . . . . . and earth are o'er; . . . . Where care and toil
3 A-cross these forms . . . . . . so frail and worn; . . . . No more shall roll
4 There Je-sus bids . . . . . . His chil-dren come; . . . . Be-yond the sea

1 of end-less day, ... Where all our tears . . . are wip'd a-way.
2 have pass'd a-way; . . . . Where wea-ry feet . . . . no more shall stray.
3 the sea of tears . . . . A-cross these hearts . . by an-guish torn.
4 the tem-pests cease, . . . There an-gels sing . . . a wel-come home.

1 of end-less day, . . . Where all our tears . . . are wip'd a-way.
2 have pass'd a-way; . . Where wea-ry feet . . . no more shall stray.
3 the sea of tears . . . A-cross these hearts . . . by an-guish torn.
4 the tem-pests cease, . . There an-gels sing . . . a wel-come home.

Beyond the Sea—*Continued*

Beyond the sea, ... the rest-less, roll-ing sea, ...
Be-yond the sea, be-yond the sea,

I hear my lov'd .... ones gent-ly call-ing me, ...
I hear my lov'd ones call-ing, gent-ly call-ing me,

I soon shall leave .... the troub-led shores of time, ...
I soon shall leave the shores of time, the shores of time,

And dwell for aye ...... in that ce-les-tial clime. ....
And dwell for aye ...... in that ce-les-tial clime

739 My Mother's Prayer

J. W. VAN DE VENTER   HANNAH L.M.D   W. S. WEEDEN

1 I nev-er can for-get the day I heard my mo-ther kind-ly say:
2 I nev-er can for-get the voice That al-ways made my heart re-joice;
3 Tho' years have gone, I can't for-get Those words of love, I hear them yet;
4 I nev-er can for-get the hour I felt the Sa-viour's cleans-ing pow'r;

1 'You're leav-ing now my ten-der care; Re-mem-ber child, your mo-ther's pray'r.'
2 Tho' I have wan-der'd God knows where, Still I re-mem-ber mo-ther's pray'r.
3 I see her by the old arm-chair, My mo-ther dear, in hum-ble pray'r.
4 My sin and guilt He can-cell'd there; 'Twas there He an-swer'd mo-ther's pray'r.

REFRAIN

1-3 When-e'er I think of her so dear, I feel as if   she still were here;
4   O praise the Lord for sav-ing grace! We'll meet up yon-der, face to face,

1-3 A voice comes float-ing on the air, Re-mind-ing me of mo-ther's pray'r.
4   The home a-bove to-geth-er share, In an-swer to my mo-ther's pray'r.

The tune MARMORA is on the following page.

739 My Mother's Prayer

J. W. VAN DE VENTER   MARMORA L.M.D   E. H. SWINSTEAD

1 I nev-er can for-get the day I heard my mo-ther kind-ly say:
2 I nev-er can for-get the voice That al-ways made my heart re-joice;
3 Tho' years have gone, I can't for-get Those words of love, I hear them yet;
4 I nev-er can for-get the hour I felt the Sa-viour's cleans-ing pow'r;

1 'You're leav-ing now my ten-der care; Re-mem-ber, child, your mo-ther's pray'r.'
2 Tho' I have wan-der'd God knows where, Still I re-mem-ber mo-ther's pray'r.
3 I see her by the old arm-chair, My mo-ther dear, in hum-ble pray'r.
4 My sin and guilt He can-cell'd there; 'Twas there He an-swer'd mo-ther's pray'r.

REFRAIN

1-3 When-e'er I think of her so dear, I feel as if she still were here;
4 O praise the Lord for sav-ing grace! We'll meet up yon-der, face to face,

1-3 A voice comes float-ing on the air, Re-mind-ing me of mo-ther's pray'r.
4 The home a-bove to-geth-er share, In an-swer to my mo-ther's pray'r.

Music by permission of E. H. SWINSTEAD   The tune HANNAH precedes this one

740 The Very Friend I Need

E. E. HEWITT   DUET   W. J. KIRKPATRICK

1 When I'm sad and heav-y la-den, Burden'd with the weight of sin,
2 When I'm strugg-ling with temp-ta-tion, When my strength shall al-most fail,
3 When I drink the cup of sor-row, When I tread the path of grief,
4 When I reach the sil-ent riv-er, When I wait be-side the tide,

1 Je-sus is the ver-y Friend I need; To the blood-stain'd Cross He points me,
2 Je-sus is the ver-y Friend I need; For His arm will bring de-liv-'rance,
3 Je-sus is the ver-y Friend I need; In His Word is con-so-la-tion,
4 Je-sus is the ver-y Friend I need; He will bear me o'er the bil-lows

1 And He gives me peace with-in, Je-sus is the ver-y Friend I need.
2 And His grace will still pre-vail, Je-sus is the ver-y Friend I need.
3 In His pres-ence sweet re-lief, Je-sus is the ver-y Friend I need.
4 To the ra-diant morn-ing-side, Je-sus is the ver-y Friend I need.

REFRAIN

O He is the best of Friends! For His good-ness nev-er ends, And His

love will ev-'ry hu-man tho't ex-ceed; Let me love Him more and more,

The Very Friend I Need—*Continued*

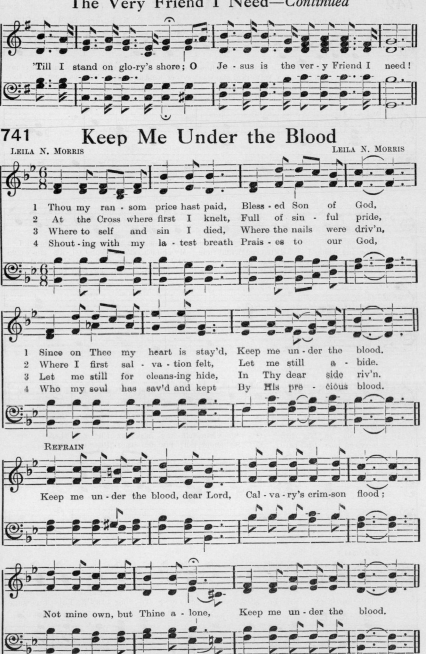

'Till I stand on glo-ry's shore; O Je-sus is the ver-y Friend I need!

741 Keep Me Under the Blood

Leila N. Morris   Leila N. Morris

1 Thou my ran-som price hast paid, Bless-ed Son of God,
2 At the Cross where first I knelt, Full of sin-ful pride,
3 Where to self and sin I died, Where the nails were driv'n,
4 Shout-ing with my la-test breath Prais-es to our God,

1 Since on Thee my heart is stay'd, Keep me un-der the blood.
2 Where I first sal-va-tion felt, Let me still a-bide.
3 Let me still for cleans-ing hide, In Thy dear side riv'n.
4 Who my soul has sav'd and kept By His pre-cious blood.

REFRAIN

Keep me un-der the blood, dear Lord, Cal-va-ry's crim-son flood;

Not mine own, but Thine a-lone, Keep me un-der the blood.

742   Tell Mother

CHARLES M. FILLMORE   C. M. F., *arr.* E. W. MACGILL

1 When I was but a lit-tle child, how well I re-col-lect, How I would grieve my
2 Tho' I was of-ten way-ward, she was ev-er kind and good, So pa-tient, gen-tle,
3 When I be-came a prod-i-gal, and left the old roof-tree, She al-most broke her
4 One day a mes-sage came to me, it bade me quick-ly come, If I would see my

1 mo-ther with my fol-ly and ne-glect; And now that she has gone to heav'n, I
2 lov-ing, when I ac-ted rough and rude, My child-hood's griefs and tri-als she would
3 lov-ing heart in mourn-ing af-ter me, And day and night she pray'd to God to
4 mo-ther ere the Sa-viour took her home; I prom-is'd her, be-fore she died, for

1 miss her ten-der care; O Sa-viour, tell my mo-ther I'll be there!
2 glad-ly with me share; O Sa-viour, tell my mo-ther I'll be there!
3 keep me in His care; O Sa-viour, tell my mo-ther I'll be there!
4 heav-en to pre-pare; O Sa-viour, tell my mo-ther I'll be there!

REFRAIN

Tell mo-ther I'll be there, in an-swer to her pray'r; This mes-sage,

Tell Mother—*Continued*

bless-ed Sa-viour, to her bear; . . Tell mo-ther I'll be there, heav'n's

joys with her to share; Yes, tell my dar-ling mo-ther I'll be there.

743
The Whosoever

JAMES NICHOLSON

JNO. R. SWENEY

1 I praise the Lord that one like me, For mer-cy may to Je-sus flee;
2 I was to sin a wretch-ed slave, But Je-sus died my soul to save;
3 I look by faith and see this word Stamp'd with the blood of Christ, my Lord;
4 I now be-lieve He saves my soul, His pre-cious blood hath made me whole;

1—4 He says that who-so - ev - er will May seek and find sal - va-tion still.

REFRAIN

D.S.

My Sa-viour's pro-mise fail - eth ne -ver, He counts me in the Who-so - ev - er.

744 Some Day

Victor M. Staley

Chas. H. Gabriel
Arr. P. J. Mansfield

1 Some day 'twill all be o - ver, The toil and cares of life; Some
2 Some day I'll see the man-sions Of hea - ven's ci - ty fair; Some
3 Some day I'll see the Sa - viour, And know Him face to face; Some

1 day the world be vanquish'd With all this mor-tal strife; Some day, the jour-ney
2 day I'll greet with plea-sure The dear ones wait-ing there; Some day I'll hear the
3 day re - ceive un - measur'd, The bless-ings of His grace; Some day He'll smile up-

1 end - ed, I'll lay my bur - den down; Some day, in realms su - per - nal, Re -
2 voi - ces Of God's an - gel - ic throng; Some day I'll join the cho - rus In
3 on me From that white throne a - bove; Some day I'll know the full-ness Of

Refrain

1 ceive at last my crown. Some day, . . . some hap-py day, . . .
2 heav'n's im-mor-tal song. some hap-py day, some hap-py day,
3 His un - dy - ing love.

Some Day—*Continued*

The Lord will wipe all tears a - way, ... And I shall go to dwell with
all tears a - way,

Him, ... To dwell with Him . . . . some hap-py day.
To dwell with Him, To dwell with Him some hap-py, hap-py day.

745

Don't Stay Away

ANON

NEGRO MELODY

Bro-ther, don't stay a - way, Bro-ther, don't stay a - way, Bro-ther, don't stay a -

way, don't stay a - way. My Lord says there's room e-nough, room e - nough

in the heav'ns for you, My Lord says there's room e-nough, don't stay a - way.

746 He Will Lead

F. R. Havergal

ANON

1 He who hath led will lead All through the wild-er-ness;
2 He who hath made thee whole Will heal thee day by day;
3 He who hath made thee nigh Will draw thee near-er still;
4 He who hath won thy heart Will keep it true and free;

1 He who hath fed will sure-ly feed; He who hath bless'd will bless;
2 He who hath spo-ken to Thy soul Hath many things to say;
3 He who hath giv'n the first sup-ply Will sat-is-fy and fill;
4 He who hath shown thee what thou art Will show Himself to thee.

1 He who hath heard thy cry Will nev-er close His ear;
2 He who hath gent-ly taught Yet more will make thee know;
3 He who hath giv'n thee grace Yet more and more will send;
4 He who hath bid thee live, And made thy life His own,

1 He who hath mark'd thy faint-est sigh Will not for-get thy tear.
2 He who so won-drous-ly hath wrought Yet great-er things will show.
3 He who hath set thee in the race Will speed thee to the end.
4 Life more a-bun-dant-ly will give, And keep it His a-lone.

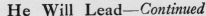

He Will Lead—*Continued*

Alternative Tune when the Refrain is used alone

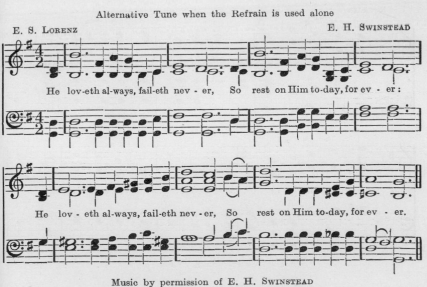

Music by permission of E. H. SWINSTEAD

He Cares

747

JOHNSON OATMAN   EPIMEL 8.5.8.5.D   J. HOWARD ENTWISLE

1 When your spi-rit bows in sor - row   From the load it bears,
2 Have your feet be-come en - tan - gled   In the temp-ter's snares?
3 Have you been by grief o'er - tak - en,   Strick-en un - a - wares?
4   Is your bod - y fill'd with an - guish, With the pain it bears?
5 Loss of friends and loss of for - tune, Life a dark look wears;
6   So a-mid life's cares and strug - gles, Blend-ing songs with pray'rs,

1 Go and tell your heart to Je - sus, Don't you know He cares?
2 There is One who died to save you, Don't you know He cares?
3 Yet ye will not be for - sak - en, Don't you know He cares?
4 Think of how the Sa-viour suf - fer'd, Don't you know He cares?
5 Yet the Sa-viour still is with you, Don't you know He cares?
6 Al-ways put your trust in Je - sus, Don't you know He cares?

REFRAIN

Yes, there is One who bears your bur-dens, Ev - 'ry sor - row shares;

Go and tell it all to Je - sus, Don't you know He cares?

The Tune MERIMNA is on the following page

747 He Cares

JOHNSON OATMAN   MERIMNA 8.5.8.5.D   E. H. SWINSTEAD

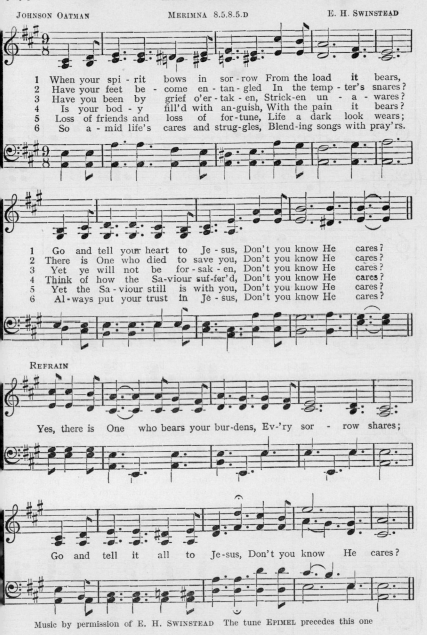

1 When your spi-rit bows in sor-row From the load it bears,
2 Have your feet be-come en-tan-gled In the temp-ter's snares?
3 Have you been by grief o'er-tak-en, Strick-en un-a-wares?
4 Is your bod-y fill'd with an-guish, With the pain it bears?
5 Loss of friends and loss of for-tune, Life a dark look wears;
6 So a-mid life's cares and strug-gles, Blend-ing songs with pray'rs.

1 Go and tell your heart to Je-sus, Don't you know He cares?
2 There is One who died to save you, Don't you know He cares?
3 Yet ye will not be for-sak-en, Don't you know He cares?
4 Think of how the Sa-viour suf-fer'd, Don't you know He cares?
5 Yet the Sa-viour still is with you, Don't you know He cares?
6 Al-ways put your trust in Je-sus, Don't you know He cares?

REFRAIN

Yes, there is One who bears your bur-dens, Ev'-ry sor-row shares;

Go and tell it all to Je-sus, Don't you know He cares?

Music by permission of E. H. SWINSTEAD   The tune EPIMEL precedes this one

748

A Clean Heart

Walter C. Smith

Fred. H. Byshe

1 One thing I of the Lord de - sire, For all my path hath mi - ry been:
2 If clear - er vis - ion Thou imp - art Grate-ful and glad my soul shall be;
3 Yea, on - ly as this heart is clean May lar - ger vis - ion yet be mine,
4 I watch to shun the mi - ry way, And staunch the springs of guil - ty thought;

rit.

1 Be it by wa - ter or by fire, O make me clean! O make me clean!
2 But yet to have a pur - er heart Is more to me, is more to me.
3 For mir-ror'd in its depths are seen The things di-vine, the things di - vine.
4 But, watch and strug-gle as I may, Pure I am not, pure I am not.

rit.

REFRAIN

So wash me, Thou, with - out, with - in, Or purge with
Wash me Thou, with - out, with - in, Or

A Clean Heart—*Continued*

fire,   if that must be ;   No mat-ter how,   if on-ly

purge with fire,   if   that must be ;   A - ny - how,   if

rit.

sin   Die out   in   me,   die out   in   me.

on - ly sin Die out   in   me,   die out, die out   in   me.

Die in   me,

rit.

749 The Load Lifted

E. E. HEWITT

WM. J. KIRKPATRICK

1 The trust-ing heart to Je-sus clings, Nor an-y ill fore-bodes,
2 The pass-ing days bring man-y cares, 'Fear not,' I hear Him say,
3 He tells me of my Fa-ther's love, And ne-ver slum-b'ring eye;
4 When to the throne of grace I flee, I find the pro-mise true,

1 But at the Cross of Cal-v'ry sings, Praise God for lift-ed loads.
2 And when my fears are turn'd to pray'rs, The bur-dens slip a-way.
3 My ev-er-last-ing King a-bove Will all my needs sup-ply.
4 The might-y arms up-hold-ing me Will bear my bur-dens too.

REFRAIN

Sing-ing I go a-long life's road, Prais-ing the Lord, prais-ing the Lord,

rit. ad lib.

Sing-ing I go a-long life's road, For Je-sus has lift-ed my load.

An alternative Tune is on the following page

749 The Load Lifted

E. E. Hewitt

E. H. Swinstead

1 The trust-ing heart to Je-sus clings, Nor an-y ill fore-bodes,
2 The pass-ing days bring man-y cares, 'Fear not,' I hear Him say,
3 He tells me of my Fa-ther's love, And nev-er slum-b'ring eye;
4 When to the throne of grace I flee, I find the pro-mise true,

1 But at the Cross of Cal-v'ry sings, Praise God for lift-ed loads.
2 And when my fears are turn'd to pray'rs, The bur-dens slip a-way.
3 My ev-er-last-ing King a-bove Will all my needs sup-ply.
4 The might-y arms up-hold-ing me Will bear my bur-dens too.

REFRAIN

Sing-ing I go a-long life's road, Prais-ing the Lord, prais-ing the Lord,

Sing-ing I go a-long life's road, For Je-sus has lift-ed my load.

Music by permission of E. H. Swinstead An alternative Tune precedes this one.

750 The Promise to Mother

INA DULEY OGDON

F. S. FEARIS

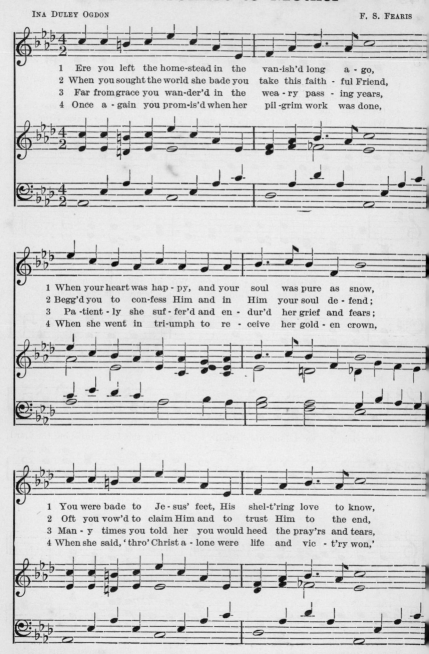

1 Ere you left the home-stead in the van-ish'd long a-go,
2 When you sought the world she bade you take this faith-ful Friend,
3 Far from grace you wan-der'd in the wea-ry pass-ing years,
4 Once a-gain you prom-is'd when her pil-grim work was done,

1 When your heart was hap-py, and your soul was pure as snow,
2 Begg'd you to con-fess Him and in Him your soul de-fend;
3 Pa-tient-ly she suf-fer'd and en-dur'd her grief and fears;
4 When she went in tri-umph to re-ceive her gold-en crown,

1 You were bade to Je-sus' feet, His shel-t'ring love to know,
2 Oft you vow'd to claim Him and to trust Him to the end,
3 Man-y times you told her you would heed the pray'rs and tears,
4 When she said, 'thro' Christ a-lone were life and vic-t'ry won,'

The Promise to Mother—*Continued*

1-4 Don't for - get the pro - mise made to mo - - - ther.

Refrain

Don't for-get those ten-der hands that sooth'd your cares a -way; Don't for-get that gen - tle face, those tress -es thin and grey; And don't for - get her Sa-viour. who is call-ing you to-day; Don't for-get the pro-mise made to mo - ther.

751 That Means Me

JOHNSON OATMAN

ADAM GEIBEL

1 I read that who-so - ev - er May from wrath flee; God will re-
2 His blood is ef-fi - ca-cious, His love is free; To sin-ners
3 Christ died for ev - 'ry na - tion On Cal - v'ry's tree; He died for
4 I read the pro-mise giv - en, That o'er death's sea We'll live with

REFRAIN

1 ject me nev - er, For that means me.
2 He is gra-cious, And that means me.
3 our sal - va - tion, And that means me.
4 Him in hea - ven, And that means me.

For that means me, Yes

that means me; When I read who-so - ev - er, Then that means me.

752 In Summer Land

W. B. WILLIAMS

SUMMER LAND 6.4.6.4.6.6.6.4

POWELL G. FITHIAN

1 The sun will nev - er set In Sum-mer Land; No eyes with tears
2 No one will lose the way In Sum-mer Land; Nor ev - er go
3 No death is ev - er known In Sum-mer Land; For life is on

In Summer Land—*Continued*

1 are wet   In Sum - mer Land;   No shade of dark-'ning night   Will shut the
2 a - stray   In Sum - mer Land;   No moun-tain hard to climb,   Yet all is
3 the throne In Sum - mer Land;   No mourn-ing for the dead,   No hea-vy

pp rit.

1 view from sight,   Nor e'er be-cloud the light   In Sum - mer Land.
2 grand, sub - lime,   With end-less sum - mer clime   In Sum - mer Land.
3 hearts like lead,   But end-less joy in - stead   In Sum - mer Land.

W. B. WILLIAMS   ST. MARGARET 6.4.6.4.6.6.6.4   F. A. MANN

1 The   sun will nev - er set   In Sum-mer Land;   No   eyes with tears
2 No   one will lose the way   In Sum-mer Land;   Nor   ev - er go
3 No   death is   ev - er known   In Sum-mer Land;   For   life is on

1 are wet   In Sum-mer Land;   No shade of dark-'ning night   Will shut the
2 a - stray   In Sum-mer Land;   No moun-tain hard to climb,   Yet   all is
3 the throne   In Sum-mer Land;   No mourn-ing for the dead,   No   wea-ry

1 view from sight, Nor   e'er be-cloud the light   In Sum-mer Land.
2 grand, sub - lime, With   end - less sum - mer clime   In Sum-mer Land.
3 hearts like lead, But   end - less joy in-stead   In Sum-mer Land.

753 Beautiful Isle

JESSIE B. POUNDS

J. S. FEARIS

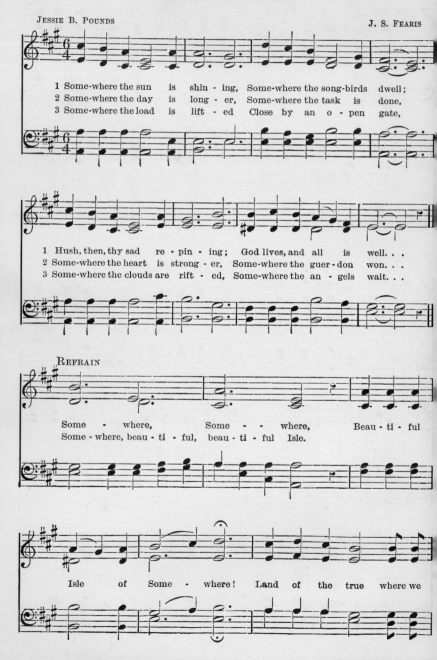

1 Some-where the sun is shin-ing, Some-where the song-birds dwell;
2 Some-where the day is long-er, Some-where the task is done,
3 Some-where the load is lift-ed Close by an o-pen gate,

1 Hush, then, thy sad re-pin-ing; God lives, and all is well...
2 Some-where the heart is strong-er, Some-where the guer-don won...
3 Some-where the clouds are rift-ed, Some-where the an-gels wait...

REFRAIN

Some - where, Some - - where, Beau - ti - ful
Some - where, beau - ti - ful, beau - ti - ful Isle.

Isle of Some - where! Land of the true where we

Beautiful Isle—*Continued*

live a - new, Beau - ti - ful Isle of Some - where.

754 We will Follow Jesus

ANON   FOLLOW JESUS 7.6.7.6.7.7.7.6   OLD MELODY

When the world and sin op - pose, We will fol - low Je - sus;

He is great - er than our foes, We will fol - low Je - sus.

On His pro - mise we'll de - pend; He'll be with us to the end,

He will guard us and de - fend; We will fol - low Je - sus.

755

In Thy Courts

EFFIE S. BLACK

ARTHUR WILTON

1. Both weak and blind, dear Lord, I am, For now Thy face I
2. But I can feel Thy gen - tle touch, And I can read Thy
3. Till then, dear Lord, but lead me on, And guide me in the
4. And when at last my jour - ney's o'er, Earth's hea - vy bur - dens

1. can - not see, But I can hear Thy gen - tle voice Speak
2. bless - ed word, And with Thy might - y, throb - bing love My
3. bet - ter way, Lest grop - ing in the dark - ness here My
4. are laid down, When tears are changed to pearls of joy, My

CHORUS.

1. words of love to me.
2. lone - ly heart is stirred.   O some day I shall
3. feet should go a - stray.
4. cross to jew - elled crown.   O some day, some day I shall

see, And some day clasp Thy hand, Yes,
see, I shall see, And some day, some day clasp Thy hand, clasp Thy hand, Yes,

some day see Thy face, When in Thy courts I stand.
some day, some day see Thy face, see Thy face,

756   I Can't Tell it All

LEILA N. MORRIS   LEILA N. MORRIS

1. { Oh, I can't tell it all, of the won-der-ful love, How, when
   { With a heart full of love, how He came from a - bove, Threw His

2. { Oh, I can't tell it all, how He free - ly for - gave; How the
   { O'er my lost, guilt - y soul, how it cleansed and made whole, While

3. { Oh, I can't tell it all, what a Friend He has been; How He's
   { How He saves me to - day, bids the clouds chase a - way, How He

1st time.

1. lost in my sins Je - sus found me; strong arms of mer-cy a - round me.
2. blood flowed with won-der-ful heal - ing; low at the cross I was kneel - ing.
3. borne all my sor-rows and sad - ness; turns all my mourning to glad - ness.

2nd time.

CHORUS.

Oh, I can't tell it all; No, I can't tell it all; But my

heart is so full of His glo - ry, That wher - ev - er I go in this

wide world be - low, I am tell - ing the won - der - ful sto - ry.

4. Oh, I can't tell it all, but His love you may know,
You may have Him, this wonderful Saviour;
You may taste of His bliss, you may say, I am His,
And He is my portion for ever.

5. Oh, I can't tell it all, but as long as I've breath
I will still tell the wonderful story;
When my life work is done and a crown I have won,
I will tell it for ever in glory.

757   When I Behold Him

ELLA M. PARKS   H. L. GILMOUR

1 Af - ter the earth - ly   sha-dows have lift - ed, And o'er the hill - tops
2 Help-less He found me,   lift - ed me to Him; Whis-per'd of par - don a -
3 Now in His pres - ence,   dai - ly I'm liv - ing, Walk-ing by faith where mine

1 morn - ing I   see,   Sweet-est of pros - pects,   I shall be - hold Him, Je-sus, the
2 bun - dant and free; Breath'd He His peace o'er my sin-strick-en spi - rit; Point-ed my
3 eyes can - not see;   For He is guid - ing   home to that cit - y, Built for His

ritard.............   REFRAIN

1 Sa - viour of sin - ners like me.
2 vis - ion to Cal - va - ry's tree. } When I be - hold Him, Christ, in His beau-ty,
3 lov'd ones—sav'd sin-ners like me.

When with the ran - som'd His face I shall see,   O how my heart in

ritard..............

rap - ture will praise Him! Praise Him for sav - ing a   sin - ner like me.

758

Book Divine

JOHN BURTON   BOOK DIVINE 7.7.7.7.D   E. O. EXCELL

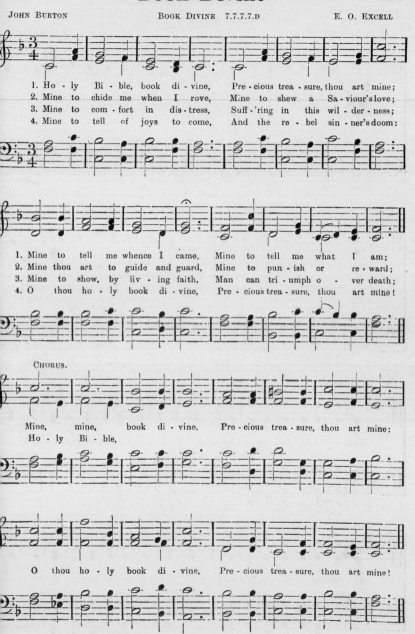

1. Ho - ly Bi - ble, book di - vine,   Pre - cious trea - sure, thou art mine;
2. Mine to chide me when I rove,   Mine to shew a Sa - viour's love;
3. Mine to com - fort in dis - tress,   Suff - 'ring in this wil - der - ness;
4. Mine to tell of joys to come,   And the re - bel sin - ner's doom:

1. Mine to tell me whence I came,   Mine to tell me what I am;
2. Mine thou art to guide and guard,   Mine to pun - ish or re - ward;
3. Mine to show, by liv - ing faith,   Man can tri - umph o - ver death;
4. O thou ho - ly book di - vine,   Pre - cious trea - sure, thou art mine!

CHORUS.

Mine,   mine,   book di - vine,   Pre - cious trea - sure, thou art mine:
Ho - ly Bi - ble,

O thou ho - ly book di - vine,   Pre - cious trea - sure, thou art mine!

32

759 What Hinders?

Duet—Alto and Tenor.

Julia H. Johnston   S. D. Goodale

1. What hinders your coming to Jesus, What hinders your coming to-day?
2. If pleasures and earthly enjoyment Have hindered your coming before,
3. The fearful, the troubled and doubting, May lovingly lean on His breast;
4. What hinders your coming to Jesus? The fear that you may not hold out?

1. He offers His grace and His pardon, Tell Jesus what stands in the way.
2. O tarry no longer but prove Him, Who offers you joy evermore.
3. O trust Him who offers salvation, Come now to His arms and be blest.
4. His mercy endureth for ever, O how can you linger in doubt?

CHORUS.

What is it that hinders your coming? You may find this salvation to-day;

The Saviour is ready and waiting, O why do you longer delay?

Seeking the Wandering

1. Far from home and kin - dred, Wan - der - ing a - way,
2. Far he may be stray - ing From the heaven - ly fold,
3. Ah! no heart can har - den So He can - not teach;
4. May the bells of hea - ven Ring for Him with joy;

1. Where is he I think of, Pray for, day by day? Once home's brightest
2. Yet the ten - der shep - herd, With a love un - told, And a great com -
3. And no sheep can wan - der Where He can - not reach: So I keep on
4. May re - joic - ing an - gels Smile up - on my boy; May the Fa - ther

1. sun - shine, Once its joy and light, Still his mo-ther's dar - ling, Where is
2. pas - sion, Fill - ing all His mind, Will be following af - ter, Seek-ing
3. pray - ing, Where - so - e'er he be, Bring him home, Good Shepherd, Bring him
4. meet him Com - ing back a - lone, Say - ing, "Loved and lost one, Welcome,

CHORUS.

1. he to - night!
2. till He find. } For the Shep - herd, Je - sus, Leaves the rest be -
3. back with Thee.
4. wel - come home!"

hind, Seeks the lost and wand'ring, Seeks un - til He find,

761 His Loving Arms

ELLA M. PARKS

CLARENCE B. STROUSE

1 I was far a-way from Je-sus, dead in
2 Then he whis-per'd to me par-don thro' the
3 Day by day He guides and keeps me in the
4 In the hour of deep-est tri-al when all
5 O this bless-ed life in Je-sus! sin-ner,

1 tres-pas-ses and sin, And I thought for one so
2 all a-ton-ing blood Which He shed for my trans
3 bless-ed nar-row way, From the ban of sin and
4 earth-ly com-fort fails, And no cheer-ing ray of
5 won't you hear His call? From the pow'r of sin's do

1 vile no hope could be; But the bless-ed Lord of
2 gres-sions on the tree; And the bless-ed peace of
3 death He makes me free; There's no e-vil can be
4 sun-shine I can see, Then to Him I bring my
5 min-ion He can free; Yield thy heart to Him this

1 Glo-ry stoop'd and rais'd me to Him-self, And He put
2 hea-ven came in-to my wea-ry soul, As He pu
3 fall me while I'm rest-ing in His grace, And He ha
4 sor-row, and He wipes a-way my tears As He put
5 mo-ment, and with joy thou'lt sure-ly find That He'll pu

His Loving Arms—*Continued*

1–4 His lov-ing arms a - round me. He put His
5 His lov-ing arms a - round thee. He'll put His

1–4 lov - ing arms a - round me, He put His lov-ing arms a -
5 lov - ing arms a - round thee, He'll put His lov-ing arms a -

1–4 round me, I look'd in - to His face, it beam'd with ten - der
5 round thee, Look up in - to His face, it beams with ten - der

1–4 grace As He put His lov-ing arms a - round .. me.
5 grace, And He'll put His lov-ing arms a - round .. thee.

762 I Belong to Jesus

E. S. Lorenz   E. S. Lorenz

1 With ev - 'ry pow'r, with heart and soul,   I   be - long   to   Je - sus;
2 What tho' temp-ta - tions sore be - set,   I   be - long   to   Je - sus;
3 In   vain the world my heart al - lures,   I   be - long   to   Je - sus;
4 No threat-'ning dan - ger then I   see,   I   be - long   to   Je - sus;

1 He   shall my ev - 'ry thought con-trol,   I   be - long   to   Je - sus.
2 What tho' earth's cares an - noy and fret, I   be - long   to   Je - sus.
3 In   weak-ness this my soul as - sures,   I   be - long   to   Je - sus.
4 Thro' time and thro' e - ter - ni - ty,   I   be - long   to   Je - sus.

REFRAIN

I   be - long   to   Je - sus,   I   be - long   to   Je - sus,

I   be - long   to   Je - sus, He be - ongs to   me.

An alternative Tune is on the following page

762

I Belong to Jesus

E. S. Lorenz

E. H. Swinstead

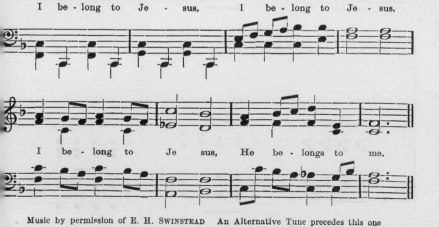

1 With ev-'ry power, with heart and soul,   I be-long to Je-sus;
2 What tho' temp-ta-tions sore be-set,   I be-long to Je-sus;
3 In   vain the world my heart al-lures,   I be-long to Je-sus;
4 No threat-'ning dan-ger then I   see,   I be-long to Je-sus;

1 He shall my ev-'ry thought con-trol,   I be-long to Je-sus.
2 What tho' earth's cares an-noy and fret,   I be-long to Je-sus,
3 In weak-ness this my soul as-sures,   I be-long to Je-sus.
4 Thro' time and thro' e-ter-ni-ty,   I be-long to Je-sus.

REFRAIN

I be-long to Je-sus, I be-long to Je-sus,

I be-long to Je-sus, He be-longs to me.

Music by permission of E. H. SWINSTEAD   An Alternative Tune precedes this one

763   Christ, our Rock

P. B.

P. BILHORN

1. When wea - - - - ry and faint - - ing and rea - - - dy to
2. When thirst - - ty and parch'd . . with the heat . . . . of the
3. Though bil - - lows of sor - - row a - round . . . me may

1. die, ... To the Rock . . . in the des - - ert for
2. day, ... To the Rock . . . that was smit - - ten I'll
3. roll, ... And dan - - gers of mid - - night may

1. safe - - ty I fly, ... There 'neath . . . its cool
2. haste . . . me and say, ... "Give me . . . . a cool
3. trou - - ble my soul, ... I'll haste . . . to the

Christ, our Rock—*Continued.*

1. shel - - ter from storms . . . I would hide; . . . My
2. drink . . . from Thy boun - - ti - ful store," . . . And
3. Rock . . . that is high - - er than I, ... And

1. soul . . . is re - fresh'd . . as in Him I a - bide. . .
2. quick - ly and free - ly the life - wa - ters pour. . .
3. safe - ly I'll rest . . . till the night pass - eth by. . .

CHORUS.

O come, all ye wea - ry, and bliss - ful - ly prove. . .

That Christ is the Rock, And His sha - dow is . . love. . .

764 I Belong to the King

IDA L. REED

MAURICE A. CLIFTON

Solo or Duet

1. I belong to the King, I'm a child of His love, I shall dwell in His palace so fair; For He tells of its bliss in yon heaven above, And His children its splendours shall share.
2. I belong to the King, and He loves me, I know, For His mercy and kindness so free, Are unceasingly mine, wheresoever I go, And my refuge unfailing is He.
3. I belong to the King, and His promise is sure, That we all shall be gathered at last In His kingdom above, by life's water so pure, When this life with its trials is past.

CHORUS.

I belong to the King, I'm a child of His love, And He never forsaketh His own; He will call me some day to His palace above, I shall dwell by His glorified throne.

765 What Wilt Thou?

B. A. R.

P. P. BILHORN

1. Lord, Thou hast granted sal - va - tion to me, What wilt Thou have me to do?
2. Since I am saved by the Cru - ci - fied One, What wilt Thou have me to do?
3. Par - don is granted thro' Him who hath died, What wilt Thou have me to do?
4. Read - y and will - ing Thy voice to o - bey, What wilt Thou have me to do?

1. From Sa - tan's bond-age at last I am free, What wilt Thou have me to do?
2. I would point o - thers to God's on - ly Son, What wilt Thou have me to do?
3. I am so hap - py with Thee at my side, What wilt Thou have me to do?
4. Bid me to fol - low Thee day un - to day, What wilt Thou have me to do?

CHORUS. Faster.

What wilt Thou have me to do? Where wilt Thou have me to go?

Je - sus, my Mas - ter, Thy will shall be mine, What wilt Thou have me to do?

766 **Some Glad Day**

C. J. B.

CHAS. J. BUTLER

1. I shall lay the cross a - side, Some day, some glad day;
2. I the sin - ner's friend shall see, Some day, some glad day:
3. I shall meet the friends of yore, Some day, some glad day;
4. I shall lean on Je - sus' breast, Some day, some glad day;

1. Safe - ly pass to Canaan's side, Some day, some glad day;
2. See the wounds once made for me, Some day, some glad day;
3. And with them the Lamb a - dore, Some day, some glad day;
4. Find a sweet, a per - fect rest, Some day, some glad day;

1. If I live a life of pray'r, And the cross for Je - sus bear,
2. I shall press close to His side Who for me was cru - ci - fied,
3. There at Je - sus' sa - cred feet Saints of ev - 'ry clime I'll meet,
4. On that bright e - ter - nal shore All our sor - rows will be o'er,

1. I a glo - ri-ous crown shall wear, Some day, some glad day.
2. And shall then be sat - is - fied, Some day, some glad day.
3. Hold with them com - mun - ion sweet, Some day, some glad day.
4. We shall meet to part no more, Some day, some glad day.

Nat. Anthem 631

535 omit V.2

767 The Friendship of Jesus

IDA M. BUDD

CHAS. H. GABRIEL

1. Have you ac-cept-ed the friend-ship of Je - sus? Do you
2. Dear as a moth-er, or sis-ter or broth-er, To His
3. Ser-vants no long-er, but friends He doth call us, If we

1. walk with Him day by day, Rest-ing se-cure in His
2. in-fin-ite heart of love Is He that do-eth the
3. do what His love com-mands, Yes-ter-day, now, and for-

1. bless-ed as-sur-ance, "Lo, I am with you al - way?"
2. will of the Fa - ther. Seek-ing for strength from a - bove.
3. ev - er His prom-ise, Fixed and un-change-a - ble stands.

CHORUS.

By and by, by and by, They who walk with Him here be-low,
in the home ov - er yon-der,

In His glo-ri-fied likeness a-wak-ing, As they are known, shall they know.

768   Lead Me Gently Home

1. Lead me gent-ly home, Father, Lead me gently home, When life's toils are ended, And
2. Lead me gent-ly home, Father, Lead me gently home: In life's darkest hours, Father

1. part - ing days have come; Sin no more shall tempt me, Ne'er from Thee I'll
2. When life's troubles come, Keep my feet from wan-d'ring, Lest from Thee I

1. roam, If Thou'lt on - ly lead me, Fa-ther, Lead me gent - ly home.
2. roam, Lest I fall up - on the way-side, Lead me gent - ly home.

Lead Me Gently Home—*Continued.*

REFRAIN.

Lead me gent-ly home, Fa-ther, Lead me gent-ly,

Lead me gent-ly home, Fa-ther, Lead me gent-ly home, Fa-ther,

Lest I fall up-on the way-side, Lead me gent-ly home.
Lead me gent-ly, gent-ly home.

769

Jesus of Nazareth

JOHN R. CLEMENTS.

H. P. DANKS.

1. Je-sus of Naz-a-reth, heal-er of men, Cur-er of halt and of blind;
2. Je-sus of Naz-a-reth, cur-er of sin, Seek-er for lost and de-filed;
3. Je-sus of Naz-a-reth, dy-ing for all, Hanging in pain on the tree;

1. Worker of won-ders a-gain and a-gain, Seeking the sad ones to find. . . .
2. Striving so kind-ly the straying to win, Lov-ing each pen-i-tent child. . . .
3. Suff'ring so meek-ly that we who may call, Par-don thro' Him may have free. . . .

REFRAIN.

Je-sus of Naz-a-reth, Tell it a-gain, Died on the cross For sin-ful men.

770   I Come to Thee

LEILA N. MORRIS   LEILA N. MORRIS

1. Just as I am I come to Thee, My-self I can-not bet-ter make;
2. Just as I am, yet this I know, The blood will all-suf-fi-cient be;
3. Just as I am I come to-day, My hungry soul cries out for Thee;
4. Just as I am, my Life, my Love, My soul here finds a per-fect rest;

1. The pre-cious blood my on-ly plea, Oh, save me for Thy mer-cy's sake.
2. I shall be whi-ter than the snow, Made ful-ly whole in trust-ing Thee.
3. I can no long-er stay a-way, Thine, whol-ly Thine, I long to be.
4. While, like the wea-ry, wand'ring dove, Safe fold-ed in Thy love I rest.

CHORUS.

Just as I am, Just as I am I come to Thee;
Just as I am, Just as I am, I come to Thee

Oh, hear me, bless me, save me, Lord, Just as I am I come to Thee.

He Bore our Sins

771

F. TYLER.

CHAS. REEVES

1. Oh, aw - ful load for that bow'd Head, Ter - rif - ic weight for that marr'd form,
2. Transferred to Him the guilt-less, see Your guilt, in blood your debt was paid;
3. Be - lieve, be-lieve, thou guil-ty one; That all thy sins de - serv-ed doom

1. He bore *your* sins, *your* burden dread, And brav'd *your* judgment's fearful storm.
2. Be - hold, to set the cap-tive free, Je - sus the great sin-off-'ring made.
3. Was borne by Christ; God's Ho-ly Son For thee has bow'd Him to the tomb.

CHORUS.

Thy death, Lord Je - sus, ev - er - more . . . . Shall

be our song on yon-der shore, . . We'll praise the blessed One who

bore Our load of sin up-on the tree. . . . .

772 Make the Courts Ring

JOHNSON OATMAN
JOHN R. SWENEY

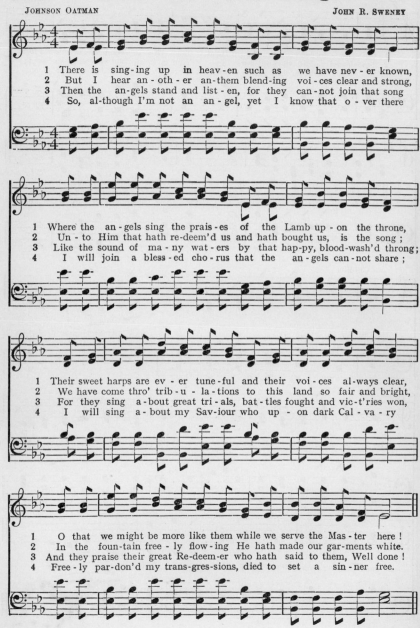

1 There is sing-ing up in heav-en such as we have nev-er known,
2 But I hear an-oth-er an-them blend-ing voi-ces clear and strong,
3 Then the an-gels stand and list-en, for they can-not join that song
4 So, al-though I'm not an an-gel, yet I know that o-ver there

1 Where the an-gels sing the prais-es of the Lamb up-on the throne,
2 Un-to Him that hath re-deem'd us and hath bought us, is the song;
3 Like the sound of ma-ny wat-ers by that hap-py, blood-wash'd throng;
4 I will join a bless-ed cho-rus that the an-gels can-not share;

1 Their sweet harps are ev-er tune-ful and their voi-ces al-ways clear,
2 We have come thro' trib-u-la-tions to this land so fair and bright,
3 For they sing a-bout great tri-als, bat-tles fought and vic-t'ries won,
4 I will sing a-bout my Sav-iour who up-on dark Cal-va-ry

1 O that we might be more like them while we serve the Mas-ter here!
2 In the foun-tain free-ly flow-ing He hath made our gar-ments white.
3 And they praise their great Re-deem-er who hath said to them, Well done!
4 Free-ly par-don'd my trans-gres-sions, died to set a sin-ner free.

Make the Courts Ring—*Continued*

REFRAIN

Ho - ly, ho - ly, is what the an - gels sing, And I ex -

pect to help them make the courts of hea - ven ring; But

when I sing re-demp-tion's sto - ry they will fold their wings, For

an - gels nev - er felt the joys that our sal - va - tion brings.

773   # At Calvary

WM. R. NEWELL   GAMBIA 9.9.9.4. D   D. B. TOWNER

1. Years I spent in van-i-ty and pride, Car-ing not my
2. By God's Word at last my sin I learn'd; Then I trem-bled
3. Now I've giv'n to Je-sus ev-'ry-thing, Now I glad-ly
4. O the love that drew sal-va-tion's plan! O the grace that

1. Lord was cru-ci-fied, Know-ing not it was for me He died
2. at the law I'd spurn'd, Till my guilt-y soul im-plor-ing, turned
3. own Him as my King, Now my rap-tur'd soul can on-ly sing
4. brought it down to man! O the might-y gulf that God did span

REFRAIN

1. On Cal-va-ry.
2. To Cal-va-ry.
3. Of Cal-va-ry.
4. At Cal-va-ry.

Mer-cy there was great and grace was

free, Par-don there was mul-ti-plied to me, There my

bur-den'd soul found li-ber-ty at Cal-va-ry.

The tune CROSSHILL is on the following page

At Calvary

773

Wm. R. Newell

CROSSHILL 9.9. 9.4. D

E. H. SWINSTEAD

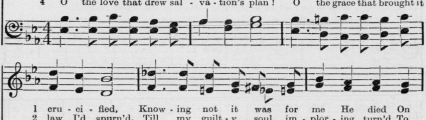

1 Years I spent in van-i-ty and pride, Car-ing not my Lord was
2 By God's Word at last my sin I learn'd; Then I trem-bled at the
3 Now I've giv'n to Je-sus ev-'ry-thing, Now I glad-ly own Him
4 O the love that drew sal-va-tion's plan! O the grace that brought it

1 cru-ci-fied, Know-ing not it was for me He died On
2 law I'd spurn'd, Till my guilt-y soul, im-plor-ing, turn'd To
3 as my King Now my rap-tur'd soul can on-ly sing Of
4 down to man! O the might-y gulf that God did span At

REFRAIN

1-4 Cal - va - ry, Mer - cy there was great and grace was

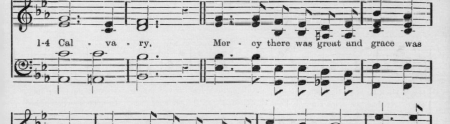

free, Par - don there was mul-ti-plied to me, There my

bur-den'd soul found li-ber-ty, at Cal - va - ry.

Music by permission of E. H. SWINSTEAD

The Tune GAMBIA precedes this one

774 He'll Never Forget

F.A. GRAVES

F.A. GRAVES

TENOR AND ALTO DUET.

1. My Father has many dear children; Will He ever forget to keep me?
2. Our Father remembers the sparrows, Their value and fall He doth see;
3. The words of the Lord are so priceless, How patient and watchful is He;
4. O brother, why don't you accept Him? He offers salvation so free;

1. He gave His own Son to redeem them, And He cannot forget to keep me.
2. But dearer to Him are His children, And He'll never forget to keep me.
3. Tho' mother forget her own offspring, Yet He'll never forget to keep me.
4. Repent and believe and obey Him, And He'll never forget to keep thee.

REFRAIN.

1, 2, 3. He'll never forget to keep me (keep me), He'll never forget to keep me (keep me);
4th v. He'll never forget to keep thee (keep thee), He'll never forget to keep thee (keep thee);

1. He gave His own Son to redeem me, And He'll never forget to keep me.
2. But dearer to Him are His children, And He'll never forget to keep me.
3. Tho' mother forget her own offspring, Yet He'll never forget to keep me.
4. Repent and believe and obey Him, And He'll never forget to keep thee.

775 Lost and Found

J. H. SAMMIS

CARL FISCHER

1. What were we when mer - cy found us? Captives un - to death and sin;
2. What are we since mer - cy found us? Blameless, spotless in His sight;
3. What we shall be? That's a sto - ry Nev - er uttered, or ex - pressed!

1. Clouds and darkness closed a - round us, All was hopeless night with - in.
2. Sons and saints His word has crowned us, Called to walk with Him in light.
3. We shall see Him in His glo - ry, And be fold - ed to His breast.

CHORUS.

We were lost, but Je - sus found us, Burst the bonds of death that bound us,

Wrapt the robe of grace a - round us, And the heirs of glo - ry crowned us.

776 Unanswered Yet?

R. Browning
DUET.

CHARLIE D. TILLMAN

1. Un - an-swered yet? The pray'r your lips have plead - ed In a - go - ny
2. Un - an-swered yet? Tho' when you first pre - sent - ed This one pe - ti
3. Un - an-swered yet? Nay, do not say "un - grant - ed;" Per-haps your part
4. Un - an-swered yet? Faith can - not be un - an - swered; Her feet are firm

1. of heart these ma - ny years? Does faith be - gin to fail? Is hope de - part - ing?
2. tion at the Father's throne. It seemed you could not wait the time of ask - ing,
3. is not yet whol - ly done; The work be - gan when first your prayer was ut - tered,
4. ly plant - ed on the Rock; A - mid the wild - est storms she stands un - daunt - ed,

1. And think you all in vain those fall - ing tears? Say not the Fa - ther
2. So ur - gent was your heart to make it known. Tho' years have passed since
3. And God will fin - ish what He has be - gun, If you will keep the
4. Nor quails be - fore the loud - est thun - der shock. She knows Om - nip - o -

1. hath not heard your prayer, You shall have your de - sire, some - time, some-
2. then, do not des - pair; The Lord will an - swer you, some - time, some-
3. in - cense burn - ing there, His glo - ry you shall see, some - time, some-
4. tence has heard her prayer, And cries, "It shall be done," some - time, some-

Unanswered Yet?—*Continued*

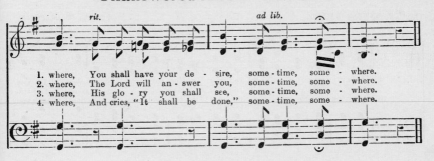

1. where, You shall have your de - sire, some-time, some - where.
2. where, The Lord will an - swer you, some-time, some - where.
3. where, His glo - ry you shall see, some-time, some - where.
4. where, And cries, "It shall be done," some-time, some - where.

777 Prodigal Child

Ellen H. Gates

W. H. Doane

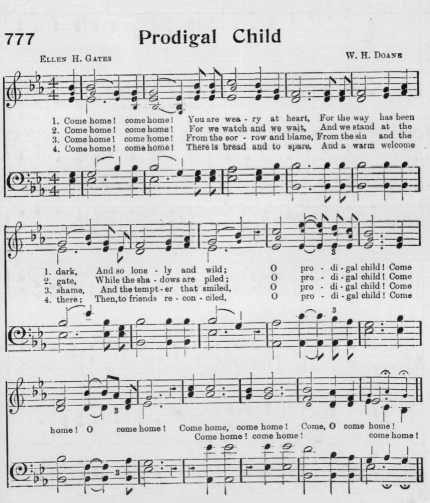

1. Come home! come home! You are wea - ry at heart, For the way has been
2. Come home! come home! For we watch and we wait, And we stand at the
3. Come home! come home! From the sor - row and blame, From the sin and the
4. Come home! come home! There is bread and to spare, And a warm welcome

1. dark, And so lone - ly and wild; O pro - di - gal child! Come
2. gate, While the sha - dows are piled; O pro - di - gal child! Come
3. shame, And the tempt - er that smiled, O pro - di - gal child! Come
4. there; Then, to friends re - con - ciled, O pro - di - gal child! Come

home! O come home! Come home, come home! Come, O come home!
Come home! come home! come home!

778 I am Coming Back

J. WAKEFIELD MACGILL

Arr. E. W. MACGILL

1. There is something strangely ten - der In His part - ing words so sweet, "Do not
2. Ah, those words, so strangely ten - der, Still keep ech - o - ing all round, And tho'
3. Don't you hear the words so ten - der? Don't they ech - o in your heart? Don't they

1. let your heart be trou - bled, For we by - and - bye shall meet In the home of ma - ny
2. they have gone to glo - ry, And have reach'd the hallow'd ground, The sweet promise has not
3. woo you from this poor life, That with which you soon must part? Those who wait His coming

1. man - sions, Which I go now to pre - pare, And when I am read - y, dear ones, I will
2. failed them, They are with their Lord to - night, We shall find them read - y wait - ing Just with-
3. glo - rious Then will form His roy - al train, Oh, the rapturous hour of meet - ing When the

CHORUS.

1. come and take you there."
2. in the gates of light.
3. Lord comes back to reign.

"Ah," He whisper'd, when He left them, "I am com - ing back a -

gain, And will take you to your new home, Ev - er near Me to re - main."

He Knows it All

779

OPHELIA ADAMS.

C. M. DAVIS.

1. I love to think my Fa-ther knows Why I have missed the path I chose,
2. I love to think my Fa-ther knows The thorns I pluck with ev'-ry rose,
3. I love to think my Fa-ther knows The strength or weak-ness of my foes,

1. And that I soon shall clearly see The way He led was best for me.
2. The dai-ly griefs I seek to hide From the dear souls I walk be-side.
3. And that I need but stand and see Each conflict end in vic-to-ry.

REFRAIN.

He knows it all, ... He knows it all, ... My Fa-ther
He knows it all, He knows it all,

knows, ... He knows it all: . . . . Thy bit-ter tears, . . . how
My Fa-ther knows, He knows it all; Thy bittter tears

fast they fall! He knows, My Fa-ther knows it all.
how fast they fall!

780 I am Happy in Him

E. O. E.

E. O. Excell

1. My soul is so hap-py in Je - sus, For He is so precious to me;
2. He sought me so long ere I knew Him, When wand-'ring a - far from the fold;
3. His love and His mer-cy surround me, His grace like a riv-er doth flow;
4. They say I shall some day be like Him, My cross and my burden lay down;

1. His voice it is music to hear it, His face it is hea-ven to see. . . .
2. Safe home in His arms He hath bro't me, To where there are pleasures un - told. . .
3. His Spi - rit, to guide and to com-fort, Is with me wher-ev-er I go. . . .
4. Till then I will ev-er be faithful, In gath - er - ing gems for His crown.

CHORUS.

I am happy in Him, ... I am happy in Him; . . .
I . . . . am happy in Him, I . . . . am happy in Him;

My soul with de-light He fills day and night, For I am happy in Him.

781 Channels Only

MARY E. MAXWELL   CHANNELS ONLY 8.7.8.7. D   ADA ROSE

1. How I praise Thee, precious Sa-viour, That Thy love laid hold of me;
2. Just a chan-nel, full of bless-ing, To the thirst-y hearts a-round;
3. Emptied that Thou shouldest fill me, A clean ves-sel in Thine hand;
4. Wit-ness-ing Thy power to save me, Set-ting free from self and sin;
5. Je-sus, fill now with Thy Spi-rit Hearts that full sur-ren-der know;

1. Thou hast sav'd and cleans'd and filled me, That I might Thy chan-nel be.
2. To tell out Thy full sal-va-tion, All Thy lov-ing mes-sage sound.
3. With no pow'r but as Thou giv-est Gracious-ly with each com-mand.
4. Thou hast bought me to pos-sess me, In Thy ful-ness, Lord, come in.
5. That the streams of liv-ing wa-ter From our in-ner man may flow.

CHORUS.

Channels on-ly, bless-ed Mas-ter, But with all Thy wondrous power,

Flow-ing through us, Thou canst use us Ev-'ry day and ev-'ry hour.

782   The Old-Fashioned Way

JOHNSON OATMAN   E. O. EXCELL

1. I am on the Gos - pel high - way, Pressing for - ward to the goal,
2. From the snares of sin - ful plea - sure, Here my feet are al - ways free;
3. Ma-ny friends have gone be - fore me, They have laid their ar - mour down,
4. Just a few more steps to fol - low, Just a few more days to roam;

1. Where for me a rest re - main - eth, In the home - land of the soul:
2. Tho' the way may be called nar - row, It is wide e - nough for me;
3. With the pil - grims and the mar - tyrs Have obtained a robe and crown;
4. But the way grows more de - light - ful As I'm draw - ing near - er home;

1. Ev - 'ry hour I'm mov - ing on - ward, Not a mo - ment to de - lay;
2. It was wide e - nough for Dan - iel, And for Da - vid in his day;
3. On this road they fought their bat - tles, Shouting vic - t'ry day by day;
4. When the storms of life are o - ver, And the clouds have rolled a - way,

1. I am go - ing home to glo - ry In the good old-fashioned way.
2. I am glad that I can fol - low In the good old-fashioned way.
3. I shall o - ver-come and join them In the good old-fashioned way.
4. I shall find the gates of hea - ven In the good old-fashioned way.

The Old-Fashioned Way—*Continued*

Chorus.

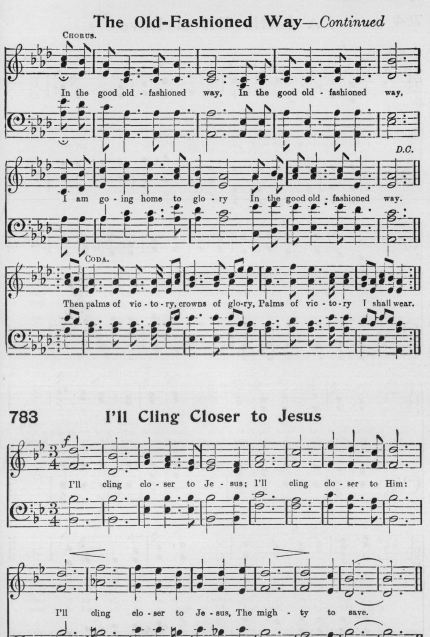

In the good old - fashioned way, In the good old - fashioned way,

D.C.

I am go - ing home to glo - ry In the good old - fashioned way.

Coda.

Then palms of vic - to - ry, crowns of glo - ry, Palms of vic - to - ry I shall wear.

783   I'll Cling Closer to Jesus

I'll cling clo - ser to Je - sus; I'll cling clo - ser to Him:

I'll cling clo - ser to Je - sus, The migh - ty to save.

784 A Little Bit of Love

E. O. E.

E. O. EXCELL.

1. Do you know the world is dy-ing For a lit-tle bit of love?
2. From the poor of ev-'ry ci-ty, For a lit-tle bit of love,
3. Down be-fore their i-dols fall-ing, For a lit-tle bit of love,
4. While the souls of men are dy-ing For a lit-tle bit of love,

1. Ev-'ry-where we hear their sigh-ing For a lit-tle bit of love;
2. Hands are reach-ing out in pi-ty For a lit-tle bit of love;
3. Ma-ny souls in vain are call-ing For a lit-tle bit of love;
4. While the chil-dren, too, are cry-ing For a lit-tle bit of love;

1. For the love that rights a wrong, Fills the heart with hope and song;
2. Some have bur-dens hard to bear, Some have sor-rows we should share;
3. If they die in sin and shame, Some one sure-ly is to blame
4. Stand no long-er i-dly by, You can help them if you try;

1. They have wait-ed, oh, so long! For a lit-tle bit of love.
2. Shall they fal-ter and des-pair For a lit-tle bit of love?
3. For not go-ing, in His name, With a lit-tle bit of love.
4. Go, then, say-ing, "Here am I," With a lit-tle bit of love.

A Little Bit of Love—*Continued*

REFRAIN.

1. For a lit - tle bit of love, For a lit - tle bit of love;
2. For a lit - tle bit of love, For a lit - tle bit of love;
3. With a lit - tle bit of love, With a lit - tle bit of love;
4. With a lit - tle bit of love, With a lit - tle bit of love;

1. They have wait-ed, O so long, For a lit - tle bit of love.
2. Shall they fal - ter and des - pair For a lit - tle bit of love?
3. For not go - ing, in His name, With a lit - tle bit of love.
4. Go, then, say-ing, "Here am I," With a lit - tle bit of love.

85 Only a Word

J. M. DUNGAN.

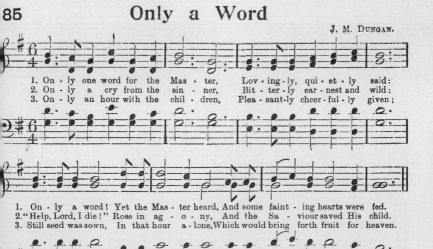

1. On - ly one word for the Mas - ter, Lov - ing-ly, qui - et - ly said:
2. On - ly a cry from the sin - ner, Bit - ter-ly earn - est and wild;
3. On - ly an hour with the chil - dren, Plea - sant-ly cheer - ful - ly given;

1. On - ly a word! Yet the Mas - ter heard, And some faint - ing hearts were fed.
2. "Help, Lord, I die!" Rose in ag - o - ny, And the Sa - viour saved His child.
3. Still seed was sown, In that hour a - lone, Which would bring forth fruit for heaven.

786 A Starless Crown

GRANT COLFAX TULLAR STARLESS CROWN L.M.D I. H. MEREDITH

1. There is a land mine eyes shall see When I shall
2. The gains of earth are all but loss,— E - ter - nal
3. For - bid it, Lord, that I should be Con - tent to

1. lay life's ar - mour down; But all its bliss is not for
2. joys are all for me When I by faith up - lift the
3. live for self a - lone. Oh, may some soul I win for

CHORUS.

1. me, If I must wear a star - less crown.
2. cross And lead one soul, dear Lord, to Thee.
3. Thee A - dorn my crown when life is done.

A star - less crown, when life is done, No glit - t'ring gems which I have won?

Rit.

For - bid it, Lord, that there should be A star - less crown in Heav'n for me.

87 Anchored

Johnson Oatman   Anchored 8.7. 8.7. d   George G. Hugg

1 Once up - on the tide I drift - ed   With no guide to yon-der shore ;
2 Let the storms sweep o'er life's o - cean,   They can do me no more harm ;
3 Here my peace flows like a ri - ver,   Here my soul o'er-flows with song ;
4 When this life be - low is end - ed,   I shall an - chor on that shore ;

1 But I've found a side once rift - ed,   Where I'm safe for - ev - er - more.
2 An-chor'd far from their com-mo-tion   I am rest-ing 'neath His arm.
3 Pray'r and prais-es to the Giv - er   Fill my glad heart all day long.
4 Where my prais-es will be blend-ed   With ten thous-and thous-and more.

REFRAIN

I am an-chor'd, safe-ly an - chor'd,   An-chor'd, nev-er-more to roam,

An-chor'd by the side of Je - sus,   An-chor'd in the soul's bright home.

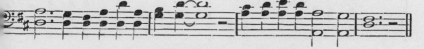

788   Peace, Wonderful Peace

W. D. Cornell

W. G. Cooper

1. Far a-way in the depths of my spi-rit to-night Rolls a
2. What a trea-sure I have in this won-der-ful peace, Bur-ied
3. I am rest-ing to-night in this won-der-ful peace, Rest-ing
4. And me-thinks when I rise to that ci-ty of peace, Where the
5. Ah, soul! are you here without com-fort and rest, March-ing

1. mel-o-dy sweet-er than psalm; In ce-les-tial-like strains it un
2. deep in the heart of my soul, So se-cure that no pow-er can
3. sweet-ly in Je-sus' con-trol; For I'm kept from all dan-ger by
4. Au-thor of peace I shall see, That one strain of the song which the
5. down the rough pathway of time? Make Je-sus your Friend ere the

1. ceas-ing-ly falls O'er my soul like an in-fi-nite calm.
2. mine it a-way, While the years of e-ter-ni-ty roll!
3. night and by day, And His glo-ry is flood-ing my soul.
4. ran-som'd will sing In that heav-en-ly king-dom will be.
5. shad-ows grow dark; O ac-cept of this peace so sub-lime.

CHORUS.

Peace! peace! won-der-ful peace, Coming down from the Fa-ther a-bove,

o-ver my spi-rit for ev-er, I pray, In fath-omless billows of love!

789 # Beyond Thy Love

IDA L. REED   LYNESS C.M.D.   WM. J. KIRKPATRICK

1 I can - not drift be - yond Thy love, Be - yond Thy ten - der care ;
2 I can - not drift be - yond Thy sight, Dear Lord the thought is sweet ;
3 I can - not drift a - way from Thee, No mat - ter where I go ;

1 Wher - e'er I stray, still from a - bove Thine eye be - holds me there.
2 Thy lov - ing hand will guide a - right My wea - ry, wan - d'ring feet.
3 Still Thy dear love doth glad - den me, Thou all my way dost know.

1 I can - not drift so far a - way But what Thy love di - vine
2 When rough and dark my lone - ly way, I shall not be for - got,
3 Wher - e'er I jour - ney Thou art there, In wind and wave I hear

1 Up - on my path, by night and day, In mer - cy sweet doth shine.
2 Thro' all life's change - ful, sha - dow'd day Thou wilt for - sake me not.
3 Thy voice, in tones of mus - ic rare, And know that Thou art near.

790 # The Haven of Rest

H. L. GILMOUR　　　　　　　　　　　　　　　GEORGE D. MOORE

1 My soul in sad ex - ile was out on life's sea, So bur-den'd with
2 I yield - ed my - self to His ten - der em - brace, And faith tak - ing
3 The song of my soul, since the Lord made me whole, Has been the old
4 How pre - cious the thought that we all may re - cline, Like John, the be -
5 O come to the Sa - viour! He pa - tient - ly waits To save by His

1 sin and dis - tress'd, Till I heard a sweet voice say-ing, 'Make Me your
2 hold of the word, My fet - ters fell off, and I an-chor'd my
3 sto - ry so blest, Of Je - sus, who'll save who - so - ev - er will
4 lov - ed and blest, On Je - sus' strong arm, where no tem - pest can
5 pow - er di - vine; Come, an - chor your soul in the Ha - ven of

D.S.—The tem - pest may sweep o'er the wild, storm-y

FINE　　REFRAIN

1 choice'; And I en - ter'd the Ha - ven of Rest.
2 soul; The Ha - ven of Rest is my Lord.
3 have A home in the Ha - ven of Rest.
4 harm, Se - cure in the Ha - ven of Rest.
5 Rest, And say, 'My Be - lov - ed is mine.'

I've an-chor'd my

deep, In Je - sus I'm safe ev - er - more.

D.S.

soul in the Ha - ven of Rest, I'll sail the wide seas no more;

791 Welcome for Me

Fanny J. Crosby   Wm. J. Kirkpatrick

1. Like a bird on the deep, far a-way from its nest, I had
2. I am safe in the ark; I have fold-ed my wings On the
3. I am safe in the ark; and I dread not the storm, Tho' a-

1. wander'd, my Sa-viour, from Thee; But Thy dear lov-ing voice called me
2. bo-som of mer-cy di-vine; I am filled with the light of Thy
3. round me the sur-ges may roll; I will look to the skies, where the

1. home to Thy breast, And I knew there was wel-come for me.
2. pre-sence so bright, And the joy that will ev-er be mine.
3. day nev-er dies, I will sing of the joy in my soul.

CHORUS.

Welcome for me, Saviour, from Thee; A smile and a welcome for me,

Thee.

Now, like a dove, I rest in Thy love, And find a sweet re-fuge in Thee, in Thee.

Thee.

792 My Father Knows

S. M. I. HENRY   E. O. EXCELL

1 I know my heav'n-ly Fa-ther knows The storms that would my way op-pose;
2 I know my heav'n-ly Fa-ther knows The balm I need to soothe my woes;
3 I know my heav'n-ly Fa-ther knows How frail I am to meet my foes;
4 I know my heav'n-ly Fa-ther knows The hour my jour-ney here will close,

1 But he can drive the clouds a-way, And turn my dark-ness in-to day.
2 And with His touch of love di-vine He heals this wound-ed soul of mine.
3 But He my cause will e'er de-fend, Up-hold and keep me to the end,
4 And may that hour, O faith-ful Guide, Find me safe shel-ter'd by Thy side,

REFRAIN

1 And turn my dark-ness in-to day.
2 He heals this wound-ed soul of mine.
3 Up-hold and keep me to the end.
4 Find me safe shel-ter'd by Thy side.

He knows, He
My Fa-ther knows—

knows   The storms that would my way op-pose; He
I'm sure He knows   that would my way op-pose;

pp rall.

knows,   He knows,   And tem-pers ev-'ry wind that blows.
My Fa-ther knows—   I'm sure He knows,   the wind that blow

793

The Pearly Gates

OLD MELODY

1. I have giv'n up all for Je-sus, This vain world is nought to me, All its
2. When the voice of Je-sus calls me, And the an-gels whis-per low, I will
3. Just beyond the waves of Jor-dan, Just be-yond its chill-ing tide, Blooms the

mf

1. pleasures are for-gotten In rememb'ring Cal-va-ry; Though my friends despise, for-
2. lean up-on my Saviour, Through the val-ley as I go; I will claim His precious
3. tree of life im-mor-tal, And the liv-ing wa-ters glide; In that hap-py land of

1. sake me, And on me the world looks cold, I've a Friend that will stand by me When the
2. promise, Worth to me the world of gold, "Fear no e-vil, I'll be with thee When the
3. spi-rits Are there stores of bliss un-told, And the an-gels are a-waiting Where the

f CHORUS.

pear-ly gates un-fold. Life's morn will soon be waning, And its evening bells be

toll'd, But my heart will know no sad-ness When the pear-ly gates un-fold.

794 The Debt Unknown

R. Murray McCheyne

D. B. Towner

1 When this pass-ing world is done, When has sunk yon glow-ing sun,
2 When I stand be-fore the throne Dress'd in beau-ty not my own,
3 When I hear the wick-ed call On the rocks and hills to fall,
4 When the praise of heav'n I hear Loud as thun-ders to the ear,

1 When we stand with Christ in glo-ry, Look-ing o'er life's fin-ish'd sto-ry,
2 When I see Thee as Thou art,.. Love Thee with un-sin-ning heart,
3 When I see them start and shrink On the fier-y del-uge brink,
4 Loud as man-y wa-ters' noise, Sweet as harp's me-lo-dious voice,

REFRAIN

Then, dear Lord, shall I ful-ly know, Not till then, how much I owe,

Then, dear Lord, shall I ful-ly know, Not till then, how much I owe.

795 His Grace is Enough

J. BRUCE EVANS — J. BRUCE EVANS

1. Just when I am dis-hearten'd, Just when with cares op-press'd, Just when my
2. Just when my hopes have vanish'd, Just when my friends for-sake, Just when the
3. Just when my tears are flow-ing, Just when with an-guish bent, Just when temp-

1. way is dark-est, Just when I am dis-tress'd, Then is my Sa-viour near me,
2. fight is thick-est, Just when with fear I shake, Then comes a still small whisper,
3. ta-tion's hard-est, Just when with sadness rent, Then comes a thought of comfort,

1. He knows my ev'ry care; Je-sus will ne-ver leave me, He helps my burdens bear.
2. "Fear not, my child, I'm near," Jesus brings peace and comfort, I love His voice to hear.
3. "I know my Father knows." Je-sus has grace suf-fi-cient To con-quer all my foes.

CHORUS.

His grace is enough for me, for me, His grace is enough for me;

Thro' sor-row and pain, Thro' loss or gain, His grace is enough for me.

796 Jesus Understands

BIRDIE BELL

WM. J. KIRKPATRICK
Arr. P. J. MANSFIELD

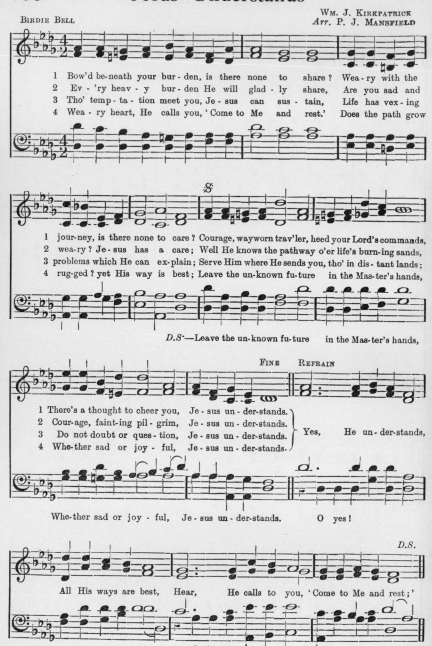

1 Bow'd be-neath your bur-den, is there none to share? Wea-ry with the
2 Ev - 'ry heav - y bur-den He will glad - ly share, Are you sad and
3 Tho' temp - ta - tion meet you, Je - sus can sus - tain, Life has vex - ing
4 Wea - ry heart, He calls you, 'Come to Me and rest.' Does the path grow

1 jour-ney, is there none to care? Courage, wayworn trav'ler, heed your Lord's commands,
2 wea-ry? Je - sus has a care; Well He knows the pathway o'er life's burn-ing sands,
3 problems which He can ex-plain; Serve Him where He sends you, tho' in dis - tant lands;
4 rug-ged? yet His way is best; Leave the un-known fu-ture in the Mas-ter's hands,

D.S.—Leave the un-known fu-ture in the Mas-ter's hands,

FINE   REFRAIN

1 There's a thought to cheer you, Je - sus un - der-stands.
2 Cour-age, faint-ing pil - grim, Je - sus un - der-stands.
3 Do not doubt or ques - tion, Je - sus un - der-stands.
4 Whe-ther sad or joy - ful, Je - sus un - der-stands.

Yes,   He un - der-stands,

Whe-ther sad or joy - ful, Je - sus un - der-stands.   O yes!

D.S.

All His ways are best, Hear, He calls to you, 'Come to Me and rest;'

O hear!

797 # Higher Ground

JOHNSON OATMAN   HIGHER GROUND 8.8.8.8.D.   CHAS. H. GABRIEL

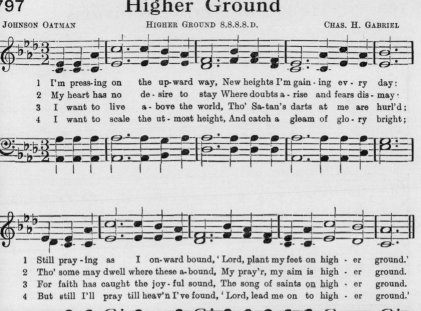

1 I'm press-ing on   the up-ward way, New heights I'm gain-ing ev-ry day:
2 My heart has no   de-sire to stay Where doubts a-rise and fears dis-may:
3 I want to live   a-bove the world, Tho' Sa-tan's darts at me are hurl'd;
4 I want to scale   the ut-most height, And catch a gleam of glo-ry bright;

1 Still pray-ing as   I on-ward bound, 'Lord, plant my feet on high-er ground.'
2 Tho' some may dwell where these a-bound, My pray'r, my aim is high-er ground.
3 For faith has caught the joy-ful sound, The song of saints on high-er ground.
4 But still I'll pray till heav'n I've found, 'Lord, lead me on to high-er ground.'

REFRAIN

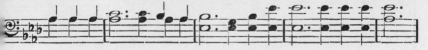

Lord, lift me up and let me stand By faith on heav-en's ta-ble-land;

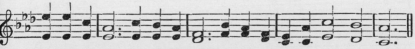

A high-er plane than I have found, Lord, plant my feet on high-er ground.

798 House of Many Mansions

E. Norman Gunnison

George C. Stebbins

1 O house of ma - ny man - sions! Thy doors are o - pen wide,
2 O house of ma - ny man - sions! My wea - ry spi - rit waits
3 O house of ma - ny man - sions! O house not made with hands!

1 And dear are all the fa - ces Up - on the o - ther side;
2 And longs to join the ran - som'd With - in thy pear - ly gates;
3 I sigh for thee while wait - ing With - in these bor - der lands;

1 Thy por - tals they are gold - en, And those who en - ter in
2 Who en - ter thro' thy por - tals The man - sions of the blest;
3 I know that but in dy - ing Thy thresh - old is cross'd o'er;

1 Shall know no more of sor - row, Of wea - ri - ness and sin.
2 Who come to thee a - wea - ry, And find in thee their rest.
3 There shall be no more sor - row In thy for - ev - er - more.

REFRAIN

O house of ma - ny man - sions! Thy doors are o - pen wide,

House of Many Mansions—*Continued*

And dear are all the fa - ces Up - on the o - ther side.

E. NORMAN GUNNISON   THE HOMELAND 7.6.7.6.D.   ARTHUR S. SULLIVAN

1 O house of ma - ny man - sions! Thy doors are o - pen wide,
2 O house of ma - ny man - sions! My wea - ry spi - rit waits
3 O house of ma - ny man - sions! O house not made with hands!

1 And dear are all the fa - ces Up - on the o - ther side;
2 And longs to join the ran - som'd With - in thy pear - ly gates;
3 I sigh for thee while wait - ing With - in these bor - der lands;

1 Thy por - tals they are gold - en, And those who en - ter in
2 Who en - ter thro' thy por - tals The man - sions of the blest;
3 I know that but in dy - ing Thy thresh - old is cross'd o'er

1 Shall know no more of sor - row, Of wea - ri - ness and sin.
2 Who come to thee a - wea - ry, And find in thee their rest.
3 There shall be no more sor - row in thy for - ev - er - more.

799 It Never Grows Old

JOHN H. YATES

M. L. McPHAIL

1 How dear to my heart is the sto - ry of old,
2 It came to my heart when, all fet - ter'd by sin,
3 It comes to my soul when the temp - ter is nigh
4 When sor - row is mine, and on pil - lows of stone
5 When down in the val - ley and sha - dow of Death

1 The sto - ry that ev - er is new, . . .
2 I sat in the pris - on of doubt: . . .
3 With snares for my way - wea - ry feet; . . .
4 My ach - ing head seeks for re - pose, . . .
5 I en - ter the gloom of the grave, . . .

1 The mes - sage that saints of all a - ges have told,
2 Like an - gel of old the glad sto - ry came in,
3 It tells of the rock that is high - er than I,
4 This sto - ry brings com - fort and peace from the throne,
5 I'll tell the old sto - ry with life's lat - est breath

It Never Grows Old—*Continued*

1 The mes - sage so ten - der and true. . . . .
2 And led me tri - umph - ant - ly out. . . . .
3 And leads to its bliss - ful re - treat. . . . .
4 My des - ert blooms forth like the rose. . . . .
5 Of Christ and His pow - er to save. . . . .

REFRAIN

The sto - ry that nev - er grows old, . . . Though o - ver
that nev - er grows old,

and o - ver 'tis told; . . . . The sto - ry so dear, bring - ing
'tis told;

hea - ven so near, Sweet sto - ry that nev - er grows old. . . .

800 He Keepeth His Promise

S C. Kirk

HERBERT J. LACEY

1 The Lord hath de-clar'd and the Lord will per-form; Be-hold! I am
2 Who seek Him shall find Him, shall find Him to-day, The word is to
3 Tho' oft-en my toil seems but la-bour in vain, I leave with the
4 My heart may sink low in the depths of its woe, But nev-er, He
5 The bonds that u-nite us in earth's dear-est ties The rude hand of

1 near to de-liv-er, A re-fuge and fort-ress, a co-vert in storm;
2 all, who-so-ev-er! No soul that en-treat-eth He turn-eth a-way;
3 Lord my en-deav-our! I pa-tient-ly wait for the sun-shine and rain,
4 tells me, O nev-er! The frail, bruis-ed reed will He break; and I know
5 time will dis-sev-er; But we shall re-new them a-gain in the skies;

REFRAIN

1-5 He keep-eth His pro-mise for-ev-er. For-ev-er! for-ev-er! O

not for a day! He keep-eth His pro-mise for-ev-er; To all who

be-lieve, to all who o-bey, He keep-eth His pro-mise for-ev-er.

801 They shall be Comforted

E. E. Hewitt

Wm. J. Kirkpatrick

1. They shall be com-fort-ed; sor-row-ing heart, Soon ev-'ry cloud will for-
2. They shall be com-fort-ed; Je-sus says so, True and e-ter-nal His
3. They shall be com-fort-ed; yea, e-ven here, Bless-ed the mourn-er whom
4. They shall be com-fort-ed; rise, then, and shine, Shine in the beau-ty of

1. ev-er de-part; Joy, wondrous joy, in that beau-ti-ful day, When God shall
2. promise we know; Gen-tle His smile, and how ten-der His voice, Bid-ding His
3. Je-sus shall cheer; Sunbeams of glo-ry thro' time's fleeting show'rs, Heaven a-
4. love so di-vine; Let o-thers find where the "still waters" flow, They may be

1. wipe ev-'ry tear-drop a-way, When God shall wipe ev-'ry tear-drop a-way.
2. chil-dren in Him to re-joice, Bid-ding His chil-dren in Him to re-joice.
3. round us—this Sa-viour is ours! Heav-en a-round us—this Sa-viour is ours!
4. com-fort-ed, Je-sus says so, They may be com-fort-ed; Je-sus says so.

CHORUS. mf

Nev-er a sor-row, nev-er a fear, Nev-er a shadow, nev-er a tear,

They shall be comforted in that sweet day, When God shall wipe ev'ry teardrop away.

802 # Thy Boundless Love

Neil A. McAuley   Boundless Love 8.6.8.6.6.6.8.6   Chas. H. Gabriel

1 Be - hold the prec - ious Lamb of God, Who died up - on the tree,
2 Be - hold the heal - ing streams of grace That from His side did flow,
3 Be - hold the Cross He bore for me, Where-by He sav'd my soul;

1 That guil - ty sin - ners such as I Might thro' His grace be free.
2 I plung'd be-neath the crim - son flood That wash - es white as snow.
3 His match-less grace shall be my theme While count-less a - ges roll.

Refrain

Thy bound - - less love I'll sing, Thy grace............ so full and free,
Thy bound-less, bound-less love I'll sing, Thy grace, Thy grace so full and free,

'Tis un - der Thy pro - tect - ing wing My soul de-lights to be.................
de-lights to be.

The tune St. Louis is on the following page

802 Thy Boundless Love

NEIL A. McAULEY   ST. LOUIS 8.6.8.6.6.6.8.6   LEWIS H. REDNER

1 Be - hold the prec - ious Lamb of God, Who died up - on the tree,
2 Be - hold the heal - ing streams of grace That from His side did flow,
3 Be - hold the Cross He bore for me, Where - by He sav'd my soul;

1 That guil - ty sin - ners such as I Might thro' His grace be free.
2 I plung'd be-neath the crim - son flood That wash - es white as snow.
3 His match-less grace shall be my theme While count-less a - ges roll.

REFRAIN

Thy bound - less love I'll sing, Thy grace so full and free,

'Tis un - der Thy pro - tect - ing wing My soul de - lights to be.

The tune BOUNDLESS LOVE is on the previous page

803 Under the Blood

ELISHA A. HOFFMAN · ELISHA A. HOFFMAN

1 I have per-fect peace to-day, All my sins are wash'd a-way;
2 What a work the Lord hath done! What a work of grace be-gun!
3 Won-drous is God's grace to me, Mak-ing me for ev-er free,
4 So in glad-ness I go on Till the Mas-ter's work is done,

1 Hid-ing 'neath the crim-son blood; I am re-con-cil'd to God.
2 All my sins are cov-er'd o'er; He re-mem-bers them no more.
3 Sanc-ti-fy-ing me to God Thro' the all-pre-vail-ing blood.
4 Trust-ing in a-ton-ing blood, Walk-ing in the love of God.

REFRAIN

Un-der the blood, un-der the blood, Par-don and cleans-ing I

found un-der the blood; Un-der the blood, un-der the blood,

There I for ev-er will hide, un-der the blood.

Jesus is Precious

804

Grant Colfax Tullar

I. H. Meredith

805   I Know not the Hour

FANNY J. CROSBY   WM. J. KIRKPATRICK

1. I know not the hour of His com-ing, Nor how He will
   speak to my heart; Or whe-ther at morn-ing or mid-day My
   spi-rit to Him will de-part.

2. I know not the bliss that a-waits me, At rest with my
   Sa-viour a-bove; I know not how soon I shall en-ter, And
   bathe in the o-cean of love,

3. Per-haps in the midst of my la-bour A voice from my
   Lord I shall hear; Per-haps in the slum-ber of mid-night Its
   mes-sage may fall on my ear.

4. I know not, but O I am watch-ing! My lamp ev-er
   burn-ing and bright; I know not if Je-sus will call me At
   morn-ing, at noon, or at night.

REFRAIN

But I know........ I know I shall wake in the like-ness Of Him.......... Of Him I am long-ing to see; I know......... I know that mine eyes shall be-hold Him, Who died................. Who died for a sin-ner, for a sin-ner like me.

806 ## Hidden Peace

J. S. BROWN

L. O. BROWN

1. I can-not tell thee whence it came, This peace with-in my breast;
2. Be-neath the toil and care of life, This hid-den stream flows on;
3. I can-not tell the half of love, Un-feigned, su-preme, di-vine,
4. I can-not tell thee why He chose To suf-fer and to die;

1. But this I know, there fills my soul A strange and tranquil rest.
2. My wea-ry soul no long-er thirsts, Nor am I sad and lone.
3. That caused my dark-est in-most self With beams of hope to shine.
4. But if I suf-fer here with Him, I'll reign with Him for aye.

CHORUS.

There's a deep, set-tled peace in my soul (in my soul),

There's a deep, set-tled peace in my soul (in my soul); Though the

bil-lows of sin near me roll, He a-bides, Christ a-bides.

807

'Tis Jesus

S. C. KIRK HANWELL 8.8.8.7.D ALFRED JUDSON

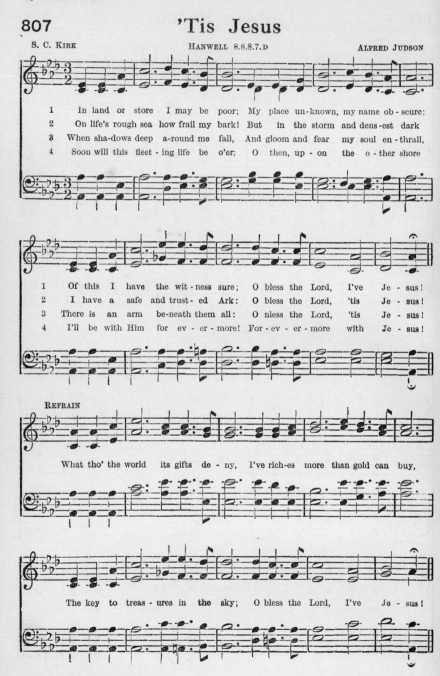

1 In land or store I may be poor; My place un-known, my name ob-scure;
2 On life's rough sea how frail my bark! But in the storm and dens-est dark
3 When sha-dows deep a-round me fall, And gloom and fear my soul en-thrall,
4 Soon will this fleet-ing life be o'er; O then, up-on the o-ther shore

1 Of this I have the wit-ness sure; O bless the Lord, I've Je-sus!
2 I have a safe and trust-ed Ark: O bless the Lord, 'tis Je-sus!
3 There is an arm be-neath them all: O nless the Lord, 'tis Je-sus!
4 I'll be with Him for ev-er-more! For-ev-er-more with Je-sus!

REFRAIN

What tho' the world its gifts de-ny, I've rich-es more than gold can buy,

The key to treas-ures in the sky; O bless the Lord, I've Je-sus!

808 Since I Found My Saviour

E. E. HEWITT   JOHN R. SWENEY

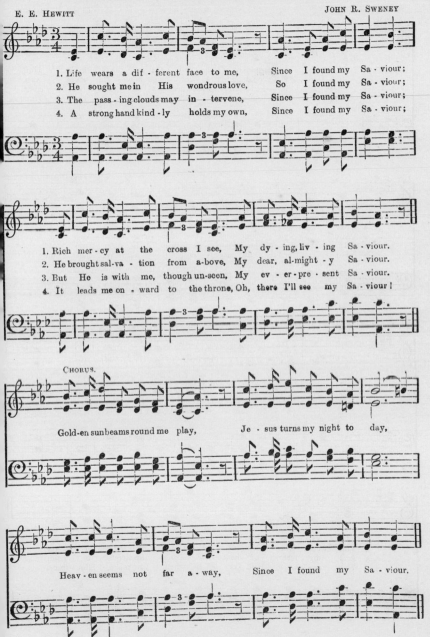

1. Life wears a dif-ferent face to me, Since I found my Sa-viour;
2. He sought me in His wondrous love, So I found my Sa-viour;
3. The pass-ing clouds may in-tervene, Since I found my Sa-viour;
4. A strong hand kind-ly holds my own, Since I found my Sa-viour;

1. Rich mer-cy at the cross I see, My dy-ing, liv-ing Sa-viour.
2. He brought sal-va-tion from a-bove, My dear, al-might-y Sa-viour.
3. But He is with me, though un-seen, My ev-er-pre-sent Sa-viour.
4. It leads me on-ward to the throne, Oh, there I'll see my Sa-viour!

CHORUS.

Gold-en sunbeams round me play, Je-sus turns my night to day,

Heav-en seems not far a-way, Since I found my Sa-viour.

809 Could I Tell It

INA DULEY OGDON

PETER P. BILLHORN

1 If I could on - ly tell Him as I know Him,
2 If I could on - ly tell you how He loves you,
3 If I could tell how sweet will be His wel - come
4 But I can nev - er tell Him as I know Him:

1 My Re - deem - er who has bright - en'd all my way;
2 And if we could thro' the lone - ly gar - den go,
3 In that home whose match - less beau - ty ne'er was told;
4 Hu - man tongue can nev - er tell all love di - vine;

1 If I could tell how pre - cious is His pre - sence,
2 If I could tell His dy - ing pain and par - don,
3 Thy Fa - ther's man - sions stand by liv - ing wa - ters,
4 I on - ly can en - treat you to ac - cept Him;

1 I am sure that you would make Him yours to - day.
2 You would wor - ship at His wound - ed feet, I know.
3 And the trees of heal - ing shade the streets of gold.
4 You can know Him on - ly when you make Him thine.

Could I Tell It — *Continued*

REFRAIN

Could I tell . . . . it, Could I tell . . . . it,
Could I tell it, yes, I would, Could I tell it as I should,

How the sun - shine of His pre - sence lights my way;

I would tell . . . . it, I would tell . . . . it,
I would tell you, yes, I would, I would tell you if I could,

And I'm sure that you would make Him yours to - day.

810 The Joy-Bells Ringing

ELIZA E. HEWITT   JOY-BELLS RINGING 8.7.8.7. D   JOHN R. SWENEY

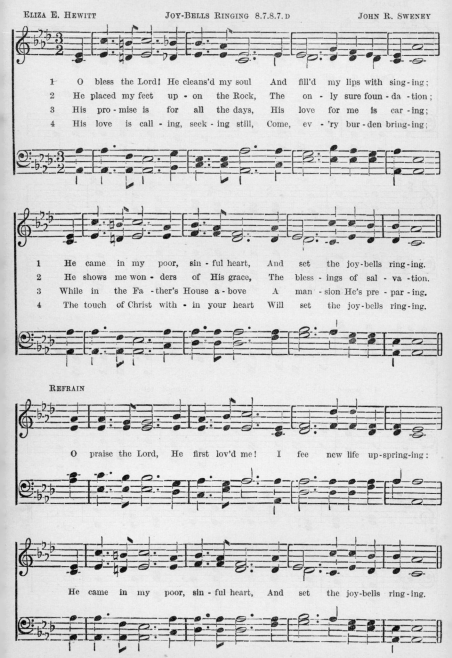

1   O bless the Lord! He cleans'd my soul   And fill'd my lips with sing-ing;
2   He placed my feet up-on the Rock,   The on-ly sure foun-da-tion;
3   His pro-mise is for all the days,   His love for me is car-ing;
4   His love is call-ing, seek-ing still,   Come, ev-'ry bur-den bring-ing;

1   He came in my poor, sin-ful heart,   And set the joy-bells ring-ing.
2   He shows me won-ders of His grace,   The bless-ings of sal-va-tion.
3   While in the Fa-ther's House a-bove   A man-sion He's pre-par-ing.
4   The touch of Christ with-in your heart   Will set the joy-bells ring-ing.

REFRAIN

O praise the Lord, He first lov'd me! I fee new life up-spring-ing:

He came in my poor, sin-ful heart, And set the joy-bells ring-ing.

811 God's Promise is True

Leila N. Morris   Leila N. Morris

1 For God so lov'd this sin-ful world His Son He free-ly gave,
2 I was a way-ward wan-d'ring child, A slave to sin and fear,
3 The who-so-ev-er of the Lord I trust-ed was for me;
4 E-ter-nal life be-gun be-low Now fills my heart and soul:

1 That who-so-ev-er would be-lieve E-ter-nal life should have.
2 Un-til this bless-ed prom-ise fell, Like mu-sic on my ear.
3 I took Him at His gra-cious word, From sin to set me free.
4 I'll sing His praise for ev-er-more, Who has re-deem'd my soul.

REFRAIN

'Tis true, O yes! 'tis true, . . . God's won-der-ful
'Tis true. O yes! the prom-ise is true, God's won-der-ful

prom-ise is true; . . . For I've trust-ed, and test-ed, and
                        'tis true;

tried it, And I know God's prom-ise is true.
                                            'tis true.

812 When I Survey

ISAAC WATTS

ALEXANDER LEE

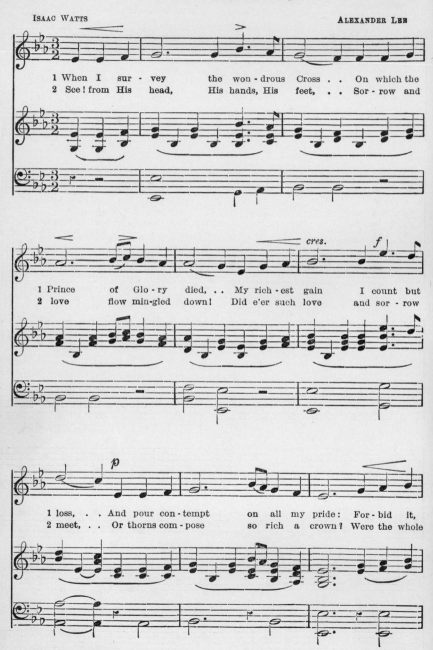

1 When I sur - vey the won - drous Cross . . On which the
2 See! from His head, His hands, His feet, . . Sor - row and

1 Prince of Glo - ry died, . . My rich - est gain I count but
2 love flow min - gled down! Did e'er such love and sor - row

cres. f

1 loss, . . And pour con - tempt on all my pride: For - bid it,
2 meet, . . Or thorns com - pose so rich a crown? Were the whole

When I Survey—*Continued*

1 Lord. that I should boast, Save in the death of Christ my
2 realm of na-ture mine, That were an off - 'ring far too

1 God; All the vain things that charm me
2 small; Love so a - maz - - - ing, so di -

1 most . . I sa - cri - fice them to His blood.
2 vine, . . De - mands my soul, my life, my all.

For the ORDINARY TUNE see No. 573

34

813 Doing His Will

LEILA N. MORRIS

LEILA N. MORRIS

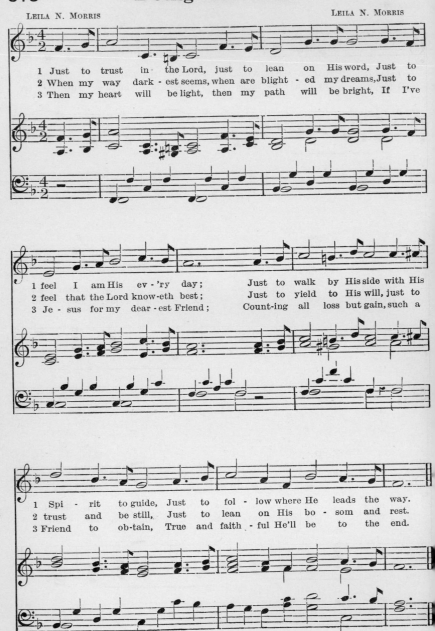

1 Just to trust in the Lord, just to lean on His word, Just to
2 When my way dark-est seems, when are blight-ed my dreams, Just to
3 Then my heart will be light, then my path will be bright, If I've

1 feel I am His ev-'ry day; Just to walk by His side with His
2 feel that the Lord know-eth best; Just to yield to His will, just to
3 Je-sus for my dear-est Friend; Count-ing all loss but gain, such a

1 Spi - rit to guide, Just to fol - low where He leads the way.
2 trust and be still, Just to lean on His bo - som and rest.
3 Friend to ob-tain, True and faith - ful He'll be to the end.

Doing His Will—*Continued*

Just to say what He wants me to say,

Just to say what He wants, what He wants me to say,

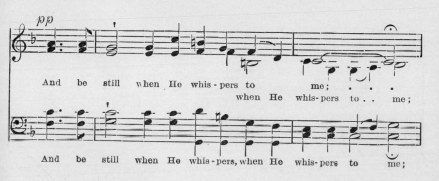

And be still when He whis-pers to me;

when He whis-pers to . . me;

And be still when He whis-pers, when He whis-pers to me;

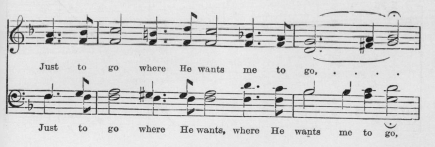

Just to go where He wants me to go, ...

Just to go where He wants, where He wants me to go,

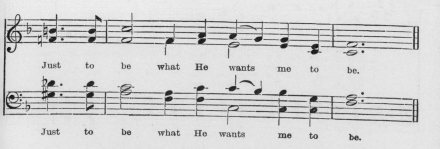

Just to be what He wants me to be.

Just to be what He wants me to be.

814 He Loves Even Me

E. E. HEWITT

WM. J. KIRKPATRICK

1. On the cross my Sa-viour bought me, In the wil-der-ness He sought me,
2. Soft as ev-'ning dew-drops fall-ing, Is His voice so sweet-ly call-ing,
3. Since that hap-py day He found me, Ev-er-last-ing arms sur-round me;
4. All my needs to Him I'm bring-ing, To His keep-ing hand I'm cling-ing,
5. Tho' the ills of life may grieve me, Yet I know He'll nev-er leave me,

1. To His bless-ed fold He brought me, For He loves e-ven me,
2. More and more my soul en-thral-ling, For He loves e-ven me,
3. With His mer-cies He hath crowned me, For He loves e-ven me,
4. And my heart for joy is sing-ing, For He loves e-ven me,
5. To His glo-ry He'll re-ceive me, For He loves e-ven me,

1. For He loves e-ven me, He loves e-ven me;
2. For He loves e-ven me, He loves e-ven me;
3. For He loves e-ven me, He loves e-ven me;
4. For He loves e-ven me, He loves e-ven me;
5. For He loves e-ven me, He loves e-ven me;

1. To His bless-ed fold He brought me, Je-sus loves e-ven me.
2. More and more my soul en-thral-ling, Je-sus loves e-ven me.
3. With His mer-cies He has crowned me, Je-sus loves e-ven me.
4. And my heart with joy is sing-ing, Je-sus loves e-ven me.
5. To His glo-ry He'll re-ceive me, Je-sus loves e-ven me.

815 I Know He's Mine

JOHNSON OATMAN

B. FRANK BUTTS

1 There's One a-bove all earth-ly friends Whose love all earth-ly love trans-cends,
2 He's mine be-cause He died for me, He sav'd my soul, He set me free;
3 He's mine be-cause He's in my heart, And nev-er, nev-er will we part;
4 Some day up-on the streets of gold Mine eyes His glo-ry shall be-hold,

1 It is my Lord and Christ di-vine, My Lord, be-cause I know He's mine.
2 With joy I wor-ship at His shrine, And cry, 'Praise God, I know He's mine.'
3 Just as the branch is to the vine I'm join'd to Christ; I know He's mine.
4 Then, while His arms a-round me twine, I'll cry for joy, 'I know He's mine.'

REFRAIN

I know He's mine, ... this Friend so dear, ... He lives with
  I know He's mine,   this Friend so dear,

me, ... He's ev-er near; . . . . . Ten thou-sand
  He lives with me,   He's ev-er near;

charms . . a-round Him shine, . . . And, best of all, I know He's mine.
Ten thou-sand charms   a-round Him shine,

816 Poor as the Poorest

Frank H. Mashaw

J. Lincoln Hall

1 I was poor as the poor-est out-cast from the fold, I sank by the way-side with
2 I was poor as the poor-est, I shrank from the throng, I hid in the dark-ness that
3 I was poor as the poor-est, I wan-der'd a-lone, No dwell-ing had I, and my
4 I was poor as the poor-est, no rich-es had I, But Je-sus, my Saviour, came
5 I was poor as the poor-est till Je-sus stoop'd low, And wash'd me and cleans'd me as

1 hun-ger and cold; But He bade me look up, all His rich-es be-hold;
2 dwelt with me long; But He came like the morn-ing with sun-light and song,
3 pil-low a stone; But I heard some-one whis-per, 'I'll make thee My own;'
4 down from the sky, And He went to the Cross there to suf-fer and die,
5 white as the snow, I have bath'd in the blood, I am un-der the flow,

D.S.—And a man-sion a-bove that will nev-er grow old,

FINE REFRAIN

1 O the wealth of the world is Je-sus!
2 Now the light of my life is Je-sus.
3 Now the peace of my heart is Je-sus.
4 And my soul was re-deem'd by Je-sus.
5 O the pow-er to save is Je-sus!

I was poor as the poor-est out-

For the wealth of the world is Je-sus.

D.S.

cast from the fold, But He gave me great trea-sures of sil-ver and gold,

817

Grace, Enough for Me!

E. O. E.

E. O. EXCELL

1. In look - ing through my tears one day I saw Mount Cal - va - ry;
2. While standing there my trembling heart, Once full of a - go - ny,
3. When I be - held my ev - 'ry sin Nailed to the cru - el tree,
4. When I am safe with - in the veil, My por - tion there will be

cres.

1. Beneath the cross there flowed a stream Of grace, enough for me.
2. Could scarce believe the sight I saw Of grace, enough for me. (enough for me.)
3. I felt a flood go thro' my soul Of grace, enough for me.
4. To sing thro' all the years to come Of grace, enough for me.

CHORUS.

Grace is flowing from Cal - va - ry, Grace as fathomless as the sea,
Grace is flowing from Cal - va - ry, for me, Grace as fathomless as the rolling sea,

Rit.......

Grace for time and e - ter - ni - ty, Grace, enough for me!
Grace for time and e - ter - ni - ty, A - bun - dant grace I see, enough for me!

By permission of the CHARLES M. ALEXANDER COPYRIGHTS TRUST

818 Serving Thee Best

FLORA KIRKLAND   CHAS. H. GABRIEL

1 Where shall I go, Lord, where shall I go? Wis-dom to guide me Thou wilt be-stow;
2 What shall I say, Lord, what shall I say? Thou art my Teach-er, teach me to-day;
3 What shall I read, Lord, what shall I read? Here Thy pro-tec-tion ev-er I need;
4 Pur-chas'd by Thee, Lord, now I am Thine, Time, thought, and effort nev-er-more mine;

1 Help me to go, Lord, where Thou dost lead,   Trust-ing Thy pro-mise, Grace for all need.
2 On-ly and ev-er help me to be   Speak-ing for Thee, Lord, speak-ing for Thee.
3 Led by Thy Spi-rit sent from a-bove,   E'en thro' temp-ta-tion safe-ly I'll move.
4 Thou hast re-deem'd me, help me to be   Shin-ing for Thee, Lord, on-ly for Thee.

REFRAIN

What shall it be, ... Lord, what shall it be?
What shall it be,

How can I serve Thee, serve Thee best? Speak un-to
How can I serve Thee, serve Thee best?

me, Lord, speak un-to me, Help me to shrink from no test.

819 Bearing the Cross

Mary E. Maxwell

Ada Rose

1. The way of the Cross means sac-ri-fice, As to God you yield your all,
2. As the voice of song and prayer we raise, How easy to say, "We give all!"
3. Do you fal-ter then, or, true to death, Just die on the Cross in the way,
4. 'Tis the plan of life—for you die to live—One with Je-sus cru-ci-fied;

1. To be laid on the al-tar, the place of death, Where fire will sure-ly fall.
2. Till some rougher Cross lies just be-fore, And stern-er is du-ty's call.
3. Till tho ful-ness of life from the Liv-ing One Is filling you day by day?
4. With the life a-lone to be lived thro' you, Of the risen, the glo-ri-fied?

CHORUS

'Tis the way of the Cross, are you will-ing for this? What does bearing the Cross mean to you? You who've given yourself, your all to God! To God are you whol-ly true?

820   To Me, Dear Saviour

H. H. BOOTH   H. H. BOOTH

1. To me, dear Saviour, yes, to me, Speak out Thy ut-most will,
2. To me, dear Saviour, yes, to me, Thy gra-cious par-don shew,
3. To me, dear Saviour, yes, to me, The flood-gates o-pen wide,
4. To me, dear Saviour, yes, to me, To me, the least of all,
5. To me, dear Saviour, yes, to me, Thy sav-ing power be given,

1. What Thy great love doth bid me do, I sure-ly can ful-fil,
2. That not one sin I've ev-er sinned May un-for-giv-en go,
3. That e-ven I may stoop and wash With-in the crim-son tide,
4. With all my consciousness of guilt, Thou hast for me a call,
5. Then shall I know why I have lived, And what on earth is heaven,

1. What Thy great love doth bid me do, I sure-ly can ful-fil,
2. That not one sin I've ev-er sinned May un-for-giv-en go,
3. That ev-en I may stoop and wash With-in the crim-son tide,
4. With all my consciousness of guilt, Thou hast for me a call,
5. Then shall I know why I have lived, And what on earth is heaven,

1. What Thy great love doth bid me do, I sure-ly can ful-fil.
2. That not one sin I've ev-er sinned May un-for-giv-en go.
3. That e-ven I may stoop and wash With-in the crim-son tide.
4. With all my consciousness of guilt, Thou hast for me a call.
5. Then shall I know why I have lived, And what on earth is heaven.

To Me, Dear Saviour—*Continued*

CHORUS.

There is not in my heart left one trea-sure, dear Lord, That I would not yield glad - ly to Thee, . . On - ly let, in Thy mer - cy, Thy pleadings be heard, They shall glad - ly be answered by me. . . .

821 He Never will Forsake Me

1. No, no, no, He nev-er will for-sake me, No, no, no, no e-vil can o'er-take me; His
2. No, no, no, He nev-er will de-ceive me, No, no, no, His words shall never grieve me; I
3. No, no, no, He nev-er will de-sert me, No, no, no, no grief can ev-er hurt me; For
4. No, no, no, He nev-er will re-ject me, No, no, no, His blood will e'er protect me; And

1. love will ev - er last, Till all of earth is past, Oh, no, He nev-er will for-sake me.
2. know His love is true, And what He says He'll do, Oh, no, He nev-er will de-ceive me.
3. on His throbbing breast I can most sweetly rest, Oh, no, He nev-er will de-sert me.
4. when be-fore His throne, I shall not stand a-lone, No, no, He nev-er will re-ject me.

822 The Sweetest Old Story

IRVIN H. MACK, *Arr.* ADAM GEIBEL

DUET

1 Tell me a-bout the Mas-ter, I am wea-ry and worn to-night, .. The
2 Tell me a-bout the Mas-ter, Of the wrongs He for us for-gave; .. Of
3 Yet what I know of sor-row And temp-ta-tions that oft be-fall, .. The

1 day lies be-hind me in sha-dow, And on-ly the ev'n-ing is light: ..
2 love and of ten-der com-pass-ion, Of love, that was might-y to save: ..
3 in-fi-nite Mas-ter had suf-fer'd, And know-eth and pit-i-eth all: ..

QUARTET

1 Light with a ra-di-ant glo-ry That lin-gers a-bout the West, My poor
2 Sad is my heart and a-wea-ry Of woes and the trials of life, Of the
3 Tell me the sweet-est old sto-ry, That falls on each wound like balm, And my

ritard

1 heart is a-wea-ry, a-wea-ry, And longs like a child for rest. ..
2 wrongs that are stalk-ing in noon-day, Of false-hood, and sin, and strife. ..
3 heart that was bruis-ed and bro-ken Shall grow well, and strong, and calm. ..

823 ## Jesus will Keep

JOHNSON OATMAN   W. G.

1. If waves of af - flic - tion should o - ver thee roll, Tho' tem-pests a -
2. Whene'er thou art wea - ry, and long seems the road, If lad - en with
3. If thou hast been pray-ing for more of His grace, Hast pray'd to know
4. Thy dear, lov - ing Saviour has gone to pre - pare A mansion in

round thee may sweep. No storms on life's o - cean can in - jure thy soul,
care thou art press'd, Thy Sa - viour has promised to car - ry thy load,
more of His will, Hast pray'd to be held in His lov - ing em - brace,
glo - ry for thee, He's promised to take thee to live with Him there,

CHORUS,

The Sa - viour has pro - mised to keep.
Has pro - mised to give thee His rest.
He's pro - mised such pray'rs to ful - fil.
If Thou on - ly faith - ful wilt be.

Hold thy faith stea - dy,

be not a - fraid, Je - sus will keep ev - 'ry pro - mise He's made,

824 The Raven He Feedeth

L. E. JONES

L. E. JONES

1 In ten - der com - pas - sion and won - der - ful love The
2 His arm is a - bun - dant - ly a - ble to save, His
3 No need have I ev - er to trou - ble my breast, Or

1 Fa - ther looks down from on high; He know - eth the ra - ven hath
2 eye is a guide to my feet; Since love sought and found me I
3 fear what the mor - row may bring; The heart of the Fa - ther is

1 need of its food, And hear - eth in mer - cy its cry.
2 con - stant - ly dwell With Him in com - pan - ion - ship sweet.
3 plan - ning my way, And I am the child of a King.

The Raven He Feedeth—*Continued*

REFRAIN

The ra - ven He feed - eth, then why should I fear?

To the heart of the Fa - ther His chil - dren are dear;

So, if the way dark - ens or storms ga - ther o'er,

I'll sim - ply look up - ward and trust Him the more.

825 Remembered No More

FRANK M. DAVIS

FRANK M. DAVIS

1 Tho' your sins may be red and like scar-let, Out-
2 Hear the voice that in love now en-treats you To
3 At the door of your heart Christ is knock-ing, He

1 num-b'ring the sands on the shore, Yet thro' Christ and His
2 en-ter the wide o-pen door, That will lead to the
3 oft-en has knock'd there be-fore, Let Him in, He'll for-

1 in-fi-nite mer-cy They're cleans'd and re-mem-ber'd no more.
2 king-dom of hea-ven Where sins are re-mem-ber'd no more.
3 give your trans-gres-sions, And they'll be re-mem-ber'd no more.

REFRAIN ritard a tempo

1-3 Re-mem-ber'd no more, Re-mem-ber'd no more, Yet thro' Christ and His

in-fi-nite mer-cy Your sins are re-mem-ber'd no more.

I Shall See Him

326

Frank E. Graeff

J. Lincoln Hall

1 When my heart is sad with life's cares and toils I will hush my trou-bled
2 When the path is rough and the way is hard, And no rest-ing for my
3 When the day grows dark and the clouds o'er-hang, And they close out all the
4 Then my heart be brave and my soul re-joice, For His pro-mise stand-eth

1 spi-rit's an-xious cry; For the day is com-ing fast when my
2 wea-ry feet is nigh; I will brave-ly press a-long sing-ing
3 sun-shine from the sky; Tho' in dark-ness I a-bide He is
4 sure—on it re-ly; And for all the care and pain there shall

1 cares shall all be past, I shall see Him, I shall see Him by and by.
2 still my hope-ful song, I shall see Him, I shall see Him by and by.
3 still my faith-ful Guide, I shall see Him, I shall see Him by and by.
4 be e-ter-nal gain When I see Him, When I see Him by and by.

REFRAIN

I shall see Him, My Re-deem-er, O my heart, be brave, be strong!

I shall see Him,

I shall see Him, and I'll praise Him With an ev-er-last-ing song.

827 Safe in the Hollow

Leila N. Morris

Leila N. Morris

1 Blest rev-e-la-tion, won-drous sal-va-tion, God in love doth for the lost
2 Noth-ing can harm me, naught can a-larm me, Fierce-ly tho' the tem-pest rage
3 Come all ye bur-den'd and hea-vy la-den! With-out doubt-ing all your cares

1 earth pro-vide; . Sins like a moun-tain lost in the foun-tain, Cal-v'ry's stream
2 sea and land; . Wak-ing or sleep-ing safe in His keep-ing, Kept with-in
3 on Him roll; . Gra-cious for-ev-er, strong to de-liv-er, Ye shall sure

Refrain

1 ev-er flows, a cleans-ing tide. } Safe in the hol-low of His hand, . .
2 hol-low of His migh-ty hand. } of His hand,
3 find sweet rest un-to your soul. } Safe in the hol-low of His hand,

Safe in the hol-low of His hand, . . . To His pro-mise cling-in

Safe in the hol-low of His hand, To His pro-mise cling-in

p slower

ev-er-more I'm sing-ing; I am safe with-in the hol-low of God's hand.

The Reaping

328

GEORGE F. HOPKINS

W. A. POST

1 Af - ter the sow-ing of   sin is all done,   Af - ter the glo - ry of
2 Af - ter the pleasures of sin are all past, Af - ter the wealth of the
3 Come to the Sa-viour of sin-ners, come home ! Why will you long - er so
4 Cease from thy waywardness, Je - sus in - vites, List to the Bride who with

1 earth has been won,   Af - ter the sands of thy life have all run, O
2 world is a - mass'd, When the death-an - gel you face at the last, O
3 aim - less - ly roam ? While He is plead-ing, O wan-der - er, come ! The
4 plead-ing u - nites, While the blest Spi - rit to pray'r now in - cites, The

REFRAIN

1, 2 what shall thy reap - ing be !   Sow - ing, sow - ing, Sow - ing in
3, 4 Mas - ter is waiting for thee. Come home, come home, Like as a

rit.

1, 2 Sa - tan's might ; Reap - ing, reap - ing, Reap-ing e - ter - nal night.
3, 4 wea - ry dove, Come home, come home, Un - to thy Fa - ther's love.

829 O Tell Me More!

ELIZA E. HEWITT

PETER P. BILHORN

1 O tell me more of Christ, my Sa - viour
2 O tell me more of love's sweet sto - ry!
3 O tell me more! How waves of sor - row
4 O tell me more! And I re - peat - ing

1 On this glad theme dwell o'er and o'er;
2 If you would cheer and com - fort me;
3 Shall hear His voice say, 'Peace, be still;'
4 The hap - py news shall spread the joy;

1 His bound - less grace, His sav - ing fa - vour,
2 How Je - sus wept, the King of Glo - ry,
3 How af - ter night bright dawns the mor - row,
4 Come, bless - ed Lord, Thy work com - plet - ing,

O Tell Me More!—*Continued*

1 His pre - cious name,   O tell me more!
2 Those ten - der tears   of sym - pa - thy.
3 To those who trust   His bless - ed will.
4 Till songs of praise   our lips em - ploy.

REFRAIN

O tell me more! So much I need His pow'r to keep,

His hand to lead; O tell me more of Him I

love! Un - til I see His face a - bove. . . .
face a-bove.

830   The Burden Bearer

M. R. Boyd and F. P. Wood

Marianne R. Boyd, *Arr.* P. J. Mansfield

1 Is there a heart that is will-ing to lay
2 Is there a heart that is lone-ly to-day
3 Is there a heart that has fail'd to o'er-come
4 Is there a heart that is long-ing to bring

1 Bur-dens on Je-sus' breast? He is so lov-ing and
2 Need-ing a faith-ful Friend? Je-sus will al-ways keep
3 Sin with its might-y pow'r? Je-sus is strong-er than
4 Bless-ing to some lost soul? Je-sus is will-ing the

1 gen-tle and true, Come un-to Him and rest.
2 close by your side, Lov-ing you to the end.
3 Sa-tan and sin, Trust Him this ve-ry hour,
4 weak-est to use, Let Him Thy life con-trol.

rall.

The Burden Bearer—*Continued*

Lord, it is I who need Thy love! . . Need Thy strength and

pow'r; . . O keep me, use me, and hold . me

fast! Each mo-ment, . each day, . . each hour.

831 Enough of Thee

W. SPENCER WALTON

SPENCER 8.6.8.8.6.6.

L. S. CHAFER

1 I can-not breathe e-nough of Thee, O gen-tle breeze of love! More fra-grant than the myr-tle tree, The Rose of Shar-on is to me The balm of heav'n a-bove, The balm of heav'n a-bove.

2 I can-not gaze e-nough on Thee, Thou Fair-est of the fair! My heart is fill'd with ec-sta-sy, As in Thy face of ra-dian-cy I see such beau-ty there, I see such beau-ty there.

3 I can-not work e-nough for Thee, My Sa-viour, Mas-ter, Friend; I do not wish to go out free, But ev-er, al-ways, will-ing-ly, To serve Thee to the end, To serve Thee to the end.

4 I can-not sing e-nough of Thee, The sweet-est name on earth; A note so full of mel-o-dy Comes from my heart so joy-ous-ly, And fills my soul with mirth, And fills my soul with mirth.

5 I can-not speak e-nough of Thee, I have so much to tell; Thy heart it beats so ten-der-ly, As Thou dost draw me close to Thee, And whis-per: 'All is well,' And whis-per: 'All is well.'

By permission of the SOUTH AFRICA GENERAL MISSION

The tune VESPER is on the following page

331

Enough of Thee

W. SPENCER WALTON   VESPER No. 3, 8.6.8.8.6.   HENRY BAKER

1 I can - not breathe e - nough of Thee, O
2 I can - not gaze e - nough on Thee, Thou
3 I can - not work e - nough for Thee, My
4 I can - not sing e - nough of Thee, The
5 I can - not speak e - nough of Thee, I

1 gen - tle breeze of love! More fra - grant
2 Fair - est of the fair! My heart is
3 Sa - viour, Mas - ter, Friend; I do not
4 sweet - est name on earth; Thy heart so
5 have so much to tell; Thy heart it

1 than the myr - tle tree, The Rose of Shar - on
2 fill'd with ec - sta - sy, As in Thy face of
3 wish to go out free, But ev - er, al - ways,
4 full of mel - o - dy Comes from my heart so
5 beats so ten - der - ly As Thou dost draw me

1 is to me The balm of heav'n a - bove.
2 ra - dian - cy I see such beau - ty there.
3 will - ing - ly, To serve Thee to the end.
4 joy - ous - ly, And fills my soul with mirth.
5 close to Thee, And whis - per: 'All is well.'

Music by permission of Miss CONSTANCE MORLEY HORDER

The tune SPENCER is on the preceding page

832 I Shall be Changed

H. L. Brooks

H. L. Brooks

1 Fill'd with my sin to the Sa - viour I came,
2 Chang'd all my grief to a heart full of song,
3 When through the por - tals of glo - ry I've pass'd,

1 This pow - er has chang'd me, all praise to His Name;
2 And now I'm con - fid - ing in Him all day long;
3 I then shall be chang'd to His im - age at last;

1 Grace all suf - fi - cient He gives me each day,
2 Ten - der com - pas - sion and love He has shown,
3 I shall be like Him in beau - ty to shine,

1 Trust - ing I fol - low where He leads the way.
2 Cleans'd me and heal'd me and call'd me His own.
3 Ev - er to live in His pres - ence di - vine.

I Shall Be Changed—*Continued*

REFRAIN

O . . . . what a change . . since He came .
O what a change! . . won - der - ful change since He came in -

to my heart! . . . O . . what a change . .
to my heart! . . O what a change! . . mar - vell-ous change

since He bade . sin de - part! . . . O . . what a
since He bade all sin de - part! . . O what a change! .

change . . Je - sus wrought in my soul! . . .
glo - ri-ous change . . . He wrought in my soul! .

O . . what a change since His blood makes me whole! . . .
O what a change! what a change since His blood makes me whole, makes me whole!

833

All for Jesus

MARY D. JAMES   ALL FOR JESUS 8.7.8.7.D.   ASA HULL

1 All for Je-sus! all for   Je-sus!   All my be-ing's ran-som'd pow'rs
2 Let my hands per-form His   bid-ding,   Let my feet run in His   ways;
3 World-lings prize their gems of   beau-ty,   Cling to gil-ded toys of   dust,
4 O what won-der! how a-maz-ing!   Je-sus, glo-rious King of   kings!

1 All my thoughts and words and do-ings,   All my days and all my   hours.
2 Let my eyes see Je-sus on-ly,   Let my lips speak forth His   praise.
3 Boast of wealth, and fame, and pleas-ure;   On-ly Je-sus will I   trust!
4 Deigns to call me His be-lov-ed,   Lets me rest be-neath His   wings.

REFRAIN

1 All for Je-sus! . all for Je-sus! .   All my days and all my   hours,
2 All for Je-sus! . all for Je-sus! .   Let my lips speak forth His   praise.
3 On-ly Je-sus! . on-ly Je-sus! .   On-ly Je-sus will I   trust!
4 All for Je-sus! . all for Je-sus! .   Rest-ing now be-neath His   wings.

rit.

1 All for Je-sus! . all for Je-sus! .   All my days and all my   hours.
2 All for Je-sus! . all for Je-sus! .   Let my lips speak forth His   praise.
3 On-ly Je-sus! . on-ly Je-sus! .   On-ly Je-sus will I   trust.
4 All for Je-sus! . all for Je-sus! .   Rest-ing now be-neath His   wings.

The tune MORIAH is on the following page

All for Jesus

333

MARY D. JAMES   MORIAH 8.7.8.7.D.   WELSH HYMN MELODY

1 All for Je-sus! all for Je-sus! All my
2 Let my hands per-form His bid-ding, Let my
3 World-lings prize their gems of beau-ty, Cling to
4 O what won-der! how a-maz-ing! Je-sus,

1 be-ing's ran-som'd pow'rs; All my thoughts and words and do-ings,
2 feet run in His ways! Let my eyes see Je-sus on-ly,
3 gil-ded toys of dust, Boast of wealth, and fame, and pleas-ure;
4 glo-rious King of kings! Deigns to call me His be-lov-ed,

REFRAIN

1 All my days and all my hours. All for Je-sus! all
2 Let my lips speak forth His praise. All for Je-sus! all
3 On-ly Je-sus will I trust! On-ly Je-sus! on-
4 Lets me rest be-neath His wings. All for Je-sus! all

1 for Je-sus! All my days and all my hours.
2 for Je-sus! Let my lips speak forth His praise.
3 ly Je-sus! On-ly Je-sus will I trust!
4 for Je-sus! Rest-ing now be-neath His wings.

The tune ALL FOR JESUS is on the preceding page

834 Coming Home To-night

JAMES ROWE

PETER P. BILHORN

1 If you are sad and wea - ry and bur-den'd down with care, And
2 The Sa - viour loves you dear - ly, and longs your soul to win, His
3 He of - fers you for - give - ness, and peace, and joy, and rest, He

1 feel that you have wan -der'd from the right; Tho' all your life seems drear - y,
2 pre-cious love would make your bur - den light; Heed now His ten - der plead - ing,
3 wants to make your path-way fair and bright; His lov - ing arms are o - pen

1 Your load seems hard to bear; Just tell Him you are com-ing home to - night.
2 And turn a - way from sin; Just tell Him you are com-ing home to - night.
3 To fold you to His breast; O tell Him you are com-ing home to - night!

REFRAIN

Just tell Him you are com - ing home to - night, Just tell Him

you are com-ing home to - night; If, wea - ry and dis - tressed, You

Coming Home To-night—*Continued*

long for peace and rest, Just tell Him you are com-ing home to-night.

835

Master, Speak!

Frances R. Havergal   Ottawa 8.7.8.7.7.7   Lowell Mason

1 Mas-ter, speak! Thy ser-vant hear-eth, Wait-ing for Thy gra-cious word,
2 Speak to me by name, O Mas-ter! Let me know it is to me;
3 Mas-ter, speak! tho' least and low-est, Let me not un-heard de-part;
4 Mas-ter, speak! and make me read-y, When Thy voice is tru-ly heard,

1 Long-ing for Thy voice that cheer-eth, Mas-ter, let it now be heard!
2 Speak, that I may fol-low fast-er With a step more firm and free,
3 Mas-ter, speak! for O Thou know-est All the yearn-ing of my heart!
4 With o-bed-ience glad and stead-y, Still to fol-low ev-'ry word;

1 I am list-'ning, Lord, for Thee: What hast Thou to say to me?
2 Where the Shep-herd leads the flock In the sha-dow of the rock.
3 Know-est all its tru-est need; Speak! and make me blest in-deed.
4 I am list-'ning, Lord, for Thee: Mas-ter, speak, O speak to me!

836
Time for Prayer

EDITH H. KINNEY

GEO. O. WEBSTER

1. Should the new dawn, breaking, a bur-den bring, That your soul deems hard to bear,
2. With a lift of heart let the day be-gin, And a mo-ment res-pite spare,
3. When your wea-ry feet fal-ter on the path, Tho' to pause you do not dare,
4. When the late light dies with the set-ting sun, Would you taste a balm for care?

rit.

1. Seek a boon of grace for a lit-tle space; There is al-ways time for pray'r.
2. Ere you press a-long with the toil-ing throng; There is al-ways time for pray'r.
3. Would you find the stress of the noon grow less? There is al-ways time for pray'r.
4. With a lift of heart let the day de-part; There is al-ways time for pray'r.

CHORUS.

There is al-ways time in the morning's prime, And the gold-en noon-tide fair;

rit.

There is al-ways time 'neath the e-ven-chime, There is al-ways time for pray'r.

837   Holy Spirit, Come In!

J. Wilbur Chapman   P. P. Bilhorn

1. My soul cri-eth out for the Spi-rit, I'm hun-g'ring and
2. O Spi-rit of God and of Je-sus, Blest Tr-n-i-ty,
3. My bo-dy make meet for Thy tem-ple, My heart make Thou
4. Oh, ye that are thirst-ing for ful-ness, Make room by for-

1. thirst-ing to know The ful-ness of bless-ing He giv-eth; Now
2. come and pos-sess My bo-dy, my soul, and my spi-rit, And
3. whit-er than snow; My spi-rit make lov-ing and gen-tle— Oh,
4. sak-ing all sin; Sur-ren-der to Him your whole na-ture, By

Chorus.

1. fill me while hum-bly I bow. . .
2. fill me with Thy ho-li-ness. . .
3. fill me while hum-bly I bow. . .
4. faith let the Spi-rit come in. . .

Come in, come in! Ho-ly
Spi-rit, Thy work of great bless-ing be-gin; By faith I lay
hold of Thy pro-mise, And claim com-plete vic-t'ry o'er sin. .

Copyright by Bilhorn Brothers

35

838   Anchored to the Rock

J. W. B.

JOSEPH W. BURGESS.

1. When the waves are roll-ing fast, And I face the threat'ning blast, And a
2. Sa-tan tries by ev-'ry art, And with ma-ny a fier-y dart, To af-
3. I am wait-ing for a day When the storms have passed a-way, And the

1. dark, for-bid-ding cloud my bark en-folds; Tho' the billows round me roll, There's a
2. fright me from the Christ my faith be-holds; But I trust Him more and more, And I've
3. ha-ven of sweet rest my eye be-holds; When my voy-age is com-plete, And I

1. calm with-in my soul, Hal-le-lu-jah! praise the Lord, my an-chor holds.
2. proved Him o'er and o'er, Hal-le-lu-jah! praise the Lord, my an-chor holds.
3. bow at Je-sus' feet, Praise the Lord for ev-er-more, my an-chor holds.

CHORUS.

I can face the tem-pest's shock, For I'm an-chored to the Rock, And His

might-y arm my fee-ble strength up-holds; Tho' the billows round me roll, There's a

Anchored to the Rock—*Continued*

calm with-in my soul, Hal-le-lu-jah! praise the Lord, my an-chor holds.

839 Somebody

JOHN R. CLEMENTS   GOLDEN DEED 8.8.8.8.6.6   W. S. WEEDEN

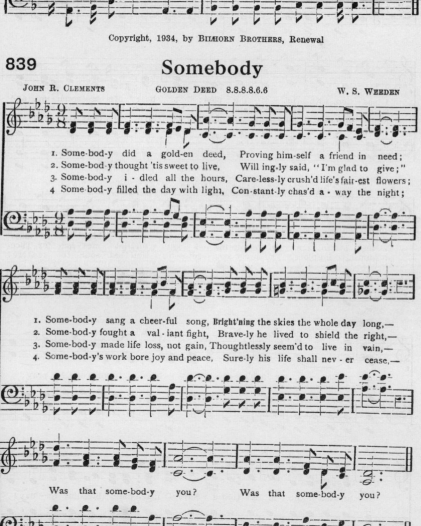

1. Some-bod-y did a gold-en deed, Proving him-self a friend in need;
2. Some-bod-y thought 'tis sweet to live, Will-ing-ly said, "I'm glad to give;"
3. Some-bod-y i-dled all the hours, Care-less-ly crush'd life's fair-est flowers;
4. Some-bod-y filled the day with light, Con-stant-ly chas'd a-way the night;

1. Some-bod-y sang a cheer-ful song, Bright'ning the skies the whole day long,—
2. Some-bod-y fought a val-iant fight, Brave-ly he lived to shield the right,—
3. Some-bod-y made life loss, not gain, Thoughtlessly seem'd to live in vain,—
4. Some-bod-y's work bore joy and peace, Sure-ly his life shall nev-er cease,—

Was that some-bod-y you? Was that some-bod-y you?

Make Me a Blessing

IDA SCOTT TAYLOR

W. H. DOANE

1 O soft - ly the Spi - rit is whisp'-ring to me, With ten - der com -
2 Some heart may be long-ing for on - ly a word, Whose love by the
3 Some soul may be plung'd in the dark-est des-pair, Whose sha-dows would

1 pas - sion, with pit - y - ing plea; I hear His be - seech - ing, and
2 Spi - rit s quick-en'd and stirr'd; Now grant, bless-ed Sa - viour, this
3 melt in the sun-light of pray'r; O give me, dear Sa - viour, I

1 ear-nest - ly pray That Je - sus will make me a bless-ing to - day.
2 ser - vice to me. Of speak-ing a com - fort-ing mes-sage for Thee.
3 hum-bly im-plore, The sweet con - sol - a - tion that soul to re-store!

REFRAIN

Lord, make . . me a bless-ing to-day, A bless-ing to some one, I pray;
Lord, make me a bless-ing, I pray;

In all that I do, in all that I say, O make me a bless-ing to - day!

841 May God Depend on You?

W. C. Martin   Ira B. Wilson

1. In the war-fare that is rag-ing For the truth and for the right,
2. See they come on sa - ble pin-ions, Come in strong Sa-tan-ic might,—
3. From His throne the Fa-ther sees us; An-gels help us to pre-vail;

1. When the con-flict, fierce, is rag-ing With the pow-ers of the night;
2. Pow-ers come and dark do-min-ions From the re-gions of the night,
3. And our lead-er true is Je-sus, And we shall not, can-not fail;

1. God needs work-ers brave and true,   May He, then, de-pend on you?
2. God re-quires the brave and true,   May He, then, de-pend on you?
3. Tri-umph crowns the brave and true,   May the Lord de-pend on you?

work - ers brave and true,

Chorus.

May the Lord . . depend on you? . . Loy-al-ty . . . is but His due, . .
May the Lord de - pend on you? Loy-al-ty is but His due,

Say, O spi - rit, brave and true,   That He may de-pend on you.

spi rit, brave and true,

842 He is Coming Again

P. P. BILHORN

P. P. BILHORN

1. Saved by grace, oh, won-der-ful sto - ry, Je - sus, the Sa - viour, has
2. Saved by grace, and just-i-fied free - ly, Je - sus, the Cru - ci - fied,
3. Saved by grace, and sanc - ti - fied through Him, Christ, the As - cend - ed, now

1. come from on high: Saved by grace, an heir to His glo - ry,
2. rose from the grave; Saved by grace, oh, mar - vel - lous deal - ing,
3. pleads for His own; Saved by grace, I sing hal - le - lu - jah!

CHORUS. *Joyful.*

1. I shall in - her - it it by - and - bye.
2. Life ev - er - last-ing to me He gave.   Saved by grace, oh, won-der-ful
3. I shall be - hold Him up - on His throne.

sto - ry, Sing it o'er and o'er a - gain; . . Saved by grace, oh,

tell of His glo - ry, Je - sus is com - ing, com-ing a - gain.

843 Love so Abundant

G. C. T.

Grant Colfax Tullar

1. Je - sus the Sa - viour, dy - ing on Cal - v'ry, Purchased my
2. Oh, what a Sa - viour, ten - der and lov - ing, Guard-ing my
3. Constant Com - pan - ion, leav - ing me nev - er, Bid - ding me

1. par - don, set - ting me free: Love so a - bun - dant,
2. foot - steps lest I should stray: Love so a - bun - dant,
3. fol - low close by His side: He is my Re - fuge,

1. should I not serve Him, When He so glad - ly suf - fer'd for me?
2. lead - ing me ev - er, Out of the dark - ness in - to the day.
3. safe - ly I shel - ter, Know-ing He loves me, what-e'er be - tide.

Lord, . . . I am Thine, . . . Sa - - viour Di - vine! . .
Lord, I am Thine, Lord, I am Thine, Saviour Divine, Saviour Divine!

Oh, ... what a joy . . . just to know . . . Thou art mine! . . .
Oh, what a joy, oh, what a joy just to know Thou art mine!

844   His Love is all My Song

GEORGE O. WEBSTER

GRANT COLFAX TULLAR

1 I have a might-y Sa - viour, His love is all my song,
2 No friend so kind and ten - der, And none so true as He;
3 I would that you might know Him, As Friend and Sa - viour too!
4 Some day in realms of glo - ry I'll see Him face to face,

1 And since His grace re - deem'd me I praise Him all day long,
2 Un - wor - thy of His good - ness, His grace my song shall be.
3 For what He is to o - thers He'll sure - ly be to you.
4 And sing thro' end - less a - ges Of His re - deem-ing grace.

REFRAIN

He brought me out of dark - ness, He turned my night to day,

rit.

For when I knew His par-d'ning love The sin clouds rolled a - way.

845 My Times are in His Hands

E. E. HEWITT

E. S. LORENZ

1. My times are in my heav-'nly Father's hands, Their changeful scenes I should not
2. My times are in my heav-'nly Father's hands, The joy He sends a bless ing
3. My times are in my heav-'nly Father's hands, Used for His glo - ry may they

1. fear; The rea - son why, He ful - ly un - der-stands, He
2. brings; His light will spar - kle on life's gold - en sands; I'll
3. be; Un - til, in that most beau - ti - ful of lands, I'll

CHORUS.

My times are in His

1. will not cause a need - less tear.
2. hide be - neath His shel - t'ring wings.
3. sing of Him Who died for me.

My times are in my

hands, What's best for me He un - der-stands, I'll

heav'nly Father's hands, What's best for me He ev - er ful - ly un-der-stands, I'll

ev - er trust in His un-changing love, 'Twill lead me to my home a - bove.

846 Jesus Fully Saves

LEILA N. MORRIS   LEILA N. MORRIS

1. I had heard the gos - pel call, of - f'ring par - don free for all, And I
2. Now the load of sin is gone, and by faith I tra - vel on, And I
3. From the mire and from the clay, Je - sus took my feet a - way, And He

1. hearkened to the bless - ed in - vi - ta - tion; Laid my sins at Je - sus'
2. rest no long - er un - der con - dem - na - tion; For the blood has been ap -
3. placed them on the Rock, the sure Foun - da - tion; Whether now I live or

1. feet, tast - ed there re - demp - tion sweet, And He saved me with an
2. plied, and my soul is sat - is - fied With this full, and free, this
3. die, this shall be my con - stant cry, Je - sus saves me with an

CHORUS.

1. ut - ter - most sal - va - tion. } Je - sus saves, full - y saves, Je - sus
2. ut - ter - most sal - va - tion. }
3. ut - ter - most sal - va - tion. } Je - sus saves, full - y saves,

Jesus Fully Saves—*Continued*.

saves me with an ut-ter-most sal-va - tion; Tho' I can-not tell you how,

Je-sus full - y saves me now, With a full, and free, an ut-ter-most sal-va - tion.

347 ## Thy Spirit's Might

A. M. LLOYD   REQUEST 8.8.8.6   A. M. LLOYD

1. Lord, fill us with Thy Spi-rit's might, That we may live as in Thy sight, And
2. Lord, cleanse our hearts from ev-'ry sin, And let Thy love so dwell with-in That
3. As we for oth-ers in-ter-cede, Lord, let Thy power be felt in-deed, And

1. teach us how to pray a-right; We ask in Je-su's name.
2. Thou canst use our lips to win Some souls for Je-su's name.   A - MEN.
3. some from Sa-tan's grasp be freed; We ask in Je-su's name.

4. On all children lay Thy hand,
That each may live as Thou hast planned,
To serve in home or foreign land;
We ask in Jesus's name.

5. The prayers that we have offered, Lord,
In Faith, according to Thy word,
We thank Thee, Father, Thou hast heard,
And praise in Jesu's name.

848 Be Careful what You Sow

DANIEL W. WHITTLE   SOLO OR DUET   CHARLES C. CASE

1. Be care-ful what you sow, For seed will sure-ly grow; The
2. Be care-ful what you sow, For seed will sure-ly grow; Where
3. Be care-ful what you sow, The weed you plant will grow; The
4. Then let us sow good deeds, And not the briars and weeds; Then

1. dew will fall, The floods will come, The clouds grow dark, And then the sun,
2. it may fall You can-not know, In sun or shade, 'Twill sure-ly grow,
3. scat-tered seed From thoughtless hand, Must gath-ered be, By God's com-mand,
4. har-vest time Its joys shall bring, And when we reap Our hearts shall sing,

1. And he who sows good seed to-day Shall reap good seed to-mor-row;
2. And he who sows good seed to-day Shall reap good seed to-mor-row;
3. And he who sows wild oats to-day Must reap the crop to-mor-row;
4. And he who sows good seed to-day Shall reap good seed to-mor-row;

1. And he who sows good seed to-day Shall reap with joy to-mor-row.
2. And he who sows good seed to-day Shall reap with joy to-mor-row.
3. And he who sows wild oats to-day Shall reap with tears to-mor-row.
4. And he who sows good seed to-day Shall reap with joy to-mor-row.

Be Careful what You Sow--*Continued.*

CHORUS.

Be care-ful what you sow, For seed will sure-ly grow, And
what seed you sow, will sure-ly grow,

he who sows good seed to-day Shall reap with joy to-mor-row.

849 Lead Us by Thy Hand

J. M. DUNCAN   DARAK 6.6.6.6   J. M. DUNCAN

1. Je - sus, Thy strength we need, Sow - ing Thy pre - cious seed;
2. May we this hour be led In right-eous paths to tread;
3. As this brief fleet - ing day Pass - es so swift a - way,
4. And when the hour draws nigh When death shall dim our eye,

1. In thought, or word, or deed, Oh, lead us by Thy hand.
2. And, by Thy man - na fed, Oh, lead us by Thy hand.
3. May we from Thee not stray,—Oh, lead us by Thy hand.
4. Take us to Thee on high,—Oh, lead us by Thy hand.

850 ## The Whispers of Jesus

JAMES ROWE

E. S. LORENZ

1. When the storm is rag-ing and the heart is sad, List-en for the whis-
2. When be-neath a bur-den you are bend-ing low, List-en for the whis-
3. When the night seems end-less, when for cour-age pressed, List-en for the whis-

1. pers of Je - sus; Sure - ly you will hear them and they'll make you glad,
2. pers of Je - sus; When your friends forsake you and the sad tears flow,
3. pers of Je - sus; When the soul is wea - ry and you sigh for rest,

CHORUS.

List - en for the whis - pers of Je - sus. List-en . . . .
List-en for the whis-pers!

Listen! . . . List-en for the whis-pers of Je - sus! Sure-ly you will
Listen for the whispers!

hear them and they'll make you glad, List-en for the whispers of Je - sus!

851   In that City

CHARLES J. BUTLER   CHARLES J. BUTLER

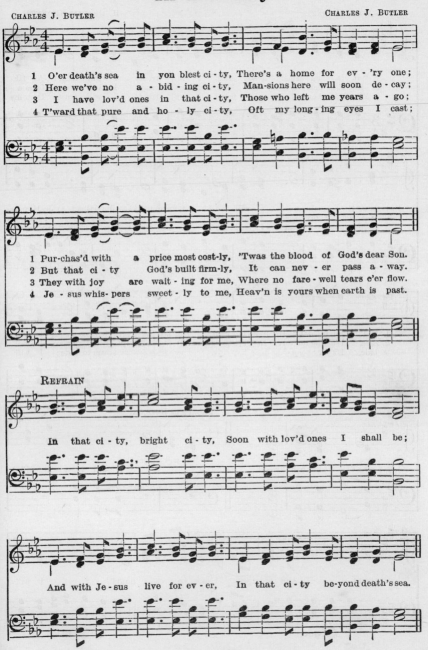

1 O'er death's sea in yon blest ci - ty, There's a home for ev - 'ry one;
2 Here we've no a - bid - ing ci - ty, Man-sions here will soon de - cay;
3 I have lov'd ones in that ci - ty, Those who left me years a - go;
4 T'ward that pure and ho - ly ci - ty, Oft my long - ing eyes I cast;

1 Pur-chas'd with a price most cost-ly, 'Twas the blood of God's dear Son.
2 But that ci - ty God's built firm-ly, It can nev - er pass a - way.
3 They with joy are wait - ing for me, Where no fare - well tears e'er flow.
4 Je - sus whis - pers sweet - ly to me, Heav'n is yours when earth is past.

REFRAIN

In that ci - ty, bright ci - ty, Soon with lov'd ones I shall be;

And with Je - sus live for ev - er, In that ci - ty be-yond death's sea.

852

I Will Trust!

H. GRATTAN GUINNESS   H. GRATTAN GUINNESS

1. "It is fin-ished!" Jesus cries, I will trust! I will trust! As He
2. Je-sus, hear my cry to Thee, I will trust! I will trust! Thou a-
3. Wherefore should I doubt or fear? I will trust! I will trust! Thou, my

1. bows His head and dies! I will trust! I will trust! All my load on Him was
2. lone art all my plea; I will trust! I will trust! In Thy hands I leave my
3. Lord, art ev-er near: I will trust! I will trust! May I close to Thee a-

1. laid; All my debt He free-ly paid; He my peace with God has made; I will
2. case, Trusting ful-ly in Thy grace; All my hope in Thee I place; I will
3. bide, Ev-er keep-ing near Thy side, There from ev-'ry storm to hide: I will

CHORUS or REFRAIN.

I will trust!

1, 2, 3. trust! I will trust! I will trust! I will

trust! And I will not be a-fraid! I will

I will trust! be a-fraid!

I Will Trust!—*Continued.*

trust!   I will trust!   And I will not be a-fraid!

I will trust!   I will trust!

853   I've been Redeemed!

Arr. by A. F. I.

1. I've been re - deemed, all glo - ry to the Lamb, Je - sus has
2. O sin - ner, lis - ten, I once was lost like you, But Je - sus
3. I am so glad I've found the way of life, Free from all
4. I'm go - ing home, all glo - ry to the Lamb, Je - sus will

CHORUS.—I've been re - deemed, yes, I have been re - deemed, Glo - ry to

1. loved me, I'm saved, I know I am; O wondrous love that
2. found me, and saved me thro' and thro'; Now He is waiting for
3. sor - row, from sin, and from strife; I am so glad I'm
4. take me now just as I am; Soon I'll be there with

Je - sus! 'Tis sweet for me to know; I've been re - deemed, yes,

D.C. for CHORUS.

1. caused my Lord to die, Now will I serve Him, then reign with Him on high.
2. you to make a start, Come to Him quickly and choose the better part.
3. in this ho - ly way, O hal - le - ju - jah! I'm hap - py night and day.
4. friends who've gone before, O hap - py meeting! we'll meet to part no more.

I have been re-deemed, O hal - le - lu - jah! my soul is white as snow.

854 Somebody Cares

Irene Durfee

W. Stillman Martin

1. Nev-er a-lone in this earth-ly way, Somebody cares, Somebody cares,
2. When I am sing-ing a hap-py song, Somebody cares, Somebody cares,
3. When I am wea-ry and long for rest, Somebody cares, Somebody cares,

1. I have a Help-er each bu-sy day; Somebody cares, 'tis Je-sus.
2. When I am fight-ing a-gainst the wrong, Somebody cares, 'tis Je-sus.
3. When by the temp-ter I'm sore-ly pressed, Somebody cares, 'tis Je-sus.

1. Somebod-y cares when the clouds hang low, Cares when my heart is o'er-
2. Somebod-y cares when I stand a-lone, Cares when the plea-sures of
3. Somebod-y cares, and what-e'er be-tide, Walks ev-'ry hour by the

1. whelm'd with woe, Cares and is marking my path be-low. Somebody cares, 'tis Je-sus.
2. earth are gone, Cares when my false hopes with wings have flown, Somebody cares, 'tis Je-sus.
3. Christian's side, Love so a-maz-ing will e'er a-bide, Somebody cares, 'tis Je-sus.

Refrain

Some-bod-y cares for me, Some-bod-y cares for me,
Somebody cares, yes, Somebody cares, yes, He cares for me,

Somebody Cares—*Continued.*

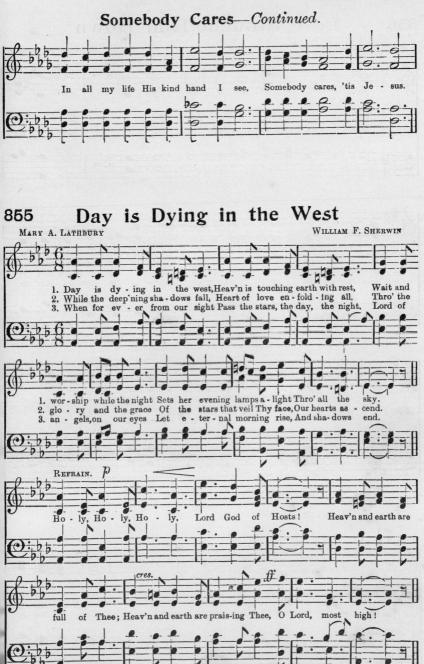

In all my life His kind hand I see, Somebody cares, 'tis Je - sus.

855 Day is Dying in the West

MARY A. LATHBURY WILLIAM F. SHERWIN

1. Day is dy - ing in the west, Heav'n is touching earth with rest, Wait and
2. While the deep'ning sha - dows fall, Heart of love en - fold - ing all, Thro' the
3. When for ev - er from our sight Pass the stars, the day, the night, Lord of

1. wor - ship while the night Sets her evening lamps a - light Thro' all the sky.
2. glo - ry and the grace Of the stars that veil Thy face, Our hearts as - cend.
3. an - gels, on our eyes Let e - ter - nal morning rise, And sha - dows end.

REFRAIN. *p*

Ho - ly, Ho - ly, Ho - ly, Lord God of Hosts! Heav'n and earth are

cres. *ff*

full of Thee; Heav'n and earth are prais-ing Thee, O Lord, most high!

856   Love Brought Him Down

J. WAKEFIELD MacGILL

Arr. P. J. MANSFIELD

1 Came . He to Beth-le-hem's man - ger, . . In - fant,
2 Pass'd . He the fie-ry temp - ta - tion? . . Was . He
3 Went . He to Pi-late and He - rod? . . Bore . He

1 yet glo-ri-ous Lord? . . . Stood . He in Tem-ple and
2 the home-less and lone? . . . Was . He de-spis'd and re-
3 the lash and the nail? . . . Pray'd . He His Fa-ther to

1 ut - ter'd . . Won - drous and mys-ti-cal word? . . .
2 ject - ed? . . Claim'd He dark sor-row His own? . . .
3 par - don? . . Died He with a-gon-y's wail? . . .

1 ut - ter'd . .
2 ject - ed? . .
3 par - don? . .

1 Toil'd . He in work-shop, and low - ly . . Bore . He the
2 Came . He to O-li-vet's gar - den? . . Drank . He the
3 Lay . He in grave of the stran - ger? . . Rose . He in

Love Brought Him Down—*Continued*

1 bur-den of life . . . Calm - ly, and sweet-ly, and
2 dregs of the cup? . . . Say, . was that ho - ly cheek
3 ma - jes - ty grand? . . . Went . He to claim as a

1 pure - ly? . . Mix'd . He in an-ger or strife? .
2 sul - lied! . . Gave . He His pre-cious life up? .
3 vic - tor . . Tro - phies as count-less as sand? .

REFRAIN

Love . bro't Him down from the glo - ry, . . Love . made Him

come from the sky, . . . Love . in His heart for the

sin - ner . . Led . Him to suf - fer and die. . . .

857 God Will Take Care

Eliza E. Hewitt　　　　　MELO 6.4.6.4.6.6.6.4.　　　　Wm. J. Kirkpatrick

1 God will take care of me; Here will I rest,
2 God will take care of me; Hush - ing my fear;
3 God will take care of me; Hold - ing the helm;

1 Trust - ing His prom - ise true, . Safe on His breast;
2 When dan - gers 'round I see, . His voice I hear;
3 Storms that may sweep the sea . Will not o'er - whelm;

1 Change - ful may be my lot, His mer - cy chang - eth not;
2 Then let my soul be brave, High tho' the wind and wave,
3 Soon, ev - 'ry bil - low pass'd, I shall my an - chor cast,

1 No child of His for - got, In Je - sus, blest.
2 Great - er His pow'r to save, Ten - der - ly near.
3 Safe, safe at home at last, In joy's bright realm.

The tune CROYDON is on the following page

857 God Will Take Care

ELIZA E. HEWITT   CROYDON 6.4.6.4.6.6.6.4.   SAMUEL CHING

1 God will take care of me; Here will I rest,
2 God will take care of me; Hush - ing my fear;
3 God will take care of me; Hold - ing the helm;

1 Trust - ing His prom - ise true, Safe on His breast;
2 When dan - gers 'round I see, His voice I hear;
3 Storms that may sweep the sea Will not o'er - whelm;

1 Change - ful may be my lot, His mer - cy chang - eth not;
2 Then let my soul be brave, High tho' the wind and wave,
3 Soon, ev - 'ry bil - low pass'd, I shall my an - chor cast,

1 No child of His for - got, In Je - sus, blest.
2 Great - er His pow'r to save, Ten - der - ly near.
3 Safe, safe at home at last, In joy's bright realm.

The tune MELO is on the preceding page

858 Tell Some One

ADA BLENKHORN DUET IRA B. WILSON

1. There's joy in the home-land, there's plen - ty and peace, A wel - come for
2. The sin - ful and wea - ry find par - don and rest, The lame may be
3. For love like the Mas-ter's, for wis - dom to win, For pa - tience and
4. The part - ing com-mand-ment of Je - sus, your King, Be ear - nest and

* AIR.

1. souls gone a - stray; Glad songs o - ver sin-ners re - turn-ing to God!— Tell
2. healed in the way; Be - liev - ing in Je - sus, each soul may be blest;— Tell
3. ten - der - ness pray; And, weep-ing, go forth to the high-ways of sin;— Tell
4. swift to o - bey; To help the good Shep-herd His "o - ther sheep" bring, Tell

CHORUS.

some one the sto - ry to - day. Tell some one the sto - ry to - day,...
Tell some one the wonder - ful sto - ry to-day,

Tell some one,... tell some one;... Tell some one the
Tell some one from Je - sus, the Sa - viour, a - stray;

sto - ry, 'twill add to His glo - ry; Tell some one the sto - ry to - day.

* Air in Tenor, but can also be sung by Soprano

A Friend so True

859

Harriet Fithian

Ira B. Wilson

1. I have a dear Sav-iour who loves me I know, And whose
2. This won-der-ful Friend is a help-er in-deed; He has
3. He soothes me in sor-row with songs in the night, And in-
4. His love is a fount-ain of bless-ing so pure, Ev-er

1. will I de-light to do; He's pre-sent to cheer me wher-ev-er I go;
2. prom-is'd to lead me through, And clo-ser He comes than a bro-ther in need;
3. spires me with hopes a-new; He fills me with cour-age my bat-tles to fight;
4. flow-ing for me, for you; His pow'r is un-fail-ing, His pro-mise is sure;

Refrain

Was there ev-er a Friend so true? Was there ev-er a Friend so true? Was there ev-er a Friend so true? I oft-en have prov'd Him, I ev-er will love Him; Was there ev-er a Friend so true?

860 Because of His Love

O. C. Scott

Jas. L. Gilbert

1 Be-cause of His love the Sav-iour died, For sin of the world was
2 Be-cause of His love, O bless-ed thought! Were won-der-ful deeds of
3 Be-cause of His love, His blest com-mand, We'll send the glad word to

1 cru-ci-fied; With His own blood our ran-som paid, And for our
2 mer-cy wrought; The wind and wave o-bey'd His will, Hush'd by His
3 ev-'ry land; His Name, a-bove all names we'll sing, And crown Him

REFRAIN

1 souls de-liv-'rance made.
2 won-drous, 'Peace, be still.' } Be-cause of His love, His sac-ri-fice;
3 Sa-viour, Priest, and King.

cres.

Be-cause of His love, O what a price! He suf-fer'd and died,

f   dim.

was cru-ci-fied, Be-cause of His love, Be-cause of His love.

Show Me the Way

861

ALLIE TOLAND CRISS   ALLIE TOLAND CRISS

1 Show me the way, dear Sav-iour! The sha-dows are fall-ing fast, And
2 Show me the way, dear Sav-iour! The night is so wild and dark; I
3 Show me the way, dear Sav-iour! My cour-age is fail-ing fast; My

1 thro' the clouds a-bove me No ray of light is cast;...... The storm is wild-ly
2 can-not stem the cur-rent Un-less Thou guide my bark;...... O fierc-er grows the
3 storm-toss'd bark is sink-ing, But I'll be sav'd at last;...... Come near-er, near-er

1 rag-ing, The thun-ders loud-ly roar, The rest-less waves are dash-ing A-
2 tem-pest, And wild-er rolls the sea, Help! help me, O my Sa-viour, I
3 to me, And speak the word of peace That stills the an-gry wa-ters, And

REFRAIN

1 gainst the wreck-strewn shore.
2 trust a-lone in Thee. } Show me the way, dear Sa-viour, That Thou wouldst have me
3 bids the tem-pest cease.

go; Show me the way, dear Sav-iour, For Thou a-lone dost know.

862 Is it Nothing to You?

John R. Clements   May Whittle Moody

1. Is it noth-ing to you that heav - en's King Came down to this world of woe, That He suffered and bled and rose from the dead, That e - ter - nal life you might know?

2. Is it noth-ing to you that by and by You must trav - el death's dark vale, Where Jor - dan's waves the path - way laves, And all but Christ doth fail?

3. Is it noth-ing to you that some sweet day In the heav - en - ly land so fair You may join the song that the ran - somed throng Are for - ev - er sing - ing there?

REFRAIN.

Is it nothing to you that grace is free, And that God in His love doth call? Is it nothing to you? Is it noth-ing to you? Is it noth-ing, noth-ing to you?

Songs by Night

863

John B. Clements

Ferd. Degen
Arr. by P. P. Bilhorn

1 Are you with some sor-row burd-en'd, On your way no ray of light?
2 Paul and Si - las, pris-on-fast-en'd, Shook the jail with earth-quake might;
3 It is oft in sad-dest mo-ments That our souls take high-est flight;

1 Strain your ear, all hea-ven's watch-ing; God can give you songs by night.
2 Bands were rent and doors were o-pen'd; God had giv - en songs by night.
3 And to strains of sweet-est mu - sic God doth set the songs by night.

REFRAIN

Wea - ry soul,............ cease thy re - pin - ing, Burd-en'd
O wea - ry soul, cease thy re - pin - ing,

one............ God's ways are right, Ev' - ry cloud......... has sil - ver
O burd-en'd one, God's ways are right! Yes ev'-ry cloud

lin - - ing; God can give......... you songs by night........
has sil - ver lin-ing; God can give you songs by night, songs by night.

864 Anchored at Last

LEILA N. MORRIS

LEILA N. MORRIS

1. O so long was my bark toss'd a-bout on life's sea, But I've anchor'd in
2. Safe-ly moor'd to the Rock which no tem-pest can shake, I have anchor'd in
3. In the har-bour of faith there is safe-ty and rest, I have anchor'd in
4. Deeper grow-eth my peace as I'm near-ing the shore, I have anchor'd in

1. Je-sus at last; And I heard a sweet voice gent ly call-ing to me, And I've
2. Je-sus at last; Tho' the billows in fu - ry a-round me may break, I have
3. Je-sus at last; And a deep settled peace now is fill-ing my breast, I have
4. Je-sus at last; And by sim-ply be - liev - ing I'm safe ev - er - more, I have

CHORUS.

anchor'd in Je-sus at last. At last! . . . at last! . . .
I've anchor'd in Je - sus, I've anchor'd at last,

All my doubt-ings are o - ver, my struggling is past, And the load of my

sin at His feet I have cast, I have anchor'd in Je-sus at last. at last.

865 Make Me Understand

KATHERINE A. M. KELLY   K. A. M. KELLY

1 Give me a sight, O Sav - iour! Of Thy won - drous love to me, ..
2 Was it the nails, O Sav - iour! That bound Thee to the tree? .
3 O won - der of all won - ders! That through Thy death for me ..
4 Then melt my heart, O Sav - iour! Bend me, yea, break me down ..

rall.

1 Of the love that bro't Thee down to earth To die on Cal - va - ry. ...
2 Nay, 'twas Thine ev - er - last - ing love, Thy love for me, for me. ...
3 My o - pen sins, my se - cret sins, Can all for - giv - en be. ...
4 Un - til I own Thee Con - quer - or, And Lord and Sov - 'reign crown, ..

REFRAIN

O make me un - der - stand it! Help me to take it in! . What it

meant to Thee, the Ho - ly One, To bear a - way my sin. .

By permission of the NATIONAL YOUNG LIFE CAMPAIGN

866　　In the Upper Garden

C. Austin Miles

C. Austin Miles, *Arr.* P. J. Mansfield

1　Just be-yond the riv-er Jor-dan, . . . Just a-cross its chill-ing
2　Grow-ing in the Up-per Gar-den, . . . Flow'rs the earth too rude-ly
3　There the buds from earth trans-plant-ed, . . . For our com-ing watch and

1　tide, . . . There's a land of life e-ter-nal, . . . Thro' its
2　press'd, . . In that land shall reach per-fec-tion . . . By the
3　wait: . . . In that Up-per Gar-den grow-ing, . . . Just with-

1　vales sweet wa-ters glide: . . . By the crys-tal riv-er flow-ing
2　heav'n-ly Gard-'ner dress'd, . . . Where the flow-ers bloom for-ev-er,
3　in the gold-en gate, . . . Tho' our hearts may break with sor-row,

1　Grows the tree of life so fair, . . Ma-ny lov'd ones wait our
2　Death can find no en-trance there: . . All is life and light e-
3　By the grief so hard to bear, . . We shall meet them some glad

In the Upper Garden—*Continued*

1 com - ing . . . In the Up-per Gar-den there. . . .
2 ter - nal, . . . All is joy be-yond com - pare. . . .
3 morn - ing . . . In the Up-per Gar-den there. . . .

REFRAIN

We . shall meet them some bright morn-ing . . . . .
We shall meet them some bright morn-ing
We . shall . meet them some bright morn - ing, some bright morn-ing,

Rest - ing by the wa-ters fair, . . . They are wait-ing for our
Rest-ing by . . the wa-ters fair; . . . They are wait - ing for our

com - ing, ... In . . the Up-per Gar-den there. . .
com - ing, . . . In the Up-per Gar - den there. . .
com - ing, our com - ing, In the Up-per Gar-den there.

com - ing, In the Up - per Gar - den there.

867 O Touch Him Too!

M. COLQUHOUN   SELAFO L.M.D.   M. COLQUHOUN

1 She came to Je-sus, one of old; Who sent her He has not re-veal'd;
2 She heard, she came, she touch'd the hem Of His loose gar-ment in the way;
3 I came with all my guilt and sin; Knelt in con-tri-tion at His feet;
4 O come to Him, and rest as-sur'd! What-e'er thy sin He'll wel-come thee;

1 This on-ly are we plain-ly told, How she by sim-ple faith was heal'd.
2 Im-med-iate-ly thro' her weak frame She felt the thrill of health that day.
3 The Ho-ly Spi-rit en-ter'd in, And wrought in me a change com-plete.
4 Who-ev-er came to Him was cur'd, And from all doubt and fear set free.

REFRAIN

O touch Him too! O touch Him too! There's vir-tue still in Christ for thee;

His blood can cleanse, His pow'r can save, Tho' crim-son-dyed your sins may be.

The tune JULIAN is on the following page

867   # O Touch Him Too!

M. COLQUHOUN   JULIAN L.M.D.   F. C. MAKER

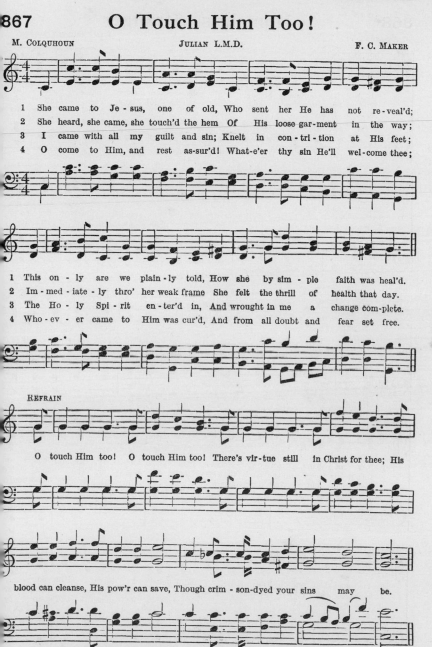

1 She came to Je - sus, one of old, Who sent her He has not re-veal'd;
2 She heard, she came, she touch'd the hem Of His loose gar-ment in the way;
3 I came with all my guilt and sin; Knelt in con - tri - tion at His feet;
4 O come to Him, and rest as-sur'd! What-e'er thy sin He'll wel-come thee;

1 This on - ly are we plain - ly told, How she by sim - ple faith was heal'd.
2 Im - med - iate - ly thro' her weak frame She felt the thrill of health that day.
3 The Ho - ly Spi - rit en - ter'd in, And wrought in me a change com-plete.
4 Who - ev - er came to Him was cur'd, And from all doubt and fear set free.

REFRAIN

O touch Him too! O touch Him too! There's vir-tue still in Christ for thee; His

blood can cleanse, His pow'r can save, Though crim - son-dyed your sins may be.

The tune SELAFO is on the preceding page

868 A Homeless Stranger

ANON.   MAY WHITTLE MOODY

1. A home-less Stranger a-mongst us came To this land of
2. And then from this sad and sor-row-ful land, This land of
3. And I must a-bide where He a-bode, And fol-low His

1. sin and mourn-ing; He walked in a path of sor-row and shame,
2. tears He de-part-ed; But the light of His eyes, and the touch of His hand
3. steps for-ev-er; His peo-ple, my peo-ple; His God, my God,

1. Thro' in-sult, and hate, and scorn-ing: A Man of Sor-rows, of
2. Had left me bro-ken-heart-ed: And I clave to Him as He
3. In the land be-yond the riv-er: His face in glo-ry I'll

1. toils, of tears, An out-cast man and lone-ly, But He looked on
2. turn'd His face From the land that was mine no long-er, The land I'd
3. soon be-hold. And dear ones who've gone be-fore me, With the blood-bough

1. me, and thro' end-less years, Him must I serve, Him on-ly
2. loved in the gold-en days, ere I knew the love that was strong-er
3. throng in that heav'n-ly fold, I'll sing Re-demp-tion's sto-ry

869 ## Shipwrecked, but not Lost

H. L. G.

H. L. Gilmour

1. O ship-wrecked soul, far out on sin's dark wave, With no help
2. O ship-wrecked soul, no wave can drown the voice Of Him who
3. O ship-wrecked soul, He waits with pity-ing eye Be-hold-ing

1. near no life-line thrown to save; No boat to launch, no
2. speaks to make thy soul re-joice; 'Midst tem-pest swirl, make
3. thee; He'll hear thy help-less cry; O ven-ture now, trust

ritard . . . .

1. crew with cour-age brave; Thy on-ly help is Je-sus.
2. Je-sus now thy choice; Thy on-ly help is Je-sus.
3. ful-ly, He is nigh; Thy on-ly help is Je-sus.

CHORUS.

Je-sus has conquer'd the storm-toss'd sea, Walk'd the wild bil-lows of

ritard.

Ga-li-lee; He is the Sa-viour for you, and me: Je-sus on-ly Je-sus.

870 The Hope of the Coming

D. W. WHITTLE

MAY WHITTLE MOODY

1. A lamp in the night, a song in time of sor - row; A great glad hope which
2. A star in the sky, a bea-con bright to guide us; An an-chor sure to
3. A call of command, like trumpet clear-ly sound-ing, To make us bold when
4. A word from the One to all our hearts the dear-est, A part-ing word to

1. faith can ev-er bor-row To gild the pass-ing day with the glo-ry of the mor-row,
2. hold when storms betide us; A ref-uge for the soul, where in qui-et we may hide us;
3. e-vil is sur-round-ing; To stir the sluggish heart, and to keep in good a-bound-ing,
4. make Him aye the near-est; Of all His precious words, the sweetest, brightest, clearest,

CHORUS. *tempo.*

1. Is the hope of the com-ing of the Lord.
2. Is the hope of the com-ing of the Lord.
3. Is the hope of the com-ing of the Lord.
4. Is the hope of the com-ing of the Lord.

Blessed hope, blessed hope, blessed hope,

Blessed hope, blessed hope, blessed hope,

Bless-ed hope of the com-ing of the Lord; How the ach-ing heart it cheers;

The Hope of the Coming—*Continued*

How it glistens thro' our tears, Blessed hope of the com-ing of the Lord.

871   I Remember Calvary

W. C. MARTIN   TRUEST FRIEND L.M.D.   J. M. BLACK

1. Where He may lead me I will go, For I have learn'd to trust Him so,
2. O I delight in His command, Love to be led by His dear hand,
3. Onward I go, nor doubt nor fear, Hap-py with Christ, my Saviour near,

And I re-mem-ber 'twas for me, That He was slain on Cal-va-ry.
His divine will is sweet to me, Hallowed by blood-stained Cal-va-ry.
Trusting some day that I shall see, Je-sus, my Friend of Cal-va-ry,

REFRAIN.

Je-sus shall lead me night and day, Je-sus shall lead me all the way;

He is the tru-est Friend to me, For I re-mem-ber Cal-va-ry.

872 Every Step with Jesus

J. W. MacGill

Anon. Chorus, M. S. Sloane

1. Ev - 'ry *step* with Je - sus Thus we love to go,
2. Ev - 'ry *day* with Je - sus When the morn-ings break,
3. Ev - 'ry *nerve* for Je - sus Strained in might - y toil,
4. Ev - 'ry *man* for Je - sus, What a might - y throng,

1. Down life's sha - dy path - way In - to ev - 'ning's glow.
2. Whis - per - ing life's se - crets E'er the road we take.
3. Just to bring the Mas - ter Heaps of gold - en spoil.
4. Then would swell the cho - rus Of the vic - tor's song!

Chorus.

Ev - 'ry power for Je - sus, Brain and heart and will, Used at high - est

pres - sure Till the pulse be still: Crown of Glo - ry wait - ing,

On the fur - ther shore, Sing with glad re - joic - ing, Praises ev - er - more.

For Jesus' Sake

873

Colin Stern

H. Ernest Nichol

1 Will you come and help us in our work, For Je - sus' sake? *Org.* Will you
2 Will you make the homes of dark-ness bright For Je - sus' sake? Will you
3 Will you curb the quick and an - gry word For Je - sus' sake? Will you
4 Will you turn from ev' - ry ev - il way For Je - sus' sake? Will you

1 fight with en - e - mies that lurk, For Je - sus' sake? *Org.* The pow'rs of e - vil
2 be an ev - er shin - ing light For Je - sus' sake? A - gainst all forms of
3 bear the yoke of our dear Lord For Je - sus' sake? When work is hard and
4 climb up high - er day by day For Je - sus' sake? A - mid the stress of

1 stronger grow, With-in, with - out, we meet the foe; Will you lend a hand to strike a blow, For
2 dead - ly sin, Against all e - vil thoughts within, Will you strike as one who means to win, For
3 du - ty dry, And ea - sy seems the tempt-ing lie, Will you speak the truth, although you die, For
4 earth-ly strife, A - mid a world with e - vil rife, Will you try to live the high - er life, For

REFRAIN *cres.*

Je - sus' sake? For Je - sus' sake, For Je - sus' sake, What will you do for

dim.

Je - sus' sake? Let each one bring some worthy thing For Je - sus' sake.

By permission of H. Ernest Nichol

874   Launch Out

J. B. MACKAY   JNO. R. SWENEY

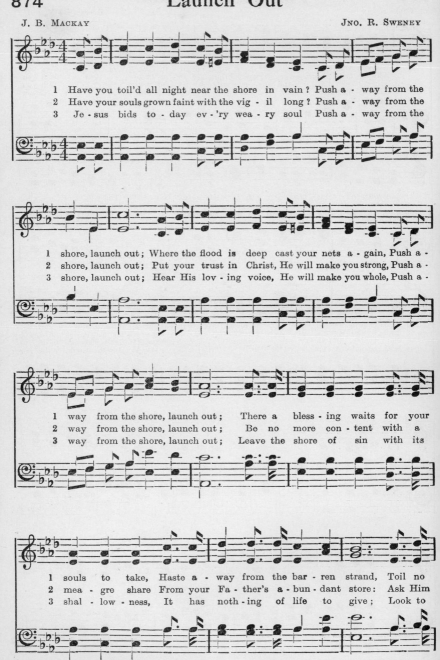

1 Have you toil'd all night near the shore in vain? Push a - way from the
2 Have your souls grown faint with the vig - il long? Push a - way from the
3 Je - sus bids to - day ev - 'ry wea - ry soul Push a - way from the

1 shore, launch out; Where the flood is deep cast your nets a - gain, Push a -
2 shore, launch out; Put your trust in Christ, He will make you strong, Push a -
3 shore, launch out; Hear His lov - ing voice, He will make you whole, Push a -

1 way from the shore, launch out; There a bless - ing waits for your
2 way from the shore, launch out; Be no more con - tent with a
3 way from the shore, launch out; Leave the shore of sin with its

1 souls to take, Haste a - way from the bar - ren strand, Toil no
2 mea - gre share From your Fa - ther's a - bun - dant store: Ask Him
3 shal - low - ness, It has noth - ing of life to give; Look to

Launch Out—*Continued*

1 more in vain where the sur - ges break, Launch out is your Lord's com-mand.
2 large - ly now, He will hear your pray'r, And give till you want no more.
3 Je - sus now, who a - lone can bless, Launch out on His grace and live.

REFRAIN

Launch out, launch out, Push a - way from the
Launch out, launch out,

shore, Launch out, God's grace flows free, like a
Launch out,

might - y sea, And the Mas - ter calls, 'Launch out!'

875 The Seed of the Kingdom

FRED. A. FILLMORE   FRED. A. FILLMORE

1. Are you sow-ing the seed of the king-dom, brother, In the morn-ing
2. Are you sow-ing the seed of the king-dom, brother, In the still and
3. Are you sow-ing the seed of the king-dom, brother, All a-long the

1. bright and fair? Are you sow-ing the seed of the king-dom, brother,
2. sol-emn night? Are you sow-ing the seed of the king-dom, brother,
3. fer-tile way? Would you glean gold-en sheaves in the har-vest, brother,

CHORUS.

1. In the heat of the noonday's glare?
2. For a har-vest pure and white?
3. Come and join the ranks to-day.

} For the har-vest time is com-ing

on (coming on), And the reap-ers' work will soon be done (soon be done); Will your sheaves be

man-y, will you gar-ner an-y For the gath'ring at the har-vest home?

An Alternative Tune is on the following page

875 The Seed of the Kingdom

FRED. A. FILLMORE

E. H. SWINSTEAD

1 Are you sow-ing the seed of the king-dom, *bro-ther, In the morn-ing
2 Are you sow-ing the seed of the king-dom, bro-ther, In the still and
3 Are you sow-ing the seed of the king-dom, bro-ther, All a-long the

1 bright and fair ? Are you sow-ing the seed of the king-dom, *bro-ther,
2 sol-emn night ? Are you sow-ing the seed of the king-dom, bro-ther,
3 fer-tile way ? Would you glean gold-en sheaves in the har-vest, bro-ther ?

REFRAIN

1 In the heat of the noon-day's glare ? }
2 For a har-vest pure and white ? } For the har-vest time is com-ing on,
3 Come and join the ranks to-day.

And the reap-ers' work will soon be done ; Will your sheaves be man-y, Will you

gar-ner an-y For the gath-'ring at the har-vest home ?

*king-dom.
har-vest.

Music by permission of E. H. SWINSTEAD An Alternative Tune precedes this one
* If desired, the word 'brother' may be omitted, and the preceding word sung
as shown at the end of the tune

876

With Heart and Voice

LIZZIE DE ARMOND   SAMUEL W. BEAZLEY

1. Praise the Lord with heart and voice, Joy - ful - ly serv - ing your King, Come and
2. Praise the dear Redeemer's name, Crown Him with beauty and light, Just and
3. Praise the Lord with heart and voice, Ev - er a - dor - ing - ly raise Hal - le

1. wor - ship at His throne, Lov - ing - ly, grate - ful - ly sing; Hap - py ev - 'ry
2. true are all His ways, Won - der - ful, boundless, His might; Glad ho - san - nas
3. lu - jahs sweet and strong, Un - to the "Ancient of Days;" Shout with ac - cla -

1. hour, trust - ing in His pow - er, Un - to the Giv - er of our sal - va - tion
2. swelling, loud His good - ness tell - ing, Fountain of bless - ing our joy e - ter - nal,
3. mation, hail Him all cre - a - tion, Worship Je - ho - vah, O come re - joic - ing,

CHORUS. *Unison.*

1. prais - es bring.
2. day and night. } Praise Him! sing with me - lo - dy, Heart and voice,
3. sound His praise.

Praise Him ev - er - last - ing - ly, Come, re - joice; Hail Him,

With Heart and Voice—*Continued*

Lord, most glo - ri - ous, Might - y One vic - to - ri - ous, Praise His

ho - ly name. . . . . Praise Him, heav'nly com - pa - ny,

An - gels bright, . . Crown Him now and ev - er - more,

Lord . . of light; Praise Him, all cre - a - tion, God of our sal -

va - tion, Boundless in maj - es - ty, King e - ter - nal; Praise His name.

877

Forward!

Mrs. Frank A. Breck

Grant Colfax Tullar

1. Christ, our mighty Cap-tain, leads against the foe; We will nev-er fal-ter
2. Sa-tan's fear-ful on-slaughts cannot make us yield, While we trust in Christ, our
3. Let our glorious ban-ner ev-er be unfurled— From its mighty stronghold
4. Fierce the bat-tle ra-ges, but 'twill not be long, Then triumphant—shall we

1. when He bids us go; Tho' His righteous pur-pose we may nev-er know
2. Buckler and our Shield; Pressing ev-er on— the Spi-rit's sword we wield,
3. e-vil shall be hurled; Christ, our mighty Cap-tain, o-ver-comes the world,
4. join the bless-ed throng, Joy-ful-ly u-nit-ing in the vic-tor's song—

CHORUS.

1. Yet we'll fol-low all the way.
2. And we fol-low all the way.
3. And we fol-low all the way.
4. If we fol-low all the way.

For-ward! for-ward! 'tis the Lord's command,

For-ward! for-ward! to the promised land; For-ward! for-ward!

let the cho-rus ring: We are sure to win with Christ, our King!

878 Lifetime is Working Time

Carrie E. Breck
E. S. Lorenz

1. Life-time is working time, Spend no i-dle days; Je-sus is call-ing thee
2. Life-time is working time, Learn where duty lies; Grasp ev-'ry passing day
3. Life-time is working time, Do thy ho-nest part; Tho' in discouragements

1. On the harvest ways. Working with a will-ing hand, Sing a song of praise;
2. As a precious prize, Glad to help the sor-row-ing, Glad to sym-pa-thize;
3. Bear a cheerful heart. Trusting Je-sus as thy Friend, Ne'er from Him de-part,

CHORUS

Work, ev-er work for Je-sus! Swift-ly the hours of
Work, work, work, work! Work, work, work, work!

la-bour fly, Freight-ed with love let each pass by! There is joy in
Work, work, work, work! Work, work, work, work! Work, work, work, work!

la-bour for the struggling neighbour, Work, ev-er work for Je-sus!

879

Reapers are Needed

C. H. G.

CHAS. H. GABRIEL

1. Standing in the mar - ket pla - ces all the sea - son through, Id - ly say - ing
2. Ev - 'ry sheaf you ga - ther will be - come a jew - el bright In the crown you
3. Morning hours are pass - ing, and the ev'n - ing fol - lows fast; Soon the time of

1. "Lord, is there no work that I can do?" O how ma - ny loi - ter, while the
2. hope to wear in yon - der world of light. Seek the gems im - mor - tal that are
3. reap - ing will for ev - er - more be past, Emp - ty handed to the Master

1. Mas - ter calls a - new—"Reapers! reap - ers! Who will work to-day?
2. precious in His sight! "Reapers! reap - ers! Who will work to-day?
3. will you go at last? "Reapers! reap - ers! Who will work to-day?

CHORUS.

Lift thine eyes and look up - on the fields that stand
Lift thine eyes and look up - on the fields that stand all read - y,

Lift thine eyes to fields that stand all

Ripe and read-y for the will - ing glean - er's hand, Rouse ye, O
Ripe and ready for the will - ing glean - er's hand, O rouse ye,

Read - y for the glean - er's hand, O

Reapers are Needed *Continued*

880

Message of Mercy

T. H.

THORO HARRIS

1. Come to the ark of re - fuge, Come to the place of rest;
2. Come to the heart that loves thee, Come to the soul's true home,
3. Christ is the soul's sure re - fuge: When breaks the world's fierce blast,

1. Safe in this qui - et har - bour, Naught can thy peace mo - lest;
2. Come while the Lord in - vites thee, Come while there yet is room;
3. He will pro - tect His chil - dren Till all is o - ver - past;

1. Come with thy guilt to Je - sus, Wea - ry and sore dis - trest;
2. Tell Him thy ev - 'ry sor - row, Naught from this Friend with - hold;
3. When storms without are rag - ing Rest and be not a - fraid;

rit.

1. List to His plea, "Come un - to Me, And I will give you rest."
2. He'll hear thy prayer, Thy bur - den bear: Trust in His love un - told.
3. Look to the Lord, Hope in His word, Trust, and be un - dis - mayed.

He is calling thee.

CHORUS. *Unison.* (*Alto part may be sung, or played by cornet.*)

O message of mer - cy! Un - bounded, un - known! He died to re -

Message of Mercy—*Continued*

rall. a tempo.

deem thee; O make Him now thine own! By faith in His mer - cy,

By trust in His grace; With saints in His kingdom, He'll give thy soul a place.

881

What Did He Do?

JAMES M. GRAY   DEEMSTER   WILLIAM OWEN

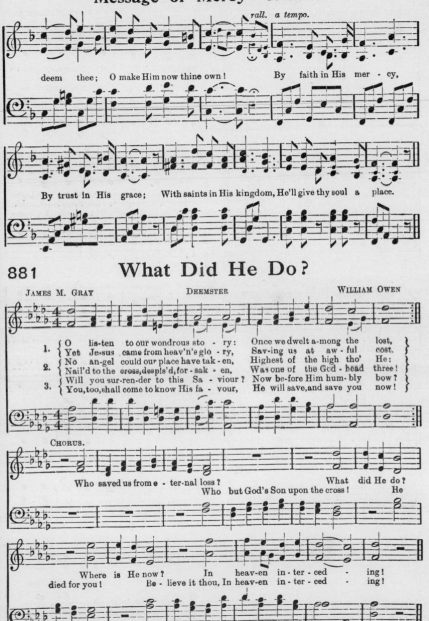

1. { O lis-ten to our wondrous sto - ry: Once we dwelt a-mong the lost, }
   { Yet Je-sus came from heav'n's glo - ry, Sav-ing us at aw - ful cost. }
2. { No an-gel could our place have tak - en, Highest of the high tho' He: }
   { Nail'd to the cross, despis'd, for-sak - en, Was one of the God - head three! }
3. { Will you sur-ren-der to this Sa - viour? Now be-fore Him hum- bly bow? }
   { You, too, shall come to know His fa - vour, He will save, and save you now! }

CHORUS.

Who saved us from e - ter-nal loss?   What did He do?
Who but God's Son upon the cross!   He

Where is He now?   In heav-en in-ter-ced - ing!
died for you!   Be - lieve it thou, In heav-en in-ter-ced - ing!

882 The Way of the Cross

JESSIE BROWN POUNDS

CHAS. H. GABRIEL

1. I must needs go home by the way of the cross, There's
2. I must needs go on in the blood-sprink-led way, The
3. Then I bid fare-well to the way of the world, To

1. no oth-er way but this; I shall ne'er get sight of the Gates of Light,
2. path that the Sa-viour trod, If I ev-er climb to the heights sub-lime,
3. walk in it nev-er-more; For my Lord says, "Come," and I seek my home,

CHORUS.

1. If the way of the cross I miss.
2. Where the soul is at home with God. } The way of the cross leads
3. Where He waits at the o-pen door.

home, The way of the cross leads home, It is sweet to
leads home; leads home;

know, as I on-ward go, The way of the cross leads home.

883   I Love the Gospel Story

N. A. McAulay   John P. Hillis

1. I love the gos-pel sto-ry, 'Tis God's re-deem-ing love, It
2. I love the gos-pel sto-ry, It keeps me ev-'ry hour; For
3. I love the gos-pel sto-ry, It cheers me day by day; My

1. comes with light and glo - ry From Him who reigns a-bove. I love the bless-ed
2. Christ, the Prince of glo - ry Im-parts His sav-ing pow'r. I love the bless-ed
3. hope, my joy, my glo - ry, I own its gen-tle sway. I love the bless-ed

1. sto - ry, Its theme the Lamb of God, Who left His home in glo-ry, For
2. sto - ry, 'Tis man-na to my soul; The balm of life and glo-ry, It
3. sto - ry, My por-tion ev-er-more; 'Twill be my theme in glo-ry, When

Chorus.

1. me to shed His blood. }
2. makes my spi-rit whole. } I love the gos-pel sto-ry, It nev-er can grow
3. earth-ly cares are o'er. }

old; It helps me on to glo-ry, The more I hear it told.

884
C. H. G.

Abide, Abide with Me

CHAS. H. GABRIEL

1. Dear Lord, I need Thy saving care a-bout me; In - to Thine arms of refuge would I
2. When foes without, and foes within as-sail me, And I am tossed upon a troubled
3. When o'er my way the sun is brightly shin ing, My Counsellor, my Guide and Keeper
4. When I am near the dark and unknown riv - or, Lord, who in earth or heav'n can save but

1. Dear Lord, I need Thy saving care about me; In-to Thine arms of

flee; .... I could not live—I dare not die with - out Thee, In
sea, ... When, in my weakness, hope and courage fail me, In
be; .... And in the hour of sor-row and re - pin ing, In
Thee ?.... 'Tis Thou a - lone hath power to de - liv - er, In

refuge would I flee; I could not live— I dare not die without Thee In

CHORUS.

mer - cy then a - bide, a - bide with me. ...
mer - cy then a - bide, a - bide with me. ... A - bide with me,— I
mer - cy then a - bide, a - bide with me. ...
mer - cy then a - bide, a - bide with me. ...

mer - cy then a - bide, a - bide with me. A - bide, a-bide with me,—I

need Thee ev'ry hour; A - bide with me, I fear the tempter's pow'r, A -
need Thee ev-'ry hour; A-bide, a-bide with me, I fear the tempter's pow'r; A-

Abide, Abide with Me—*Continued*

bide with me, in sunshine and in show'r; In life, in death, O Lord, abide with me.
bide, abide with me, in sunshine and in show'r; In life, in death, O Lord, abide, a-bide with me.

885 Home to the Land Above

FRANK M. DAVIS   CHAS. K. LANGLEY

1. By the way of the Cross we're go - ing, Home to the Land a - bove;
2. By the way of the Cross we're go - ing; Je - sus has gone be - fore;
3. By the way of the Cross we're go - ing; Rough tho' the path may be;

1. We will fear not the hosts of e - vil, Kept by a Fa-ther's love.
2. We will fol - low our Master's foot - steps Home to the gold - en shore!
3. There's a hand that will guide us safe - ly, Home, bles-sed Lord, to Thee!

REFRAIN.

Home, home, home, Home to the Land a - bove,
Go - ing home, go - ing home, the Land a - bove,

By the way of the Cross we're go - ing, Home to the Land of love.

886 Who are the Soldiers?

COLIN STERNE

H. ERNEST NICHOL

1 Who are the sol-diers of Je - sus Christ? Who, who are they?
2 Who are the sol-diers of Je - sus Christ? Who, who are they?
3 Who are the sol-diers of Je - sus Christ? Who, who are they?
4 Who are the sol-diers of Je - sus Christ? Who, who are they?

1 What is the fight that they wage on earth? Why do they watch and pray?
2 Are they the he - roes of earth-ly war, Ea - ger to smite and slay?
3 Are they the lov - ers of emp - ty joys, Things that will pass a - way?
4 Are they the rich and the great of earth, Hold-ing a migh-ty sway?

TREBLES ONLY

1 Ah! they are God's own chil-dren; He is near them, He will cheer them;
2 No, they are some-thing no-bler; And the sto - ry Of their glo - ry
3 No, they would lead for ev - er Lives of beau-ty, Lives of du - ty,
4 No, in a grand-er king-dom, Ev - er fair - er, Ev - er rar - er,

ALL IN UNISON   HARMONY

1 Truth is the cause for which they strive In bat - tle fray.
2 Rings with the pow'r of faith and love That lights their way.
3 Lives that are hid with Christ in God, No more to stray.
4 Bring with the crown of end - less life, They'll shine like day.

Who are the Soldiers?—*Continued*

CHORUS, TREBLES ONLY

They are step-ping brave-ly on - ward, They are ea - ger with the hope of

HARMONY

youth, They nev - er fear the foe, But strike a gal - lant blow For

UNISON

God and the cause of truth; They are ev - er climb-ing

HARMONY

home - ward, They are look-ing un - to high - er things,

Free as the flag that waves o'er-head, Sol - diers of the King of kings.

By permission of H. ERNEST NICHOL

887

Loyalty unto Christ

C. H. G.

CHAS. H. GABRIEL

1. "Loy-al-ty un-to Christ" the trum-pet now is sound-ing, And the
2. "Loy-al-ty, faith and works, in ho-ly con-se-cra-tion, Shall the
3. "Loy-al-ty un-to Christ!" O what a might-y pow-er, Were the

1. ech-oes an-swer from the fields of sin; Na-tions are a-wak-ing,
2. scat-tered na-tions un-to Him re-store; Then the world shall own Him,
3. hosts of God u-ni-ted in His name! Then would an-gels greet us,

FINE.

1. I-dol thrones are shaking, For the great mil-len-ni-um is com-ing in
2. And with joy enthrone Him, King of kings and Lord of lords for ev-er-more.
3. Christ Himself would meet us, And baptise us with the Pen-te-cost-al flame.

SOLO OR DUET.

1. Like . . . . . a might-y arm-y, The heralds of the cross are
2. See . . . . . the darkness rift-ing! The gos-pel light of truth is
3. Then . . . . . would come the tri-umph, And Christ be known and lov'd, His

1. marching o-ver land and sea, Bear . . . . ing thro' the
2. spread-ing to the per-fect day! Clouds . . . . are backward
3. praise be sung from shore to shore, Earth . . . . . would then, in

Loyalty unto Christ —*Continued*

1. dark - ness, The light that lead - eth to sal-va - tion, full and free.
2. drift - ing! Re - new en - dea - vour! for the King prepare the way!
3. glo - ry, Be - come the king-dom of the Lord for ev - er - more.

CHORUS.

Long and loud, "Loy - al - ty un - to Christ" we sing; Till

ev - 'ry hu - man tongue, Shall hear His prais - es sung!

Let the hills, val - leys and des - ert pla - ces ring, With

"Loy - al - ty un - to Christ, our Lord and King." . . . .
our King."

888 The Kingdom of Heaven

Colin Sterne

H. Ernest Nichol

Trebles and Altos

mf 1 What are you seek-ing day by day, Work-ing with heart and hand ?
mf 2 What are you seek-ing day by day ? Is it for some-thing new ?
mf 3 What are you seek-ing day by day, Com-rade so brave and true ?
mf 4 En - ter the King-dom, child of truth, Seek-ing the Sa-viour's face ;

1 Is it for hon-our in the fray ? Is it for wealth or land ?
2 Is it for plea-sures bright and gay, Brief as the morn-ing dew ?
3 Is it for some great thing to say ? Some no-ble deed to do ?
4 En - ter the King-dom, maid and youth, Come in your strength and grace ;

1 Turn from the ea-ger long-ing thirst, Turn from the world's great strife,
2 Seek ye the King-dom ev-er-more, Joys shall be add-ed then,
f 3 Give to the Mas-ter heart and hand, Fol-low in truth and love,
cr 4 En - ter the King-dom one and all, Cease from the path to stray,

cr 1 Seek ye the King-dom of Hea-ven first, Seek ye e-ter-nal life.
cr 2 Great-er than all that you felt be-fore, Ev-er re-new'd a-gain.
3 So shall you share in His work and stand Crown'd in the life a-bove.
4 Hear ye the voice of the Mast-er call, 'I am the liv-ing Way.'

The Kingdom of Heaven—*Continued*

CHORUS FOUR PARTS

mf For the King-dom of Heav'n is bet-ter Than pearls of a price-less worth, Than trea-sures great, or pomp of state, *cr.* Than the

worth, Than trea-sures great,

UNISON

king-dom of all the earth. *f* It ev-er a-bid-eth with-

HARMONY

in you, This home of the life di-vine, *cr.* Let the dark clouds roll from your heart and soul, Let the Light of the King-dom shine.

By permission of H. ERNEST NICHOL

889 Hark! 'Tis the Clarion

JOSEPH BROWN MORGAN

G. DONIZETTI

1 Hark! 'tis the cla - rion sound-ing the fight, Turn from each si - ren charm - er;
2 Haste to the res - cue, souls in their need Loud for re - lief are call - ing;
3 Soon 'twill be o - ver, dan - ger all past; End - ed the march - es drea - ry;

1 Ban - ners are wav - ing, swords gleam-ing bright, Gird on the heav'n-ly ar - mour:
2 Must they for ev - er hope - less - ly plead? None hear the cry ap - pal - ling?
3 Af - ter the war - fare rest comes at last, Sweet rest for sol - diers wea - ry:

1 Stern is the con - flict, fierce is the foe; Cow-ards and trait-ors will back-ward go:
2 Brok - en in spi - rit, wound-ed by sin, Foe-men a-round them, and fear with - in;
3 Crown aft - er con - flict, ease aft - er pain; Part-ing shall nev - er be known a - gain:

1 Brave men are want-ed, hearts all a-glow, Want-ed to bat-tle for Je - sus.
2 Speed ye to help them free-dom to win; Speed with the Gos-pel of Je - sus.
3 Joy ev - er-last - ing all shall ob - tain; All who are faith-ful to Je - sus.

Hark! 'Tis the Clarion—*Continued*

REFRAIN

Sol - diers of God, we join you to - day, Join in your

grand en - dea - vour; Sol - diers of God . ad - vance

to the fray, For the truth is tri - umph - phant for ev - er.

CODA FOR SOLO VOICE

Sol - diers of God, we join you to - day, . Join in your

Hark! 'Tis the Clarion—*Concluded*

grand en - dea - - vour; . Sol - diers of God ad -

vance to the fray, for the truth is tri - umph - ant for ev - er.

REFRAIN (2nd time)

Sol-diers of God we join you to-day, Join in your grand en - dea - vour; Sol-diers

of God ad - vance to the fray, For the truth is tri-umph-ant for ev - er.

390 Christian, Rise and Shine!

JUBILEE SINGERS

O Chris - tian, rise and shine, and give God the glo - ry! Chris - tian, rise and shine, and give God the glo ry; Chris - tian, rise and shine, and give God the glo - ry; Chris - tian, rise, rise and shine! Do you want to be a real - ly hap - py Chris - tian? Do you

Christian, Rise and Shine!—*Continued*

want   to   be   a   real - ly   hap - py   Christ - ian?   Do   you

want   to   be   a   real - ly   hap - py   Christ - ian?   Full   of

joy,   joy   di - vine?   Yes,   I   want   to   be   a

real - ly   hap - py   Christ - ian!   Yes,   I   want   to

be   a   real - ly   hap - py   Christ - ian;   Yes,   I

Christian, Rise and Shine!—*Concluded*

want to be a real - ly hap - py Christ - ian? Full of

joy, joy di - vine. Then you must rise and shine, and

give God the glo - ry; You must rise and shine, and

give God the glo - ry; You must rise and shine, and

give God the glo - ry; You must rise, rise and shine!

891

On to the Front!

C. H. G.

CHAS. H. GABRIEL

1. On to the front, for the fight is on! This is not the time for dream - ing!
2. On to the front, nor the dan - ger fear, Satan's forc-es can - not harm you;
3. On to the front! He who smote the sea, And its an-gry waves di - vid - ed,

1. See! on the breeze of the ear - ly dawn, Banners of the foe are stream - ing!
2. Let not the hordes that are pressing near In their proud array a - larm you;
3. Is thy Com-mander, and sure - ly He For the vic-t'ry hath pro - vid - ed.

1. In - to po - si - tion for bat - tle drawn, And with weapons brightly gleam - ing,
2. Be not dismayed by the foemen's cheer, Let no e - vil power dis - arm you;
3. Trust in His pow - er, and ev - er be By His love and wis-dom guid - ed;

1. Now from the hill - top of vantage ground, Loud their battle cries re - sound.
2. Trust in the Lord for your strength to win O - ver all the ranks of sin.
3. Keep up the fight till the whole world sings Praise un - to the King of kings.

CHORUS.

On - ward to the con-flict! Fearless, like a sol - dier true;
on - ward! Fear - less like a sol - dier true;

On to the Front—*Continued*

Press in-to the bat - tle, Your Com-mand-er calls for you,
bat - tle, for - ward,

892 Bring Wanderers Home

B. MANSELL RAMSEY

B. MANSELL RAMSEY

1 Lord, bring some wan-d'rers home to-night—Some who have gone a - stray;
2 May none Thy mer-cy spurn to-night, Thy Ho-ly Spi - rit grieve;
3 Let none un-blest de - part to-night, Un-saved and un-for - giv'n;

1 O give them grace to come to-night! Let them no more de - lay.
2 May pro-di-gals re - turn to-night; May sin-ners now be - lieve.
3 O-ver some yield-ing heart to-night Let there be joy in heav'n.

REFRAIN

To - night, Lord! to - night, Lord! Bring wan-d'rers home to - night:

P e rall.

To - night, Lord! to - night, Lord! Bring wan-d'rers home to - night.

By permission of J. CURWEN & SONS, LTD.

893   Conquerors are We

LEILA N. MORRIS   LEILA N. MORRIS

1 Con-quer-ors and o-ver-com-ers now are we, Thro' the pre-cious blood of Christ we've
2 In the name of Is-rael's God we'll on-ward press, O-ver-com-ing sin and all un-
3 Un-to him that o-ver-com-eth shall be giv'n Here to eat of 'hid-den man-na'

1 vic-tor-y, If the Lord be for us, we can ne-ver fail; Noth-ing 'gainst His
2 right-eous-ness; Not to us, but un-to Him the praise shall be For sal-va-tion
3 sent from heav'n; O-ver yon-der he the vic-tor's palm shall bear And a robe of

REFRAIN

1 migh-ty pow'r can e'er pre-vail. Con - quer-ors are we, thro' the
2 and for blood-bought vic-tor-y. Con-quer-ors are we, con-quer-ors are we,
3 white and gold-en crown shall wear. Con-quer-ors are we,

blood; thro' the blood; God will give us vic-tor-y, thro' the
thro' the blood, thro' the blood, God will give vic-tor-y,

blood; thro' the blood, Thro' the Lamb for sin-ners slain, Yet who lives and
thro' the blood, thro' the blood,

Conquerors are We—*Continued*

reigns a-gain, More than con-quer-ors are we, More than con-quer-ors are we.

894   Love Found Me

H. L. GILMOUR   *Arr.* H. L. GILMOUR

1   When out in sin and dark-ness lost,   Love found me;   My faint-ing soul was
2   The Spi - rit roused me from my sleep,   Love found me;   Con - vic-tion seized me
3   I'll praise Him while He gives me breath,   Love found me;   For sav - ing from an
4   And when I reach the gold-paved street,   Love found me;   I'll sit a - dor-ing

1   tem-pest tossed, Love found me;   I heard the Sa-viour's words so blest, Love found me;
2   strong and deep, Love found me;   Al-though I long with-stood His grace, Love found me;
3   end-less death, Love found me;   Christ is my Ad - vo - cate a - bove, Love found me;
4   at His feet, Love found me;   And sing ho - san - na round the throne, Love found me;

REFRAIN

1   Come, wea - ry, hea - vy - la - den, rest,   Love found me.   O 'twas love,
2   He wooed me to His kind em-brace,   Love found me.
3   I'm yoked to Him in per-fect love,   Love found me.
4   Where I shall know as I am known,   Love found me.   O 'twas love; 'twas

love,   Love that moved the might-y God, Love, love, 'twas love found me.
won-drous love.

895   Soldiers of the Master

COLIN STERNE   H. ERNEST NICHOL

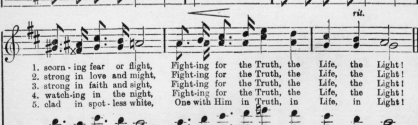

1. Where the flag is fly - ing, where the fight is keen, Where the trumpet
2. Where the dark - ness reign - eth, where the pow'r of sin, Binds the heart of
3. Where the doubts are thick - est, where the strength of youth, Falls be-neath the
4. Where the pal - lid suf - frer, wea - ry, worn, and weak, On his bed of
5. Where from an - gel - cho - rus thro' the heav'n - ly dome, Rings a song of

1. call is ring - ing, There you find the sol - diers, stea - dy and se - rene,
2. man in sad - ness, There you find the sol - diers, wait - ing souls to win,
3. chains of er - ror, There you find the sol - diers, with the lamp of truth,
4. pain is ly - ing, There you find the sol - diers, words of hope to speak,
5. tri - umph splen - did, There you find the sol - diers en - ter - ing their home,

1. There you hear the sound of sing - ing. Ser-vants of the Mas - ter,
2. Bring-ing them to light and glad - ness. Ser-vants of the Mas - ter,
3. Free - ing men from thoughts of ter - ror. Ser-vants of the Mas - ter,
4. Com - fort - ing the sick and dy - ing. Ser-vants of the Mas - ter,
5. By the heavenly hosts at - tend - ed. Ser-vants of the Mas - ter,

rit.

1. scorn - ing fear or flight, Fight-ing for the Truth, the Life, the Light!
2. strong in love and might, Fight-ing for the Truth, the Life, the Light!
3. strong in faith and sight, Fight-ing for the Truth, the Life, the Light!
4. watch-ing in the night, Fight-ing for the Truth, the Life, the Light!
5. clad in spot - less white, One with Him in Truth, in Life, in Light!

Soldiers of the Master—*Continued.*

CHORUS. *Unison.*

Sol-diers of the Mas-ter, onward tread, Tell-ing out the grand old sto-ry!

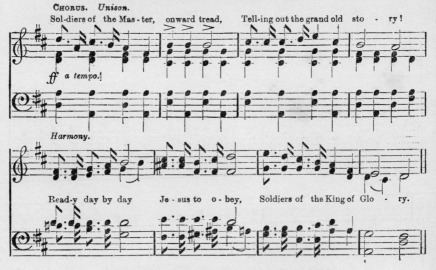

Read-y day by day Je-sus to o-bey, Soldiers of the King of Glo-ry.

By permission of the NATIONAL SUNDAY SCHOOL UNION

896 Wait a Little While

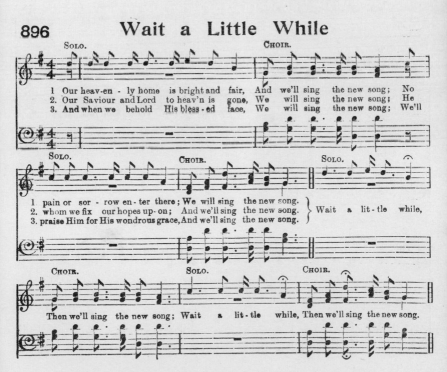

SOLO. CHOIR.

1 Our heav-en-ly home is bright and fair, And we'll sing the new song; No
2. Our Saviour and Lord to heav'n is gone, We will sing the new song; He
3. And when we behold His bless-ed face, We will sing the new song; We'll

SOLO. CHOIR. SOLO.

1 pain or sor-row en-ter there; We will sing the new song.
2. whom we fix our hopes up-on; And we'll sing the new song.
3. praise Him for His wondrous grace, And we'll sing the new song.

Wait a lit-tle while,

CHOIR. SOLO. CHOIR.

Then we'll sing the new song; Wait a lit-tle while, Then we'll sing the new song.

897 The Call of the Roll

D. W. WHITTLE

JAMES M'GRANAHAN

1. Sad - ly from the field of con - flict, Where the wound-ed and the slain
2. On the ground we softly laid him, Thinking he no more will wake,
3. Oh! from many a field of bat - tle Ear-nest pray'r has gone to God,

Lay with pale and
When, with eyelids
From the lips of

1. Lay with pale and up-turn'd fa - ces, Some in peace and some in pain, Slow we
2. When, with eye - lids wide - ly o - pen, Point-ing up - ward, thus he spake: "Comrades,
3. From the lips of dy - ing sol - diers, As their life-blood drench'd the sod; And to

1. up - turned fa - ces,
2. wide - ly o - pen,
3. dy - ing sol - diers,

1. bore a dy - ing sol - dier, Who had fall - en in the fight, And to
2. lis - ten! don't you hear it, Hear the roll - call there on high? Hark! my
3. ma - ny came the mes - sage: Son, thy sins are all for - giv'n, And their

1. us he faint - ly whis - per'd, "Comrades, let me sleep to - night."
2. name the Sa - viour's call - ing, "Je - sus, Cap - tain, here am I?"
3. lips with joy re - spond - ed, When the roll was called in heav'n.

The Call of the Roll—*Continued*

CHORUS.

1 & 2. Let him sleep,   calm-ly sleep,   While the days and the years go by,
3. Now they sleep,   calm-ly sleep,   While the days and the years go by,

1 & 2. Let him sleep,   calm-ly sleep, While the days and the years go by,
3. Now they sleep,   calm-ly sleep, While the days and the years go by,

1 & 2. Let him sleep,   sweet-ly sleep,   Till the call of the roll on high.
3. Now they sleep,   sweet-ly sleep,   Till the call of the roll on high.

1 & 2. Let him sleep,   sweet-ly sleep, Till the call of the roll on high.
3. Now they sleep,   sweet-ly sleep, Till the call of the roll on high.

1 & 2. Let him sleep,   calm-ly sleep,   While the years go by.
3. Now they sleep,   calm-ly sleep,   While the years go by.

dim.

1 & 2. Let him sleep,   calm-ly sleep, While the years go by.
3. Now they sleep,   calm-ly sleep, While the years go by.

* These last four measures may be omitted until after last verse, if thought best.

898

Jesus! Blessed Name

Je-sus! blessed name,   Je-sus! still the same,   I will sing it more and more, Till we meet on heaven's shore.
blessed name,   still the same,

899 Homeward

ADA POWELL

CHAS. H. GABRIEL

1. Home-ward I go re - joic - ing! O love - ly promised land,
2. Home-ward to meet my Sa - viour On that e - ter - nal shore,
3. Home-ward I go be - liev - ing That there shall be no night

1. Far in the dis - tance gleam - ing, I see Thy shin - ing strand.
2. Won - der-ful land of Ca - naan, Where sor-rows come no more.
3. In that e - ter - nal cit - y, Where God Him - self is light!

CHORUS.

Homeward, to join the ransomed, Beyond the borders of the crystal sea;
Homeward bound, to join the ransomed ones,

We're

Homeward, to joys e - ter - nal, And oh, how sweet the rest will be!
Homeward bound to joys, e - ter - nal joys,

900　Jesus, the Best Friend

H. G. SMYTH

H. G. SMYTH

1. There is One who un - derstands our hearts, Je - sus, the best Friend of all;
2. He will soothe and com - fort in dis - tress, Je - sus, the best Friend of all;
3. In temp-ta - tion He will help thee stand, Je - sus, the best Friend of all;
4. There is One who died for you and me, Je - sus, the best Friend of all;

1. And for ev - 'ry need His grace im - parts, Je - sus, the best Friend of all.
2. He will sym - pa - thize, and help, and bless, Je - sus, the best Friend of all.
3. Will sup-port thee with His strong, right hand, Je - sus, the best Friend of all.
4. He will give us par - don full and free, Je - sus, the best Friend of all.

CHORUS.

Je-sus, the best Friend of all; the best of all; Je-sus, the best Friend of all, the best of all,

He knows our ev - 'ry care, And will ev - 'ry burden bear, Je-sus, the best Friend of all.

901 The Love of the Father

COLIN STERNE

H. ERNEST NICHOL

TREBLES ONLY (OR SOLO)

1 We sing of a sto-ry the Mas-ter told Of God's great love,
2 O all who have wander'd a-way and fed On husks of sin;
3 That house of the Fa-ther is full of light, Our home a-bove,

1 A love that can ne-ver grow faint or cold, Wher-e'er we rove;
2 O ye who are faint for the Liv-ing Bread, And sad with-in;
3 There waits you a robe of im-mor-tal white, A ring of love.

1 A love that waits to wel-come us When from our sins we turn,
2 Whose thoughts are turn-ing long-ing-ly To-wards the Fa-ther's home,
3 O Fa-ther grant us all Thy grace To leave our sin be-hind,

rall.

1 Whose depth and height are in-fi-nite, Whose ful-ness none can learn.
2 No lon-ger stay, make no de-lay, For Je-sus bids you come.
3 To en-ter straight the nar-row gate, And seek Thee till we find.

The Love of the Father—*Continued*

CHORUS HARMONY

mf
Then a - rise and come to the Fa - ther! He will meet you on the

way; . . . All the lost to His arms He will ga - ther In His

UNISON

home of e - ter - nal day; . . . . For the bells of the ci - ty of

HARMONY

God shall ring, And the choirs of heav'n shall sing,   'Let

joy a-bound, let songs re - sound, For the lov'd and lost is found.'

By permission of H. ERNEST NICHOL

902 To the Harvest Field

CHARLES H. GABRIEL   DUET   CHARLES H. GABRIEL

1. A band of faith-ful reap-ers we, . . Who ga-ther for e-ter-ni-ty . The gold-en sheaves of rip-en'd grain From ev-'ry val-ley, hill and plain; . . Our song is one the reap-ers sing, . In hon-our of their Lord and King: . The Mas-ter

2. We are a faith-ful glean-ing band, . . And la-bour at our Lord's com-mand, . Un-yield-ing loy-al, tried and true, For lo! the reap-ers are but few; . Be-hold the wav-ing har-vest field . A-bun-dant with a gold-en yield; . And hear the

3. The gol-den hours like mo-ments fly, . . And har-vest days are pass-ing by; . Then take thy rust-y sick-le down And la-bour for a fade-less crown; . Why will you id-ly stand and wait? . Be-hold, the hour is grow-ing late! . Can you to

To the Harvest Field—*Continued*

1 of the har-vest wide, Who for a world of sin-ners died. . .
2 Lord of har-vest say To all: 'Go reap for me to-day.' . .
3 judg-ment bring but leaves, While here are wait-ing gol-den sheaves? . .

REFRAIN

To the har-vest field a-way . For the Mas-ter call-eth;

There is work for all to-day . Ere the dark-ness fall-eth;

Swift-ly do the mo-ments fly, . Har-vest days are go-ing

by, . Go-ing, . go-ing, . go-ing, go-ing by. .

903 The Fight is On

LEILA N. MORRIS

LEILA N. MORRIS

1 The fight is on, the trum-pet sound is ring-ing out, The cry, To
2 The fight is on, a-rouse ye sol-diers brave and true; Je-ho-vah
3 The Lord is lead-ing on to cer-tain vic-to-ry, The bow of

1 arms! is heard a-far and near; . . The Lord of hosts is
2 leads, and vic-t'ry will as-sure; . . Go buck-le on the
3 prom-ise spans the east-ern sky; . . His glo-rious name in

1 march-ing on to vic-to-ry, The tri-umph of the right will soon ap-pear.
2 ar-mour God has giv-en you, And in His strength un-to the end en-dure.
3 ev-'ry land shall hon-our'd be, The morn will break, the dawn of peace is nigh.

REFRAIN *Unison*

The fight is on, O Chris-tian sol - dier! And face to face in

The Fight is On—*Continued*

stern ar - ray, . . With ar - mour gleam - ing, . and col - ours

stream - ing, . . The right and wrong en - gage to - day. . .

Harmony

The fight is on, but be not wea - - - ry, Be strong and

in His might hold fast; . . If God be for us,
vic - t'ry!

The Fight is On—*Concluded*

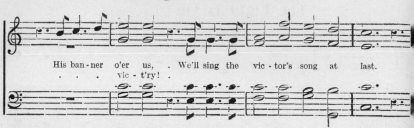

His ban - ner o'er us, . We'll sing the vic - tor's song at last.
. . . vic - t'ry!

904   ## Jesus, Precious Saviour

WILLIAM LUFF   TIMIOS 8.8.8.6   CHARLES REEVES
Arr. P. J. MANSFIELD

1 When dark-'ning clouds ob-scure our sky, And friends are
2 Friends, bask-ing in . the sum-mer ray Of bright-er
3 When hopes, like Au-tumn leaves, are dead, And ev-'ry
4 Je-sus hath died . thine heart to win, His pre-cious
5 O let Him fold . thee to His breast! There find a

1 few, and trou-bles nigh, . . On One a-lone we
2 hours, have pass'd a-way; . . But One is left in
3 joy of earth is fled, . . Sweet pil-low—rest for
4 blood a-tones for sin, . . His lov-ing arms would
5 true, a per-fect rest, . . And thou shalt be for

1 may re-ly, . . Je-sus! pre-cious Sa - - viour!
2 sor-row's day, . . Je-sus! pre-cious Sa - - viour!
3 heart and head, . . Je-sus! pre-cious Sa - - viour!
4 take thee in; . . Je-sus! pre-cious Sa - - viour!
5 ev - er blest. By Je-sus! pre-cious Sa - - viour!

905 Onward, Ever Onward!

Marian Wendell Hubbard   Charles H. Gabriel

1 Christ has need of sol-diers, brave and staunch and true;
2 Sa - tan would op-pose us, tempt our souls to stray,
3 Let us then with cour-age press our up-ward way,

1 Christ has need of sol - diers, . brave and staunch and true;
2 Sa - tan would op-pose . us, . tempt our souls to stray,
3 Let us then with cour - age . press our up-ward way,

1 In the front of bat - tle there's a place for you; . . .
2 But through Him who loves us we shall win the day; . . .
3 With our gaze on Je - sus, ev - er watch and pray; . . .

1 In the front of bat - tle there's . a . place for you; .
2 But through Him who loves us we . shall . win the day; .
3 With our gaze on Je - sus, ev - er . watch and pray; .

1 Ev - er march-ing on - ward through a world of sin,
2 Oth - er val - iant sol - diers in the a - ges past
3 Bla - zon'd on our ban - ner, 'Christ, the Lord of all,'

1 Ev - er march-ing on - ward through a world of sin,
2 Oth - er val - iant sol - diers . in the a - ges past
3 Bla - zon'd on our ban - ner, 'Christ, the Lord of all,

Onward, Ever Onward!—*Continued*

1 For the heav'n - ly coun - try is the prize we win. . . . .
2 O'er this up - ward path - way reach'd their home at last. . . . .
3 While we shout, Ho - san - na! Sa - tan's hosts must fall. . . . .

1 For the heav'n - ly coun - try is . the . prize we win. . .
2 O'er this up - ward path - way reach'd their . home at last. .
3 While we shout, Ho - san - na! Sa - tan's . hosts must fall. .

REFRAIN

On - - ward! . . . . . sol - diers of the Cross, Doubt - ing

On - ward, ev - er on - ward! sol - diers of . the . Cross, . .

nev - er, . . trust - ing ev - er; . . .

To the cause be true, . . . Je - sus calls for you, .

On - - ward! . . . sol - diers of the Cross,

On - ward, ev - er on - ward! sol - diers of . the . Cross.

Onward, Ever Onward!—*Concluded*

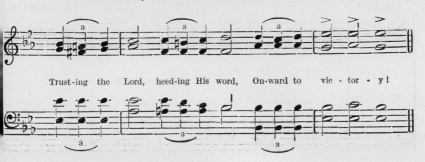

Trust-ing the Lord, heed-ing His word, On-ward to vic - tor - y!

906 Never Mind the Scoffs

Let us nev-er mind the scoffs or the jeers of the world For we

all have a cross to bear; It will on - ly make the crown the

bright - er to shine, When we have the crown to wear.

907 The Harvest Field

J. T. ALMY

J. C. BEAZLEY

1 A - way to the har - vest field, toil - ers, a - way; Go,
2 Be - hold how the ri - pen'd grain bends to the earth! The
3 O say not, 'No work of this sort can I do,' For
4 And when the last sheaf to the gar - ner has come, And

1 ga - ther the gold - en grain whilst it is day, Strength meet for thy
2 har - vest is rea - dy, O why such a dearth Of la - bour - ers
3 some kind of toil there is e - ven for you, For if the keen
4 saints join with an - gels to shout, 'Har - vest home'; When la - bour is

1 la - bour thy Lord will be - stow: A - way to the har - vest field'
2 rea - dy and will - ing to toil? Will they list - less - ly suf - fer the
3 sic - kle thy hand may not wield, Bind to - geth - er the sheaves, or else
4 o - ver, then rest and re - ward, And the wel - come, 'Well done,' from the

1 la - bour - ers, go, For now is the time to be do - ing thy
2 rich grain to spoil? No, it must not be so; to the field hie a -
3 glean in the field: If you fol - low the reap - ers o - ver the
4 lips of the Lord: A - way to the har - vest field, toil while you

The Harvest Field—*Continued*

1 best, Soon, soon will be com-ing . the sea-son for rest. .
2 way With heart and with hand to . work whilst . it is day. .
3 ground, Full man-y a rich gold-en ear . shall be found. .
4 may, Soon, soon will be end-ed . the bright har-vest day. .

REFRAIN

A-way, . . a-way, . . a-
. . A-way, a-way, a-way,

way, . . a-way, . . For soon . . will be
a-way, a-way, a-way, . . For soon will be

end-ed . The bright, the bright har-vest day.

908

Tell the Saviour All

JOHNSON OATMAN, Jr.   TELL HIM ALL 8.5.8.5.D   MORGAN, *Arr.* P. J. MANSFIELD

1 Make the Lord a full con - fess - ion When on
2 Not a - lone the great temp - ta - tions That the
3 For the Eye that guards cre - a - tion Sees a

1 Him you call, . . Do not car - ry half the bur - den;
2 heart ap - pal; . . But the lit - tle cares and bur - dens;
3 spar - row fall; . . All your trou - bles will not tire Him;

REFRAIN

1 Tell the Sa - viour all. .
2 Tell the Sa - viour all. . Tell the Sa - viour all, .
3 Tell the Sa - viour all. .
tell Him all,

Tell . the Sa - viour all, tell Him all; . Make to Him a

full con - fess - ion, Tell . the Sa - viour all. . .

The tune ELLISON is on the following page

908   Tell the Saviour All

JOHNSON OATMAN, JR.   ELLISON 8.5.8.5.D   DAVID CARYLL

1 Make the Lord a full con-fess-ion When on
2 Not a-lone the great temp-ta-tions That on the
3 For the Eye that guards cre-a-tion Sees a

1 Him you call, . . Do not car-ry half the bur-den;
2 heart ap-pal, . . But the lit-tle cares and bur-dens;
3 spar-row fall; . . All your trou-bles will not tire Him;

REFRAIN

1 Tell the Sa-viour all. . . } Tell the Sa-viour all, . . . tell Him all,
2 Tell the Sa-viour all. . .
3 Tell the Sa-viour all. . .

Tell . the Sa-viour all, ... Make to Him a
tell . Him all;

full con-fess-ion, Tell the Sa-viour all. . .

The tune TELL HIM ALL is on the preceding page

909 Marching Beneath the Banner

COLIN STERNE

H. ERNEST NICHOL

TREBLES AND ALTOS ONLY.

1 Hark to the sound of voi - ces! Hark to the tramp of feet!
2 Out of the mist of er - ror, Out of the realms of night,
3 Out of the bonds of ev - il, Out of the chains of sin,
4 On then, ye gall - ant sold - iers, On to your home a - bove!

1 Is it a mighty ar - my Treading the bu - sy street?
2 Out of the pride of learn - ing, Seek-ing the home of light;
3 Ev - er they're pressing on - ward, Fighting the fight with-in;
4 Yours is the truth and glo - ry, Yours is the pow'r and love.

FOUR PARTS

1 Near - er it comes and near - er, Sing-ing a glad re - frain:
2 Out of the strife for pow - er, Out of the greed of gold,
3 Hold - ing the pass - ions und - er, Rul - ing the sense with soul,
4 Here are ye trained for he - roes, Yon - der ye serve the King;

1 List what they say as they haste a - way To the sound of a mar-tial strain :—
2 On - ward they roam to their heavenly home, And the treasure that grows not old.
3 Wielding the sword in the Name of the Lord, As they march to their heav'nly goal.
4 March to the light 'neath the banner white, With the song that ye love to sing:

In verses 1, 2 and 3, the effect should be produced of the gradual approach from the distance of a band of soldiers.

Marching Beneath the Banner—*Continued*

f " Marching beneath the ban - ner, Fighting beneath the Cross,

Trusting in Him who saves us, Ne'er shall we suffer loss !

ff Sing-ing the songs of home - land, Loud - ly the cho - rus rings, We

march to the fight in our armour bright At the call of the King of kings."

By permission of H. ERNEST NICHOL

910 Beautiful Words of Jesus

Eliza E. Hewitt

I. H. Meredith

1 Beau-ti-ful words of Je-sus Spo-ken so long a-go,
2 Beau-ti-ful words of Je-sus, Cheer-ing us day by day;
3 Beau-ti-ful words of Je-sus, To-kens of end-less rest,

1 Yet, as we sing them o-ver, Dear-er to us they grow,
2 Throw-ing a gleam of sun-shine O-ver a cloud-y way;
3 When, by and by, we en-ter In-to His pre-sence blest;

DUET *Ladies' Voices*

1 Call-ing the heav-y la-den, Call-ing to hearts op-press'd,
2 Cast-ing on Him the bur-den We are too weak to bear,
3 There shall we see His beau-ty, Meet with Him face to face;

All Voices

1 'Come un-to Me, ye wea-ry, Come, I will give you rest.'
2 He will give grace suf-fi-cient, He will re-gard our pray'r.
3 There shall we sing His glo-ry, Prais-ing His match-less grace.

Beautiful Words of Jesus—*Continued*

REFRAIN *Unison*

Hear the call of His voice so sweet; Bring your load to the Saviour's feet;

Beautiful Words of Jesus — *Concluded*

Lean . your . heart . on His
lov - ing . breast, . . Come, O .
come! and He will give thee rest. .

911 ## Will You Meet Us?

Say, . bro-ther,* will you meet . us, Say, . bro-ther, will you meet . us, Say, . bro-ther, will you meet . us On Ca-naan's hap-py shore? By the grace of God we'll meet . you, By the grace of God we'll meet . you, By the grace of God we'll meet you On Ca-naan's hap-py shore!

* May be sung as sister, children, or other appropriate word

912   Build on the Rock

COLIN STERNE

H. ERNEST NICHOL

1 What are you building, bro-ther, So bu-si-ly day by day?
Is it a migh-ty cas-tle of stone?
Is it a house of clay?
Whose is the plan you build on?
What are the stones and lime?
Is it based on the build on?

2 What are you building, bro-ther, You work at it ev-'ry day;
Something is add-ed, something is changed,
Some-thing is cast a-way.
Is it a house of pleas-ure?
Is it a house of sin?
Or a tem-ple di-pleas-ure?

3 Bro-ther, a time is com-ing When all shall be tried by fire:
Storms of the world shall beat on your house,
Winds of a fierce de-sire.
Then, if you based it wrong-ly,
Great will the ru-in be;
But if built on the wrong-ly,

4 Build on the Rock, then, bro-ther, How grandly it towers a-bove!
Pierc-ing the clouds and the star-ry skies,
Lost in the heights of Love!
Hea-ven and earth shall per-ish,
Grow like a gar-ment old;
But the Rock is the per-ish,

Unison

Build on the Rock—*Continued*

rall.

1 Rock of e - ter - ni - ty, Or the sands of the shores of time?
2 vine for the Light of lights To de - scend and a - bide with - in?
3 firm and un - chang-ing Rock It will stand for e - ter - ni - ty.
4 same, and it shall not fail, Thro' the a - ges of time un - told.

CHORUS *ff*
Harmony a tempo.

Then build on the Rock, the Rock that ev - er stands, O build on the

Rock, and not up - on the sands! You need not fear the storm or the

Chorus may be repeated in Unison

earth-quake shock, You're safe for ev - er - more if you build on the Rock.

By permission of H. ERNEST NICHOL

913 The Cloud and Fire

C. Austin Miles   C. Austin Miles

1 As of old, when the hosts of Is - ra - el Were com-pell'd in the wil-der-ness to dwell,
2 To and fro, as a ship with-out a sail, Not a com-pass to guide them thro' the vale,
3 All the days of their wand'rings they were fed; To the land of the pro-mise they were led;

1 Trust-ing they in their God to lead the way To the light of per - fect day.
2 But the sign of their God was ev - er near, Thus their faint-ing hearts to cheer.
3 By the hand of the Lord in gui-dance sure They were brought to Canaan's shore.

REFRAIN UNISON

So the sign of the fire by night, And the sign of the cloud by day,

Hov-'ring o'er, just be-fore, As they jour-ney on their way,

Shall a guide and a lead-er be Till the wil - der - ness be past.

The Cloud and Fire—*Continued*

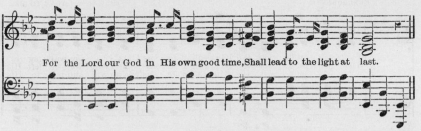

For the Lord our God in His own good time, Shall lead to the light at last.

914

That Fair Land

C. F. ALEXANDER   SILKSWORTH 7.5.7.5.7.7   CHARLES VINCENT

1 Ev - 'ry morn - ing the red sun Ris - es warm and bright;
2 Ev - 'ry spring the sweet young flow'rs O - pen fresh and gay;
3 Lit - tle birds sing songs of praise All the sum - mer long;
4 Christ our Lord is ev - er near Those who fol - low Him;
5 Who shall go to that fair land? All who love the right;

1 But the ev - 'ning com - eth on, And the dark cold night:
2 Till the chil - ly au - tumn hours Wi - ther them a - way:
3 But in cold - er, short - er days They for - get their song:
4 But we can - not see Him here, For our eyes are dim:
5 Ho - ly child - ren there shall stand In their robes of white;

1 There's a bright land far a - way . . Where 'tis nev - er - end - ing day.
2 There's a land we have not seen . . Where the trees are al - ways green.
3 There's a place where an - gels sing . . Cease - less prais - es to their King.
4 There's a hap - py, glor - ious place . . Where His peo - ple see His face.
5 For that heav'n so bright and blest . . Is our ev - er - last - ing rest.

Music by permission of the PSALMS AND HYMNS TRUST

915 The King called Jesus

F. G. BURROUGHS

ADAM GEIBEL

1 What will you do with the King call'd Je - sus? Ma - ny are wait-ing to
2 What will you do for the King call'd Je - sus? He who for you left His
3 What will you do with the King call'd Je - sus? Who will sub-mit to His

1 hear you say; Some have de-spis'd Him, re - ject - ing His mer - cy, What will you
2 throne a - bove, Here 'mid the low - ly and sin - ful to la - bour, Dai - ly un -
3 gen - tle sway? Where are the hearts rea-dy now to en-throne Him? Who will His

1 do with your King to - day? What can you wit -ness con-cern -ing His good-ness?
2 fold - ing His Fa-ther's love: Look on the fields white al - rea - dy to har-vest,
3 kind com - mands o - bey? Come with your oint-ments most cost-ly and pre-cious,

1 Who died to save you from sin's bit - ter thrall; Who will de-clare Him the
2 Who now is will - ing to toil with the few? What will you do for the
3 Pour out your gifts at the dear Sa-viour's feet; Ren - der to Him all your

1 fair - est of thou-sands? Who now will crown Him the Lord of all?
2 dear Sa - viour, Je - sus? Lo, He is wait - ing, He calls for you!
3 loy - al de - vo - tion; Seek to ex - alt Him by prais - es meet.

The King called Jesus—*Continued*

What will you do with the King call'd Jesus? What, O what, will you do with Je-sus?

Voices in parts

He waits to bless all who hum-bly con-fess Faith in His blood and right-eous-ness.

916   **By-and-Bye**

ANON.

OLD MELODY

By-and-bye we'll see the King, By-and-bye we'll see the King, By-and-bye we'll

see the King, And crown Him Lord of all, And crown . . Him Lord of all, And crown

Him Lord of all, And crown . . Him Lord of all, And crown Him Lord of all.

917 **The Victorious Army**

Colin Sterne

H. Ernest Nichol

Choir, or Men in Unison

The Victorious Army—*Continued*

CHORUS. ALL, IN UNISON

mf
We've en - list - ed in the cause vic - tor - ious, Of the ev - er - last - ing Lord, We are march - ing in the ranks all - glo - rious, Re - splen-dent with the shield and sword. Christ is our Cap - tain, Christ our might, So we fight, Seek - ing right; Christ is lead - ing us to light In the all - vic - tor - ious ar - my.

HARMONY

ff

UNISON

By permission of H. ERNEST NICHOL

918 When the King Comes

E. S. ELLIOTT

E. S. ELLIOTT

1 They come and go the sea-sons fair, And bring their spoil to
2 The floods have lif-ted up their voice: The King hath come to His
3 A ran-som'd earth breaks forth in song, Her sin-stain'd a-ges
4 O bro-thers, stand as men that wait! The dawn is purp-ling

1 vale and hills; But O there is wait-ing in the air! And a
2 own, His own; The lit-tle hills and vales re-joice: His
3 o-ver-past, Her yearn-ing, 'Lord, how long, how long?' Ex-
4 in the East, And ban-ners wave from heav'n's high gate; The

1 pas-sion-ate hope the spi-rit fills: Why doth He tar-ry, the
2 right it is to take the crown: Sleep-ers a-wake, and
3 chang'd for joy at last, at last: An-gels car-ry the
4 con-flict now, but soon the feast: Mer-cy and truth shall

1 ab-sent Lord? When shall the King-dom be re-stor'd, And
2 meet Him first! Now let the mar-riage hymn out-burst, And
3 roy-al com-mands; Peace beams forth through-out all the lands; The
4 meet a-gain; Wor-thy the Lamb that once was slain! We can

When the King Comes—*Continued*

1 earth and heav'n with one ac - cord Ring out the cry that the
2 pow'rs of dark - ness flee, dis - pers'd; What will it be when the
3 trees of the field shall clap their hands; What will it be when the
4 suf - fer now, He will know us then; What will it be when the

REFRAIN *a tempo*

1-4 King . . comes! What will it be when the King comes!

What will it be when the King comes! What will it be when He

when He
When He

comes! . . Slower

comes, when He comes! What will it be when the King . . comes!

comes!

919 My Redeemer Liveth

JESSIE H. BROWN   J. H. FILLMORE, *arr.* P. J. MANSFIELD

1 I know that my Re-deem-er liv - - eth, And on the
2 I know His pro-mise nev-er fail - - eth, The word He
3 I know my man-sion He pre-par - - eth That where He

1 earth . . . a - gain shall stand;
2 speaks . . . it can - not die;
3 is . . . there I may be;

1 And on the earth a - gain shall stand;
2 The word He speaks it can - not die;
3 That where He is there I may be;

1 I know e - ter - nal life He giv - - eth, That grace and
2 Tho' cru - el death my flesh as - sail - - eth, Yet I shall
3 O won-drous thought! for me He car - - eth, And He at

1 pow'r . . . are in His hand.
2 see . . . Him by - and - bye.
3 last . . . will come for me.

1 That grace and pow'r are in His hand.
2 Yet I shall see Him by - and bye.
3 And He at last shall come for me.

My Redeemer Liveth—*Continued*

REFRAIN

I know, I know . . . that Je - sus liv - eth,
I know, I know that Je - sus liv - eth,

And on the earth . . . , a - gain shall stand;
And on the earth a - gain shall stand;

I know, I know . . . . that life He giv - eth,
I know, I know that life He giv - eth,

That grace and pow'r . . . are in His hand.
That grace and pow'r are in His hand.

920 My Shepherd Leads

MARY S. LEONARD

F. A. CLARK

1 In - to the val - leys of bless - ing My Shep - herd leads; . .
2 In - to the ways that are wea - ry My Shep - herd leads; . .
3 In - to the land all im - mor - tal My Shep - herd leads; . .

1 Peace is my spi - rit pos - sess - ing, My soul He feeds. .
2 Dark tho' the skies be and drear - y, He knows my needs. . .
3 Un - to the glo - ri - ous por - tal My way He heeds. . .

1 Pas - tures so green are a - round me, Wa - ters of life shall flow; . .
2 Hea - vy the load I am bear - ing, Love hath my path - way plann'd; . .
3. Man - sions of heav - en - ly splen - dour Wait me when I shall come, . .

Slowly

con affeto

1 Fair - est of flow - ers sur - round me, Ev - er I on - ward go. . .
2 Trust - ing, I'm still for - ward far - ing, Led by my Shep - herd's hand . .
3 Led by my Shep - herd so ten - der Un - to my Fa - ther's home. .

My Shepherd Leads—*Continued*

REFRAIN *Slowly*

My Shep-herd leads a - long the way, Kept by His care I can - not stray;

Slowly and tenderly

In ten-der love, To realms a - bove, My Shep-herd leads me home. . .

921 The Place of Rest

J. WAKEFIELD MacGILL   J. WAKEFIELD MacGILL

There is a place of rest, . The sweet-est and the best, . The saints have found it

down the a - ges hoar - y; . . Life that is hid in Him . . is

full right to the brim Of love, and peace, and ec-sta-sy, and glo - ry . . .

922 The Other Shore

W. H. CLARK

POWELL G. FITHIAN

1. When we have reached the heav'nly plains, And joined the hosts a - bove,
2. While years e - ter - nal roll a - long, Their ev - er cease - less round,
3. Then we shall see as we are seen, And know as we are known,

1. One song shall swell the rapturous strain, The song of Je - sus' love.
2. Like o - cean's waves shall swell the song, The glad, tri - um - phant sound.
3. And walk the fields of fade - less green, While gaz - ing on the throne.

1. When we have reached the pearl - y gate, And passed its por - tals through,
2. There life's fair riv - er, broad and deep, Re - flects its gold - en ray;
3. And when are tuned the harps of gold To ev - 'ry bliss - ful sound,

1. The saints, with ho - ly joy e - late, Shall tune their harps a - new.
2. Where eyes have nev - er learned to weep, Where joys shall ne'er de - cay.
3. And a - ges long have on - ward rolled, Je - sus shall king be crowned.

CHORUS.

Rejoice, Rejoice, for Christ Himself is near, His wondrous love I feel,

Rejoice, rejoice, is near, I feel,

The Other Shore—*Continued*

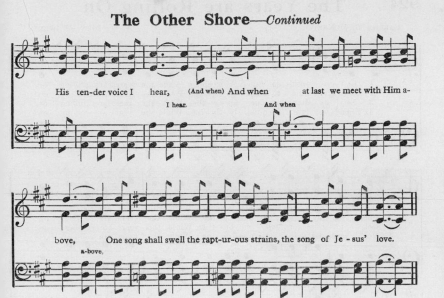

His ten-der voice I hear, (And when) And when at last we meet with Him a-
I hear. And when

bove, One song shall swell the rapt-ur-ous strains, the song of Je - sus' love.
a-bove,

923 ## God Answers Prayer

B. P. HEAD   PONDOLAND 7,7,7,5   ANON

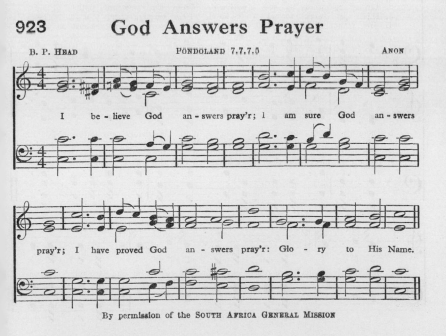

I be - lieve God an - swers pray'r; I am sure God an - swers

pray'r; I have proved God an - swers pray'r: Glo - ry to His Name.

By permission of the SOUTH AFRICA GENERAL MISSION

924 The Years are Rolling On

HARRIET B. McKEEVER

JOHN R. SWENEY

1. In a world so full of weeping, While the years are roll-ing on,
2. There's no time to waste in sighing, While the years are roll-ing on!
3. Let us strengthen one an-o-ther, While the years are roll-ing on!
4. Friends we love are quick-ly fly-ing, While the years are roll-ing on!

1. Chris-tian souls the watch are keeping, While the years are roll-ing on!
2. Time is fly-ing, souls are dy-ing, While the years are roll-ing on!
3. Seek to raise a fall-en bro-ther, While the years are roll-ing on!
4. No more part-ing, no more dy-ing, While the years are roll-ing on!

1. While our jour-ney we pur-sue, With the ha-ven still in view,
2. Lov-ing words a soul may win From the wretched paths of sin;
3. This is work for ev-'ry hand, Till, throughout cre-a-tion's land,
4. In the world be-yond the tomb Sor-row nev-er more may come,

1. There is work for us to do, While the years are roll-ing on!
2. We may bring the wan-d'rers in, While the years are roll-ing on!
3. Arm-ies for the Lord shall stand, While the years are roll-ing on!
4. When we meet in that blest home, While the years are roll-ing on!

CHORUS.

Are roll-ing on! (Are roll-ing on!) Are roll-ing on! (Are roll-ing on!)

The Years are Rolling On—*Continued*

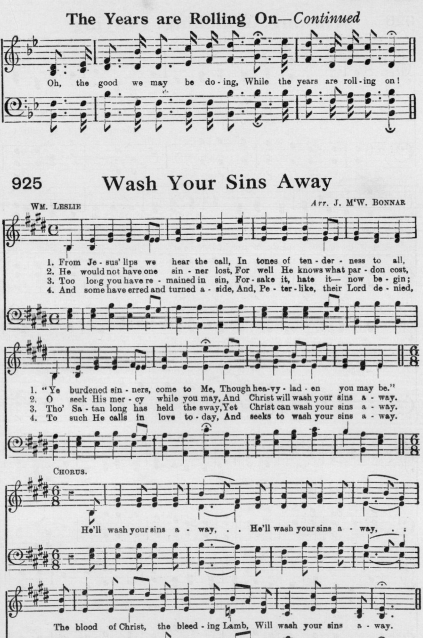

Oh, the good we may be do-ing, While the years are roll-ing on!

925 Wash Your Sins Away

WM. LESLIE

Arr. J. M'W. BONNAR

1. From Je-sus' lips we hear the call, In tones of ten-der-ness to all,
2. He would not have one sin-ner lost, For well He knows what par-don cost,
3. Too long you have re-mained in sin, For-sake it, hate it— now be-gin;
4. And some have erred and turned a-side, And, Pe-ter-like, their Lord de-nied,

1. "Ye burdened sin-ners, come to Me, Though hea-vy-lad-en you may be."
2. O seek His mer-cy while you may, And Christ will wash your sins a-way.
3. Tho' Sa-tan long has held the sway, Yet Christ can wash your sins a-way.
4. To such He calls in love to-day, And seeks to wash your sins a-way.

CHORUS.

He'll wash your sins a-way, . . He'll wash your sins a-way, . .

The blood of Christ, the bleed-ing Lamb, Will wash your sins a-way.

926 Working, Watching, Praying

Frank A. Breck   Powell G. Fithian

1. Go forth, go forth for Je - sus now! Be work - ing! Be watch - ing! The
2. Go forth, go forth to all the world! O stay not! De - lay not! But
3. Go forth, let hearts and hands be strong! Be work - ing! Be watch - ing! O
    Go forth!   Go forth!

1. Lord Him - self will teach you how To watch and pray; 'Tis not for thee thy
2. let love's ban - ner be un-furl'd, And grace be told; O let re-deem - ing
3. stay the might - y pow'r of wrong Where - e'er ye may! Equipped with love and

1. field to choose, No work He gives must thou re - fuse; Be work - ing! Be
2. love be sung, A song of joy on ev - 'ry tongue! Be work - ing! Be
3. strength di - vine, The vic - to - ry is sure - ly thine; Be work - ing! Be

CHORUS.

watch-ing! Be pray - - ing! Go forth to work, to watch and pray! 'Tis Je - sus who
    Go forth!

calls thee; The harvest waits for thee to-day, Go bring some sheaves for God!
Go forth!

927 # The Friend who Cares

FRANK M. DAVIS   JOHN THOMPSON

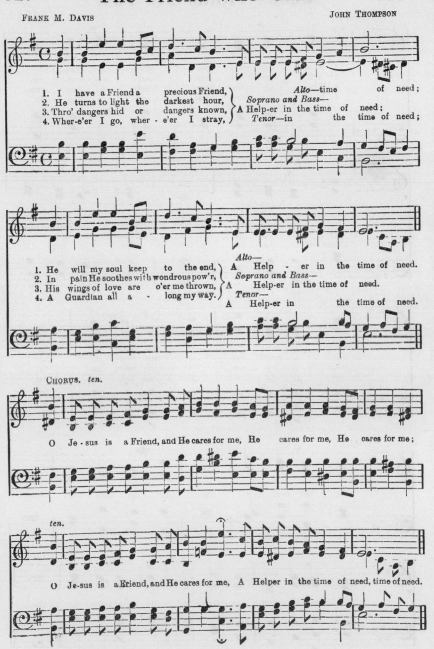

1. I have a Friend a precious Friend,
2. He turns to light the darkest hour,
3. Thro' dangers hid or dangers known,
4. Wher-e'er I go, wher-e'er I stray,

*Alto—*time of need;
Soprano and Bass—
A Help-er in the time of need;
*Tenor—*in the time of need;

1. He will my soul keep to the end,
2. In pain He soothes with wondrous pow'r,
3. His wings of love are o'er me thrown,
4. A Guardian all a - long my way.

Alto—
A Help - er in the time of need.
Soprano and Bass—
A Help-er in the time of need.
Tenor—
A Help-er in the time of need.

CHORUS. *ten.*

O Je - sus is a Friend, and He cares for me, He cares for me, He cares for me;

ten.

O Je-sus is a Friend, and He cares for me, A Helper in the time of need, time of need.

928   # Jesus Holds Me Fast

R. F. BEVERIDGE   R. F. BEVERIDGE

1 When my steps are slow and wea - ry,
2 Oft when storms and clouds sur - round me,
3 When my faint heart dreads the mor - row,
4 When the sum - mons, "Come up high - er,"

1 Shad - ows o'er me cast, And the way seems
2 He has held me fast; With His strong right
3 He will hold me fast: When my spir - it
4 Reach - es me at last, Face to face I'll

1 long and drear - y, Je - sus holds me fast.
2 arm a - round me Je - sus holds me fast.
3 bows in sor - row, Je - sus holds me fast.
4 see my Sa - viour: He has held me fast.

REFRAIN

He will hold me fast Till my jour - ney's past:

Ran - som'd by His pre - cious blood, Je - sus holds me fast.

By permission of the Composer

929   Go Tell It

LAURENE HIGHFIELD

JOHN P. HILLIS

1 If you have heard that our God is love, Go tell it, go tell it;
2 If you can sing the dear Saviour's praise, Go sing it, go sing it;
3 If you can turn o-ther hearts to God, Go do it, go do it;

Go tell it, go tell it;
Go sing it, go sing it;
Go do it, go do it;

1 That He is reign-ing in hea-ven a-bove, Go tell of His love to-day...
2 Un-to Him glad-ly your voi-ces now raise, Go sing of His love to-day...
3 Bid them to fol-low where Je-sus has trod, Go do what you can to-day...

REFRAIN

Tell of a Sa-viour so kind and true, Tell of His love and His mer-cy too,

Tell of the good He would have us do, Go tell of His love to-day...

930   Onward! Christian Soldiers

S. BARING-GOULD   ADAM GEIBEL
Unison

1 On-ward! Chris-tian sol - diers, march-ing as to war,
2 At the Name of Je - sus Sa - tan's host doth flee;
3 Like a might - y arm - y moves the Church of God:
4 Crowns and thrones may per - ish, king - doms rise and wane;
5 On-ward, then, ye peo - ple! join our hap - py throng;

1 Look-ing un - to Je - sus who is gone be - fore;
2 On then, Christ-ian sol - diers, on to vic - tor - y!
3 Bro-thers, we are tread - ing where the saints have trod;
4 But the Church of Je - sus con - stant will re - main;
5 Blend with ours your voic - es in the tri - umph song:

1 Christ, the Roy - al Mas - ter, leads a - gainst the foe;
2 Hell's found-a - tions quiv - er at the shout of praise:
3 We are not di - vid - ed, all one bo - dy we,
4 Gates of hell can nev - er 'gainst that Church pre - vail;
5 'Glo - ry, praise, and hon - our un - to Christ the King!'

Onward! Christian Soldiers—*Continued*

1 For-ward in - to bat - tle, see! His ban - ners go. . .
2 Bro-thers, lift your voic - es, loud your an - thems raise. . .
3 One in hope and doc - trine, one in cha - ri - ty. . .
4 We have Christ's own pro - mise, and that can - not fail. . .
5 This, thro' count-less a - ges, men and an - gels sing. . .

REFRAIN

On - - ward! Chris - tian sol - diers, march - ing
On - ward! on - ward!

as to war, . . Look - ing un - to

Je sus who is gone be - fore.

Words by permission of J. CURWEN & SONS LTD.

931

Hark, Hark! My Soul!

F. W. Faber

Adam Geibel

1 Hark, hark! my soul! .. an - gel - ic songs are swell - ing
2 On - ward we go, .. for still we hear them sing - ing,
3 Rest comes at length, .. though life be long and drea - ry,
4 An - gels, sing on! your faith - ful watch - es keep - ing;

1 O'er earth's green fields .. and o - cean's wave - beat shore; ..
2 Come, wea - ry souls! .. for Je - sus bids you come; ..
3 The day must dawn, .. and dark - some night be past; ..
4 Sing us sweet frag - ments of the songs a - bove; ..

1 How sweet the truth .. those bless - ed strains are tell - ing
2 And through the dark, .. its e - choes sweet - ly ring - ing,
3 Faith's jour - ney ends .., in wel - come to the wea - ry,
4 Till morn - ing's joy .. shall end the night of weep - ing,

1 Of that new life when sin shall be no more. ..
2 The mu - sic of the Gos - pel leads us home. ..
3 And heav'n, the heart's true home, will come at last,
4 And life's long sha - dows break in cloud - less love. ..

Hark, Hark! My Soul!—*Continued*

REFRAIN

Male Voices in Unison. Altos to join Male Voices to last two verses

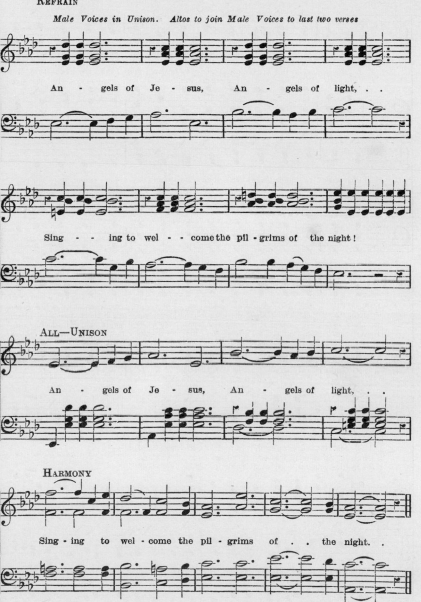

An - gels of Je - sus, An - gels of light, . .

Sing - - ing to wel - - come the pil - grims of the night!

ALL—UNISON

An - gels of Je - sus, An - gels of light, . .

HARMONY

Sing - ing to wel - come the pil - grims of . . the night. .

932 The New Glory Song

Samuel D. Smith   Samuel D. Smith

1. There's a ci - ty of such beau - ty Mor - tal eye hath nev - er seen,
2. There the ran - somed dwell e - ter - nal, Out of tri - bu - la - tion come,
3. Would you see this heaven-ly ci - ty? Would you drink its rap - ture in?
4. "Un - to Him that o - ver - com - eth," Is the pro - mise full of love;

1. Filled with ra-diance bright - er than the noon - day sun (noon - day sun).
2. Undreamed the ran - mu - sic fills the soul thro' end - less day (end - less day).
3. There's a place pre - pared for all who will be - lieve (will be - lieve).
4. Fi - ery tri - al in the fur - nace proves the gold (proves the gold).

1. Streets of gold and streams of crys - tal, Trees of ev - er - liv - ing green,
2. Hope so dear and as - pi - ra - tions Down on earth there free - ly bloom,
3. Je - sus ear - nest - ly in - vites you, He will guide you, cleanse your sin,
4. Aft - er con - quest in life's con - flict Faith sus - tained by grace a - bove,

CHORUS.

1. Je - sus reigns ex - alt - ed One, in glo - ry land.
2. Life's real trea-sures ne'er de - cay in glo - ry land.
3. And a man-sion free - ly give in glo - ry land.
4. Comes the vic - tor's joy un - told in glo - ry land.

} Then crowns of glo - ry

palms of vic - to - ry, Harps of gold tri - umphant anthems blend, Ho - san-nahs ringing,

The New Glory Song—*Continued*

prais - es sing-ing, We shall come, our tro-phies bring-ing, in that glo - ry land.

933 Abundance of Rain

WM. LESLIE   OLD MELODY

1 Our ser-vice for God has been bar-ren and dry, And bar-ren it still shall re-main,
2 The pro-phets of Pride and the priests of De - sire Are call-ing and cut-ting in vain;
3 The al-tars of God that our sins have de-stroy'd We must build with the things that remain;
4 To each may the faith of E - li - jah be giv'n, To pray till the an-swer we gain,

1 Un - til we are blest with the fire from on high, And sound of a - bun-dance of rain. . .
2 The halt-ing are wait-ing for wit-ness of fire, And sound of a - bun-dance of rain. . .
3 And prove to the world that no pro-mise is void By sound of a - bun-dance of rain. . .
4 And sin-ners ac-know-ledge the wit-ness of heav'n, And sound of a - bun-dance of rain. . .

REFRAIN

There's sound of a - bun-dance of rain, . . There's sound of a - bun-dance of rain; . .

To God we draw near, and by faith we can hear The sound of a - bun-dance of rain. . .

934 Bear the Message

FRANK A. BRECK   *Unison.*   SAMUEL W. BEAZLEY

1. Go tell to souls be-night-ed, of the Lord who came, Speak His name—
2. In lands be-yond the roll-ing of the o-cean foam, Wan-d'rers roam—
3. Go bear the joy-ful mes-sage ev-'ry-where you may, Work and pray—

1. love pro-claim; Go tell the gos-pel sto-ry, that the lost may know,
2. bring them home; O lead them to the Sa-viour and His par-d'ning love—
3. day by day; Lift bur-dens from the wea-ry, cheer the griev-ing heart—

1. Bring sal-va-tion near. O bid them come re-pent-ing, bid them
2. He will give them rest. And they who long have wandered soon will
3. Walk where Je-sus trod. O be a beam of sun-shine that re-

1. come to-day, Help them say, "I o-bey." Bear the bless-ed mes-sage,
2. learn to see How to be tru-ly free, Liv-ing for the king-dom
3. flects His light, Pure and bright, in the night, Help-ing ma-ny sin-ners

Rit. ad lib. . . . . . . CHORUS. *Harmony.*

1. has-ten now to go, Go with love sin-cere. } Press on-ward
2. of the land a-bove, Safe and glad and blest.
3. choose the "bet-ter part" In the love of God. ev-er on-ward

Bear the Message—*Continued*

ere the night is fall - ing, On - ward, hear the Sa-viour call - ing,
Ev - er on - ward,

Hear Him gent - ly, sweet - ly say, "I will be with thee al - way,"

Peace and joy to bring, Press on - ward, nev - er dan - ger fear-ing,
ev - er on - ward,

On - ward, bright-est hope is near - ing, Dark-ness shall no more en-thrall,
Ev - er on - ward,

Christ our light shall shine for all, He shall reign our King.

935 Sing Me the Song

J. Wakefield MacGill

J. Bland

1 Sing me the song that tells of Je - sus, That is the song which has music's sweet-est tone, Com - ing from heav - en like per - fume on breez-es Fills all my soul with the joy that is His own: Bears me in spi - rit to bright realms of glo - ry, Holds me en-rap - tur'd with vi - sions

2 This song has wings like ea - gle's pin - ions, Oft has it borne me to God's own par - a - dise, There I have sung with an - gels in chor-us, Knows not my soul of a trance of joy like this: But when re-turn - ing to life's din and bat - tle, Spells still are o'er me and sounds are

3 Wor - thy the Lamb Who died to save us, Wor - thy the Lamb, let it sound thro' earth and sky, 'Wor - thy the Lamb' sing the an - gels in chor-us, 'Wor - thy the Lamb' our re - demp-tion draw-eth nigh: Wor - thy of hon - our from high - est arch-an - gels, Wor - thy of glo - ry the un - i -

Sing Me the Song—*Continued*

1 of de - light;   Gives me to hear what the saint dar'd not
2 in mine ear,   Tak - ing the glare from the earth - ly and
3 verse a - round,   Wor - thy of ma - jes - ty, pow'r, a - dor -

1 ut - ter   When he re-turn'd to the sha - dow and the night.
2 fleet - ing,   Fill - ing my life with . . what the an - gels hear.
3 a - tion,   Worth - y the Lamb, the . . lov'd and lost are found.

REFRAIN

Sing me the song that tells of Je - sus, Sing to this heart

and bid its throb-bing cease, Sing me that song for it chas - tens my

spi - rit, Calm - ing my soul with its mag - ic spell of peace.

936 A Thousand Tongues

CHARLES WESLEY   LYNGHAM 8.6.6. 8.6.6.6.   T. JARMAN

1 O for a thou — sand tongues to sing My great Re-deem-er's praise! My great — Re - deem - er's praise! The glo - ries of — my God — and King,

2 My gra - cious Mas — ter and my God As - sist me to pro - claim, As - sist — me to pro - claim And spread through all — the earth a - broad

3 Je - sus! the Name that charms our fears, That bids our sor - rows cease, That bids — our sor - rows cease; 'Tis mu - sic in — the sin - ner's ears,

4 He breaks the pow'r — of can - cell'd sin, He sets the pris - 'ner free, He sets — the pris - 'ner free; His blood can make — the foul - est clean,

A Thousand Tongues—*Continued*

The tune EXPECTATION is on the following pages

936 A Thousand Tongues

CHARLES WESLEY EXPECTATION 8.6.8.8. 6.6.6. S. L. ARMITAGE

1 O for a thou - sand tongues to sing
2 My gra - cious Mas - ter and my God
3 Je - sus! the Name that charms our fears,
4 He breaks the pow'r of can - cell'd sin,

1 My great Re - deem - er's praise! The
2 As - sist me to pro - claim, And
3 That bids our sor - rows cease, 'Tis
4 He sets the pris - 'ner free, His

1 glo - ries of my God and King,
2 spread through all the earth a - broad,
3 mu - sic in the sin - ner's ears,
4 blood can make the foul - est clean,

1 The glo - ries of my God and King,
2 And spread through all the earth a - broad
3 'Tis mu - sic in the sin - ner's ears,
4 His blood can make the foul - est clean,

A Thousand Tongues—*Continued*

The tune LYNGHAM is on the preceding pages

937 Little Raindrops

LAURA M. WINSLOW   FOR CHILDREN'S CHOIRS   J. S. FEARIS

1 When God sees the flow- ers   Need His ten-der care,   He sends lit-tle   rain-drops
2 We are lit-tle   rain-drops,   God has sent us   here   From His fount of   bless- ing
3 Ev-'ry drop re- flect- ing   God's most ten-der   love   Helps to light the   path- way
4 Tho' we are but   rain-drops   We are glad to   know   That we have a   mis- sion

REFRAIN

1 With a bless-ing   there.
2 Bring-ing hope and   cheer.
3 To the home a - bove.
4 In this world be - low.

Bus-y lit-tle   rain-drops Let us be to-day

As we strive to scat-ter bless-ings All a-long the   way: Help-ful lit-tle

rain-drops Will we be to- day,   Do-ing work for   Je-sus In a   rain-drop's way.

938   Hallelujah! Grace is Free

James Fraser   R. F. Beveridge

1 I love to think of Christ, my King, Who did sal - va - tion free-ly bring;
2 O won-drous is the crim - son flood! O pre-cious is the cleans-ing blood!
3 What great-er love could ev - er be To die up - on the cru - el tree,
4 And when I reach that sil - ver strand, And join that ho - ly, hap-py band,

1 So while I live I mean to sing, Hal - le - lu - jah! grace is free.
2 My Je - sus as my sure - ty stood, Hal - le - lu - jah! grace is free.
3 And ran-som such a wretch as me? Hal - le - lu - jah! grace is free,
4 This song I'll sing in that bright land, Hal - le - lu - jah! grace is free.

REFRAIN

O Hal - le - lu - jah! grace is free, This my song shall ev - er be:

Je - sus died to set me free, Hal - le - lu - jah! grace is free.

By permission of R. F. Beveridge

939

All Will be Well

MARY PETERS   SOUTHGATE 8.4.8.4.8.8.8.4   T. B. SOUTHGATE

1 Thro' the love of God our Sa - viour, All will be well;
2 Tho' we pass thro' tri - bu - la - tion, All will be well;
3 We ex - pect a bright to - mor - row; All will be well;

1 Free and change-less is His fa - vour, All, all is well:
2 Ours is such a full sal - va - tion, All, all is well:
3 Faith can sing thro' days of sor - row, All, all is well:

1 Pre - cious is the blood that heal'd us; Per - fect is the grace that
2 Hap - py still in God con - fid - ing; Fruit - ful if in Christ a -
3 On our Fa - ther's love re - ly - ing, Je - sus ev - 'ry need sup -

1 seal'd us; Strong the hand stretch'd forth to shield us, All must be well.
2 bid - ing; Ho - ly, thro' the Spi - rit's guid - ing; All must be well.
3 ply - ing, Or in liv - ing or in dy - ing, All must be well.

TUNE AR HYD Y NOS is on next page

939   All Will be Well

MARY PETERS   AR HYD Y NOS   8.4. 8.4. 8.8. 8.4   WELSH AIR

1 Thro' the love of God our Sa - viour, All will be well;
2 Though we pass thro' tri - bu - la - tion, All will be well;
3 We ex - pect a bright to - mor - row; All will be well;

1 Free and change-less is His fa - vour, All, all is well:
2 Ours is such a full sal - va - tion, All, all is well:
3 Faith can sing thro' days of sor - row, All, all is well:

1 Pre - cious is the blood that heal'd us! Per - fect is the grace that seal'd us;
2 Hap - py still in God con - fid - ing; Fruit-ful if in Christ a - bid - ding;
3 On our Fa-ther's love re - ly - ing, Je - sus ev - 'ry need sup - ply - ing,

1 Strong the hand stretch'd forth to shield us, All must be well.
2 Ho - ly, thro' the spi - rit's guid - ing; All must be well.
3 Or in liv - ing or in dy - ing, All must be well.

Tune SOUTHGATE is on previous page

940   Good Night!

KATE SACHS   GOOD-NIGHT 10.10.10.6.   CHARLES H. GABRIEL

1. The night draws near, our day of praise is o'er, Our songs, our
2. The day of life has oft times dark-en'd been, Fierce storms have
3. The task will soon be o'er, how-ev-er hard, The lone-ly
4. Go forth in ear-nest, stead-fast lives to prove Thy teach-ing
5. Good night! The long-est day must have an end, The hap-piest

1. hearts, up-lift-ed rise once more, As at Thy feet, O
2. raged, with fit-ful lights be-tween; But still at ev-en,
3. strug-gle, watch'd still by the Lord; With Him is thine ex-
4. true: deep root-ed in His love, Fruits bud-ding here, to
5. hours will to their clos-ing tend, Be-yond, a-far, th' e-

1. Lord! our off-'rings pour, And then, Good night, Good night!
2. o'er the chang-ing scene, Has come, sweet word, Good night!
3. ceed-ing great re-ward— Till then, Good night, Good night!
4. rip-en soon a-bove, Where none shall say: Good night!
5. ter-nal day we'll spend— Good night, Good night, Good night!

941   Never say, Good-bye!

E. W. CHAPMAN   J. H. TENNEY

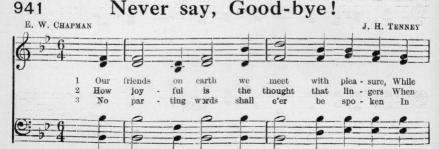

1. Our friends on earth we meet with plea-sure, While
2. How joy-ful is the thought that lin-gers When
3. No par-ting words shall e'er be spo-ken In

Never Say, Good-bye!—*Continued*

1 swift the mo - ments fly; . Yet ev - er comes the
2 lov'd ones cross death's sea, . That when our la - bours
3 that bright land of flow'rs, . But songs of joy and

1 thought of sad - ness That we must say, Good - bye. . .
2 here are end - ed, With them we'll ev - er be. . .
3 peace and glad - ness Shall ev - er - more be ours. . .

REFRAIN

We'll ne - ver say, Good - bye, in heav'n, We'll ne - ver say, Good - bye, . .

Good-bye,

For in that land of joy and song We'll ne - ver say Good - bye: . .

Softly

For in that land of joy and song We'll ne - ver say, Good - bye. . .

942

God be with You

Jeremiah E. Rankin   Wm. G. Tomer

1 God be with you till we meet again! By His coun-sels guide, up-
2 God be with you till we meet again! 'Neath His wings pro-tect-ing
3 God be with you till we meet again! When life's per-ils thick con-
4 God be with you till we meet again! Keep love's ban-ner float-ing

1 hold you, With His sheep se-cure-ly fold you; God be
2 hide you, Dai-ly man-na still pro-vide you: God be
3 found you, Put His arms un-fail-ing round you; God be
4 o'er you, Smite death's threat'ning wave be-fore you; God be

REFRAIN

1-4 with you till we meet a-gain! Till we meet!............... Till we

Till we meet! Till we

meet! Till we meet at Je-sus' feet; Till we

meet a-gain! Till we meet!

God be with You—*Continued*

meet! .... Till we meet! God be with you till we meet a-gain!

Till we meet! Till we meet a-gain!

J. E. RANKIN   RANDOLPH 9.8. 9.8   RALPH VAUGHAN WILLIAMS

1 God be with you till we meet a-gain, By His
2 God be with you till we meet a-gain, 'Neath His
3 God be with you till we meet a-gain, When life's
4 God be with you till we meet a-gain, Keep love's
5 Till we meet, ... till we meet a-gain, Till we

1 coun-sels guide, up-hold you, With His sheep se-cure-ly
2 wings pro-tect-ing hide you, Dai-ly man-na still pro-
3 per-ils thick con-found you, Put His arms un-fail-ing
4 ban-ner float-ing o'er you, Smite death's threat'ning wave be-
5 meet at Je-sus' feet; ..... Till we meet, ... till we

1 fold you: God be with you till we meet a-gain!
2 vide you: God be with you till we meet a-gain!
3 round you: God be with you till we meet a-gain!
4 fore you: God be with you till we meet a-gain!
5 meet: ..... God be with you till we meet a-gain!

By permission of the OXFORD UNIVERSITY PRESS

943

Gloria Patri

CHARLES MEINEKE

Glo - ry be to the Fa - ther, and to the Son, and to
the Ho - ly Ghost; As it was in the be - gin - ning, is
now, and ev - er shall be, world with-out end. A - men, A - men.

R. WOODWARD

Glory be to the Father, | and to the | Son, and | to the
Ho - ly | Ghost; As it was in the beginning, is now, and |

Gloria Patri—*Continued*

ev - er | shall be, World without | end, — A - men.

944 Father, in High Heaven

GEORGE RAWSON   EVENING HYMN 8.8.7.8.8.7   W. JACKSON

1 Fa - ther, in high hea - ven dwell-ing, May our ev' - 'ning
2 This day's sins, O par - don, Sa-viour! E - vil thoughts, per -
3 From en - tice - ments of the de - vil, From the might of
4 Whilst the night dews are dis - till-ing Ho - ly Ghost, each

1 song be tell - ing Of Thy mer - cy large and free;
2 verse be - hav-iour, En - vy, pride, and van - i - ty;
3 spi - rits e - vil, Be our shield and pan - o - ply;
4 heart be fill - ing with Thine own se - ren - i - ty;

1 Through the day Thy love hath fed us, Through the day Thy
2 From the world, the flesh, de - li - ver, Save us now, and
3 Let Thy pow'r this night de - fend us, And a heav'n - ly
4 Soft - ly let our eyes be clos - ing, Lov - ing souls on

1 care hath led us, With di - vin - est char - i - ty.
2 save us e - ver, O Thou Lamb of Cal - va - ry!
3 peace at - tend us, And an - gel - ic com - pan - y.
4 Thee re - pos - ing, Ev - er bless - ed Trin - i - ty.

945 Lord, Dismiss Us

JOHN FAWCETT   DISMISSAL 8.7.8.7.8.7   W. L. VINER

1 Lord, dis - miss us with Thy bless-ing, Fill our hearts with joy and peace ;
2 Thanks we give, and a - dor - a - tion, For Thy Gos-pel's joy - ful sound ;
3 So when-e'er the sig - nal's giv - en, Us from earth to call a - way,

1 Let us each, Thy love poss-ess-ing Tri - umph in re-deem-ing grace :
2 May the fruits of Thy sal - va - tion In our hearts and lives a-bound ;
3 Borne on an-gels' wings to hea - ven, Glad the sum-mons to o - bey,

1 O re - fresh us, O re - fresh us, Trav-'lling through this wil - der - ness !
2 May Thy pre-sence, may Thy pre-sence With us ev - er - more be found !
3 We shall sure - ly, we shall sure - ly Reign with Christ in end-less day.

JOHN FAWCETT   REDEMPTION 8.7.8.7.8.7   C. F. GOUNOD

1 Lord, dis - miss us with Thy bless-ing, Fill our hearts with joy and peace ;
2 Thanks we give, and a - dor - a - tion, For Thy Gos-pel's joy - ful sound ;
3 So when-e'er the sig - nal's giv - en, Us from earth to call a - way,

Lord, Dismiss Us—*Continued*

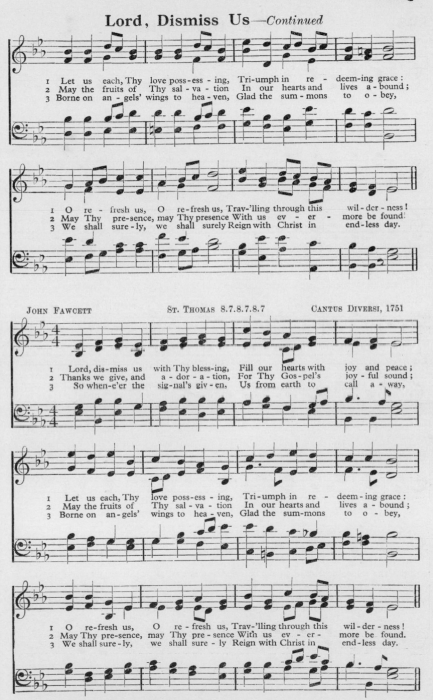

1 Let us each, Thy love poss-ess - ing, Tri-umph in re - deem-ing grace :
2 May the fruits of Thy sal-va - tion In our hearts and lives a-bound ;
3 Borne on an - gels' wings to hea - ven, Glad the sum - mons to o - bey,

1 O re - fresh us, O re-fresh us, Trav-'lling through this wil - der - ness !
2 May Thy pre-sence, may Thy presence With us ev - er - more be found!
3 We shall sure - ly, we shall surely Reign with Christ in end-less day.

JOHN FAWCETT   ST. THOMAS 8.7.8.7.8.7   CANTUS DIVERSI, 1751

1 Lord, dis-miss us with Thy bless-ing, Fill our hearts with joy and peace ;
2 Thanks we give, and a - dor - a-tion, For Thy Gos-pel's joy - ful sound ;
3 So when-e'er the sig-nal's giv - en, Us from earth to call a - way,

1 Let us each, Thy love poss-ess - ing, Tri-umph in re - deem-ing grace :
2 May the fruits of Thy sal - va - tion In our hearts and lives a-bound ;
3 Borne on an-gels' wings to hea - ven, Glad the sum-mons to o - bey,

1 O re-fresh us, O re - fresh us, Trav-'lling through this wil - der - ness !
2 May Thy pre-sence, may Thy pre - sence With us ev - er - more be found.
3 We shall sure - ly, we shall sure - ly Reign with Christ in end-less day.

946

The Tie that Binds

JOHN FAWCETT

DENNIS S.M.

H. G. NAGELI

1 Blest be the tie that binds Our hearts in Chris - tian love;
2 Be - fore our Fa - ther's throne, We pour our ar - dent pray'rs;
3 We share our mu - tual woes; Our mu - tual bur - dens bear;
4 When we a - sun - der part, It gives us in - ward pain;

1 The fel - low - ship of kin - dred minds Is like to that a - bove.
2 Our fears, our hopes, our aims are one— Our com - forts and our cares.
3 And oft - en for each oth - er flows The sym - pa - thiz - ing tear.
4 But we shall still be join'd in heart, And hope to meet a - gain.

JOHN FAWCETT

DONCASTER S.M.

SAMUEL WESLEY

1 Blest be the tie that binds Our hearts in Chris - tian love;
2 Be - fore our Fa - ther's throne, We pour our ar - dent pray'rs;
3 We share our mu - tual woes; Our mu - tual bur - dens bear;
4 When we a - sun - der part, It gives us in - ward pain;

1 The fel - low - ship of kin - dred minds Is like to that a - bove.
2 Our fears, our hopes, our aims are one— Our com - forts and our cares.
3 And oft - en for each oth - er flows The sym - pa - thiz - ing tear.
4 But we shall still be join'd in heart, And hope to meet a - gain.

Tune GEORGE SQUARE is on next page

946 The Tie that Binds

JOHN FAWCETT   GEORGE SQUARE S.M.D.   H. E. DIBDIN

1 Blest be the tie that binds Our hearts in Christian love,
2 We share our mutual woes; Our mutual burdens bear;

1 The fellowship of kindred minds Is like to that above.
2 And often for each other flows The sympathizing tear.

1 Before the Father's throne, We pour our ardent pray'rs;
2 When we asunder part, It gives us inward pain;

1 Our fears, our hopes, our aims are one, Our comforts, and our cares.
2 But we shall still be joined in heart, And hope to meet again.

Tunes DENNIS and DONCASTER are on previous page

947 Sun of My Soul

JOHN KEBLE   HURSLEY L.M.   *Katholisches Gesangbuch*

1 Sun of my soul. Thou Sa - viour dear,
2 When the soft dews of kind - ly sleep
3 A - bide with me from morn till eve,
4 If some poor wand - 'ring child of Thine
5 Watch by the sick, en - rich the poor
6 Come near and bless us when we wake.

1 It is not night .. if Thou .. be near;
2 My wear - ied eye - lids gent - ly steep,
2 For with - out Thee .. I can - not live:
4 Have spurn'd to - day .. the voice .. di - vine,
5 With bless - ings from .. Thy bound - less store,
6 Ere through the world .. out way .. we take;

1 O may no earth - born cloud a - rise
2 Be my last thought, how sweet to rest
3 A - bide with me .. when night is nigh,
4 Now, Lord, the gra - cious work be - gin;
5 Be ev - 'ry mour - ner's sleep to - night,
6 Till, in the o - cean of Thy love,

1 To hide Thee from .. Thy ser - vant's eyes!
2 For ev - er on .. my Sa - viour's breast.
3 For with - out Thee .. I dare .. not die.
4 Let him no more .. lie down .. in sin.
5 Like in - fant's slum .. bers, pure .. and light.
6 We lose our - selves .. in heav'n a - bove.

The tunes BIRLING, ABENDS, and OTTERBURN are on the following pages

947 **Sun of My Soul**

JOHN KEBLE   BIRLING L.M.   From a 19th Century MS.

1 Sun of my soul, Thou Saviour dear,
2 When the soft dews of kindly sleep
3 Abide with me from morn till eve,
4 If some poor wand'ring child of Thine
5 Watch by the sick, enrich the poor
6 Come near and bless us when we wake.

1 It is not night if Thou be near;
2 My wearied eyelids gently steep,
3 For without Thee I cannot live:
4 Have spurn'd today the voice divine,
5 With blessings from Thy boundless store,
6 Ere through the world our way we take;

1 O may no earthborn cloud arise
2 Be my last thought, how sweet to rest
3 Abide with me when night is nigh;
4 Now, Lord, the gracious work begin;
5 Be ev'ry mourner's sleep tonight,
6 Till, in the ocean of Thy love,

1 To hide Thee from Thy servant's eyes!
2 For ever on my Saviour's breast.
3 For without Thee I dare not die.
4 Let him no more lie down in sin.
5 Like infant's slumbers, pure and light.
6 We lose ourselves in heav'n above.

Music by permission of the OXFORD UNIVERSITY PRESS
The tune HURSLEY precedes, and the tunes ABENDS and OTTERBURN follow this one

947 Sun of My Soul

JOHN KEBLE   ABENDS L.M.   H. S. OAKELEY

1 Sun of my soul, Thou Saviour dear,
2 When the soft dews of kindly sleep
3 A - bide with me from morn till eve,
4 If some poor wand - 'ring child of Thine
5 Watch by the sick, en - rich the poor
6 Come near and bless us when we wake,

1 It is not night if Thou be near;
2 My wear - ied eye - lids gent - ly steep,
3 For with - out Thee I can - not live:
4 Have spurn'd to - day the voice di - vine,
5 With bless - ings from Thy bound - less store;
6 Ere through the world our way we take;

1 O may no earth - born cloud a - rise
2 Be my last thought, how sweet to rest
3 A - bide with me when night is nigh,
4 Now, Lord, the gra - cious work be - gin;
5 Be ev - 'ry mourn - er's sleep to - night,
6 Till, in the o - cean of Thy love,

1 To hide Thee from Thy ser - vant's eyes!
2 For ev - er on my Sa - viour's breast.
3 For with - out Thee I dare not die.
4 Let him no more lie down in sin.
5 Like in - fant's slum - bers, pure and light.
6 We lose our - selves in heav'n a - bove.

The tunes HURSLEY and BIRLING precede, and OTTERBOURNE follows this one

947 Sun of My Soul

JOHN KEBLE   OTTERBOURNE L.M.   J. TURLE, *from* HAYDN

1. Sun of my soul, Thou Saviour dear,
It is not night if Thou be near;
O may no earth-born cloud arise
To hide Thee from Thy servant's eyes!

2. When the soft dews of kindly sleep
My wearied eyelids gently steep,
Be my last thought, how sweet to rest
For ever on my Saviour's breast.

3. Abide with me from morn till eve,
For without Thee I cannot live;
Abide with me when night is nigh,
For without Thee I dare not die.

4. If some poor wand'ring child of Thine
Have spurn'd to-day the voice divine,
Now, Lord, the gracious work begin;
Let him no more lie down in sin.

5. Watch by the sick, enrich the poor
With blessings from Thy boundless store;
Be ev'ry mourner's sleep to-night,
Like infant's slumbers, pure and light.

6. Come near and bless us when we wake,
Ere through the world our way we take;
Till, in the ocean of Thy love,
We lose ourselves in heav'n above.

The tunes BIRLING, HURSLEY, and ABENDS are on the previous pages

948

Abide with Me

H. F. LYTE   EVENTIDE 10.10.10.10   W. H. MONK

1 A - bide with me! fast falls the e - ven - tide;
2 I need Thy pre - sence ev - 'ry pass - ing hour;
3 Swift to its close ebbs out life's lit - tle day;
4 I fear no foe with Thee at hand to bless;

1 The dark - ness deep - ens; Lord, with me a - bide;
2 What but Thy grace can foil the temp - ter's pow'r?
3 Earth's joys grow dim, its glo - ries pass a - way
4 Ills have no weight, and tears no bit - ter - ness

1 When o - ther help - ers fail, and com - forts flee,
2 Who like Thy - self my guide and stay can be?
3 Change and de - cay in all a - round I see;
4 Where is death's sting? where, grave, thy vic - tor - y?

1 Help of the help - less, O a - bide with me!
2 Thro' cloud and sun - shine, O a - bide with me!
3 O Thou, who chang - est not, a - bide with me!
4 I tri - umph still if Thou a - bide with me!

The tune EVENTIDE (Pope) is on the following page

948 Abide with Me

H. F. LYTE   EVENTIDE 10.10.10.10.   G. A. POPE

1 A - bide with me! fast falls the e - ven - tide;
2 I need Thy pre - sence ev - 'ry pass - ing hour;
3 Swift to its close ebbs out life's lit - tle day;
4 I fear no foe with Thee at hand to bless;

1 The dark - ness deep - ens; Lord, with me a - bide;
2 What but Thy grace can foil the temp - ter's power?
3 Earth's joys grow dim, its glo - ries pass a - way;
4 Ills have no weight, and tears no bit - ter - ness:

1 When o - ther help - ers fail, and com - forts flee,
2 Who like Thy - self my guide and stay can be?
3 Change and de - cay in all a - round I see:
4 Where is death's sting? where, grave, thy vic - tor - y?

1 Help of the help - less, O a - bide with me!
2 Thro' cloud and sun - shine, O a - bide with me!
3 O Thou who chang - est not, a - bide with me!
4 I tri - umph still if Thou a - bide with me!

Music by permission of A. W. FORD & CO., LTD.
The usual tune EVENTIDE (Monk) is on the preceding page

949 The Day Thou Gavest

JOHN ELLERTON   ST. CLEMENT 9.8.9.8   C. C. SCHOLEFIELD

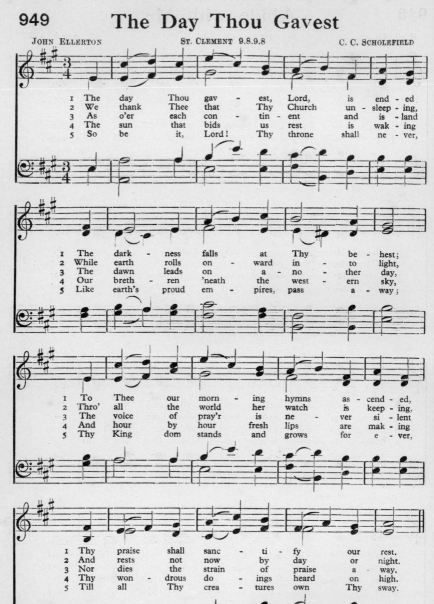

1 The day Thou gav - est, Lord, is end - ed.
2 We thank Thee that Thy Church un - sleep - ing,
3 As o'er each con - tin - ent and is - land
4 The sun that bids us rest is wak - ing,
5 So be it, Lord! Thy throne shall ne - ver,

1 The dark - ness falls at Thy be - hest;
2 While earth rolls on - ward in - to light,
3 The dawn leads on a - no - ther day,
4 Our breth - ren 'neath the west - ern sky,
5 Like earth's proud em - pires, pass a - way;

1 To Thee our morn - ing hymns as - cend - ed,
2 Thro' all the world her watch is keep - ing,
3 The voice of pray'r is ne - ver si - lent,
4 And hour by hour fresh lips are mak - ing
5 Thy King - dom stands and grows for e - ver,

1 Thy praise shall sanc - ti - fy our rest.
2 And rests not now by day or night.
3 Nor dies the strain of praise a - way.
4 Thy won - drous do - ings heard on high.
5 Till all Thy crea - tures own Thy sway.

The tune RADFORD is on the following page

949   The Day Thou Gavest

JOHN ELLERTON   RADFORD 9.8.9.8   S. S. WESLEY

1. The day Thou gavest, Lord, is ended;
   The darkness falls at Thy behest;
   To Thee our morning hymns ascended,
   Thy praise shall sanctify our rest.

2. We thank Thee that Thy Church unsleeping,
   While earth rolls onward into light,
   Thro' all the world her watch is keeping,
   And rests not now by day or night.

3. As o'er each continent and island
   The dawn leads on another day,
   The voice of pray'r is never silent,
   Nor dies the strain of praise away.

4. The sun that bids us rest is waking
   Our brethren 'neath the western sky,
   And hour by hour fresh lips are making
   Thy wondrous doings heard on high.

5. So be it, Lord! Thy throne shall never,
   Like earth's proud empires, pass away;
   Thy Kingdom stands and grows for ever,
   Till all Thy creatures own Thy sway.

Tune ST. CLEMENT is on the previous page

950 Grant Us Thy Peace

JOHN ELLERTON   ELLERS 10.10.10.10   E. J. HOPKINS

1 Sa - viour, a - gain to Thy dear Name we raise, With one ac-
2 Grant us Thy peace up - on our home-ward way; With Thee be-
3 Grant us Thy peace, Lord, thro' the com - ing night, Turn Thou for
4 Grant us Thy peace through - out our earth - ly life, Our balm in

1 cord our part - ing hymn of praise; We stand to bless Thee
2 gan, with Thee shall end the day; Guard Thou the lips from
3 us its dark - ness in - to light; From harm and dan - ger
4 sor - row and our stay in strife; Then, when Thy voice shall

1 ere our wor-ship cease, Then, low - ly kneel - ing, wait Thy word of peace.
2 sin, the hearts from shame, That in this house have called up - on Thy Name.
3 keep Thy chil-dren free, For dark and light are both a - like to Thee.
4 bid our con-flict cease, Call us, O Lord, to Thine e - ter - nal peace.

JOHN ELLERTON   AUTUMN 10.10.10.10   FRANCIS DUCKWORTH

1 Sa - viour, a - gain to Thy dear Name we raise, With one ac-
2 Grant us Thy peace up - on our home-ward way; With Thee be-
3 Grant us Thy peace, Lord, thro' the com - ing night, Turn Thou for
4 Grant us Thy peace through-out our earth - ly life, Our balm in

Grant Us Thy Peace—*Continued*

1 cord our part-ing hymn of praise; We stand to bless Thee
2 gan, with Thee shall end the day; Guard Thou the lips from
3 us its dark-ness in-to light; From harm and dan-ger
4 sor-row and our stay in strife; Then, when Thy voice shall

1 ere our wor-ship cease, Then, low-ly kneel-ing, wait Thy word of peace.
2 sin, the hearts from shame, That in this house have called up-on Thy Name.
3 keep Thy chil-dren free. For dark and light are both a-like to Thee.
4 bid our con-flict cease, Call us, O Lord, to Thine e-ter-nal peace.

By permission of FRANCIS DUCKWORTH

951   Praise God

THOMAS KEN   OLD HUNDREDTH L.M.   FRENCH PSALTER

Praise God, from whom all bless-ings flow; Praise Him, all crea-tures here be-low;

Praise Him a-bove, ye heav'n-ly host, Praise Fa-ther, Son, and Ho-ly Ghost!

952 On the Shining Shore

Emma Pitt

Wm. J. Kirkpatrick

1 I hope to meet you all in glo - ry When the storms of life are o'er;
2 I hope to meet you all in glo - ry By the tree of life so fair;
3 I hope to meet you all in glo - ry Round the Sa-viour's throne a - bove;
4 I hope to meet you all in glo - ry When my work on earth is o'er;

1 I hope to tell the dear old sto - ry On the bless - ed shin - ing shore.
2 I hope to praise our dear Re - deem - er For the grace that bro't me there.
3 I hope to join the ran - som'd ar - my Sing-ing now re - deem - ing love.
4 I hope to clasp your hands re - joic - ing On the bright e - ter - nal shore.

REFRAIN

On the shin - ing shore, On the gold - en strand, In our Fa - ther's home, In the hap - py land: I hope to meet you there! I hope to meet you there! A crown of vic - t'ry wear, In glo - ry.

CHORUSES

1

I am the Door

JOHN X. 9

I am the Door, I am the Door, By Me if an-y man en-ter in

He shall be sav'd, he shall be sav'd, he shall be sav'd.

JOHN X. 9

CECIL J. ALLEN

I am the Door, I am the Door, By Me if

an-y man en-ter in He shall be sav'd, . he shall

rall.

be sav'd. If an-y man en-ter he shall be sav'd.

Music by permission of the Composer

2 Something More than Gold

JOHN MARTIN JOHN MARTIN

1 A cer-tain man of whom we read Who lived in days of old,
2 It hap-pen'd on a cer-tain day This lit-tle man was told
3 He climb'd a tree a-bove the crowd So that he might be-hold
4 The Sa-viour came a-long the way, And saw him on the tree,
5 So he o-bey'd, and soon he found The half had not been told,

1 Though he was rich he felt his need Of some-thing more than gold.
2 That Je-sus soon would pass that way With some-thing more than gold.
3 The bless-ed One with pow'r to give . some-thing more than gold.
4 Then call-ing to him Je-sus said: 'I must a-bide with thee!'
5 The bless-ing Je-sus brought to him Was bet-ter far than gold.

REFRAIN

O yes, my friend! there's some-thing more, some-thing more than gold,

To know your sins are all for-giv'n is some-thing more than gold.

By permission of REID BROTHERS, LTD.

3

Look to Him Now

Look to Him now, look to Him now, Je - sus

is wait - ing to save; . . Look to Him now,

look to Him now, Je - sus is wait - ing to save. .

4

Who'll be the Next?

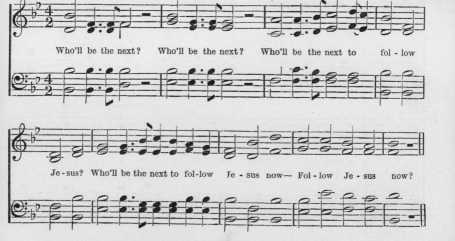

Who'll be the next? Who'll be the next? Who'll be the next to fol - low

Je - sus? Who'll be the next to fol-low Je - sus now— Fol - low Je - sus now?

5 Tell the Saviour All

Tell the Sa - viour all, . . . tell Him all, Tell the
Sa - viour all, . . . tell Him all; Make to Him a
full con - fes - sion, Tell the Sa - viour all. . .

6 and 7 Come (Steal) Away to Jesus

JUBILEE SINGERS

1 Come a - way, come a - way, Come a - way to
2 Steal a - way, steal a - way, Steal a - way to

1 Je - sus; . Come a - way, come a - way home! For
2 Je - sus; . Steal a - way, steal a - way home! For

Come (Steal) Away to Jesus—*Continued*

1 Je - sus waits to save you. My Lord calls me, He
2 Je - sus waits to save you. My Lord calls me, He

1 calls me by the thun - der, The trum - pet sounds it
2 calls me by the light - ning, The trum - pet sounds it

1, 2 in my soul; I hain't got long to stay here.

1, 2 Steal a - way, steal a - way, Steal a - way to Je - sus,

1, 2 Steal a - way, steal a - way home! For Je - sus waits to save you.

8 Eternity !

E. A. HOFFMAN

ANON.

E - ter - ni - ty! e - ter - ni - ty! Where will you

spend e - ter - ni - ty? E - ter - ni - ty! e - ter - ni -

ty! Where will . . you spend e - ter - ni - ty?
Where will you spend e - ter - ni - ty?

THE USUAL TUNE

E. A. HOFFMAN

J. H. TENNEY

1 E - ter - ni - ty! e - ter - ni - ty!
2 E - ter - ni - ty! e - ter - ni - ty!
3 E - ter - ni - ty! e - ter - ni - ty!

1 Where will you spend e - ter - ni - ty?
2 Lost through a long e - ter - ni - ty!
3 Sav'd through a long e - ter - ni - ty!

9   O Glory !

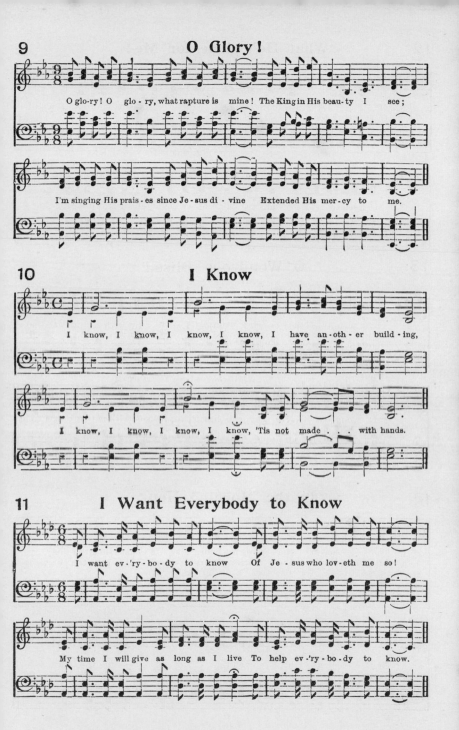

O glo-ry! O glo - ry, what rapture is mine ! The King in His beau-ty I see ;

I'm singing His prais-es since Je-sus di - vine Extended His mer-cy to me.

10   I Know

I know, I know, I know, I know, I have an-oth-er build-ing,

I know, I know, I know, I know, 'Tis not made . . . with hands.

11   I Want Everybody to Know

I want ev-'ry-bo-dy to know Of Je-sus who lov-eth me so!

My time I will give as long as I live To help ev-'ry-bo-dy to know.

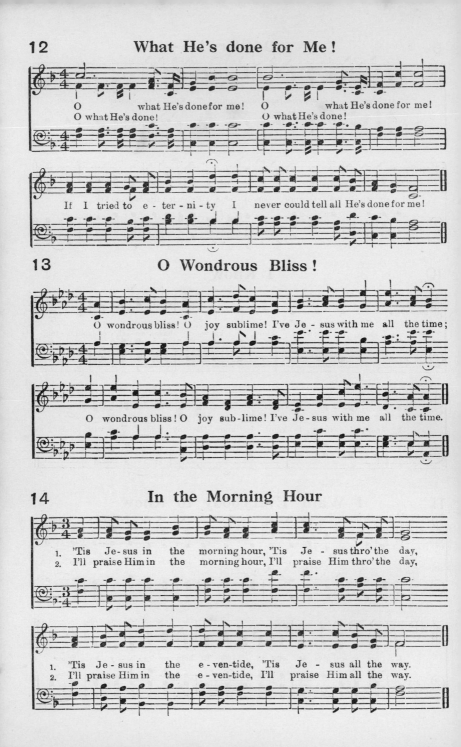

12

What He's done for Me!

O   what He's done for me!   O   what He's done for me!
O what He's done!   O what He's done!

If I tried to e - ter - ni - ty   I   never could tell all He's done for me!

13

O Wondrous Bliss!

O wondrous bliss! O joy sublime! I've Je - sus with me all the time;

O wondrous bliss! O joy sub-lime! I've Je - sus with me all the time.

14

In the Morning Hour

1. 'Tis Je - sus in   the   morning hour, 'Tis Je - sus thro' the day,
2. I'll praise Him in   the   morning hour, I'll   praise Him thro' the day,

1. 'Tis Je - sus in   the   e - ven-tide, 'Tis Je - sus all the way.
2. I'll praise Him in   the   e - ven-tide, I'll   praise Him all the way.

Get Right with God

Get right with God, ... Get right with God, ... Oh, do not let the
Get right with God, Get right with God,

Spi - rit now de - part, ... Get right with God, ...
do not let Him now de - part, Get right with God,

Get right with God, ... And grant Him glad ad-mis-sion to thy heart.
Get right with God,

16   Saved, Saved, oh Glory to God!

Saved, saved, oh glo - ry to God! I have the as - sur-ance di - vine;

Saved, saved, oh glo - ry to God! His Spi - rit bears witness with mine.

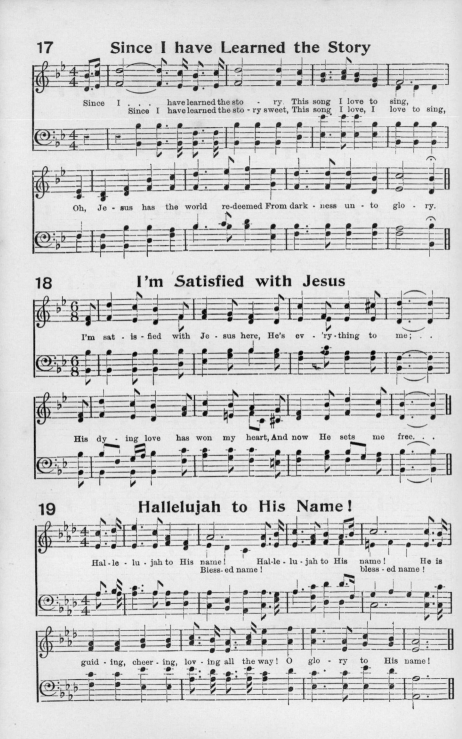

17 Since I have Learned the Story

Since I . . . have learned the sto - ry. This song I love to sing,
Since I have learned the sto - ry sweet, This song I love, I love to sing,

Oh, Je - sus has the world re-deemed From dark - ness un - to glo - ry.

18 I'm Satisfied with Jesus

I'm sat - is - fied with Je - sus here, He's ev - 'ry -thing to me; . .

His dy - ing love has won my heart, And now He sets me free. . .

19 Hallelujah to His Name!

Hal -le - lu - jah to His name! Hal -le - lu - jah to His name! He is
Bless - ed name!   bless - ed name!

guid - ing, cheer - ing, lov - ing all the way! O glo - ry to His name!

20 The Lamb, the Lamb, the Bleeding Lamb

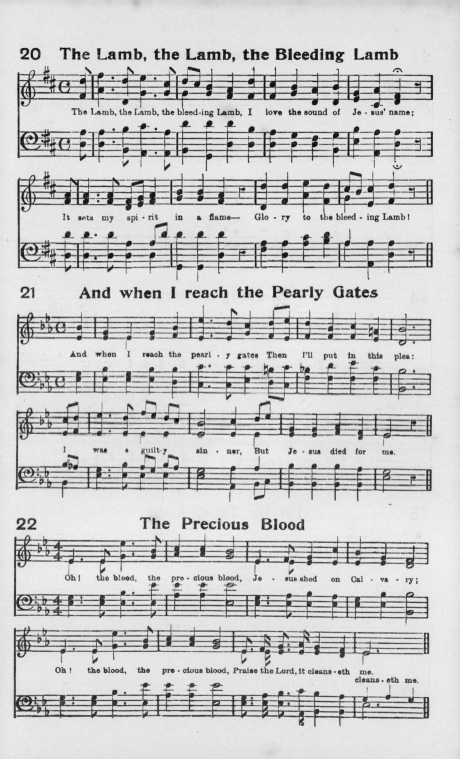

The Lamb, the Lamb, the bleed-ing Lamb, I love the sound of Je-sus' name;

It sets my spi-rit in a flame— Glo-ry to the bleed-ing Lamb!

21 And when I reach the Pearly Gates

And when I reach the pearl-y gates Then I'll put in this plea:

I was a guilt-y sin-ner, But Je-sus died for me.

22 The Precious Blood

Oh! the blood, the pre-cious blood, Je-sus shed on Cal-va-ry;

Oh! the blood, the pre-cious blood, Praise the Lord, it cleans-eth me.

cleans-eth me.

23 Every Step of the Way

Ev - 'ry step of the way, my Lord, yes, ev - 'ry step of the way,

Thy all is mine, and I am Thine, for ev - 'ry step of the way.

24 I'm going through

I'm go-ing thro', Je-sus, I'm go-ing thro', I'll pay the price what-ev-er oth-ers do;

I'll take the way with the world-despis-ed few, I've start-ed out, Je-sus, I'm go ing thro'.

25 I'll be True, Lord

I'll be true, Lord, to Thee, I'll be true, Lord, to Thee, And what-

e'er be - fall, I shall con - quer all, If I'm on - ly true to Thee.

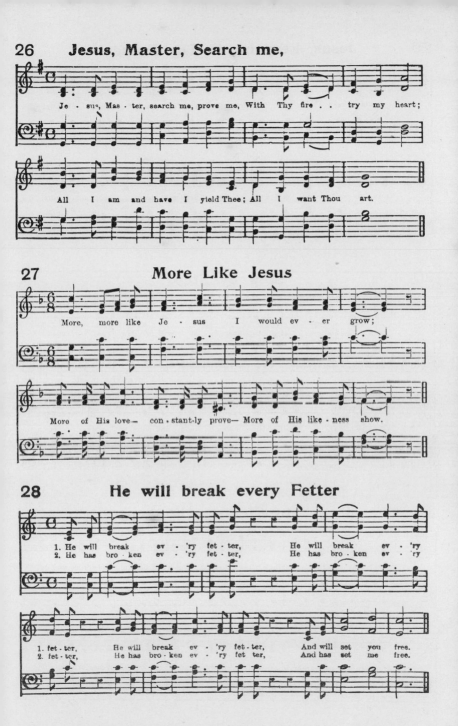

26 Jesus, Master, Search me,

Je - sus, Mas - ter, search me, prove me, With Thy fire . . er try my heart;

All I am and have I yield Thee; All I want Thou art.

27 More Like Jesus

More, more like Je - sus I would ev - er grow;

More of His love— con - stant-ly prove— More of His like - ness show.

28 He will break every Fetter

1. He will break ev - 'ry fet - ter, He will break ev - 'ry
2. He has bro - ken ev - 'ry fet - ter, He has bro - ken ev - 'ry

1. fet - ter, He will break ev - 'ry fet - ter, And will set you free.
2. fet - ter, He has bro - ken ev - 'ry fet - ter, And has set me free.

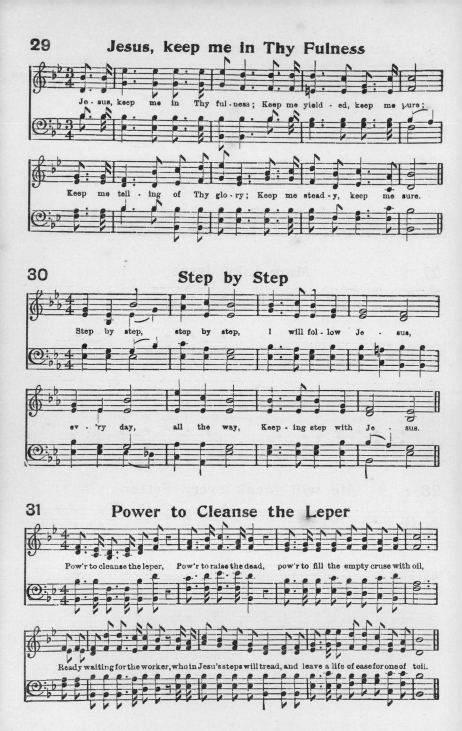

29 Jesus, keep me in Thy Fulness

Jesus, keep me in Thy fulness; Keep me yielded, keep me pure;
Keep me telling of Thy glory; Keep me steady, keep me sure.

30 Step by Step

Step by step, step by step, I will follow Jesus,
every day, all the way, Keeping step with Jesus.

31 Power to Cleanse the Leper

Pow'r to cleanse the leper, Pow'r to raise the dead, pow'r to fill the empty cruse with oil,
Ready waiting for the worker, who in Jesu's steps will tread, and leave a life of ease for one of toil.

32   Nearer, yes, Nearer

Near-er, yes, near-er, my Sa-viour, Oh draw me yet near-er to Thee!

rit.

Near-er, yes, near-er, my Sa-viour, And per-fect Thy like-ness in me!

33   Thy Love, Thy Boundless Love

Thy love, Thy love, Thy bound-less love; Thy love, Thy love, all-con-q'ring love,

Shed in, shed in my heart a-broad; Give me this per-fect love.

34   Nothing too Hard

1. There's no-thing too hard for Thee (dear Lord), There's nothing too hard for
2. I'm trust-ing a-lone in Thee (dear Lord), I'm trust-ing a-lone in

1. Thee; No-thing, no-thing, There's no-thing too hard for Thee.
2. Thee; Trust-ing, trust-ing, I'm trust-ing a-lone in Thee.

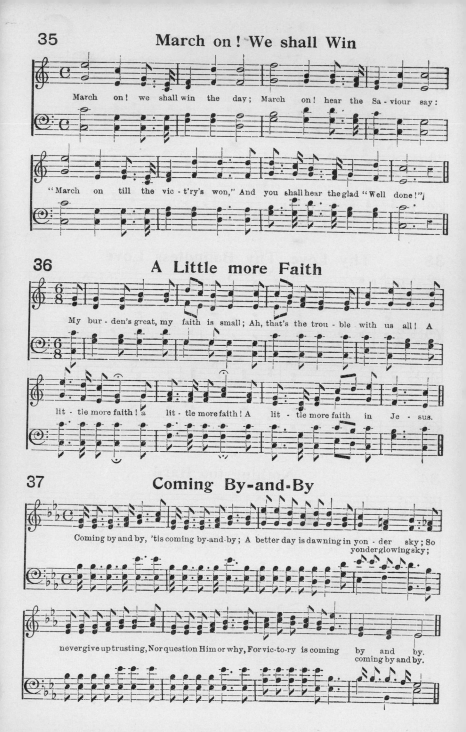

35 March on ! We shall Win

March on! we shall win the day; March on! hear the Sa - viour say:

"March on till the vic - t'ry's won," And you shall hear the glad "Well done!"

36 A Little more Faith

My bur - den's great, my faith is small; Ah, that's the trou - ble with us all! A

lit - tle more faith! a lit - tle more faith! A lit - tle more faith in Je - sus.

37 Coming By-and-By

Coming by and by, 'tis coming by-and-by; A better day is dawning in yon - der sky; So
yonder glowing sky;

never give up trusting, Nor question Him or why, For vic-to-ry is coming by and by.
coming by and by.

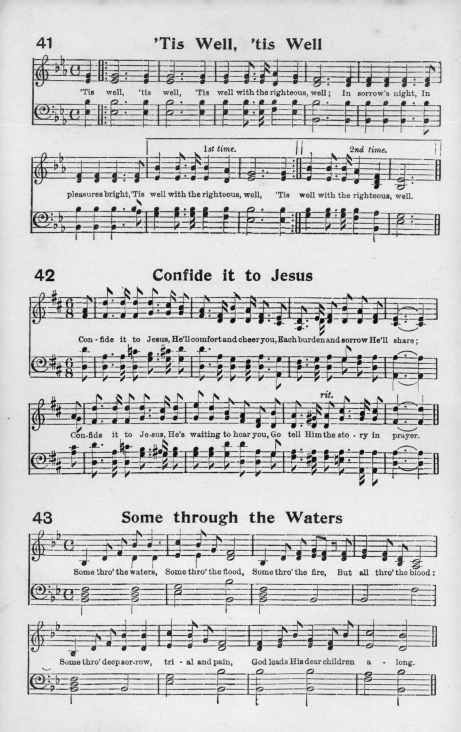

41

'Tis Well, 'tis Well

'Tis well, 'tis well, 'Tis well with the righteous, well; In sorrow's night, In

1st time. *2nd time.*

pleasures bright, 'Tis well with the righteous, well, 'Tis well with the righteous, well.

42

Confide it to Jesus

Con-fide it to Jesus, He'll comfort and cheer you, Each burden and sorrow He'll share;

rit.

Con-fide it to Je-sus, He's waiting to hear you, Go tell Him the sto-ry in prayer.

43

Some through the Waters

Some thro' the waters, Some thro' the flood, Some thro' the fire, But all thro' the blood:

Some thro' deep sor-row, tri-al and pain, God leads His dear children a-long.

44 Jesus Bled and Died for Me

Some - thing whis - pers, can it be   There is
can it be

hope   for   one   like   me? .   I   will   seek   His
like   me?

mer - cy   full   and   free,   Je - sus   bled   and   died   for   me.

45 In Tune with Thee

In   tune with Thee,   .   .   .   in   tune with Thee;
In   tune with Thee,   in   tune with Thee;

Lord,   keep   my   heart   in   tune   .   .   .   with   Thee.
in   tune   with   Thee.

Since I have been Forgiven

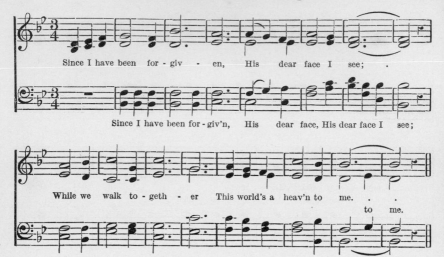

Since I have been for-giv - en, His dear face I see; .

Since I have been for-giv'n, His dear face, His dear face I see;

While we walk to-geth - er This world's a heav'n to me. . .

to me.

47 A Little Talk with Jesus

A. L. ASHLEY

H. WRIGHT

A lit - tle talk with Je - sus makes things right, all

right; A lit - tle talk with Je - sus makes things right, all

right; Thank God! I al - ways find In trou-ble of ev - 'ry

kind   That a   lit-tle talk with Je-sus makes things right,   all   right.

48   Determined to Hold Out

I   am   de-ter-min'd   to   hold out   to the   end,

Je-sus   is   with me,   on   Him   I   can   de-pend;   And   I

know   I   have   sal-va-tion   for   I   feel   it   in   my   soul;

I   am   de-ter-min'd   to   hold   out   to   the   end.

Index of Choruses

These appear throughout the Hymn Book

INDEX OF CHORUSES

Index of Choruses and Refrains

Those marked c *are in the Chorus Section at the end of the Hymns; those marked* H *are among the Hymns; and those marked* R *are Refrains of Hymns.*

INDEX OF CHORUSES AND REFRAINS

Alphabetical Index of Tunes

ALPHABETICAL INDEX OF TUNES

Metrical Index of Tunes

Staincliffe	540
Totland	555
Undershaft ..	588
Walton 481, 540,	588
Wareham .. 499,	555
Warrington ..	72
Winchester New ..	312
Winscott	602

L.M.D.

Calvary's Brow ..	153
Canaan's Land ..	478
Hannah	739
Hour of Prayer ..	560
Julian	867
Lacrima	573
Marmora	739
Merthyr Tydfil ..	253
Redemption Ground	30
Repose	253
Selafo	867
Starless Crown ..	786
Truest Friend ..	871

4.8.8.4.4

Door of Hope ..	583

5.4.5.4.D

St. Cecilia New ..	45
Theodora	45

5.5.6.5.6.4.6.4

Gleniffer	660
Little Candle ..	660

5.5.7.5.5.7

Golden Key ..	572

6.4.6.4

Frogmore	148
Nain	148

6.4.6.4.D

Lathbury	2
Overtown	2

6.4.6.4.6.6.4

Excelsior	569
Horbury	569
Nenthorn	569

6.4.6.4.6.6.6.4

Croydon	857
Feast	113
Fenwick	578
Melo	857
St. Margaret ..	752
St. Nicholas ..	548
Summer Land ..	752
Tryst	548

6.4.6.4.6.7.6.4

Happy Land ..	680

6.5.6.5.D

Aspiration	590
Goshen	667
Kirkbraddan ..	667
Mamre	564

6.5.6.5.6.5.D

Anything for Jesus	393
Armageddon 8,	460
Forward	669
Hermas .. 8,	668
Himself Alone ..	393
Our Watchword ..	669
Rachie .. 8,	668
St. Gertrude ..	460
Wye Valley ..	418

6.6.4.6.6.6.4

Greenwood ..	580
Light	652
Malvern	652
Moscow	652
Olivet	580

6.6.6.5.D

Ashland	254
Broughton ..	254

6.6.6.6

Darak	849

6.6.6.6.6.6

Baca	570

6,6,6,6,8,6

Water Street ..	571

6.6.6.6.8.8

Warsaw	629

6.6.6.6.8.8.8

Lenox .. 69,	629

6.6.8.4.D

Covenant	18
Leoni	18
Priory	19

6.6.11.D

Jewels .. 523,	659

6.7.8.7

Ever Thine ..	593

7.5.7.5.7.7

Moel Llys ..	644
Silksworth ..	914

7.6.7.5.D

Diligence	429

7.6.7.6

Aule	132
Knecht	279
St. Victor ..	279

7.6.7.6.6.6.7.6

Near the Cross ..	390

7.6.7.6.7.6.7.5

Rutherford ..	411

7.6.7.6.D

Angels' Story ..	656
Ariel	576
Aurelia	50
Cruger	533
Day of Rest ..	51
Eden Grove ..	149
Ellacombe	533
Ellon	656
Endless Praise ..	11
Ewing	372
Greenland	626
Herrnhut (Cruger)	11
Just a Word ..	609
Meirionydd ..	576
Missionary 281,	626
Morning Light ..	52
Penlan	149
Pilgrimage ..	281
Refuge	663
Salvation's Story ..	380
Sheltered	723
The Homeland ..	798

7.6.7.6.7.6.D

Wir Pflugen ..	39
Wondrous Sight ..	438

7.6.7.6.7.7.7.6

Follow Jesus ..	754
Heavenly Home ..	190
Jesus Saves ..	200

7.6.8.6.D

Alford	43

7.7.7.3

Vigilate	484

7.7.7.5

Pondoland ..	923

7.7.7.5.D

Rawlins	283

Index of First Lines and Titles

First Lines in ordinary type; TITLES in SMALL CAPITALS

INDEX OF FIRST LINES AND TITLES

INDEX OF FIRST LINES AND TITLES

INDEX OF FIRST LINES AND TITLES

INDEX OF FIRST LINES AND TITLES

INDEX OF FIRST LINES AND TITLES

INDEX OF FIRST LINES AND TITLES

INDEX OF FIRST LINES AND TITLES

INDEX OF FIRST LINES AND TITLES

INDEX OF FIRST LINES AND TITLES

INDEX OF FIRST LINES AND TITLES

The Lord's Prayer

RICHARD LANGDON

Our Fa-ther, which art in heav'n, hal-low-ed be Thy name, Thy king-dom come, Thy will be done in earth as it is in heav'n; Give us this day our dai-ly bread, and for-give us our tres-pass-es, as we for-give them that tres-pass a-gainst us: And lead us not in-to temp-ta-tion, but de-

Carolyn Gregg

Christmas 1967